Hans von Bülow

Hans v. Bülow

17.

Hans von Bülow in 1886. A photograph by E. Bieber.

Hans von Bülow

A Life and Times

ALAN WALKER

OXFORD
UNIVERSITY PRESS
2010

OXFORD
UNIVERSITY PRESS

Oxford University Press, Inc., publishes works that further
Oxford University's objective of excellence
in research, scholarship, and education.

Oxford   New York
Auckland   Cape Town   Dar es Salaam   Hong Kong   Karachi
Kuala Lumpur   Madrid   Melbourne   Mexico City   Nairobi
New Delhi   Shanghai   Taipei   Toronto

With offices in
Argentina   Austria   Brazil   Chile   Czech Republic   France   Greece
Guatemala   Hungary   Italy   Japan   Poland   Portugal   Singapore
South Korea   Switzerland   Thailand   Turkey   Ukraine   Vietnam

Published by Oxford University Press, Inc.
198 Madison Avenue, New York, New York 10016

www.oup.com

Oxford is a registered trademark of Oxford University Press

Library of Congress Cataloging-in-Publication Data
Walker, Alan, 1930–
Hans von Bülow : a life and times / Alan Walker.
   p.   cm.
Includes bibliographical references and index.
ISBN 978-0-19-536868-0
1. Bülow, Hans von, 1830–1894. 2. Conductors (Music)—Germany—Biography. I. Title.
ML422.B9W36 2009
780.92—dc22[B]   2008039701

9 8 7 6 5 4 3 2 1

Printed in the United States of America
on acid-free paper

To the memory of
Marie von Bülow
Keeper of the flame

Acknowledgements

Hans von Bülow's vast legacy, scattered across a wide variety of locations, reflects a life of ceaseless travel. He is known to have given more than 3,000 concerts during his career as a pianist and conductor. His long and arduous tours took him through a dozen or more countries, and left a complex trail of paper in their wake—programmes, newspaper reviews, photographs, reminiscences, diary entries, and correspondence. Much of this material is esoteric and remains unpublished. But it is not possible to write a reliable account of Bülow's life without taking it into account. It is my pleasant duty to thank all those colleagues who helped me along the way.

I have elsewhere spoken of the 'geography of biography', of the absolute necessity for biographers to visit the places about which they write, without which it is virtually impossible for the spirit of times past to penetrate their work. A single walk across Dresden's venerable Augustus Bridge, which spans the river Elbe, did more to stimulate my recalcitrant pen into capturing the details of Bülow's childhood than did the perusal of a dozen articles in remote libraries. Equally memorable were my visits to Bülow's impressive grave in Hamburg's Ohlsdorf Cemetery, and the great St. Michaelis Church where the funeral ceremony itself was held. Several accounts of Bülow's obsequies have come down to us, of course, but for me they refused to leap from the page until I had experienced these geographical locations for myself.

As for such cities as Berlin and Meiningen, with whose orchestras Bülow achieved his greatest triumphs, they are an indispensable part of the biographer's itinerary—even though a number of places associated with his career were destroyed during World War II. My guide on all these visits to Germany was Dr. Horst Förster, who lavished the same attention on my work as if it had been his own, and he opened doors for me, particularly in Berlin and Hamburg, which might otherwise have remained closed. I remain grateful to him.

By far the largest Bülow archive is held in the Deutsche Staatsbibliothek in Berlin. It was deposited there by Bülow's second wife, the actress Marie Schanzer, in several installments between the two world wars. On various visits to the Staatsbibliothek I was helped by the music archivist Frau Ute Nawroth, herself a Bülow specialist, and by her colleagues. Documents that might have taken days for me to uncover in this largely uncatalogued collection were made readily available for my inspection, and simplified my work.

My visits to the Meininger Museen and the Meininger Staatsarchiv were likewise made easier for me by the support I received from Frau Maren Goltz, the chief music archivist. Bülow spent five years of his life in Meiningen, directing the Court Orchestra and bringing it to the forefront of Europe's musical life. The archive, which is housed in the ducal castle, contains a rich supply of memorabilia, to which I was given free access.

Many other organizations supported me in my work, of course, together with individual members of their respective staffs, and it is a pleasure to acknowledge them here. Among the most important were: Fran Barulich and the New York Public Library for the Performing Arts; Jane Gottlieb and the Juilliard School of Music Library; Catherine C. Rivers and the Music Division of the Library of Congress; Donald Manildi and the International Piano Archives, University of Maryland; Mária Eckhardt and the Liszt Museum and Research Centre, Budapest; Robert Parker and the Music and Rare Books Division of the British Library; Jonathan Summers and the British Library Sound Archives; Paul Collen and the Centre for Performance History at the Royal College of Music, London; Sally-Anne Coupar and The Hunterian Museum, University of Glasgow; and Rosemary Johnson and the Royal Philharmonic Society, London. Among other individuals who helped in important ways were Professor William Renwick, who designed the music examples; Professor Hans Schulte and Professor Gabriele Erasmi who served as linguistic consultants; and Laura Siegel, Dominique Caplier, Nadejda Vlaeva and Peter Förster, who dealt with a medley of musicological inquiries arising from my biographical narrative. I am likewise grateful to Professor Alan McComas, in the Department of Neurology at McMaster University, Canada, for throwing light on many of the baffling symptoms associated with Bülow's terminal illness and death, and encouraging me to explain them in terms that a layman could understand. There could be few better guides through the maze that constitutes Bülow's family tree than Anna Gravina, one of his direct descendants, and I greatly appreciate her assistance in helping me to fill in some gaps in the genealogical table on pp. xxvi–xxvii. To Peggy Findlay, Helen Creedon, and the staff of the Inter-Library Loans Services at McMaster University, I extend my special thanks. The care they expended on my numerous requests for assistance, over a very long period of time, was exemplary.

My colleague William Wright was generous to a fault in his support of my project across the years. He not only helped me put the finishing touches to my account of Bülow's visits to Scotland (the details of which still remain a closed book to many scholars), but also drew my attention to a rich variety of unpublished sources, some of which I was able to integrate into my text. He also read through the entire book in typescript, a heroic task, and made a number of practical suggestions along the way. The help I received from Lisa Yui must also be acknowledged. She spent many a difficult hour in the mustiest corners of New York's research libraries, in pursuit of materials having to do with Bülow's American tours. More than once these scholars struck gold, and the fruits of their work have left their impression on my narrative.

To Gregor Benko I owe a particular debt. He generously made available to me the important run of unpublished letters from Bülow to his last amour, Cécile Mutzenbecher, which throws new and unexpected light on the musician's complex emotional life. Dick Anderson's familiarity with the Steinway archives in New York came more than once to my rescue, and he referred me to a number of unpublished documents connected to Bülow that might otherwise have passed me by. To Professor Jim Lawson my thanks are especially due for going through my German translations. Bülow's prose is often dense and labyrinthine, and it sometimes branches out in unexpected directions. Few are the letters of Bülow that do not contain either a series of esoteric puns or a display of verbal fireworks so brilliant that they are liable to dazzle even the native German speaker. Professor Lawson saved me from wandering down more than one blind alley and led me back to the essential points at hand.

Finally I want to place on record my indebtedness to my research assistant of many years standing, Pauline Pocknell, who passed away very suddenly after she had already begun to help me with this project. Pauline was irreplaceable, and was therefore not replaced. I can only hope that from whatever coign of vantage she occupies in that heaven which is surely set aside for scholars of her calibre, she will accept this accolade, and survey the pages that follow with friendly tolerance—an attitude that I actively discouraged her from extending towards my work during her lifetime.

Contents

Illustrations

The Bülow Chronicles

A severe winter in Dresden, 1830 ~ the river Elbe freezes over ~ Bülow's birth on January 8, 1830 ~ his childhood marred by chronic 'brain fever' ~ discovers his talent for music, aged nine, together with his photographic memory ~ first piano lessons with Cäcilie Schmiedel ~ youthful encounters with the eccentric Henry Litolff, who lives with the Bülow family ~ enrolls at the Dresden Lyceum, where he studies Greek and Latin ~ attends the premier performance of Richard Wagner's *Rienzi* in the Dresden Royal Opera House (October 20, 1842) and becomes a confirmed Wagnerian ~ friendship with the Ritter family ~ an early encounter with Franz Liszt ~ studies at the Leipzig Conservatory of Music, where his teachers are Louis Plaidy for piano and Moritz Hauptmann for theory ~ his youthful repertoire includes Bach, Beethoven, and Chopin ~ a memorable encounter with Felix Mendelssohn ~ the turbulent marriage of his parents ~ a sojourn in Stuttgart, 1846–1848 ~ friendship with the Molique family ~ a boyhood prank ~ Wagner praises some of his youthful compositions ~ becomes an unwilling law student at Leipzig University ~ the Dresden Uprising, May 1849 ~ his parents divorce ~ he transfers to Berlin University ~ an excursion to Weimar ~ meets Liszt and sees him conduct *Fidelio* ~ back in Berlin he begins to write polemical articles for the press and makes enemies.

With Liszt in Weimar   49

Bülow witnesses Liszt conduct the world premier of Wagner's *Lohengrin* (August 1850) ~ despite parental opposition he gives up the study of law in favour of music ~ Wagner and Liszt intervene in his behalf ~ Wagner secures temporary conducting posts for him in Zurich and St. Gall ~ Bülow then moves to Weimar and studies the piano with Liszt ~ a description of Weimar and Liszt's musical reforms there ~ he meets the members of Liszt's masterclasses ~ a trip with Liszt to the Ballenstedt Music Festival (June 1852) ~ the First Berlioz Week in Weimar (November 1852) and Bülow's role in it ~ the 'War of the Romantics' ~ Bülow's article against Henriette Sontag and its repercussions ~ it causes a rift with his father ~ with Liszt's support, Bülow sets out on his first concert tour of Germany, Austria, and Hungary ~ a setback in Vienna, a success in Pest.

The death of Eduard von Bülow ~ Hans dashes from the Karlsruhe Festival to Ötlishausen to attend the funeral ~ his letters of condolence to his mother and sister ~ he returns to the Karlsruhe Festival and receives an ovation for his performance of Liszt's Fantasie on Motifs from Beethoven's 'Ruins of Athens' ~ meets Count Theodore Myscielski in Dresden, who invites him to teach his four daughters at the family castle in Chocieszewice, Poland ~ Berlioz visits Dresden (April/May, 1852) and conducts his *Damnation of Faust* and other works ~ Bülow spends much time in the composer's company ~ he undertakes to make a four-hand arrangement of Berlioz's *Benvenuto Cellini*.

Bülow takes up his teaching post at Chocieszewice, October 1854 ~ his droll descriptions of life in his 'Polish swamp' ~ after several weeks of dull routine he visits Berlin and attempts to ignite a new career there ~ he gives a concert in the Singakademie, which loses money, but he forms useful connections with the city's leading musicians ~ Julius Stern offers him the post of head of the piano department at the Stern Conservatory to replace Theodor Kullak ~ he returns to Poland for a few more weeks before beginning a new life in Berlin.

Franziska joins Bülow in Berlin, and finds a new apartment for them both ~ he begins teaching at the Stern Conservatory ~ his teaching routine and methods described ~ some early connections with Prussian royalty help his career ~ Bülow reacts against the stilted musical life of Berlin and forms his own concert series, the 'Trio-Soirées' ~ he gives the first performance of Liszt's Sonata in B minor, January 22, 1857, and presents the new Bechstein grand piano at the same concert ~ his declining relations with the Berlin press ~ an explosion in the Singakademie, January 14, 1859 ~ *Die Ideale*: 'I achieved victory under this sign'.

The 'War of the Romantics' and its ramifications ~ Brendel calls a 'Congress of Musical Artists' in Leipzig, June 1859 ~ in his keynote speech he withdraws the designation 'Music of the future' hitherto used to describe the works of Liszt and Wagner, and instead calls these composers and their acolytes 'the New German School' ~ in response Brahms and Joachim draw up a 'Manifesto' dissociating themselves from such a school, condemning its principles as 'contrary to the innermost spirit of music'.

The arrival in Berlin of 'the Erlking's daughters', Blandine and Cosima Liszt ~ Bülow is charged with giving them piano lessons ~ the early childhood and youth of these girls ~ Liszt's fretted relations with their mother, Countess Marie d'Agoult ~ Liszt's life in Weimar with Princess Carolyne von Sayn-Wittgenstein ~ Bülow and Cosima declare their love for each other ~ Liszt is not entirely in favour of this match, and asks the couple to wait before marrying ~ the Catholic wedding finally takes place at St. Hedwig's Church, Berlin, on August 18, 1857 ~ they spend their honeymoon by Lake Geneva, and visit Wagner in Zurich ~ three weeks of music making with Wagner at the 'Asyl' ~ married life in Berlin ~ the incompatibility of Cosima and Franziska von Bülow ~ Daniel Liszt sees Bülow conduct in Prague ~ Daniel visits the Bülows in Berlin and falls ill ~ his death and funeral.

The marriage of Hans and Cosima begins to founder ~ the birth of Daniela ~ Cosima falls ill and begins a lengthy convalescence at Bad Reichenall ~ the death of her sister Blandine Liszt, and the effect of this loss on Cosima ~ a second daughter, Blandine, is born to Cosima: the harrowing circumstances surrounding the delivery of this child ~ Wagner and Cosima meet in Berlin and 'amidst sobs and tears' declare their love for each other during a ride in the Tiergarten, November 28, 1863 ~ their respective woes contrasted and compared ~ Cosima's disturbed frame of mind considered ~ her earlier 'suicide pact' in Geneva with Karl Ritter becomes known to Wagner, together with the unhappy state of her marriage to Bülow ~ a catastrophe looms.

Catastrophe in Munich, 1864–1869   115

The newly crowned eighteen-year-old King Ludwig of Bavaria brings Wagner to Munich ~ he installs Wagner in the Villa Pellet by Starnberger See ~ Wagner invites Bülow and Cosima to join him there ~ Wagner procures for Bülow the position of *Vorspieler* to the king ~ Cosima becomes pregnant by Wagner with their first child, Isolde ~ in June 1914 the Bayreuth *Landesgericht* is asked to rule on the paternity of this child, but concludes that the matter cannot be determined beyond reasonable doubt ~ after Bülow discovers that Cosima and Wagner are lovers, he suffers a breakdown and moves into a Munich Hotel ~ Liszt arrives in Munich ~ he warns Wagner to terminate the relationship with Cosima on pain of losing his friendship ~ Ferdinand Lassalle's visit to Munich, and his dramatic death by duelling ~ Bülow and Cosima return to Berlin (September 1864) and make arrangements for their permanent transfer to Munich ~ another visit from Liszt.

The University of Jena bestows on Bülow the degree of doctor of philosophy, February 13, 1864 ~ the convocation programme features Bülow as pianist and conductor ~ the Bülow family returns to Munich (November 24) and takes up residence on Luitpoldstrasse ~ Wagner resides on Briennerstrasse, where Cosima spends much time in his company ~ Bülow gives a royal command concert in Munich's Odeon Theatre, and conducts model performances of Wagner's *Flying Dutchman* ~ Wagner's plans for the creation of a Royal Music School ~ his lavish lifestyle becomes a drain on the royal treasury and arouses hostility ~ the Munich press lampoons Wagner and Bülow and a newspaper war breaks out ~ rehearsals for *Tristan* begin on April 10, 1865, and Cosima gives birth to Isolde the same day ~ Bülow's 'Schweinhunde' remark gets him into trouble with the press ~ Wagner chooses Ludwig Schnorr von Carolsfeld as his first 'Tristan' and Ludwig's wife, Malvina, as his first 'Isolde' ~ dogged by misfortune, the first performance of *Tristan* is postponed until June 10 ~ the death of Ludwig Schnorr and the 'curse' of *Tristan* ~ Wagner dabbles in Munich politics and is banished from Bavaria.

Wagner moves to Tribschen in Switzerland, and continues his relationship with Cosima ~ her infidelity is reported in the Munich press, and Bülow challenges the editor of the *Volksbote* to a duel ~ King Ludwig visits Tribschen incognito ~ Wagner and Cosima persuade the king to publish a letter in their defence and in so doing perjure themselves ~ Cosima gives birth to Eva on February 17, 1867, her second child by Wagner ~ the episode marks a crucial turning point in Bülow's relations with Wagner ~ Liszt confronts Wagner at Tribschen and breaks off all connection with him ~ Malvina Schnorr conveys to the king some intimate details of Cosima's relationship with Wagner: the king realizes for the first time that he has been duped ~ Bülow conducts the first performance of *Die Meistersinger* ~ his growing conflict with Wagner ~ Cosima decides to leave Bülow and flee to Wagner ~ she informs Liszt who removes his blessing from her ~ Bülow tenders his resignation from Munich, begins divorce proceedings, and moves to Florence.

Book Two: Ascending the Peak, 1870–1880

First sight of Florence: 'a dream of wonder' ~ meets again his childhood friend, Jessie Laussot ~ he acquires an apartment on the Borgo S. Frediano ~ the ballerina Elvira Salvioni beguiles him and he dedicates to her his *Il Carnevale di Milano*, op. 21 ~ an infatuation with Giulia, 'the seventeen-year-old star in my life' ~ a benefit concert for the victims of the Pisa floods, January 1870 ~ his Bechstein piano at last arrives from Munich, but his practicing disturbs the neighbours ~ travels to Berlin in pursuit of a Protestant divorce from Cosima ~ spends time with Carl Tausig ~ the Franco-Prussian War of 1870, and Bülow's reaction to it ~ a Beethoven Centennial Festival in Milan, November–December 1870 ~ Tausig dies and Bülow writes his obituary notice for the Leipzig *Signale* ~ visits Liszt in Rome to celebrate the latter's sixtieth birthday, October 22, 1871 ~ completes work on his edition of Beethoven's piano music, which he dedicates to Liszt 'as the fruits of his teaching' ~ announces a farewell concert in Florence (December 28, 1871) and embarks on his European concert tours ~ within three months he gives more than sixty recitals, and by year's end has raised almost 100,000 francs, much of it for the support of his children.

Bülow crosses Albion's shores in April 1873 ~ of musical life in England, and its absence ~ J. W. Davison 'the music monster' of newspaper criticism ~ Bülow makes his debut with the Philharmonic Society, playing Beethoven's *Emperor* Concerto ~ he is awarded the Society's Gold Medal, May 26, 1873 ~ he also appears as a conductor, directing the Prelude and Liebestod from Wagner's *Tristan* ~ after spending the summer in Baden-Baden he returns to London, in November 1873, and plays at the Crystal Palace ~ his subsequent tour of the English provinces takes him to such cities as Manchester, Liverpool, Bristol, Birmingham, and Newcastle, en route to Scotland ~ he accuses his agent, George Dolby, of swindling him ~ his extended tours take him to eastern Europe, as far afield as Vilnius, Kiev, Odessa, and Kursk ~ Carl Bechstein supplies him with pianos along the way ~ Bülow's mixed commentaries to Bechstein on these instruments ~ he objects to being used as 'a commercial traveller' ~ in Moscow he meets his old fellow student Karl Klindworth, who is working on his vast piano reduction of Wagner's *Ring* cycle ~ visits the dying Countess Marie von Mouchanoff-Kalergis in Warsaw and plays Chopin to her as she slips into the arms of death ~ during a brief return to Italy he excoriates Verdi's newly composed *Requiem,* an action he later regrets and for which he apologizes ~ his English pupil Elizabeth Beesley ~ the reminiscences of Laura Rappoldi-Kahrer ~ of cold baths and water cures ~ a sojourn in Glasgow and a success with the Glasgow Choral Union ~ returns to London and conducts at one of the 'Walter Bache Concerts' ~ suffers a mild stroke, but succeeds in giving three 'farewell' recitals in London ~ returns to Germany with a partial paralysis of the right hand ~ he establishes contact with a new agent, Bernard Ullman, who plans his American tour.

First Tour of America, 1875–1876   211

Bülow draws up a will and sets out for America ~ first concerts in Boston's Music Hall ~ he gives the world premier of Tchaikovsky's Piano Concerto in B-flat minor, October 25, 1875 ~ he fires his conductor, Carl Bergmann, for 'incompetence' ~ an unfortunate interview in *The New York Sun* ~ a letter from Tchaikovsky ~ concerts and contretemps in New York ~ Chickering versus Steinway ~ Bülow inaugurates Chickering Hall, November 15, 1875 ~ some ear-witness accounts of his playing ~ his impressions of Midwest America ~ an interview in the *Chicago Times* ~ considers becoming an American citizen ~ becomes infatuated with Baroness Romaine von Overbeck, who does not return his advances ~ Bülow and the young singer Lizzie Cronyn ~ he abandons his gruelling American tour in a state of exhaustion after giving 139 concerts ~ returns to Germany and seeks a cure at Bad Godesberg ~ Liszt on Bülow's physical condition ~ Hans von Bronsart offers Bülow the conductorship of the Hanover Court Theatre.

A Scottish Interlude, 1877–1878:   237
Bülow and the Glasgow Choral Union

Bülow is invited to direct the Glasgow Choral Union ~ his connections with the critic Thomas Logan Stillie ~ meets the Scottish composer George Macfarren ~ inaugural concert in St. Andrew's Hall, November 16, 1877 ~ impressions of the organist W. T. Best ~ Bülow's 'Saturday Popular Concerts' ~ Alexander Mackenzie's description of Bülow on the podium ~ a farewell concert before an audience of more than 3,000 people ~ he is presented with an inscribed baton by the organizers of the Choral Union ~ returns to his position in Hanover.

At Hanover, 1877–1879   247

Misfortunes of the Hanover Court Theatre ~ Bülow takes command ~ his reforms are not well received ~ he introduces Brahms's newly published Symphony no. 1, in C Minor (October 20, 1877) and dubs it 'Beethoven's Tenth' ~ Liszt visits Hanover ~ with Liszt at the annual festival of the Allgemeiner Deutscher Musikverein in Erfurt, June 22–26, 1878 ~ Bülow plays Bronsart's Piano Concerto in F-sharp minor, with Liszt conducting ~ returns briefly with Liszt to Weimar ~ tours England as a pianist once more and raises money for the Bayreuth Deficit Fund ~ his gift of 40,000 marks is returned by Wagner ~ a Beethoven recital in

London's St. James's Hall ~ a failure in Glasgow ~ he plays in the English provinces ~ an alcoholic concert in Birkenhead ~ Bülow loses his luggage as he crosses the English Channel en route to Hanover ~ some fabled confrontations with the heldentenor Anton Schott ~ Bülow dubs him 'the Knight of the Swine' ~ resigns from Hanover, and Schott follows two years later.

BOOK THREE: VISTAS FROM THE SUMMIT, 1880–1894

The orchestral tours continue ~ the twenty-three-year-old Gustav Mahler hears the orchestra in Cassel (January 1884) and is electrified ~ Mahler's letter to Bülow ~ Brahms's music is regularly featured ~ Brahms is invested by Georg II with Meiningen's 'Grand Cross' ~ the orchestra creates a sensation with three concerts in Berlin's Singakademie (February 1884) ~ Bülow conducts the Berlin Philharmonic in a 'Popular Concert', and in a legendary speech from the podium insults the Berlin Royal Opera House, calling it the 'Hülsen circus' ~ Baron von Hülsen retaliates by stripping Bülow of his title of 'Prussian Court Pianist', whereupon Bülow styles himself 'the People's Pianist' ~ Bülow's interest in his young acolyte Richard Strauss ~ Strauss makes his traumatic conducting debut with the Meiningen Orchestra ~ Bülow appoints the twenty-one-year-old Strauss as his assistant conductor at Meiningen ~ some Strauss anecdotes of Bülow on the podium ~ Bülow gives recitals in Paris (April 1885) and introduces the piano music of Brahms ~ some mixed reviews ~ in Versailles he meets Cosima's half-sister Claire de Charnacé and they recollect some past family crises ~ after a disagreement with Brahms, Bülow resigns from Meiningen ~ Strauss follows him a year later ~ Marie Schanzer is fired from the Meiningen Theatre ~ a brief sojourn in St. Petersburg where Bülow conducts a season of concerts for the 'Russian Music Society' ~ a farewell appearance in Meiningen, January 29, 1886.

Dr. Joseph Hoch leaves his fortune for the creation of the Hoch Conservatory of Music in Frankfurt ~ Joachim Raff is appointed the first director ~ Raff dies prematurely ~ his funeral and burial in Frankfurt ~ he leaves his family in straitened circumstances ~ Raff's successor is the conservative Bernhard Scholz ~ a 'revolution' ensues at the Conservatory and a number of the faculty break away ~ they form the Raff Conservatory of Music and bring in Bülow as its honorary president ~ the tensions between the two institutions ~ for four summers (1884 through 1887) Bülow gives masterclasses at the Raff Conservatory to raise money for a monument to Raff ~ the classes described ~ some Bülow aphorisms on the piano and its technique ~ some anecdotes from the classes ~ a lesson with Laura Kahrer ~ Walter Damrosch becomes a conducting student ~ Damrosch describes his time with Bülow ~ Bülow takes over Liszt's masterclass in Weimar and has some confrontations with the pupils ~ Broadwood & Sons presents the Raff Conservatory with one of its Imperial grand pianos, 1884 ~ Bülow's editions considered ~ Clara Schumann's reaction to them: 'I have always forbidden my students to use these editions.'

Bülow bids farewell to Meiningen and settles in Hamburg ~ a description of this Hanseatic city and its artistic and commercial promise ~ Bülow develops his famous Beethoven Cycle, to be given across four successive evenings ~ presents it for the first time in the Leipzig Gewandhaus, in October 1886 ~ Hugo Wolf hears it in Vienna and attacks Bülow for a 'Beethoven massacre' ~ Daniela marries Henry Thode in Bayreuth ~ Bülow takes up a new position as director of the Hamburg

Subscription Concerts ~ a description of the city's 'Convent Garden' concert hall ~ begins to feature Brahms's music in Hamburg, its 'most illustrious musical son' ~ Bülow is invited by Bernhard Pollini to take on an ambitious series of thirty operas in the Stadttheater ~ a landmark production of *Carmen* ~ Weingartner's criticisms of Bülow's conducting; his crusades against Bülow and their origins considered ~ Bülow's clandestine love affair with Cécile Gorrisson-Mutzenbecher ~ he terminates the relationship at the request of Marie von Bülow ~ Bülow is invited to take over the ailing Berlin Philharmonic Orchestra.

The Berlin Philharmonic, 1887–1892: I: The Eagle's Wings

Bülow tells his manager, Hermann Wolff, 'I can only justify my existence [in Berlin] by introducing reforms' ~ first concert in the Philharmonie (October 21, 1887) arouses enthusiasm ~ his preoccupation with programme-building ~ emphasis on the German classics ~ world-famous soloists appear with him on the platform ~ the Paderewski saga ~ the lights go out while Teresa Carreño plays the Tchaikovsky Concerto ~ the old Philharmonie and its history ~ Bülow's conducting style ~ the young Bruno Walter witnesses his first Bülow concert and decides to become a conductor ~ Nikisch and Furtwängler compared with Bülow ~ Max Kalbeck and Felix Weingartner among Bülow's severest critics ~ the special relationship between Bülow and Richard Strauss ~ Bülow introduces some of Strauss's orchestral works to Berlin, including *Macbeth, Aus Italien,* and *Don Juan* ~ he rehearses *Death and Transfiguration* ~ Bülow creates an endowment fund for the Berlin Philharmonic ~ he opens his rehearsals to the general public ~ more Bülow anecdotes ~ Bülow conducts Beethoven's *Choral* Symphony twice in one evening, March 6, 1889.

Return to America, 1889 and 1890

March 14, 1889: Bülow sets sail for America on the steamship SS *Saale* which docks in New York eight days later ~ he agrees to play exclusively on Knabe pianos ~ New York and its many marvels ~ Bülow and his colourful manager, Frederick Schwab ~ makes his first appearance as a conductor in America on March 27 in the Metropolitan Opera House ~ W. J. Henderson's description in the *New York Times* ~ a dispute over the Menuetto of Beethoven's Eighth Symphony ~ Henry Krehbiel of the *Tribune* weighs in ~ Bülow gives his four-part Beethoven Cycle in the Broadway Theatre for the first time in America, April 1 to 5, 1889 ~ plays the Fugue from the *Hammerklavier* Sonata as an encore ~ takes his Beethoven Cycle to Boston ('a modern Athens') ~ makes a cylinder recording for Thomas Edison of a Chopin Nocturne ~ describes Edison's invention as 'an acoustical marvel' ~ plays in Philadelphia before returning to New York for his final concert in the Metropolitan Opera House ~ a contretemps over a contrabassoon ~ records the *Eroica* Symphony for Edison: an account in *The Century Magazine* ~ departs America on May 5 ~ signs a contract with the impresario Leo Goldmark to return the following year.

March 12, 1890: crosses the Atlantic for a second time ~ a storm at sea, 'not without its dangers' ~ a blizzard in Boston ~ the opening concert in Boston's Music Hall is delayed ~ Bülow learns of the dismissal of his political hero Chancellor Bismarck: 'my patriotism has suffered badly' ~ gives piano recitals in New York,

Chicago, Cincinnati, Philadelphia, Pittsburgh, and Washington ~ conducts a farewell concert in the Metropolitan Opera House on May 10, with d'Albert as soloist in Brahms's B-flat major Piano Concerto ~ returns to Germany on the SS *Fulda*.

Bülow returns to the Philharmonic despite ill health ~ he seeks a variety of cures, including 'galvanic' treatments ~ he receives the Freedom of the City of Hamburg on February 22, 1892 ~ on March 28, 1892, he gives his last official concert with the Philharmonic ~ he delivers a postconcert speech in which he 're-dedicates' the *Eroica* Symphony to Bismarck, which causes a political uproar in Berlin and beyond ~ he meets Bismarck in Hamburg (April 1) and conveys his greetings to the former chancellor on the occasion of the latter's seventy-seventh birthday ~ the concert he conducts that evening is described by Gustav Mahler as 'supreme perfection' ~ the relationship between Mahler and Bülow considered ~ Bülow admires Mahler the conductor but fails to understand Mahler the composer ~ Bülow's disastrous introduction to Mahler's *Resurrection* Symphony ~ he writes a letter of atonement to Giuseppe Verdi, who graciously replies ~ resigns the conductorship of the Berlin Philharmonic after five years and fifty-one concerts ~ an emotional return to Italy where he is reunited with his daughter Blandine and meets his three grandchildren for the first time ~ his portrait is painted by Lenbach.
   The cholera epidemic in Hamburg and its impact on daily life ~ 17,000 citizens are infected and the wealthier inhabitants flee the city ~ the Bülows repair to the Danish resort of Skodsborg and then move on to Berlin ~ Bechstein Hall is opened on October 4, 1892, and Bülow gives the inaugural recital ~ it is his swansong as a pianist ~ he conducts the Berlin Philharmonic one last time in benefit of the orchestra's pension fund ~ too weak to give a speech, he plays instead a snatch of music from Mozart's *Zauberflöte:* 'Auf wiedersehen, until we meet again.'

Enters Berlin's Pankow Hospital for nervous diseases ~ undergoes experimental treatments ~ becomes a patient of Freud's colleague Dr. Wilhelm Fliess ~ criticizes the medical experts and discharges himself from Pankow ~ travels to Bavarian watering places in search of a cure ~ cholera breaks out again in Hamburg ~ a refuge in Aschaffenburg, in the Black Forest ~ Marie and Bülow set out for Cairo in search of a 'miracle-cure' ~ death of Bülow in Cairo, February 12, 1894 ~ an autopsy is performed the following day ~ the body is returned to Hamburg and lies in state at the city's St. Michaelis Church ~ the funeral service, in which Gustav Mahler participates ~ Mahler is inspired to complete his *Resurrection* Symphony ~ last farewells and cremation at Ohlsdorf ~ Bülow's second will ~ Marie von Bülow's final years in Berlin ~ she edits Bülow's letters.

Bülow's Family Tree

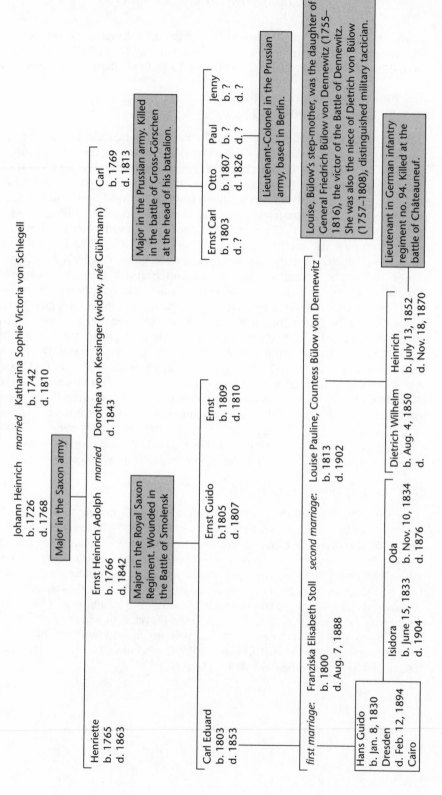

first marriage: Cosima Francesca Gaetana Liszt
b. Dec. 24, 1837
d. April 1, 1930

second marriage: Marie Amalie Katherina Josefa Schanzer
b. Feb. 12, 1857
d. Aug. 30, 1941

Hans von Bülow could trace his lineage back to the thirteenth century. According to the 'family book', compiled in 1858 by his father's cousin Paul von Bülow, a Lieutenant-Colonel in the Prussian army, the founder of the line was the knight Gottfried von Bülow, who was known to be alive in the year 1231. This more remote part of the family tree may be found in RHB.

Daniela Senta
b. Oct. 12, 1860
d. July 28, 1940

married

Henry Thode
b. Jan. 13, 1857
d. Nov. 10, 1920

Blandine Elisabeth
b. March 20, 1863
d. Dec. 4, 1941

married

Count Biagio Gravina
b. Dec. 5, 1850
d. Sept. 14, 1897

Manfredi
b. June 6, 1883
d. Sept. 19, 1932

Maria Cosima
b. Sept. 19, 1886
d. 1929

Gilberto
b. Oct. 17, 1890
d. Nov. 23, 1972

Guido
b. Feb. 1, 1896
d. Jan. 1931

first marriage

Klara Voigt
b. 1883
d. 1931

Hans Amadeus
b. Nov. 20, 1919
d. Dec. 16, 1950

second marriage

Dorothea Briggs
b. April 5, 1905
d. July 11, 1990

Christopher Manfredi
b. July 21, 1934
d. March, 1994

Michael Francis
b. May 5, 1936

Timothy James
b. 1942

PROLOGUE

From Alpha to Omega

From Alpha to Omega, he is Music personified.
—Franz Liszt[1]

In Art there are no trivial things.
—Bülow[2]

I

Hans von Bülow once arrived in a small German town to give a piano recital. He was informed by the somewhat nervous organizers that the local music critic could usually be counted on to give a good review, provided that the artist first agreed to take a modestly priced lesson from him. Bülow pondered this unusual situation for a moment, and then replied, 'He charges such low fees he could almost be described as incorruptible'. On another occasion Bülow got back to his London hotel after dark. As he was climbing the dimly lit staircase, he collided with a stranger hurrying in the opposite direction. 'Donkey!' exclaimed the man angrily. Bülow raised his hat politely, and replied, 'Hans von Bülow'![3]

Volumes could be filled with the wit and wisdom of Hans von Bülow, and the biography that follows teems with examples. His banter was woven into the very weft and weave of his complex personality. He had, moreover, the enviable gift of instant retort. A gentleman eager to be seen in his company once observed Bülow taking a morning stroll. He overtook the great musician, but was unsure of how to introduce himself. Finally he thought of something to say. 'I'll bet you don't remember who I am.' 'You just won your bet', replied Bülow, and walked on. Equally withering were Bülow's observations on the follies of everyday life. Having

---

1. WLLM, p. 397.
2. *Weimarer Zeitung*, issue of December 16, 1880.
3. These and other Bülow anecdotes have come down to us in a variety of forms and from a variety of sources. The main ones will be found in BBLW, pp. 276–91; and BA, pp. 210–16.

heard that an eligible young bachelor wanted to improve his social station through marriage, he observed, 'It will never work. The young lady wants to do the same thing'.

On orchestral players Bülow could be particularly hard, especially if he felt that they were incompetent. He once berated a trombone player who was failing to deliver the right kind of sound, and told him that his tone resembled roast beef gravy running through a sewer. In Italy, during a rehearsal of Beethoven's Ninth Symphony, Bülow found himself confronted by a timpanist who simply could not master the intricate rhythms of the Scherzo. There comes a moment in this dynamic movement when the timpanist must break through with force, hammering out the basic rhythm of the main theme. Bülow strove with might and main to pound the pattern into the poor man's head, but to no avail. Suddenly the solution occurred to him. *Timp-a-ni! Timp-a-ni! Timp-a-ni!* he kept yelling. A smile of comprehension slowly dawned on the player's face, as he caught the rhythm of the one word with which he was familiar, and in no time at all he was playing the passage in the correct manner.[4]

Bülow could also be severe on fledgling composers, particularly if he suspected that they wanted him to endorse their music. During a visit to Boston, in the spring of 1889, a local composer of modest talent sent Bülow one of his compositions and was bold enough to request an opinion. The piece was titled 'O Lord, hear my prayer!' Bülow glanced briefly at the manuscript and wrote beneath the title, 'He may, if you stop sinning like this!'[5]

A more famous case was that of Friedrich Nietzsche who, in the summer of 1872, was indiscreet enough to send Bülow an ambitious orchestral composition of his own—a 'Manfred Meditation'—for the conductor's critical appraisal. It was one of the philosopher's major blunders. He had witnessed Bülow conduct *Tristan* at the Munich Royal Opera House a few weeks earlier, and by way of thanking him for 'the loftiest artistic experience of my life' he had sent Bülow a copy of his newly published 'The Birth of Tragedy'. When he heard that Bülow was sufficiently impressed with the book to carry it with him everywhere, he was emboldened to

---

4. DMML, pp. 83–84. This concert took place in Milan, on December 4, 1870, as part of the city's Beethoven centennial festival.

5. *Boston Evening Transcript,* April 1, 1890, referring to Bülow's visit of the previous year.

send him his 'Manfred Meditation', doubtless hoping that the famous conductor would favour him with the usual assortment of platitudes that professionals are sometimes apt to offer distinguished amateurs. If Nietzsche thought to secure some fine phrases from Bülow, proffered by virtue of who he was, rather than by virtue of what the music itself was worth, he was sadly mistaken. Bülow looked at the 'Manfred Meditation' and knew that he must do his duty. He told Nietzsche that his score was 'the most unedifying, the most anti-musical thing that I have come across for a long time in the way of notes put on paper.' Several times, Bülow went on, he had to ask himself if it were not some awful joke. Having inserted the blade, Bülow now twisted the hilt and used Nietzsche's own philosophical precepts against him. 'Of the Apollonian element I have not been able to discover the smallest trace; and as for the Dionysian, I must say frankly that I have been reminded less of this than of the "day after" a bacchanal.' In brief, Nietzsche's score had produced in Bülow a hangover.[6]

Schadenfreude, too, was never far from the surface, for like most of us Bülow found occasional joy in the misfortune of others. Two of his orchestral players, named Schulz and Schmidt, were slowly driving him to distraction because of their evident inability to understand what he required of them. One morning he got to the rehearsal only to be met with the sad news that Schmidt had died during the night. 'And Schulz?' he inquired.

It would demean Bülow to be remembered by such anecdotes alone. He strode across the world of nineteenth-century music like a colossus. Bülow was music's great reformer. He set out to make a difference. His career, as we shall see, was epoch making, and it unfolded in at least six directions simultaneously. He was a renowned concert pianist; a virtuoso orchestral conductor; a respected (and sometimes feared) teacher; an influential editor of works by Bach, Mendelssohn, Chopin, and above all of Beethoven, in the performance of whose music he had no rival; a scourge as a music critic, whose articles resembled the spraying of antiseptic on bacteria; and last, he was a composer whose music, while it is hardly played today, deserves a better fate than benign neglect. The tales with which his life has become encumbered can easily divert attention from his real achievements. When Bülow's second wife, the Meiningen actress Marie Schanzer, was invited to provide some recollections about her late husband for the influential journal *Die Musik,*[7] some sixteen years after his death, she at first declined, and for rather similar reasons. She knew what the world wanted to read, and instinctively realized that Bülow

---

6. Bülow's devastating critique may be consulted in full in BB, vol. 4, pp. 552–554.
7. Issue of January 1910/11, Heft 7, pp. 210–212.

the jester and provocateur, however entertaining these aspects of his personality might be to the general reader, must not obscure a musical legacy that was possibly unique.

II

Hans von Bülow's stature first impressed itself upon me while I was writing my three-volume biography of Franz Liszt. There, of course, he inevitably played a supporting role, first as Liszt's most gifted piano pupil and later as his son-in-law, the husband of Liszt's daughter Cosima. Bülow's life touched on Liszt's at a hundred different points, and it is hardly possible to tell the one story without reference to the other. Nonetheless, Bülow must needs remain on the sidelines as far as the story of Liszt's life is concerned. In the standard biographies of Richard Wagner his position is marginalized still further. Bülow dutifully enters Wagner's life just in time to help propel the composer onto the international stage by conducting unforgettable world premiers in Munich of *Tristan* (1865) and *Die Meistersinger* (1868). Meanwhile, as the whole world knows and is weary of being reminded, Wagner seduces Cosima, impregnates her with three of his children while she is still Bülow's wife, and encourages her to leave hearth and home to join him in Switzerland. Bülow then obligingly disappears from view, his mission accomplished. Yet this most musical of musicians went on to enjoy a remarkable career, quite independent of those of Liszt and Wagner, from both of whom he broke free.

It has been well said that we burn a page of history even as we read it. To Hans von Bülow that observation applies with peculiar force. So much that was once known and admired about him has been forgotten, his narrative consigned to the ashes of the past. Until now there has never been a full-scale biography of Bülow in English. The present book not only fills the void, but presents much that is new.

If we had to find a single phrase to sum up Bülow's exceptional career it would surely be 'The pursuit of excellence'. All his joys and all his sorrows flowed from this primary goal. Excellence achieved was a day of rejoicing. Excellence denied was a day of sorrow and even of retribution, both for himself and for others. He knew that in order to better the future he must disturb the present. That disturbance forms one of the more graphic aspects of his story.

We remarked that Bülow's career unfolded in several directions simultaneously. Before turning to the main narrative it would be helpful to review them here.

III

Bülow came to be regarded as the greatest classical pianist of his time, renowned for his fidelity to the score. His creed was never in doubt. The role of the performer was to be the servant of the composer, not his master. Today such a view is commonplace, but it was not commonplace in Bülow's time. Bach and Beethoven dominated his repertoire, but he also played a lot of music by Chopin, Schumann, Mendelssohn, Liszt, and in later years much Brahms.[8] When Bülow confronted a musical masterpiece he believed that he was in the presence of greatness. And he expected his listeners to share his sense of reverence. When they did not, he chastised them. Like the prophets of old, the interpreter was a chosen one, there to be ushered into the presence of God in order to take back the Word to the people. Nor is the biblical analogy inappropriate, for Bülow himself was always making them. His aphorism 'In the beginning was rhythm' is an obvious modification of the opening verse of the book of Genesis. He once described Bach's 48 Preludes and Fugues as the Old Testament of music, and Beethoven's 32 Piano Sonatas as the New. To which observation he added, 'We must believe in both'.[9] And in an interview that he gave to *The Etude,* he observed, 'I believe in Bach the father, Beethoven the son, and in Brahms the holy ghost of music'.[10] The abandon and excess that sometimes characterized the playing of his great rival Anton Rubinstein, with its self-indulgent departures from the text, was for him a form of blasphemy—as if the Bible itself was being used to justify a personal opinion. He believed that no performance could be as perfect as the work it interpreted. For the performer, Parnassus must always be just beyond reach.

The only two pianists in the second half of the nineteenth century with whom Bülow could be compared were Carl Tausig and Anton Rubinstein. (Liszt had retired from the concert platform in 1847, at the height of his powers.) Tausig died young, and Bülow's fine obituary notice of the Polish virtuoso testifies to the high regard in which he held him. A year before Tausig's demise, in fact, Bülow heard him perform privately in Berlin and was stunned. He confided to his Italian pupil Giuseppe Buonamici, 'Tausig is surely the greatest pianist in the world—he has attained the most ideal perfection that I ever imagined'.[11] Rubinstein falls into a different category. He was seen as Bülow's great contender, his nemesis even, and comparisons were constantly being made between them. Their performing styles, to say nothing of their platform personalities, were quite dissimilar. Rubinstein ambled onto the platform like a great bear. Bülow appeared on stage rapidly, 'like someone afraid that the bank will close before he can make his deposit'.[12] Bülow complained that 'Rubinstein

8. The full extent of Bülow's vast repertoire, both as a pianist and as a conductor, may be seen in HMIB, pp. 458–515.

9. BAS (part 2), p. 273.

10. Issue of May 1889, p. 73.

11. BC, unpublished letter dated June 26, 1870.

12. *Chicago Times,* February 6, 1876.

Bülow at the piano. A silhouette by Hans Schliessmann.

can make any number of errors during a performance and nobody is disturbed. If I make a single mistake, it will be noticed immediately by everyone in the audience, and the effect will be spoiled'.[13] The observation was well founded. Rubinstein was described during his celebrated tour of America as a storm-king at the piano, riding the instrument as he would a war-charger. His errors in technique were concealed beneath a thunder of sound, or else atoned for by the superb eloquence of his expression. Bülow was exactly the opposite—a precise, careful, uncompromising, studious technician. He was the Swiss watchmaker of pianists. The jewelled perfection of his playing was a thing to behold. Everything was so tightly sprung that he could not afford to make an error.[14]

But the comparison runs deeper than that. Rubinstein and Bülow represented the twin archetypes of piano playing which remain with us today. They are best described as the 'Dionysian' and the 'Apollonian'.[15]

13. MMML, p. 238.

14. Sir Alexander Mackenzie, who attended Bülow's recitals in Scotland, made a similar distinction in his memoirs. 'Rubinstein could at times behave like a whirlwind; Bülow impressed by a brilliant technique, but even more by the surgeon-like skill with which he laid bare the composer's intentions . . .' MMN, p. 88.

15. Dionysius and Apollo, the gods of fertility and intellectual organization respectively, have often been invoked to describe the opposite sides of human nature. The one represents through his Bacchanalian revels the passionate side of humanity; the other represents the supreme authority in matters of intellectual organization, his notable interests being archery, medicine—and music.

It was said that unless one had heard Rubinstein, one could not appreciate Bülow; that unless one had heard Bülow, one could not esteem Rubinstein. The one served as a foil for the other. With Rubinstein the text was the starting point. It served as an entrance into a world of imagination, in which the performance was borne aloft on the wings of fantasy, constrained only by the mood of the moment and the taste of the player. The electricity generated by Rubinstein's recitals was partly due to the unexpected, which lay in wait for the audience (and possibly for Rubinstein, too) at every touch and turn.

For Bülow the unexpected was anathema. Such was his respect for the composer that his goal was to reproduce the text down to the smallest detail. He would have agreed with Stravinsky that to violate the letter was to violate the spirit. He once said, 'Learn to read the score of a Beethoven symphony *accurately* first, and you will have found its interpretation'.[16] Bülow's idea of perfection was to play with such clarity that if the performance were to be taken down from dictation the result would conform in every respect to the printed score. Since such an ideal is beyond the reach of most mortals, the pursuit of perfection for Bülow consisted in reducing the distance, however short, that separated sight from sound. And he would have argued that his was by far the harder task, as indeed it was. By the very nature of the difficulty, in fact, Bülow knew that he could never rest content.

Eduard Dannreuther used the words 'passionate intellectuality' to describe Bülow's playing, and they have often been quoted. Others found it cold and devoid of imagination. Clara Schumann called it 'wearisome', disliking Bülow's analytical approach to music that she herself played with distinction. During his fabled American tour of 1875–1876 the critic of *The Music Trade Review* longed for a false note, such as Rubinstein and even Liszt were known to strike. But Bülow rarely obliged his audience with such a symptom of vulnerability. Seated at the piano his posture was restrained. He was memorably described by Richard Strauss, his acolyte and admirer, as 'marble from the wrists up'. Bülow had small hands, and could hardly stretch beyond an octave—providing yet another instructive example to pianists that nimbleness and dexterity may yet compensate for a small grasp.[17]

Bülow's ability to sight-read was also something to behold. He was completely at home when confronting a full orchestral score, replete with its transposing instruments and a medley of clefs spread across twenty staves or more. Wagner was amazed when he witnessed Bülow play *prima*

---

16. SRR, p. 121.
17. The casts of Bülow's hands, made during his lifetime, are preserved in the Bülow archives of the Deutsche Staatsbibliothek. See the photograph reproduced on p. 339.

vista from the pencil sketches of the composer's still-unpublished opera *Siegfried*. He kept peering over Bülow's shoulder, while Bülow, his eyes glued to the page, kept exclaiming 'Colossal!' 'Unique!' 'Fit for the next century!'[18]

Bülow was one of the first pianists to devote an entire recital to one composer—Bach, Chopin, and above all Beethoven, whose last five sonatas were regularly presented by him during a single evening. Even more striking was the great Beethoven Cycle that he began to present in public around 1886, in which he played all the important sonatas and sets of variations, from the A major Sonata, op. 2, no. 2, right through to the *Diabelli* Variations, across four consecutive evenings. And everything was performed from memory, an important point to which we propose to return. Largely forgotten today is that Bülow was the first pianist to devote an entire recital to the music of Brahms. Such a proposal was at first considered dubious, even by Brahms, but Bülow overcame the opposition and achieved a conspicuous success. Bülow was the thinking man's pianist and he came to prominence at a time when the concert platform stood in danger of being taken over by a generation of 'light entertainers'— Leopold de Meyer, Louis Gottschalk, and (later) Vladimir de Pachmann among them—who laced their programmes with paraphrases of popular operas and potpourris of favourite melodies. With this sort of programme the mature Bülow would have nothing to do. The care that he took in creating his recitals and orchestral concerts, especially in his later years, is still a model that can be followed with profit today. He understood that a good programme, like a good piece of music, is greater than the sum of its parts, that each piece could and should throw light on the others. In an age when many programmes lasted for three hours or more, and consisted in the main of a smorgasbord of pieces put together on a whim, Bülow's concerts became memorable for their musical logic. The individual pieces were like members of one family, bound together by biography, history, genre, and sometimes by their key-schemes—golden threads that ran from one composition to the next.

Bülow's piano technique was obtained and kept up at great physical expense. It was nothing for him to practise for five or six hours a day while preparing for a concert tour. Bernard Boekelmann expressed it well when he pointed out that 'at the piano Bülow was never free . . . his mental organization was inflexible . . . he was rigid in mind and body'.[19] This

---

18. That was in August 1857, when Bülow and Cosima visited Wagner in Zurich. For Wagner's account of the visit see WML, p. 669; also MCW(2), p. 29.

19. BRAB, p. 502. Boekelmann, an admirer of Bülow, was a Dutch pianist and teacher who is chiefly remembered for his unique editions of Bach's 48 Preludes and Fugues and the Two-Part Inventions, in which he prints the different voices in contrasting colours, to indicate the part-writing, an idea worthy of Bülow himself.

stood in such marked contrast to the fire, dash, and freedom of his conducting that it led many to say that the orchestra, not the piano, was his natural instrument.

IV

Bülow was, in fact, the first virtuoso conductor. It was his work with the Meiningen Court Orchestra, in the 1880s, that allowed him to claim this title. The story of how he took a small forty-eight-piece orchestra, and fashioned it in his own image, has entered the history books. That part of his narrative, at least, has not turned to ashes. At Meiningen, Bülow the conductor emerged as an extension of Bülow the pianist. After rigorously rehearsing the orchestra on a daily basis for three months, Bülow had the ensemble play all nine Beethoven symphonies from memory. He then took the orchestra on tour. The capital cities of Berlin and Vienna had never witnessed such discipline in an orchestra, and it made them look to their laurels. When the entire string section played Bülow's orchestral arrangement of Beethoven's Grosse Fuge from memory, standing up, audiences were astonished. But that was before ten of the violins returned to the stage and played Bach's unaccompanied Chaconne from memory, in unison. Bülow would doubtless have justified such radical demands by observing that he was not asking the players to accept anything that he himself was unwilling to do.[20]

Some of the best descriptions of Bülow at rehearsal we owe to Richard Strauss, who became Bülow's assistant conductor in Meiningen in 1884. 'The gracefulness with which he handled the baton', wrote Strauss, 'the charming manner in which he used to conduct his rehearsals—instruction frequently taking the form of a witty epigram—are unforgettable; when he suddenly turned away from the rostrum and put a question to the pupil reading the score, the latter had to answer quickly if he were not to be taunted with a sarcastic remark by the master in front of the assembled orchestra'.[21]

Nor was Strauss alone in his admiration of Bülow. Conductors as diverse as Bruno Walter, Gustav Mahler, and Walter Damrosch witnessed the passion and fire he could draw from an orchestra, and they wrote about it. So did other musicians, including composers Alexander Mackenzie, Charles Villiers Stanford, and above all Tchaikovsky—whose bold

---

20. Bülow's reforms often caught the attention of the press. A typical article in the *Boston Musical Herald* informed its readers that 'Hans von Bülow is continually making innovations on the customs of conductors. Not satisfied with requiring members of the orchestra perfectly to memorize their parts throughout, he is now training them so to observe marks of tempo and expression as to be able to play satisfactorily without the guidance of the conductor's baton.' Issue of January 1885, p. 6.

21. SRR, pp. 120–121.

letter in support of Bülow deserves to be better known.[22] Felix Weingartner was deeply impressed when he first witnessed Bülow conducting the
Meiningen Orchestra in Eisenach. Later he became one of Bülow's severest critics, accusing him of self-aggrandizement and of having done damage by creating 'a lot of little Bülows', those aspiring conductors who
aped the choreography of their hero while not possessing a sliver of his
talent. 'Sensation-mongering in music began with Bülow', Weingartner
wrote caustically in his widely read treatise *On Conducting*.[23] These remarks, as we now know, were written in a spirit of revenge. They were
calculated to damage Bülow, and we shall eventually come to understand
that they arose from autobiographical considerations.[24]

We may safely leave the last word with Liszt's pupil Frederic Lamond,
who had also studied with Bülow and was intimately acquainted with
the European scene from the 1880s up to World War II. 'He was the greatest conductor who ever lived—not even Toscanini approaching him',
Lamond wrote. 'I have seen and heard them all. No one, Nikisch, Richter,
Mahler, Weingartner, could compare with him in true warmth of expression, which is the soul and substance of all art'.[25]

Bülow's appointment as artistic director of the recently formed Berlin
Philharmonic Orchestra, in 1887, garnered international acclaim both
for him and for the city. Within five years he raised what was at that time
a modest group of players in search of leadership to an ensemble of world
stature. There were many ear-witnesses to what Bülow accomplished in
Berlin, and we have devoted substantial portions of our narrative to those
golden years. His Berlin audiences packed the old Philharmonie to capacity, for they understood that they were witnessing history. Bülow's
public rehearsals, and his postconcert speeches, which were filled with
the wittiest observations, sent everyone home in anticipation of the next
concert. On the podium Bülow was a figure of enormous authority,
bouncing with energy. His arm gestures were wide, and his baton described the most eloquent arcs, bringing the entire ensemble into its
orbit. He was described as having 'a singing baton'. His body would sway
back and forth as he attempted to capture that most elusive quality called
tempo rubato (elusive, that is, to orchestras). Attending to the shape of
every phrase, Bülow would dart here and there, piercing the players with

22. The Paris *Figaro*, issue of January 13, 1893. See also TLF, p. 529.

23. WMC, pp. 22–23; and WBR, p. 163.

24. Weingartner's observations had an unfortunate influence on both David Ewen (EMB)
and Gunther Schuller (SCC), in their respective books on conductors and conducting. Both
authors seem unaware that Weingartner held two irreconcilable opinions about Bülow, one
before January 1887 and one afterwards. The significance of that date, which represented a
dramatic turning point in the personal relationship between Weingartner and Bülow, is dealt
with at length on pp. 364–66.

25. LM, p. 43.

his gaze and drawing from them music of deep intensity. His mental equipment for a conductor was complete. His ear was infallible, as was his memory, which had no boundary line.

Bülow's memory. All roads lead to this topic, and it would be negligent not to touch on it here. It was a gift of nature and had been his from childhood. He had the ability to imprint on his memory whole pages of a musical score that he had seen but once, and reproduce them at the piano. This has always been a rare possession, and there is probably no one in the profession of music today who can lay claim to it, which is why it provokes disbelief. Even Toscanini's well-known ability to recall orchestral scores in detail pales by comparison. Among the many anecdotes that have come down to us, one that can do duty for the others was recorded by Bülow's admirer, the Irish composer Charles Villiers Stanford.

During a concert tour of Britain, Stanford tells us, Bülow encountered the Irish composer George Osborne opposite Lamborn Cock's old music shop in Bond Street, London. Bülow remarked that he was about to leave for Brighton where he was to play a recital that same evening. 'Of course, you are going to play something of Sterndale Bennett's?' remarked Osborne. 'Why?' queried Bülow. 'Because it is his birthday', retorted Osborne. 'I don't know anything of Bennett's,' observed Bülow, 'tell me something'. 'We are at his publisher's door', replied Osborne. 'Come in and choose for yourself'. After rummaging through various items, Bülow selected Bennett's *Three Musical Sketches,* op. 10: 'The Lake', 'The Mill Stream', and 'The Fountain'. He then left the shop, went to the railway station, and learnt them on the train journey from London to Brighton. That same evening he played them from memory.[26]

Whatever the score, and whatever its complexity, Bülow rarely had a note of music in front of him, not merely at the concerts but more impressively at the rehearsals as well. He usually knew better than the players what was on the printed page before them, and sometimes better than the composer too. He was once rehearsing an orchestral piece of Liszt, in Liszt's presence, when Liszt stopped him with the observation that a certain note should have been played *piano*. 'No', replied Bülow, 'it is

---

26. SPD, pp. 263–264. Because this account of Bülow's memory, as told by Osborne, struck Stanford as being so extraordinary, he searched for someone who had actually witnessed Bülow walk onto the platform in Brighton that evening without any printed notes before him, as opposed to someone who had merely seen Bülow buying the scores in a London music shop earlier in the day. He found a witness whom he identified as 'a musician, the late Dr. Sawyer', a resident of Brighton who had attended the concert and confirmed that Bülow had played everything from memory. The most likely time for this concert to have taken place would have been towards the end of April 1873, during Bülow's first visit to England. Sterndale Bennett's birthday fell on April 13, more than a week before Bulow arrived in the country, so Osborne's own memory of the incident was not entirely reliable. Stanford was wise to subject the matter to more careful scrutiny.

sforzando'. Liszt suggested that Bülow should look at the score, which was duly produced. It turned out that Bülow was right. The orchestra began to applaud and in all the excitement one of the brass players lost his place, creating further uncertainty. 'Look for a B-flat in your part' said Bülow, who had once more thrown the score aside. 'Five measures further on I wish to begin'.[27]

One thing remains to be said, for it is the bane of orchestras everywhere. Few are the players who actually enjoy their work, who draw from it that spiritual satisfaction that lured them to music in the first place. From childhood they labour to conquer the technical difficulties posed by their instruments, and eventually learn to express their artistic selves through them, only to discover that the thing they have come to treasure most—their musical individuality—is the one thing not required of an orchestral player. This surrender of self, this loss of musical identity for the good of the group, is a trauma from which the player may never recover. Whatever individual impulses remain are quickly suppressed by the conductor, as he strives to impose his own view of the music on everybody else. And this view changes as each visiting conductor does his best to obliterate the interpretations left by his predecessors. In such a depressing context, the player becomes part of an ever-changing soundscape, so to say, which is never quite his own, and which may even have a compulsory visual component attached to it—with all the strings bowing together, and all the winds breathing together, a picture-perfect image redolent of soldiers on the parade ground.

By the same token, few are the conductors who are able to convince the player of the rightness of their view, and so inspire them that they draw the best from them. Conversion, not compulsion, seems to be the key. One thinks of Furtwängler and of Beecham, of Bruno Walter and of Leopold Stokowski, but the list is painfully short. To this roll call we must add the name of Bülow, whose players in the Meiningen and Berlin Philharmonic orchestras came to identify so completely with his world of sound that they willingly played as one. Of course there were conflicts, as the pages that follow amply demonstrate. But the rank and file were won over. It is sufficient for us to recall that when Bülow resigned from the Berlin Philharmonic, his players signed a petition urging him to stay, and referred to him as 'our great teacher'.

V

Teaching, in fact, was one of Bülow's lifelong activities, although he came to detest institutionalized instruction. When he was only twenty-five years old he was appointed head of the Piano Department of the Stern

27. BRAB, p. 502.

Conservatory of Music in Berlin (taking the place of the renowned pedagogue Theodor Kullak), a position he held for nine years. Later, at the
behest of King Ludwig II of Bavaria, and in collaboration with Richard
Wagner, Bülow took charge of the fledgling Royal Music School in Munich, and helped to draw up its first curriculum. It was to his summer
masterclasses at the Raff Conservatory in Frankfurt, however, that an international cast of pupils flocked. They included Frederic Lamond, Vianna
da Motta, Giuseppe Buonamici, Laura Kahrer, and Theodor Pfeiffer, all of
whom left vivid accounts of those days. Bülow, they all agreed, was a
teacher to be revered, but also feared.

Unlike Liszt, who cast a benevolent ray of light on all his pupils, however poorly they played, Bülow took it to be his mission to drive the worst
of them out of the profession. The concert hall of the Raff Conservatory
was filled with young hopefuls each summer. Bülow was fond of making
little speeches from the platform, filled with paradox and humour. 'Piano
playing is very difficult', he warned his audience. 'First we have to learn
to make all the fingers equal. Then later, in playing music with several
independent voices, we have to learn to make them unequal again. That
being so, it seems best not to practice the piano at all—and that is the advice I give to many'.[28] Because he could not abide incompetence, those
pupils who played badly through sheer nervousness, or were simply not
prepared, had reason to fear his sarcasm. He once listened to a young lady
and, with the whole class looking on, turned to her with a deep bow and
the caustic comment, 'I congratulate you, Mademoiselle, upon playing
the easiest possible passages with the greatest possible difficulty'. To another pupil, whose Beethoven playing lacked contrast, he remarked drily,
'If you play the second bar exactly like the first, the public will say, "Good
God, he is practicing!"'[29]

VI

Closely linked to Bülow's activity as a pedagogue was his work as an editor. He understood that a deep study of a musical text is as important for
the performer as the study of fingerprints is for the detective. The printed
page was like the bars of a prison behind which the composer held his
muse captive. Those bars had to be removed. His editions of Bach, Mendelssohn, Chopin, and above all of Beethoven show the great detective
at work. Every page of his edition of the Beethoven sonatas, for example,
contains footnotes and commentaries on the text that are both exhaustive and exhausting. And they have but one purpose: to help the player
release the ghost that the composer has imprisoned inside the machine.

28. PSB, p. 14.
29. ZMB, p. 37.

Bülow's editions do not meet the requirements of modern scholarship. They betray their time and place, as for that matter do the editions of Liszt, Tausig, Klindworth, Busoni, Schnabel, and countless others who died before the Age of the Urtext was ushered in. Nor should we forget that they are performing rather than scholarly editions. Their chief fascination for us is that they illuminate Bülow's own interpretations. If they were to be published today, some enterprising publisher would doubtless suggest that they be accompanied by a CD, in which Bülow himself would give some practical illustrations at the keyboard. Because recordings were unavailable to him, his detailed verbal injunctions were the only substitute.

Bülow was also a critic who did not hesitate to dip his pen in vitriol in defence of things he thought worthwhile. His early articles in the Leipzig *Signale* often created mayhem. One or two of them—his fulminations against the soprano Henriette Sontag, for example, and his attacks against the British musical establishment—brought him notoriety, and even resulted in an occasional death threat. But they all served the same purpose. They reminded the public that 'in Art there are no trivial things'.

VII

Finally, what of Bülow the composer? In a brief note on Bülow's compositions, Frederick Niecks delivered an opinion from which posterity has scarcely wavered. 'So supremely eminent as an interpreter, both as a pianist and as a conductor, Bülow was sterile as a composer'.[30] That was a harsh judgement. There are more compositions than are generally supposed, although it is true that they are hardly ever played today. During Bülow's lifetime his Orchestral Fantasy *Nirwana,* and his incidental music to *Julius Caesar* were frequently to be heard. And works for solo piano, songs, chamber music, and choral music abound in his catalogue of works. His suite of piano pieces called *Il Carnevale di Milano,* op. 21, his Ballade for Piano, op. 11, and his *Mazurka-Fantasie,* op. 13 (dedicated to Cosima), are worth reviving. (A complete list of Bülow's compositions will be found in Appendix II to the present volume.) When Bülow himself was asked why he so rarely featured his own music in his programmes, he replied with uncharacteristic modesty that 'others have written much better things than mine'. Bülow was not the first musician to sacrifice his career as a composer in order to concentrate on promoting the works of others, but he may have been the most prominent. He saw his situation with clarity when he proposed the following device, which shows his name being supported by those of his three great contemporaries— Berlioz, Liszt, and Wagner—whose music he spent a lifetime promoting at the expense of his own.

30. NPM, p. 481.

B	Ü	L	O	W
e		i		a
r		s		g
l		z		n
i		t		e
o				r
z				

VIII

As for Bülow the man, he was complex, difficult, always living on a knife-edge, and intolerant of much that he observed around him in humanity at large. He had no small talk. Normal conversation for Bülow took the form of debate. Disputation was the only way to arrive at a satisfactory conclusion. And he would continue an argument for as long as it took, finally wearing down his interlocutor. He would have made a brilliant lawyer, a profession for which he was at first intended but soon abandoned. His sharp intelligence was placed instead in the service of music, a discipline which he spent a lifetime attempting to transform, wishing to rid it of incompetents and ne'er-do-wells wherever he found them. Bülow might well have said of himself, what the French statesman Lazare Carnot once said of Talleyrand, 'If he despised men so much, this is because he had studied himself so deeply'.

Bülow had a hasty tongue, and rarely bothered to varnish his remarks; he therefore made enemies who retaliated. Constance Bache, the English translator of some of his early letters, was not wrong to describe him as the 'best abused' musician of his time—with the exception of Wagner.[31] He was often asked to write his memoirs, but usually turned down the request with such ripostes as 'life is too short for reflection', or 'it is better to use such time for fresh work'.[32]

IX

Any discussion of Bülow the man raises a matter that cannot be allowed to go by default. It is impossible to read his letters without observing the vein of anti-Semitism that runs through them.

His correspondence is laced with mindless references to 'Jew-ridden Berlin', a 'Jewish conspiracy', and even distasteful mention of a 'Jew's greasy face' (this last being an observation about his one-time agent Julius Steinitz, who, in the 1870s, after their common expenses had been met, was extracting a usurious 25 percent commission from what remained). We call such language 'mindless' because in nineteenth-century Germany

31. BEC, p. ix.
32. BB, vol. 1, p. vi.

comments of this kind were part of the *lingua franca,* picked up and thrown about with abandon by the population at large.

There can be no reasonable reply to the observation that it is not the job of a modern biographer to thrust his head through the canvas of history and give whomever he finds back there a lesson in political correctness. It has been well said that the past is a foreign country: they do things differently there. This thorny topic has in any case been dealt with in commendable detail by Bülow's most recent German biographer Frithjof Haas, and it would be a pity to waste another word on it.[33] We are nonetheless obliged to raise a fundamental question: was Bülow simply reflecting the temper of the times or helping to create it? To put the matter bluntly, was he the ventriloquist or the dummy? Like hundreds of thousands of Europeans, and not just Germans, Bülow was a thoughtless mouthpiece for individuals with dangerous ideas.

A very good example of this was his readiness to sign the petition against the Jews drawn up by the anti-Semitic agitator Dr. Bernhard Förster (1843–1889), whose other claim to fame was that he was Nietzsche's brother-in-law. Förster was a schoolteacher and author. In 1880 he drew up a petition against the Jews in Germany, addressed to Chancellor Bismarck, which quickly acquired 250,000 signatures. It was titled 'Petition in der Judenfrage, an Fürst Bismarck', and was published in the *Berliner Bewegung.* German society, it warned, was being undermined by wave upon wave of Jewish immigrants who were crossing the German borders without restriction from Eastern Europe, and changing the fabric of the nation. Bülow signed it, along with all the others, but regretted having done so when he discovered that Wagner had declined Förster's request. In Cosima Wagner's Diary we learn: '[Wagner] reads aloud the ridiculously servile phrases and the dubiously expressed concern, "And I am supposed to sign that!" he exclaims'.[34] The best that can be said for Bülow's position in this sorry affair is that he tried to have his signature withdrawn, to no avail. Bismarck, incidentally, would have nothing to do with the petition.

Not long after signing Förster's appeal, Bülow went to Vienna and was asked about his action by his Jewish colleague, the publisher and concert promoter Albert Gutmann, who used to arrange occasional concerts for him in the imperial capital. Gutmann noticed that Bülow had included a group of Mendelssohn's 'Songs without Words' in one of his recitals, and challenged him: 'I heard that you signed the anti-Semitic petition in

33. HHB, pp. 312–322.
34. WT, vol. 2, p. 506.

Berlin. How come that with such a disposition you put Mendelssohn into your programme?' 'Very simple!' Bülow replied. 'Because Mendelssohn was a Jew—like Christ!'[35]

Bülow, in fact, was a perfect example of the great paradox that so often entangles individuals in possession of those supreme artistic and intellectual gifts that were his. While condemning Jews as a group, he enjoyed warm and vital friendships with individual Jewish intellectuals and artists, friendships in which one finds no trace of the abrasive utterances he reserved for Jews in general. The two contemporary pianists he most admired—Carl Tausig and Anton Rubinstein—were both Jews. Among conductors, the one for whom he reserved the greatest praise was Gustav Mahler. Above all violinists he esteemed Joachim, and was proud to share the concert platform with him. He was the great defender of Felix Mendelssohn, whom he had revered from his youth. He also appointed Jewish musicians to the Hamburg and Berlin Philharmonic orchestras, basing such appointments on merit. For the last fifteen years of his life he entrusted every aspect of his public career to Hermann Wolff, his Berlin-based Jewish agent, who became far more than a business colleague, but a family friend as well. In politics, one of his heroes was the left-wing socialist Ferdinand Lassalle, 'the Jew from Breslau', and a follower of Karl Marx. It was for Lassalle's 'German Workers Party' that Bülow composed a rousing anthem, to be sung at their rallies. And this raises a prospect of a somewhat different kind. If Bülow had been alive in Hitler's time, he would almost certainly have been sent to the gas chambers for his support of Lassalle and for his radical left-wing political views.

Were Bülow to revisit us today, he would surely marvel at the distance we have managed to place between ourselves and the prejudices of his time, and we suspect that he might want to argue with us about it. He would doubtless point out that long after his own demise, such luminaries as Franklin D. Roosevelt, Charles Lindbergh, H. L. Mencken, Henry Ford, Ezra Pound, and Mark Twain[36]—the list is long—were uttering infractions far worse than the ones for which Bülow himself is properly brought before the bar of history, and he would be right to insist that they join him there, as indeed they have.

---

35. GAW, p. 16. Bülow was referring to the fact that Mendelssohn's father, Abraham Mendelssohn, had brought up his family of four children as Christians. They were baptised and received into the Protestant Church in 1816, the name 'Bartholdy' being affixed to their own, at the time of their conversion.

36. Mark Twain's essay 'Concerning the Jews' is widely interpreted as an anti-Semitic document, although he himself always denied it. It first appeared in *Harper's Monthly Magazine,* September 1899.

X

We do well to recall that for much of his life Bülow suffered from a variety of neurological symptoms which, while they did not succeed in diverting him from his chosen path, often resulted in friction with his fellow human beings, who usually had no idea of his physical tribulations. Yet there were times when to be in Bülow's company was to bask in the full nobility of a superior character. Toni Petersen, the daughter of the mayor of Hamburg, who knew Bülow well, put it best of all when she remarked ruefully, 'When one is friends with Bülow, one has wonderful moments but sorrowful years'.[37]

Descended from a distinguished military family in Germany, whose lineage can be traced back to the thirteenth century, personal discipline and the need to excel were instilled into Bülow from childhood. He spoke four modern languages—German, French, Italian, and English—and was well versed in the classics, writing both Greek and Latin. He was deeply read in the philosophy of Schopenhauer, whose pessimistic view of the world appealed to him. Optimism for Bülow was an impossibility, a preposterous principle on which to base one's life. 'Pessimism', he once observed, 'has made me more light-hearted, more philanthropic, more tolerant, more at ease, than that other absurd doctrine'.[38] He daily looked the world in the face and saw it for what it was: a ridiculous tragedy over which one has little control. For Bülow there was no promise of anything at the end of the difficult road that life had marked out for him. But, good Schopenhauerian that he was, he found redemption in one simple idea: it was not enough to have life, one must live it. And live it he did. Bülow packed so much activity into his relatively brief span of years, that there are times when the biographer can hardly keep pace with him. Nonetheless, the complex pleasures of his company make the journey well worthwhile.

---

37. S-WWW, p. 71.
38. BB, vol. 5, p. 75.

Bülow's Family Background

'All the Bülows are honourable'. From the Bülow
family coat of arms.

On the morning of August 17, 1812, Napoleon's Grande Armée paused
on its long march towards Moscow, and began a terrifying barrage of

artillery against the Russians defending the old city of Smolensk. The battle continued all day, and part of the next, and involved more than 110,000 soldiers. By nightfall the 'holy city', with its historic spires and golden domes, was on fire. Napoleon roused his exhausted equerry General Caulaincourt from his slumbers in order to admire the spectacle through his spy-glass. 'It's an eruption of Vesuvius!', exclaimed Napoleon. 'Is it not a fine sight?' 'It is horrible, sire', replied the general. 'Bah!' replied Napoleon. 'Remember, gentlemen, this adage of a Roman emperor: "the corpse of a dead enemy always smells good."'[1] At dawn the following day, as the first French scouts clambered over the shattered masonry and zig-zagged their way along rubble-strewn streets littered with dead bodies, it was the smell that many of them remembered. The carnage had been appalling. In the Battle of Smolensk, the French lost 9,000 men, the Russians 11,000.

Among the wounded German officers was Baron Ernst von Bülow, a major in the Royal Saxon regiment fighting in support of Napoleon. He was decorated for valour, and was bestowed with the Royal Saxon Order of Henry from his own commanders and the Imperial Order of the Legion of Honour from Napoleon. After the war he was pensioned off and lived in Dresden until his death in 1842. He was the grandfather of Hans von Bülow. Hans knew him well, and during his childhood he must often have listened enthralled as grandfather Ernst relived his military campaign under Napoleon. The Bülow family book describes Ernst as a man of 'punctuality and orderliness', qualities that remained with this professional soldier for life. 'The love for his princely house, the courteous behaviour of a nobleman towards the rest of mankind, and his goodness of heart, were recognized by all.'[2] Ernst had earlier married Dorothea von Kessinger, a widow, who brought to the marriage a castle at Eilenberg, which is where she gave birth to their three sons, only one of whom survived infancy. This was Eduard von Bülow, the father of Hans. He was born on December 17, 1803.

Destined by his soldier-father for a career in business, Eduard was put to work in various banking houses, but he found the experience so distasteful that he rebelled, and when he was only twenty-three he acquired a publishing business in which he invested money and still greater hopes. The venture failed and he enrolled at the University of Leipzig in order to study the classics. In 1828 he married Franziska Elisabeth Stoll, who was born in 1800, and took her back with him to live in Dresden. This marriage was an act of pure chivalry on Eduard's part. When he first met her, Franziska was trapped in an unhappy union to a Dresden banker named

1. CM, vol. 1, pp. 393–95.
2. BAB, p. 1.

Kastel. According to Du Moulin Eckart the twenty-five year old Eduard 'freed her from these unworthy bonds'—by methods that have not become part of the scholarly record.[3] We shall have more to say about Franziska presently.

In Dresden, Eduard pursued his preferred life of scholar, writer, and poet. The Bülow home became a meeting point for an important artistic and literary circle, which included Baron von Lüttichau (Intendent of Dresden's Royal Opera House) and his talented artist-wife Ida; Countess Pauline Bülow-Dennewitz and her daughter Louise; and Eduard's friend, the German romantic novelist Ludwig Tieck. Music played a conspicuous role on these occasions. Franziska was a good amateur pianist and she often took part in performances of chamber music with local players.

Eduard published a number of books that were well regarded in their day.[4] Perhaps his most colourful narrative was a biography devoted to his distant relative, the great military tactician Baron Heinrich Dietrich von Bülow (1757–1808), whose life reads like a novel, and ought one day to become the basis for one.[5] In his account of Heinrich's work Eduard wrote that 'given greater luck, Baron Heinrich might have earned the name of genius in his chosen profession of military theorist.'[6] Heinrich had joined the Prussian army in 1773 but resigned his commission in 1790 in order to travel to France, then in the turmoil of revolution, where he studied the battlefield tactics of the French and came to admire Napoleon. When he got back to Germany he devoted himself to his main work, 'Geist der neuern Kriegssystems' ('Spirit of the new system of warfare') (1799), which attracted attention. In 1805 he published two further books on battlefield tactics called 'Lehrfätze der Strategie' ('Practical rules of Strategy') and 'Neue Taktik der Neueren: wie sie sein sollte' ('Latest Tactics of the Innovator: how they should be'). Based on precise mathematical principles, Heinrich's theories attempted to transform warfare into an exact science. In these texts he laid down the rules of battle as if he were explaining a game of cricket, and illustrated his expositions with complex diagrams resembling a field of play, with shells taking the place of cricket-balls. All one had to do was to follow the rules of geometry and the war would be won. The trouble with such a 'choreography of a battlefield', as Heinrich's

3. MHB, pp. 19–20.
4. Among them are: 'Simplicissimus' (1836); 'Ein Fürstenspiegel' (1849); 'Der arme Mann von Tockenburg' (1852); and the first German translation of Alessandro Manzoni's patriotic novel 'I promessi sposi'.
5. The book is subtitled 'Military accounts and various writings of Heinrich Dietrich von Bülow, with a critical introduction by Eduard von Bülow and Wilhelm Rüstow' (1853). Eduard provided the biographical material, while Rüstow supplied the statistics. Eduard's greatest work remained unfinished at his death: a massive biographical lexicon of all the famous personalities of antiquity.
6. BRM, p. 1.

critics were quick to point out, is that you could not expect your adversaries to conform to it, and the law of unforeseen consequences would intervene. He had a somewhat arrogant attitude towards his peers and once declared, 'I am writing for posterity, not for my contemporaries. I do not like to cast my pearls before swine.'[7] Unfortunately for Heinrich his ideas were never taken up by the Prussian generals, perhaps because they suspected that they themselves might be the swine before whom he was reluctant to cast his pearls. During the Napoleonic campaign of 1805, Heinrich was accused of being implicated in a covert effort to raise money to help bring about a French invasion of England—a favourite idea of his, which he discussed too freely. An arrest warrant was issued by the Prussians, who went to his house but failed to find him there. They eventually located him 'in the arms of a young maiden who loved him',[8] and a criminal process was begun against him. He was declared insane (his battlefield tactics presumably being part of the evidence against him), handed over to the Russians, and died in prison in Riga, possibly as a result of ill-treatment by his captors. These and other stories about this Hoffmanesque character were often retailed within the Bülow family circle, and played a vibrant role in the development of young Hans's personality.

II

Before her marriage to Eduard, Franziska had lived for some years in the Leipzig home of her sister Henriette, who was twelve years her senior and married to Kammerrath Christian Gottlob Frege, the head of Leipzig's great banking house and a man of high social standing in the city.[9] Kammerrath Frege had powerful connections both to the Royal Saxon Court in Dresden and to the hierarchy of the Church. His political views were those of the conservative right, and the maintenance of social order was for him a primary duty. This patrician home was famous for its support of the arts. Among its distinguished visitors were writers, painters, and musicians, including Goethe, Herder and Auerbach, as well as Mendelssohn and Schumann. During the early years of their marriage the Freges lost several infant children to illness, and looked to Franziska to help them protect the welfare of those who remained. She became a surrogate mother to their son Woldemar, who in later life always praised his aunt Franziska

---

7. Ibid., p. 25.
8. Ibid., p. 37.
9. The venerable Frege banking house had been established in the 18th century by the head of the family, Gottlob Frege (1715–81), who had come into a sudden fortune when the German currency was de-valued. He had gone on to increase his family's wealth through his weaving and lace-manufactory, and was given the title 'Kammerrath' by the Saxon court for himself and his heirs in perpetuity. His sons later joined him in the banking business.

for her loyalty to him and for her devotion to the Frege family. After giving up this home, and settling down to married life with Eduard in Dresden, Franziska continued to visit the Frege family during the holidays, and often took her two small children Hans and his sister Isidora to meet their cousin Woldemar and his growing family in Leipzig.

Woldemar was twenty years older than Bülow, and by the time of these holiday visits (1840–45) he was a professor of law at Leipzig University. He had married the soprano Livia Gerhardt on her eighteenth birthday, and brought her into the Frege household, the newly-weds living in one part of the spacious dwelling and Woldemar's parents in another. This gifted singer had already appeared in prominent roles at the Leipzig Theatre and the Royal Opera House in Berlin. Mendelssohn thought highly enough of her to dedicate some of his songs to her. Livia even entertained thoughts of becoming a professional musician, but marriage and motherhood intervened, and she devoted much time to the welfare of their son Arnold. The influence of the Frege family on the young Bülow cannot be overestimated. We shall have reason to mention them frequently in the course of our narrative.

III

Despite its starry-eyed beginnings, the marriage of Eduard and Franziska was a turbulent one and ended in an acrimonious divorce when Bülow was nineteen years old. Eduard was an intellectual for whom the life of the mind was paramount. Franziska had a more passionate nature and could be abrasive when crossed, unable to compromise with those around her. She was, moreover, intensely religious, something that helped to alienate her from her free-thinking husband. When she was already eighty-four years old her implacable character forced her to renounce her Protestant religion, with some of whose tenets she had become disillusioned, and convert to Roman Catholicism.[10] More important than these religious differences were the political ones. Eduard was a social liberal, an opponent of the oppressive clerical and state parties then in power in Saxony. His political sympathies lay with the left wing reformers, who were springing up across Germany and clamouring for change. Franziska, forever loyal to the conservative views of the Frege family, found Eduard's position intolerable. It required one event of significance to rip the marriage apart, and that was provided by the Dresden Uprising of 1849, which found the couple on opposite sides. They parted company soon afterwards, and a Protestant divorce followed.

---

10. On January 28, 1884, Bülow wrote to his daughter Daniela, 'Tomorrow your grandmamma is to enter the Roman Catholic Church at Coblenz, which means that I have to send five hundred marks to the poor of St. John's parish. There's news for you.' (BNB, p. 616).

Eduard married again almost at once. His new bride was Franziska's young friend Countess Louise Bülow-Dennewitz, whom he had met as a regular guest in his home. Louise was the daughter of General Friedrich Wilhelm Bülow-Dennewitz, the victor of the Battle of Dennewitz and a distinguished veteran of the Napoleonic wars. The General was the brother of the aforementioned military strategist Heinrich von Bülow, who was therefore Louise's uncle—yet another labyrinthine connection within the Bülow family circle. Louise herself was a product of General von Bülow's second marriage. His first wife, Marianne Auguste, whom he had led to the altar in 1802, died after only five years of marriage, in 1807. The following year, when he was already fifty-three years old, the General took Marianne's eighteen-year-old sister Pauline as his second wife, and she bore him three children, a son and two daughters, the elder of whom was Louise. After Countess Pauline was widowed, in 1816, she moved with Louise to Dresden where they mingled in the Bülow circle.

Following their marriage, in 1849, fate allowed Louise and Eduard a respite of four brief years together. Eduard suffered a massive stroke in September 1853, and died shortly afterward. He left behind him a grieving widow and two small sons, named Heinz and Willi. In keeping with the military traditions of the family, Heinz joined the army, but was killed in the Franco-Prussian War of 1870. Bülow always stood by his extended family. His relationship with his stepmother and his two stepbrothers was characterized by loyalty, respect, and unconditional support, whatever their endeavours. Louise in turn took an exceptional interest in Bülow's career, and we have her to thank for providing us with many personal observations, especially about his early life.

The military traditions within Bülow's family helped to mould his character, and may also have influenced the way in which he was perceived by friend and foe alike. Warlike imagery was frequently used to describe Bülow's bearing on the podium and the authority with which he commanded the orchestra—his troops. When the Scottish composer Alexander Mackenzie first beheld the dapper figure of Bülow on the platform, with his neatly clipped moustache and goatee beard, he was reminded of a *Garde Offizier en miniature*—an image that was reinforced by the brisk choreography Bülow employed to marshal the rank-and-file. Franz Liszt, tongue-in-cheek, promoted Bülow to the rank of 'General' after he had witnessed the conductor lead his small band of Meiningers to a European victory over much larger 'battalions' in Leipzig and Berlin, in the 1880s. Bülow was not displeased with such descriptions, and even added to them. Shortly after assuming command of three orchestras simultaneously—Bremen, Hamburg, and Berlin—he surveyed the coming season in much the same way as Napoleon had once surveyed Smolensk through his spy-glass, and spoke of it memorably as 'my musical winter campaign in three cities'.[11]

At the moment of Eduard's death, the title of 'Baron' passed to Hans, together with the honour of heading a family that could trace its origins back to the thirteenth century. And he did his best to uphold the motto that runs beneath its coat-of-arms—*'Alle Bülow'n ehrlich'* ('All the Bülows are honourable')—sometimes against almost impossible odds.

11. BB, vol. 7, p. 164.

BOOK ONE

On the Slopes of Parnassus, 1830–1869

The Early Years

He learned with the utmost rapidity what to other boys cost great labour and pains.

—Louise von Bülow[1]

I

The winter of 1829–1830 was spectacularly cold, with bone-chilling temperatures that regularly hovered around minus 20 degrees Celsius. No one could recall a winter of such severity. As the celebrations of Christmas and then of the New Year waxed and waned, with no relief in sight, it became hazardous to venture out of doors for long. The river Elbe was frozen solid, and the citizens of Dresden were able to skate from one bank to the other, a distance of more than 900 feet, bypassing the venerable Augustus Bridge, which was clogged with snow and ice. On Friday, January 8, 1830, the thermometer dropped to minus 37.5 degrees Celsius, a murderous level that threatened both man and beast. It was on that day that Hans von Bülow chose to make his entrance into the world. He was born in the family home at 19 Kohlmarkt (later 12 Körnerstrasse) diagonally opposite the birth-house of the German nationalistic poet Theodor Körner. His arrival took everyone by surprise. The previous evening his mother had been with friends, and had given no sign that she was about to go into labour. Swift may have been the delivery, but it was not without complications, and Franziska's firstborn was so weak that few thought the infant would survive. It was to be his first victory over adversity.[2]

Three years after Bülow was born, Franziska gave birth to a daughter, Isidora, who was likewise afflicted with delicate health in her youth. A third child, a barely remembered daughter named Oda, who was mentally retarded, was born in 1834. She was transferred into the care of the Moravian Brethren during infancy and brought up in their closed community

1. BB, vol. 1, p. 11.
2. On the eve of his forty-sixth birthday, which he celebrated in New York, Bülow referred with mock humor to 'my poor mother [who] had a bad quarter-of-an-hour bringing me into the world'. Ibid., vol. 5, p. 332.

in Niesky, a small village in Saxony not far from Dresden, close to the Polish border, where she died in 1876.[3]

Bülow's childhood was marred by chronic illness. From his earliest years he was under the regular care of doctors. He succumbed no fewer than five times to what his mother called 'brain fever', a condition that no amount of medical attention seemed to cure. He himself tells us that until he was nine years old he had neither much talent for nor interest in music.[4] This changed in a dramatic way after a serious illness, probably meningitis, and then to a phenomenal degree. During his convalescence the boy lay propped up in bed, silently reading the scores of Beethoven and Bach, and as an amusement trying to engrave each note on his memory. What began as a pastime soon turned into an obsession. Bülow discovered that he possessed a photographic memory, which eventually extended to the total recall of full orchestral scores.

Hans was barely in his fourth year when his father, Eduard von Bülow, began setting him the task of committing to memory the entire series of fifty so-called 'Speckter Fairy-tales' for children, and of learning the little verse of poetry attached to each of them. Every Saturday night before going to bed, Hans would present himself to Eduard and recite these stories down to the last detail, together with the accompanying poem.[5] Franziska's own special contribution to her son's mental development was to teach him French, a language of which she was especially fond, and in which both he and his sister Isidora had become bilingual by their late teens.

3. Always small in number, the Moravians were known across Germany for their charitable work, which included caring for the sick and the homeless, and educating young children according to Christian precepts. Their religious ancestors had been the Hussites. It was Count Nicholas von Zinzendorf (1700–1760), who had given the Brethren land on his Bohemian estates, and had galvanized them into forming their own brand of social evangelism. The Moravian Brethren and Sisters also ran hospitals within their own communities and they trained their own nurses. Although they lived in isolated groups, they worked closely with the Lutheran Church, which supported their activities. The Moravian community in Niesky, into whose care Oda was placed, had been there since the middle of the eighteenth century and would have been well known to the religious-minded Franziska.

4. See Bülow's 'Autobiographical Sketch', which covers the years from his birth until 1858. We do not know for what purpose this Sketch was prepared, but it may have been destined for a biographical dictionary which failed to materialize. BB, vol. 3, pp. 166–173.

5. BAB, p. 4. Commonly called 'Otto Speckter's Fable Book', this illustrated collection of animal stories was written by the German poet Wilhelm Hey. Bülow told his daughter Daniela that the excellence of his memory was due to her grandfather Eduard having forced him to use it while young. 'I have always been grateful to him,' he added (BNB, p. 306). And he urged Daniela to commit as many things as possible to memory in order to develop this most precious of human faculties. He often pressed on his pupils the idea that 'memory is not a special gift; it may be trained and exceedingly strengthened' (ZMB, p. 41). It was a wrenching experience for Bülow to witness his mother's decline into senility, and, with the onset of extreme old age, the loss of her memory.

Bülow, an engraving based on a watercolour by Frau
Ida von Lüttichau.

Not until he was nine years old did Bülow begin to receive his first
music lessons—from a local cellist named Henselt, who happened to be
an occasional chamber partner of his mother's. Despite this relatively
uncertain start, the boy soon outstripped his teacher and he became a
pupil of Fräulein Cäcilie Schmiedel for piano and Max Eberwein for theory. Fräulein Schmiedel aroused in him an abiding love of the classics, and
under her guidance he was soon playing with fluency some of Bach's 48
Preludes and Fugues, and some of the sonatas of Beethoven and Mozart.

Fräulein Schmiedel died young, and Bülow remembered her with affection. He later wrote, 'I have her to thank for my first training in my so-
called specialty'.[6] Another early influence was the composer-pianist Henry
Litolff, whom the growing teenager saw on an almost daily basis in the
home of his parents during the period 1844–1845.[7]

6. BB, vol. 3, p. 169.
7. The English-born Litolff's association with the Bülow family cannot be glossed over. He
had arrived in Dresden with a nervous condition, and because they found much to admire

Bülow often went across to the nearby Catholic church to listen to the organ and choral music, and when he came home he was able to reproduce at the piano whatever pieces had particularly pleased him. Although music absorbed much of his time, his parents made sure that his academic studies were not neglected. He was enrolled at the Dresden Gymnasium where, according to Louise von Bülow, who later became his stepmother, 'he learned with the utmost rapidity what to other boys cost great labour and pains'.[8] He became well grounded in Greek and Latin, and thanks to the influence of his father he also excelled in the history of antiquity. In light of his advanced general education, and his obvious intellectual gifts, it never occurred to either of his parents to allow their son to become a professional musician. Music might be a useful social adornment, but could not be considered as a means of earning a livelihood. Thus began Bülow's long struggle against his parents to pursue a career in music, the only profession that meant anything to him.

II

Bülow's childhood and adolescence were not happy. The ill-starred marriage of his parents cast a shadow over his teenage years. His mother, Franziska, was, in the words of Du Moulin Eckart, 'a hard woman' who exercised a tyrannical domination over her gifted son, even after he had come to world prominence and she herself had entered old age.[9] Franziska held the profession of music in low esteem, and she placed many obstacles in his path. She believed that something more stable and secure

---

in him as an artist, the Bülows offered him the sanctuary of their home. There he spent many hours daily in the company of the young Bülow, who came to admire his precocious piano playing and compared it with that of the greatest virtuosi. The family was well aware of the reckless life that Litolff insisted on leading, a life which may well have contributed to his sad and highly public condition—an uncontrollable twitching of the face which, in the words of Bülow, 'affects strangers so unpleasantly' (BB, vol. 1, pp. 185–186). When he was only seventeen, Litolff had eloped to Gretna Green with a sixteen-year-old English girl named Elisabeth Etherington. After marrying in haste Litolff had time to repent at leisure. While attempting to procure a divorce, he was arrested, heavily fined, and sent to jail. He escaped from prison by employing skills similar to the ones that had sent him there in the first place: by seducing the jailor's daughter. In Germany he eventually married the widow of his business partner, Gottfried Meyer, and went on to found his highly successful publishing firm, the Henry Litolff Verlag. This second marriage too, ended in divorce. Undeterred by this melancholy quest to find conjugal bliss, Litolff married for a third time, a union that seems to have brought him thirteen years of relative calm, terminated only by the death of this particular wife, in 1873. Litolff married for a fourth time—a seventeen-year-old girl who had nursed him back to health the previous year. When Bülow first met Litolff, the older man still had much of his chequered past in front of him, so to say. In a great understatement Bülow once described Litolff's private life as an 'adventurous destiny' (ibid., vol. 1, p. 44).

8. Ibid., p. 11.
9. BNB, p. xxviii.

was required for her delicate 'Hänschen' than to go through life as a musician. The young boy's letters tell their own sad story. 'I should be very glad', he wrote wistfully to his mother, 'if I had a little encouragement in my piano playing. . . . Today I am not very well, with some giddiness and headache'.[10] Such pleas to maternal solicitude were brushed aside, and it was determined that Hans should study jurisprudence, a subject for which his bright intelligence and industrious nature seemed to suit him. Long after he had established himself in Germany with his first successful concerts, a feat of which any normal mother would have been proud, we find Franziska still railing against the career of her son. 'At last, a letter from Hans! . . . Tonight he is playing to the students at Breslau. On Sunday there is to be a monster-concert at which he plays, and where he hopes to make some money. God grant it, if one may trouble God about such a thing'.[11] A few weeks later she writes, 'To have such a child rushing about the world in all sorts of adventures, is truly no sinecure'. And she added gratuitously, 'As our shoemaker recently said, the Herr Sohn has become a genius'.[12]

Bülow's father, Baron Eduard von Bülow, had a softer nature and a more sympathetic attitude towards his son's profession. The religious and political differences that separated him and Franziska slowly poisoned their union. When the revolutionary struggles of 1849 swept across Germany they found themselves on opposite sides of an unbridgeable divide, and their marriage, already dead in everything but name, fell apart. Bülow was a daily witness to the domestic fights that erupted between his dysfunctional parents. Many years later he wept in the presence of his close friend and fellow Liszt pupil Hans von Bronsart. 'You cannot imagine what impressions my delicate childhood made on me', he told Bronsart. 'I was forced to experience every day how my father and mother fought incessantly, becoming a deadly sickness to one another'.[13]

Bülow inherited leading qualities from both parents: an acerbic tongue from his mother, and a love of intellectual pursuits from his father. To Eduard, too, he owed his democratic political views, which he carried with him to the end. Two other legacies from those traumatic times can be observed. Bülow was ravaged by headaches, a functional symptom which struck him down whenever the problems of life overwhelmed him. He also became self-conscious about his appearance; his short stature, high forehead, and slightly bulging eyes gave the impression that he was glaring at everyone, and caused him youthful embarrassment. Eventually he learned to protect himself from the hostility of the world, both real and

---

10. BB, vol. 1, p. 109.
11. Ibid., vol. 2, p. 331.
12. Ibid., p. 332.
13. BAB, p. 4.

imagined, through his trenchant use of language, which became the scourge of his enemies and the despair of his friends.

III

During these early years in Dresden, Bülow formed a number of friend-ships that remained with him for life. One of Fräulein Schmiedel's piano pupils was the thirteen-year-old Jessie Taylor from England, who later found a niche in the history books because of her brief love affair with Richard Wagner, and for the financial support she and her first husband, Eugene Laussot, gave the impecunious composer during the difficult years of his exile in Switzerland. Three years older than Bülow, Jessie be-came a surrogate sister to him, and it was to her that he frequently turned for support and advice whenever adversity struck. At the time of his dark-est hour she offered him a temporary sanctuary.[14] Other important friend-ships were formed with the teenage brothers Karl and Alexander Ritter, whose mother, Frau Julie Ritter, a well-to-do widow from Narwa, in Esto-nia, had settled in Dresden with her young family after the death of her merchant husband. Frau Ritter, too, is remembered today for the generous support she extended to Wagner.

Richard Wagner, the Kapellmeister of Dresden's Royal Opera House, was the musical hero of Bülow's adolescence. When the boy was twelve years old he was given a free ticket by the orchestra's concertmaster, Karol Lipiński, to attend the premier performance of *Rienzi*. The event took place on October 20, 1842, and, as Bülow himself put it, that was the date on which he became a confirmed Wagnerian. More than forty years later he told his daughter Daniela that he longed to throw himself at the feet of the pale little man in the brown coat who came forward at the end of the final act to acknowledge the applause. Bülow subsequently wrote that 'the performances of operas by Gluck and Mozart, as well as the Bee-thoven symphonies under Wagner, belong to my most cherished musi-cal memories'.[15] With Wagner's interpretation of Beethoven's Ninth Sym-

---

14. See pp. 163–64.

15. BB, vol. 3, p. 171. To this performance of *Rienzi* was attached an important child-hood reminiscence. During the third act the twelve-year-old boy went completely deaf and saw the characters moving about the stage in total silence. Until that evening, his experience of opera had been confined to Mozart and the Italian school, with its light, transparent scor-ing. The rich colours of Wagner's orchestration overwhelmed Bülow's sensitive ears, and provoked a traumatic reaction. By the beginning of the fourth act his hearing had returned (RWHB, p. iv). Two years later (in February 1844) the boy heard *Rienzi* again. Liszt was in the audience, and Bülow was afterwards taken over to the Hotel de Saxe to meet the pianis-tic legend. When Bülow himself came to conduct *Rienzi*, thirty-six years later, Liszt was once again in the audience, and Bülow was not one to let such coincidences go unremarked. His amusing characterization of the situation in which he found himself on that later occasion will be found on page 252.

phony Bülow was especially enthralled, and in later life he freely admitted incorporating many of its features into his own rendition of the work.[16]

Bülow also got to know Liszt at this time. The great pianist was giving concerts in Dresden, and because he was already casually acquainted with Franziska and Eduard von Bülow, he was invited into their home. The conversation naturally turned on the musical talents of their twelve-year-old son, which had just begun to manifest themselves. Liszt remembered that conversation because on his next visit to Dresden, a few weeks later, he invited Hans to attend a concert he was about to give in the neighborhood. Despite the late hour—Hans was in bed—the youngster was roused from his slumbers and taken to hear Liszt. It was his first glimpse of a man whom he shortly came to venerate, and with whose destiny his own was to become inextricably bound.

IV

Now that he was ready for more advanced instruction in music, Bülow's parents allowed him to enroll at the Leipzig Conservatory of Music, on condition that he also pursue his general education at the Gymnasium in readiness for the university there. The problem of where the boy would live was easily settled. For the next several years he became part of the Frege household and was looked after by his aunt Henriette and his older cousins, Woldemar and Livia Frege, whose acquaintance we made on an earlier page. Hans was given his own room, the use of the family piano (a rather derelict upright Klemm, about which he often complained), and was able to walk the short distance back and forth to the Conservatory. His chief teachers were the well-known pedagogue Louis Plaidy, who helped to lay the foundations of his piano technique, and the theorist Moritz Hauptmann, with whom he studied harmony and counterpoint.

Bülow soon began to display those twin qualities of discipline and determination for which he later became renowned. He rose early, and by 6:00 a.m. was already at the keyboard practising trills, scales, chromatic exercises of every kind, together with studies for what he called 'throwing

16. Wagner brought Beethoven's Ninth Symphony to Dresden on Palm Sunday, April 5, 1846, and worked like a galley slave with both the orchestra and the choir to make the performance possible. He acquired the parts from Berlin, coached the four soloists, and drove the large ensemble through one rehearsal after another, refusing to accept anything less than the highest musical results. He even had the platform of the old Dresden Opera House rebuilt in order to accommodate his preferred seating plan for the performers. Dresden, like the rest of the world at that time, considered the Ninth Symphony to be incoherent, the final outburst of a musical genius gone mad. The moving success that Wagner achieved on this occasion proved that this most intractable of symphonies was capable of stirring the crowd.

the hands'. As he told his mother, *'Je travaille comme un nègre'*.[17] He embarked on a conquest of Chopin's Studies (which he admitted were at first difficult for him) and some of the Beethoven sonatas, including the ones in D minor (*Tempest*) and C-sharp minor (*Moonlight*). In later years he produced celebrated editions of these pieces. By the time he was fifteen years old, he had learnt Hummel's Concerto in A minor and John Field's Concerto in A major. For basic technical training he turned to the studies of Ignaz Moscheles and Leopold de Meyer, and above all to Czerny's 'School of Velocity'.[18] Mendelssohn and Adolf Henselt were a regular part of his regimen as well. By the age of fourteen he was already learning Mendelssohn's *Rondo Capriccioso,* a work he was later to play to perfection. Bach's 48 Preludes and Fugues he eventually mastered in their entirety. He informs us that he used to practice the two-part Fugue in E minor (Book One) with each hand in octaves, an interesting idea that he got from Otto Goldschmidt, a fellow student at the Conservatory and a former pupil of Mendelssohn.[19]

It was an impressive repertoire for a boy in his mid teens, and he appears to have acquired it on the basis of little more than two or three hours' practice a day, begun shortly after dawn, because his general studies at the Leipzig Gymnasium took up most of the rest of his time.

There was one other teacher whose influence must not be overlooked. Bülow received some instruction in Dresden from Friedrich Wieck (the father of Clara Schumann), whose pupil he briefly became in the summer

17. BB, vol. 1, p. 41.
18. Ibid.
19. Ibid. Bülow does not identify the fugue, but the one in E minor (Book I) is the only one in the entire set of '48' for two voices.

of 1845. This encounter is scarcely remembered today, so we do well to recall the glowing tribute that Bülow paid to his old master many years later: 'You were the one who first . . . taught my ear to hear, who impressed upon my hand the rules of correct formation, and who led my talent from the twilight of the unconscious into the bright light of the conscious'. To which Bülow added the generous words, 'He who fosters the invisible seed with such unusual conscientiousness, care, and love, may claim a co-creator's share in the developed fruit'.[20]

V

At the heart of Leipzig's musical life stood Felix Mendelssohn. When he was only twenty-six years old and already a composer of European distinction, this young genius had been appointed conductor of the Gewandhaus concerts. Under his inspired leadership the Gewandhaus became a musical shrine at which the faithful regularly gathered to hear the masterpieces of Beethoven, Schubert, and Bach brought to life by this incomparable musician. Schumann called Mendelssohn 'the Mozart of the nineteenth century' and in everything that he did the composer lived up to this designation.

Bülow's private encounters with Mendelssohn were among his cherished teenage memories. He was about fourteen years old when he first heard Mendelssohn play the piano in the home of the Frege family. On several occasions he also witnessed Mendelssohn rehearsing the Gewandhaus Orchestra. At about this time, too, Mendelssohn gave Bülow a private lesson. Bülow recalled that Mendelssohn was very patient during the period of instruction, which lasted for several hours, and from which he learned much in matters of form and style. The two pieces that occupied the lesson were the composer's own *Rondo Capriccioso,* op. 14, and the *Capriccioso Brillant* in B minor, with orchestral accompaniment, op. 22. This encounter impressed itself on the boy, and years later he recalled that 'the power of the magical personality of the master came to the rescue of the relative immaturity of the would-be student'.[21]

VI

In the summer of 1846 Eduard moved his family to Stuttgart where they spent the next eighteen months. The reason for this unexpected step is

20. Ibid., vol. 3, p. 554. Because so many biographical sketches of Bülow claim that he took piano lessons from Wieck from the age of nine, let us recall that Bülow himself has told us that he did not receive instruction from this pedagogue until 1845—that is, when he was fifteen years old—and it ended the following year. Ibid., vol. 3, p. 169.

21. Thirty-five years later Bülow captured this reminiscence in the foreword to his edition of Mendelssohn's *Rondo Capriccioso* (1880), reprinted in BAS (part 2), pp. 206–209.

unknown, but may have been connected to Eduard's historical research. Hans felt unable to leave Dresden without meeting in the flesh the man he adored and had so far been able to worship only from a distance. In the company of concertmaster Lipiński he journeyed to nearby Gross-Graupe, where Richard Wagner was on holiday, working on the sketches of *Lohengrin*, and was introduced to his idol.[22] He begged Wagner to write something in his album, who inscribed it with these winged words:

> If there gleams in your breast the sincere, pure glow of art, assuredly the lovely flame will some day burst forth: but it is knowledge that nourishes this glow and turns it into strong, pure flame.[23]

Buoyed by such encouragement, the sixteen-year-old sent Wagner some of his juvenile compositions and awaited the master's reply.

Hans was meanwhile enrolled in the Stuttgart Gymnasium where he continued to outstrip his peers and graduated with a baccalaureate diploma when he was eighteen years old. The family lived on the ground floor of 22 Alleestrasse, a house that belonged to the painter Franz Stirnbrand. Stuttgart possessed a well-developed theatre and a symphony orchestra, whose leader was the distinguished violinist Bernhard Molique. Bülow spent much time in the Molique household and became attached to Molique's four daughters (the 'four-leafed clover', as they were fondly called). Clara Molique, one of the younger girls, left an affectionate reminiscence of Bülow's visits to her house. Dwelling on the boy's gifts as a pianist, she recalled, 'There was nothing angular or helpless about Bülow. When he was at the piano, one soon saw that it was a young *master* who was in command of the instrument'.[24] Bülow often played Beethoven, Mendelssohn, and Hummel to his audience of female admirers; and he presented the eldest daughter, Caroline Molique, with two of his juvenile compositions: one was a short character-piece for her album, and the other was a song called 'Klinge, kleines Frühlingslied'. Caroline was an accomplished pianist who sometimes joined her father and his colleagues at their Sunday afternoon concerts, where they performed chamber music. On one such occasion Bülow heard the group play Molique's newly composed Piano Trio, op. 27, which he later put into his own repertoire. Once Bülow's skills as a pianist were recognized by Molique, he invited the sev-

---

22. This first historic meeting between the sixteen-year-old Bülow and Richard Wagner took place on July 29, 1846.

23. Quoted in NLRW, vol. 1, p. 458.

24. BB, vol. 1, p. 52.

enteen-year-old to accompany him, and Bülow had the joy of playing a number of chamber works with the great violinist, including one or two of the Beethoven violin sonatas.

At Molique's house Bülow met a number of influential musicians, including the conductor Julius Benedict, the violinist Max Bohrer, and the pianist Wilhelm Kruger, all of whom left their varying impressions on him. It was in Stuttgart, too, that he made the acquaintance of Joachim Raff, who became his lifelong friend. Raff was eight years older than Bülow, and for a time he was not only his companion but also his mentor. He had recently lost his job in a music shop in Cologne because of some outspoken remarks he had made in the *Wiener Allgemeine Musik-Zeitung,* and had moved to Stuttgart. On Mendelssohn's recommendation Raff had already had some of his early piano compositions published in Leipzig, and Bülow, on the cusp of his own musical career, saw much to admire in his older friend. Later they were both drawn to Liszt, and lived in close proximity to each other in Weimar.

Bülow also kept in touch with his friend Alexander Ritter, who still lived in Dresden. The two teenagers not only exchanged letters but also their respective musical compositions, offering each other friendly advice. One day Bülow received a package containing some of Ritter's music—a group of songs, a portion of a string quartet, and a piano sonata dedicated to Bülow. With these manuscripts was enclosed a letter from Wagner, commenting on the various compositions that Bülow had sent him after their meeting in Gross-Graupe. We learn that Wagner was in the Dresden opera house dealing with visitors when Ritter approached him in the artists' room, unannounced. Wagner detached himself from the group, and handing Bülow's manuscripts back to Ritter, whispered, 'an undeniable talent'. Wagner's message to the young composer ran:

> Dresden, September 2, 1847. Your works, dear Herr von Bülow, have given me much pleasure; I did not wish to give them back to your friend Ritter without accompanying them with a cheering word to you. I do not add a criticism to them, for you will have enough of criticism without me; and I feel all the less disposed to pick out weaknesses and other things which did not please me, as I see from all that remains that you will soon be completely able to criticize your earlier attempts for yourself.
>
> Go on trying, and let me soon see something more.[25]

Bülow preserved the letter as a sacred relic.

25. RWHB, p. 1.

VII

To Clara Molique we owe a charming story which adds detail to Bülow's early character. In order to celebrate the *Dreikönigsfest* (Epiphany, or 'Twelfth Night') on January 6, 1848, three of the Molique sisters were invited round to Bülow's house, together with Mimi and Gerhardine von Gall, the daughters of the theatre intendant. The children began to enjoy themselves on this magical evening and Hans ('always the electrifying centre-point of our little society of friends') was full of delightful humour and unstoppable banter. They became rambunctious and began to make a lot of noise. Suddenly, Clara tells us, the adjoining door opened and the imposing figure of Eduard von Bülow appeared. In tones of frustration he told the children that they had disturbed his writing and they must keep quiet. He withdrew as suddenly as he had appeared, and closed the door. The children were left sitting at the beautifully decorated table, over which Franziska von Bülow presided, doing their best to remain subdued. Calm was restored when Frau von Bülow brought in a large, beautifully decorated French bean-cake surrounded with a paper crown in celebration of the *Dreikönigsfest,* and placed it on the table.

The children ate the cake with care. They knew that it contained two French beans, as hard as bullets, and that the first finder would become king for the entire evening, and not only get to wear the paper crown that surrounded the cake but also to choose his queen. It was a time-honoured ritual that went back hundreds of years. Clara tells us that although the children crammed every last crumb into their mouths, their bewilderment was great because not a single bean could be found. Suddenly, Clara continued, Hans got up from the table, and 'as quiet as a mouse', stole over to the stove, where he pretended to busy himself with something or other, and returned to the table with the beaming countenance of a lucky finder, which at once identified him as the demolisher (*der Vertilger*) of the beans. 'We felt very deprived', she added, 'but he found the joke so capital and laughed so heartily, that we joined in his laughter and our wrath evaporated. Hans had once again played a practical joke on us!'[26] Bülow had crowned himself king for the evening—a point of psychological interest to anyone familiar with the way in which he dominated both orchestras and audiences in later years. The child was father to the man.

Bülow made his first public appearance as a pianist in Stuttgart. On January 1, 1848, not yet eighteen years old, he appeared with Bernhard Molique and other artists in the royal theatre for a concert in benefit of 'the Widows and Orphans of the Court Orchestra and Theatre'. His con-

---

26. BB, vol. 1, pp. 49–50.

tribution was a performance of Raff's recently composed Concert Fantasie on Friedrich Kücken's *Le Prétendant,* op. 42, a notable choice, because all his life Bülow was to champion the music of Raff. Noteworthy, too, was the fact that this was a charity concert. Bülow frequently placed himself and his talent in the service of things he thought worthwhile—an unsung aspect of his long career as a performer.

In the spring of 1848, Eduard's sojourn in Stuttgart came to an end, and he took his family back to Dresden. When Hans went to bid farewell to the Molique family, the four sisters were suffering from measles, and the members of 'the four-leaved clover' were all in quarantine. Bülow always regretted that he could not take his formal leave of a family to whom he had become so attached.

VIII

In an effort to placate his parents, Bülow reluctantly agreed to study jurisprudence, and in the autumn of 1848 he enrolled as a law student at Leipzig University, taking courses as well in philology, history, and literature. He chafed beneath these constrictions, which got in the way of his musical studies, and within a year he had resolved to transfer to Berlin's Friedrich Wilhelm University. This decision was made somewhat easier for him by the political upheavals in Saxony, culminating in the Dresden Uprising of May 1849, in which many people were killed during the street fighting, and martial law was imposed. Richard Wagner, who had helped to design the street barricades, was forced to flee the city with a price on his head. For young Bülow the failure of the Uprising was a disaster, and Wagner's exile a catastrophe. In an anguished state of mind, he wrote to his mother that studying and music making were at the moment quite impossible for him, suggesting that one or the other had to go.[27] Bülow was also unhappy at being forced to live in Leipzig with his uncle and aunt, the highly conservative Henriette and Christian Frege, whose right-wing political views he found so intolerable that there were frequent arguments. His cousin Woldemar used to walk out of the room whenever Bülow played *Tannhäuser;* equally disappointing to him was the behaviour of Woldemar's young wife Livia, who reneged on a promise to go through the same score with him, because she took the music to be either 'bad or crazy'. The nineteen-year-old was subjected to a nighttime curfew during these troubled times, and had to be indoors by 8:30 p.m., lest he become involved in the growing number of street demonstrations. He became convinced that the Frege family regarded him as a 'resident spy' for the democrats. Uncle Christian was even begged by the rest of the family

27. Ibid., pp. 163–64.

to guard his tongue in Bülow's presence, in case the young man passed on information of value to the revolution! Doubtless this most patrician of families, with its banking interests and its ties to the royal court, felt vulnerable, but Bülow was nonetheless hurt that his own relatives had come to regard him as an outsider. By early May the clamour and chaos of the Dresden Uprising had reached Leipzig. On May 6 eight people were killed and several more wounded in the vicinity of the Frege house. 'Now that they know my opinions they [the Freges] dare to implicate me in it all', he told his mother angrily. 'I cannot stand being in this house any longer', he wrote, and begged to be allowed to leave. 'If only I could come to you and hear a few friendly, tolerant words'. And he exclaimed in anguish, 'If only Wagner does not get shot!' Just how close that fear was to becoming fact was only made known to Bülow later on. The royal warrant for Wagner's arrest, his narrow escape from a Dresden execution squad, his flight to Chemnitz, and from there to Weimar where he found a temporary refuge with Liszt before moving on to a Swiss exile with borrowed money and a forged passport, is a well-worn tale whose further telling would add little to the story of Bülow's own life.[28]

In Dresden, where the bulk of the fighting had taken place, it was a time of personal upheaval for Bülow's parents as well. Eduard and Franziska finally brought their tumultuous marriage to an end, and they divorced in the autumn of 1849. Almost at once Eduard married Countess Louise Bülow-Dennewitz, whose acquaintance we made at an earlier point in our story, and departed with his bride for Switzerland, and the haven of a castle at Ötlishausen in the Canton of Thurgau, just across the German border. Meanwhile, Bülow promised his mother that he would remain in the Frege household until the end of the term, after which he would pursue his law studies in Berlin.

IX

It is an indication of Bülow's unsettled frame of mind that at the end of May 1849, just before moving to the Prussian capital, he made a brief excursion to Weimar in order to renew his acquaintance with Liszt, and seek his advice. He rented a room at the Russischer Hof Hotel, intending to stay for a couple of days, but found the experience of meeting Liszt so stimulating that he remained in Weimar for more than a week. Because he did not have enough money to pay his bills, he had to beg his mother to send him a further three Reichsthaler to cover the cost. Liszt greeted Bülow with warmth and affection. They went for a long walk in the

---

28. My own detailed account of Wagner's fate during this time of political upheaval may be found in WFL, vol. 2, pp. 113–119.

Goethe Park and chatted about the exiled Wagner, about Bülow's own future, and about Liszt's work in progress. Liszt introduced the young man to some of the artists in his circle and brought them to dine with him and Bülow at the Russischer Hof. He not only heard Bülow play the piano, but arranged for his young visitor's newly composed string quartet to be performed a day or two after his arrival at one of the Altenburg matinees.[29] Bülow attended a rehearsal of *Fidelio* in the Court Theatre and was impressed by Liszt's style of conducting, which was much freer than anything he had witnessed in Dresden or Leipzig. But it was Liszt's piano playing that left the deepest impression. Liszt played two of his new and still unpublished concert paraphrases on Wagner's *Tannhäuser:* Wolfram's song 'O du mein holder Abendstern', and the famously difficult Overture.[30] As the nineteen-year-old observed Liszt's unbridled approach to interpretation, he became aware of a chief defect in his own playing: a lack of abandon. Bülow had presented himself to Liszt as a perfect representative of the Leipzig school—classical, correct, conservative. These qualities were not to be despised, especially when they were covered with a veneer of professional polish that Bülow was now bringing to all his performances, but they were not enough. Bülow was simply a good soldier whose playing lacked the *feu sacré*. He sensed at once what was required of him. 'I must completely cure myself of a certain angular want of freedom in conception. . . . When I have conquered the technical difficulties of a piece, in modern pieces especially, I must *let myself go* more, according to how I feel at the moment'.[31]

X

It was a difficult time for the young man. He would have preferred to stay in Weimar and bask in the company of Liszt and his circle, but he was duty bound to take up his law studies in Berlin. Franziska and the sixteen-year-old Isidora travelled with him to the Prussian capital, and they all lived briefly in the city *en famille*. Franziska sought out two of Eduard's influential cousins, Ernst and Paul von Bülow, the first a member of the Prussian government, the second a lieutenant-colonel in the Prussian army. These were important contacts who eventually helped ease Bülow

---

29. Although Bülow mentions this string quartet several times in his correspondence, it does not show up in any catalogue of his works.

30. BB, vol. 1, pp. 178–179. The pianist who has confronted Liszt's 'Paraphrase de Concert' of the Overture to *Tannhäuser*, and pondered its technical difficulties, will take heart from the fact that it often gave Liszt himself some trouble. On this occasion, as he neared the end of the piece, Liszt stopped from sheer exhaustion for a moment before continuing. He turned to Bülow and remarked, 'You can write down today in your diary that I have played the *Tannhäuser* Overture to you'.

31. Ibid., p. 180.

into the upper echelons of Berlin society. That the young man would have made an excellent lawyer was evident in everything that he now said and did. His ability to cut through intellectual dross and get to the heart of the matter was already evident, as were his tendencies toward radical socialism. Bülow criticized the monarchy, favoured the creation of a German republic, and eventually came to admire Bismarck as the saviour of the nation. These views were hardly calculated to win friends and influence people, especially in the Prussian capital, whose own royal family had looked on nervously as the revolutionary fervour of 1848 had rocked a number of nearby principalities.

During these first few months in Berlin, Bülow also tried his hand at music criticism. It came about almost by default. He noticed that not a single Berlin newspaper had bothered to review Wagner's recently published essays *Art and Revolution* and *The Art-Work of the Future,* so he himself wrote a series of articles about them which he submitted to leading newspapers. Much to his annoyance they were rejected, and it is not hard to see why. Wagner had just begun his long Swiss exile, with a price on his head, and he was presently the object of a conspiracy of silence by the Prussian press. Refusing to be muzzled, Bülow turned to the left-leaning *Abendpost: Demokratische Zeitung,* to which two of his fellow university students were at that time connected. The names of Adolf Mützelburg and Eduard Fischel, who were both youthful followers of Karl Marx, are barely remembered today, but they were important footnotes in the story of Bülow's early life, for they managed to get the *Abendpost* to open its columns to him.[32]

On February 26, 1850, Bülow fired his opening salvo with a review of Beethoven's *Fidelio,* which the ever-conservative Royal Opera House had just brought to Berlin—almost forty-five years after its first performance in Vienna. Bülow told his readers that the capital had waited a long time for the appearance of such a fine opera, but its arrival, he went on, had nothing to do with the theatre administration's appreciation of art. Rather *Fidelio* had been mounted as a benefit concert for Frau Köster (a passing diva of the day), whose local reputation explained the packed house and all the flowers and bouquets that rained down on her in acknowledgement of her performance of the title role. Chivalry having been served, Bülow then went to work with a will. 'Mantius [the shackled Florestan] played with his chain as audibly as he ought to have sung', he remarked

---

32. Bülow tells the story of these early years in an obituary notice that he devoted to Eduard Fischel, written on the occasion of the latter's unexpected death in 1863. Fischel was run over by an omnibus in Paris in the summer of that year. See BAS (part 2), pp. 17–25.

caustically. 'Both performance and declamation were ridiculously emotional'.[33] As for the venerable conductor of the Royal Opera House, Wilhelm Taubert, he and the orchestra sometimes went their separate ways, and Bülow observed drily, 'Under Taubert's direction, the orchestra did not achieve what one had a right to expect of it: they were weak, and lacking in precision and fire. The director should beat time rather less and rehearse somewhat more'.[34] With this article Bülow killed three birds with one stone: the theatre administration, the leading tenor, and the conductor. Although Bülow signed this and similar articles with the solitary initial 'B', the readers soon fastened on to his identity. And there would be consequences: despite his stellar reputation as an opera conductor in later life, Bülow was never invited to conduct in the opera house that he had insulted.

Bülow also formed with his young friends on the *Abendpost* a 'League of Youth', whose chief goal was to foment political dispute. Marie von Bülow called the newspaper an 'anarchistic organ', and suppressed Bülow's political commentaries when she republished his early writings in her collected edition of his letters and articles. Bülow used his position not only to promote the music of Liszt and Wagner but also to settle some old scores against those newspapers which had earlier refused to print his articles. He declared war on their accredited music critics, whom he accused of smugness and ignorance. In particular he pilloried Ludwig Rellstab and the conservative *Vossische Zeitung* that employed him in a satirical article called 'Aunty Voss's Fossilized Critics'.[35] In a very short time Bülow had become *persona non grata* in Berlin's musical circles. The polluted atmosphere in which he was soon to find himself, at a time when he was struggling to launch his own career as a performer, was a completely foreseeable response on the part of those whose hostility he had aroused through his work on the *Abendpost*.

---

33. Issue of February 26, 1850.
34. Ibid.
35. This article was published by the *Abendpost* in February 1850. When Bülow came to prepare his reflections, in 1863, he was unable to find a single surviving copy, because every issue appeared to have been destroyed. Among the other newspapers for which the young Bülow wrote during the 1850s were The *Berliner Feuerspritze, Die Fackel,* the *Neue Berliner Musik-Zeitung, Deutschland,* and *Das Echo.*

With Liszt in Weimar

> I love him as if he were my own son, and I regard myself as if I were
> his father. And it will be the same, ten years from now.
> —Liszt to Franziska von Bülow[1]

I

In the spring of 1850 Franziska and Isidora departed from Berlin and returned to Dresden, leaving Bülow to continue his law studies in the Prussian capital. He applied himself diligently to jurisprudence, but the topic brought him little pleasure. It was music, and the memory of his recent encounter with Liszt in Weimar, that held him in thrall. In August 1850, Bülow persuaded his mother to meet him in Weimar in order to attend the Herder Festival. There he witnessed Liszt conducting the world premier of Wagner's *Lohengrin,* a major turning point for him. He knew that he must abandon law in favour of music. Since he lacked the means to support himself, his first priority was to come to an understanding with his father. He travelled down to Ötlishausen on September 10 in order to begin the difficult process of converting Eduard to his point of view. His sister Isidora happened to be there on a family visit, and he shared his hopes and aspirations with her as well. He also spent time in the company of his new stepmother, Louise, who later recalled these days of agitation. 'We often went for walks in the beautiful neighborhood', she reminisced, 'but the pleasant time in Ötlishausen did not last long. One morning Hans had vanished. He was absent from breakfast, dinner, and supper. All inquiries were unsuccessful'.[2]

For an explanation of Hans's dramatic disappearance from his father's home we have to turn to Richard Wagner's *Mein Leben.*[3] Hearing that Hans

---

1. BB, vol. 1, p. 483.
2. Ibid., p. 244.
3. WML, pp. 549–552.

was in Switzerland, Wagner tells us that he had despatched Karl Ritter to the Bülow villa in Ötlishausen with a letter inviting Hans to join him in Zurich as an assistant conductor of the opera there, a position which Hans would share with Ritter himself. It transpired that Wagner was not entirely happy with the performance of this young acolyte, who had shown signs of inexperience at the podium, and he decided that Ritter's job, and his salary, ought to be divided with someone of superior calibre. His choice fell on Bülow whom he remembered from the Dresden days. The duties included rehearsing the orchestra, and conducting whatever operas Wagner was not inclined to direct himself. For Bülow it was a gift from heaven. Fearing to inform his father, he had set out on foot for Zurich in Ritter's company, a journey that took them two days. When Eduard discovered what had happened he pursued Hans to Zurich. According to Louise, Hans fell at the feet of his father and implored him to let him become a musician. His father gradually yielded, Louise continued, 'but on condition that his mother agreed to it. I did my best to calm [Eduard]. And my endeavours were not without result'.[4]

Now began a series of negotiations with his parents that resulted in one of Bülow's greatest psychological victories. In a long and wrenching letter to Franziska he explained that his love of music was greater than his love of the law, a profession which he called 'indescribably hateful'. And by way of stressing the irrevocable nature of his decision, he added, 'My views I cannot sacrifice for the love of you'.[5]

Knowing full well the pressures to which Bülow was being subjected by his parents, Wagner stepped in with a diplomatic letter to Franziska, which was meant to remove whatever doubts she might harbour about music as a suitable profession for her son. After explaining in detail the various circumstances that had led him to offer Bülow a position at Zurich, Wagner came to the nub of the matter:

Zurich
September 19, 1850

... Will you now permit a man who has attained to riper years, and who has been accustomed, as far as his power lay, to think and act not by halves, but fully—will you permit him to give his opinion on this point? I have followed the youthful, developing period of your son's life with cognizance and sympathy, without exercising

4. BB, vol. 1, p. 244.
5. Ibid., p. 247.

any other influence upon him than that of my example as an artist, and my most cautious advice. I have observed that his love of Art, and especially of music, is based upon no mere transient excitement, but upon great, indeed uncommon, powers. It was with my special concurrence, and indeed at my suggestion, that he went on with his law studies with undiminished zeal, as there is nothing so repugnant to me as a musician who is that alone, without any higher general culture. At the wish of his family he applied himself also to the study of Jurisprudence; full of devotion to his mother he tried hard to take an interest in this study, which in reality went dreadfully against the grain. And now what is the perfectly clear and evident result of all his pains and experience? Simply the outspoken and absolute conviction that the more he sets the one thing against the other the more he feels that it is Art alone—in other words, Music—that he can love unceasingly. This one thing, my dear Lady, stands first and foremost as an undeniable fact, and I cannot doubt that, when once you yourself are convinced of this wish of your son to devote himself entirely to music, you will make it your own wish also.

. . . Pardon the candour and plain-speaking of my letter! I address myself to no one to whom I may not venture to speak plainly and candidly, but I do so to you in a special and sacred cause, in which I am convinced that the happiness of a human being—or rather, considering your deep love to him, of two human beings— is at stake, whom I would fain see happy.

With deep respect and devotion, I am

Yours,

Richard Wagner.

For all its fine phrases this important letter did little to assuage Franziska's fretted feelings. The painful reality for her was that Hans had temporarily removed himself from her sphere of influence, had been proffered a modest income in Zurich, and was poised to become independent. This had never been a part of her plan. Almost before she had time to catch her breath, she received a second missive, this time from Franz Liszt:

Weimar

September 28, 1850

Madame La Baronne:

Several friends of your son's have spoken to me (unknown to him, as I believe), to beg me respectfully to submit a request to you. Little as I am fitted to serve as an intermediary with you for wishes and hopes—a noble and legitimate ambition—yet I confess that the knowledge of the duty, as well as the sincere affection I bear your son, will not permit me to put these pressing requests entirely aside, requests which, I do not doubt, are in accordance with your son's vocation. Whatever decision you may come to with regard to the future of his career, pray excuse, Madame, the liberty I am taking in meddling thus with questions of a nature at once so serious and so delicate, and do not impute to this letter any motive contrary to my habits and convictions.

Hans is evidently gifted with a musical organization of the rarest kind. His executive talent will easily place him in the front rank of the greatest pianists, and his essays at composition denote quite exceptional qualities of imagination, of individuality, and of conception. Besides, Hans has taken an antipathy to every career which would sever him from Art . . . . Permit me, then, to confide to your motherly love the happy solution of the noble struggle between his natural vocation and that destined for him, however bright and alluring it might be; and, in view of the sentiments which dictate this letter, pray pardon the intercession I have ventured to make to you today.

I have the honour to be, Madame la Baronne, with deep respect,

Your devoted servant,

F. Liszt

To receive two letters within nine days from two of the greatest musicians of the nineteenth century, glowing with praise for the musical gifts of her son, was without precedent. Yet Franziska remained implacably opposed to his choice of profession for years.

II

The three months that Hans spent in Zurich gave his life a new impetus. He worked with Wagner on a daily basis, and was entrusted by him with many practical duties at the opera house, including directing some of the orchestral rehearsals for Wagner himself. It would have been a remarkable opportunity for any young man standing on the threshold of a conducting career. For Bülow, at this time of crisis in his life, it was nothing less than a godsend. Among the operas he conducted were Lortzing's *Czar and Zimmerman,* Rossini's *Barber of Seville,* and Auber's *Fra Diavolo.* On occasion Wagner allowed Bülow to coach some of the leading singers, an experience that led to the young man's downfall. Bülow quarrelled with the husband of one of the leading ladies who subsequently gave notice that she would no longer sing under Bülow's direction, and in early December the Zurich appointment was abruptly terminated by the management. Wagner expressed it more euphemistically when he wrote that 'the management consented to free us from our irksome duties'.[6] As far as Bülow was concerned it was a harbinger of similar incidents to come. He never learned to control his acerbic tongue.

Eduard von Bülow, furious that his son could not even hold down his first important job, told Hans to 'freeze in the cold'.[7] Lurking in the background of the Zurich episode was the distrust that both parents had for Richard Wagner. The Dresden circle was still reeling from the fact that its erstwhile Royal Kapellmeister was now a fugitive in neutral Switzerland, with a price on his head, a result of his participation in the failed uprising the previous year. To Bülow and many of his young acquaintances, Wagner was a political hero. To Franziska and Eduard, however, the left-leaning Wagner was anathema. They were deeply concerned lest Hans had aligned himself with a fugitive from justice, a connection from which they felt no good would emerge.[8]

Hans sprang to Wagner's defence, and wrote a defiant letter to Eduard:

> I am a musician, and intend to remain one. I am a follower—now a pupil—of Wagner's, and shall prove this by my actions. That is irrevocably decided. . . . Save yourself reproaches until I have done something really wrong, I do implore you! If you withdraw your love from me because I place Wagner, whom I love and honour more every hour, above everything, then with tears I must say to you, "Well, do it then, and give it all to your Willi,[9] to whom I on my side will give all a brother's love in place of my filial love". But believe me that *I am so steadfast* that I am not afraid of anything, and take the consequences of my actions upon myself with my eyes open.[10]

---

6. WML, p. 552.

7. BB, vol. 1, p. 288.

8. In a little-known letter that Eduard wrote about this time to his cousin Ernst von Bülow in Berlin, we get a glimpse of some of the anxieties with which the Bülow family had been afflicted as a result of the 1849 Uprising. 'Let me disabuse your mind of one other error; you, as a good Prussian, will naturally have been anxious, like myself, lest Hans should through and through be republicanised by Wagner, and brought up as an arch-traitor. Therefore I give you my word of honour that Hans was only bitten by the political mania whilst he was wavering between two professions, as he was in Berlin. Once fixed in his true calling, as he is now, he thinks and dreams of nothing else but music . . .' (ibid., p. 295).

9. Willi was Hans's half-brother, now just a few months old, and the elder son of Eduard's second marriage.

10. BB, vol. 1, pp. 276–277.

It was Wagner who nonetheless came once more to Bülow's rescue by providing him with the necessary references to procure an appointment as conductor of the opera for a limited season at nearby St. Gall. Bülow's reputation had preceded him, and the good people of St. Gall seemed to be pleased that they had captured a kapellmeister from Zurich, a welcome change from losing their own best people to the country's commercial hub. The orchestra consisted almost entirely of *dilettanti*—a few merchants, lawyers, and some local officials—and Bülow at first despaired of doing anything worthwhile with such a motley group. 'What sort of animals I have to deal with in my orchestra it would pass the powers of natural history to imagine', he observed caustically.[11]

There were two bassoonists in the orchestra who always kept Bülow on tenterhooks. They were so enthusiastic that they were ready to make an entry at the slightest provocation, and Bülow had constantly to make signs to them not to come in ('Not yet! Not yet!'). This placed him in a very awkward position when they *had* to come in. But even these players paled by contrast with the drummer, who suffered from the opposite problem. So accurate was his timekeeping that whenever he had nothing to do, during those long stretches of idleness which composers often create for percussion players, he would repair to the local café and inwardly count his rests while taking his refreshment, then return to his post in time for his next entry. He never once jeopardized the ensemble. Thirty-five years later, when Bülow was at the height of his fame as a pianist, he returned to St. Gall to give a recital, at the conclusion of which he made a little speech to the audience about his 'first winter campaign' there, and the many anxious moments that the orchestra had given him.[12] Eventually Bülow managed to pull everything together, and went on to produce a notable performance of Weber's *Der Freischütz*, which he conducted from memory before a packed house. It pleased him greatly that his father attended this production and was able to observe his local triumph. During his tenure at St. Gall he gave a piano recital which did much to increase his local stature, and was attended by Wagner. The highlight of the programme was Liszt's demanding arrangement of Wagner's *Tannhäuser* Overture, which in Wagner's own words 'caused quite a sensation'. Up to that point he admitted that he had not paid sufficient attention to Bülow's piano playing, and was astounded at his execution.[13]

The season at St. Gall ended in April 1851, and Bülow found himself once more unemployed. He returned temporarily to his father's abode in

11. BB, vol. 1, p. 286.
12. Ibid., vol. 1, p. 287. This visit to St. Gall took place on February 25 and 26, 1886.
13. WML, p. 554.

Ötlishausen, the rupture with his mother not yet having been repaired. Eduard von Bülow, enthused by Hans's recent successes in St. Gall, had meanwhile approached Liszt for some advice, and had been impressed with the very detailed response that Liszt had given him. Liszt made no attempt to sugar the pill, and even warned Eduard of the folly of anyone trying to earn a living in Germany, either as a conductor or as a composer. But he felt certain that Hans could easily attain a high position as a piano virtuoso, and he assured Eduard that despite the obvious hardships of the profession he was willing to help Hans in whatever way that he could. 'As soon as ever an occasion arises, be assured that I shall neglect nothing which can prove to you the sincerity of my attachment to your son', Liszt told him. And he added that he would be glad to talk things over the next time Hans cared to come to Weimar.[14] This letter proved to be decisive. After staying for another month in Ötlishausen, Hans took his leave of his father and stepmother, and set out for Liszt in early June 1851.

III

When Bülow arrived in Weimar, he found that Liszt had left town for several weeks for the watering spa of Bad Eilsen, because of an illness of his companion, Princess Carolyne von Sayn-Wittgenstein. Informed that the young man now awaited him in Weimar, and was meanwhile encamped at the Altenburg (Liszt's large house on the hill just beyond the town centre), Liszt wrote to Bülow from Eilsen on June 21, 'I was delighted to hear of your safe arrival in Weimar, and since I must renounce the pleasure of receiving you there for several more weeks, let me at least bid you welcome there'.[15]

Bülow was allotted his own rooms in the Altenburg and the use of a piano. He himself tells us that he practised from eight to ten hours a day. He rose at 6:00 a.m., went straight to the keyboard in his dressing gown, 'and set to work at my hammering with a calm and peaceful soul'. Liszt's valet cleaned his shoes and pressed his clothes, while the cook prepared his breakfast. At 1:30 p.m. he went into town and had his midday meal at the Erbprinz Hotel. Then he walked for a couple of hours. By 4:00 p.m. he was back in his 'hole', as he put it, and practised until 9:00 p.m. His evening meal he would take at one of the local taverns. Back at the Altenburg he would 'improvise by moonlight, or in the dark—it makes no difference'.[16] As there was no spare door key, he would, if he got back late, often clamber over the wall and get into the house through a side window that he had discovered how to open from the outside, in order to avoid

---

14. Liszt's letter is dated 'Eilsen, January 4, 1851'. BB, vol. 1, pp. 292–294.
15. LBLB, p. 1.
16. BB, vol. 1, p. 332.

The Altenburg. A pencil drawing by Friedrich Preller.

disturbing the servants. This simple routine suited Bülow's monk-like devotion to art. Within a few short days he had mastered a difficult piano trio by Raff ('one with which even Liszt had to take no end of trouble') and was able to play it with two of Weimar's best string players, both of whom had recently been brought to Weimar by Liszt—the cellist Bernhard Cossmann and the violinist Joseph Joachim, who led the court orchestra.[17]

Bülow must have complained to someone about the poor condition of the piano that Liszt had placed at his disposal, for Liszt told him, 'I am sorry that you found such a bad piano in the rooms I beg you to consider yours at the Altenburg. If, as I would like, you prolong your stay in Weimar, it would be necessary for you to have a better instrument sent to you from Leipzig or elsewhere, for keyboards like Mr. Hippe's [a local manufacturer] ruin the fingers. For the first weeks, the damage will not be great, but in the long run it could happen that your performance might be affected unfavourably'.[18]

Liszt got back to Weimar on Sunday, October 12, and the lessons began the next day. Master and pupil worked on the last sonatas of Beethoven, the more significant compositions of Chopin and Schumann, and the newer works of Liszt himself. Liszt promised to help Bülow build a reper-

17. Ibid., p. 330.
18. LBLB, p. 1.

toire 'that no other pianist could show'.[19] Since Liszt never taught technique, Bülow was left very much to his own devices in this area, and he chose to continue working on Czerny's *School of Velocity* and the studies of Adolf Henselt, on which 'I crucify, like a good Christ, the flesh of my fingers, in order to make them obedient, submissive machines to the mind as a pianist must'.[20] To make the 'crucifixion' yet more severe, Bülow installed in his rooms a piano with a particularly stiff keyboard, and he drilled his fingers on this instrument daily.

IV

Liszt had lived in Weimar for about three years. He had taken up residence in this small town of 12,000 souls in 1848, after retiring from a virtuoso career unmatched in musical history. In one recital after another he had brought audiences to their feet as he swept through the major concert halls of Europe. And when he walked away from it all he was only thirty-five years old. Having secured his reputation as Europe's greatest pianist, he wanted leisure to compose. As early as 1842 he had been invited to take up the position of Kapellmeister to the court of Weimar, but he was unable to free himself from the yoke of a public performer until five years later. Many things attracted Liszt to Weimar. It was one of the more cultured centres in Germany. It throve under the benign patronage of the Grand Duchess Maria Pawlowna of Saxe-Weimar, sister of Tsar Nicholas I of Russia. And it could boast more than a century's unbroken association with the arts. Bach had lived and worked there; so, too, had Goethe and Schiller. Moreover it possessed a good orchestra and an opera house. Liszt's intention was to turn Weimar into a vanguard of modern music. Conservative cities like Vienna, Berlin, Leipzig, and Paris had put modern music into a straitjacket and made it virtually impossible for younger composers to gain a foothold. A new generation of musicians now turned to Liszt and Weimar for leadership. With characteristic generosity he placed himself and his resources wholeheartedly at their service. Overnight, Weimar became a mecca of contemporary music, and a steady stream of artists converged on the small town. Not only composers such as Wagner, Brahms, Rubinstein, and Berlioz descended on Weimar; but painters, sculptors, poets, dramatists, scientists, and politicians were frequent visitors, attracted there by Liszt's magnetic personality.

By the time that Bülow got to Weimar, Liszt's masterclasses were a fixture of musical life there. They were held in the music room of the Altenburg two or three times a week. His first generation of pupils included Karl Klindworth, Dionys Pruckner, Hans von Bronsart, the American pianist

19. BB, vol. 1, p. 343.
20. Ibid., p. 381.

Liszt in 1858. A photograph by Franz Hanfstaengl.

William Mason, and eventually the young Polish prodigy Carl Tausig. Bülow got to know them all in time, and formed bonds of collegiality that were severed only by death. To this magic circle we must add the names of composer Peter Cornelius, the Tiefurt organist Alexander Gott-schalg, the editor of the *Neue Zeitschrift für Musik* Franz Brendel, and above all Bülow's old friend Joachim Raff, who had been brought to Weimar by Liszt to help him orchestrate the early drafts of his symphonic poems. As to Bülow's keyboard studies, Liszt did not offer piano lessons in the con-ventional sense of the term. His classes were described as 'more like con-versations about music'. A student would play a work to the others—a Bach fugue or a Beethoven sonata, perhaps, a Chopin Ballade or some pieces by Schumann—with Liszt presiding at a second piano. A general discussion would then ensue, not only about the piece and its interpre-tation but also about the composer and his background. Refreshments would be served, anecdotes would flow, and a whole world of fresh ideas about music and musicians would be opened up to these young musi-cians. Liszt never charged a penny for his services. 'Génie oblige!' ('Genius carries obligations!') was his watchword. It was an example to which Bülow himself would often defer, both in his teaching and in his concerts.

Bülow was in any case more privileged than the other students because he often played to Liszt privately. And it was not mere piano instruction that Liszt offered the young man. During that first season in Weimar, Bülow spent much time with Liszt in the opera house and observed him conduct new productions of operas as diverse as Verdi's *Ernani,* Auber's *Carlo Broschi,* Spohr's *Faust,* and Flotow's *Indra*—works that were hardly performed elsewhere in Germany. When Liszt travelled out of town he sometimes took Bülow with him. In June 1852, for example, Liszt was invited to direct the Ballenstedt Music Festival, and he engaged Bülow as the soloist in Beethoven's Choral Fantasy, op. 80, a work that the young man would one day make very much his own. Liszt also procured solo engagements for his youthful protégé in nearby Erfurt and Jena.

For Bülow the great musical event of 1852 was the First Berlioz Festival, which Liszt mounted in the Weimar Opera House during the week of November 14 to 21. The fiery Frenchman himself came to Weimar to be fêted by Liszt and to hear some of his music performed. Berlioz shared the podium with Liszt. Among the works featured were *Roméo et Juliette, La Damnation de Faust,* and the revised version of Berlioz's opera *Benvenuto Cellini,* the first time that the work had been performed since its abysmal failure at the Paris Opéra fifteen years earlier—after which the French had taken to dismissing the work as 'Malvenuto Cellini'. Liszt had difficulty in recruiting enough orchestral players for *La Damnation,* so he invited some of his pupils to help out: Bülow played the bass drum, Dionys Pruckner the triangle, and Klindworth the cymbals. Berlioz declared himself satisfied—as well he might, because they were possibly the most distinguished percussion section ever assembled to perform his music. At the conclusion of the Festival, Berlioz was invested with the Order of the White Falcon by Grand Duke Carl Friedrich, and given a reception in the town hall, with more than eighty guests in attendance.

This was the heady atmosphere that the young Bülow inhaled during his time as Liszt's pupil. There were new ideas in the air, some of which he had hardly considered. What sort of language is music? What does music express? What is the difference between Absolute Music and Programme Music? Are there any underlying connections between music and the other arts? Does the symphony have a future, or must it be jettisoned in favour of newer forms such as the symphonic poem? Musicians had started to take sides on such issues. The resulting conflict, the so-called 'War of the Romantics', developed into one of the great cultural battles of the mid-nineteenth century, with progressive Weimar leading the revolution, and conservative cities such as Leipzig, Dresden, and Vienna providing the opposition. Bülow entered the fray with relish, and became one of Weimar's chief protagonists. He never forgot these halcyon days, and remained grateful to Liszt. The personal bond between master and pupil was to be tested later on, and Bülow eventually came to regret that he had identified so completely with the Weimar School during his headstrong years. But he also knew that the debt he owed to Liszt was incalculable, and could not be erased.

V

In Weimar Bülow continued to flex his muscles as a music critic. His motive for taking up the pen once more was at first financial. The life of genteel poverty into which he found himself slowly sinking made it necessary for him to turn his literary talents into money. He had a few piano students, but not enough to pay his way. Although he lived in the Altenburg as one of the family with Liszt and the princess, we find him complaining to his father that his clothes were in a neglected condition and he sometimes had to forgo his evening meal. Franziska sent him an allowance, but it was never enough to make ends meet. Liszt would doubtless have kept his young pupil solvent, but Bülow was too ashamed of his poverty to ask, so he pawned his watch instead.[21] The journals for which Bülow started to write—the *Neue Zeitschrift,* the Leipzig *Signale, Deutschland,* and later on the *Berliner Feuerspritze* and the *Neue Berliner Musikzeitung* —paid him little, but somehow enabled him to eke out a modest existence. More important, they made his name known across Germany. One article written under Liszt's roof brought him such notoriety that it has meanwhile entered the annals of music criticism.

In January 1852 the forty-six-year-old coloratura soprano Henriette Sontag turned up on the Weimar stage, presenting herself in three of her most famous roles: as 'Marie' in Donizetti's *The Daughter of the Regiment,* as 'Rosina' in Rossini's *The Barber of Seville,* and as 'Martha' in Flotow's *Martha.* Sontag brought much history to Weimar. In earlier years she had dominated the European operatic stage, her chief rival being Malibran. She had created the title role of Weber's *Euryanthe* when she was only seventeen, and a year later she had sung the soprano part in the premier performances of Beethoven's Ninth Symphony, as well as his *Missa solemnis.* Sontag's triumphs in London, Vienna, and Paris had, by the time she was in her mid-twenties, consolidated her position as one of the great singers of her time. In 1826, with Berlin at her feet, she had been satirized by the German critic Ludwig Rellstab in a pamphlet titled *Henriette, oder die schöne Sängerin.* Her fans were so outraged that Rellstab was tried for libel

---

21. Ibid., p. 444.

and served three months in Spandau Prison. A secret marriage to the diplomat Count Carlo Rossi in 1827, followed by a secret confinement, had not impeded her meteoric rise to fame, and more to the point it had not compromised Count Rossi's own career in the Sardinian diplomatic service either, as it so easily could have done had it been uncovered: Sontag was of low birth, so public exposure of such a marriage would have led to Rossi's certain ruin. But when in 1830 the king of Prussia, ravished by her singing, bestowed a title on Sontag, her station in life soared and she was able to live openly with her husband in the Hague as his equal, but in consequence was obliged to renounce her career for the man she loved. She was only twenty-four years old. For almost nineteen years Sontag rested on her laurels, appearing mainly before small diplomatic circles, a legend in her lifetime. (When Tsar Nicholas heard her, he took pleasure in calling her a '*Rossi*-gnol'—a nightingale—a designation that could hardly have originated with him who was much more at home with generals than with poets.) In 1849, as a result of the political upheavals sweeping Europe, the king of Sardinia abdicated, and Rossi's career in the diplomatic service was abruptly terminated. The Rossis were soon deeply in debt, partly the result of their lavish lifestyle and partly the result of the count's gambling habits, and Sontag had to make money. The impresario Benjamin Lumley came to the rescue and put 'the nightingale' on display at Her Majesty's Theatre in London for the phenomenal sum of £6,000 for a six-month season, and Sontag followed this with successful appearances in various parts of Europe, even though her voice was past its prime.

It is worth dwelling on these details because by the time that Sontag walked onto the Weimar stage in January 1852, they were known to the whole world, including Bülow, who turned up expecting to hear the miracle resurrected. He had, moreover, a special task, assigned to him by Franz Brendel, the editor of the *Neue Zeitschrift:* namely, to capture the essence of the evening in prose and give posterity a permanent reminder of what it was like to be in the presence of greatness. What Brendel got was an article of such virulence and sarcasm that it must have given him pause. For a time he even wondered whether he should print it. In the end he published it anonymously, thereby inadvertently creating another problem that we will come to presently.

What had Bülow said? He told his readers that Sontag could no longer lay claim to the title of a luminary of the first magnitude, for the simple reason that she was no longer a luminary of the second magnitude. Her return to the stage, Bülow went on, was the quickest way in which she could gather some necessary lucre. He described her as 'an artist of achievements which are no more achieved'. From any musical or even dramatic

Bülow as a young man. A lithograph.

standpoint she was past it. Her voice, he admitted, was still quite wonderful, but it did not contain a shred of poetry or genuine feeling, her emotional range spanning the distance between the soubrette and the coquette. He even drew the attention of his readers to her makeup, which was there to cover the cracks in what had once doubtless been a beautiful face. And he finished the process of demolition by referring to her unflatteringly as 'the Thalberg of song'. Bülow was shrewd enough to understand that since Sontag had been received rapturously by the general public, his own response was that of a minority. So that is what he called his polemic: 'The Opinion of the Minority'.[22]

A torrent of abuse was levelled against the *Neue Zeitschrift,* and a determined effort was made by Sontag's fans to identify the source of the article. In the absence of a name, the 'nightingale's' adherents provided one: Franz Liszt. They were quickly disabused by Brendel, who must have been genuinely concerned that the protective mantle of anonymity he had so obligingly thrown around Bülow now served the entirely unexpected purpose of pointing the finger of suspicion in a completely different di-

22. Published without attribution in the NZfM on February 13, 1852.

rection. But far worse lay in store for Bülow. Sontag, deeply offended by the article, appeared in Leipzig and Dresden, where she began an effective whispering campaign against him. These were the very cities associated with the Bülow family and their relatives, the powerful Frege clan, who were mortified to think that Sontag had been publicly ridiculed by one of their own, and they rallied round their famous guest. This was a major embarrassment for Bülow, who now found himself fighting battles on two fronts. His combative personality had no trouble in dealing with the venom directed against him through the columns of the Weimar and Leipzig newspapers; both *Deutschland* and the *Leipziger Tageblatt* carried articles against him, the latter even addressing an open letter to Liszt, saying in effect that his continued silence would be interpreted as complicity in the slanders of 'his pupil and protégé'.[23] What Bülow was unprepared for, and hardly knew how to cope with, was the injury inadvertently inflicted on his father, who criticized the article in the harshest terms, together with the brouhaha surrounding it. For a time, in fact, Eduard broke off relations with his son because of it. Bülow, deeply contrite, was forced to explain himself:

> Weimar, May 25, 1852
> Dearest Father:
> If you have a spark of affection left for a son who, though his actions speak against him, has never for a moment ceased to think of you with the deepest love, I do beg you, above everything in the world, not to be angry with me any longer for the unhappy time now (thank the gods) past, but to forgive and forget.
> . . . Had Liszt known of my intention he would at all events have tried to dissuade me from it; but he did not see the article till it was in print and too late to recommend me to write more moderately. As regards the calumny which touched himself he said nothing, and thereby gave me a lesson and an example of how I ought to behave towards injuries to myself. By this calm and resolute silence I have been able to preserve a demeanour that is in my favour, and I am sure I have thus avoided many unpleasantnesses. I have made a collection of the most violent attacks in the papers here, and from Leipzig, etc.; if you were to read those you would understand in what a state of perpetual excitement and embitterment the long dragging on of these affairs has placed me; though at the same time I did receive a few very flattering, but not very comforting sign of recognition of my courage. Not merely people such as Robert

---

23. Ibid., February 22, 1852.

Franz, Wagner, Herwegh, but even quite respectable Philistines, have given me to understand that they entirely approve of what I had done.

After offering several more pages of self-justification, he signed the letter 'Your loving son, Giovanni Penitente'.[24] By summoning such distinguished witnesses as Robert Franz, Wagner, and the poet Georg Herwegh to his defence, it is clear that whatever lamentations and supplications were now pouring from his pen, 'the Penitent One' remained secretly proud of his article. He had hoped all along that it would create a commotion. This is borne out by a letter to his young colleague Theodor Uhlig, written shortly after the article was finished, in which he said:

> It is the best article I have yet written. It will create a scandal that is not an article of luxury, but of necessity. If you read it before you have heard Sontag you will think that it is reeking of impudence, but afterwards you will see that it is only full of truth and moderation. What a lot of good puns I could have put into it also![25]

To his sister Isidora he was even more boastful. He wrote to her that if she had an opportunity to hear Sontag, not to take it. Then he provided her with this interesting anecdote. A few days earlier he had bumped into Johann Eckermann, who had attended Goethe in his final years and whose book *Conversations with Goethe* had made him famous. It was pouring with rain, but Eckermann walked along the cobbled streets of Weimar, through the mud and the downpour with his umbrella up, in order to have a fifteen-minute chat with Bülow about Sontag. Eckermann told Bülow that Goethe himself had held negative views about the singer. 'When I had discovered what kind of creature [Sontag] was', Goethe was supposed to have told Eckermann, 'and had got sufficiently enraged over the bad taste of the public, I took both my grandchildren, in spite of their resistance, and led them, one in each hand, out of the theatre, just as Lot fled with his two daughters from Sodom and Gomorrah when his wife was turned into a pillar of salt'. To which Bülow added, 'Eckermann forgot to publish this [in his *Conversations*], so now boast that you know it'.[26]

As for Liszt, he understood Bülow through and through and admired the young man's readiness to stand in harm's way. Early one morning,

24. BB, vol. 1, pp. 441–443.
25. Ibid., p. 420.
26. Ibid., p. 425.

and at the height of the scandal, he called on Bülow and presented him with a special gift. It was a stick, 'most original and full of meaning. . . . It is to me like a badge of the Order of Liszt of the Altenburg'.[27] This was tantamount to having Liszt's authority to go on beating those artists who appeared to place themselves above the art that they were supposed to serve.

There the matter might have rested. Alas for Sontag (and for Bülow, too) the storm surrounding the article returned to buffet them both the following year. When she arrived in New York she found Bülow's polemic waiting for her, translated into English and published on the front pages of *The Musical World*, where it was openly (and possibly deliberately) attributed to Liszt.[28] In the end, this piece of malice probably brought more grief to Bülow than to Sontag. The rest of the saga is soon told. Her relentless pursuit of lucre led her to Mexico City, performing *The Daughter of the Regiment* in the afternoons and *Lucrezia Borgia* in the evenings. It was an impossible workload. She contracted cholera on June 11, and died on June 17, 1854, aged forty-eight.

There was a lesson for Bülow in the Sontag affair, but he stubbornly failed to benefit from it. He curbed neither his pen nor his tongue, and in consequence brought much retribution down on his head. It would take us far afield to examine the abysmal state of music criticism in the mid-nineteenth century, and the increasing concerns that musicians harboured against journalists who could demolish them with a stroke of the pen, while lacking any training in the art of music. Liszt spoke for the entire profession when he said that 'the field of musical literature is far too little cultivated by practising artists. If they continue to neglect it they will have to bear the consequences and pay *their* damages'.[29] Bülow was simply taking his master's words to heart by presuming that his position as a 'practising artist' endowed him with the authority to set the necessary standards. Robert Schumann, the founding editor of the *Neue Zeitschrift,* was the shining example for everybody, and as the nineteenth century unfolded he was joined by Berlioz, Wagner, Hugo Wolf, and Liszt himself —all of whom made memorable contributions to music criticism. Later would come Debussy. Whether there is a conflict of interest in having 'practising artists' act as their own judge and jury, or whether there is something to be said for an independent commentary is still an open question.

27. Ibid., p. 423.
28. Issues of March 19 and 26, 1853.
29. LLB, vol. 1, p. 197.

VI

Within eighteen months Liszt felt that Bülow was ready to make his public debut, and he encouraged his twenty-three-year-old protégé to undertake a short concert tour, first to Vienna and then to Pest, Dresden, and Leipzig. The itinerary was a good one. Liszt had solid contacts in all these cities, and as 'a pupil of Liszt' many doors were opened for the young man that might otherwise have remained closed. Liszt nonetheless followed Bülow's journey with some trepidation, for he knew that much hinged on the outcome. At first the news from Vienna was bad. The hall was not full and Bülow had to make good the deficit out of his own pocket. Worse, the Viennese critics found his playing frigid. Part of the trouble was that he was billed as a 'Pianist aus Weimar'. To the conservative Viennese this would have been a provocation; the 'War of the Romantics' was in full swing, the music of Liszt much criticized. After reading their reviews Bülow fell into a depression, developed one of his famous headaches, and retired to his hotel bedroom. Franziska von Bülow foresaw a disaster-in-the-making for her son, and worked herself into a hysteria. 'God forgive those who led him to it' she told Liszt, doubtless lacking the courage to blame him directly for her son's misfortune.[30] Liszt was magnanimity itself. He told Franziska to be patient, reminding her of Hans's boundless talent which would guarantee for him 'a good and fine career'. He then wrote to Bülow himself, advising him to remain in the imperial city for a while in order to strengthen his contacts there. He also got in touch with his uncle Eduard Liszt, a prominent Viennese lawyer who looked after Liszt's own investments, instructing him to advance Bülow 100 florins for ongoing expenses, and keep another hundred in reserve for him.

Meanwhile, Eduard von Bülow observed the development of his son's musical career with silent satisfaction. In a letter to cousin Ernst, he wrote:

> Hans has ended his musical education. His first compositions have just appeared in Leipzig, and he is about to begin his first great concert tour of Vienna and Pest.
>
> Liszt has the greatest expectations of his success.
>
> In his basic political beliefs—I say thank God!—he remains unchanged. He only has to learn to control himself and to remain silent—until better times.[31]

'Silent—until better times'. Eduard's anxieties were rooted in the political uncertainties of the day, and in his son's penchant for direct speech. Four

---

30. BB, vol. 2, pp. 9–10.
31. Ibid., vol. 1, p. 505.

years earlier Hungary's ill-fated War of Independence against Austria had been crushed, and the nation brought to its knees as the Austrians occupied the country and carried out massive retribution. Bülow had never travelled beyond Germany's borders (save for his fleeting trip to Switzerland), and Eduard was concerned for the personal safety of his son. The Compromise of 1867, and with it the emergence of the Austro-Hungarian Empire, was to change everything. But in 1853, Hungary was likened to a graveyard, with the Austrians as the grave diggers.

Bülow's first real success came in Hungary. To ensure that the young man's appearance in Pest went smoothly, Liszt had written ahead of time to a number of his powerful friends there. On June 1, 1853, Bülow walked onto the stage of the Hungarian National Theatre and played Liszt's Fantasie on themes from Beethoven's 'Ruins of Athens', for piano and orchestra, with Ferenc Erkel conducting, and received a standing ovation. Bülow wrote to his mother that the occasion was 'an unparalleled triumph', a view that was confirmed by Liszt. 'He was called back for an encore ten times, and at the end of the concert he was forced to replay *in full* a very long piece (the Fourteenth Hungarian Rhapsody) . . . for which I had given him the manuscript'.[32] While he was in Hungary the newly founded publishing firm of Rózsavölgyi, doubtless wishing to capitalize on his successful collaboration with Erkel, invited him to compose a concert piece for solo piano, based on Erkel's own national opera *Hunyadi László*. Bülow chose to paraphrase the 'Marche héroïque', a part of the opera which was already widely popular with the Hungarian public, and which was designed to show off his powers as a virtuoso. This unabashed showpiece would hardly merit our attention today, were it not for the fact that its unauthorized republication in New York nearly twenty-five years later created a minor scandal during Bülow's first tour of America.[33]

Bülow's early concert tours had fulfilled their promise, and had brought him to national attention. Thanks to Liszt, he was poised to embark on the life of a piano virtuoso. He possessed the repertoire, the technique, and above all, the imprimatur of his master. Liszt bestowed on Bülow the highest possible praise when he observed, 'I do not consider him my *pupil*, but rather my heir and successor'.[34]

32. Unpublished letter to an unknown correspondent dated 'Weimar, June 8, 1853' (AWC, box 30). The Fourteenth Hungarian Rhapsody, arranged here for piano and orchestra under the title 'Fantasie on Hungarian Folk-themes' (S.123) was receiving its world premier. It is dedicated to Bülow, together with the version of this Rhapsody for solo piano (S.244, no. 14).

33. See pp. 216–17.

34. CLBA, p. 42.

The Growing Virtuoso,
1853–1855

In the diadem of virtuosity, [Bülow] gleams like a solitaire, the most
precious crown jewel in the world of piano playing.

—Ludwig Rellstab[1]

I

On September 16 Eduard von Bülow died in Switzerland after suffering a
stroke. More than a week elapsed before the news reached Bülow, because
no one had a precise idea of where he was. His concert tours had taken
him to Karlsruhe, and it was not until September 25, just as he was about
to leave the city, that he was handed the fateful letters from his mother
and his sister, informing him of his father's demise. News of the tragedy
shattered him. His reply to his mother, written the next day, reveals the
depth of his loss:

Karlsruhe, September 26, 1853
Dearest Mother:
I am quite inconsolable. Nothing could ever have affected me more
deeply; *never* could a blow be harder than this, unexpected as it
was, indeed not even feared.

I was so infinitely happy at the prospect of travelling with Liszt
in Switzerland after the [Karlsruhe] musical festival, and of then
visiting him who can never know how truly and deeply I have
loved him. So without a farewell—for ever! His fatherly look, which
since yesterday has been constantly in my mind's eye—dust!

It is terrible. As yet I can scarcely realize it. So many hopes shattered for ever! That of your reconciliation, lost;—That of the discourse which I now first thought to begin with him, over;—I myself

1. *Vossische Zeitung,* December 8, 1854.

an orphan, deprived henceforth of the father, whose happiness, would that I could say together with yours, would have compensated me for my past and probably future misfortunes!

My father's love—I recognize its immeasurable, unique value just as it is lost to me for ever. The sacred connection between him and me broken—no father for me any more!

No one in the whole world who was from the depths of the heart so determined to be, and was, '*my best friend;*' that he exists no more for me, I, no more for him, I dead to him—yes, that also is death!

It is terrible, and so quickly too, so entirely without warning! . . . Farewell, dear mother . . .

Your deeply afflicted son,

Hans[2]

Two days later Bülow arrived in Ötlishausen, where he braced himself for the sad task of comforting his stepmother, Louise, and his two small step-brothers, Heinz and Willi. He commissioned a memorial stone to mark his father's remains in the local burial chapel, and began the process of cataloguing Eduard's vast collection of books. Louise later made a gift of this library to Bülow, an act of generosity which overjoyed him and helped further to cement the cordial relations he enjoyed with her for the rest of his life.[3]

In the midst of these sad rituals, he wrote to his sister, Isidora:

Ötlishausen, September 28, 1853

My dear, beloved sister:

I am too violently shaken, too painfully smitten, so stupefied, I might say, in mind and strength, that I am unable to answer your beautiful letter (which I received just as I was leaving Karlsruhe) as it deserves—to give you, or rather to return to you, anything like what you have given me. The tears which flowed down my cheeks as I read your sad words had so relieved and strengthened me that I was able to take the very fatiguing journey in my overwrought condition, without injury to my health . . .

[My father] would really have had much happiness in me; I pictured to myself our discourse after the Karlsruhe festival as so delightful, so soothing and enlivening for me—for I was quite determined to surprise him then by a pretty long visit . . . I should

2. BB, vol. 2, pp. 89–91.
3. BNB, pp. 535–556.

have told him minutely of all my joys and sorrows, small and great; he would probably have listened to me gladly and patiently; I should have collected all the printed signs and traces of my first artist-journey which were of but little value to me; to please me he would have played the role of Virtuoso-Papa . . .
Your deeply stricken brother,
Hans[4]

Distraught though he was, Bülow was unable to linger in Ötlishausen. The Karlsruhe Festival, which this year was directed by Liszt, was about to begin, and Bülow had promised to play Liszt's Fantasie on Themes from Beethoven's 'Ruins of Athens' on October 5, conducted by Liszt himself. 'And I will do it', he told his mother stoically, determined not to let his master down. 'I shall have recovered myself by that time'.[5] This sojourn in Karlsruhe, in fact, did Bülow a world of good. He was reunited with his old Weimar companions Cornelius, Joachim, and Pruckner; and Liszt's presence was a steadying influence. The streets of the venerable city had been decked out with bunting, and the music festival had been combined with a *Volksfest,* featuring a fireworks display and a torchlight procession, with manifold attractions for the townspeople. There was even a spectacular release of air-balloons which filled the sky with colour. As for the musical side of the festival, it was one of the most ambitious that had ever been mounted in Germany up to that time. It included performances of Beethoven's Ninth Symphony, Schumann's *Manfred* Overture, Joachim's Violin Concerto (with Joachim himself as soloist), excerpts from Wagner's *Lohengrin* and Mendelssohn's unfinished opera *Die Lorelei,* as well as the second part of Berlioz's dramatic symphony *Romeo and Juliet* and works by Meyerbeer and Mozart, all of them conducted by Liszt.[6] Bülow's performance of the Fantasie went so well that he later claimed that it was at Karlsruhe that his name first became properly known in Germany.[7] Nonetheless, this triumph was tinged with sadness, coming so hard on the heels of the death of a father unable to witness it.

II

Bülow spent the spring and summer of 1854 in Dresden with his mother. His letters of this period show that he enjoyed good connections with a number of wealthy Polish aristocrats who regularly spent their summer

4. BB, vol. 2, pp. 91–96.
5. Ibid., pp. 90–91.
6. By far the best account of the Karlsruhe festival was written by 'Liszt's bulldog', the critic Richard Pohl, in PGS, vol. 2, pp. 5–45.
7. See Bülow's autobiographical sketch, BB, vol. 3, pp. 167–168.

holidays in the old city, not far from the Polish border. To one such family—Countess Kamienska and her daughter Helene, who had a fixed home in Dresden—Bülow was especially close, and he often took part in the soirées that they arranged in their stylish apartments for their fellow Poles. It was here that Bülow met Count Theodor Mycielski, who asked him to give his four daughters music lessons during their six-month stay in the city. Bülow needed the money and readily agreed. The arrangement was so successful that the Count further proposed that starting in the autumn Bülow should accept the position of permanent music-master to the Mycielski household, and take up residence in the family castle at Chocieszewice, situated near Kröben in the Polish duchy of Poznań, an area somewhat removed from the civilized world. This unusual offer gave Bülow pause. There was nothing in it to advance his career as a pianist—nothing, that is, save the salary which might at least enable him to put aside enough money to pay for future concerts in Paris, a trip that Liszt had been urging on him as a necessary next step in his career. Bülow described Count Mycielski's proffer as 'three or four hundred crowns a year, with room and board', in exchange for which he had to give 'three or four lessons a day, and amuse the people in the evening with my playing'.[8] Because he was in debt to his mother, and wanted to find some way to repay her, he accepted his fate. But the prospect of a Polish exile, beginning in October, was not one that he relished.

Meanwhile, the spring of 1854 was enlivened for Bülow by the welcome arrival in Dresden of Hector Berlioz. The French composer was in the middle of a tour of Germany, which had taken him to Hanover and Brunswick, and brought him to Dresden during the third week of April. We recall that the two musicians had already met in Weimar, in November 1852, during the weeklong 'Berlioz Festival' that Liszt had mounted in honour of the composer. But nothing had prepared Bülow for the overwhelming impression made on him as he witnessed Berlioz rehearsing his own music in the old Dresden Opera House, the scene of so many of his childhood memories, and with a somewhat better orchestra than the one that Liszt had been able to muster. It was like a return of the glory days when Richard Wagner had been in charge. Altogether Berlioz conducted four concerts in Dresden, and the first of them, devoted to a performance of *The Damnation of Faust,* on April 22, got the series off to a spectacular start. At the conclusion of the concert the theatre intendant, Baron von Lüttichau, came on stage and invited Berlioz to repeat the work, a performance which took place three days later, on April 25. The other concerts featured the *Romeo and Juliet* Symphony, *The Flight into*

---

8. BB, vol. 2, p. 212.

Das alte Dresdener Hoftheater

The old Royal Opera House, Dresden. A lithograph.

Egypt (from 'The Childhood of Christ'), and the *Roman Carnival* and *Benvenuto Cellini* overtures. This was difficult music that had been the undoing of many orchestras. But the Dresden players rose to the occasion and played magnificently under their distinguished visitor. This had the rather peculiar effect of upsetting Kapellmeister Karl Krebs, who had taken over the Royal Opera House Orchestra after Richard Wagner had fled Dresden in 1849. 'Can you imagine it?' Bülow complained to Liszt. 'Last week Krebs . . . bitterly rebuked the orchestra for having played so splendidly for a "foreigner". What a public humiliation for the local conductors, under whose direction it never managed to play with such zeal and ardour!'.[9] So enthusiastic were the players and singers in their praise of Berlioz that they wanted to keep him in Dresden as their musical director 'following five years of sterility', as Bülow put it. Lüttichau broached this intriguing possibility to Berlioz himself. When Berlioz pointed out that the job was not vacant, Lüttichau replied, 'It could become so'.[10] In the event, Berlioz left Dresden with this matter unsettled; his life took on a different direction, and Lüttichau never returned to the topic in subsequent correspondence with Berlioz.

III

The bile with which Krebs flavoured his comments about Berlioz can only be understood within the broader context that was already in place before the composer arrived in town. It was widely accepted that the work

9. LBLB, p. 78.
10. CB, vol. 2, p. 538.

of the disaffected Kapellmeister was marked by ineptitude. Bülow was convinced that Krebs could not read the simplest score without difficulty, and after enduring a number of third-rate productions under his baton he was ready to expose him publicly. Fortunately he was spared the trouble. That task was taken over by Richard Pohl, who wrote music criticism in support of Liszt and the New Music under the aggressive pseudonym of 'Hoplit'—a heavily armed infantry soldier of ancient Greece, equipped with helmet, breastplate, sword, and shield. Dismayed at the sharp decline in musical standards since Wagner's departure from the Dresden Opera House, Pohl subjected Krebs to a regular pounding in the columns of the *Neue Zeitschrift*. He even made comical allusion to the name 'Krebs' (which means crab in German), implying that opera in Dresden was moving sideways and even backwards, but never forwards. Goaded beyond endurance Krebs replied, not in the *Neue Zeitschrift,* with its relatively limited circulation, but in the columns of two of Germany's national newspapers—the widely read *Deutsche Allgemeine Zeitung* and the *Constitutionelle Zeitung.* Pohl found his remarks so insulting that he was urged to seek satisfaction by challenging Krebs to a duel. Even Liszt became involved in the matter. 'Such a coarse public insult absolutely calls for pistols. . . . Only a drunken stable-boy could approve of Krebs's behaviour towards you', Liszt assured his acolyte. 'Police intervention in the matter must be carefully avoided, but you certainly cannot dispense with the satisfaction due to you'.[11] It would not have been the first time that Art and Criticism had bloodied themselves on a field of honour; but on this occasion a physical confrontation was avoided. Pohl appealed to an *Ehrengericht* (a citizen's court set up to examine disputes in which the integrity of one or more of the parties was impugned) which ruled in his favour. It was from this decision that Krebs was still smarting when Berlioz arrived in town.

Because Bülow spoke fluent French and Berlioz spoke no German, the two musicians established a unique rapport during the latter's stay in Dresden, which resulted in a subsequent correspondence between the pair.

11. WLP, p. 196. Pohl had fired his opening salvo in the columns of the NZfM on August 20, 1852, under the provocative headline 'Die Dresdner Oper und ihr Verfall'—'the Dresden Opera-house and Its Decline'. He followed through with twelve more articles, each one more critical than the last, which appeared in successive issues of the NZfM dated October 29, November 12 and 19, December 17, 1852; January 14, May 27, October 7, 1853; February 10, March 17, April 7, June 23, July 14, 1854. Krebs was left with little choice but to respond. He wrote a letter of protest to the NZfM, and when it did not appear he sent it to the *Constitutionelle* instead. He accused Pohl of having 'endeavoured with all his usual arrogance to place my activities in the worst possible light', and recommended that after reading his letter, Pohl should impose on himself 'a year-long silence due to a man of honour', namely to Krebs himself.

Bülow had already written two long articles about *Benvenuto Cellini*, for the *Neue Zeitschrift* and *Deutschland*, respectively,[12] so Berlioz had every reason to be grateful to him. The younger man also translated into French some local criticisms from the Dresden newspapers that pleased Berlioz. Berlioz in turn found time to hear Bülow play the piano. He told Bülow that if his plans to come to Paris materialized, he would do everything possible to facilitate the visit. It must have been on one of these private encounters that Bülow offered to undertake a four-hand piano arrangement of the Overture to *Benvenuto Cellini*, which was as yet unpublished, and he began work on it almost as soon as Berlioz had departed Dresden. Bülow accomplished this task with so much alacrity that when the manuscript arrived in Paris, just a few weeks later, a delighted Berlioz observed, 'It is a charming surprise that you have given me, and your manuscript is all the more welcome as Brandus, the publisher, who is at this moment engraving *Cellini*, had already chosen a somewhat obscure and sixth-rate pianist to arrange the Overture'.[13]

Berlioz left Dresden in early May and caught the night train to Weimar, where he spent the next four days with Liszt, making arrangements for a performance of the newly completed oratorio *L'Enfance du Christ* to take place in the Weimar Court Theatre the following year.[14] From there he returned to Paris in a state of exhilaration that his music had been so well received in Germany.

IV

By early October 1854, Bülow was en route for Chocieszewice, and his Polish 'exile'. The first stage of the long journey, which took him from Dresden to Breslau, was, in Bülow's words, 'horrible', involving poor roads and overnight travel. He was impressed with the musical life of Breslau, however, and witnessed 'a very decent performance' of Meyerbeer's *Robert le diable*. Then followed another overnight journey from Breslau to the small Polish town of Rawicz, where he arrived at six o'clock in the morning. Because he was carrying such a lot of extra luggage he was charged an additional fee, with the result that he could not afford to continue his journey and had to prevail on the good offices of the woman in charge of the coach-line at Rawicz to let him continue his journey and send the

12. NZfM, vol. 36, issues of April 2 and 30, 1852. The *Deutschland* article was spread across four consecutive days, on November 18, 19, 20, and 21, 1852.

13. BB, vol. 2, p. 225. Bülow would later supply the piano accompaniments for six 'Lyric Pieces' from the opera itself. Later still, in 1879, he would revive this ill-fated opera and mount a full production of the work in Hanover.

14. It duly occurred on February 21, 1855, during the Second Berlioz Festival arranged by Liszt.

bill to Count Mycielski. The coach finally pulled into the entrance of Chocieszewice Castle at 10:30 a.m., having weathered a bitterly cold storm, with Bülow 'gone all to pieces'. The journey Bülow described as 'contemptible'. As a final indignity, there was no one at the castle to greet him, the count having left with his contingent of daughters and their governess to visit some relatives for a few days. Bülow told his mother that he was so displeased with the treatment he had received so far, that if things did not improve when the count returned, he would be unable to endure such horrors for more than a month.[15]

The castle Bülow found quite grand, and he was especially impressed with its spacious dining halls and salons, which were of royal proportions. But the rooms were so cold, he observed, that one needed a Slavonic temperament to withstand the frigid air. His own room was damp, the recent inundations having penetrated the walls. The first thing he had to do was to light the stove which, so he was assured by the old Polish valet assigned to him, would throw out enough heat to dry him out. The service offered by this manservant, who understood hardly any German, functioned in Bülow's words at the same level as that of a prison jailor, both as regards quantity and quality. Although Bülow needed no money for living expenses, he was obliged to appeal to his mother for certain luxuries—a bottle of hair-oil, a small pair of scissors, and a supply of his favourite Russian cigarettes, which he instructed her to buy in Dresden and then mail to the castle.

During the temporary absence of the count, Bülow was left in the dubious care of the countess, a woman of aimless disposition who was the count's second wife, with daughters of her own, and who distracted him with her idle chatter. After dinner she prevailed upon him to charm her with his piano playing, which he did with frozen fingers in the cold music room, while the countess accompanied him with her ceaseless conversation. Deliverance from this bondage came with the return of the count, who introduced some order into Bülow's life, and reviewed his main duties. He replaced the Polish valet with one from Dresden, with whom Bülow could at least converse in German; he had his carpenter build Bülow a proper wardrobe for his clothes, which had hitherto been randomly draped across the furniture; and he even passed along the latest newspapers to Bülow, after he himself had read them—the *Indépendance,* the *Schlesische Zeitung,* and Bülow's favourite, the satirical *Kladderadatsch.*

In this unlikely environment Bülow settled into a daily routine. He rose at 7:00 a.m. and had breakfast. From 9 to 11 he was expected to give

15. BB, vol. 2, p. 243.

A youthful picture of Bülow. A pencil drawing by Stein.

two music lessons, during which he instilled into the count's unwilling daughters some Czerny studies, Döhler's *Tarantella,* and Willmers' popular *Schwalben* study. He described the experience as analogous to 'the national torture of Persia', the wrong notes dripping into his ears like the constant drops of water on the skull of a convict. A daily walk at noontime in the surrounding park helped him to recover his composure. He then practised the piano for a couple of hours. At 2:00 p.m. came the main meal of the day, followed by more 'aimless conversations', this time in French. Because the count insisted on grounds of health that the temperature inside the castle's main rooms should hover around the freezing point, Bülow was forced to go outside to get warm. From 4:00 p.m. to 5:00 p.m. came more piano practice and from 5:00 p.m. to 6:00 p.m. he gave the third lesson of the day. After a hot supper he repaired to his room, where he cheered himself up by reading Gervinus's *Literaturgeschichte des deutschen Mittelalters* and Berlioz's *Soirées d'Orchestre*. One topical souvenir to emerge from these bleak months was his salon piece Mazurka-Impromptu, op. 4, 'dedicated to Countess Elisa Mycielska'.

V

It has been well said that geography determines destiny. Bülow knew that unless he made the effort to seek a wider public, preferably in Berlin, he might moulder indefinitely in what he had taken to calling his 'Polish swamp'. With not much time left before the Christmas season brought everything to a standstill, he secured a short leave of absence from Chocieszewice, and with barely sufficient funds to pay for the trip, set out for the Prussian capital.

Bülow arrived in Berlin on November 30 and booked a room in Meinhardt's Hotel, on the Unter den Linden. The first thing he did was to call on a number of prominent people to enlist their support. With all the brashness of his twenty-four years he approached Ludwig Rellstab, the powerful critic of the *Vossische Zeitung,* who, much to Bülow's chagrin, threw him a sop and gave him just one line in the newspaper announcing his upcoming concert.[16] Baron Boto von Hülsen, the intendant of the Berlin Opera, to whom Bülow sent his card, also showed him scant courtesy; it was the beginning of Bülow's lifelong enmity towards this particular administrator, which would result in some memorable confrontations across the years. His meeting with the composer and theorist Adolf Marx went more smoothly. Marx was well acquainted with Liszt, took an active interest in Bülow, and provided the young man with a lot of useful information about musical life in Berlin. Together with Theodor Kullak and Julius Stern, Marx had earlier founded the Berliner Musikschule, now known as the Stern Conservatory of Music, a leading establishment for the training of professional musicians. These personal contacts aside, Bülow's immediate concern was to find an instrument on which to practice, and after a search that took him the better part of a day, he settled for a grand piano by Eck of Cologne, whose rich tone pleased him. All these perambulations through the damp winter streets of Berlin gave him a cold, the last thing he needed before making his solo debut in the capital.

If Bülow was to make any impact at all on the Berlin public, and receive some badly needed press coverage, he knew that a simple piano recital in a simple venue would not be enough. He would have to appear as a concerto soloist, and for that he would have to engage a symphony orchestra. His choice fell upon Carl Liebig's orchestra, then considered to be the best in the city. That in turn meant finding a suitable hall, so Bülow rented the well-known Singakademie. To make sure of an audience, and as an additional enticement for the critics, Bülow asked Johanna Wagner (the celebrated opera singer, and niece of Richard Wagner) to appear with him.[17]

---

16. Rellstab could hardly have forgotten that four years earlier he had been the butt of Bülow's humour, in the *Abendpost.*

17. By bringing in another name to add lustre to his own, Bülow was simply following established practice. Artists who were unknown had to bear all the costs, and tried to recover them by adding other box office attractions.

As a final precaution, he arranged for the concert to be managed by the publishing house of Bote and Bock. This cost money, and the young man found himself turning yet again to his mother for help. To add to his worries, Clara Schumann, who was presently in Breslau, announced that she was coming to Berlin to give concerts of her own.[18] Bülow lived in daily anguish that the two events would clash, and rob him of an audience. Small wonder that he exclaimed, 'It is impossible that, among pianists, there can be a man more worried than I am'.[19]

Bülow's programme is almost forgotten today, and no handbills have survived. But from an advertisement in the *Vossische Zeitung* (December 6, 1854), it is possible to reconstruct the details.

CHERUBINI	Overture to *Les Abencerrages*
BEETHOVEN	Piano Concerto no. 5, in E-flat major (*Emperor*), op. 73
RAIMONDI	Aria with Orchestra
	soloist, Johanna Wagner
BACH-LISZT	Prelude and Fugue in A minor
CHOPIN	Ballade no 1, in G minor, op. 23
	Intermission
BÜLOW	Lieder[20]
	soloist, Johanna Wagner
WEBER	Polonaise brillante, op. 72
	arr. for piano and orchestra by Liszt
LISZT	Fantasie on Hungarian Folk-themes, for Piano and Orchestra (dedicated to Bülow)

Half-an-hour before he walked onto the concert platform, Bülow received 'a dear, dear letter from Liszt' which in his words 'raised and strengthened me to an uncommon degree'.[21] The audience was small but distinguished, and included some of Berlin's musical elite—composers Friedrich Truhn and Emil Nauman; pianists Theodor Kullak and Julius Stern; the music pedagogue Adolf Marx; and the philosopher Bruno Bauer, who had been a student of Hegel. More important, a phalanx of music critics turned up, including Ludwig Rellstab (*Vossische Zeitung*); Otto Gumprecht

18. Clara Schumann was at that moment on a tour of Germany. Her husband, Robert, had been incarcerated in Endenich earlier in the year, after a failed suicide attempt, and she had meanwhile picked up the threads of her former career as a concert pianist in order to support her large family.

19. BB, vol. 2, p. 296.

20. We surmise that these were the Six Songs, op. 1, settings of poems by Heine and Sternau, for soprano with piano accompaniment, composed about eighteen months earlier under Liszt's supervision, and published by Kahnt of Leipzig. Bülow mentions them in a letter to his father (ibid., vol. 1, p. 466–447).

21. Ibid., vol. 2, p. 303.

(*Nationalzeitung*); and Ernst Kossak, who reported for a variety of newspapers throughout Prussia, encompassing Berlin, Königsberg, and Breslau. The press coverage was more than Bülow could have hoped for, and brought him to national attention. He was angered by Rellstab, however, who came forward privately to praise his performance of the *Emperor* Concerto and then happily 'ate his own words' by saying the opposite in his public column. Rellstab had reached that most mournful stage in the life of a music critic, where every positive reaction has to be set against a negative one in order to create a semblance of balance. Nonetheless, when Rellstab described Bülow as 'standing alone among the modern virtuosi',[22] he was offering the young pianist the highest praise his particular lexicon could provide.

Artistically, the concert had been a success. Financially, Bülow was chagrined to find himself in debt to the tune of 122 thaler. He was also incensed at what he considered to be an act of gamesmanship on the part of Clara Schumann, who advertised her own concert on the very day that he gave his own. He admitted to being somewhat envious when he learned that she was to share her concert with Joachim. That event took place a day or two after his own, on December 11. Despite his ruffled feelings Bülow attended her concert, and afterwards he gallantly presented Clara with a bouquet, but reported that her playing in the *Kreutzer* Sonata was 'rough'. He was, however, impressed with her performance of music by Robert Schumann. The relationship between Bülow and Clara Schumann was already marked by mutual misgiving.

VI

Bülow now had to turn his thoughts to the immediate future. The prospect of returning to the drudgery of Chocieszewice, where both his salary and his security presently lay, filled him with disquiet. He had almost resigned himself to his fate when Adolf Marx invited him to lunch and offered him the position of principal piano teacher at the Stern Conservatory in place of Theodor Kullak, who was about to resign because of a disagreement with his colleagues.[23] There had been talk of offering this important job to Clara Schumann, and Bülow was flattered that Marx now offered it to him. The appointment brought with it a salary of 300 thalers a year with a promise of more later on, and it carried a light teaching load of ninety minutes each day. As Bülow pointed out to his mother,

---

22. Ibid., pp. 308–309.
23. Kullak went on to form his own institution, the Neue Akademie der Tonkunst, which specialized in the training of advanced pianists. It eventually became the largest private music institute in Germany, numbering well over 100 teachers and 1,100 pupils.

he could easily make up any shortfall in his salary by taking private pupils who would not be hard to find in Berlin, now that he was better known. The contract specified that he would have to start teaching on April 1, 1855.

So Bülow girded himself to return to his 'herring's pond of Polish solitude', at least for a while, and in order to complete the terms of his contract there. He then bade farewell to Count Mycielski and his family, who were doubtless disappointed to lose their distinguished music teacher after so brief a tenure, and travelled back to Germany and a new life in Berlin.

Berlin, 1855–1864

I: A City of Mingled Chimes

A great city is what Hans requires
—Franziska von Bülow[1]

But this job is killing me . . . what is best in me is dying
because of the chores of teaching.
—Bülow[2]

I

Bülow's appointment as head of the piano department at the Stern Conservatory was the first secure position he had enjoyed. Although he looked forward with trepidation to the routine of institutionalized teaching, it was an important situation and he knew that it would bring him to prominence in the Prussian capital. Shortly before taking up his duties, he wrote to his mother, telling her that if he was going to be condemned to waste his life in Berlin as a piano teacher, the least she could do for him would be to move to Berlin in order to look after him. 'You must make this sacrifice for me', he told her.[3] Whether the remark was made half in jest, or whether it was made in all sincerity, even Bülow himself may not have known. Franziska did not require a second invitation; she closed down her home in Dresden, and joined her son in his bachelor's apartment at no. 4 Behrenstrasse. The fact is, Bülow was incapable of regulating his own establishment. The notion of a man of his cast of mind dealing on a daily basis with the butcher, the baker, and the candlestick-maker provokes mirth. Almost before she had unpacked, Franziska began a search

1. BB, vol. 2, p. 369.
2. LBLB, p. 187.
3. BB, vol. 2, pp. 338–339.

Bülow age twenty-five. An oil painting by Wilhelm
Streckfuss.

for a more spacious apartment for herself and her son, and Bülow found
himself moving yet again—this time to quarters on Berlin's fashionable
Wilhelmstrasse. Because the Stern Conservatory was also situated on Wilhelmstrasse, he was able to walk easily back and forth between his home
and his teaching studio. Franziska's arrival in the city, while timely, introduced many complications into his life, as we shall discover.

During the nine years that Bülow spent at the Stern Conservatory, he
stored up a wealth of experience through his day-to-day teaching that
he later put to good use in those standard editions of piano works for
which he became renowned. Bülow himself has left a detailed account of
his daily grind, the particulars of which need not detain us.[4] It is enough
to know that the repertoire he taught his young charges ranged from the
quite simple to the highly advanced. In the advanced class he had a
pupil, Herr Ludwig Kortmann, who was assigned Chopin's Etudes, op. 10,

4. Ibid., vol. 3, pp. 1–15. A complete list of Bülow's students, during the decade that he
taught at the Stern Conservatory (1855–1864), may be consulted at the Deutsche Staatsbibliothek, together with his many handwritten annotations as to their progress—or lack
of it—under the call number 'Mus. NL HvBülow F IV, 6'.

together with a Liszt transcription of one of the numbers from Wagner's *Lohengrin*—a clear enough indication that he was a top student. In the lowest class, which Bülow described as 'for beginners', Fräulein Strahl was assigned the first movement of a Mozart Sonatina in C major, and some of the *Kinderstücke* of Mendelssohn. This division of pieces into simple and difficult eventually met with Bülow's disapproval, and he abandoned it. It later drew from him one of his thought-provoking maxims, 'There are no easy pieces, they are all difficult'.[5]

During that first spring and summer in Berlin, Bülow met a number of influential people who were helpful to his career. Because of a chance invitation from the duchess of Sagan, Bülow found himself playing to the inner members of the Prussian royal family. So impressed were the prince and princess of Prussia with his virtuosity, that they asked him to give some occasional piano lessons to their daughter, Princess Louise. Such contacts opened further doors for him, and Bülow was soon acquainted with a large number of established personalities, including the historian Hermann Grimm, the singer Madame Decker, the court painter Wilhelm Hensel, the composer Giocomo Meyerbeer, and the pianist Karl Bronikowski. In 1858, when Bülow's significance to the musical life of Berlin had become apparent to everybody, he was appointed 'Royal Court Pianist', a title he held until 1884, when it was summarily removed from him for publicly insulting Baron von Hülsen, the intendant of the Royal Opera House.

II

The musical life of Berlin in those days was underdeveloped. It could not be compared with such sophisticated centres as Leipzig, Dresden, and Vienna. At the court no one was interested in Wagner's music; he was considered a left-wing revolutionary whose day was done. As for concerts and operas, they provided little more than a smorgasbord of popular entertainment. Italian music dominated the repertory. Ever since Spontini's forced dismissal in 1841 as director of the Royal Opera House for alleged corruption (which had nearly earned him a prison sentence), the institution had been clouded by intrigue. The appointment of Meyerbeer to replace Spontini ensured only that the Berlin public now heard more Meyerbeer. Botho von Hülsen was Wagner's adversary, and he used his position as the intendant of the opera house to cast a protective mantle over his colleagues, the court conductors Heinrich Dorn and Wilhelm Taubert, whose own works were ushered onto the stage with a frequency that was out of all proportion to their talents.

5. BAS (part 2), p. 275.

It was against this stilted background that Bülow launched his own concerts. They began in a modest way in the assembly rooms of the Englisches Haus Hotel, in November 1856, and moved after two seasons to the more spacious location of the Hôtel de Russie. These so-called 'Trio-Soirées' (presented in collaboration with Bülow's two chamber music partners, violinist Ferdinand Laub and cellist Heinrich Wohlers) were meant to offer Berliners music that they could not hear elsewhere in the city. The strategy was evangelical. Modern composers such as César Franck, Robert Volkmann, Liszt, and Schumann, were smuggled into the series by placing them cheek by jowl with Mozart, Bach, and Beethoven in order to make them more palatable. Bülow took a calculated risk when, in 1860, he rented Berlin's prestigious Singakademie for all his subsequent concerts. Within three short seasons they had become central to what passed for Berlin's musical life at that time, and started to attract critical attention, not all of it positive. Bülow frequently found himself locked in conflict with the city's conservative music critics, who did not always approve of the modern music he wanted them to hear. One of these concerts, and the critical reception it received, has passed into legend.

III

On the evening of January 22, 1857, Bülow delivered the world premier of Liszt's Sonata in B minor in the Englisches Haus Hotel. The Sonata had taken him more than two years to prepare, most recently under the guidance of Liszt himself.[6] Bülow had not proceeded very far before certain gentlemen of the press experienced signs of distress. The Sonata appeared to them to be in no fixed key, with thematic contrasts that were so extreme they gave the impression of being non sequiturs. Two of these critics remained stubborn opponents of the work. One was Otto Gumprecht of the *Nationale Zeitung,* and the other was Gustav Engel of the *Spener'sche*

---

6. Bülow had made his first acquaintance with the Sonata in 1854, shortly after Liszt had sent him a newly printed copy (LBLB, p. 75). The following year, on July 21, 1855, Bülow had heard Liszt play it to a group of friends at the Altenburg, among whom were Liszt's thirteen-year-old prodigy pupil Carl Tausig and the boy's father (HLSW, p. 68). It is evident that by then Bülow had already embarked on a serious conquest of the work, because the following month he gave it a preliminary run-through to Niels Gade in Berlin (LBLB, p. 141). On August 1, 1856, came the moment when Bülow was able to play it to his master for the first time. We know that Liszt was pleased with the performance, because the following day he wrote to his disciple Richard Pohl, 'Bülow played several pieces for me quite wonderfully, among other things both my Polonaises and the Sonata' (WLP, p. 197).

Liszt did not attend the premier of his pianistic masterwork. He was ill in Weimar, hardly able to walk, and was obliged to remain at home under medical care. For several weeks he had been suffering from a form of blood poisoning. His feet were covered in abscesses, and whenever he left his bed he was obliged to hobble around on crutches, his painful condition made worse by the application of saltpetre at the insistence of his Weimar physician, Dr. Goullon.

Zeitung. A few days after the performance Gumprecht wrote that the Sonata was 'an invitation to hissing and stamping', while Engel informed his readers that 'not only had it nothing to do with beauty, but it conflicted with nature and logic'.[7] It is tempting to adjust some words of Charles Ives and remark that 'their ears were on wrong'. But they expressed a majority opinion that was to prevail for a generation or more. Later they would be joined by Eduard Hanslick of Vienna's *Neue Freie Presse* who, after hearing Bülow play the Sonata in Vienna in 1881, famously described it as 'a steam-driven mill which nearly always runs idle'.[8]

The next morning, in the first flush of enthusiasm, Bülow told Liszt, 'I am writing to you the day after a great day. Yesterday evening I played your Sonata for the first time before the Berlin public, which applauded me heartily and called me back'.[9] Then came the published reviews and the negative comments, which enraged Bülow and marked a new low in his toxic relations with the press. For the next several years he engaged in a bitter newspaper war with the Berlin critics, with Liszt's compositions at the centre, until Liszt himself appealed to his old pupil to calm himself and desist from such a useless activity.[10]

The date January 22, 1857, was important for another reason. That evening Bülow inaugurated the Bechstein grand piano, an instrument he eventually came to admire above all others.[11] Its action and its responsive touch, and above all its rich sound, were qualities he valued. Thereafter, he became a 'Bechstein artist', and he and Carl Bechstein developed a close friendship which was sundered only by death. He called Bechstein his *'Beflügler'*—the man who gave him his wings.[12]

IV

Bülow's dogged promotion of modern music sometimes got him into trouble with the Berlin public as well as the critics. On January 14, 1859, a distinguished audience assembled in the Singakademie to hear him conduct works by Berlioz, Raff, Beethoven, Wagner, and Liszt, a concert in which he also appeared as a soloist. Among those present were some

7. *Spener'sche Zeitung*, issue of January 30, 1857.

8. RLS, vol. 2, p. 62. See the concert billing reproduced on p. 292.

9. LBLB, p. 188.

10. The background to Bülow's tussle with the press will be found in BB, vol. 3, pp. 63–68.

11. According to Bülow, this particular instrument had been built especially for him by Carl Bechstein, who had just opened his own factory, having earlier learned his craft at the Berlin firm of Perau, where he had been made foreman at the early age of twenty-one.

12. This is a typical Bülow pun. In German the word *Flügel* means both a grand piano and a wing.

of Berlin's elite aristocrats, including an entourage from the royal household headed by the prince and princess of Prussia, come to hear their 'court pianist' once more in action. Bülow scored a notable triumph with his performance of Beethoven's Piano Concerto in G major, for which he had recently composed his own virtuoso cadenzas. The trouble began when he returned to the podium to conduct Liszt's symphonic poem *Die Ideale,* the first time the work had been heard in Berlin. It was poorly received and hissing broke out. This situation Bülow could not take calmly. The disturbance catapulted him back onto the podium, and facing the audience he said in an angry voice, 'I ask all the hissers to leave the hall. It is not permitted to hiss here!'[13] It may well have been the first time that a conductor had asked a section of his audience to leave the building. The princess of Prussia disappeared into her box and ordered a cup of tea. Prince Friedrich likewise sank into the shadows, but the literature does not record what he drank. An oppressive blanket of silence descended over the hall; one waited for an explosion, but nothing happened. It was already 9:00 p.m. before Bülow decided to continue the concert by giving selections from Wagner's *Lohengrin* and *Tannhäuser,* which were absorbed by the subdued listeners without further mishap. Bülow had scored another victory for modern music; the hissers had been silenced, if only temporarily.[14]

Bülow never forgot the turbulence surrounding that concert of January 14, 1859. He later had a photograph taken of himself at a conductor's desk, in commemoration of that evening, displaying a copy of Liszt's *Die Ideale.* Beneath the picture he printed a Latin inscription: *Sub hoc signo*

---

13. BB, vol. 3, p. 203. In a trenchant defence of his actions, Bülow later argued that he had both a moral and a legal right to attack the audience. He told Liszt that the audience always assumed that because it paid for its tickets, it had purchased the right to judge the product and was entitled to declare itself for or against. But this argument was false, Bülow informed a doubtless bemused Liszt. 'By paying for the hall and the musicians with my own money, I am the master of it for those few hours, and retain the right to chase the vultures out of the building . . .'. And he added that he would be perfectly entitled to tell the audience, 'You are only my guests, my invited people. By paying your Thaler you are just making a formal gesture, you are a decoration, assisting a philanthropic, charitable event' (LBLB, p. 260). The argument has some merit, and makes us regret once again that Bülow never appeared as counsel for the defence in a court of law. He described the hissing and booing of music in public as mob rule, or in his words as 'Lynch-Justice'.

14. The storm of newspaper criticism that broke over Bülow's head, as well as a number of anonymous letters containing personal abuse, promised still worse things to come at his next orchestral concert on February 27, which included whistling and stamping. When Liszt heard what his embattled acolyte was having to endure, he came to Berlin and conducted a repeat performance of *Die Ideale* himself. Both he and Bülow thought that the best reply to the critics was to offer them a second helping of the very music which had offended them in the first place. With Liszt himself on the podium, incidentally, *Die Ideale* was well received.

Bülow in Berlin. A photograph inscribed 'Sub hoc
signo vici, nec vincere desistam'.

vici, nec vincere desistam, which might be translated as, 'I achieved victory under this sign, and I shall not desist from further conquests'. The photograph bears the dedication 'to his master, to his artistic Ideal, with thanks and respect from a full heart'. It was sent to Liszt on the latter's fifty-second birthday.

Pictures sometimes symbolize a career. This one appears to have been taken and sent to Liszt for just that purpose. By the early 1860s Bülow had become the undisputed leader of the musical avant-garde in Berlin. His concerts regularly featured the music of Berlioz, Liszt, Wagner, and Schumann. As if this were not bad enough for the conservative Berliners, Bülow insisted on sprinkling his concerts with liberal helpings of completely unknown works by Eduard Lassen, Joachim Raff, Felix Draeseke, Anton Rubinstein, Adolf Henselt, and Friedrich Kiel as well. The establishment trembled, and Bülow often found himself at odds with the press. The newspaper wars that erupted, and the polemical articles that Bülow wrote in defence of his programmes, are hardly remembered today. But the essence of it all was enshrined in a little-known brochure by Bülow's former colleague on the old *Demokratische Zeitung,* the writer Adolf Müt-zelburg: 'Hans von Bülow und die Berliner Kritik'.[15] It remains required reading for anyone interested in revisiting the rough-and-tumble of those times.

V

Like many commanders on the field of battle, Bülow, from his limited vantage point, seemed to think that the outcome of the musical war in which he was currently engaged was entirely in his hands. But Berlin was only one sector in a conflict that had been launched in Weimar ten years earlier and had meanwhile assumed European dimensions. Other acolytes of Liszt and Wagner had secured tactical positions across Germany, and were fighting similar battles on a variety of fronts. There was Leopold Damrosch in Breslau, Karl Klindworth in London, Alexander Ritter in Stettin, and Carl Tausig in Vienna. Tausig's brief tenure as a conductor is hardly remembered today, but in the early 1860s he temporarily abandoned his fledgling career as a concert pianist and moved to Vienna, where he emulated Bülow's example, directing a series of orchestral concerts devoted to modern music, including some of his own still-unpublished symphonic poems.

The underlying issues that fanned the flames of the War of the Romantics have already been touched on.[16] It is enough to recall that a solid wall of resistance to revolutionary Weimar, and its promotion of 'programme music' and the symphonic poem, was now in place at the conservative cities of Leipzig, Frankfurt, and Vienna. The idea that the symphonic poem was a 'reply' to the classical symphony, and might even signal its demise, was anathema to those who upheld the traditions of the First Viennese School. Ten years earlier, Liszt's music had been somewhat arbitrarily described as *Zukunftsmusik,* or 'music of the future', and the phrase had frequently been taken up by his young acolytes and held aloft by them like a banner.[17] Predictably, such provocation acted on conservative

15. See MBB.

16. See pp. 59–60.

17. The phrase was coined by Liszt's companion, Princess Carolyne von Sayn-Wittgenstein, in the early 1850s. (See her unpublished comments in GSA, Kasten 338, no. 2.) She herself later told Lina Ramann how the term came to be introduced into Liszt's circle. A number of them had gathered in the Altenburg after a performance of Wagner's *Lohengrin* and the conversation turned on Wagner's recently published 'Art Work of the Future'. Brendel lamented the fact that the work was 'premature', and in advance of its time, because the present was unable to understand it. 'Very well', interrupted the princess, 'then we are making music for the *future!*' Ramann reports the story in the third volume of her life of Liszt, RLKM, vol. 3, p. 69n2.

musicians like a red rag to a bull. As the dust and din of battle showed few signs of abating, it became evident that nothing short of a national forum would do to air the issues now confronting the world of music.

On June 1, 1859, the first meeting of the Tonkünstler-Versammlung ('Congress of Musical Artists') was convened in Leipzig. The moving spirit behind the Congress was Franz Brendel. Its initial impulse was the celebration surrounding the twenty-fifth anniversary of the *Neue Zeitschrift für Musik*, the journal he had acquired from its founder Robert Schumann, in 1844. During the intervening years Brendel had turned the *Zeitschrift* into a mouthpiece for Weimar and the 'music of the future'. Many people complained that the journal had been hijacked for a cause that Schumann himself would never have supported. Brendel was sensitive to the criticism and resolved to make amends during the Congress. More than 300 musicians travelled to Leipzig from such diverse places as Berlin, Schwerin, Breslau, Dresden, Merseburg, Prague, St. Petersburg, Stockholm, and even New York.[18] Richard Pohl was there, his pencil poised, ready to record the proceedings for posterity. His comprehensive account of the Congress may be found in his 180-page brochure *Die Tonkünstler-Versammlung zu Leipzig, am 1. bis 4. Juni 1859,* which was published later that year and provides many details not obtainable elsewhere. Liszt arrived a day or two before the event got underway, and was joined by Bülow, eager to support his old master. Bülow, in fact, performed Bach's *Italian Concerto* for the Congress on June 4. By far the greatest excitement was generated by Wagner's Prelude to *Tristan,* which Liszt conducted from the manuscript at the opening concert on June 1. This music had never been heard in Germany before. Liszt had long harboured a desire to conduct the world premier, but that honour had fallen to Bülow, who had earlier included the Prelude in a *Zukunftskonzert* in Prague on March 12.

The day before the Congress began there was a full-scale production of Schumann's opera *Genoveva* in honour of the composer, who had died three years earlier. It was meant to be a conciliatory gesture on Brendel's part. On the first day of the Congress, Brendel gave the keynote address and went out of his way to pay tribute to Schumann and to offer an olive branch to the opponents of *Zukunftsmusik.* He admitted that the term

---

18. The crowd that Brendel mustered in Leipzig was soon to be transformed into the Allgemeiner Deutscher Musikverein, which became one of the most powerful musical organizations in Germany. Its declared purpose was 'to promote the welfare of musicians and improve musical conditions through the union of all groups and parties'. Liszt was the first to sign its new charter, and he allowed himself to be appointed president for life, a position he held for twenty-five years. After his death this influential office was taken over by Richard Strauss. The ADMV survives to this day.

had done the cause of modern music little good, and proposed that henceforth the phrase 'New German School' should be used instead. This historic name is still the one by which Liszt and the Weimar circle is recognised today.

Poor Brendel meant well, but he had little idea of what he was proposing when he minted this phrase. When the text of his keynote address appeared in the next issue of the *Zeitschrift,*[19] it was widely assumed to be a formal constitution adopted by the Congress itself. Incensed by Brendel's comments, and angered by the presumption that the symphonic tradition of the Viennese classics had had its day, Brahms and Joachim drew up a 'constitution' of their own. This was the origin of the famous 'Manifesto' which amounted to a formal declaration of war against the New German School. The text of the document was written by the twenty-seven-year-old Brahms, and his Hamburg address was used as the collection point for the signatures that were canvassed from across Germany. Many were promised but only four signatories had attached their names to the document when it inexplicably found its way into the editorial offices of the *Berliner Musik-Zeitung Echo* and was published prematurely on May 6, 1860:

> The undersigned have long followed with regret the pursuits of a certain party, whose organ is Brendel's *Zeitschrift für Musik.*
>
> The above journal continually spreads the view that musicians of more serious endeavour are fundamentally in accord with the tendencies it represents, that they recognize in the compositions of the leaders of this group works of artistic value, and that altogether, and especially in northern Germany, the contentions for and against the so-called Music of the Future are concluded, and the dispute settled in its favour.
>
> To protest against such a misrepresentation of facts is regarded as their duty by the undersigned, and they declare that, so far at least as they are concerned, the principles stated by Brendel's journal are not recognized, and that they regard the productions of the leaders and pupils of the so-called New German School, which in part simply reinforce those principles in practice and in part again enforce new and unheard-of theories, as contrary to the innermost spirit of music, strongly to be deplored and condemned.

JOHANNES BRAHMS   JULIUS OTTO GRIMM
JOSEPH JOACHIM   BERNHARD SCHOLZ[20]

19. NZfM, June 10, 1859.
20. *Berliner Musik-Zeitung Echo,* May 6, 1860.

The appearance of such a document, with only four names to support it, was a major embarrassment for Brahms. His chagrin was complete when a copy of the text was prematurely leaked to the *Neue Zeitschrift für Musik*, and Brendel came out with a parody of it on May 4,[21] two days before the text itself appeared in *Das Echo*. Although more than twenty musicians eventually came forward to support the 'Manifesto'—including Bargiel, Bruch, Dietrich, Hiller, Kirchner, and Reinecke—the long delay in collecting signatures proved to be its undoing.

As for Brahms, he drew an important lesson from this episode. Never again would he meddle in musical politics. Henceforth he rose above the fray and let his music speak for itself. The wisdom of this policy was proved when Bülow himself was won over to Brahms's side. One day Bülow would call Brahms the greatest composer since Beethoven, and become his finest interpreter.

21. Under the rubric 'Kleine Zeitung. Correspondenz'. See also the letter that Bülow wrote to Felix Draeseke about the 'Manifesto' on May 6, 1860, the day of its publication (BB, vol. 3, pp. 312–313). Bülow also pilloried the document for its ponderous style and lack of humour in a letter to Louis Köhler, written one week later. 'The Declaration of the Hanoverians has not made the least sensation here. [They] have not even enough wit mixed with their malice to have done the thing in good style, and to have launched it at a well chosen time, such as the beginning or the end of the season' (BB, vol. 3, p. 317). Bülow's original text referred to 'the Crétins', for which Marie von Bülow substituted the neutral 'they' in the published version of the letter. Brahms's uneasy relationship with the New German School is surveyed in detail in FBZ, pp. 159–169.

Berlin, 1855–1864

II: Marriage to Cosima

> For me Cosima is superior to all women . . .
> —Bülow to Liszt[1]

I

During his first turbulent years in Berlin, Bülow's private life had undergone a profound change. In July 1855, barely four months after Franziska von Bülow had joined him in the Prussian capital, the household was transformed by the arrival of Liszt's two daughters, Blandine and Cosima, who took up residence there as well. Blandine was nineteen years old and Cosima was two years her junior. They were alive with energy and humour, and they filled the apartments on Wilhelmstrasse with their laughter. The active minds and boisterous behaviour of these two young women posed a constant threat to the strict domestic routine which Franziska liked to impose on her son. Bülow was entranced by both girls, and referred to them affectionately as 'the Erlking's daughters'. At Liszt's request he gave them piano lessons, and was particularly impressed with Cosima's accomplished playing; she already performed the standard sonatas of Beethoven and a variety of compositions by Chopin with confidence.[2] But

---

1. BBLW, p. 67.
2. Cosima's disposition as a pianist remains an unheralded aspect of her career. Before coming to Berlin she had been a piano student in Paris of Liszt's old colleague François Seghers, and during her teens had appeared at a number of soirées, playing difficult pieces by Weber and Hummel. She took especial pleasure in writing to her father that she had embarked on a study of Hummel's B minor piano concerto, a work which she knew had been one of Liszt's own war-horses during his youth. There was even talk of Cosima becoming a professional musician, and her mother, Marie d'Agoult, was convinced that she could have become a second Clara Schumann, but Liszt resisted the idea.

what were these girls doing in Berlin, and why had Franziska been charged with their care? The story is complex, but it must be told at this point in the narrative because it changed the course of Bülow's destiny.

From their early childhood the two girls had lived in Paris, together with their younger brother Daniel. These three children were the progeny of Liszt and his first mistress Countess Marie d'Agoult and they had all been born during his years of pilgrimage through Switzerland and Italy, in the mid- to late 1830s. In order to elope with Liszt and bear his children Marie had abandoned hearth and home, as well as her position in Parisian society, leaving her husband Count Charles d'Agoult to look after their surviving daughter Claire.[3] The relationship ended in 1844, amidst much acrimony and mutual recrimination, at which point Liszt sought legal advice, legitimized the children, and became responsible for their welfare. Because he was absent for much of their childhood, pursuing those great concert tours of Europe on which his fame as a pianist ultimately rested, the children were raised in Paris by Liszt's mother, Anna, who brought them up as her own, and lavished much love and affection on them.

II

In 1847, Liszt's tours had taken him to Kiev, where he met the Polish-born Princess Carolyne von Sayn-Wittgenstein, and became enamoured of her. Carolyne was twenty-eight years old, and separated from her husband, Prince Nicholas, by whom she had a daughter, Princess Marie. She was enormously wealthy, having inherited from her father vast estates in the province of Podolia in Polish Ukraine. More than 30,000 serfs toiled on her domains, which took several days to traverse on horseback. After giving the last of his recitals, in Elisabetgrad, in September 1847, Liszt accepted her invitation to join her for an extended period at her estate in Woronince.

This was a honeymoon in everything but name, and within three short months Carolyne had decided to throw in her lot with Liszt's. In February 1848 she followed him to Weimar when he took up the position of Kapellmeister-in-Extraordinary to the court of Weimar, offered to him some years earlier. One of the last things that Carolyne did before setting

---

3. Claire d'Agoult (1830–1912). Marie's elder daughter Louise (b. 1828) had died in infancy. Claire, under her married name of Countess de Charnacé, makes frequent appearances in Cosima's life story, and her unpublished archives contain material relevant to Bülow as well.

out for Germany was to file an application for an annulment of her marriage with the Catholic authorities in St. Petersburg.[4] In order to keep up appearances, Liszt lived for a time in the Erbprinz Hotel, while Carolyne and her daughter rented a large house overlooking the river Ilm and the old part of the city, called the Altenburg. Carolyne wished to do nothing to offend the church authorities. In this small Protestant city it was still a punishable offence for unmarried couples to live together without benefit of clergy. After a year Liszt put an end to the façade, moved into the Altenburg, and established a formal *ménage à deux* with Carolyne. It was in this house, as we have seen, that Bülow first met Liszt, in 1851. That same year the dwelling was purchased for Liszt's exclusive use by Maria Pawlowna, the Grand Duchess of Weimar. The social tensions which whirled around Liszt as a result of his association with the princess were considerable. But they are a part of Liszt's story, not Bülow's. All we need to know is that for the next ten years Carolyne turned the Altenburg into a shrine memorializing Liszt, replete with paintings, furniture, and memorabilia from his years as a touring pianist. Among the roll-call of musical luminaries who passed through Weimar, to which glancing reference has already been made, the names of Wagner, Brahms, Anton Rubinstein, and Berlioz were preeminent; all of them were houseguests at one time or another. Nor was Liszt's circle confined to musicians. The writers George Eliot and Hans Christian Andersen were visitors; as were the painters Wilhelm von Kaulbach and Friedrich Preller.

From this brilliant life in Weimar, Liszt's children were excluded. The presence of his offspring from an earlier union, while he himself now lived openly with another woman and her child, would have strained the patience of both church and state. Although Liszt's children spent an occasional holiday with their father in Weimar, the prospect of offering them a permanent home there was never contemplated.

In 1855 all that changed when Liszt learned that the children had been seeing their mother in Paris against his wishes. He summoned them to Weimar on the pretext of giving them a 'holiday', and then informed his two daughters that they were to be removed to Berlin, where they would live with the Bülows until their majority. Daniel was sent to Vienna to study law at the University of Vienna, and live under the protection of Liszt's lawyer-uncle, the distinguished jurist Eduard Liszt.

---

4. The story of Carolyne's long struggle to secure an annulment in order to marry Liszt was locked in the Vatican's archives until recent times. See the documents published in WELC.

III

The dramatic story of how Cosima and Hans declared their love for each other commands attention. On October 19, 1855, about six weeks after Cosima and Blandine arrived in Berlin, Hans conducted an orchestral concert that included the first performance in Berlin of the Overture and Venusburg Music from *Tannhäuser.* The entire household turned out to support him—Cosima, Blandine, Franziska—and Liszt himself journeyed from Weimar to attend the event. At the conclusion of the concert, hissing and booing broke out in the audience. Bülow stalked off the rostrum, livid with rage. In the artists' room his feelings overcame him, and he fainted dead away. Liszt and a group of Bülow's local supporters stayed with him until he recovered, while the three ladies returned to Wilhelmstrasse. Cosima insisted that it was their duty to stay up until Hans got back. As midnight chimed, Franziska and Blandine went to bed, leaving Cosima to stand vigil. At two o'clock in the morning, Liszt finally pushed Hans through the front door and returned to his hotel. As Hans entered the living room he found Cosima waiting for him. The atmosphere was emotion laden, and they sat down and talked. Hans unburdened himself and told Cosima that she had become indispensable to him. Her simple reply told him that she already loved him. This fateful night marked the beginning of their long betrothal.

Liszt was not entirely in favour of the match. Cosima was only seventeen years old and too young, he thought, to contemplate matrimony. Moreover, the couple barely knew each other. But Liszt may have had deeper reservations. Despite the praise that he constantly heaped on Hans, particularly with regards to his musical gifts, he was aware of the manic-depressive qualities of his pupil's personality, and he knew that Cosima would find them hard to bear. Once Liszt had assured himself of the depth of his daughter's feelings, however, he gradually dropped his objections, asking of the young couple only that they wait for at least one year.

The extraordinary letter that Bülow wrote to Liszt on April 20, 1856, represented his Rubicon.

> I feel for her more than love. The thought of moving nearer to you encloses all my dream of whatsoever may be vouchsafed to me on this earth, you whom I regard as the principal architect and shaper of my present and future life. For me Cosima is superior to all women, not only because she bears your name but because she resembles you so closely, being in many of her characteristics a true mirror of your personality . . .[5]

5. BBLW, p. 67.

We call the letter 'extraordinary' because Bülow appears to be saying that one reason he wanted to marry Cosima had to do with his love for Liszt. It is as if he were attempting to win the hand of the daughter through the most outrageous flattery of the father. Bülow then went on to offer Liszt a solemn promise:

> I give you my word of honour that however much I am bound to her by my love, I would never hesitate to sacrifice my happiness to her, and release her were she ever to feel that she had made a mistake with regards to me.[6]

These were prophetic words. He would be called upon to redeem this pledge under circumstances so harrowing that they almost ended his life. Did Cosima herself ever see this letter? It seems inconceivable that she did, otherwise she would have realized from the start that she was not loved entirely for herself but because of her resemblance to her father.[7] The relationship was already flawed. Liszt took the letter seriously enough to suggest that he and Bülow should meet in Merseburg on May 11, where they could discuss everything at leisure.[8] During this meeting the conversation turned on Hans's poverty, of which it emerged he was deeply ashamed. Liszt would certainly have mentioned the generous dowry that he had set aside for his daughters. And because he had always insisted that they marry only for love, abhorring the idea of arranged marriages, he also wanted to be sure of the depth of Hans's feelings towards Cosima. Having satisfied himself that they were genuine, he took the young man back to Weimar to stay with him and Princess Carolyne at the Altenburg for a week, and make provisional plans for a wedding next year. The fact that Bülow was a Protestant was not regarded as an impediment, either by him or by the deeply Catholic Liszt. Bülow was not particularly religious, and he appears to have been ready enough to yield on doctrinal matters regarding mixed marriages. Having procured Liszt's blessing, Hans took the good news back to Berlin where Cosima had been anxiously waiting for him. During the period of their betrothal, Hans tactfully moved into nearby bachelor quarters at no. 10 Eichhornstrasse.

Opposition to the marriage came from a predictable quarter. When she heard about it, Cosima's mother, Marie d'Agoult, tried to intervene. She

---

6. Ibid., p. 68.

7. The letter was not published until 1925, by which time Cosima was eighty-eight years old and suffering from Alzheimer's disease.

8. Liszt was in Merseburg to attend the premier performance of his 'Prelude and Fugue on the name BACH', on May 16, played by his pupil Alexander Winterberger. He arrived in the city a few days early in order to help Winterberger with the complex registrations of this virtuoso piece.

sent her daughter Claire de Charnacé (Cosima's stepsister) to Berlin to reason with her and have the marriage indefinitely postponed. Claire stayed in the Hôtel de Rome for a part of April 1856, but eventually had to return to Paris with the news that Cosima could not be swayed. Cosima told Claire, 'I am determined to marry Hans; I am well aware that it is a bad match, that it does not please mother'. To which Blandine, who was also a party to these discussions, added, 'She loves him. What can be done about that?'[9] These choice disclosures come to us from the unpublished Charnacé archives, from which one other piece of information also captures our attention. During her visit to Berlin Claire learned that Bülow had been so nervous at the prospect of breaking the news to Liszt that he prevailed upon his mother to do it for him, who then claimed that 'it was Cosima's idea'.[10] This revelation, so unexpected at first, fits in perfectly with the characters of Hans and Cosima, as posterity has come to know them: she, bold and aggressive in the pursuit of her interests; he, weak and uncertain in his dealings with the opposite sex.

One other small matter had to be settled before the marriage could take place. Bülow was not yet a naturalized Prussian subject. He was still a citizen of Saxony, a displaced person of the revolution of 1848–49, who had chosen Berlin as his place of residence, and several months had to elapse before the necessary formalities were completed. After consulting Liszt, the wedding date was set for mid-August 1857. This allowed Liszt to complete a water cure at Aachen, which lasted for several weeks and which he refused to postpone, and from there he travelled to Berlin.[11]

On the morning of August 18, 1857, Bülow led his nineteen-year-old bride to the altar of St. Hedwig's Church, Berlin, and entered into matrimony with her in accordance with the rites of the Roman Catholic Church. Liszt himself gave his daughter away, and was the only member of Cosima's family to be present. Bülow was attended by his relative Lieutenant-Colonel Paul von Bülow. Because Bülow's relations with the Berlin press were so poor, he feared that his father-in-law's presence at the ceremony would create a spectacle, so news of the wedding was kept as quiet as possible. Immediately after the service, however, Liszt circulated this terse notice:

9. VMA, p. 13. Many years later, when Claire came to reflect on her fruitless visit to Berlin, she said of Franziska, 'How ridiculous and intolerable that woman was in 1856!'

10. Ibid.

11. For several months Liszt had suffered from abscesses on the feet and legs which had occasionally immobilized him. After undergoing a series of medical treatments in Weimar, he was advised to take the sulphuric waters of Aachen, a time-consuming cure that his doctors did not want him to abandon.

I have the honour to announce herewith
the marriage which took place today at the
CHURCH of ST. HEDWIG, BERLIN
between my daughter
COSIMA LISZT
and
HERR VON BÜLOW

Berlin, August 18, 1857   FRANZ LISZT

The newlyweds left on honeymoon that same day. They accompanied Liszt as far as Weimar, lingered for a while in Baden-Baden, and then reached their ultimate destination, Lake Geneva. There the honeymoon might have ended without further ado. But in nearby Lausanne the young couple encountered Hans's old school friend Karl Ritter, Wagner's erstwhile conducting assistant in Zurich, who had himself just got married. The four honeymooners decided that it was too good an opportunity not to visit the exiled master in his retreat in Switzerland; accordingly, they all set out at the beginning of September. Wagner was at that time living with his wife, Minna, in a house called the Asyl ('Refuge') on the estate of his wealthy benefactor, Otto Wesendonck, not far from Zurich. The story of his secret love affair with Frau Mathilde Wesendonck, which even then was being conducted behind the backs of their respective spouses, is so well known that it need not be retailed here. The main point to bear in mind is that when Bülow and Cosima turned up on his doorstep, Wagner's genius was in full flood, either because of Mathilde or despite her. He had already completed the first two acts of *Siegfried* and was now embarked on *Tristan*. Wagner insisted that Bülow and Cosima stay at the Asyl as his houseguests, and he lost no time in putting Bülow's pianistic talents to work. *Das Rheingold* and *Die Walküre* were both brought to life under Bülow's fingers (in Klindworth's 'atrocious' arrangement, as Wagner later described it), with Wagner singing the leading parts. Wagner also took the opportunity to treat his guests to daily readings of his newly completed *Tristan und Isolde* poem. Bülow made a separate copy of it for Cosima, who read and reread it late into the night. It made such a deep impression on her that she occasionally came down in the morning with a tear-stained face. Did she see in this poem of star-crossed lovers a portent of her own destiny? Wagner observed of her that she seemed 'strangely troubled' and 'reserved'. Whatever the case, we know that she took the *Tristan* poem back to Berlin as a precious token of her stay in the Asyl.

IV

By mid October Hans and Cosima had settled into their new apartment at no. 11 Anhalterstrasse. Franziska was tactfully removed into an apartment of her own, but still in the neighborhood. Cosima possessed natural gifts as a hostess, and the Bülow home became known as a place where Berlin's intelligentsia could gather to discuss the issues of the day, both artistic and political. Musicians such as Carl Tausig, Ludwig Ehlert, Carl Bechstein, Ferdinand Laub, and Adolf Marx frequently assembled there. The Russian critic Alexander Serov and the composer Giacomo Meyerbeer were honoured dinner guests. Politicians, too, were included in the Bülows' circle, including Ferdinand Lassalle, the left-wing political thinker and cofounder of the German Workers' Party (who was briefly jailed for his views, and was later killed in a duel over a love affair).[12] Chief among the scientific celebrities was the astronomer Giovanni Schiaparelli, the discoverer of the imagined 'canals' on Mars. Distinguished academics such as the historian and biographer Varnhagen von Ense were also among the guests who descended on Anhalterstrasse and enriched the social fabric of Bülow's life. During these early years Cosima's ambition was to help develop the manifold gifts of her 'great man', ease his path, and move with him to the forefront of Berlin's cultural life. In this noble quest she was doomed to reap a harvest of discontents.

Aside from his students at the Stern Conservatory, Bülow had a number of private piano pupils. One of them was a young woman barely out of her teens named Ellen Franz, who became a close friend of Cosima. Ellen, who was also studying to be an actress, later enjoyed success on the German stage. After joining the Meiningen Theatre, she was spotted by the Duke of Meiningen, and entered into a morganatic marriage with him. From her newly elevated position as the Baroness Helene von Heldburg, she never ceased trying to attract Bülow to the Meiningen Court and have him take over the orchestra there. She realized her ambition many years later, with spectacular results both for Meiningen and for Bülow himself.

Bülow's concerts kept him occupied, and they often drew him away from home. Aside from his Trio-Soirées, which were now a fixture in Berlin, Bülow appeared in such diverse cities as Leipzig, Stettin, Löwenberg, Baden-Baden, Hamburg, Königsberg, and Danzig, all within the first few months of his marriage. Cosima was not well suited to a life of isolation.

---

12. Bülow retained some lively recollections of Lassalle, and years later wrote that whenever he visited Lassalle's house, 'I had neither eyes nor ears for anyone but the heroic man who was so sympathetic to me–all the others present were for me merely extras, walk-ons, shadows, daytime ghosts' (BB, vol. 3, p. 345). An intriguing example of the political support that Bülow gave Lassalle, and the German Worker's Party he headed, may be found in Bülow's four-part male-voice chorus, 'Bundeslied des Allgemeinen deutschen Arbeitervereins', a setting of words by Georg Herwegh, which was adopted by the Party as its anthem. It was composed in 1863 and published a year later under the pseudonym 'W. Solinger'. For the colourful context of Lassalle's death through duelling, see pp. 124–25.

In the absence of any indication from Bülow himself about his choice of the name 'Solinger' as his *nom de plume*, we surmise that he took it from the German town of Solingen, long famous for the quality of its knives and sabres.

Until recently she had enjoyed the daily companionship of Blandine, to whom she could turn in any emergency. But Blandine had meanwhile attained her majority, and at the time of Cosima's marriage had already returned to Paris. There she met and, after a whirlwind courtship, married the rising French lawyer and politician Emile Ollivier, who later became prime minister of France under Napoleon III. Cosima and Blandine had never been parted since their infancy, and Cosima's sense of loneliness was difficult for her to bear. Her growing frustration with Franziska, and eventually with Bülow himself, began to overwhelm her. The fissures in the Bülows marriage, which were there from the start, began to widen as their union was subjected to one extremity after another, until it finally collapsed. And the first of these extremities was almost upon them.

V

In March 1859, Daniel Liszt, who was pursuing his law studies in Vienna, heard that Bülow was about to conduct an orchestral concert in Prague. The nineteen-year-old youth desperately wished to travel there, especially since Bülow was to introduce three of Liszt's symphonic poems to the city, but he told his father that he lacked the funds. Princess Carolyne replied by return post from Weimar with the money. Daniel rushed off to Prague and attended not only the concert (on March 23), but the three rehearsals leading up to it. He had never seen Bülow conduct before, and was impressed by the swiftness with which the conductor imposed his authority on the players, who were grappling with unfamiliar pieces. Afterwards he wrote to his father, 'Bülow confirmed yet again Philippe's witticism: "Better a lion at the head of fifty stags than a stag at the head of fifty lions".'[13]

In August 1859 Daniel arrived in Berlin in order to spend his summer holidays with Hans and Cosima. He travelled via Dresden, where he had begun to feel vaguely unwell. When Cosima saw him she was struck by the change in his physical appearance. He looked weak and undernourished, and complained of dizziness. Despite all the ministrations that Cosima lavished on him, Daniel took to his sickbed and by the autumn he lay seriously ill, unable to return to his university. He was already doomed, suffering from the galloping consumption that would claim him a few months later. Cosima now started to wear herself out and suffer from lack of sleep, because she insisted on keeping all-night vigils by her brother's bedside. By November, the strain had started to take its toll on the small household. Bülow moved out, so that he could practice without disturbing the patient. Meanwhile, news of Daniel's deteriorating condition reached Liszt, who travelled to Berlin to visit his son, staying at the Brandenburg

13. BA(2), unpublished letter dated April 1, 1859.

Bülow toward the end of the 1850s. A photograph.

Hotel. He was badly shaken when he first observed Daniel's wasted condition. Dr. Bücking, the family physician, arrived. Liszt took him aside and asked for a frank diagnosis, telling Bücking that he expected the worst. Bücking, in the finest traditions of the medical profession, was unable to offer any firm assurances. Cosima accompanied Liszt back to his hotel before returning to her nightly vigil. The following morning, December 13, Bülow came round to Liszt's hotel in tears. His sad mission was to break the news that 'all hope was lost'. For nearly twelve hours Liszt took turns with Cosima and Hans to sit by Daniel's side, who slipped into the arms of death towards midnight. He was twenty years old.

Cosima washed the body herself, and dressed it in a burial shroud. Before the coffin lid was closed, she placed beside Daniel's corpse a portrait of Pascal, his favourite philosopher, whose thoughts had preoccupied him during his final weeks.[14] The sad group of mourners—Liszt, Cosima, Hans, and a group of pallbearers—then set out on the long journey from Anhalterstrasse to the Catholic cemetery beyond the Oranienburg Gate, where Daniel was buried.

Daniel's death ravaged the family, and Cosima never shook off the feeling of guilt that she might have been able to do more to save her brother, unreasonable though that feeling was. As for Bülow, he never stopped working throughout the long ordeal. His lessons at the Stern Conservatory went on as usual. He even travelled to Hamburg and Stralsund on the Baltic coast to give recitals, leaving Cosima to tend her dying brother as best she might. Two days before Daniel passed away, in fact, Bülow gave a major recital in Berlin's Singakademie for the benefit of the Schiller Society. At moments of crisis, it was Bülow's way to shut himself off and present a marble exterior to the outside world. Nevertheless, when a marble exterior is presented to one's kith and kin it can be particularly hard to bear. Did Cosima understand the threat that such a lack of empathy posed to her marriage? There is ample evidence to suggest that she did, and it was eventually to sound the death knell of their union. Years later, after she had deserted hearth and home for Richard Wagner, she told Bülow that she would never have left him if she had felt that she could have been the slightest use to him.

Within four weeks of Daniel's passing, Cosima became pregnant. This first daughter, named Daniela in memory of Cosima's recently deceased brother, was born on October 12, 1860. Cosima recuperated from the birth slowly, and the child was not baptized until December 1. The local Catholic priest conducted the ceremony in the same room in which Daniel had died almost a year earlier, and Liszt came up from Weimar for the service. Bülow made an indifferent father, and often fell prey to depression followed by outbursts of verbal violence. Cosima bore his moods in silence, because she knew that they did not represent his innermost nature. She shrugged off her own weakened condition, not wishing to alarm him. By January she was in need of medical attention. At Liszt's insistence she stayed with him in Weimar for ten days, but her inability to sleep and her dry, hacking cough, alarmed him and for a time he genuinely feared that she might be carried off by the same illness that had brought about her brother's demise a year earlier. It was Blandine who alerted Liszt to Cosima's true plight by telling him bluntly that the Bülow

14. These details of Daniel's death and funeral may be found in a long letter that Liszt wrote to Princess Carolyne, two or three hours after the burial service. LLB, vol. 4, pp. 500–507.

household was the last place in the world for Cosima to convalesce. She was frank in her criticism of both Bülow and his mother. 'Cosima could die in six months if she has only these people around to persuade her to take care of herself. You are the only one who can save her'.[15]

These words Liszt took to heart. He persuaded Cosima to spend part of the summer of 1861 in a sanatorium at Bad Reichenall, in the Bavarian Alps. Consumption was diagnosed and the 'whey cure' prescribed. The clear mountain air, and the long country walks, slowly restored Cosima to health. Meanwhile Liszt begged Bülow not to give in to his 'migraine moods', and assured him that he was someone, with something to do in the world. Although our existence is sometimes unbearable, he counselled Bülow, it is a question of using life well. 'Continue to go on, and live with what you are'.[16] This was sound advice, but Bülow did not, or could not, accept it. In a dexterous understatement Liszt would later remark, 'Bülow lacks the talent to be a husband'.[17]

A further sorrow was inflicted on the Bülows when they learned of the death of Blandine, who passed away on September 11, 1862, at the early age of twenty-six, a few days after giving birth to her first child in the south of France. Blandine did not die in childbirth, a notion that has become something of a fixture in the Liszt literature; the birth of her son Daniel (named after Blandine's dead brother) was swift and virtually painless. She died as a result of medical malpractice at the postnatal stage, and a hopeless struggle against the septicemia that overwhelmed her after her doctor had surgically removed an abscess on the left breast, without the use of anaesthetic. Cosima would have known none of these dreadful details, which were, in fact, kept from the Liszt family by Blandine's anguished husband, Emile.[18]

VI

To this catalogue of outcries and asides one more entry must be made. The harrowing circumstances surrounding the birth of Cosima's second daughter represented a breaking point for her. After returning from Bad Reichenall, and her course of treatment at the sanitarium there, she resumed her daily life with Bülow in Berlin. In the summer of 1862 she again became pregnant. She later confessed, 'I hardly dared tell [Hans] that I was pregnant, so unfriendly was his reaction, as if his comfort were being

15. OCFL, p. 271.
16. LBLB, p. 291.
17. SZM, p. 425.
18. The entire, appalling medical procedure to which Blandine was subjected was dealt with in depth in the third volume of my Liszt biography, WFL, vol. 3, pp. 47–50.

disturbed'.[19] On March 20, 1863, Cosima gave birth to a second daughter, Blandine, named in memory of Cosima's deceased sister. The circumstances surrounding this child's entry into the world almost defy belief. Franziska and Hans were in another part of the house, unaware that Cosima was in the final stages of labour. Cosima tells us that she paced back and forth across the room, all by herself, wriggling like a worm and whimpering. One cry of pain she could not suppress, and it roused the household. Bülow and his mother got her to bed just as the baby was born. By the time the midwife arrived it was all over. Cosima never spoke to anyone of the dreadful neglect to which she had been subjected, but committed the episode to her diary six years later, on the anniversary of her suffering. And she added these graphic words: 'I cannot think without shuddering of that night in Berlin which serves to make utterly clear to me the subsequent course of my destiny'.[20]

VII

The 'destiny' to which Cosima refers was the unexpected arrival in Berlin of Richard Wagner, in November 1863. He was in the middle of a conducting tour, undertaken for the urgent purpose of replenishing his depleted resources, and a desperate attempt to stave off bankruptcy. Wagner's long political exile from Germany had ended in March 1862 when the King of Saxony granted him a full amnesty for his part in the Dresden Uprising. His burning ambition was to find a suitable German theatre in which to mount the first production of *Tristan*. Wagner toyed in turn with the possibilities of Weimar, Karlsruhe, and even Dresden itself, but all these plans had come to naught. It was Vienna that seemed to offer the best prospect, and Wagner moved to the Austrian capital in the summer of 1862 in order to supervise the production. As is well known, the opera proved to be so formidable an undertaking that it was abandoned after seventy-seven rehearsals; Vienna was not to hear *Tristan* until after Wagner's death. Bülow's stalwart role in preparing the piano reduction of the full score, undertaken at Wagner's express request, had by now been widely acknowledged. He had toiled for months over this task. The intricacies of Act II, in particular, had nearly overwhelmed him, and he had more than once turned to Liszt for some professional advice.[21] The massive

---

19. WT, vol. 1, pp. 75–76.
20. Ibid., p. 76.
21. We need look no further than the letters Bülow wrote to Liszt on August 14 and October 16, 1859, to appreciate the anguish he endured for much of that late summer and autumn as he attempted to bring Wagner's mammoth score under the control of ten fingers (LBLB, pp. 269 and 274). Shortly after he had begun this travail he also wrote to his friend Hans von Bronsart about the intricacies of the task, and provided Bronsart with some tantalizing music examples meant to whet the latter's appetite (BB, vol. 3, pp. 255–257).

piano score, finally published in November 1860, had meanwhile become a primary source for the study of Wagner's masterpiece. For this toil Bülow received from Breitkopf the paltry sum of twenty pounds. Aside from Wagner himself, Bülow's knowledge of the opera remained unmatched by anyone. No wonder that Wagner now began to see in Bülow a conductor who would one day serve him well and help him present *Tristan* to the world.

That Cosima was ready to be swept off her feet by Wagner will be obvious to anyone who has followed the story so far. Bülow was completely wrapped up in his own work and had become a stranger to her; the apartment on Anhalterstrasse was little more than a place of stifling routine. The difficult experiences of her recent pregnancy were still fresh in her mind and made her vulnerable. According to Wagner, he and Cosima first declared their love for each other on November 28, 1863, while taking a ride through Berlin's Tiergarten, and amidst 'much sobbing and weeping we sealed our confession to belong to one another alone'.[22] The question is rarely asked, but where was Bülow at that moment? When Cosima's first act of betrayal took place, he was at the Singakademie rehearsing an orchestral concert that included his newly composed orchestral ballade *Des Sängers Fluch* ('The Minstrel's Curse'), based on a poem by Johann Uhland, which he conducted that same evening. The gods must have laughed aloud as they gazed down on the spectacle they had helped to create. While Cosima and Wagner were exchanging their secret vows, Bülow was conducting the perfect background music from an auditorium less than two miles away.[23]

Only the most naive of observers could suppose that this emotional encounter in the Tiergarten took the parties by surprise. That Cosima and Wagner were somehow the innocent victims of Cupid's arrows, drawn from his quiver just as the random pair drove past his coign of vantage, is a romantic notion that Wagner himself might well have wished pos-

---

22. WML, p. 876. This sentence was expunged by Cosima in the first public edition of *Mein Leben,* which appeared in 1911. Until modern times it was to be found only in the private printing of eighteen copies that Wagner arranged for distribution among his friends during the 1870s.

23. Uhland's dark tale of the seductive power of music is set in olden times. The elderly king, in whose castle the minstrel has sung his siren song to such magical effect, observes his beautiful young queen throw the handsome singer a rose from her bosom, as if spellbound. 'You have seduced my people', raves the king, 'Do you now entice my wife?' He draws his sword and kills the minstrel, piercing the singer's breast. The stream of golden song is turned into a river of blood. A curse from heaven is invoked. The castle and its marbled halls collapse in ruins; its beautiful gardens fall into neglect. Where there was once life, everything is now barren. 'That is the minstrel's curse', laments the poet.

terity to cultivate. But it would stretch credulity to the point where fact ends and fiction begins, were we to assume that the couple had begun their drive through the park in a spirit of amiable collegiality, chatting about this and that, only to emerge a couple of hours later as star-crossed lovers in the grip of forces they could not understand but had no alternative but to obey. A retrospective glance at the evidence proves the opposite.

VIII

Cosima had had much to grieve over since the honeymoon that she and Bülow had spent in Zurich, six sorrowful years earlier. One positive memory had remained to illuminate the bleak landscape that now constituted her daily life with Bülow, and that was the portion of the honeymoon spent as guests of Wagner and his wife, Minna, in the Asyl. Even then Cosima had fallen under the spell of Wagner's personality and his *Tristan* poem. Nor had she failed to notice the daily tensions between Wagner and Minna, and a marriage in turmoil. The next summer, in July 1858, the Bülows had once again descended on the Asyl and had walked into the middle of a violent quarrel between Wagner and Minna, who was filled with resentment at his continued relationship with Frau Mathilde Wesendonck, the depth of which had only recently dawned on her. She had intercepted a love letter that Wagner had sent to Mathilde, and having first confronted Wagner about it went on to confront Mathilde, who, offended at being accused of harbouring secrets from her husband, promptly informed him.[24] The atmosphere between the two women was toxic. Wagner later wrote that 'the Bülows really seemed to me to have been providentially sent for the purpose of quelling the horrible excitement that prevailed in the house'.[25] Providence, in fact, did not have a great deal to do with it. The Bülows had actually gone to Geneva to meet Cosima's mother, Countess Marie d'Agoult, who had not yet been introduced to her new son-in-law. Bülow was enchanted both by Marie d'Agoult's beauty and by her intelligence, and he could not help comparing her with Liszt's present companion, Princess Carolyne, whom he termed 'a caricature of a woman'. He was delighted when Wagner invited them all to come to Zurich and stay with him at the Asyl; the Bülows moved in on July 21, and Marie d'Agoult followed a few days later. Wagner doubtless hoped that, surrounded by such stimulating friends, he and Minna might raise themselves from their daily slough of despond and regain some semblance of normality, for however brief a span of time. That did not happen,

24. The letter is often referred to in the literature as the 'Morning Confession', an appellation that Wagner himself gave to his long epistle. It remains a topic of endless discussion among Wagnerians. The best summary of the affair is to be found in SLRW, pp. 167–168.
  25. WML, p. 687.

and throughout the three-week ordeal that followed, Cosima and Hans witnessed Minna and Wagner slowly tearing each other to pieces, until it became evident to everybody that a permanent rupture must follow.

IX

During this visit a disturbing episode took place, about which the literature remains tantalizingly obscure. There was another guest staying at the Asyl, Bülow's old friend Karl Ritter, who had recently separated from his young wife after only a year of marriage, and was suffering some torments of his own. As Marie d'Agoult was about to take her leave, Cosima decided to accompany her as far as Geneva and Karl Ritter announced that he would like to go along with them. Arrived in Geneva, and finding himself alone with Cosima, Ritter unburdened himself of his private sorrows. Cosima, in despair at what she had witnessed of Wagner's problems, and all too aware of the corrosive effect that Bülow's migraine moods were having on her own marriage, suddenly became agitated, almost hysterical, and she begged Ritter to kill her. When he refused, she threatened to drown herself in the lake, and was deterred only when he vowed to do the same if she carried out her threat. This 'suicide pact' would have to be dismissed as romantic fiction were it not for the fact that it was reported in some detail shortly afterwards by Wagner in a letter to Mathilde Wesendonck, and that he could only have received the story from Ritter himself. But Wagner did not stop there. In a letter written a few years later to the German novelist Eliza Wille, who was his Zurich neighbour at the time of the Ritter episode, he disclosed that Cosima 'only a year after their marriage . . . tried to take her own life in her despair at having committed the error of marrying'.[26] And he added that she went on to make repeated attempts to contract various fatal illnesses in the vain hope that she might succumb to one or another of them. For the final word on this we must turn to Cosima herself. Long after all the parties were dead—Bülow, Wagner, and Ritter—she told her biographer Du Moulin Eckart that 'in the very first year of my marriage I was in such despair at our misunderstandings that I wanted to die'.[27]

When Cosima got back to the Asyl, Wagner noticed that she 'was in a strangely excited state which showed itself in a convulsively passionate tenderness towards me'.[28] There has been speculation that Ritter had

---

26. This passage was censored from the first published edition of the Wille-Briefe (MW, 1935), and was only restored in 1987. See SLRW, p. 621.

27. MCW(1), vol. 1, p. 428.

28. Letter to Mathilde Wesendonck, September 4, 1858, suppressed from the official run of letters, RWMW.

fallen in love with Cosima, and that she was torn over how to respond to his advances. In her highly emotional state, she may well have transferred to Wagner all the pent-up feelings to which Bülow never responded and that she was unable to offer Ritter. It is a fact that within three weeks she had sent a letter to Ritter telling him to forget about the Geneva episode, of which she was now ashamed. Ritter, mortified that he had revealed so much of himself to Cosima while receiving so little from her in return, felt rebuffed and never replied to her.

Hans and Cosima stayed on at the Asyl to the bitter end. Hans was present when Wagner went over to settle some business matters with Otto Wesendonck, and was with Wagner when the latter took his final leave of Mathilde, who appears to have realized too late what a devastating effect her relationship with Wagner had had on Minna, leading to the breakup of Wagner's home. On August 16, as the Bülows said farewell to Wagner before returning to Berlin, 'Hans was bathed in tears and his wife Cosima was gloomy and silent'.[29] The following day Wagner himself left Switzerland. Because Germany was still barred to him, he travelled to Venice in the company of Karl Ritter, in search of that solitude so necessary for him to complete *Tristan;* he stayed there until March 1859, and it was in the city of canals and bridges that he brought the second act of the opera to a conclusion. By mutual agreement Minna stayed on at the Asyl for a few more days in order to supervise the sale of their few effects, and then rejoined her kin in Saxony. She vexed Wagner considerably when he discovered that she had advertised in the local newspapers that their belongings were for sale at a reduced price 'because of a hasty departure'.[30]

It is worth pausing for a moment to reflect on the mournful mood that pervaded the Asyl during that woebegone summer of 1858. The marriage of Wagner and Minna was collapsing in full view; Karl Ritter's attempts at matrimony had ended in a separation after a few short months, and he was wrapped in gloom; Hans and Cosima were in a constant state of mutual misunderstanding; and Marie d'Agoult had arrived with emotional problems of her own, spending much time (part of a nostalgic tour reliving the memories of her earlier romantic life with Franz Liszt in Switzerland and Italy) in private tears and quiet anguish.[31] Small wonder, then,

29. WML, p. 688.
30. Ibid., p. 689.
31. Did Cosima know of the symptoms of insanity regularly exhibited by her mother? The prevailing view is that she did. Since 1848 Marie d'Agoult had been an occasional patient of Dr. Emile Blanche, who treated her for 'spleen' (a romantic appellation for melancholy) in his clinic on the rue Berton in Passy. Once or twice she had been plunged into an emotional crisis so severe that she had been placed in a straitjacket by Blanche's assistants

that Cosima returned to Berlin in a state of profound unease. And the turbulent episodes described earlier in our narrative—the deaths of Daniel and Blandine, the trauma surrounding the birth of her second daughter, and her battle with tuberculosis—still lay before her.

X

With Wagner's marriage in its last throes and his financial resources depleted, his inner circle of friends took to contemplating his fate among themselves. From Venice, and with bankruptcy staring him in the face, he sent out a stream of appeals for money. One of them almost cost him his friendship with Liszt, from whom he demanded an annual pension of 'two or three thousand thalers . . . I cannot do with less'.[32] The request came at a bad time for Liszt (who had in any case sent Wagner large sums of money across the years), and he replied by promising to send Wagner copies of his *Dante* Symphony and his *Gran* Mass. Wagner had expected the usual bank-draft, and when it did not come, his response to Liszt was boorish in the extreme. 'Why should I put up with such open contempt

---

and taken to Passy for observation. Marie's attempts at suicide have not been well documented, and Lisztians especially are always taken by surprise when they read about them. But one such episode reminds us forcibly of Cosima's pact with Ritter in Geneva. Twenty-six years earlier Marie had been on holiday with Count d'Agoult and her elder daughter Louise in that same city, and had become suicidal. She wanted to throw herself into the lake, but her frightened husband restrained her, crying, 'They will say that it is I who killed you!' She was admitted to the city hospital and Count d'Agoult and Louise had to leave Geneva without her. This information comes to us from Marie's younger daughter Claire de Charnacé (DMSJ, vol. 2, p. 288n76), and it is unthinkable that Claire would not have passed the story and others like it, to her half-sister Cosima at some point in their long friendship. Cosima would also surely have known that her aunt Augusta de Flavigny, Marie's sister, had twice tried to commit suicide (once by stabbing herself and the other by drinking poison) and finally succeeded when she flung herself into the river Main and drowned. (VCA, vol. 1, pp. 18–19). The extent to which Cosima's knowledge that insanity ran in her family, and its possible effect on her imagination, has never been fully explored. Further evidence of Marie's battles against mental derangement may be found in the memoirs of Marie-Thérèse, the second wife of Emile Ollivier, who knew Marie well. See OASE, pp. 151–152.

It would take us far afield to examine the role of Ritter's psychopathology in all this, and its baleful influence on Cosima. But we must not forget that it was Ritter whose poem 'Nirvana' ('Extinction') inspired Bülow to compose his orchestral fantasy *Nirwana*, op. 20. The work was even known as the 'Suicide Fantasy' among Bülow's inner circle of acquaintants, and its title page bears a dedication to Ritter. Wagner showed an unusual fascination with Bülow's score, and anyone familiar with its main ideas will see that they left their mark on the Prelude to *Tristan*. The long critique that Wagner sent to Bülow about *Nirwana*, before he had penned a note of *Tristan*, may be found in RWHB, pp. 59–64. He told Bülow that he did not recall his mood ever having been so deeply disturbed by a recent piece of music as by *Nirwana*. Bülow conducted his orchestral fantasy for the first time on February 27, 1859, in the Berlin Singakademie.

32. BWL, vol. 2, p. 231; KWL, vol. 2, p. 243.

on your part? . . . No money? . . . I can see that you simply do not know what hardship is, you lucky man!'[33]

Even from distant Berlin, Cosima remained well enough informed about Wagner to understand not only that he was emotionally wracked, but that his separation from Minna held out no hope of a divorce, for Minna resolutely refused to grant him one.[34] Whether Cosima also knew of the various affairs with which Wagner now began to compensate himself as a reward for his loveless marriage is uncertain. But after leaving the Asyl, he fluttered around a number of women, of whom Cosima was just the latest, including the Viennese actress Friederike Meyer, in whose arms he appears to have sought solace during the dark days of the collapse of the *Tristan* production in the Vienna Opera House, in 1862. As for the twenty-nine-year-old Mathilde Maier of Mainz, and Frau Henriette von Bissing (a wealthy widow from Löwenburg who had pledged to bail him out of his financial difficulties, but later reneged), they need no introduction to Wagnerians long steeped in tales of their hero's amours. Wagner would almost certainly have been willing to marry one or the other of these ladies had not the inconvenient business of severing his bonds with Minna been beyond his capacity to resolve. Such was his state of mind at this point in his life that according to one biographer it was not improbable that 'Wagner hoped one day simultaneously to enjoy the security of Henriette as a wife and the pleasure of young Cosima as his mistress'.[35]

This was the position in which Cosima and Wagner found themselves, on that chill November afternoon in 1863, as they began their fateful drive through the Tiergarten. The carriage was freighted with powerful memories of the past and the attendant emotions could not be contained. The 'sobbing and weeping' that accompanied the couple along the way was not staunched by journey's end. It welled up frequently in the months ahead, until all three parties—Cosima, Wagner, and Bülow himself—found themselves adrift on a sea of sorrows.

33. This letter, dated December 31, 1858, was omitted from BWL, but restored in KWL, vol. 2, pp. 237–238.
34. The situation remained unchanged until the night of January 25, 1866, when Minna suffered a fatal stroke, and Wagner was finally freed from the shackles of matrimony.
35. GRW, p. 226.

Catastrophe in Munich, 1864–1869

You have no idea what has been going on. I could scarcely make
you comprehend verbally [let alone in a letter], the horror
and weirdness of what I have undergone.
—Bülow to Joachim Raff[1]

I

On March 10, 1864, Wagner's declining fortunes experienced a dramatic reversal. Maximilian II of Bavaria died, and his eighteen-year-old son Ludwig ascended the throne. Ludwig was still a student, a romantic dreamer, more interested in music and theatre than in the military or politics— the usual enthusiasms for royalty. He was already a fervent admirer of Wagner. When he was thirteen years old, one of his private tutors had presented him with a copy of Wagner's essay *Opera and Drama*. Fascinated by the *Lohengrin* saga, and especially by Wagner's operatic treatment of it, the boy was thereafter on the lookout for anything that issued from Wagner's pen. In 1863, a year before he became king, Ludwig got hold of one of the privately printed copies of Wagner's poem of *The Ring of the Nibelungen*. The story held him in thrall; but it was the preface that compelled his immediate attention. There Ludwig read of Wagner's despair at the impossibility of finding a German theatre capable of mounting such complexities as were to be found in his tetralogy. To be sure there were gifted singers in Germany, Wagner wrote, but they were scattered around various theatres; and the stage designers and machinists, required to solve mechanical problems not yet faced by any opera house, would have to be trained afresh if they were to help bring his gigantic conception to fruition. Then came the prophetic words that had for months pursued Ludwig like some Hound of Heaven. Only a German prince, with an interest in the

---

1. BB, vol. 4, p. 143.

theatre and sufficient resources, could bring everything together and help Wagner realize his dream. 'Will this Prince be found?' Wagner asked. And he ended with a flourish of words from Goethe's *Faust:* 'In the Beginning was the Deed!'

One of the first things that Ludwig did was to search out Wagner and summon him to Munich. The composer was at that moment living an itinerant life, running from his creditors. He was tracked down in Stuttgart by the monarch's private secretary, Franz von Pfistermeister, and handed a letter from Ludwig bidding him come to Munich for an interview. Their first encounter took place on May 4. 'Our meeting yesterday was one great love-scene which seemed as though it would never end', Wagner reported.[2] Among the many matters they discussed were possible productions of *Tristan* and of the as yet unfinished *Die Meistersinger;* the erection of a model theatre to contain these and other operas of Wagner; and the creation of a Royal Music School for the training of the singers and players who would make performances of Wagner's music possible. The young monarch gave Wagner an immediate gift of 4,000 gulden to settle his most pressing debts, and placed at his disposal the Villa Pellet, a spacious dwelling on the shores of Lake Starnberg, just outside Munich.[3] Then, his head filled with dreams which the king had promised to make reality, Wagner left on a hurried two-day visit to Vienna with further cash in hand to keep his creditors at bay.

II

Wagner moved into the Villa Pellet on May 15. Unable to look after such an expansive residence alone, he began to yearn for female companionship, without which his life was never complete. His thoughts turned first to the object of an earlier affection, the thirty-one-year-old Mathilde Maier. He sent her Ludwig's letter to read, the better to impress her with his newfound prospects, and implored her to join him at Starnberg as his housekeeper and companion. Mathilde lived in Mainz with her mother, Josephine, from whom she was reluctant to be parted. Wagner had met her three years earlier in the home of Franz Schott, the publisher, and had found her sympathetic and attractive; his initial overtures had been discouraged because it was thought that Mathilde's incipient deafness might be an impediment to a satisfactory life with someone outside her family circle. It was nonetheless a compliment to Mathilde's character that Wag-

---

2. SLRW, p. 600.

3. Additionally the king gave Wagner an annual stipend of 4,000 gulden, soon to be raised to 6,000. On June 10 he handed Wagner a further gift of 16,000 gulden. And later that year he purchased the rights to Wagner's uncompleted *Ring* Cycle for 30,000 gulden.

ner continued to find her appealing. 'I must have someone here to run my house for me', he wrote to her on June 22.[4] Impatient to receive an answer, Wagner wrote a lengthy letter to Frau Josephine Maier, on June 25, which he sent first to Mathilde, asking her to read it before showing it to her mother. With winged words he assured Josephine that his motives were honorable; that he knew what a sacrifice it would be to part with her daughter; that Mathilde would have separate living quarters on the second floor of the Villa; that the relationship would remain chaste; that had Mathilde been younger he would have liked to have adopted her in order to make the arrangement more acceptable in the eyes of the world; that in the event of his wife, Minna's, death he would be happy to sue for Mathilde's hand in marriage. 'Would you have the courage to face the world and enough confidence in me to entrust your daughter to me?' he inquired of her.[5]

Josephine never saw this letter. Four days later, on June 29, Wagner wrote in haste to Mathilde, begging her not to reveal it under any circumstances. 'There can be *no* question for now of any change in our mutual position,[6] he informed her. What had happened to bring about such an abrupt change of mind? Earlier that day Cosima had unexpectedly arrived at Starnberg in the company of her two small daughters and their nursemaid. Her appearance on his doorstep brought Wagner's negotiations with Mathilde to a grinding halt. He had not seen Cosima since with 'sobs and tears' they had sealed their relationship in Berlin a few months earlier. But why was she at Starnberg at all?

III

While making advances to Mathilde, Wagner had thought it expedient to start a correspondence with the Bülows on the same topic: namely, their transfer to Munich to come and live with him there. He wrote to Bülow about his transformed situation on June 1, inviting him and Cosima to participate in the Munich paradise that the king was willing to create for him. 'You can stay with me and live with me here as long as you wish', he told Bülow. 'My domestic arrangements are such that you won't disturb me for a moment'.[7] Bülow's reply has not survived, but he appears at first to have shown little enthusiasm for the idea of giving up Berlin for Munich. Wagner was not about to be deterred, so he directed his siren song towards Cosima—his real quarry in this matter. On June 10 he wrote

4. SLRW, p. 613.
5. Ibid., p. 616.
6. Ibid., p. 618.
7. Ibid., p. 610.

her a long letter in which he sought to justify his wish to have them both at his side. He told Cosima that he knew of Hans's dissatisfaction with life in Berlin; of his wish to escape the daily drudgery of giving piano lessons; of his rumoured quarrel with Julius Stern at the music conservatory; of his secret regret at never having been offered an appointment as Kapell-meister in some large metropolis more appreciative than Berlin of his talents; and even of his desire to retire from the hustle and bustle of life in the Prussian capital, where he was in constant conflict with the critics, and settle in some peaceful backwater, such as Gotha! While these may well have been among the private grievances that Hans had vouchsafed to Wagner during their conversations across the years, they have not become part of the official record. After playing on Cosima's emotions for awhile, and telling her that for the first time in his life he was in a position to help her and Hans instead of constantly having them help him, Wagner comes to the nub of the matter. The young king, he tells Cosima, lacks a musical education; he knows only Wagner's works, and nothing by Beethoven or other composers. While the monarch longs to make good this defect in his musical education, Wagner goes on, he is too old to begin learning a musical instrument, and Wagner himself lacks the ability to play for him:

> How divinely and utterly uniquely Hans can do so! I told [the king] of this: he now yearns for refreshment from this font of instruction. The Cabinet Secretary Pfistermeister, who is very much the basis upon which the security of my relationship exists, is urging me to bring Hans here. What this means is simply that Hans will remain here, as performer to the King, at a salary of *at least* 1500 florins.[8]

The prospect of having to do nothing more than occasionally play the piano for the king and help Wagner prepare the world premier of *Tristan* was difficult for Bülow to resist. Unable to free himself immediately from his duties in Berlin, Bülow readily allowed Cosima to travel ahead of him. He himself did not arrive at Starnberg until July 7, one week after Cosima herself got there. He may well have thought that she had gone ahead to inspect Wagner's new residence, and make sure that it would be comfortable enough for the family's two-month stay there. As we now know, Cosima went to Starnberg for one reason only: to give herself to Wagner.

It has for long been a commonplace in the Wagner literature to pose the question, 'What did Bülow know of Cosima's deception, and when did

---

8. Ibid., p. 612.

he know it?' It used to be generally supposed that he knew nothing, and continued to know nothing, until well after Cosima had given birth to Wagner's first child, Isolde, the following April, and Wagner's unmistakable features had imprinted themselves on the young girl's face. This picture of Bülow as a husband innocent of all knowledge of his wife's adulterous behaviour, even while the rest of the world was laughing about it behind his back, was never convincing and can no longer be sustained. Bülow first became aware that Cosima and Wagner were lovers shortly after she and the children arrived at the Villa Pellet, on June 29, 1864. The evidence now lies readily to hand.

IV

In June 1914, Isolde petitioned the Bayreuth *Landesgericht* to rule that she was not Bülow's child but Wagner's. She was forty-nine years old. Why bring a legal case at such a time? Isolde had married in 1900, and did not want her thirteen-year-old son Franz Wilhelm Beidler excluded from the possibility of one day taking over the Bayreuth Festival in succession to her brother Siegfried Wagner. She had good reason to fear that this would happen. Isolde's young husband, the conductor Franz Beidler, had been appointed a minor member of the music staff at Bayreuth, but was eventually disliked by Siegfried who pushed him out. So Isolde went to court to re-assert her family connection. This was a particularly painful trial in which a great deal of family linen was washed in public. Sworn depositions were taken by the court, including one from Cosima, who testified that between June and October 1864 she had sexual relations only with Wagner.

Cosima's testimony was undermined by that of an unexpected witness: Wagner's old housekeeper Anna Mrazék, who, together with her husband, Franz, had answered Wagner's call to leave Vienna and run his domestic affairs in Starnberg. Anna placed some sensational details before the court. Chief among them was the fact that Cosima sometimes shared Wagner's bedroom, and on one occasion was caught there by Bülow, who tried to enter but found the door blocked. Her sworn deposition, which was absorbed into the official court transcript, runs:

From July 7 1864 the Bülows stayed in the Villa Pellet as guests of Richard Wagner. According to the statement of the witness Mrazék, who obviously delivered it with the greatest conscientiousness, the Bülows stayed at Starnberg for at least four weeks. In the last days before the departure for Berlin, Bülow stayed in Munich; he was at that time somewhat ill. The witness Mrazék figured that the Bülows stay was perhaps somewhat too short. She was not certain of it. In the first, especially inclement days of July, there was no visit to the Villa Pellet. Soon thereafter, however, the Bülows came. The time that the Bülows lived together in the Villa Pellet may have lasted up to the end of August, or not so long. In any case, the period lay within the time of conception [*Empfängniszeit*].

The Bülows occupied a common bedroom on the first floor. The 3-year-old Daniela also slept in the same bedroom. There was a living-room adjoining the bedroom. Blandine, who was only half-a-year old, slept in a different room with her young nursemaid. Hans von Bülow quite often visited Munich during the day, but regularly spent the nights in the bedroom of his wife. The witness quickly noticed that a close relationship had developed between Richard Wagner and Cosima von Bülow.

Hans von Bülow did not appear to be suspicious [!]. Several weeks after the arrival of the Bülows, the husband of the witness (Herr Franz Mrazék) noticed the following: Frau Cosima von Bülow had gone to Wagner in his bedroom. After some time, Hans von Bülow likewise wanted to go into the bedroom, but he found the door blocked. He obviously knew that his wife was in the bedroom with Wagner. Bülow returned quietly back to his bedroom. Once there he lost his self-control. He threw himself to the floor and lashed out with his hands and feet. Herr Mrazék immediately informed his wife, who was busying herself downstairs, about what he had just observed. The Mrazéks believed that a stormy scene was about to develop. But the participants [*die Beteiligten*] showed the greatest restraint, so that it appeared as if nothing had taken place. The Bülows also retained their shared bedroom. Accordingly, it was certain that when the conception took place, the Bülows were living together for a great part of that time.[9]

This last point was crucial. It led the court to conclude that because Cosima was sharing the bedrooms of both Bülow and Wagner, the identity of the father could not be determined beyond reasonable doubt. Here the court erred on the side of caution. But Cosima was surely telling the truth when she testified, under oath, that she had no other sexual partner than Wagner while she was at Starnberg. And Anna Mrazék's testimony makes one thing abundantly plain. Bülow not only knew of Cosima's infidelity, but covered it up, 'as if nothing had taken place'.

Doubt about Isolde's paternity is not a sentiment that we find in the unpublished diary of Claire de Charnacé, Cosima's half-sister, with whom she had kept in touch during the difficult days in Berlin. Claire writes

9. CB-K, p. 89.

Cosima by Franz von Lenbach.

that while 'Cosima never confessed anything to me, looking at the dates I know that a monstrous seduction had taken place. . . . Since Bülow was unable to leave [Berlin] immediately, Cosima went on ahead of him and went to talk to Wagner in a hotel. Nine months later to the day, Isolde was born! During that time Cosima calmly organized in Munich a life as a threesome'.[10] Even to Claire, 500 miles away in Versailles, Cosima's success in changing the course of a life that no longer held any meaning for her was manifestly obvious. Cosima had created a *ménage à trois* for herself, and for the next several years she passed back and forth between Bülow and Wagner.

---

10. VMA, F859, carton 11. The agitation of the legal process, and the scandal it provoked, ravaged Isolde and she died in February 1919 aged fifty-four, after a difficult illness. Her long-promised vindication *Erinnerungen an meinen Vater, R. Wagner,* failed to appear. One wonders what further revelations it might have contained.

Why did Bülow accept his situation? Quite simply, he did not wish to lose Cosima. And as long as that was the case, he was willing to defend her and the Bülow family honour before the world. We are left with only one conclusion: Bülow had entered into a compact with Cosima, had forgiven her, and had accepted Wagner's child as his own in exchange for her remaining within the marriage. He always referred to 'our three daughters in common' (Daniela, Blandine, and Isolde), assumed fiscal responsibility for Isolde without discrimination, and eventually left her a substantial and equal share in his will. When in later years Wagner tried to adopt Isolde, Bülow rebuffed him, a volatile topic which we take up on a later page. This idea of a compact with Cosima is reinforced when we consider Bülow's very different response to the birth of Eva in 1867, Cosima's second daughter by Wagner, a betrayal that he found so grave that it opened the door to divorce proceedings. Bülow's position, of course, was made yet more appalling by the knowledge that the source of his misery was his chief mentor, a man whom he had hitherto admired above all others. Equally fascinating was Wagner's own position. For self-serving reasons he, too, wanted a wall of silence placed around his affair with Cosima. Had word of it reached the ears of the king, he might have lost all standing in Munich, and his grand plans for *Tristan* and *Meistersinger* would have been jeopardized. It so happens that his fears were well founded, because the eventual discovery by the king of Wagner's duplicity in this matter did, in fact, lead to a temporary breach in their relationship, and a postponement of some of their projects. At the moment, however, silence was a preferred option for all three of them. The alternative, as they knew, pointed towards catastrophe. In the end, it was catastrophe that they got.

V

Unable to bear the tensions aroused in him by the discovery of Cosima's infidelity, Bülow left the Villa Pellet on August 19, and moved into the Bayerischer Hof Hotel, in Munich, in a state of near collapse.[11] There he lay prostrate, a victim of an entire medley of neuralgic pains, and possibly of a minor stroke as well, because his symptoms included a temporary paralysis of both legs and then of his left arm. Cosima, thoroughly alarmed at his condition, paid a hurried visit to Karlsruhe, in order to 'explain' Hans's absence from the annual Tonkünstler Festival which was in full swing, and in which he had been expected to participate as conductor. And that was not all she explained. From an entry in Wagner's 'Brown

---

11. 'Hans to Munich: ill and raging in hotel', observed Wagner in his Annals. SBM, p. 40.

Book' we gather that Cosima told her father, who was also attending the Festival, that her marriage to Hans was threatened and that she was in the middle of an affair with Wagner. An agitated Liszt accompanied Cosima back to Munich in order to help her patch things up with Bülow. Liszt did not expect to encounter Wagner, and may well have preferred to avoid him. On August 25, King Ludwig's birthday, Wagner had gone to pay homage to the young monarch and his family at Hohenschwangau, and had taken with him the score of his newly completed *Huldigungsmarsch* as a birthday gift.[12] Instead of staying overnight as the king's guest, Wagner unexpectedly returned to Munich where he ran into Liszt. What were the thoughts that passed through the minds of the two old friends? They had not seen each other for three years, and the reunion was tempered on both sides by the magnitude of the problems facing them.

Liszt visited Hans in his hotel room, and observed the gravity of his son-in-law's condition for himself. For two days he barely left Bülow's side.[13] He knew full well that Bülow was prone to attacks of 'floating rheumatism', which often came upon him unbidden, but he rightly held Cosima and Wagner to be responsible for the intensity of this particular ordeal. At Starnberg he also spent many hours in conversation with Wagner. Again, Wagner's 'Brown Book' fills in some of the important pieces of the dialogue. We learn that Liszt admonished Wagner in the severest manner, telling him that no good would come of it if he persisted in having an affair with Cosima. And he went further. He warned Wagner that if he ignored this advice, he would hold him in contempt and break off their relationship.[14] This blunt admonition having been delivered, Liszt spent the rest of the time allowing himself to be beguiled by the beauties of Wagner's opera-in-progress *Die Meistersinger,* parts of which he played on the piano. Even on the basis of such a fleeting encounter with the work, Liszt described it as 'a masterpiece of humour, wit, and lively grace'.[15] Wagner then showed him some of the letters he had received from King Ludwig, and Liszt observed, 'Solomon was wrong. There truly is something new under the sun!'[16]

---

12. The March was first performed for the monarch in Munich on October 5. Roiled as he was, Bülow dutifully made two piano transcriptions of the piece, one for two hands and the other for four.

13. LLB, vol. 6, p. 36.

14. RWBB, p. 65. Liszt admonished Cosima as well. When Wagner saw her, after her return from Karlsruhe and more than a week in Liszt's company, he observed that she was 'sleepless, restless, weak, frail, miserable, lacerated'. SBM, p. 41.

15. LLB, vol. 6, p. 41.

16. Ibid., p. 36.

VI

Among the random guests who arrived at Starnberg, and unwittingly walked into the drama unfolding at the Villa Pellet, was Bülow's old socialist friend Ferdinand Lassalle. He was presently in the middle of a well-publicized love affair of his own with Helene von Dönniges, the daughter of the Bavarian *chargé d'affaires* in Geneva. Helene's father wanted nothing to do with Lassalle, who was almost twice his daughter's age, and was an active supporter of Karl Marx. Ambassador von Dönniges took the only prudent step he could think of. He confined his daughter to her room and opened all her letters, even though she had by now reached her majority. To compound Lassalle's problems, there was a rival suitor on the scene, Prince Janko von Racowitza, who was determined to wrest Helene's affections away from a man perceived by many to be little better than a left-wing agitator. By mid-August, Lassalle was desperate for some sort of resolution to the impasse that he and Helene faced. Learning that Bülow was at Starnberg, he conceived the absurd idea that Wagner, perhaps with some prodding from Bülow, might persuade King Ludwig to intercede in the matter, and induce his *chargé d'affaires* back in Switzerland to see reason. Fortunately for Wagner, who took an almost instant dislike to Lassalle, the king had left Munich, and Lassalle was obliged to return to Switzerland with nothing but an empty promise from Wagner to 'do something about it' upon the king's return. A few days later Lassalle sent a cable to Wagner withdrawing his request for help, citing as his reason the 'total unworthiness of the person', namely Helene herself. Her love, we gather, had been temporarily withdrawn from Lassalle, doubtless at the instigation of her father, whose campaign of vilification again 'the Jew from Breslau' was now in full throttle and included slander. Lassalle took the only option open to him, and challenged the ambassador to a duel. Dönniges fled the country in fear of his life, leaving Janko Racowitza to take his place and ensure that the family honour was not stained. Early on the morning of August 28, the rivals faced each other on a field of honour, and Lassalle was fatally shot. Three days later, after lingering in agony, he was dead.[17]

17. This story reads like a novel and later became the basis for one. The informed reader will doubtless recall that George Meredith's *The Tragic Comedians: A Study in a Well-Known Story,* is a fictionalized account of this real-life drama. It was published in 1880, and Meredith drew his information from a primary source, namely Helene's own account, which she had published under the title *Meine Beziehungen zu Ferdinande Lassalle.* In the novel her identity is masked as Clothilde who falls deeply in love with Alvan (Lassalle). Alvan's rival for her affections is called Marko (Prince Racowitza).

Towards the conclusion of the novel, Meredith writes: 'Alvan was dead. The shot of his adversary, accidentally well directed, had struck him mortally. He died on the morning of

VII

It is hard to imagine the purgatory that Bülow endured at Starnberg. Even in July, before the main crisis broke and drove him to seek refuge in the Bayerischer Hof Hotel, he was plagued by neuralgia. Somehow he managed to travel back and forth between Starnberg and Munich, on an almost daily basis, in order to familiarize himself with the opera house, meet some of the musicians, and become acquainted with the administrators with whom he would have to work. On four separate occasions he went over to meet King Ludwig in the monarch's private residence, playing the piano for him, and even dining with him *tête-à-tête*. On July 29 Bülow was appointed *Vorspieler* to the king at 2,000 gulden per annum—more than four times his salary in Berlin, and considerably more than the sum that Wagner had promised him.[18]

At the beginning of September, Bülow emerged from his hotel with the fixed notion that only the 'Roman baths' in Berlin would relieve his nervous condition. On Saturday evening, September 3, Cosima somehow got him to the Munich railway station, where he walked up and down the platform waiting for the train, cursing the world in general and his doctor in particular. Wagner accompanied them to the station and saw them off. All three participants in the saga knew that their destiny was sealed. Wagner had acquired a mistress; Bülow was bound to the Munich court.

---

the third day after the duel. There had been no hope that he could survive, and his agonies made a speedy dissolution desirable by those most wishing him to live'.

Unless the facts that lie beneath the fiction of this passage are brought out, the drama loses some of its savour. The twenty-year-old Janko had never before held a pistol in his hands, and he spent the afternoon before the duel firing 150 practice bullets down the shooting range in an attempt to improve his aim. Lassalle, by contrast, who was thirty-nine years old, and no stranger to firearms, slept soundly on the eve of the duel and, so we are told, even drank a cup of tea before being accompanied by his seconds and a surgeon to the field of honour. Janko, trembling with nerves, shot first, and fatally wounded Lassalle, who returned the shot but missed his adversary. Bülow and Wagner were well informed about what had happened, although we doubt that the news put their own troubles into better perspective. The day before the duel Lassalle drew up his will. Much of his patrimony he left to the German Workers' Party that he had helped to found. There were several other provisions having to do with the dispersal of his personal effects, among which was a handsome marble statue of Apollo which he bequeathed to Bülow.

Helene went on to marry Prince Racowitza, who was thoughtless enough to die within a few months of the wedding, leaving few doubts that it was Helene's disillusion with her brief and childless union that fuelled her desire to offer her story to the world, with Lassalle as the real hero. The best account in English of this regrettable affair may be found in Elizabeth E. Evans's *Ferdinand Lassalle and Helene von Dönniges: A Modern Tragedy* (1897).

18. The king's formal offer reached Bülow later, after he had returned to Berlin. It was contained in a letter from Cabinet Secretary Franz von Pfistermeister, dated 'September 12, 1864', and reproduced in BB, vol. 3, pp. 598–599.

And Cosima? Cosima was two months' pregnant, and had succeeded in creating a threesome, the chief reason she had come to Starnberg in the first place. The Bülows spent the next few weeks closing down the Berlin apartment, bidding farewell to their circle of friends, and making the necessary arrangements for their transfer to Munich and an uncertain life.

In the middle of this turmoil, a well-intentioned Liszt unexpectedly turned up in Berlin on September 5, in what was the first of several determined attempts to save the Bülows' marriage. He and Cosima visited the tomb of Daniel Liszt. Then, in early October, Cosima accompanied her father to Paris, where she was reunited first with her grandmother Anna Liszt and then with her own mother, Marie d'Agoult. The pair then set out for Saint-Tropez where they visited the grave of Cosima's sister, Blandine, in the company of Emile Ollivier, Blandine's still-grieving husband. It was a valiant attempt on Liszt's part to wean Cosima away from what he regarded as Wagner's pernicious influence and bind her more closely to the fabric of her family. But it was undermined by one simple fact: Cosima's physical condition was a daily reminder to her that the child she was carrying was Wagner's. The dilemma she faced was acute. To tell her father or not to tell him? In the end she remained silent, and Liszt never learned for sure that his granddaughter Isolde was Wagner's child, although he later came to believe that she was.

VIII

It is a relief at this juncture to turn to some details of an uplifting episode that had taken place in Bülow's professional life earlier in the year.

On February 13, 1864, the University of Jena conferred on Bülow the degree of doctor of philosophy (*honoris causa*). In learned language the citation referred to his renown throughout Germany as a famous 'setter of tones', to his skill in 'the art of orchestral conducting', and to his outstanding accomplishments as 'a creator of harmony'.[19] Bülow was then formally robed with the doctor's cap and gown, in full convocation. The occasion was crowned by an ambitious concert, featuring Bülow both as conductor and as pianist:

Liszt	Psalm 19, for Choir and Orchestra
Bach	Chromatic Fantasy and Fugue in D minor

---

19. The diploma, prepared the day before the ceremony, was dated 'February 12, 1864', and signed by the Grand Duke Carl Alexander of Weimar (Rektor); jurist Wilhelm Endemann (Pro-Rektor); and Professor Karl Snell (physicist and mathematician, Dean of the Faculty of Philosophy).

SCHUMANN	'Das Glück von Edenhall', for soloist, chorus, and orchestra, op. 143
BEETHOVEN	Sonata in F minor (*Appassionata*), op. 57
HANDEL	Bass Aria from *Alexander's Feast*
BEETHOVEN	Sonata in A major, op. 101
SCHUBERT	'Nachtgesang im Walde', for Male-voice chorus and horns
MOZART-LISZT	*Don Juan* Fantasy.[20]

The happy idea of giving Bülow an honorary degree had much to do with Hof-Justizrat Dr. Carl Gille, who had been in correspondence with Bülow about it for several weeks. Gille was a close friend of Liszt, and had followed Bülow's career closely across the years. Although Gille was not on the university faculty, he served in an advisory capacity on a commission established to preserve and develop the cultural life of the institution.[21] In his letter of thanks, dated 'Berlin, February 19, 1864', Bülow told Gille, 'The doctorate has not worked a Whitsuntide miracle—on the contrary every tongue becomes foreign to me! But it has brought endless joy to me, and for all my immediate plans it is above all an extremely mighty lever'.[22] Bülow knew that this 'extremely mighty lever' would help him command respect once he took up his new duties in the Bavarian capital.

IX

On November 24 Bülow and his family took up residence in Munich and settled into a modest apartment on Luitpoldstrasse. Wagner's quarters, by contrast, were opulent. He had persuaded the king to rent a splendid mansion for him, the former Hôtel Jochum, at 21 Briennerstrasse, a dwelling that Ludwig eventually bought for the composer. Cosima divided her time between the two establishments, often on a daily basis. At Luitpoldstrasse she was Frau von Bülow, the wife of Hans and the mother of three children. At Briennerstrasse she shed this mundane role and became a completely different creature. She was Wagner's secretary, adviser, and confidante. She helped him deal with his correspondence, gave orders to his domestic servants, and protected him from the petty officials connected to the court theatre. It was in this house that she began on July 17, 1865, to take down from Wagner's dictation the story of his life, in response to a request from the king.

20. BKHB, p. 46.
21. SLBG, p. xxix, Leipzig, 1903.
22. BAB, p. 184. Bülow's reference to 'a Whitsuntide miracle' comes from Acts, chap. 2, v. 4: 'And they were all filled with the Holy Ghost, and began to speak with other tongues, as the Spirit gave them utterance'.

Bülow still had to establish himself in the eyes of the Bavarians as some-one worthy of the king's interest. A command performance was therefore announced for Christmas Day, 1864, which was given in Munich's Odeon Theatre in the presence of the monarch. Bülow played Mozart's C minor Fantasie, Bach's Organ Prelude and Fugue in A minor (arranged by Liszt), and Beethoven's *Emperor* Concerto. It was the only occasion on which Ludwig was known to have attended a purely instrumental concert. In response to the king's further requests Bülow conducted two model per-formances of Wagner's *Flying Dutchman* on December 4 and 8, the first time that the opera had been staged in Munich.

Almost from the moment that Bülow arrived in the Bavarian capital, he and Wagner had become deeply engaged in drawing up plans for a Royal Music School, a proposal dear to the king's heart. Into this enter-prise Bülow threw himself heart and soul. Whatever doubts he harboured about 'institutionalized music education' were temporarily banished, be-cause for the first time he sensed that he might be in a position to realize some of his best ideals, given the limitless support that King Ludwig seemed prepared to bring to the project. At Wagner's urging, the king appointed Bülow the director of the school, which opened its doors the following year.[23] Ludwig even told Cosima that 'we will bid the age of Pericles arise once more', and talked in grandiose terms of 'other peoples of the earth paying homage to the spirit of the German nation'.[24] This was the heady climate that prompted Wagner to bring in both Cornelius and Rheinberger as teachers, while Franz Wüllner was authorized to or-ganize a department of choral singing. Bülow himself headed the piano department, and was assisted by several younger teachers. It was King Ludwig's firm conviction that without such a flourishing music school to replenish both talent and resources, his opera house would remain 'a costly toy'. The architect Gottfried Semper was commissioned to design a splendid new festival theatre for Munich, of which the school was to

23. The Wagner devotee, of course, will always maintain that it was Wagner himself who laid the foundations for the Royal Music School, proposed a strategy for its future di-rection, and drew up a detailed budget for King Ludwig's consideration. But none of it could have happened without Bülow. It was not until the early part of 1865 that Wagner was able to put forward a formal proposal to King Ludwig in the form of a *Report to His Majesty King Ludwig II of Bavaria upon a German Music School to be founded in Munich*. While it may bear Wagner's imprimatur, the bulk of the document was the work of Bülow, a fact admitted by Wagner to King Ludwig in his letter to the monarch of January 21 (KLRWB, vol. 1, p. 51). Moreover, after a couple of years in Munich, Wagner was so beleaguered by musical and po-litical problems, largely of his own making, that he had no time left for the daily supervision of the School, and his interest waned. The task of making everything work fell on Bülow's shoulders.

24. NLRW, vol. 4, pp. 39–40.

become an integral part, to be completed within five years. In the event, not a single shovelful of earth was turned in pursuit of this dream.

It was entirely typical of Wagner that having first assured Bülow that he would be released from the bondage of teaching once he had severed his ties with unfriendly Berlin, he went on to place him in a far worse position in Munich. The music school became an albatross around Bülow's neck, prolonging his connection with Munich long after Wagner and Cosima had left the city and he himself had no other reason to stay. To Bülow was left the burden of not only directing the faculty, but drawing up the curriculum as well—which included auditions, end-of-term examinations, student concerts, and a hundred-and-one other mundane things that fall to a director's lot. As head of the piano department (an additional encumbrance) Bülow spent countless hours preparing some 'instructive editions' for the use of the piano students. One or two of these publications went on to enjoy a wide posterity, notably his selection of studies by J. B. Cramer. It bears the topical inscription 'with instructive remarks written for the use of the Pianoforte Students in the Royal Conservatory at Munich'. Another such volume was the series of 'Twelve Easy Pieces' selected from the keyboard music of Handel.

X

Once word had spread in Munich of plans to create a Royal Music School, with resources unmatched anywhere, a dozen vested interests felt themselves threatened. The very idea of the school provoked enmity among the local music teachers and the resident orchestral players who saw themselves brushed aside, unworthy to be a part of Wagner's master plan, and a whispering campaign was begun against him. At first the jokes that made the rounds of Munich's beer halls were harmless enough, directed as they were against the pair of peacocks that roamed around the gardens of the Briennerstrasse residence (Wagner had named them Wotan and Frigge, the old Nordic spelling of Fricka), and against the opulence of its furnishings. Wagner had brought in his Viennese milliner Bertha Goldwag, who, with the help of a team of decorators, had turned the place into what has been described as a whorish fantasy of silks, satins, velvets, and laces. Through its rooms wafted the aroma of expensive perfumes specially imported from Paris. One of the main salons became known as the 'Satin Room'. It was sixteen feet long and fourteen-and-a-half feet wide, its walls covered entirely with a fine yellow satin, the floor with an expensive Smyrna carpet.[25] In the middle was a sofa on which Wagner could

25. In the account that Bertha Goldwag later gave to the world when she reflected on this adventure, she wrote, 'I travelled [from Vienna] incognita on Wagner's instructions. At

recline whenever he wished to commune with his muse. Hardly surprising, then, that the scornful nickname 'Lolette' became attached to Wagner. Old King Ludwig I was still alive, and memories of his dalliance with the dancer Lola Montez, the scandal of which had helped to bring about his abdication, was fresh in everyone's mind. It was well known that his grandson Ludwig II showed no interest in women, and the young man's powerful attachment to Wagner carried unmistakable implications. If Ludwig I had his 'Lola', why not Ludwig II his 'Lolette'? Would Wagner, like Lola Montez before him, be hounded out of town? The groundswell of public opinion against Wagner began to look perilous.

Chief among Wagner's enemies were the Munich civil servants within the Residenz, who resented his influence over the king and were determined to staunch the flow of money from the royal treasury. They did what civil servants always do when faced with a challenge to their authority: they closed ranks. They smiled, bowed, uttered the usual platitudes, and waited patiently for Wagner to bring about his own downfall. And through his native arrogance and willful recklessness Wagner obliged them. At the beginning of 1865 he indiscreetly referred to Ludwig as 'Mein Junge' (My boy) in the presence of Cabinet Secretary Pfistermeister, who conveyed the remark to the king. An offended Ludwig denied Wagner an audience. The royal displeasure was further exacerbated when Pfistermeister informed the king that a portrait of Wagner by the painter Friedrich Pecht, which the monarch had received from Wagner in the belief that it was a gift, was actually going to cost Ludwig 1,000 gulden, a piece of news that is said to have enraged him. Wagner angrily claimed to have misunderstood royal protocol governing the conveyance of gifts to the Residenz, and ended up paying for the portrait himself; but much damage was done. On February 19 the Augsburg *Allgemeine Zeitung* came out with an anonymous article under the headline 'Richard Wagner and Public Opinion', gilding a number of stories about Wagner already in general circulation—his fall from royal favour, his profligate ways, his disdain for the musicians of Munich, and the episode of the Pecht painting which Wagner is described as having deposited in the king's antechamber together with a bill for 1,000 gulden. The article was actually the work of the Munich poet Oskar von Redwitz, who was connected to the scheming world of civil servants running the Residenz, and was al-

---

Salzburg, during the customs declaration, I made out that the silk shirts, the dressing gowns, the counterpanes and so forth were actually intended for a countess in Berlin' (KBWP, p. 29). Wagner was unable at first to pay Bertha's bill, which came to 10,000 gulden. He gave her an advance of 500 gulden, while awaiting further benefactions from King Ludwig.

most certainly reflecting their views. It ended with a broadside. 'Wagner and his associates with connections to the court are thrusting themselves between us Bavarians and our beloved King'.

Such a comment could not be allowed to pass. Bülow, who was itching to get into the fight, was the first to fire back, claiming that because he alone had the honour of being an 'associate' of Wagner with connections to the court, to him belonged the right to brand the writer of the article an 'infamous slanderer'.[26] The editor of the *Allgemeine Zeitung* obligingly published Bülow's letter on February 21, promising to keep the issue alive until Wagner himself had responded.

That response reached the newspaper the following day in the form of an open letter. Wagner wrote it in consultation with Bülow, Cornelius, and Pecht, and the aggrieved quartet stayed up until one o'clock that morning putting the finishing touches to the document. Wagner begins by protesting against the intrusion of the press into his private affairs. He points out that in times past, both in London and Paris, the press had attacked his art and his theories, but never his person. Only in Munich, a city to which he has been summoned by the king himself, has he been placed in the public pillory as a man. He denies that he is a burden on the royal purse, explaining that the large advance for *The Ring* was payment to compensate him for work lost while he completed his magnum opus. He pours scorn on the colourful story of the Pecht painting, advising his critic to consult the appropriate office in the Residenz, which might offer a less colourful account of the affair. Wagner's long rejoinder is a masterpiece of circumlocution, and he himself doubtless hoped that it would silence his adversaries. But the press, which then as now took it to be its primary function to pull down anyone whom circumstance has lifted above the common herd, had other ideas.

Less than a week after the open letter appeared, Munich's satirical journal *Punsch* lampooned him in an article titled 'A Morning in the Life of a New German Composer'. A peal of laughter rippled across Munich as the reading public devoured what was, in effect, a burlesque designed to puncture Wagner's vanity. He is depicted as 'Rumorhäuser, the great composer', and the action takes place in his magnificent bedroom on Briennerstrasse, replete with velvet hangings, silk curtains, and a mirrored ceiling

---

26. That Bülow knew from the start that he was dealing with Redwitz is evident from the derisive poem he wrote against this adversary, in twelve stanzas no less, and published in the satirical magazine *Kladderadatsch* a week or two later. Bülow makes a glancing reference to the poem in a letter to Carl Bechstein. BNB, p. 176.

with frescoes by Pecht and Kaulbach. 'Rumorhäuser' is in bed, from which location he tugs on the bellpull. The trumpet signal from *Lohengrin* is heard. His valet appears and the pair engage in a banal conversation as to which one of his many coloured dressing gowns he will wear that day, how to solve the vexed question of making a proper selection from among so many new pairs of socks, and which one of his coloured servants, the black or the mulatto, will serve his coffee—a duty that depends on the shade of the coffee itself. Only his white valet may serve white coffee— an unmistakable reference to Wagner's racial prejudices.

Punsch had already unmasked its batteries in 1864 when it published a cartoon showing a Bavarian military officer drawing bags of coin from a chest marked 'Royal Bavarian Treasury' to support the army's necessary expenditures. Wagner is standing next to him, saying, 'Dear Friend, don't take it *all* out. Leave a few gulden to cover the cost of my Conservatoire of the Future'.[27] Now that Wagner's spendthrift ways had become the talk of the town, *Punsch* returned to the attack and published a cartoon showing Wagner playing the organ while moneybags, each marked '1000', dance to his endless melody. The caption explains that the Orpheus of old was able only to move rocks, whereas the new Orpheus casts a spell over metal itself.[28]

XI

This was the witch's brew of slander, parody, recrimination, and carica- ture in which Bülow began the first rehearsals of *Tristan,* at ten o'clock on the morning of April 10. By one of those bizarre coincidences that regu- larly attached themselves to Wagner's biography and gave it the appear- ance of a romantic novel, Cosima had given birth to his daughter Isolde only two hours earlier. Had this child been a boy, Cosima, with her blind attachment to Wagner and his world, would surely have named the in- fant 'Tristan'. Bülow soldiered on, despite the buzz of gossip surrounding the paternity of the newborn infant. Every morning he supervised an or- chestral rehearsal in the small Residenz Theatre, followed by a piano re- hearsal for the singers at Wagner's house in the evenings, during which he himself naturally presided at the keyboard. Wagner, who had mean- while returned to royal favour, was engaged in a detailed correspondence with King Ludwig about the best location for the presentation of his mas- terpiece. He at first favoured the intimate Residenz Theatre, which had good acoustics. The king, however, was adamant that only the Royal Opera House itself could offer the space and seating capacity that such a

27. KFW, p. 34.
28. Ibid., p. 40.

large work demanded. In the end the king prevailed, so Bülow moved his forces into the larger building.[29]

In the course of rearranging everything, Bülow expressed the need for more space for the orchestral players. The theatre machinist Joseph Penk-mayr told him that it would mean removing thirty stalls. Bülow, at the end of his tether, barked back, 'What does it matter whether we have thirty *Schweinehunde* more or less in the place!' His intemperate remark was overheard by eavesdroppers in the darkened auditorium and reported in the *Neueste Nachrichten* on May 7, which archly invited Bülow to explain himself. Two days later it printed an unusually muted apology from Bülow, in which he regretted his 'most unparliamentary expression', a phrase, he told his readers, that probably conveyed 'a more brutal sense' in cultivated Munich than elsewhere. It was not his intention to insult the refined members of the Munich public, he went on ingratiatingly, without whose support opera could not survive. That still left the rest un-accounted for. The prospect of thirty *Schweinehunde* removed from the Court Theatre was too good an image for *Punsch* to forgo, and it duly came out with a cartoon showing several rows of hound dogs sitting on their stalls, baying forlornly in the foyer. Above the picture runs the cap-tion, 'Transmigration of living bodies'; beneath it, 'A few rows of Bülow's stalls'.[30]

The *Nachrichten* accepted Bülow's explanation of the Schweinehunde remark with grudging grace, but other newspapers would not let it go.

---

29. Bülow's ability to contain within himself the chaos of his private life, and wall it off completely from his public activity, was nowhere on better display than at this time. Just days after the birth of Isolde, and beleaguered with a multitude of problems arising from the forthcoming *Tristan* production, Bülow set out for The Hague, and on April 15 gave the world premier of Liszt's *Totentanz*. When did he find the time to prepare this difficult work? With Bülow such a question is largely irrelevant, because when his workload appeared to be on the point of implosion, he simply increased his working day until his labours were done. A copy of the manuscript of *Totentanz* had been in his possession since the previous year, and Liszt had corresponded with him about a possible performance (LBLB, p. 329). Liszt did not hold out much hope of success for this work, a virtuosic set of variations on the plainchant *Dies Irae*, and he tried to discourage Bülow from going ahead with it. That was all Bülow required to move forward, and he arranged to play it at The Hague under the Dutch conductor Johannes Verhulst. In the event, Liszt was proved right, and the negative effect produced on the public prompted Liszt to tell Bülow that he deeply regretted that his 'wretched little work has caused you some unpleasantness'. Under different conditions Liszt himself might have directed the orchestra. But he was in Rome, about to enter Holy Orders, and on April 25 he received the tonsure. For the rest, the irony of playing a piece bearing the title 'The Dance of Death' would not have escaped Bülow, who returned to Munich and his *Tristan* rehearsals, only to find that the turmoil he had left behind him was about to in-crease exponentially. *Totentanz* was published later that same year with a glowing dedica-tion from Liszt: 'To the high-souled Herald of our art—Hans von Bülow'.

30. KFW, p. 37.

The *Volksblatt* was particularly aggressive and called him a 'typical specimen of truly Prussian self-esteem', warning that if he had made his offending remark in the beer halls of Munich, the 'Zervierteln' would be the least of his worries. The best advice it could offer Bülow, if he wished to avoid being 'quartered', was to consider the motto of the old Müncheners: 'Go abroad'. This was the cue for which the *Neuer Bayerischer Kurier* had been waiting. Every day for a week it displayed the headline 'Hans von Bülow Is Still Here!' in letters which increased in size with each issue. That the object of this campaign of vilification against Bülow was to drive him out of Munich and bring the preparations for the *Tristan* premier to a standstill was obvious to everybody. But Bülow had no intention of going anywhere. By May 11 he had already directed twenty-one rehearsals, driving himself to the brink of exhaustion. At one rehearsal he had actually fainted. Meanwhile, Wagner announced that *Tristan und Isolde* would make its formal appearance on May 15.

XII

There had never been much doubt in Wagner's mind that the only two singers capable of doing justice to the title roles were the tenor Ludwig Schnorr von Carolsfeld, and his wife, the soprano Malvina. They were presently attached to the Dresden Court Theatre, on which they had begun to reflect much glory. Ludwig had already sung *Tannhäuser* and *Lohengrin* to critical acclaim in Dresden, and had even begun to study *Tristan,* but had found the role so taxing that, partly on the advice of his wife, he abandoned it. In the summer of 1862 that changed when he and Malvina met Wagner in Biebrich and sang parts of the opera to him. Wagner knew at once that in Ludwig Schnorr he had found his perfect 'Tristan'; the great singer seemed to fit the role as if to the manner born. Wagner described Schnorr's voice as 'full, soft, and gleaming'. Schnorr, in turn, wrote that 'Wagner's influence on me is immeasurable'.[31] It was an artistic match of the rarest kind. In response to a request from King Ludwig, the King of Saxony agreed to the Schnorrs' temporary transfer to Munich, and the couple arrived in the city in February to meet Bülow and hold some preliminary rehearsals. When King Ludwig first set eyes on Schnorr, he expressed some reservations that the singer's excessive girth might make him an unsuitable choice for the role; but a private performance of *Tannhäuser,* arranged at short notice for the monarch's benefit on March 5, had Ludwig joining in the general chorus of praise, not only for the beauty of Schnorr's voice but also for the intelligence of his acting. As for Bülow, he was filled with veneration for the singer, whose work in the opera house he summed up as 'admirable'—a high accolade,

31. GIS, p. 217.

coming from someone whose critical lexicon was filled with many more words of invective than of praise.

Before the rehearsals for *Tristan* got underway, Wagner asked the king to confer on Bülow the title of 'Court Kapellmeister for Special Services'. Wagner privately claimed to be physically unequal to the task of conducting *Tristan*. This may have been a veiled acknowledgement that his memory was not always reliable, despite his enormous experience in earlier years conducting opera in Dresden and elsewhere. But as usual with Wagner, there was a self-serving reason behind his request. Had he taken over the baton formally, the incumbent conductor at the Munich Theatre, Franz Lachner, would have become his deputy; and in the event of Wagner himself falling victim to some hazard or other, Lachner would have assumed control of *Tristan*. This prospect Wagner was unwilling to entertain. From the start, it was to be Bülow's privilege to present *Tristan* to the world.[32]

The twenty-first rehearsal on May 11 was actually a full dress affair given in the presence of the king and 600 specially invited guests. Before it began Wagner came onto the stage and delivered a speech. In a voice charged with emotion he thanked the players and the singers for the many sacrifices they had made, and apologized for the fact that his indifferent health prevented him from directing the work himself. He assured them and the audience that he had complete confidence in Bülow, whom he described as 'my second self'. A spontaneous outbreak of applause followed his words. Bülow then spoke. He too thanked the artists for their hard work, without which, he told them, he would not have been able to fulfill the trust that Wagner had placed in him. He then lifted his baton and the first notes of *Tristan* filled the theatre. The performance lasted from ten in the morning to three-thirty in the afternoon. After each act the audience called for Wagner, but he failed to appear. As for King Ludwig, this full rehearsal on May 11 was regarded by him as so significant that he marked it by granting a pardon to all those who had participated in the 1849 Uprising.

XIII

The public premier of *Tristan,* planned for May 15, 1865, is a date widely regarded as one of the most extraordinary in the Wagner calendar. Early

---

32. Franz Lachner had been the Royal Kapellmeister in Munich since 1836, and enjoyed a solid reputation as a conductor. Wagner's arrival in the city proved to be Lachner's undoing; the two musicians frequently disagreed on a variety of musical matters. In 1865, and chiefly because of the looming *Tristan* production, Lachner departed the city on an extended leave of absence, going into permanent retirement in 1868.

in the day bailiffs broke into Wagner's house with an order to attach his furniture against the settlement of a five-year-old debt to one Madame Julie Salis-Schwabe. Cosima dashed over to the royal treasury bearing a note from Wagner in which he begged for the immediate release of 2,400 florins, which the officials there set against his salary.[33] The bailiffs had hardly left the house when there was a knock on Wagner's front door, and there stood Ludwig Schnorr with the calamitous news that his wife, Malvina, Wagner's 'Isolde', had lost her voice after taking a vapour bath that morning. The premier would have to be postponed, and an announcement to that effect was made public that afternoon. To Wagner it must have seemed that the 'curse' that had always hovered over *Tristan* would never be lifted. The wildest rumours swept the town. Malvina's voice had been ruined by Wagner's music; the orchestra, worked to the point of exhaustion, had struck for more pay; Bülow had been threatened with assassination because of his 'Schweinehunde' remarks; and so on.[34] Such gossip and innuendo were hardly new for Wagner, of course. A more serious source of embarrassment to him was that Munich had meanwhile filled up with friends and supporters from all over Europe to hear *Tristan,* and those who could not linger were forced to return home.

A new date of June 10 was set for the public premier, a postponement that gave the indefatigable Bülow the chance to get in three more rehearsals. The performance was timed to begin at 6:00 p.m. In the royal box sat the elderly King Ludwig I, his son Prince Luitpold, Duke Maximilian, and various high-ranking members of the royal household. At 6:10 p.m.

33. Once Wagner had begun to enjoy the patronage of the king, he was widely perceived to be the recipient of a river of gold, and long-forgotten creditors emerged as if from nowhere. Benefactors, sponsors, and ordinary tradespeople now descended on Wagner in droves, in hopes of exacting a share of the bounty. Madame Julie Salis-Schwabe, the rich Jewish widow of a Mancunian industrialist, was just the latest among their number. She had generously loaned Wagner 5,000 francs during the difficult days of his Paris sojourn five years earlier, following the ruinous failure of *Tannhäuser* there. As early as March 20, her Munich-based lawyer, Dr. von Schauss, had sent Wagner a friendly warning about the legal consequences of ignoring the unpaid debt, and the adverse effects the attendant publicity might have on the *Tristan* production. Wagner, through reckless indifference, chose to ignore the warning and suffered an embarrassment he could easily have avoided.

34. One rumour that came close to keeping company with the facts concerned the overburdened orchestral players. Bülow had driven them so hard that on one particularly gruelling occasion Franz Strauss, the principal horn player and father of Richard, declared that his lips were tired and he could not carry on. 'Then go and collect your pension', cried an irate Bülow from the rostrum. Whereupon Strauss senior put his horn into its case, left the orchestra pit, and went straight to the theatre intendant Baron Karl von Perfall: 'Herr von Bülow has ordered me to collect my pension', he reported. It took all Perfall's skill to sort out the tangle because he and the crestfallen Bülow knew that Strauss was indispensable. Bülow so admired the player's command of his instrument that he called him 'the Joachim of the horn'. He also knew that Strauss was married to the daughter of Georg Pschorr, one of the wealthiest brewers in Munich, and that he needed neither his pension nor his salary.

Bülow conducts *Tristan,* June 10, 1865. A caricature from Munich's *Punsch.*

the young king himself entered the royal box, and *Tristan* was officially launched. Ludwig Schnorr has described the prolonged applause that greeted the cast and the orchestra as the curtain descended on the final act, applause that he thought would never stop and which was for him and Malvina a source of justified pride. 'We have accomplished something that others cannot imitate', he wrote to his parents.[35] Two more performances took place, on June 13 and 19. Throughout the entire period Wagner was in a state of ecstasy. The impossible had been made possible, the unperformable made performable. On the twenty-first Bülow wrote to Raff, 'We are all in a dream state over the extraordinarily complete success [of *Tristan*], the greatest that a new Wagner work has had anywhere. The Schnorrs were unbelievable: all the others quite tolerable; orchestra excellent'.[36]

The 'curse' that had dogged *Tristan* was not yet lifted. As if to punish Wagner for having mounted *Tristan* at all, the fates exacted a terrible revenge. During the course of the three performances, Ludwig Schnorr

35. GIS, p. 258.
36. BB, vol. 4, p. 42.

complained of a cold draught that swept across the stage and exposed him to its chilling effect while he was singing the demanding music of Act III, bathed in perspiration. Neither Wagner nor Bülow took the complaint seriously, because Schnorr was in magnificent voice. Within days of his return to Dresden, however, he became catastrophically ill, and died on July 21. He was only twenty-nine years old. Wagner was totally unprepared for this dreadful news, and there is little doubt that he held himself partly to blame for Schnorr's death.[37] He and Bülow travelled by train to Dresden in order to attend the funeral. Wagner had asked Malvina to delay the burial by half-an-hour so that he could gaze on the face of his 'Tristan' for the last time. Because of the hot weather the body began to decompose, the coffin was closed, and the funeral was brought forward. By the time that Wagner and Bülow arrived, the ceremony had taken place. All they could do was to commiserate with the grieving widow, and hear from Malvina Schnorr's own lips a harrowing description of her husband's last moments. Schnorr's symptoms were particularly horrifying. His illness was described as *springende Gicht,* or 'leaping gout . . . that travelled from his knee-joint to his brain'. In his delirium he began to tear out his hair, which had to be sheared. Towards the end, he was roaring like a lion and three people were required to restrain him. In the absence of any other diagnosis, Schnorr's doctor let it be known that his distinguished patient had died of *Tristan.*[38]

XIV

Emboldened by the success of his masterpiece, Wagner turned his baleful eye once more towards the royal treasury. By August 1865 he had assessed his future needs and drew up a detailed schedule of expenses. These were sent to King Ludwig with an astounding request for 200,000 gulden, of which a trifling 40,000 gulden would be required immediately, the balance to be used as a trust fund into which he could dip whenever circumstances warranted. Woven into this request was an implied warning that he would have to leave Munich if it were not granted. The cabinet balked at such a brazen solicitation; Ludwig's entire disposable income amounted to no more than 300,000 gulden a year, from which was ex-

---

37. Wagner's attachment to the memory of the singer is enshrined in his moving essay *Meine Erinnerungen an Ludwig Schnorr von Carolsfeld,* which first appeared in the NZfM, issues of June 5 and 12, 1868.

38. GRW, p. 272. Such stories confirmed the growing belief in a 'curse' hovering over *Tristan.* During the rehearsals for the 1869 revival of the opera, one of Bülow's young répétiteurs, Ludwig Eberle, became so overwrought that he suffered a nervous breakdown and had to be removed to an asylum. By now even Bülow was calling *Tristan* 'a fatalistic, ominous work'. BB, vol. 4, p. 302.

tracted a large annual stipend for the support of his grandfather, the deposed Ludwig I, together with various other essential items traditionally set against the king's purse. When it became evident that Ludwig, for fear of losing Wagner, might accede to this potentially ruinous request, the politicians revolted and forced the monarch to a compromise. Wagner could have his 40,000 gulden, but not a penny more. From that moment the politicians, fearing a fiscal meltdown if Wagner continued to get his way, declared open warfare on him. They were led by Secretary Franz von Pfistermeister and the recently appointed prime minister, Baron Ludwig von der Pfordten. Wagner trivialized the pair by nicknaming them 'Pfi' and 'Pfo', but they were to prove deadly adversaries. The 40,000 gulden meanwhile awaited collection from the royal treasury, and in one of the best-known stories in the Wagner lexicon Cosima herself went there expecting to pick up a draft. The officials at the treasury had other ideas. If Wagner wanted coin of the realm, then coin of the realm he would get. They handed her sacks of coin in an attempt to embarrass her. Not to be outmaneuvered, Cosima hailed two hansom cabs and drove with the booty back to Briennerstrasse.

Wagner now made a cardinal blunder. In August 1865 he laid before the king a plan for reorganizing the Bavarian cabinet, an idea that had as its sole purpose the removal of certain people from the government who continued to vex him and stand in the way of his projects. Such an act might have been construed as treasonable had it been made public. With reckless abandon Wagner went on to accommodate his enemies. Provoked by yet another newspaper attack on him, this time from the *Volksbote*, he published an anonymous article in the *Nachrichten*, written in the third person. It purported to explain once and for all the true nature of Wagner's relations with the king, the snow-white purity of his artistic intentions for the greater good of Munich, his innocence of all those baseless charges of graft and corruption constantly levelled against him by the crowd, and above all the wickedness of certain adversaries in the cabinet who wanted to bring him down. Cosima was the chief instigator of this letter, which appeared in the *Nachrichten* on November 29, and she helped Wagner put the final polish on the text. The unmistakable style and syntax of Wagner shone through, however, and was recognized by Pfistermeister. And when he read the concluding sentence he knew that Wagner's fate was sealed.

> With the withdrawal of two or three individuals enjoying not the slightest esteem among the Bavarian people, the King and his subjects would once and for all be free of these tedious disturbances.

This was all that Pfistermeister required to raise the alarm. Here was the old left-wing rabble-rouser, the 'barricade man' of the Dresden Uprising, once again preaching the dismantling of government. The cabinet, members of the royal family, and even the archbishop of Munich rose up against Wagner, and the king himself was finally obliged to recognize that his favourite could not be allowed to remain in Bavaria. On December 6 Ludwig reluctantly signed an order for Wagner's temporary banishment. Cosima and Wagner were dining together at Briennerstrasse when the document was delivered. Wagner later reported that Cosima almost fainted when she heard the news. She knew that she would have to maintain the pretense of being Frau von Bülow in Munich while Wagner went into exile alone. Four days later Wagner left Bavaria. He was accompanied to the station only by his servant Franz Mrazék and his dog Pohl. It was five o'clock in the morning. Cosima and Cornelius were there to see him off (Bülow was away on a brief concert tour). As Wagner boarded the train, Cornelius observed that he 'looked ghostly pale, with a confused expression, and the long, loose hair quite gray . . . Cosima was completely broken. As the train pulled away, and disappeared behind the pillars, it was like the melting of a vision'.[39]

XV

After the luxury of Briennerstrasse and the daily presence of Cosima, Wagner was hard-pressed to find a suitable refuge. He spent his temporary banishment in Switzerland, where he rented a property on the outskirts of Geneva, called 'Les Artichauts'. By any standards it was an extravagant abode, but he found it difficult to compose. Cosima visited him in March 1866, and it was on one of their steamboat excursions across the Swiss lakes that they came across Tribschen, a three-story villa situated on a tongue of land jutting out over Lake Lucerne. From the moment he set eyes on the property Wagner knew that he had found his Shangri-la, a place which boasted inspirational views of the Alps, and would offer him the peace of mind to bring *Meistersinger* to completion. With the help of the king, who agreed to pay the rent, Wagner moved into Tribschen[40] in April 1866. From there he issued an invitation to Hans and Cosima to join him, offering them the ground floor and the children the third, while retaining the second one for himself. 'Hans, you will grant my request? Of course you will! For you know that I love you, and that—apart from my giddy, though wonderful relationship with this young King—nothing, nothing keeps me on this earth but you and your family'.[41] On May 12,

39. CLW, vol. 2, p. 318.

40. Wagner, with no other authority than his imagination, preferred to spell the name 'Triebschen'.

41. RWHB, p. 246.

1866, in response to Wagner's urging, Cosima travelled to Tribschen with the three children in order to help him settle in. They lived there as man and wife throughout that summer. Bülow remained in Munich, fulfilling a number of concert engagements. He did not join Cosima until June 10, one month later. What he discovered when he got to Tribschen tore him asunder and resulted in a crisis in his relationship with Wagner. The full context of that story we will come to presently.

No sooner had Wagner begun his banishment, than the king had started to pine for his return. Because that was not immediately possible, some pretext had to be found to enable Ludwig to visit Wagner; but such a re-union would have to take place in secret. Now that Wagner was installed at Tribschen, the king saw his opportunity. May 22 was the composer's fifty-third birthday, and Ludwig determined to celebrate this hallowed anniversary in Wagner's company. He travelled to Tribschen incognito, with a single aide to keep him company, and turned up at the villa disguised as 'Walther von Stolzing'—a leading character in Wagner's *Meistersinger*. Consternation broke out in the ranks of the Bavarian cabinet when it learned of this visit. The king had been expected to attend a vital cabinet meeting on May 22. Bavaria stood on the brink of war with Prussia, and the monarch had chosen to attend Wagner's birthday party rather than address a grave matter of state. His absence at a time of national crisis was something for which the politicians never forgave him. Neither did the Bavarian newspapers, and they were soon to mock him for it. During his fleeting reunion with Wagner, Ludwig observed the presence of Cosima at Wagner's side, but unlike most of the rest of the world failed to draw any conclusions from it, a symptom of his blind devotion to the composer. Cosima and her children, he believed, were simply there awaiting the arrival of Bülow, with whom they were to spend their summer holidays.

Bülow at that moment was expending much energy defending himself, and more especially Cosima, against the ongoing campaign of slander mounted by the Munich press, which seemed to know all about the goings-on at Tribschen, and rejoiced in dragging the parties through the public mire. A typical example was a scathing article that appeared in the *Neuer Bayrischer Kurier,* a journal that nicknamed Cosima 'the carrier-pigeon Madam Hanns de Bülow'—a pointed reference to her important role as go-between in the Wagner-Ludwig relationship. The worst attack, however, came once more from the *Volksbote*. In its issue of May 31, just over one week after Ludwig's visit to Tribschen, it unleashed a vitriolic offensive against Cosima, openly accusing her of being Wagner's mistress, and reminding its readers:

Less than a year has passed since the well-known 'Madame Hans de Bülow' got away in the two famous cabs with 40,000 gulden from the Treasury for her 'friend' (or what?). But what are 40,000 gulden? 'Madame Hans' ought to be looking around for more cabs, for the day before yesterday an action was entered against Richard Wagner for the recovery of debts in an amount of no less than 26,000 gulden—a fact absolutely vouched for to the *Volksbote*. Meanwhile, this same 'Madame Hans' who has been known to the public since last December by the descriptive title of 'the carrier-pigeon', is with her friend (or what?) in Lucerne, where she was during the visit of an exalted person.

Bülow was in Munich when this article appeared, with its glancing reference to the visit of the king (the 'exalted person'), and its mocking allusion to Wagner as Cosima's friend ('or what?'), and he was yet to stumble on the true state of affairs at Tribschen. Outraged by such a public attack on his wife's morals, he challenged the editor of the *Volksbote*, Dr. Zander, to a duel, which the latter declined.[42]

XVI

Bülow set out for Switzerland on June 6 with one thought on his mind: how to muzzle the Bavarian press. When he got to Zurich, en route for Tribschen, Cosima was waiting for him with the answer. The bold plan that she and Wagner had concocted, and which was intended to restore their 'good name', was nothing less than a breathtaking endeavour to draw the monarchy itself into their grand deception. Wagner had looked on with apprehension as the newspaper war against Bülow and Cosima in Munich had gathered force. With Bülow's full knowledge he despatched an urgent appeal to the palace, begging Ludwig himself to intercede in their struggle. Encouraged by the monarch's recent visit to Tribschen, Wagner pleaded with the king to affix the royal seal to a letter (that Wagner himself would draft!) so that the crown might be seen publicly defending the reputations of the threesome, and rescue them from the foul swamp of gossip through which they were forced to wade on a daily basis.

---

42. The prospect of violence against Bülow was at this time a real one. In June, when the press attacks against him were at their height, and the so-called 'Seven Weeks War' with Prussia loomed large, another Herr von Bülow from Mecklenberg sought safety in Munich, in the company of his fellow Prussians. Mistaking him for Bülow the musician, a patriotic mob broke into the poor man's house and smashed everything within sight. Bülow made light of this case of mistaken identity (BB, vol. 4, pp. 134–135). But it was nonetheless a cautionary tale that conveyed some of the underlying menace that he experienced on a daily basis in the lead-up to the war. Because of his support for Bismarck, Bülow was perceived by some in Bavaria to be the worst kind of Junker, and possibly a Prussian spy.

Ludwig, Wagner went on, must openly recognize all the good things that Bülow had done for Munich, implore him not to resign his position, and, while he was about it, compliment the spotless character of Cosima, 'his noble wife', which Ludwig had been able to observe at first hand in Tribschen just a week or two earlier. To this appeal Cosima added one of her own. She told Ludwig that she was falling on her knees before him, 'in humility and distress', entreating him to sign Wagner's letter, and so vindicate her husband's honour. Such a royal assertion, she continued, would allow her to transmit to her three children 'their father's honourable name unstained'. This last observation was a particularly bold pretense when we recall that one of these children was Wagner's.[43] Wagner concluded his brazen message with a customary piece of emotional blackmail, passed along to Ludwig's adjutant, Prince Paul. If Ludwig refused his request, Wagner would in all likelihood never see him again. Several anguished days followed as Ludwig considered what to do. Then Wagner received word from the palace that Ludwig had signed the letter, which was conveyed to Bülow. Bülow himself handed it over to the press and it was published in the *Neueste Nachrichten* on June 19 and in the *Augsburger Abendzeitung* on June 20. The trio had now committed perjury.

The *Volksbote* stuck to its guns, claiming that it could prove every allegation. It reminded its readers that the Bavarian courts had remedies for people like Bülow, and wondered archly why he had not begun legal proceedings, a clear indication of guilt. The veracity of the king's letter was barely touched on, and for good reason. On the very day that Bülow sent it to the newspapers, June 15, Bavaria entered the 'Seven Weeks War' against Prussia, and the 'Bülow question' was pushed to the sidelines. Ludwig's marionette army, led by his Gilbert and Sullivan generals, was quickly routed by the Prussians, a military embarrassment that worked to Bavaria's advantage because hardly any of the usual devastation was caused by the advancing army, and Bismarck's terms for surrender were generous, allowing Ludwig to keep his crown. Bavaria, however, must join the German Confederation. The *Volksbote* meanwhile broke off its own fight with Bülow, loftily declaring that it must occupy itself with the interests of the Fatherland, beside which the activities of a few 'foreign musicians' counted for little.

Just how directly Bülow was implicated in Wagner's devious dealings with the king has long been a matter of debate. How was it possible for Bülow, with his proud family background, and a cast of mind that placed

---

43. Cosima's letter to the king is quoted in detail by Ernest Newman in NLRW, vol. 3, pp. 548–49. He calls it 'the basest act of Cosima's whole life'.

personal integrity before everything else, to accept so passively the assortment of half-truths, misrepresentations, and outright lies that Cosima and Wagner were busily foisting on the king? The answer to our question may be found in the drama that unfolded at Tribschen during the summer of 1866.

XVII

Almost from the moment he arrived at Tribschen, Bülow's letters begin to take on a tone of anguished foreboding. In language both convoluted and searing, he writes to such old friends as Ritter and Raff in terms that leave no doubt that everything was once more collapsing around him. In an attempt to explain what was going on, a number of Wagner scholars, starting with Julius Kapp, asserted that it was at Tribschen that Bülow first stumbled across the fact that Cosima and Wagner were lovers. Kapp even expanded on an old story, derived from a comment that can be traced back to Cornelius, that on the very day that Cosima set out for Tribschen, Bülow intercepted a compromising letter to her from Wagner, and after the truth had slowly sunk in he followed her to Tribschen to have it out with the lovers.[44] But Bülow, as we learned from evidence drawn from the proceedings of the Bayreuth *Landesgericht,* and placed before the reader on an earlier page, had known for more than two years how matters stood.

There was, in fact, something else that Bülow discovered at Tribschen, which plunged him into the depths of despair. Cosima informed him that she had once more become pregnant by Wagner. Eva, the latest product of the union, was born on February 17, 1867, just nine months after Cosima got to Tribschen. It was a repetition of the Starnberg episode two years earlier. This second betrayal was for Bülow a much graver business than the first. The understanding that he had reached with Cosima after the birth of Isolde, which had helped to patch up their faltering marriage, was now in tatters. Was he supposed to accept Eva as his own, and henceforth refer to 'our *four* daughters in common'?[45] Bülow's emotional state stands revealed in his painful letter to Raff, from which we quoted at the head of this chapter, 'You have no idea what has been going on', with its strange talk of 'horror and weirdness'. And this same letter makes clear that Bülow, taking his courage in both hands, had confronted Cosima and

---

44. JKWF, pp. 246–48.

45. Astonishingly, this was the view that Bülow adopted many years later. When he came to draw up his second will (1889) he perversely named Eva as one of his daughters, knowing full well that she was not, and he left her a legacy. See pages 460–61 for some commentary on this tangled matter, and the posthumous tittle-tattle it engendered.

Wagner with the catastrophic consequences that her latest pregnancy held out for them all:

> Just as the correct formation of a problem can be regarded as half the solution, so the clear exposition of a scandalous situation is already a halfway point to relief from it', he told Raff, in labyrinthine language. 'Truly the most shameful part of the case in question was the frightful confusion, the difficulty of bringing the fellow-sufferers to a just perception, i.e. to a pessimistically calm desperation. From February 1865 I was not in the least doubt about the rottenness of things. To be sure, I never dreamed to what extent this would develop.[46]

That this latest crisis may have been deliberately driven by Wagner is a point not to be lightly set aside. Wagner's wife, Minna, had died a few months earlier, and he was now free to remarry. It is almost certain that Cosima raised with Bülow for the very first time a prospect that he dreaded and had done everything he could to prevent: the dissolution of their marriage. As a Catholic, and as the guilty party, Cosima lacked the means to sever her matrimonial bonds. The task of setting her free would therefore have to rest with Bülow. This for the present he resolutely refused to do.

XVIII

There would be little point in recounting this sorry tale, with all its destructive detail, were we to let it pass without capturing its essential meaning for Bülow himself. Bülow now saw Wagner stripped of whatever nobility and uprightness of character he had formerly attributed to his mentor. Looking back on this summer of discontent, Bülow captured the essence of Wagner's ruinous behaviour towards him in words that deserve to be better known. He called Wagner 'a scoundrel', and more witheringly 'the most cowardly of all the great men'. What we find of major psychological interest, however, especially in light of the sterling work that Bülow was later to undertake in Wagner's behalf, is his telltale description of the composer as someone who is 'as sublime in his works as he is incomparably abject in his actions'. Even in the midst of his personal turmoil, Bülow possessed the detachment to distinguish between Wagner the man, whom he despised, and Wagner the musician, whom

---

46. BB, vol. 4, p. 145. Opaque language of this kind was about the best that Bülow could do whenever he had to lay bare the sufferings of his innermost soul. His natural inclination was to cover his vulnerabilities with a protective veneer of words so sophisticated and dense that few people outside his intimate circle of friends knew how to penetrate it.

he revered. His refusal to confuse Art with the artist who created it reveals a sense of discrimination so rare among human beings that we have no hesitation in describing it as one of Bülow's finest achievements. He took the man out of the music, and it is through Bülow's devastating dichotomy that the world still deals with the complexities of Wagner's character. But there was something else gnawing at Bülow's heart, which he could not forgive. Wagner had placed him on the horns of an impossible dilemma. Bülow's own description puts it best:

> I only had the choice between two situations: that of being viewed with the most insulting pity as an individual unaware of what everyone knew; or that of being accused of infamy, as someone who had accepted the most shameful bargain as the favourite of the favourite of a King.[47]

Because he was constitutionally incapable of accepting the pity, he went for the infamy, for what he knew the world would perceive as a 'shameful bargain', and for a man of Bülow's pride that must have lacerated him.

In any case, he took his time. Tired and depressed, he lived for a few months in Basel, where, he told Raff, he hoped to find 'obscurity'. Basel was close enough to Lucerne for him to keep in touch with Cosima, who continued to flit back and forth between him and Wagner, wife to the one and mistress to the other, until her advancing pregnancy made it impossible for her to travel. Early on the morning of February 17, 1867, Bülow set out for Tribschen, and arrived in time see Cosima deliver Eva.[48] He lingered for a week, in order to cast a mantle of respectability over Cosima. Then, his duty done, he returned to a bachelor's existence in Basel, not knowing what the future might hold. Wagner, fearing that all hope of an early production of *Meistersinger* might be lost if Bülow could not be coaxed away from Basel and back to Munich, put further pressure on the king. Bülow, he told the monarch, might be persuaded to return to Munich, his good name already cleansed by royal decree, so to say, if

47. These and other damning descriptions of Wagner may be found in a very long letter that Bülow wrote to Cosima's stepsister Claire de Charnacé some three years after the Tribschen episode, explaining why the marriage had foundered and Cosima had left him. It was published in full in an earlier work of mine, WFL, vol. 3, pp. 138–142. The letter makes it clear that after the birth of Eva, Wagner's name was vinegar and bile to Bülow. The holograph may be consulted in VMA, Ms. 859, carton 3.

48. On the day that Eva was born, Bülow was reputed to have approached Cosima's bedside with the words, 'I forgive you'. To which Cosima was reputed to have replied, 'It is not necessary to forgive, it is necessary to understand'. The anecdote may well be apocryphal, but it surely represents the positions adopted by the respective parties in this ill-starred marriage.

only the following conditions could be met: (1) Bülow must be given the title of Royal Kapellmeister; (2) he must be authorized to put on *Meistersinger*, and recruit the best singers from across Germany for that purpose; (3) he must be given a full salary as director of the Royal Music School, and be empowered to carry out Wagner's dreams for that institution; and (4), he must be given a Bavarian decoration. Such was the desire of the king to have Bülow back in Munich (and by implication Wagner as well) that he agreed to each one of Wagner's demands, including the decoration.[49] Were these benefactions Wagner's 'gift' to Bülow in exchange for continued access to his wife? That is the image that has come down to posterity. But we would do well to follow the rest of the story before considering the matter closed.

Bülow and Cosima returned to the Bavarian capital in May 1867, intent on keeping up appearances as a happily married couple, justifying the king's public support for their good and upright characters. The inconvenient business of having a newborn infant to explain was quietly resolved: Eva for the time being was left behind at Tribschen. Bülow rented a spacious apartment on Arcostrasse, far too large for his own needs, and set aside two rooms for Wagner's use whenever he was in town, furnished from the composer's former Briennerstrasse residence. Armed with the plenipotentiary powers recently invested in him by the king, Bülow mounted an ambitious series of operas to sold-out audiences, including *Il Trovatore* (Verdi), *William Tell* (Rossini), *Hans Heiling* (Marschner), *Abu Hassan* (Weber), *Der Wasserträger* (Cherubini), and the incidental music to Beethoven's *Egmont*. He also put on model performances of *Tannhäuser* and *Lohengrin* in the presence of King Ludwig; and as light relief *The Merry Wives of Windsor* (Nicolai). His former adversaries 'Pfi and Pfo' had left the cabinet after the 'Seven Weeks War', and he no longer had to work against an unfriendly administration. The next two years represented the highest point of Bülow's early conducting career, and had he stayed on in Munich he would have risen to the top much faster than he did. But his present success was tarnished for him by the knowledge that he was regarded as 'the favourite of the favourite of a king'. To the Müncheners it was obvious: the *ménage à trois* was back in town, on terms that were now infinitely more favourable to Bülow.

In an attempt to hold everything together, Liszt arrived in Munich and stayed with the Bülows for three weeks during September and October 1867. It was his latest effort to help Hans and Cosima preserve the empty

---

49. Bülow was invested with the Order of the Cross of Saint Michael, First Class, in October 1867.

shell that was their marriage. Two years earlier Liszt had become an Abbé in the Roman Catholic Church and now lived in Rome, where he mixed in the highest circles within the Vatican. Bülow clearly wanted to spare his father-in-law the embarrassment of what was sure to be a highly public Protestant divorce, so he went along with Liszt's wishes and refused to contemplate one. It is unthinkable that Liszt was not in possession of the facts surrounding the birth of Eva, his latest granddaughter, although the evidence is sparse. On October 5 he made his much-discussed trip to Tribschen, in order to confront Wagner, a meeting that both men dreaded. Afterwards all that Liszt would say about it was that it was like visiting Napoleon on St. Helena. In a show of support for Bülow, whom he knew to have been cruelly wronged, Liszt carried out his earlier threat and broke off relations with Wagner for five years. It was not until 1872 that the two men put aside their differences when Wagner invited Liszt to attend the ceremonies connected to the laying of the foundation stone of the Bayreuth Festival Theatre.

XIX

Once the king's letter had been published, in June 1866, vouching for the stainless characters of Hans and Cosima, the monarch had placed himself at risk of being branded a fabricator by anyone with access to the truth and an interest in revealing it. And the revelation came from an unexpected quarter: Malvina Schnorr von Carolsfeld, Wagner's first 'Isolde'.

How this came about represents one of the strangest twists in the Wagner story, and by implication that of Bülow, too. Malvina, who was still grieving the loss of her dead husband, Ludwig Schnorr von Carolsfeld, had come to believe through her suffering in the possibility of communicating with his departed spirit. Spiritualism offered her solace and she began to attend séances. She fell under the influence of a young pupil, Isidore von Reutter, who claimed to have psychic powers. Guided by Fräulein von Reutter, Malvina wrote letters to her beloved Ludwig by day, and received his replies in her dreams at night. Isidore claimed to have received a vision revealed to her by the deceased Ludwig Schnorr himself: namely, that it was Malvina's destiny to marry Wagner, and that she, Isidore, was to become the wife of the king. The purpose of this unearthly arrangement was nothing less than to guarantee, through these crucial marriages, the king's continued largesse towards Wagner which would elevate the composer to unprecedented artistic heights and secure his place in the Pantheon. Having heard that Bülow had left Tribschen, and believing it to be a heaven-sent opportunity of finding Wagner there alone and placing this joyful news before him, she and Fräulein von Reutter arrived at Tribschen in mid-November 1866. Malvina was dumbfounded when she was greeted at the door by Cosima, whose latest pregnancy was clearly visible, and she quickly realized that Cosima was ensconced there, in charge of Wagner's domestic affairs. Wagner was at that moment working in an upstairs room, and Cosima refused to disturb him. The two visitors had in any case prepared a lengthy document, outlining Isidore's 'revelation', and this Cosima agreed to let Wagner read. He came downstairs and saw at once that Malvina was on the verge of a nervous breakdown. With difficulty he persuaded her and Fräulein Isidore to return to their Lucerne hotel for the night and he would consider the bizarre plan they had imparted to him. The next morning he despatched Cosima to Lucerne with a letter, informing Malvina that he would have no further dealings with her until she had removed herself from Isidore's malevolent influence, whom he described as a neurotic young woman and an imposter. At this Malvina broke into a torrent of verbal abuse against Cosima, and threatened 'to smash her'.[50] To Wagner she sent a letter, beneath whose conciliatory surface there lurked a veiled threat: unless he consented to see her, and allow her to disclose in greater detail the content of Isidore's 'vision', she would have no alternative but to inform Bülow that he and Cosima were lovers. In her agitated state the poor woman seems hardly to have known, or not to have cared, that this was stale news. Wagner nonetheless agreed to meet her, probably with no other thought than that of calming her agitated nerves; she was, after all, a great artist to whom he would remain forever grateful for having created the role of 'Isolde'. But he also feared that if Malvina were inclined to unburden herself to Bülow about the goings-on at Tribschen, she might in her troubled frame of mind just as easily unburden herself to the king, and that must be prevented at all costs. As Wagner listened to the divine plan that the dead Schnorr had disclosed to Malvina, he became convinced that she was temporarily unhinged, and in his anxiety he made a miscalculation. He despatched a letter to the king, alerting him to the possible arrival of a communication from the unbalanced singer, and enclosed a copy of Isidore's 'vision', with its absurd prophecy that she was destined to become the king's consort.[51] Had he done nothing, he might have been able to accommodate Malvina through quiet diplomacy. What he did not bargain for was the three-way correspondence that ensued among Malvina, himself, and the king. Malvina sent her letters via the

50. Wagner himself gave a full account of Malvina's visit to Tribschen in a long letter to August Röckel, dated November 23, 1866, KLRWB, vol. 5, pp. 46–51. It is on this highly detailed chronicle that we have based our own retelling of the story.

51. What Isidore thought that she could bring to her nuptials with the king—aside from ready access to those on the other side of the Great Divide—remains a mystery. She was not blessed with high intelligence, and appears to have been far from attractive. Wagner told Röckel that she had 'the figure of a military policeman'.

king's adjutant Captain von Sauer, and disclosed more and more information about the intimate relationship between Wagner and Cosima,
going back to the *Tristan* days. Matters came to a head on December 20,
when the king forwarded to Cosima a letter from Malvina whose contents
he described as 'shocking'. A thoroughly frightened Wagner responded,
advising the monarch to banish Malvina from Bavaria, on pain of losing
the Bavarian pension granted her after the death of Schnorr. By now it
was obvious to Malvina that Cosima and Wagner were out to discredit
her. On January 12, 1867, she sent a highly detailed letter to the king, advising him to make some private inquiries of his own about the Bülow-
Cosima-Wagner triangle, and not take their protestations at face value.
'Your royal ermine covers their shame; but consider well, my King, that
the royal ermine itself will be soiled'.[52]

By the spring of 1867, Wagner knew that the great deception was over.
Thanks to Malvina, the king was in possession of all the facts necessary
to convince him that Wagner and Cosima had deceived him for the past
three years.

XX

With the first performance of *Die Meistersinger von Nürnberg,* on June
21, 1868, Bülow's chief reason in returning to Munich was fulfilled. The
opera was set in sixteenth-century Nuremburg, the spiritual heart of Old
Germany. Everybody in Bavaria was familiar with the legends woven
around the medieval singing contests, which form the substance of the
action. Here was something from Wagner with which the Müncheners
could at last identify. Nor would Hans Sachs's jingoistic address to the audience at the end of Act I have gone unremarked: 'Honour your German
masters, would you forfend disasters!' Whatever else it was, the opera was
also a celebration of a resurgent Germany, whose appearance coincided
with a tidal wave of patriotic fervour sweeping the land, which was not
to stop until the various German states had been unified into a single
Reich. If there was any doubt about the opera's underlying political message, the speech of thanks that Wagner delivered to the artists from the
stage after the last dress rehearsal on June 19 would have put it to rest.
With the regeneration of German art, he insisted, would come the regeneration of the German people. Turning to the orchestra Wagner said,
'To you I need say nothing more. You are German musicians; we understand each other without words'.[53]

52. Malvina's letter to the king is given in full in GIS, pp. 340–47.
53. NLRW, vol. 4, p. 141.

This first performance of *Die Meistersinger* was a triumph for which Bülow must receive much credit. Wagner was later to write that it 'was the best that has ever been given of any of my works'.[54] Fifteen hundred guests from various parts of Europe filled the theatre. Wagner was invited to share the royal box with the king. There was no precedent for such an honour in the whole of Germany. Bülow marvelled at the spectacle and is said to have remarked, 'Horace at the side of Augustus'[55]—an observation that was widely reported in the newspapers. At the conclusion of the second and third acts Wagner, in a much-criticized breach of etiquette, advanced to the front of the box and acknowledged the thunderous applause, leaving the monarch in the shadows. The next morning the king sent Wagner an effusive letter signed under his old pseudonym 'Walther', in which he quoted a line from Wagner's libretto: 'Hail German art! In this sign we shall conquer'. Was this merely a piece of puffery, or was it an ominous portent? Within two years the German army was marching on France, and the slaughter of the Franco-Prussian War was in full swing.

Throughout the whole period of the *Meistersinger* rehearsals there had been signs of growing conflict between Bülow and Wagner. Wagner's 'Brown Book' contains a number of entries which reveal a state of mounting animosity between the two men. In May, at one of the piano rehearsals, Wagner recorded his 'heavy, oppressive feeling from Hans's deep hostility and estrangement'. By June, after the opera had gone into full production, we come across this blunt entry: 'Orchestral rehearsals. Serious trouble with Hans'.[56] The source of the trouble would have been clear enough to anyone, save perhaps to Wagner himself. When Bülow was together with a group of musicians in the artists' room, turning the pages of Wagner's bulky manuscript score of *Meistersinger*, a photograph of Wagner and little Eva fell out, and Bülow had to leave the room in tears. Nor was life with Wagner any better at Arcostrasse. Now that Bülow was

54. The comment is worth fastening onto. When, in later years, Bülow put the Overture to *Meistersinger* into his orchestral programmes, he was sometimes criticized for taking it too fast.

55. Perhaps only Bülow, with his knowledge of classical literature, could have minted such a phrase, and scholars of antiquity will enjoy his analogy. Horace, one of the great Latin poets, had in earlier years joined the Roman army and served under Brutus as *tribunus militum*, fighting at the Battle of Philippi against the ultimately victorious Octavian, who later became the Roman emperor Augustus. Benefitting from a general amnesty, Horace, now befriended by Augustus who admired his *Satires*, acquired land, money, and fame. Because the poet had no heirs, he bequeathed everything to Augustus. The parallels with Wagner and King Ludwig are eerily similar, even the last one. Wagner had no legal heirs. He and Cosima were not yet married, and their children were still under Bülow's lawful protection. Wagner's only legitimate 'offspring' were his compositions, the most important ones of which had already been bequeathed to Ludwig.

56. RWBB, p. 167.

Munich's Royal Kapellmeister, it was natural that he would be approached by composers of all stripes wanting their operas performed. When Wendelin Weissheimer, a follower of Liszt, turned up with the score of his opera *Theodor Werner*, Bülow generously agreed to play it through, even though Wagner had earlier turned Weissheimer down. In the middle of the run-through, the maidservant came in with a message from Wagner requesting that Bülow stop playing the piano, as the noise was disturbing his sleep. 'It was eleven o'clock in the morning!' exclaimed Weissheimer. Bülow slammed the lid of the piano shut. 'It is a high honour for me to live with the master', he barked, 'but it is often more than one can endure!'[57] We may be sure that there was more invective exchanged between Bülow and Wagner at this fractious time than the scholarly record shows.

Faced with Bülow's unusual display of independence, it comes as no surprise to learn that Wagner had quietly started to groom the twenty-three-year-old Hans Richter as a possible successor to the man he had once publicly called 'my second self'. Richter had turned up at Tribschen in the autumn of 1866 in order to help Wagner produce a fair copy of *Meistersinger,* and Wagner had at once spotted his uncommon musical talents. Richter attached himself to the composer with dog-like devotion and lived at Tribschen for six months, where he got to know Cosima and the children. Within a year Wagner had secured for the young man the position of répétiteur and chorus-master in the Munich Opera House. This inevitably brought him into contact with Bülow who, while acknowledging his musical gifts, saw in him a potential rival. Wagner, with his usual self-interest at play, had already realized that were he and Cosima to marry he would have to discard Bülow, and look to someone else to mount the world premier of *The Ring*. That honour did, in fact, fall to Richter, who directed the trilogy in Bayreuth, in the summer of 1876.[58]

---

57. WEW, pp. 392–393.

58. Bülow admired Richter's versatility. The younger conductor had an insider's knowledge of the orchestra, could play several different instruments well (especially the horn, on which he was a virtuoso), and he had retained a good voice from his boyhood years as an alto in the Vienna Court Chapel Choir. Richter's intimate knowledge of the *Meistersinger* score was put to the test when Wilhelm Fischer, who sang the role of Kothner, one of the Mastersingers, fell ill and was unable to take part in the last of the four scheduled performances, on July 16. Bülow feared that he would have to cancel the performance, but Richter declared that he knew the work so thoroughly, that he himself would sing the part of Kothner. He had never before been on the stage, but he acquitted himself so well that Bülow was completely satisfied. When Bülow resigned from Munich, he was not unhappy to learn that Richter had succeeded him as Royal Kapellmeister.

In later years the musical ideals of the two conductors diverged. When Bülow heard Richter conduct Berlioz's *Damnation of Faust* in London, in June 1888, he claimed that Richter was no longer the man he remembered, that he had come to resemble an elderly Franz

Three days after the first performance of *Meistersinger,* Wagner left Munich, resolved never to live there again, and headed back to Tribschen. He showed no interest in attending the five additional performances under Bülow's baton (on June 28, and July 2, 7, 12, 16). Eight years elapsed before he set eyes on King Ludwig once more, in Bayreuth. As for Bülow, he never saw his tormenter-in-chief again. The pair continued an essential correspondence in the course of the next few months, especially about the fate of the Royal Music School, until their letters, too, dwindled away. Bülow had ceased to be Wagner's man.

XXI

From the turbulence of his everyday life in Munich, and even from his abode on Arcostrasse, Bülow sought occasional refuge in the comfortable villa of the von Welz family, located in the 'English Garden'. Louise von Welz, the wife of a local, art-loving physician, was one of his piano pupils at the Royal Music School, and Bülow sometimes played at her soirées. A warm friendship developed between the pair, which is reflected in the more than 100 letters that passed between them in later years, preserved in the general correspondence. After Bülow left Munich, the von Welz family offered him the hospitality of their home whenever he passed through the city.

Another bond of friendship was formed with his Italian pupil Giuseppe Buonamici, who in 1868 travelled from Italy to register at the Royal Music School, eventually becoming a professor there. Buonamici's attachment to Bülow, and his abiding concern for his teacher's welfare, may be gleaned from Bülow's unpublished letters to his Italian protégé. A comparison of Buonamici's edition of the Beethoven sonatas with that of Bülow himself reveals how much the pupil learned from the master. Bülow's eventual decision to settle in Italy, and escape the mounting tensions in Munich, was due in no small measure to Buonamici's calm advice.

XXII

With Wagner's departure from Munich, but more especially from his comfortable quarters in the Bülow home on Arcostrasse where Cosima had

---

Lachner. The performance was 'pure torture' for him, Bülow said, because there was not a single correct tempo. 'I heard the work directed by the composer in Weimar, in 1852, and several times in Dresden, in 1854 . . . and [Richter's performance] completely lacked the impression made under Hallé, who was at least in possession of the tradition' (BB, vol. 7, p. 201). The mannerisms of the two conductors on the podium were also radically different. Bülow was all energy and movement. Richter was almost motionless, producing his orchestral effects while remaining immobile.

ready access to him, the Bülows' marriage entered its death throes. To track its downward spiral in dogged detail to the inevitable end would add little to what we already know of this ill-starred relationship. Of Cosima's duplicitous conduct at this time Bülow later said that 'she lied about it from morning till night'.[59] One example may serve to illustrate the others. In the summer of 1868, under the guise of visiting her sister-in-law Claire de Charnacé at Versailles, a trip for which Bülow readily granted his approval and provided money, Cosima instead joined Wagner at Tribschen and then travelled with him to Italy where they spent two weeks together in September, and were spotted by the press. Bülow learned of the deception through the newspapers along with everybody else. Once more he became the butt of local jokes and was forced to deal with the murk and moil of daily life in Munich, while maintaining before his colleagues the fiction that Cosima was indeed in Versailles with Claire de Charnacé.

Claire herself visited Munich at the beginning of November 1868, perhaps in the mistaken belief that she could help shore up the flagging marriage. She was surprised by the exceptional freedom that Cosima enjoyed at home. 'Nothing that happened there was subject to the slightest checking from her husband. Our bourgeois women would protest against that, but I honour the husband for it, and my aversion for Wagner grows proportionally'.[60] Nor did the paradoxical situation in which Claire found herself while in Munich escape her. Twelve years earlier she had travelled to Berlin in order to do her best to prevent the Bülows from marrying. And now she was in Munich doing her best to prevent them from separating. It was all too late. Cosima had already decided to abandon Hans and flee to Wagner. Hans she had told in mid-October, after returning from her Italian peregrinations with Wagner. And well before the end of the month she must have conveyed her decision to Liszt, because his blistering response is dated 'Rome, November 2':

> Where are you going? What are you telling me? What! Everything is dead for you except a single person to whom you think you are necessary; because he says he cannot do without you? Alas! I can foresee that this *necessity* will soon be an encumbrance, and by possessing you in his fashion, you will necessarily become inconvenient, annoying, contrary to him. Although you might well only want to live for him, that would not be enough at all, and would hardly be feasible because fatal poisons would begin to seep from the rock on which you aim to rest yourself.

59. VMA, Ms. 859, carton 3.
60. Ibid., Ms. 859, carton 9.

God save me from judging you wrongly. I know that 'nothing infamous, nothing low, nothing futile is subjugating you' but you have become giddy and dissipating the vital and holy forces of your soul by sealing an evil deed with approval! This perversion, this adulteration of God's gifts breaks my heart!

You speak of living alone and raising your children. How will you manage that? W's notoriety and his extremely dependent position from a material point of view will work against your best plans. After such a scandal, I doubt whether convention will allow you to live in Switzerland or Germany. Probably you will be forced to seek some refuge as far away as America. The hand of your royal friend and benefactor might slacken its grip, if not withdraw, as a consequence; embarrassment and shameful financial difficulties would dog your footsteps. Even if you were to bear them bravely, would the *other one* put up with them because of this?

And what about your children? What are you teaching them? Does not the model contain the precepts? Will they understand that one should call Evil Good, call night day, call bitter things sweet?

Yes, my daughter, what you are planning to do is bad in God's eyes and man's. Indeed, my convictions and experience protest about it to you, and I beg you by your maternal feelings to renounce this fatal plan, drive away the subtleties of sophisms, stop sacrificing [yourself] to the implacable idol. Instead of abjuring your God, fall on your knees before him; he is truth and mercy in one; invoke him with all your soul and the healing light of repentance will enter your conscience.

It is Hans to whom you are *necessary;* it is him you must not fail. You married him of your own free will, with love—and his behaviour towards you has always been so noble that on your side it calls for a different 'gegenseitige Übereinstimmung' [reciprocal agreement] than the one pleaded before the courts. What madness to ask him now to subscribe legally to your dishonour!

You are also necessary to your four children, and deserve their respect [which] must be for you the first priority. Now the more than precarious future the yoke of your passion would bestow on them exposes you to their most cruel reproaches, which your conscience will ratify. I will not speak to you about public opinion, [about] which nonetheless one should not exaggerate one's contempt to the point of absolving everything it condemns, and Jean-Jacques [Rousseau] himself warns of the danger of this contempt when it 'pushes us to the other extreme, and even makes us brave the sacred laws of decency and honesty.'

By falsely crushing the sublime, one does not change the immutable nature of duty. You must not leave the noblest of husbands; you must not mislead your children; you must not bear witness against me and plunge madly into an abyss of moral and material misery; and finally you must not deny your God.

Passion consumes itself when it is not enlivened by the sense of superior duties. It withers away or becomes poisoned in wealth, dies in poverty, and passes with frightful rapidity; but remorse remains.

Not only do I rightly condemn what you are proposing, but I am telling you this while begging you to take hold of yourself and not allow yourself to be removed from my blessing.

May God grant my prayers, and may the memory of your father make you become again the child of God our Father and our All in Eternity.

F. Liszt
November 2, 1868, Rome[61]

To the reader who has followed the story so far, the reason that compelled Cosima to abandon Bülow in November 1868 will come as no surprise. She was pregnant for a third time by Wagner. Their son Siegfried, born on June 6 the following year, was almost certainly conceived during the Italian trip two months earlier. Cosima tells us that on November 15 she 'took leave of Hans forever'.[62] The following day she set out for Tribschen, together with her two younger daughters and their nursemaid, Hermine. Daniela and Blandine she left behind in Munich at boarding school. She at first feared losing custody over these older children, but it soon became evident that Bülow was incapable of looking after them, and had no wish to deny her custody. In April 1869 the two girls joined the rest of the family at Tribschen. 'Thank your good Uncle Richard often for permitting you to live there with Mama',[63] was Bülow's advice to eight-year-old Daniela. Twelve years elapsed before he saw either Daniela or Blandine again.

Bülow began divorce proceedings against Cosima in the late summer of 1869. Uppermost in his mind was how best to handle Liszt, who wanted at all costs to rob Wagner of the satisfaction of calling Cosima his wife. Unwilling to expose himself to Liszt's influence on this topic, Bülow took the best course open to him and suspended his connections with his

---

61. Ibid., Ms. F 859, 1/3. Accompanying this letter was one from Liszt to Bülow, begging him not give Cosima a divorce.
62. We find this laconic entry in her diary, written two years later to the day (WT, vol. 1, p. 296).
63. BNB, p. 558.

father-in-law until the legal process was complete. The decision to terminate his marriage must be his alone. As he wrestled with the problem, he entered a period of severe depression. His letters to Carl Bechstein tell their own story. In July 1869 he wrote despairingly, 'Ah, my dear Bechstein, everything within me is crashing! And it had to be!'[64] By the following month he had reached a point where living was more difficult than dying. 'My situation is so incredibly and uniquely horrible, that any other way out than an exit from this world altogether requires superhuman pluck'. Later in this same letter he raises the spectre of suicide. 'The best would be for some sympathetic soul to give me the necessary dose of Prussic acid! Is there no accommodating chemist in Berlin?'[65]

XXIII

For the collapse of his marriage Bülow held himself entirely to blame, as an inspection of his letters to Cosima reveals. His language is tinged with sadness, remorse, and guilt. He proposes a proper division of their most valuable possessions; an orderly transfer of funds to be held in trust for the children; and the regular provision of money to Cosima to enable her to meet the costs of the children's education. He was determined that Wagner should not pay a penny towards the welfare of his family. In June 1869 he heard of the birth of Siegfried through the newspapers, a piece of news which, in his own cynical words, 'crowned the structure of my cuckoldry'.[66] From this heart of darkness he wrote to Cosima:

> Munich
> June 17, 1869
> . . . Since you left me, I have lost my sole support in life and in my struggle. It was your mind, your heart, your patience, indulgence, sympathy, encouragement, and advice—last and most especially, your presence, your face, your speech—which, taken all together, constituted that support. The loss of this supreme good, whose full value I recognize only after its loss, has brought about moral and artistic collapse—I am bankrupt.[67]

Those last three words speak volumes. They represent eloquent testimony from a personality on the verge of collapse.

Bülow tendered his resignation to the king, and it was refused. Ludwig was not yet ready to release his kapellmeister. At the monarch's request,

64. Ibid., p. 258.
65. Ibid., p. 259.
66. VMA, Ms. F 859, carton 3.
67. BNB, p. 477.

Im Saale der kgl. Musikschule

(Odeon, 2. Stock, Aufgang beim Hausmeister)

Samstag den 31. Juli 1869

Abends 6 Uhr

Erstes Prüfungs-Concert

der Schüler und Schülerinnen der k. Musikschule

unter Mitwirkung eines Theiles der k. Instrumentalkapelle und unter Leitung der Herren Hofkapellmeister
Dr. Hans v. Bülow & Fr. Wüllner.

— ❦ —

1. **Kyrie** aus der H-moll-Messe . . . . **J. S. Bach.**
für 5stimmigen Chor und 2 Solo-Soprane mit Orchester, ausgeführt von den beiden
obersten Classen der Chorgesangsschule; Soli: Frl. Louise Briegleb und
Josephine Roth.

2. **Erster Satz** aus dem H-moll-Concert für Piano mit Orchesterbegleitung . . . . . **J. N. Hummel.**
Camillo Giucci. op. 89.

3. **Adagio** für Flöte mit Orchesterbegleitung . . . . **W. A. Mozart.**
Carl Freitag jr.

4. **Fuge** für Streichinstrumente, comp. von Joseph Stich.

5. **Klavierstücke:** a) Ouverture und Passacaglia aus der G-moll-Suite . . . . **G. Haendel.**
Otto Hieber.
b) Toccatina, G-moll . . . . **Jos. Rheinberger.**
Paul Töpffer. op. 19.

6. **Arie** aus dem Oratorium „Josua" („Soll ich in Mamre's Fruchtgefild") . . . . . **G. Haendel.**
für Bass-Stimme mit Orgelbegleitung. Hermann Mayerhöfer, Orgel:
Heinrich Leipold.

7. **Erster Satz** aus dem 22. Concert (A-moll) für Violine mit Orchesterbegleitung . . **G. Viotti.**
Ferdinand Fernbacher.

8. **Klavierstücke:** a) Ballade (G-moll) . . . . **F. Chopin.**
Frl. Katharina Rabausch. op. 23.
b) Polonaise (As-dur) . . . . **F. Chopin.**
Frl. Eugenie Menter. op. 53.

9. **Lieder** für 4stimmigen Chor ohne Begleitung . . . . ⎫
a) Wanderers Nachtlied: „Ueber allen Gipfeln ist Ruh" (Göthe) . . . ⎬ **M. Hauptmann.**
b) „Wenn zweie sich gut sind" (nach Klaus Groth) . . . . ⎭
c) Jagdlied (Eichendorff) . . . . **F. Mendelssohn.**
ausgeführt von der obersten Chorgesangsklasse.

10. **Polonaise** für Klavier (E-dur) mit Orchesterbegleitung (bearbeitet von Fr. Liszt) **C. M. v. Weber.**
Frl. Rosa Keyl. op. 72.

Der Flügel von Bechstein in Berlin ist aus dem Magazine der Musikalienhandlung **J. Aibl.**

—————

The first Graduation Concert of students from the Royal Music School, July 1869.
A handbill.

Bülow gave two command performances of *Tristan,* in a new production, much to the dismay of Wagner who refused to sanction the revival of his masterpiece. Bülow tendered his resignation a second time, and it was reluctantly accepted. Hans Richter, who had been waiting in the wings for just such a moment, was quickly appointed to replace him. Although Bülow was done with the opera house, he was still bound to Munich through his duties as director of the Royal Music School, from which he could not disentangle himself until the end of the summer semester. Life was not made simpler for him by the dogmatic behaviour of Hans Richter's mother, Josephine, a singer of uncertain accomplishment, who had been appointed as an instructor at the Music School at Wagner's instigation a few months earlier, and now insisted on doing most of her teaching at home, all the while assuring a frustrated Bülow that her pupils were more than capable of meeting the requirements of the curriculum without having to endure the inconvenience of actually attending the building. The first graduation concert took place in the Odeon Theatre on July 31, 1869, as one of the few surviving handbills shows. On August 19 Bülow closed down the apartment on Arcostrasse and left for good. The Munich nightmare had ended.

XXIV

What of the moral question mark that Bülow himself placed over his achievements in Munich? His self-lacerating comment that he stood accused of infamy, because he had entered 'the most shameful bargain as the favourite of the favourite of a King', requires some adjustment. We must not forget that Bülow's *cri de coeur* was uttered in a moment of profound despair. Picked up by friend and foe alike, it has entered the official record as established truth. Before joining posterity's general rush to judgement, we must put the matter into the sort of perspective that Bülow himself was singularly unable to do. Let us recall that he had never wanted to leave Berlin. When he reluctantly accepted Wagner's invitation to give up his position in the Prussian capital and join him in Munich, it was to accomplish three major objectives: to help establish a royal music school; to bring *Tristan* and *Meistersinger* to the stage; and to offer a wider musical education for young King Ludwig, to which end Bülow had been appointed *Vorspieler* to His Majesty even before he took up residence in the Bavarian capital. Bülow fulfilled these obligations to a degree that Wagner could hardly have thought possible. Nowhere do we find a hint of a 'bargain' in any of this. It was only later, after the overwhelming success of *Tristan* and *Meistersinger* had brought Bülow to prominence, and Cosima's pregnancies by Wagner could not be concealed, that a whispering campaign was begun against him. To the good citizens of Munich there could be but one conclusion: Bülow had bought his success on the podium by granting Wagner access to Cosima, his main bargaining chip. When expressed in so crude a fashion, the absurdity of the equation becomes clear. When Wagner called on his services, in 1864, Bülow was the most promising conductor in Germany, and Wagner needed him far more than Bülow needed Wagner. It was only after the younger man had been drawn into Wagner's net, which started to close around him in the summer of 1866 while Cosima was living openly with Wagner at Tribschen, that he became aware of a public relations disaster from which he never found the means to extricate himself.

Determined to secure a divorce, Bülow paid a rapid visit to Berlin in order to consult advocate August Simson, a lawyer recommended to him by Carl Bechstein. The legal documents having been signed, Bülow journeyed to Wiesbaden for a brief respite at the home of his old friend Raff, one of the few people to whom he could unburden himself. Here he put the finishing touches to some future plans which had preoccupied him since Cosima had abandoned him. First, the glare of unwelcome publicity must be shut off. Second, a retreat must be found to enable him to work at his piano playing undisturbed. Finally, in the absence of any other way to bring about such conditions, he must leave Germany. For several months his thoughts had gravitated towards Italy as a possible refuge. The catalyst for this idea was his Italian pupil Giuseppe Buonamici, who had worked with Bülow at the Royal Music School for the past eighteen months, and would eventually take over his master's position as head of piano. Buonamici was born in Florence and his family still lived there. The decision to move to Italy was far from straightforward because, as Bülow told Bechstein, he was no longer in receipt of an income, his Munich pension was not yet secured, and he would have to rely on his meagre savings. By August 5 at the latest, however, the die was cast. It would be in Italy that Bülow would seek his haven, and in the ancient city of Florence his balm.

Bülow crossed the Italian frontier towards the end of September with few clothes, little money, and no piano. These things could be sent on to him later. A new life was about to begin.

BOOK TWO

Ascending the Peak, 1870–1880

Bülow in Florence

> It is really incredible that the second half of one's life should have
> no other object than to repair the follies of the first.
>
> —Bülow[1]

I

Bülow's first sight of Florence left him spellbound. He likened the old city to an incomparable dream of wonder. The houses, the streets, the churches, and the art galleries entranced him. And he rhapsodized about the weather—the warmth, the cloudless skies, the heavenly air. Italy, in a memorable phrase, he called a land above all enchantments. He was now dead to his homeland, he declared. Henceforth, he told his mother, he would live as a foreigner.[2]

From the moment he arrived in Italy, Bülow's health started to improve. He informed Carl Bechstein, 'If there is any place where I can recover, become myself again, and find the will and the power to live, it will be in this land beyond compare'. And he added expansively, 'Not to have seen Florence would haunt one in one's grave'.[3] His chief complaint was with the postal service. Some letters were never sent, others never arrived, and still more were lost. But this was a minor inconvenience to someone whose main purpose in having come to Italy at all was to find a refuge from the complications of this world. For the first couple of weeks he enjoyed the hospitality of his childhood friend Jessie Laussot, who had lived in Florence for a number of years, and now directed the Cherubini Choral Society, a group of singers she had brought together for the express purpose

---

1. BNB, p. 265.
2. BAB, p. 227.
3. BNB, p. 264.

of performing older music.[4] He eventually found accommodation at no. 10, Borgo S. Frediano, consisting of two very large rooms on the ground floor of 'a sort of palace' in the heart of the city. Through his windows he enjoyed picturesque views of a charming garden, and beyond that the river Arno.

For the time being he practised on Jessie's Bechstein grand piano. He even shed lustre on the seventy or so members of her choral society, as he put it, by giving them a few informal concerts. Before long he had also discovered a couple of gifted string players, with whom he sight-read his way through the Beethoven and Schumann piano trios; to find such polished chamber players in Florence was a surprise to him. The opera house was also far more professional than he had expected. He saw productions of Meyerbeer's *Les Huguenots,* and Verdi's *Don Carlos* and *Un Ballo in Maschera* that did not displease him.

Work was to be Bülow's redemption. In Italy he returned with renewed zeal to his piano playing, recovered his concert fingers, and laid the groundwork for the world tours that were to bring him an international audience. He also embarked on a profound study of the late Beethoven sonatas and the *Diabelli* Variations, compositions that he was to make very much his own, and which were eventually included in his edition of Beethoven's keyboard music, in 1871.

II

Bülow also began a serious conquest of the Italian language which he hoped to speak easily and fairly confidently 'within a few months'. After eight weeks he told his mother, 'The language is less easy than its ap-

---

4. We recall that Jessie Laussot (*née* Taylor), had met Bülow while they were both studying the piano in Dresden under Cäcilie Schmiedel. She had meanwhile become an ardent supporter of both Liszt and Wagner. While still in her twenties she had entered into an unhappy marriage with a wealthy wine-merchant named Eugène Laussot. The story of how the Laussots raised money to help Wagner in the 1850s, who was at that time enduring a Swiss exile for his part in the failed Dresden Uprising, and how Jessie had then become Wagner's lover and even planned to elope with him, has nowhere been better told than by Ernest Newman, in NLRW, vol. 2, pp. 133–161. After threatening to put a bullet through Wagner's head, Eugène Laussot went into a mental decline, and lost his reason. By the time that Bülow arrived in Florence, Jessie had been separated from Laussot for many years. It was not until 1879 that Eugène died, releasing her from the bonds of matrimony. She promptly married her longtime friend and companion Karl Hillebrand, the German cultural historian. Because of the turbulence in her own life, Jessie was well fitted to empathize with the storms and stresses in Bülow's, and she remained a loyal friend.

About three weeks after he arrived in Florence, Bülow was touched to receive a birthday greeting from Jessie on January 8, his fortieth anniversary. In a nostalgic reply he named her 'the Cherub of the Cherubini Society', and wondered rhetorically, 'Where would I be today without you, without your friendship?' BB, vol. 4, p. 350.

pearance leads one to expect. I practice daily for three hours and take every opportunity to stammer properly. Oddly enough the conversation and phrases of the daily material are for me more difficult than participation in a conversation about politics, music and literature.'[5] Soon he was able to tell Bechstein, 'I speak and write the language fairly fluently now. The best way to learn it is through dialogue'.[6] One person with whom he began to hold regular 'dialogues' was a young dancer with whom, so he informed Bechstein, he had fallen madly in love. She was not merely a virtuosa, he rhapsodized, but a 'toe-poetess'.[7] This was almost certainly the ballerina Elvira Salvioni who captured his imagination the moment she glided across the stage of the Florence Opera House in October 1869. She was based in Milan, and Bülow worshipped her, mainly from a distance. He appears to have met her at various social functions, however, and he asked Bechstein to withhold a sum of money he was owed because he did not want to commit any stupidities, 'not even for the most divine of dancers (one flings diamonds about in her case), or actresses . . . no follies which might cut short my stay here'.[8] Bülow understood himself well enough to realize that his emotional life was not yet stabilized, and he was vulnerable. The infatuation with Elvira was short-lived, but it had a musical consequence. She was the inspiration for Bülow's piano suite 'Il Carnevale di Milano', op. 21, a work which bears the dedication 'Alla celebre artista Signora Elvira Salvioni omaggio di ammirazione' ('To the celebrated artist Signora Elvira Salvioni with the greatest admiration'). The Suite comprises a sequence of ten dances and intermezzos, depicting various aspects of Elvira's stage persona:

Polacca
Valzer
Polka
Intermezzo fantastico: Il dormiveglia
Quadriglia
Mazurka
Intermezzo lirico: Sospiri danzanti
Tarantella
Intermezzo scherzoso
Galop

5. BAB, p. 230.
6. BNB, p. 274.
7. Ibid., p. 269.
8. Ibid., pp. 270–271. Bülow's brush with Elvira evidently created some tittle-tattle in Munich. On October 23 Cosima received an anonymous letter from someone there, telling her that Bülow was having an affair with an Italian actress whom he would have liked to marry. WT, vol. 1, p. 157.

Several months later, after his ardour for Elvira had cooled, we find Bülow referring to a 'seventeen-year-old star in my life' and wondering if she could be persuaded 'to become my permanent companion'.[9] The name of this teenager was Giulia Masetti, and Bülow confided to Jessie Laussot that she was 'a little virtuosa in love', and in a further whimsy he exclaimed, 'what Giulia has given me is indescribable . . . you have no idea of the affection of which an Italian girl is capable'.[10] He made an excursion with Giulia to Milan and Brescia, but wrapped the details of the trip in obscurity. He jestingly remarked that he would have to wait until she was nineteen years old before he could take her back to Germany— a clear reference to the fact that she had not yet reached the age of consent. These were but the first of a number of encounters with younger women that Bülow experienced as he floundered in the wake of his separation and divorce from Cosima—encounters that have hardly been chronicled, and throw unexpected light on his character.

Bülow's caution over money was understandable. Financially he was not at first secure. He had modest amounts of capital in Berlin and Munich, and some of it was sent to him whenever he requested it. Gradually he acquired some piano students, 'mostly English and American flappers' as he called them, and he charged them 15 francs a lesson. By his own calculation it amounted to 2,000 francs a quarter. This was a good income and he was able to supplement it with fees from his occasional public concerts. The pension to which he was entitled from his position in Munich had meanwhile become the object of dispute. For several months he had haggled with Baron Perfall and the treasury of Bavaria. At last he was grudgingly informed that King Ludwig had consented to give him 2,000 gulden per annum. The battle having been won, Bülow at first refused to accept the pension. It was his way of showing contempt for his adversaries, the petty court officials who insisted that he travel to Munich to claim it. Eventually the money was sent to him in quarterly installments of 500 gulden.[11]

III

The otherwise bright prospect of a new life in Florence was marred by the recurrence of a problem in his right arm. He described it as 'rheumatism', the pain of which made it difficult for him to put on his overcoat without help. He also suffered from a sprain in his right hand, forcing him to

9. BNB, p. 313.
10. BB, vol. 4, pp. 537 and 500–1.
11. See the observation he made to Claire de Charnacé on this topic (VMA, F859, carton 9, p. 12), and also his letters to Bechstein (BNB, pp. 280 and 283).

abandon his piano practicing for several days. To add to these setbacks he went down with influenza, his old enemy. More ominous was an observation he made to Buonamici. 'Neuralgia . . . afflicts the back of my head. It is hellish pain, I assure you'.[12] It was an early manifestation of the tumour that eventually helped to bring about his demise, twenty-four years later. Bülow's winter clothes had not yet arrived from Munich, the cold and the damp penetrated his apartment, and his influenza lingered. By early November it had started to pour with rain. After forty-five days of incessant downpours of biblical proportions, Florence and its environs were awash in floods. The situation in other parts of Italy was catastrophic. In January 1870, despite his physical setbacks, Bülow participated in a benefit concert for the victims of the Pisa floods. Among other things he played Liszt's *Ricordanza* and two numbers from *Venezia e Napoli,* together with the *Allegro de Concert* by Chopin.[13]

Winter clothes from Munich were not the only things that did not arrive. For weeks he had expected the delivery of his Bechstein grand piano. The move had been subjected to one delay after another, but on April 22 he was finally able to report that the instrument had arrived in Florence. 'Heaven be praised!' he told Bechstein, ' . . . it goes against the grain to exercise my fingers on a hired Pleyel here. There is only one Bechstein!'[14]

Almost from the moment he took possession of his apartments, Bülow fell foul of the other tenants at 10, Borgo S. Frediano. He had always been an early riser and after breakfast he liked to begin his daily practice by loosening his fingers on a sequence of scales and arpeggios, much to the distress of his neighbours. Out of consideration for the tenant on the floor above him, who evidently needed to rest, Bülow agreed to refrain from practicing in the mornings. Not long afterwards he was asked to keep his piano closed in the evenings. That just left the afternoons. Still the complaints continued. A female tenant who lived on the floor beneath him claimed to suffer from a minor ailment aggravated by Bülow's playing. Mindful of her distinguished neighbour's volcanic temperament, 'Madame M', as Bülow called her, lacked the courage to confront him directly, and communicated her general displeasure through the intermediary of the janitor's daughter, who, emboldened by the fact that she was a mere messenger, bluntly instructed Bülow to desist from playing in the daytime as

12. BC. Unpublished letter to Giuseppe Buonamici dated October 19, 1870. From this same source we learn that Bülow's local physician, Dr. Levier, was prescribing minute doses of arsenic to treat the pain.

13. The Italians were distinctly proud of their new arrival. Bülow was somewhat extravagantly billed as 'Giovanni de Bülow, court pianist to the sovereigns of Prussia and Bavaria'.

14. BNB, p. 286.

well. Bülow, driven beyond endurance to write a letter of complaint to his landlord Mons. Wagnière, bluntly declared:

> Frankly, it is impossible for me to obey the orders of this lady who, through the elegant intermediary of the janitor's daughter, has asked me to call a halt to my playing in the daytime, for as long as it pleases the lady to treat an ailment right below the room I occupy in your house. Please be good enough, Sir, to let me know if this slavery imposed upon me by the residents of the first floor must be strictly adhered to as a condition for having the right to live in your building.
>
> Meanwhile, with my best regards, I am
> Yours faithfully
> H. de Bülow[15]

The situation was absurd. Here was one of the century's great pianists, preparing to launch himself on a series of international tours, while his neighbours attempted to have him muzzled.

IV

Hanging like a sword of Damocles over everything that he did during these early months was his impending divorce from Cosima. After his first, fleeting, meeting with his Berlin advocate August Simson, in July 1869, Bülow had every reason to suppose that the wretched business of disentangling himself from Cosima might be accomplished by correspondence. It was a cause of apprehension when he learned towards the end of March 1870 that he would have to return to Berlin in order to sign more papers in person, and swear out an affidavit for presentation to the Prussian courts. This early return to Germany was something he had never envisaged, least of all to the Prussian capital, but since it was fraught with consequences for his future, he knew it could not be avoided. He arrived in Berlin at the beginning of April and stayed with the Bechstein family for three weeks while he dealt with Simson. It tells us much about Bülow's puckish sense of humour, which hardly ever deserted him even in the worst of times, that he took out an advertisement in the Leipzig *Signale* informing the world that during his absence from Florence any inquiries about artistic matters should be directed to 'my friend and secretary, Cavaliere Cesare Rosso, Via Santo Spirito, 31'. The so-called Cavaliere, his 'friend and secretary', was in reality Rosso the cat that belonged to Jessie Laussot's house-porter. Bülow had become greatly attached to this feline

---

15. Unpublished letter dated 'Wednesday, June 14, 1871'. In private possession.

and had recently adopted one of its kittens, which he had dubbed with the diminutive 'Rossino'.

Although Bülow made little effort to seek out his former colleagues in Berlin, there was one reunion he actively desired to bring about. Carl Tausig had just returned from a triumphal tour of Russia. The two pianists were tied together by bonds of loyalty and friendship that went back to their student days with Liszt in Weimar. Tausig had shown genuine concern for Bülow's plight. In a little-known gesture of support, he had offered to travel to Munich to spend some days with his old friend at the height of the Cosima-Wagner crisis; Bülow, while grateful for this sign of steadfastness, had declined the offer, knowing that it could serve no practical purpose. Tausig, for his part, was well acquainted with the pain of separation, having a year or so earlier parted from his own wife, the pianist Szerafina Vrabély, who now lived in Vienna. The two old friends spent a few hours together in Tausig's studio, and the master pianist played a number of pieces for Bülow, including the Schumann *Toccata*, Bach's newly published Suite in E-flat major, and some Etudes by Chopin. Bülow was astonished by what he witnessed. 'Tausig's piano playing is the most perfect that I have heard', he wrote to Jessie Laussot. 'This ultimate perfection, this exquisite beauty of tone—they are beyond all compare'.[16] Later he would write at length about Tausig's playing, and the powerful impression that it had made on him.[17] It was the last occasion on which the two pianists met. The following year Tausig was dead.

V

Now that the major part of his business with advocate Simson was concluded, Bülow left Berlin hoping for a speedy decision in his favour from the Prussian courts. He returned to Florence via Milan and Venice, and was back home by April 22. He was frustrated and despondent when he learned that it would be necessary to make a further trip to Berlin before his divorce could be finalized. The journey back to the Prussian capital took place in mid-June, and this time he remained there for six weeks, once more as a guest of the Bechstein family. Bülow was finally granted a divorce on July 18, 1870. Although he was the injured party he paid all the legal costs himself.[18]

16. BB, vol. 4, p. 407. The 'newly published Suite' by Bach was almost certainly Raff's piano arrangement of the Sonata No. 4 for unaccompanied cello (BWV 1010) which appeared in 1869.

17. In Bülow's obituary notice of Tausig, on pp. 172–73.

18. An entry in Cosima's diary runs: ' . . . In answer to my inquiry about my liabilities, [the lawyer Simson] says that Herr von B[ülow] has decided to bear all the costs of the suit. This distresses me, but there is nothing I can do about it' (WT, vol. 1, p. 267). Five weeks after the divorce was made final, Cosima and Richard Wagner exchanged wedding vows

Just ten days after Bülow had secured his divorce, and while he was still languishing in Berlin, the long-threatened war between France and Prussia broke out. Bülow followed the conflict with interest. His admiration for Prince Otto von Bismarck, the father of German unification, had increased with each passing year. He read the Iron Chancellor's war speeches, and like most Germans of his generation he greeted the four-month siege and eventual fall of Paris in January 1871 with jubilation. Bülow appreciated French culture, and his command of the language gave him an insight into French mentality that not all Germans possessed. Nonetheless he supported the war against France, and also the corresponding drive for German hegemony that took possession of Germany's political structure, a structure that became increasingly militant and proved to be the country's undoing in the two world wars that followed. Bülow has been criticized for being on the wrong side of history, but this is to introduce a double standard. Brahms, too, was on the wrong side of history, or at least that part of it having to do with German militarism, but we hear little about that. Brahms kept a picture of Bismarck hanging on the wall of his study in Vienna, crowned with a laurel wreath. And when France was finally crushed, he composed his *Triumphlied,* op. 55, a work that has meanwhile fallen into a modest obscurity—partly because of its militaristic text.

Despite the massive movement of German troops making their way to the battle lines on the western front, Bülow somehow managed to wend his way back to Florence via Vienna, where he pottered about for three or four hours taking in all the sights. He was enormously impressed with the imperial city, which had grown both in stature and beauty since he last saw it, and which he described as more like a world capital than Berlin itself. From Vienna he moved to the lake resort of Gmunden, where he had booked accommodation in the Hotel Bellevue. He was badly in need of rest after the prolonged pressures of the legal process from which he had just emerged, and he cabled his mother who was still in Munich to join him. Franziska arrived at Gmunden in the middle of August, took control of her famous offspring in her usual no-nonsense sort of way, upbraiding him and mollycoddling him in equal proportions, a process to which he was well used and to which he meekly submitted. Their ultimate destination was Venice, a city that Bülow had glimpsed but once, and which he promised to introduce to his mother. After touring upper Italy they spent ten days in Venice, enthralled by the jewel of the Adriatic. In one of those fits of boyish enthusiasm to which he was prone, Bülow observed

---

in the Protestant church of Lucerne, on August 25—King Ludwig's birthday. Bülow's terse comment was, 'Have you heard of the doings at Lucerne on the King's birthday? That was quick work . . .' (BNB, p. 293).

that the best way to render Florence ordinary was to approach it from Venice. Mother and son finally parted at Verona; she returned to Munich while he went back to Milan for a few days of sightseeing before returning to Florence with the firm intention 'to work off my long idleness'.[19] One thing that must have pleased him enormously was that in Vienna he was offered the artistic directorship of the Vienna Gesellschaft der Musikfreunde, an honour he declined. (It was later offered to Brahms, who accepted.) He was unwilling to give up Italy, which had temporarily become his adopted home.

VI

December 16, 1870, marked the one hundredth anniversary of Beethoven's birth, and Bülow was engaged to participate in the month-long Beethoven festival in Milan leading up to that important date. He participated in three chamber concerts for the *Società del Quartetto* (November 14, 21, and 25) with his regular Trio partners, Giovacchino Giovacchini (violin) and Jefte Sbolci (cello), which included a performance of the *Archduke* Trio—possibly the first time that this work had been heard in public in Italy. The festival culminated in an all-Beethoven orchestral concert, conducted by Bülow on December 4: the *Egmont* Overture, the Eighth Symphony, the Scherzo and Adagio from the Ninth Symphony, and the *Emperor* Concerto, with Bülow himself as the soloist.[20] Bülow told Bechstein that he had played everything 'with the precision of a needle-gun'—a topical reference to the new, long-distance cannon with which the Germans were presently bombarding the French, with such devastating effect, in the ongoing Franco-Prussian War.

Even while the Beethoven festival was in progress, news was brought to Bülow that his half-brother Heinz had been killed in the conflict. This eighteen-year-old youth had followed the family tradition, and had joined the German army, becoming a lieutenant in the 94th Infantry Regiment. He was killed by a French bullet at the Battle of Châteauneuf, on November 18, but news had been slow to reach Bülow, who had already left for Milan. Bülow wrote letters of consolation to his stepmother, Louise,

19. Ibid., p. 292.
20. Copies of these rare Milan programmes are preserved in the Deutsche Staatsbibliothek (Db 1815, 1870–1871). The orchestral concert was so successful that it was repeated, with slight modification, on December 8. As a result of these concerts, and the prestige they brought to the city, Bülow was approached by the administrators of La Scala opera house and asked if he was interested in becoming its artistic director. On December 5, he told his pupil Giuseppe Buonamici, 'Probably I shall be here at La Scala next year. The covert negotiations have already begun' (Hitherto unpublished letter. BC). These negotiations, in fact, went nowhere. Bülow's decision to return to his career as a touring virtuoso essentially made such an appointment unworkable.

and to his surviving half-brother, Willi. He told Louise of his affection for young Heinz, whose picture graced his writing desk in Florence. 'I cannot tell you what a really personal sorrow it is to me, and how deeply it has shaken me to see your Heinz struck from the ranks of the living', he told Louise.[21] A day or two later he wrote to twenty-one-year-old Willi:

> I have no words to tell you of my sympathy with the loss of your life-companion. . . . But, believe me, I entirely understand your feelings and entirely share your grief. That I am able to do so you will realize if you recall that bitter day, seventeen years ago, when I received the news of our dear father's death, you being too young to grasp it.[22]

Despite Bülow's support for Bismarck, and the chancellor's policy of 'blood and iron' in the service of German expansionism, the loss of Heinz on the field of battle gave him pause. He felt remorse for having so strongly supported the idea of a military career for his half-brother.

VII

The unexpected death of Tausig from typhoid fever in Leipzig, on July 17, 1871, aged twenty-nine, also had a profound effect on Bülow. Tausig was the one pianist whom Bülow venerated, and the world of music knew it. It therefore made sense for Bülow's old journal, the Leipzig *Signale,* to send him an urgent request to write an obituary notice about the pianistic legend. Bülow was not at first enthusiastic. As he himself pointed out, he had not written anything for journals of any kind for seven years, and he hardly felt up to the task. As the memories stirred, however, his pen was activated. He chained himself to his desk for two days, writing and rewriting everything until the lengthy eulogy was finished.[23] Bülow recollected that he had last met Tausig in Berlin a year earlier and had enjoyed the rare privilege of hearing the Polish pianist play to him in private. He concluded that while in former days Tausig had been a volcano, he was now transformed into a beneficent sun, spreading warmth and light. 'Hail, young Apollo!' he had proclaimed impulsively at that time. And now the gods had stepped in and reclaimed him as one of their own. Shortly after the funeral in Berlin, Tausig's effects were put up for public auction, held in his elegant apartments in Berlin. Everything was liqui-

---

21. BNB, p. 543.
22. Ibid., p. 544.
23. Ibid., p. 308. The obituary appeared in Leipzig's *Signale für die musikalische Welt* on August 22, 1871. It was translated into English and published by installments in *Dwight's Journal of Music,* in the issues of October 21 and November 18, 1871, pp. 116–117, p. 125, and p. 129.

dated. His beautiful carved oak furniture, his wardrobe of clothes including the patent leather shoes he wore on the concert platform, his paintings, his music library, and his Bechstein piano—all went under the hammer. In a touching gesture, Bechstein offered to send Tausig's piano to Bülow, but Bülow declined the offer, preferring to keep his own 'old and trusted companion', despite the persistent string-snapping from which it had suffered of late, and about which he had started to complain. Two small mementos of Tausig he did accept, however. After reading Bülow's tribute, Tausig's widow, Szerafina Vrabély, enclosed with her note of thanks a medallion of Tausig and a lock of his hair.

VIII

In October 1871, Bülow and Jessie Laussot travelled from Florence to Rome in order to be with Liszt on the latter's sixtieth birthday, October 22. It was a wonderful surprise for Liszt, who had not seen his former son-in-law for three years. Princess von Sayn-Wittgenstein and her daughter Princess Marie Hohenlohe also descended on Liszt, and they all dined in Liszt's apartments at the Santa Francesca Romana. The following day, Liszt wrote about the occasion to his friend Baroness Olga von Meyendorff:

October 23, 1871, Rome

Something really pleasant happened to me yesterday. Bülow came to convey his wishes to me on my birthday. No man is as close to my heart as he. He is practically my son and has been, for some twenty years, the most spirited and intimate of my friends. The natural nobility of his character is such that heroism seems to be a familiar condition for him.

We had not seen or written to each other in two years.[24] The painful circumstances of his separation from Cos[ima] have greatly impaired his health; but he is now recovering his full strength and intends to start on a round of performances next winter beginning with Vienna, Pest, Prague, Dresden, Berlin, Leipzig, and ending in London in May. In the fall he will be sailing to America.

Yesterday, Princess Wittgenstein and her daughter did me the honour of inviting themselves to dinner at Santa Francesca Romana. [Prince Onorato] Teano, Count Kalnoky, Father Ferrari (now archbishop of Lepanto), and Father Theiner were among our guests —and since Sgambati had taken the trouble to have a second piano

24. Here Liszt's memory is not quite correct. The two men had corresponded after Bülow's painful divorce from Cosima, and it was actually three years, not two, since they had last met.

brought to the house, we played *Mazeppa* together. I then treated the audience to some movements from the Carnevale di Milano (*Polonaise, Dormiveglia, Sospiri danzanti*) of Bülow, who also sat down at the piano thereby giving extreme pleasure to us all and to me in particular. Our little improvised concert ended with *Orpheus*, with Bülow. This morning he is offering us a Beethoven session at the Sala Dantesca and leaves again tomorrow for Florence. Mme Laussot, who accompanied him here, asks to convey to you her respectful compliments . . .
Your FL[25]

Liszt's casual reference to 'a Beethoven session' that Bülow was to give at the Sala Dantesca reveals something important. During his sojourn in Florence, Bülow had brought to completion his celebrated edition of Beethoven's keyboard music, a project he had begun in Germany and on which he had lavished a lot of care. His long correspondence with the publisher J. G. Cotta of Stuttgart yields many details of this work-in-progress, which was just about to go to the printers.[26] Bülow's original intention had been to dedicate his Beethoven edition to Wagner. On April 8, 1869, while the work was coming to fruition and before he had left Munich, he told Wagner that he had just put the finishing touches to the *Hammerklavier* Sonata 'at the cost of great exertion'. And he added, 'This work of mine will, it seems to me, be really worth something. . . . Will you allow me to dedicate this work publicly to you (with a carefully considered Preface)? It will not be an entirely unworthy contribution to your *deutsche Vortragstil*'.[27] As we now know, Bülow changed his mind and dedicated his edition to Franz Liszt instead, 'as the fruit of his teaching'. The separation and divorce from Cosima, and her subsequent marriage to Wagner, forced him to abandon all thoughts of attaching Wagner's name to the title page.[28]

25. WLLM, p. 26.

26. On November 3, 1870, Bülow told Buonamici that his Beethoven edition was 'good and finished . . . just a few hours ago'. (See BC.) This edition presents all the sonatas from op. 53 (the *Waldstein*) forward, as well as all the other later solo piano compositions of Beethoven, including the *Diabelli* Variations and the two sets of Bagatelles, opp. 119 and 126. Despite much comment to the contrary, Bülow never published a complete edition of all thirty-two Beethoven piano sonatas. Having said that, we must not forget the four early sonatas that he had edited in years past, and which had appeared separately: namely, the *Pathétique*, op. 13; the A-flat major, op. 26; the *Moonlight*, op. 27, no. 2; and the E-flat major, op. 31, no. 3. The first editions of these four sonatas are today collectors' items. Bülow's edition, incidentally, comprises volumes 4 and 5 of Cotta's 'Instructive Edition of Classical Keyboard Music'.

27. 'Your German declamatory style of execution' (BNB, p. 461).

28. Liszt was deeply touched by this dedication. See his letter to the Hungarian press (p. 291) written in the midst of Bülow's triumphs in Budapest, in 1881, shortly after the second edition had appeared.

Getting the text of the dedication right was especially important to Bülow, and it went through one or two preliminary drafts before he hit upon the exact formulation:

Dem Meister Franz Liszt
widmet diesen Interpretationsversuch
als Frucht seiner Lehre
sein
dankbarer Schuler
Hans von Bülow
[This attempt at interpretation
is dedicated to the Master Franz Liszt
as the fruit of his teaching
by his grateful student
Hans von Bülow]

Let us note Bülow's unusual description of his edition as an 'attempt at interpretation'. His work addressed the player. It was the first time in the history of Beethoven interpretation that the would-be pianist had been placed at the receiving end of such a vast array of annotations, warnings, admonitions, and injunctions of every hue. Bülow's edition, so rich in commentary, brought him both bouquets and brickbats. His chief critics included Clara Schumann and Ferdinand Hiller, both of whom accused him of beleaguering the student with so many limitations as to rob him of initiative. Bülow later explained that his annotations were there to guard against a false interpretation. And he added archly, 'I had to add the babble, not out of inner necessity, but because of the absurdity of my respected colleagues'.[29] Bülow's edition continues to absorb us, because it tells us how he himself may have played these pieces at a time when a solid performing tradition had not yet emerged.

IX

During the few hours he spent in Liszt's company, Bülow was so affected by 'the sweet and powerful emotion which filled my heart' that the moment he got back to his Roman lodgings he wrote to Cosima, with whom he had not corresponded for more than two years. 'Today, Madame, is the birthday of your father, my good and great Master'. He went on to reaffirm his determination to raise capital for the education of their daughters through his future concert tours of Britain and America, and he announced, 'I am returning on New Year's Day to my profession of

---

29. ZMB, p. 40.

virtuoso'.[30] Although he had evidently told Liszt and others that his tour of America was imminent, we now know that his departure was subjected to one delay after another, and he did not set foot in the New World until the autumn of 1875.[31]

Bülow took his leave of Florence on December 28, 1871, and gave a farewell recital in the Sala Sbolci consisting of pieces 'requested by his admirers':

J.S. Bach	Organ Prelude and Fugue in B minor (transc. Liszt)
Mendelssohn	Prelude and Fugue, op. 35, no. 6
Scarlatti	'Cat's Fugue'
Rheinberger	Andante and Toccata
Beethoven	Sonata in A-flat major, op. 110
Schumann	Faschingsschwank aus Wien, op. 28
Chopin	Two Nocturnes, op. 27
	Tarantella op. 43
	Waltz in A-flat major, op. 42
Liszt	Le lac de Wallenstadt
	Eclogue
	Au bord d'une source
	[Années de pèlerinage, 'Suisse']
	Rhapsodie espagnole
	Pianoforte: Bechstein[32]

On New Year's Day, 1872, Bülow caught the overnight train to Vienna. He arrived at the city's main railway terminus at 5:00 a.m. the following morning and was taken completely by surprise when he was greeted by Liszt, who, despite the early hour, was already at the station to welcome him.[33] Liszt, in fact, had travelled to Vienna a few days earlier in order to attend the premier performance of his 'Christmas Oratorio' (Part I of

---

30. BNB, pp. 484–485.

31. Bülow's chief reason for delaying the trip to America had to do with the fact that, by an unfortunate coincidence, Anton Rubinstein had planned his own first great tour of the New World at exactly the same time. Rubinstein gave his opening recital in New York on September 14, 1872, in the old Steinway Hall on Fourteenth Street, to a fanfare of publicity. Because Steinway had undertaken to provide Rubinstein with pianos throughout the tour, he advised Bülow that it would be impossible for him to provide a similar service to Bülow as well. He also told Bülow that he would make far more money in America if he waited until Rubinstein had left—sentiments that may be found in Bülow's letter to Bechstein, dated September 29, 1872 (BNB, p. 322).

32. A rare copy of the handbill is preserved in the British Library: RPS ms. 345ff. 108. The Sala Sbolci, where this concert took place, was located at Borgo Santa Croce 6.

33. BB, vol. 4, p. 519.

Christus), conducted by Anton Rubinstein, with Anton Bruckner officiating at the organ. Liszt, as Bülow quickly learned, had been warmly received by the audience, but the 'Christmas Oratorio' itself was now being lambasted by the critics, and especially by Liszt's nemesis, Eduard Hanslick. Bülow, with mock solemnity, described Liszt as 'his majesty', because he could not help marvelling at the regal way in which Liszt rose above the newspaper fray and showed all his usual grace under pressure. To Jessie Laussot he passed along an aphorism of Goethe's that Liszt had quoted: 'That the hounds are barking just proves that we are in the saddle'. It was a saying from which Bülow himself rarely benefitted, because whenever the hounds barked at him his first response was to bark back.

With Liszt's encouragement Bülow had planned an ambitious tour to mark his return to the concert platform. It was put together for him by the Berlin agent Julius Steinitz, who had earlier been Tausig's manager. Bülow's friends repeatedly warned him against a partnership with Steinitz, who had a reputation for sharp business practice; he charged Bülow a hefty commission of 25 percent after their common expenses had been met. This was a very great deal of money, but Bülow reasoned that he 'needed a Samson to watch over the American deal'—a clear indication that a tour of the New World remained his larger goal. In the event, Steinitz proved to be both incompetent and antipathetic. 'Samson' was later dropped for Bernard Ullman, on the recommendation of Liszt, a manager cut from very different cloth, whom we shall meet later on. Bülow was meanwhile to give dozens of recitals under the Steinitz management, which enabled him to fulfill that pledge made to Cosima on Liszt's sixtieth birthday: 'I can at least from now onwards assume the paternal obligation . . . of providing for [the children and] their material future'.

X

Bülow's opening concert in Vienna, on January 8, 1872, at which he played Beethoven's *Emperor* Concerto with the Vienna Philharmonic Orchestra, was a veritable triumph. Both Liszt and Rubinstein were in the audience. During the rehearsal the orchestral players gave Bülow an ovation. It was an unusual accolade, and represented a splendid beginning to his tour. That it occurred on his forty-second birthday made it still more memorable for him. After the concert, Bülow and Liszt boarded the overnight train to Pest where Bülow was scheduled to appear at a Philharmonic Concert, once again playing Beethoven's *Emperor* Concerto, a rendering Liszt described as 'magnificent'. Bülow also gave two mostly Beethoven recitals, of which Liszt wrote:

The Viennese and Hungarian journals are unanimous in their praise of his immense talent, and accord only to Rubinstein the honour of sharing the palm of virtuosity with him. If Tausig were still alive, there would be three great pianists towering over all the others.[34]

Liszt could not help observing the sadness that emanated from Bülow, which tinged nearly everything that the younger man did during their time together in Hungary. It prompted Liszt to compose his piano piece *Sunt lacrymae rerum: en mode hongrois,* which he dedicated to Bülow. The first part of the title is a quotation from Virgil, 'The sense of tears in mortal things'.[35]

By January 20 Bülow had reached Berlin, bracing himself for what was still to come. Within the months of January to March alone he gave sixty-one concerts, an impressive tally amounting to five or six performances a week. Among the chief highlights was his appearance in Warsaw at the Polish National Theatre, playing Beethoven's *Emperor* Concerto and Liszt's 'Fantasie on Hungarian Folk-themes'. His performances of Chopin garnered special praise from the Poles. Bülow was somewhat bemused to be offered the directorship of the Warsaw National Opera, however, a position he declined because, as he later explained to Bechstein, 'any work I did there would be entirely without influence on the actual civilized world of music'.[36] En route back to Germany he played in Königsberg, Breslau, and Danzig, a city he called 'the Venice of the North'. In Dortmund he paused to take stock of his financial position. After all his expenses had been paid, and after a mere five weeks on the road, he had netted a profit of 6,800 thalers.[37] It was a good start. On March 1 he played an all-Beethoven recital in Cologne which exceeded all his musical expectations. He wrote, 'Do you know where and when I played the best in my entire life? In Cologne, on March 1'.[38]

Bülow's first, arduous tour of Europe had lasted for four months, and consisted of well over a hundred concerts. It drew to a close with his return to Italy towards the end of April 1872. He languished in Naples for a few days before going back to Florence, and witnessed an eruption of Vesuvius on April 26, 1872. 'What a spectacle!' he wrote. 'One cannot even have an approximate idea of it!' And he added that the viewers were

34. LLB, vol. 6, p. 328.

35. From the *Aeneid,* Book I, lines 461–462. This early version of *Sunt lacrymae rerum* was later revised and included in the *Année de pèlerinage,* Book 3, published in 1883.

36. BNB, p. 320.

37. BB, vol. 4, p. 534.

38. A communication to the publisher Eugen Spitzweg (BB, vol. 4, p. 538).

Bülow gives a recital in Munich, in benefit of Wagner's
'German National Theatre', April 2, 1872.

forced to pay for it with five subsequent days of skies the colour of lead,
ash storms, fog, and a devilish dust. 'It was impossible to go out without
an umbrella and a handkerchief to veil the face'.[39] This Vesuvian fireworks display was a fitting coda to his conquest of some of Europe's
biggest cities, and a fine welcome home. On Christmas Day, 1872, when
all the receipts were in and he was able to reflect on his financial position,
he informed Jessie Laussot that his goal of raising 100,000 francs for his
family was within sight. 'Then I might be able to think a little bit about
myself'.[40]

One concert from this tour deserves special mention. On April 2, 1872,
Bülow gave a recital in Munich, in aid of the recently announced 'Foundation of a German National Theatre in Bayreuth'—Wagner's first public attempt to raise money for his operatic projects in a town that was
now his home. No one expected Bülow to give such a concert—least of
all Wagner himself. It was the first of many recitals that Bülow gave in

39. Letter written in Italian, dated 'May 4, 1872, Hotel de Genève'. Original in BC. A
heavily edited version, omitting Bülow's criticisms of local Italian musicians, was published
in BB, vol. 4, p. 544.

40. BB, vol. 5, p. 49.

support of the fledgling Bayreuth enterprise.[41] He was extremely well received and afterwards was given the diploma of the Munich-based Richard-Wagner Verein as a mark of respect. Still, this first return to Munich was the equivalent of walking back into the lion's den while still bearing the scars of earlier maulings there. The city was full of highly charged memories for him. He nonetheless agreed to return in June to conduct performances of new productions of *Tristan* and *Meistersinger,* in fulfilment of a pledge that he gave to King Ludwig. The twenty-eight-year-old philosopher Friedrich Nietzsche attended these performances and was transfixed by *Tristan,* especially, calling it 'the loftiest artistic experience of my life'.[42] Because Ludwig was prevented through illness from attending, Bülow mounted an extra performance of *Tristan* especially for the monarch on August 18.[43] These visits to Munich carried therapeutic value for Bülow, and marked the beginning of his psychological independence from the city.

For the next five years Bülow pursued the career of a wandering minstrel. It was a life he came to detest, but since it allowed him to make a very great deal of money for the support of his children, he tolerated it. He gave hundreds of concerts, not only on the European mainland, but also in Britain and later in America. His tours of the English-speaking world, especially, have never been properly chronicled. They were not without incident, and it is to them that we now turn.

---

41. In this same month of April alone Bülow gave five more benefit concerts for the establishment of a German national theatre in Bayreuth: in Mannheim (April 4), Wiesbaden (April 7), Cologne (April 8), Dresden (April 10), and Hamburg (April 12). After the Bayreuth Theatre was built, and started to lose money, Bülow once more went on the road and tried to rescue it. See pp. 254–57.

42. BB, vol. 4, p. 551. Nietzsche's gushing letter to Bülow on these performances, and his misguided attempt to arouse the conductor's interest in the orchestral score of his 'Manfred Meditation', a composition that provoked Bülow to scorn, have already been mentioned in the Prologue, pp. 4–5

43. A day or two before the performance, Bülow received a surprise. His young lover Giulia turned up in Munich, accompanied by her mother. He found the two ladies waiting for him when he got back to his hotel after midnight. 'What jubilation!' he told Buonamici, but cloaked the rest of Giulia's visit in a blanket of silence (BC, unpublished letter, dated 'August 1872'). One wonders what thoughts Giulia harboured as she watched the story of two doomed lovers unfold on the Munich stage, conducted by her present amour.

Bülow returned to the Munich Theatre on October 30, 1872, in order to direct a further performance of *Tristan.* It was the last time he conducted this work in its entirety.

First Tours of Britain—and Beyond, 1873–1875

To hell with this nomad's life, these vagrant customs, in a word,
this virtuoso occupation!
—Bülow[1]

I

When Bülow first crossed Albion's shores, in April 1873, the country was still widely regarded as 'Das Land ohne Musik'. The profession itself was generally held in low esteem, particularly by the upper classes which had never regarded music as a fitting occupation for an English gentleman. During one of Liszt's appearances in London, in 1840, Lady Blessington had inspected him through her lorgnette and had famously exclaimed, 'What a pity to put such a man to the piano!'[2] Amateurism was rife. The country had not produced a composer of major importance since Purcell. Despite the presence of the Royal Academy of Music, which had opened its doors in 1822, English musicians who wished to succeed usually went to the Continent to be 'finished', two of the favoured destinations being Paris or Leipzig, and when they returned home they often adopted foreign names in order to enjoy a better career. The Industrial Revolution had created great wealth among the middle classes, however, and foreign musicians flocked to Britain because that is where the money was to be made; they ensured that the standard of orchestral music making, especially in London, was relatively high. England's great choral tradition was different. The rest of Europe had nothing to compare with it. The oratorios of Handel and Mendelssohn, to say nothing of lesser composers, did not receive finer performances anywhere, even in Germany.

1. BBLW, p. 125.
2. ACLA, vol. 1, p. 433.

London's Oxford Street in the 1870s, looking west from Duke Street. A contemporary photograph.

J. W. Davison served as the music critic of *The Times* from 1846 to 1879, an exceptionally long period of thirty-three years. His conservative views, expressed anonymously (as was the practice at *The Times* in those days), wielded great influence and helped to stifle experiment and resist change. Davison was married to the pianist Arabella Goddard (whose pupil she had earlier become in order to study the classical composers with him), and when Davison started to promote her, the conflict of interest raised eyebrows. A French magazine pilloried the pair by saying that whenever a pianist approached the shores of England, you could be certain to see Davison standing on the cliffs of Dover shouting, 'No pianists wanted here!' Davison's harsh treatment of artists of whom he personally disapproved was notorious and has earned for him the title of 'the Music Monster'. His reputation in the history of music criticism is tarnished by the knowledge that he could be bought. After his death, his successor was besieged by presents which arrived at the front door, having been diverted from that of the deceased Davison.

Bülow's English debut took place on April 28, in St. James's Hall, London, where he played Beethoven's *Emperor* Concerto at a Philharmonic Society concert, with William Cusins conducting. He was recalled three times, and played Bach's Chromatic Fantasy and Fugue as an encore. Since the enthusiasm of the audience showed no signs of abating, Bülow returned to the platform and delivered a performance of a 'Passepied' by Bach. The Philharmonic Society was so delighted with his reception

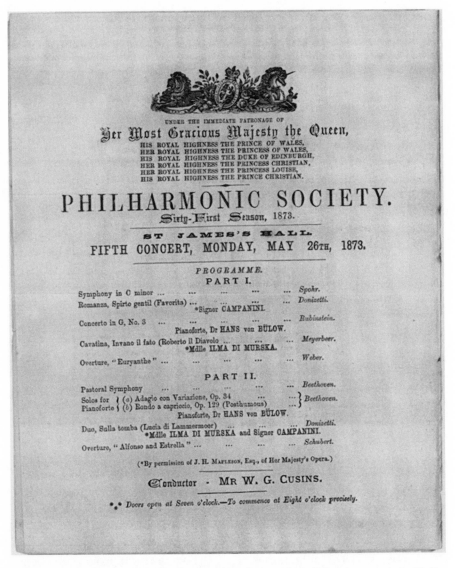

A Philharmonic Society Concert, May 26, 1873, during which Bülow is presented with the Society's Gold Medal.

that they doubled his honorarium.[3] A second appearance at a philharmonic concert followed on May 26, at which he played Rubinstein's Piano

3. Walter Bache, Liszt's most important English pupil and a staunch supporter of Bülow, sent a detailed description of the concert to Jessie Laussot. In a letter dated 'April 29, 1873', he wrote, 'He is playing better than I ever heard, and everyone agrees that no such playing has been heard in London' (BBM, p. 214).

Concerto no. 3, in G major. These two appearances prepared the way for what would become a long and fruitful relationship with the British public. At an ad hoc meeting of the directors of the Philharmonic Society, held during the intermission of the second concert, a decision was taken to bestow on Bülow the Gold Medal of the Society.[4]

Between times, on May 9, Bülow also made his British debut as a conductor, thanks to an invitation from Eduard Dannreuther. He directed a performance of the Prelude to *Tristan,* and the Introduction to Act III for the Wagner Society of London. It was the first time this music had been heard in Britain. Meanwhile, he gave solo recitals in a number of provincial cities, including Manchester, Sheffield, and Liverpool. His habit of playing and conducting everything from memory aroused universal admiration.[5]

After spending the summer of 1873 in Germany, mainly at the watering spa of Baden-Baden, Bülow returned to London in November and rented rooms at 27 Duke Street, Manchester Square. He also experienced the joy of being reunited with his sister Isidora, whom he had not seen for a number of years. She had married the diplomat Viktor von Bojanowski, consul-general to the kaiser, and they had recently moved into a spacious residence in Sydenham, with their two young children, Viktor and a daughter named Wjera. 'Uncle Hans' became a frequent visitor to their home, which represented for him a haven from what was shortly to become a sea of English troubles.[6]

II

Bülow's first concert of the new season took place at the Crystal Palace on Saturday, November 8, where yet again he scored a success with Beethoven's *Emperor* Concerto, this time under the baton of August Manns. Walter Bache took advantage of Bülow's reappearance in London by inviting him to appear as a guest conductor in Bache's 'Tenth Annual Concert', on November 27, 1873, at St. James's Hall.[7] The marathon programme began

4. Bülow's unpublished letter of thanks is dated 'June 4, 1873', and is preserved in the archives of the Royal Philharmonic Society, BL, RPS ms 337ff. 155–156.

5. The *Musical Times* went out of its way to inform its readers that 'since his arrival in England he has never had a note of music before him at his public performances . . .' (issue of June 1873).

6. Viktor von Bojanowski held several senior diplomatic postings. He had recently been transferred to London in 1873. From there he was posted to Budapest. Later (March 1888) he would be promoted to the presidency of the Imperial Patent Office in Berlin.

7. Bache had sought out Bülow in Florence two years earlier, during one of his European peregrinations in the summer of 1871. There the two musicians had struck up a lifelong friendship. Bache even rented a room in the same building as Bülow and saw him on a daily basis. 'He allows me to spend a part of every morning with him, plays to me and hears me

The Crystal Palace, London. A lithograph.

with Weber's Overture to *Euryanthe* and then went on to feature Bache himself as soloist in Liszt's arrangement for piano and orchestra of Schubert's *Wanderer* Fantasie. Two of Liszt's symphonic poems followed: *Tasso* and *Orpheus*.[8] The programme concluded with the 'Liebestod' from Wagner's *Tristan*—'repeated at the desire of many who heard the first performance in England (under Herr von Bülow's direction) at the Wagner Society Concert, May 9, 1873'. About this evening *The Monthly Musical Record* wrote:

> By installing Dr. von Bülow as conductor, Mr. Bache, who on previous occasions has given ample proof of his own remarkable skill in this capacity, made it plain that he was influenced by no motives of self-glorification, but simply by the desire to present the works selected in the most perfect manner possible. Of Dr. von Bülow's powers as a conductor, as well as those he possesses as an executant, it would be impossible to speak in too exaggerated terms. When we recall the fact that he conducted the first performances of Wagner's *Tristan, Die Meistersinger,* etc. without a score before

play' wrote Bache. 'In the evening we dine together, and I remain with him until bedtime' (BBM, p. 206).

8. This performance of *Orpheus* was a British premier. *Tasso* had already been heard for the first time by Londoners a few months earlier, when William Cusins conducted it on June 9.

him, it will be no surprise to those of our readers who were not present at Mr. Bache's concert to learn that he conducted throughout, and even accompanied the songs from memory . . .[9]

The three solo recitals he gave in St. James's Hall in November and December 1873 were notable because each one presented a late sonata of Beethoven. The recital on December 3 contained the *Hammerklavier*. This Everest among piano sonatas had not been heard by the British public since Sir Charles Hallé presented it in his Beethoven recitals, eleven years earlier. From *The Times* we learn that the Scherzo was applauded so loudly that Bülow decided to repeat it. He further obliged his audience by repeating the concluding Fugue as well, 'in reply to another demonstration'. Evidently he took the Fugue subject so fast 'as to make every hearer wonder how by any possibility the artist, great as is his executive power and prodigious his memory, could accomplish his task'.[10]

Meanwhile, Bülow gave piano recitals in Manchester and Liverpool, and was unsparing of himself in catching night trains back to London, either to ready himself for an orchestral rehearsal the following day, or to prepare for his next solo recital in the British capital. His appearances at the Liverpool Philharmonic Society concerts were numerous and well chronicled. He first appeared in the city's imposing St. George's Hall on November 25, 1873, playing Henselt's Concerto in F minor, op. 16, under the baton of Sir Julius Benedict, together with a group of solo items which included Liszt's *Waldesrauschen* and *Feux-follets,* and Chopin's Berceuse. On the strength of these performances he was invited back to Liverpool almost at once to participate in the Society's chamber concerts. On December 17 he played Sterndale Bennett's 'Maid of Orleans' Sonata (which he appropriated from under the nose of Arabella Goddard, for whom it had been composed), and then joined other artists for performances of chamber music by Rubinstein and Beethoven. This special connection with Liverpool lasted until at least February 3, 1875, when we again find Bülow in St. George's Hall, playing Beethoven's *Appassionata* Sonata, a Grieg sonata for violin and piano (with Prosper Sainton), and the Piano Quintet by Louis Spohr.

9. MMR, January 1874.

10. Issue of December 4, 1873. In his own edition of the Sonata, Bülow recommends a metronome mark of $\quarternote = 138$. This is faster than Tovey, who proposes a more modest $\quarternote = 126$. Liszt, on the other hand, follows Beethoven and calls for $\quarternote = 144$. Frederic Lamond's claim that Bülow was the first pianist to play the *Hammerklavier* Sonata in public cannot be sustained (LBS, p. 8). Liszt is known to have played it in Paris as early as 1836. However, Bülow had included the work in one of his Berlin Singakademie concerts on January 6, 1860, possibly the first time it had been heard in Germany.

His old love of languages reasserted itself, and he somehow found time to embark on a study of English. It was a repetition of his conquest of Italian two or three years earlier. Soon he was writing letters to friends and colleagues in English that show a level of polish and sophistication remarkable for their use of idiomatic expressions. He learned to pun in the language, and once wrote in the autograph album of an English friend this charming specimen of wordplay that any native Englishman would have been proud to sponsor:

In art hate respectability
And respect ability.

Bülow's constant round of activity was relieved by the Christmas holidays, which he spent in the Schloss Meiningen at the invitation of Duke Georg II of Meiningen and his new wife, Baroness Helene von Heldburg. We recall that Ellen, as she was known before her marriage to the duke, had earlier been a piano student of Bülow's in Berlin. After being elevated to the aristocracy through her morganatic marriage to Georg II she began to harbour notions of attracting Bülow to the city. Throughout Christmas and the New Year their conversations turned on the question of how best to make Bülow's transfer to Meiningen possible. He conducted the Meiningen Orchestra for the first time on December 28—an ensemble he described as 'spotless'. For the present, however, his prior commitment was to his career as a touring pianist. Seven years would elapse before Baroness Helene's dream of bringing Bülow to Meiningen in an official capacity became a reality. Meanwhile, in a private ceremony in Meiningen Castle on January 6, the duke bound Bülow more closely to his court by investing him with the Order of the Komthurkreuz (2nd Class).

Between January 2 and 8, 1874, Bülow gave concerts in Dresden and nearby Eisenach (the latter to raise money for the erection of a Bach monument in the place of the composer's birth, containing a performance of the Triple Concerto on three Bechstein pianos which were 'capitally in tune'[11]). By mid-January he had returned to England and resumed his British tour. This particular leg of his long journey across Albion's wintry terrain took him to such scattered towns as Bristol, Shrewsbury, Bath, Torquay, Liverpool, Birmingham, and Newcastle-on-Tyne, en route to Scotland. In the midst of this ceaseless travel he often asked himself whether he was awake or simply dreaming. At Liverpool he appeared at St. George's Hall once more, this time with Charles Hallé, the only English conductor

11. BNB, p. 341.

for whom he had any praise, and dubbed him 'the Joachim of the baton'. At Newcastle he faced an audience of 1,500 people ('among whom there were only 36 deadheads'), and was able to write, 'It is certain that in the English I have found my public *par excellence*'.[12] He crossed the Scottish border on January 21/22. His first glimpse of Edinburgh pleased him, and he described the city as 'one of the most beautiful in the whole of Europe'.[13] Nonetheless, he had some amusing reservations about the silence of the Scottish Sunday, which he called 'a superlative version of the English one'. In both Glasgow and Edinburgh he scored some notable successes which played an important role in his plans to return there the following year. How he found time to cross the Irish Sea and give a recital in Dublin's 'Brunswick Rooms' on the evening of January 29 remains something of a mystery. Yet the Dublin newspapers are adamant that he did.[14]

It is doubtful that Bülow could have pursued such a seamless itinerary without the help of his English agent, George Dolby, who often accompanied him on his travels. Bülow had been introduced to Dolby by the violinist Prosper Sainton, who was married to Dolby's sister, and the agent's credentials had at first seemed impeccable. Dolby had earlier managed Charles Dickens's American tours, an experience that had brought him a measure of fame and had emboldened him to launch a concert agency for musical artists, one of the first such organizations of its kind in England. Already he had a number of distinguished musicians on his books, including Joachim, Clara Schumann, and the cellist Piatti. By mutual agreement Dolby took 10 percent of Bülow's earnings—'not more!' Bülow had protested in his most chimerical vein.[15] The pianist described Dolby as 'a splendid mixture of Gentleman and Clown, Art-lover and

12. BB, vol. 5, p. 131. 'Deadheads' was Bülow's pejorative term for people who had not paid for their seats but had been placed there by the management in order to swell the crowd.

13. Ibid., p. 137.

14. See, for example, Dublin's *Freeman's Journal and Daily Commercial Advertiser*, for January 21, 1874. Bülow gave concerts in Edinburgh on January 24 and in Glasgow on the evening of January 26. Before concluding that he would have had to don Faust's mantle to be in Dublin by January 28 in order to give a concert there the following day, a glance at the timetables in the Scottish Maritime Museum might suggest an alternative mode of transport. The Stranraer-Larne Ferry got underway in 1872, and could have transported him across the Irish Sea in a couple of hours. Then would have followed the 100-mile rail journey from Belfast to Dublin, a three-hour trip, which in those days could be accomplished at a maximum speed of 40 miles per hour, with stops at various stations in between. After the evening recital in the 'Brunswick Rooms', his return journey back across the Irish Sea to the British mainland would have given him ample time to brace himself for his next major recital in Liverpool, on February 7. Bülow zigzagged his way across Britain without a great deal of logic in the planning. The plain fact is that he went where and when the money was to be made.

15. BB, vol. 5, p. 133.

Bülow in London, ca. February 1874. A photograph by
Elliot & Fry.

Business virtuoso who almost always showed good humour'. Perhaps the
highest accolade Bülow accorded Dolby came at the beginning of the
second tour when he exclaimed, 'I cannot do without him'.[16] Within a
few months all that changed when Bülow discovered that Dolby had been
systematically cheating him of some of the receipts. He called him a
Betrüger—a swindler—and considered launching a lawsuit for the recovery of his lost fees. Eventually, he thought better of it, fearing that a
threatened countersuit by Dolby for defamation of character might lead
to several months of litigation, lawyers' fees, and further wear and tear
on his already fretted nerves. He became philosophical about what had
happened. 'I have always considered money losses as reparable', was his
laconic dismissal of this unfortunate affair.[17] Before leaving London,
Bülow visited the studios of Elliot and Fry, in Baker Street, and had his

16. Ibid., p. 217.
17. BNB, p. 501.

photograph taken. The image reveals little of his autobiography as we know it to have been at that time. Beneath the calm exterior that gazes back at us, there raged a boiling caldron of discontent.

III

Out of pocket, and out of humour, Bülow left England in mid-February 1874, and without pausing for rest he embarked on a gruelling tour of eastern Europe. His itinerary took him through Warsaw, Vilnius, Viborg, Riga, St. Petersburg, Moscow, Kharkov, Kiev, Odessa, and Kursk. This difficult journey was arranged at the very last minute in order to replace one that had already been planned for Scandinavia but had fallen through because of the unexpected marriage of Marie Monbelli, a hugely popular singer at Covent Garden, with whom Bülow had agreed to share some of the concerts. In quiet desperation Bülow had handed over to Carl Bechstein the task of setting up a totally different series of concerts in eastern Europe. It was a logical solution, because Bechstein now had a network of agents spread across Poland, Russia, and Ukraine, whose primary task was to sell his pianos but who could equally well be used to arrange local concerts. Bechstein, in the finest traditions of the executive businessman, delegated the job to one Hermann Grossmann, his leading representative in Warsaw. Not to be outdone, Grossmann in turn delegated it to a Polish surrogate named 'Stanislaus'. It was a fragile chain of command, and the weakest link snapped. 'Stanislaus' decided to charge Bülow a usurious commission of 25 percent on the gross takings for doing nothing more than creating a series of blunders at every touch and turn of the tour—until Bülow fired him. In order to avoid further trouble from 'Saint Stanislaus', as Bülow dubbed him, the pianist bought him off, and abandoned this 'colossal Assinski-Dishclothiski'[18] in Vilnius, Lithuania.

Although the weather was foul, and the roads were clogged with snow, Bechstein had somehow transported a number of his best instruments through Poland and Russia, there to await the itinerant pianist's arrival. It was a commendable logistical achievement, and Bülow's letters to Bechstein tell of his delight with, and occasional disdain for, the mechanisms that greeted him. As usual with Bülow, it was the action, the repetition, the colour, and the nuances of touch, that were important, and when he could not find these qualities in the keyboard he complained. The instrument at Vilnius was not at all to his liking, and he was forthright in his condemnation:

18. 'Einen kolossiven Eselinski-Waschlapski' (ibid., p. 351).

I am quite unhappy. At this price the ease in repetition is far too dearly bought. There is nothing left under one's fingers; all the nuances of touch, colour, and shading have gone to the devil, and there is a complete lack of elasticity and impetus—in fact, it is now a mechanism for consumptive flapper virtuosi. The Warsaw pianoforte was uninspiring enough, but this one reduced me to despair last night. . . . For heaven's sake, do not send this unlucky No. 6,678 to Petersburg![19]

There were times when Bechstein's patience must have been taxed by Bülow's intemperate remarks. The piano maker went to enormous trouble to provide only the best instruments, and despatch them across barren terrain hundreds of miles from Berlin, only to be rewarded with a scathing review immediately after the concert:

Reval
March 1/13, 1874
A number of passages refuse to sound on your instruments as on those of your bad imitator Blüthner. I cannot discover the wrong principle that is at the bottom of it because I have unfortunately never had time to teach myself the laws of construction, nor did I ever find anyone to instruct me. I will gladly take the trouble, however, if you are agreeable, to write out a dozen or so of the principal passages in my repertoire which simply cannot be played on your grands, particularly the overstrung ones, or at least in accordance with the spirit of the composer.[20]

It is a pity that the 'dozen or so principal passages' that Bülow found unplayable on the Bechsteins of the 1870s have not come down to us. We could have learned much about Bechstein's instruments, to say nothing of Bülow's playing. Bechstein understood that Bülow was telling him something important, because he went on experimenting and his pianos went on improving. Even the impossibly demanding Bülow was occasionally satisfied, and when he wrote a thank-you note Bechstein knew that he meant it. The instrument on which Bülow played in Odessa, and which he identified simply as 'No. 6,645', was selected for special praise. 'It was to my mind by far the best of yours that I ever played on. Certainly it is far finer than 6,677 and 6,717, the two which were manufactured for me'.[21]

19. Ibid., pp. 348–349.
20. Ibid., p. 346.
21. Ibid., p. 357.

'To the most dangerous, to the most charming of his
rivals', Bülow's inscription for Anna Essipova.

There must have been an outbreak of joy among the workers on the
Berlin factory floor when Bechstein passed the word down the line, 'Bülow
is satisfied!'

By the middle of March, Bülow was in St. Petersburg where he encountered the twenty-three-year-old pianist Anna Essipova, a pupil (and later
the wife) of the renowned pedagogue Theodor Leschetitzsky. Charmed
both by her looks and her playing, Bülow inscribed for her a copy of his
recent London photograph, with the words, 'to the most dangerous, to
the most charming of his rivals, Hans von Bülow'.[22] Whatever the positive impressions of her playing at that time, he was soon to change his

22. It is dated in the Old and the New Style, 'St. Petersburg, March 10/22, '74'. The original photograph is located in BC, Box 1.

opinion, and later made it known that despite the polish of her salon pieces, she simply did not know how to play Beethoven. With his incorrigible habit of creating puns on people's names, Bülow went on to distort hers to 'Essigtopf'—German for vinegar-bottle—a joke taken up by the Weimar circle.

The Russian leg of the tour nearly ended prematurely when Bülow, still in St. Petersburg, discovered that both his name and his concerts were being used without his knowledge to sell the various instruments on which he played. He objected to being used as a 'commercial traveller', as he put it. The problem appeared to have originated with Grossmann who saw nothing wrong with telling prospective customers that any instrument on which Bülow played had been 'endorsed' by the famous pianist. On March 23, Bülow sent an agitated telegramme to Bechstein, bitterly complaining that his integrity had been compromised. That same day Bechstein in turn sent one to Grossman:

> *To Hermann Grossmann, Warsaw.*
> Bülow beside himself. Talks of imputations which stamp him as a commercial traveller. How can this have happened? Please put it right at once. Bülow's interests must be paramount. Your interpretation in today's letter is incorrect.
> Bechstein.[23]

Bülow eventually calmed down, but the incident put a strain on his relations with Bechstein that eased but slowly.

The physical hardships that Bülow endured as he crossed the frozen Russian landscape are difficult to imagine today. From St. Petersburg he travelled via Moscow and Kharkov all the way down to Odessa in Ukraine, a journey of more than a thousand miles. He travelled by train, mainly at night, and he passed the time by silently committing some unfamiliar scores to memory in readiness for his next concerts—Balakirev and Tchaikovsky among them. The return journey from Odessa to Moscow was a bone-crushing experience. It lasted for sixty-four hours.

In Moscow, Bülow was reunited with his old friend and fellow Liszt student Karl Klindworth, in whose 'consoling society' he relaxed for much of Russian Holy Week. Klindworth had lived in Moscow since 1868, having been appointed professor of piano at the newly opened Moscow Conservatory by its director Nikolay Rubinstein. Ever since his arrival in the city, Klindworth had been deeply involved in preparing for Wagner the official piano reduction of *The Ring* for use during rehearsals for the forth-coming world premier in Bayreuth. He had just brought his transcription of *Götterdämmerung* to completion, and played it through for an entranced Bülow. As the whole world of music knows, Klindworth had been famously obliged to make a second version of Act II, because the Russian post office had sent the first one by mistake not to Bayreuth, but to Beirut in the Middle East. Klindworth had also embarked on his celebrated edition of the *Complete Works of Chopin*,[24] a project that likewise aroused Bülow's admiration. The two pianists had so much in common—Liszt, Wagner, their student days together in Weimar, and their circle of friends in London—that when the time of parting came Bülow sincerely regretted having to say farewell to this best of colleagues.

His journey home brought him back through Warsaw, where he experienced what he called 'an unspeakable tragedy'. Countess Marie von Mouchanoff-Kalergis, who had tended Carl Tausig as the Polish pianist lay dying in a Leipzig hospital nearly four years earlier, was now herself at the point of death. She was suffering from cancer of the stomach, and the doctors could do little to relieve her excruciating condition. Marie was a gifted pianist who had in earlier years received piano lessons from Chopin, who in turn had found her playing 'truly admirable'. Liszt was still more generous in his praise and remarked that her unique interpretations were unforgettable.[25] Her avid pursuit of culture had led her to travel widely, she became a fervent supporter of both Liszt and Wagner, and was a frequent visitor to Weimar. Her brilliant salon in Baden-Baden had attracted leading intellectuals, and her love affairs with a string of celebrities had become so notorious that Heine once described her as 'a Pantheon in which so many great men lie buried'. Bülow sat by her bedside for awhile, and then, in a touching gesture, he went into an adjoining room and played Chopin for her as she lay dying.[26] It was a fitting farewell for this beautiful and talented woman.

24. Klindworth's six-volume edition of Chopin's music appeared during the period 1873–1876, and did yeoman's service up to World War II and beyond.

25. LLF, p. 150.

26. BB, vol. 5, p. 173. Bülow's observation that Marie suffered from cancer of the stomach may well be correct, although it is at odds with other accounts of her illness, which have her suffering from cancer of the leg.

A niece of the powerful Russian chancellor Count Nesselrode, Marie Kalergis, was born and reared in Warsaw. She identified with Polish causes and was active in political affairs. She once made the bold declaration, 'I believe in three infallibilities: in the Church, the Pope; in politics, Bismarck; in art, Wagner' (LLF, p. 145). Whatever Bülow may have thought of the first assertion, he certainly approved of the other two. Marie's boundless admiration for Wagner's music had prompted her to send the impecunious composer a generous gift of 10,000 francs when he was at his lowest ebb in Paris, after the ignominious failure there of *Tannhäuser*, in 1860. That gesture had drawn Bülow to Marie as had few other things. But

IV

Bülow passed quickly through Berlin, where he notably failed to call on Bechstein, who was still smarting from the pianist's telegrammes and his disparaging depiction of himself as a 'Bechstein travelling salesman'. He continued on to Munich, reaching Milan in mid-May. He had been on the road for nearly nine months.

His arrival in Milan coincided with the first performance of Verdi's *Requiem Mass,* which was conducted by the composer himself on May 22, 1874 in St. Mark's Church, Milan. Composed in memory of the Italian revolutionary politician and writer Giuseppe Mazzini, who had died on May 22 just two years earlier, this performance of the *Requiem* had attracted widespread attention. Mazzini was a national icon; the unification of Italy, for which he had fought his entire political life, was now a reality. Many dignitaries packed the church, assembled to honour his memory. They had a victorious cause to celebrate, and a life to revere.

Bülow studied the vocal score of the *Requiem,* but he did not attend the performance. Instead he stayed in his hotel room, picked up his pen, and excoriated the work in an article for the *Allgemeine Zeitung*:

> Verdi, the omnipotent corruptor of artistic taste in Italy, hopes to sweep away the last remnants of Rossini's immortality which inconvenience him. . . . [His] latest opera in ecclesiastical garb will,

---

he was also drawn to the sad story of her life, his own tribulations having given him much in common with hers. When she was only sixteen she had married in haste a Greek diplomat, Johann Kalergis, but their personalities were so diverse that they separated the following year. Shortly after the teenage Marie gave birth to their daughter, Kalergis went off to a new posting in London, leaving her behind. During the decade that followed, Marie divided her time between her elegant home in Paris and her brilliant salon in Baden-Baden, the Villa Kalergis, where she entertained many of the crowned heads of Europe, and often played the piano for them. 'When I play, even kings are silent', she used to say (LLF, p. 149). After the death of Kalergis, in 1863, Marie embarked on a second attempt at matrimony, to a Russian colonel and police-chief in Warsaw, Count Serge von Mouchanoff. This marriage, too, in the dry comment of La Mara, was not made in heaven. Marie succumbed to melancholia and returned to Baden-Baden in search of emotional stability. Liszt was entranced with her when he first met her in Warsaw, during a concert tour in 1843. Thereafter, he called her 'the good fairy in my life', and dedicated to her his 'Petite valse favorite', and later his concert paraphrase 'Salve Maria de Jerusalem' from Verdi's *I Lombardi*. A year after her death Liszt arranged a memorial concert for her in Weimar's Tempelherrenhaus where, amongst other works, his First Elegy for cello and piano (subtitled 'Slumber Song in the Grave') was played in her memory and posthumously dedicated to her. As for Wagner, he offered Marie a kind of immortality that she could well have done without when he dedicated to her the second edition of his book *Das Judenthum in der Musik* (1869) in gratitude for her unwavering support of his work across the years.

after its first pretentious compliment to the memory of the celebrated poet, be handed over to La Scala for the next three evenings, and held up for the world's admiration. After that it is supposed to be accompanied by solo singers trained by [Verdi] for its coronation in Paris, the aesthetic Rome of the Italians. A hasty, stolen glance at this latest emanation from the composer of *Trovatore* and *Traviata*, took away any desire to attend this 'Festival'.[27]

This criticism was an error of judgement which Bülow lived to regret. Brahms observed, 'Bülow has blundered since this [work] could be done only by a genius'. As the *Requiem* made its way around the world the French made Verdi a Commander of the Legion of Honour, while in Austria he was given the Order of the Emperor Franz-Josef, and Bülow began to look foolish. Many years later, when the full majesty of Verdi's masterpiece had impressed itself on Bülow, he wrote to the composer and offered an apology. 'Illustrious Maestro, Deign to hear the confession of a contrite sinner!' Verdi was generous in his reply. 'There is no shadow or sin in you, and there is no need to talk of penitence'.[28] The Italian newspapers expressed outrage at Bülow's article, and he faced physical danger simply by staying in Milan. All thoughts of giving concerts there were abandoned, and he moved quickly to Florence.

Thoroughly exhausted after such an unremitting round of concerts, to say nothing of 'the Verdi affair', Bülow rested briefly in Florence, 'the city that once gave me back my health'.[29] He did not linger, however. In mid June he somehow summoned the energy to travel down to Rome in order to spend a few relaxing days in the company of Liszt, who was staying at the Villa d'Este, in nearby Tivoli. Bülow unburdened himself of many details of his recent European tours, and he undoubtedly described in detail the last hours of Liszt's good friend Countess Marie von Mouchanoff-Kalergis—a conversation that surely prompted Liszt to compose his 'Slumber Song in the Grave' in her memory. With his old mentor Bülow also discussed plans for his long-delayed trip to America, and sought Liszt's advice. He then headed for the watering-spa of Bad Salzungen where he rented an apartment and began an extended cure, taking salt baths, drinking the waters, and subjecting himself to daily massages. From Salzungen, Bülow wrote a conciliatory letter to Bechstein, attempting to heal the

27. Reproduced in BAS (part 2), p. 137. The observant reader will not fail to notice that the date of the first performance of the Verdi *Requiem*, May 22, was also Wagner's birthday. Bülow, ever alert to such coincidences, may well have allowed his pen to run away with him for no better reason than that Verdi was not Wagner.

28. BB, vol. 7, p. 387. For the full text of their correspondence, see pp. 429–30.

29. BNB, p. 361.

breach between them. In fact, Bechstein had already smoothed the way for a rapprochement by despatching two grand pianos to the spa, in order to make it easier for Bülow to practise in readiness for his autumn concerts. It was a complete and welcome surprise for the pianist. Alas, neither he nor Bechstein had reckoned with the staircase leading to his studio on the upper floor, and the movers, in Bülow's words, 'had to smuggle it through the window of another flat on the garden side of the building'—a major inconvenience for him. As for the second piano, it was handed over to an English pupil on the ground floor who had followed him all the way from Liverpool, temporarily abandoning her husband and children, to have a course of lessons from him. 'That is quite respectable, no?' Bülow asked a doubtless bemused Bechstein. 'I will guarantee that she does not ruin your pianoforte. In the case of this one I managed things better. Its measurements were taken into account before engaging rooms. . . . It stands on the ground floor'.[30]

The name of this twenty-eight-year-old English pupil was Mrs. Elizabeth Beesley, whom Bülow had met in Liverpool earlier in the year. She remains an intriguing figure in the Bülow chronicles. He thought highly of her piano playing, and found her enthusiasm for music 'doubly remarkable in a Briton'.[31] Mrs. Beesley soon took charge of Bülow's domestic affairs, assuming the duties of his housekeeper in Bad Salzungen, a situation he evidently welcomed. When Bülow resumed his tours of England, in October 1874, he began to promote Elizabeth Beesley with zeal, describing her as the best English female pianist of her generation—Agnes Zimmermann and Arabella Goddard notwithstanding. In January 1875, for example, she appeared with him in an orchestral concert at St. George's Hall, Liverpool, performing Beethoven's *Emperor* Concerto; a few months later, Bülow managed to procure an important London engagement for her at one of his concerts in London with the New Philharmonic Orchestra (May 8), in which she distinguished herself still further in performances of Liszt's E-flat major Concerto and Bach's Concerto in C minor for two pianos, with Bülow himself presiding at the second piano.[32] After Bülow suffered a minor stroke, in January 1875 (a crisis to which we will return), Elizabeth Beesley travelled with him on some of his journeys across Britain, acting as his caregiver. In one letter, Bülow

---

30. Ibid., p. 363.
31. Elizabeth Beesley was the daughter of Thomas Edward Spinney, the Salisbury Cathedral organist, and before meeting Bülow she had been a pupil of Julius Benedict and Sterndale Bennett. She herself was soon to become organist at St. Paul's, Salisbury, and of Banbury Parish Church. Elizabeth was married to a pharmacologist, and we surmise that this gave her some knowledge of palliative care.
32. BB, vol. 5, p. 268.

wrote that she performed 'the most touching services of a sister of charity; without her my condition would have become terribly aggravated'.[33]

V

Some colourful details of Bülow's daily life in Bad Salzungen have been preserved for us by an unexpected witness. In early July, the twenty-one-year-old pianist Laura Kahrer arrived on Bülow's doorstep, accompanied by her domestic servant and chaperone Fräulein Schulz. Laura Kahrer was an advanced player who had already studied with both Liszt and Henselt. Having heard that Bülow was 'taking the waters' in her neighbourhood, she turned up and asked for lessons. Normally Bülow would not have entertained such a notion, but he had already met Kahrer, and was acquainted with her fiancé, the violinist Eduard Rappoldi, who played in the Joachim String Quartet. He was in any case already giving lessons to Elizabeth Beesley, so he accepted Laura Kahrer as well. The reminiscences that Laura later recorded of her daily encounters with Bülow throw much light on his unsettled frame of mind.[34] Laura scarcely had time to introduce Fräulein Schulz before Bülow launched into a litany of complaints about Salzungen. He was not happy with the place, it lacked comfort, the food was awful, the summer heat was frightful, etc. He went on to tell his visitors that his nerves were shattered and he had been obliged to start a regime of mineral baths. After a sufficiently long pause, which allowed his unhappiness with the world in general to descend over the room like a blanket and stifle all reasonable conversation, he turned to Laura, assured himself that she had an apartment and a piano, and then asked her, 'What do you wish to study? Do you play Beethoven's op. 106 (the *Hammerklavier*), and the organ fugues of Bach in the Liszt transcriptions?' Laura confessed that she did not know these pieces, so Bülow went on, 'You must begin at once with the most difficult things . . . always the greatest!' That was a tall order, and Laura did her best. The content of the lessons need not detain us here, however.[35] Of more immediate concern are Laura's observations about Bülow's physical health and the manner in which it affected his outlook on the world.

On one occasion he was dining with Laura Kahrer, Fräulein Schulz, and Elizabeth Beesley. He railed once more against Salzungen and declared that after his course of baths was finished he was going over to the nearby resort of Bad Liebenstein, 'in order to get away from this nest'. Evidently he managed only to consume the soup, for when he saw the eels coming

---

33. Ibid., pp. 283–284.
34. Published in R-KE, pp. 305–318.
35. They are touched on in the chapter 'Bülow the Pedagogue'. See especially pp. 337–45.

(the next course on the menu) he got up, threw a thaler onto the table, and walked away with the remark, 'Please pay my bill. I have to eat somewhere else—I'm sorry'.[36]

On August 12 Bülow fulfilled his threat and moved to Bad Liebenstein, which had superior hydropathics and specialized in cold baths. 'Here at least one can buy a tie or an umbrella', he joked, as if to justify the upheaval. He rented the same villa that Rubinstein had occupied a few years earlier, a connection that failed to bring him pleasure because he fell ill almost at once and had to take to his bed for two or three days. From there he checked into the Müller Hotel, which at least offered him room service, while continuing to give sporadic lessons both to Laura Kahrer and Elizabeth Beesley. When Laura turned up for what proved to be her last lesson with Bülow, she found him in a towering rage. He had been practising Chopin's *Allegro de Concert,* and kept breaking down, possibly as a result of some muscular problems in his right hand. He became so frustrated that he flung the music against the wall with force and the volume split into two. That same morning, according to Laura, Bülow had also destroyed two chairs in his apartment. And the cause of these explosions? It was the memory of his wedding anniversary (August 18) that had disturbed him, and for several days had given him no peace. On the eve of that anniversary, in fact, his nerves were in such a poor state that his doctor had forbidden him to practise, recommending that he rest instead.[37] From Bad Liebenstein he wrote to his Munich friends Dr. and Frau von Welz, 'In hindsight I have never spent such a disastrous summer, one so totally wasteful and regrettable. The Salzungen cure—absolutely useless'.[38]

Bülow's dog days had meanwhile been enlivened by a long correspondence with Bernard Ullman, the enterprising manager whose siren song of a great tour of America, with its promise of gold and treasure, was beginning to sound increasingly attractive to Bülow. Ullman had been recommended to Bülow by Liszt, two or three years earlier. Following the

36. R-KE, p. 314.

37. It was behaviour such as this that stoked rumours that Bülow was mentally unstable. With the benefit of hindsight, it could equally well be argued that his behaviour was perfectly normal. Consider the predicament in which he found himself. He was preparing for his great tour of America next season, and his piano practising was adversely affected by serious problems with his right hand—eventually diagnosed as a mild stroke. His promise to Cosima to raise money for the upkeep of his children was now a millstone around his neck, and he faced the prospect of a financial disaster-in-the-making. Under the weight of such stress, who would not break a couple of chairs?

38. BB, vol. 5, p. 207.

rupture with his English agent, George Dolby, Bülow had begun to look upon Ullman with favour, as someone who might actually offer him a swift salvation from a life of bondage. Bülow's main concern, then and later, was to make as much money in the shortest time possible, in order (as he put it to Ullman) to withdraw from the 'cretinizing life of a virtuoso'.[39] In the weeks and months ahead, Ullman and Bülow sparred constantly over the American contract until the details were in place and Bülow had a document to which he could attach his signature. We shall have more to say about Ullman, because during the next year or two he became the chief architect of Bülow's career. Meanwhile, it was London that once more beckoned, and Bülow finally arrived there during the first week of October 1874.

VI

As on his earlier stay, Bülow resided at 27 Duke Street. He appeared at St. James's Hall and the Crystal Palace, and made various forays into the provinces, playing in Plymouth, Torquay, and Shrewsbury. More important, he went up to Glasgow and Edinburgh again. These preliminary contacts with Scotland were to have consequences for Bülow's later career.

Bülow's arrival in Glasgow, in January 1875, came at an opportune time for the Scots, for it coincided with some ongoing discussions on the part of the board of directors of the Glasgow Choral Union. These gentlemen were eager to establish a resident orchestra which would provide a series of subscription concerts not only for the increasingly sophisticated citizens of Glasgow, but for those of Edinburgh as well. Already an ensemble of fifty players had been formed for the first season, 1874–1875, and Henry Lambeth had been appointed as the orchestra's first conductor, 'at a fee of three guineas a concert, and railway fares'.[40] Lambeth was an obvious choice for this task, because he was already the conductor of the Choral Union itself, and had a local following. The happy idea of engaging Bülow to conduct one of the orchestral concerts had come from a certain Mr. MacKay, who had organized Bülow's solo recitals in Glasgow and Edinburgh, and had been angling to have him appear as a conductor as well.[41]

---

39. Ibid., p. 288.

40. CEH, vol. 5, p. 10. The history of the founding of Glasgow's first symphony orchestra, the predecessor of today's Royal Scottish National Orchestra, is traced in some detail in A. M. Henderson's 'Musical Memories', pp. 113–133.

41. Among the piano recitals that Bülow gave in Scotland during his extended tour of Britain, the one he presented in Glasgow on March 4, 1875, in the old Trades Hall, was of more than passing interest. Sitting in the audience was the seven-year-old Frederic Lamond with his older brother David. One of the main works in the programme was Beethoven's

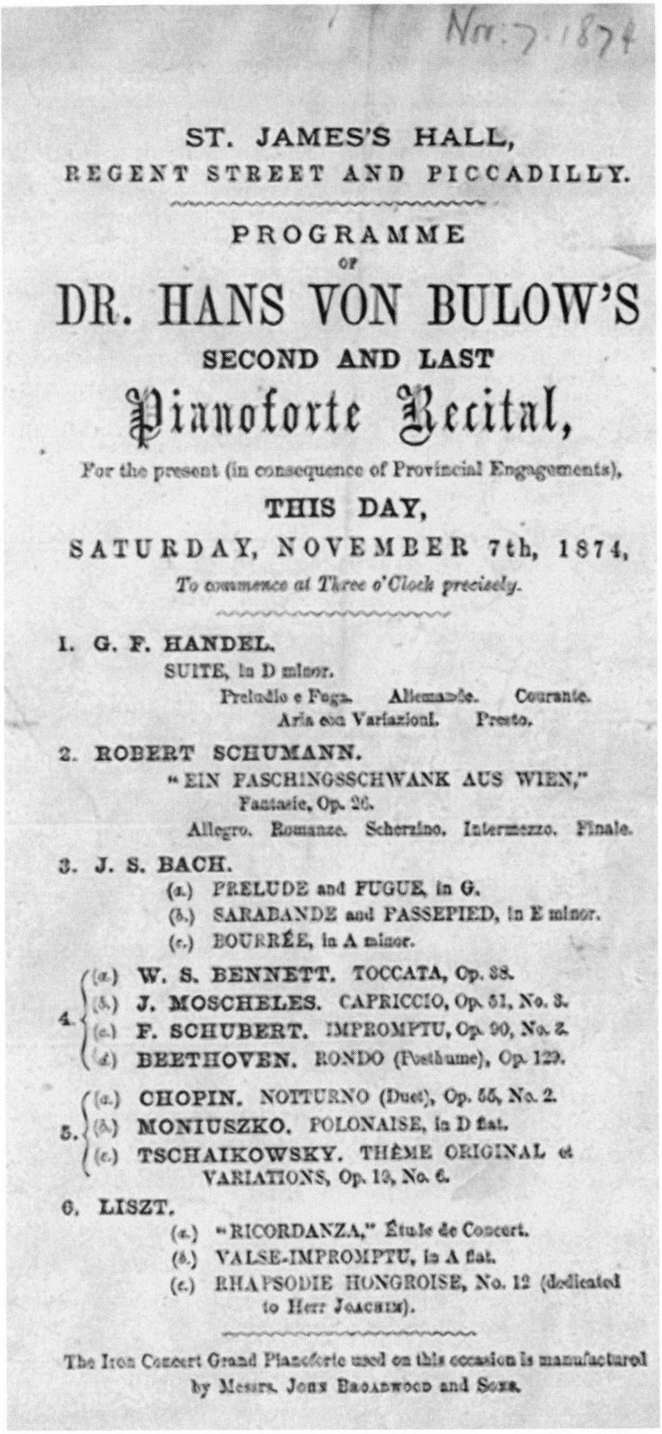

Nov: 7. 1874

ST. JAMES'S HALL,
REGENT STREET AND PICCADILLY.

PROGRAMME
OF
DR. HANS VON BULOW'S
SECOND AND LAST
Pianoforte Recital,
For the present (in consequence of Provincial Engagements),
THIS DAY,
SATURDAY, NOVEMBER 7th, 1874,
To commence at Three o'Clock precisely.

1. G. F. HANDEL.
SUITE, in D minor.
Preludio e Fuga. Allemande. Courante.
Aria con Variazioni. Presto.

2. ROBERT SCHUMANN.
"EIN FASCHINGSSCHWANK AUS WIEN,"
Fantasie, Op. 26.
Allegro. Romanze. Scherzino. Intermezzo. Finale.

3. J. S. BACH.
(a.) PRELUDE and FUGUE, in G.
(b.) SARABANDE and PASSEPIED, in E minor.
(c.) BOURRÉE, in A minor.

4. (a.) W. S. BENNETT. TOCCATA, Op. 38.
(b.) J. MOSCHELES. CAPRICCIO, Op. 51, No. 3.
(c.) F. SCHUBERT. IMPROMPTU, Op. 90, No. 2.
(d.) BEETHOVEN. RONDO (Posthume), Op. 129.

5. (a.) CHOPIN. NOTTURNO (Duet), Op. 55, No. 2.
(b.) MONIUSZKO. POLONAISE, in D flat.
(c.) TSCHAIKOWSKY. THÈME ORIGINAL et VARIATIONS, Op. 19, No. 6.

6. LISZT.
(a.) "RICORDANZA," Étude de Concert.
(b.) VALSE-IMPROMPTU, in A flat.
(c.) RHAPSODIE HONGROISE, No. 12 (dedicated to Herr Joachim).

The Iron Concert Grand Pianoforte used on this occasion is manufactured by Messrs. John Broadwood and Sons.

A Bülow recital in London's St. James's Hall, November 7, 1874.

When Bülow walked onto the platform of the Glasgow City Hall, on January 25, 1875, and faced the new ensemble, the concerts had already started to founder, and public disaffection with Lambeth was expressing itself through the box office. Bülow's concert that evening changed everything. The unpublished archives of the Choral Union, scrupulously annotated and preserved by one of its later secretaries, Robert Craig, tell their own vivid story:

> It was unanimously agreed he [von Bülow] gave the finest concert ever given in Glasgow during the present generation. The orchestra has the ability to do well when it chooses, but it needs proper drilling. . . . The orchestra were whipped up during his short stay with them. There was solidity of tone, brilliant colouring which flowed from the care and attention all were making. . . .[42]

The programme was as follows:

WEBER	Overture to *Euryanthe*
BEETHOVEN	Concerto no. 5, in E-flat major (*Emperor*), op. 73 (soloist—Hans von Bülow)[43]
SCHUMANN	Symphony no. 1, in B-flat major (*Spring*), op. 38
WAGNER	Overture to *Tannhäuser*
	Huldigungsmarsch
LISZT	Fantasie on Hungarian Folk-themes (soloist—Hans von Bülow)
WAGNER	Kaisermarsch

As we peruse Robert Craig's narrative, some graphic details come tumbling from the pages. We learn that 'the glowing reports in the Press on the morning following the Von Bülow concert stung Mr. Lambeth so severely that he immediately sent a letter to the President resigning his position as Conductor of the Choral Union'. By this time Bülow was on his way back to London, blissfully unaware of the wreckage that he was leaving in his wake. And of wreckage there was no shortage in the weeks that followed. Craig was merely paraphrasing what the Scottish press was saying

---

Appassionata Sonata. This was an augury of things to come. Lamond later became a Bülow pupil and one of the notable Beethoven interpreters of his time.

42. CEH, vol. 5, pp. 38–39.

43. The conductor for the Beethoven Concerto and the Liszt Fantasie was the English violinist John Carrodus, who had been principal violinist of the Covent Garden Orchestra, and was presently the leader of the resident orchestra.

quite brazenly. In its issue of January 26, the *Glasgow Herald* reported that 'it may be said that last night's concert was the grandest ever given in Glasgow during the present generation'.[44] Lambeth, goaded by such comparisons, turned up at the next meeting of the directors in the company of his solicitor. The Committee took fright at his strongly worded letter of resignation, which held out the prospect not only of losing the conductor of their orchestral concerts but of their Choral Union as well; at the same time the committee remained liable for the rest of Lambeth's salary and his legal expenses. With a cunning and guile rarely shown by the boards of directors of musical societies, the one in Glasgow suggested to Lambeth how he might divide and rule, and rescue them all. They persuaded the ruffled conductor to hand in a milder letter, and instructed him to write, 'The "Orchestral Concerts" being now over, I cannot be exposed to insult in connection with them',[45] and then go on to add the subtle plea that he be allowed to keep the choir if he agreed to relinquish the orchestra. The request was granted, honour was restored, and as a concession to common sense Lambeth even agreed to see the orchestral concerts through to the end of the season. This was doubtless made more pleasant for him by a supportive message he received from the entire orchestra, which expressed its complete confidence in him 'as a musician and a gentleman'. The success of Bülow's concert laid the groundwork for his engagement as conductor of the Glasgow Choral Union during the 1877/1878 season.

VII

Back in London, Bülow was invited to conduct another of the 'Walter Bache Annual Concerts', on February 25. The ambitious programme was typical of Bache's single-minded mission to bring Liszt and Wagner to the attention of the British public:

44. The *Glasgow Herald* took the unprecedented step of sending its chief music critic, Thomas Logan Stillie, to cover not only the concert, but three arduous rehearsals leading up to it, which began on Saturday, January 23.

> On Saturday, Dr. Hans von Bülow conducted two long and careful rehearsals with the full orchestra for tonight's concert. We never attended a more painstaking and thorough rehearsal. The conductor and every member of the orchestra were alike unsparing in their efforts to get the various pieces played in an exceptional style. In this they were completely successful.
>
> Another complete rehearsal is to take place this forenoon. We understand that Dr. Bülow expressed himself in terms of high admiration regarding the abilities of the orchestra. At tonight's concert, besides conducting Weber's Overture *Euryanthe*, Schumann's Symphony no. 1, and Wagner's three compositions, Dr. von Bülow will play Beethoven's Piano Concerto in E-flat, opus 73 and *Fantasia on Hungarian Melodies*. The orchestra to these will be conducted by Mr. Carrodus (*Glasgow Herald*, issue of January 25, 1875).

45. CEH, p. 49.

ST. JAMES'S HALL
Mr.
WALTER BACHE'S
Eleventh
ANNUAL CONCERT
Thursday Evening, February 25, 1875
Orchestra of sixty-eight performers.
Choir of one hundred and sixty voices.
Conductor
Dr. Hans von Bülow

LISZT	Symphonic Poem: *Festklänge*
SCHUBERT	'Gott in der Natur'—Hymn for female voices, op. 133 (orchestrated from Schubert's piano accompaniment by Hans von Bülow) 1st perf. in England.
LISZT	'Oh! quand je dors' soloist: Mr. Henry Guy (tenor)[46]
LISZT	Piano Concerto no. 2 in A major soloist: Walter Bache

Intermission

LISZT	Psalm Thirteen, for Tenor solo, Chorus and Orchestra
WEBER-LISZT	Polonaise Brillante, op. 72 soloist: Walter Bache
LISZT	'Soldatenlied', from Goethe's *Faust*
LISZT	'Chorus of Reapers', from Herder's *Prometheus*

[There will be an interval of three minutes, during which
all who do not wish to hear the last piece
are requested to leave the Hall]

WAGNER	Overture: *Tannhäuser*

NB. The doors will be Closed during the Performance of each Piece.

Bache lost more money than usual on this concert. So concerned was Bülow about the plight of his English colleague that he not only waived his fee, but generously insisted on contributing 50 pounds out of his own pocket as well.[47] In a revealing letter that Bache had written a couple of years earlier, when time was no longer on his side as far as the development of his solo career was concerned, he had observed:

---

46. The soloist was originally to have been W. H. Cummings. An insert into the programme informs the reader that 'Mr. W.H. Cummings is unfortunately suffering from a severe Cold, which prevents him singing this Evening'.

47. BBM, p. 240.

I must decide whether I shall sacrifice myself entirely to the production of Liszt's orchestral and choral works (which after all can
never be immortal as Bach, Beethoven and Wagner: here I feel that
Bülow is right). Or shall I make my own improvement the object
of my life, and not spend a third of my income in one evening?[48]

That telltale phrase 'here I feel that Bülow is right', offers a clue to the
change of heart that Bülow was undergoing with regards to his hitherto
unflinching support of Liszt. It suggests that the two acolytes were at this
moment engaged in some soul-searching about Liszt, and his place in the
wider scheme of things.

Bülow continued to feature Liszt's piano music in his solo recitals, however, and he was winning high praise from the British press. The qualified
judgements of the previous season were set aside as more and more listeners came to appreciate the subtle nuances revealed in his playing. *The
Monthly Musical Record* remarked that at his three 'Farewell Recitals', given
in St. James's Hall in April 1875, to mark his departure for America, the
large auditorium was not only comfortably filled, but contained a number of leading pianists who had 'sacrificed important engagements in
order to be present'. The journal proceeded to list this pianistic galaxy in
alphabetical order, ladies first. Among the women were Mlle Marie Krebs
(who had played the Schumann Concerto to great acclaim in London
a few days earlier) and Miss Agnes Zimmermann; among the men were
Bache, Beringer, Dannreuther, Hartvigson, Osborne, Schloesser, and Franklin Taylor.[49] These pianists were there for one reason. They had come to
hear the Swiss watchmaker at work, and marvel afresh at the jewelled precision of his playing. From others they could hear the notes at any time;
from Bülow they got the nuances. And in London, in 1875, that was magic.

The first of these 'farewell' recitals was devoted to Chopin. By modern
standards it was an impossibly long programme, containing about two-
and-a-half hours' music:

Sonata in B minor, op. 58
Variations brillantes, sur une Romance de Hérold, op. 12
Nocturne op. 37, no. 2 (by request)
Ballade no. 1, in G minor, op. 23

---

48. Ibid., p. 215. Bache was not yet affiliated with the Royal Academy of Music, and enjoyed no regular salary. When, finally, he was appointed to the piano faculty of the Academy,
on November 2, 1881, he was paid the princely sum of 10 shillings and sixpence per hour.
See the RAM Committee Minutes of that date, p. 247, presently housed in the Academy.

49. MMR, May 1, 1875, p. 73.

Prelude no. 13, op. 28
Impromptu in F-sharp major, op. 36 (by request)
Scherzo no. 4, in E major, op. 54
Three Waltzes, op. 34
Allegro de Concert, op. 46
Three Mazurkas, op. 9
Tarantella, op. 43
Berceuse, op. 57 (by request)
Polonaise in A-flat major ('the Heroic'), op. 53

This gargantuan concert was all the more impressive because a short time earlier, as many in the audience now learned from the press, Bülow had been taken ill and there had been a real possibility that he might have had to abandon his tour of America. Briefly, in January 1875 he had suffered what his 'completely ignorant' English doctors called an 'attack of gout', which had partially paralyzed his right hand and led to the cancellation of some concerts. Thoroughly alarmed at Bülow's condition, his sister Isidora arranged for him to return briefly to Germany and consult neurologists in Godesburg, near Bonn. They diagnosed his condition as an 'apoplectic stroke'. Bülow sought another opinion in Munich where his doctors told him that 'a blood vessel broke in the brain'.[50] This was the condition under which he laboured as he walked onto the platform of St. James's Hall and faced his audience. In the end it was a triumph of mind over matter, a common occurrence with Bülow. It will not escape attention that he ended his monumental programme with a performance of that most formidable of Chopin's Polonaises, the so-called 'Heroic'. It was an apt symbol of the struggle. And in case there were those in the audience who missed the point, Bülow produced an even greater *tour de force* at his second 'farewell recital' a few days later. He began with a smorgasbord of music by Bach, Schumann (the C major Fantasie), Raff, Brahms (the E-flat minor Scherzo), Rheinberger, and Beethoven (Sonata in A major, op. 101), after which most pianists would have been content to call it an evening and go off in pursuit of some relaxation. But this was Bülow, and there had to be a second half. It was devoted to Beethoven's monumental *Diabelli* Variations, 'a wondrous performance from memory', as one critic observed, which 'formed a worthy climax to his labours'.[51]

VIII

By the time that Bülow got back to Germany he was clearly very ill. His right hand continued to cause him problems and he also reported 'a par-

---

50. BNB, pp. 369 and 502.
51. MMR, May 1, 1875, p. 73.

tially paralyzed right side of the body and the left side of the face'.[52] These were potentially life-threatening symptoms which forced him to seek urgent medical attention. He also took a course of mineral baths to help, as he put it, the reabsorption of the blood into the limbs.

From a letter to Cosima, dated June 28, 1875, we also learn more about Bülow's money losses in England. He told her that he had been swindled out of the sum of 9,000 thalers, and that he had been 'a victim of the most scandalous deceptions'. The sad consequence was that he was able only to deposit the sum of 35,000 thalers with the banking firm of Frege in Leipzig, instead of an anticipated 45,000 thalers. There could be no question of retiring from the life of a wandering minstrel until he had redeemed the promise made to Cosima and his children. Reluctantly he revived his correspondence with the impresario Bernard Ullman, begun more than a year earlier, and resolved to seek his fortune in the New World without further delay.

IX

This is the place to answer the question: Who was Bernard Ullman? His name has fallen into obscurity, but he was one of the leading impresarios of his day. Born in Pest, in 1816, he had settled in the United States in the early 1840s, shrewdly sensing that money was to be made there in the burgeoning field of artist management. What Ullman lacked in musical training (in the early part of his career he had been a journalist) he more than made up for in business acumen. Fluent in English, German, French, and Spanish, he was soon masterminding the American tours of some of Europe's prominent artists, including Thalberg, Henri Herz, and Henriette Sontag, accompanying them across America and, in the case of Thalberg and Sontag, through Mexico as well. Neither rain nor sleet nor snow nor dark of night deterred him from bringing his concerts to the American heartland. Ullman himself sailed back and forth across the Atlantic so often in his quest to bring fresh talent to the New World that *Dwight's Journal* likened him to a shuttle 'weaving star after star of European theatre and concert notoriety into the great American web of Art and—speculation'.[53] It was the speculation that eventually got him into trouble, and after some disastrous forays into the world of opera in New York, he was forced to return to Europe and settle in Paris, in 1862, from where he continued to promote concerts. Liszt had come across Ullman in Pest, in November 1871, and admired the way in which this master showman had paraded a galaxy of performers before the Hungarian public with the

52. BNB, p. 512.
53. DWJ, 1856, 10:15.

aplomb of a ringmaster. He had amusingly described Ullman at that time as 'the most illustrious elephant-driver of artists from both the Old and the New World'.[54] Obviously attached to this image of a circus, Liszt went on to talk of the 'Ullman *ménagerie,* of which Mme Monbelli is the principal lioness and the Florentine Quartet and Sivori are the elephants'.[55] Beneath the spectacle of a circus, however, Liszt perceived Ullman's genius for business. With such a strong endorsement Bülow felt that he could safely place himself in Ullman's hands.

What Bülow constantly referred to as filthy lucre was the chief reason he pursued the career of a concert pianist, a career that had by now become anathema to him. That is why he pinned his hopes on Ullman, and why, in the summer of 1875, he signed an impressive contract. In exchange for giving 172 concerts in America in fewer than nine months, Ullman agreed to pay him the very large fee of 100,000 francs, plus all travel and hotel expenses, statistics which have found a niche in the annals of piano playing. During the tour of America, Bülow bound himself to give four or five recitals a week, including matinées, and traverse vast distances across the American continent.[56]

X

Toward the end of July, Bülow sought refuge at the summer resort of Ventnor, on the Isle of Wight, in order to find some necessary solitude and ready his concert fingers for America. Ventnor had lately become a retreat for the wealthy, known for its warm sea breezes, and its stately Victorian dwellings with access to the beach. His stay on the island was made more pleasurable for him by the arrival of a fine Chickering grand piano, sent from Boston at the express request of Ullman who, after months of negotiations, had secured an agreement with Frank Chickering to provide

54. LLB, vol. 6, p. 315.
55. WLLM, p. 31.
56. An entire chapter could be written on the protracted negotiations between Bülow and Ullman. One of Bülow's earliest letters to the impresario had begun with the unpromising sentence, 'Never in this world shall I agree to affix my signature at the end of such a contract. It would be better to work as a chorus director at the Augsburg Theatre. . . .' Evidently, Ullman had wanted Bülow to pay his own hotel and local travel expenses out of his fees, so the impresario had to be brought to heel. 'A contract like the one between Grau and Rubinstein I will never sign', said Bülow, referring to the tour of America that had been arranged for the Russian pianist by the agent Maurice Grau, three years earlier. By the end of the bruising battle, Bülow had not only wrested from Ullman a promise to receive his fee of 100,000 francs in gold coin (as opposed to paper currency) but had also been given a guarantee that all his travel and living expenses would be paid for as well. It was a handsome deal for Bülow, far better than the one that Rubinstein had signed with Grau; but Ullman also made money and eventually followed the pianist to America, not only to witness the triumphs, but to secure the profits.

pianos for Bülow's concerts in America, in exchange for the pianist's exclusive commitment to these instruments while he was in the New World. Bülow was delighted with the piano and told Ullman, 'I shall not be able to make so much noise on a Chickering as on a Steinway, but the tone is far more noble and distinguished, like those of Erard's'.[57] While in Ventnor he was visited by Walter Bache and his valiant pupil and caregiver Elizabeth Beesley, who wanted to accompany him to America. But as he put it, 'I cannot under any circumstances—for a thousand and one reasons—accept her offer and sacrifice'.[58] On July 29, after months of prevarication, Bülow finally picked up his pen and wrote the letter for which Ullman had been waiting. He was at last ready to embark on the great adventure of an Atlantic crossing.

57. MTR, November 18, 1875.
58. BB, vol. 5, p. 288.

The First Tour of America, 1875–1876

> . . . I must tell you how inconceivably glad I am to have crossed the ocean. The New World is to be preferred to the Old in every respect.
> —Bülow[1]

I

Before setting out on his long odyssey, Bülow drew up a will. He knew that he would be in North America for at least nine months, and he wanted to set his affairs in order before he left. His recent stroke in England had shaken him deeply, reminding him of his mortality. Most of his capital he had already transferred to Leipzig and deposited in the Frege bank under the care of his cousin Professor Woldemar Frege. The will itself was drafted in Munich during the summer of 1875 by Bülow's attorney, Dr. Jakob Gotthelf, and the disposition of his worldly goods gave Bülow some trouble. In a lengthy letter to Cosima[2] he outlined the main contents of the document, of which no original copy seems to have survived. There was a predictable division of money and personal property to the three daughters Daniela, Blandine, and Isolde (the last of whom he continued to call his own), including his library of rare books inherited from his father. Each daughter was to receive a capital sum of 56,250 francs on reaching her majority. He also bequeathed to each of them some valuable silver plate still in storage in Munich. Perhaps the most intriguing aspect of the will entailed 'a delicate, confidential mission', which he entrusted to Cosima's personal care. He told her that he proposed to leave a special gift of 5,000 francs to a person who was to remain unnamed in his will,

---

1. BNB, pp. 49–50.
2. Ibid., pp. 509–512. From a letter to his Munich friends the von Welz family, we gather that Bülow was tormenting himself over his will. He told them that he was notoriously ignorant of this branch of the law, had never seen a will in his life, and had not the faintest idea how to draw one up. 'I need to be instructed about every detail so as not to make a hash of it.' (BB, vol. 5, p. 271.)

someone who lived in a foreign country, and someone whom he was only prepared to identify after Cosima had given him a solemn undertaking that the money would reach its proper destination. This person, he went on, had been prepared to love him, but he had been forced to relinquish her affections because of the complications of his family life. He now asks Cosima for a simple 'yes' to his unusual request, and only after receiving it would he disclose the name of this young woman. Cosima, her interest thoroughly aroused, assured him that she would indeed carry out this confidential mission. Bülow then revealed that the person in question was Mlle Sophie Alexeievna de Poltovatzki who lived in Dobrokitovo, near Kursk in Russia.[3] He had evidently encountered Sophie on his Russian tour earlier in the year, when he passed through Kursk on April 17. That he had become enamoured of her was obvious, although the extent of their relationship remains unknown. This solitary mention of Sophie in his first will is all that we know of her. She never became a part of the official narrative of Bülow's life.

II

The American tour began in Boston, on Monday, October 18, 1875, after a very rough transatlantic crossing on the steamer *Parthia,* during which Bülow was seasick.[4] Immediately after his arrival in Boston, he locked himself away in his private quarters at 23 Beacon Street. The local newspapers reported that he practised for eight or nine hours a day—as well he might in view of the workload before him. The city's large Music Hall was packed for his American debut on October 18, not only with listeners from Boston itself but also from the outlying townships.[5] Even the New York newspapers sent reporters. We are told that Bülow walked onto the platform, a short, dapper figure, carrying a hat. This disconcerting appendage he proceeded to place under the piano. He also wore gloves which he ceremoniously removed before surveying the audience with his

3. Ibid., p. 512.
4. BB, vol. 5, p. 292. Bülow told his mother that from the moment he boarded the *Parthia* in Liverpool the crossing had been 'abominable' (BB, vol. 5, p. 277). Rather against his wishes Elizabeth Beesley and Bernard Ullman had accompanied him to the quayside in order to say farewell, but the strong gusts of rain and the howling winds had turned the solemn parting into a comedy. Nor did he find much sanctuary in his cabin. To add to the physical indignities brought on by the rolling vessel, Bülow found himself berthed in a cabin opposite one containing four German babies 'crying in Saxon'. It might have consoled him to know that when Rubinstein had made the crossing in the steamship *Cuba,* early in September 1872, the seas were so rough that the Russian pianist had confined himself to his cabin for the whole journey and suffered ten days of racking sickness, made worse because he could find no respite from the sound of the ship's engines and propeller blades boring into his brain.
5. Built in 1852, Boston's old Music Hall held 2,700 seats. The building still stands and is today known as the Orpheum Theatre.

usual aristocratic disdain (he called it 'exploring the local physiognomy').
After these preliminaries were over, he launched into a performance of
Beethoven's *Emperor* Concerto. The programme also contained a group
of Chopin pieces and concluded with a rendition of Liszt's 'Fantasie on
Hungarian Folk-themes'—a work dedicated to him, whose premier performance, we recall, he had given in Pest in 1853. This opening concert
was hugely successful and Bülow could not have been happier with the
press notices, although his relationship with the American newspapers
was to change as the tour unfolded. The *New York Times* accorded him a
position of preeminence among the pianists who had visited America
during the past fifteen years.[6] Bülow wrote to Ullman to thank him for
having 'morally forced me to cross the ocean'.[7] During the first few days
in Boston, Bülow gave four more concerts. But it was his appearance the
following week, on October 25, that has entered the history books. That
was the date on which he gave the world premier of Tchaikovsky's Piano
Concerto in B-flat minor, a work that the composer dedicated to him
in gratitude, after it had been famously rejected as 'unplayable' by its intended recipient, Nikolay Rubinstein. So popular was the Concerto that
Bülow was obliged to repeat the Finale, a fact that Tchaikovsky found astonishing.[8] After the intermission Bülow played Beethoven's *Moonlight*
Sonata, during which the lights of the Music Hall were lowered. These
Boston concerts were marred only by the fact that they were given with
a scratch orchestra of a mere thirty-five players. That would not have
been so bad had it not been for the incompetence of the conductor, the
German-born Carl Bergmann, who missed several rehearsals and put
Bülow in the position of having to fire him. Bülow replaced him with
Benjamin Lang, a former pupil of Liszt, and after the performance of the
Tchaikovsky Concerto he made a special point of directing the applause
toward Lang.

III

By the time Bülow got to New York, word of his problems with Bergmann
had reached the press. The large German population in Manhattan knew
all about Bülow's idiosyncrasies, and especially his habit of making negative comments about his fellow countrymen when he was abroad, and
they were waiting for him. His troubles started when he gave an interview
to the *New York Sun,* which was eager to learn why he had fired Bergmann

6. Issue of October 19, 1875. After praising his beauty of sound and the crystal clarity of
his textures, the *Times* goes on to tell us that Bülow was recalled to repeat both the Chopin
Waltz in A-flat major, op. 42, and the Prestissimo section of the Hungarian Fantasie, and he
received three curtain calls at the end of the concert.

7. BB, vol. 5, p. 292.

8. See Tchaikovsky's letter of thanks to Bülow, pp. 214–15.

so soon after making his acquaintance. Bülow obliged the *Sun* and its readers by denouncing Bergmann as incompetent. He went on to berate him for 'showing more interest in drinking beer' than in pursuing his duties as a conductor.[9] He explained that he had now hired as a replacement Leopold Damrosch, his trusted friend and colleague from the Weimar years. The interview was so outspoken that it created what *Harper's Magazine* called a 'hullabülow'. The German press gored him, calling him a great artist but a small man. That only made matters worse. Bülow went on to criticize the Germans in general as a beer-swilling crowd who drank until their brains were stupid, rendering them incapable of appreciating great music because they listened to everything through an alcoholic haze. This led to a further outcry and Bülow received the predictable crop of hostile letters.

Bülow had a further success with the Tchaikovsky Concerto in New York, where the finale had once again to be repeated. He wrote the composer a second letter bearing these good tidings. Tchaikovsky's reply is barely recalled today, which we quote in full:

Moscow 1/13 February 1876
Dear, Great Master!
I have just got back to Moscow after a short excursion to Switzerland, where I went on family business, and have found your kind letter of 13 January, in which you announce another American success that I owe to you. All my warmest thanks, dear protector of my muse, and let me express my joy on considering the enormous step forward that the propagation of my music has made, thanks to your protection.

Isn't it strange to think that between the two famous artists of our time, it is by you, who have known me only a short time, and not by Anton Rubinstein, who was moreover my master, that my music has found such a necessary and kind support. That Olympian God has never shown anything but sovereign contempt for my compositions, and I will tell you under the seal of the confessional that I have always been profoundly hurt by that. With regard to the Concerto, whose success you announced to me, let me tell you a little incident that will make you understand how great this contempt is. When, a few years ago, I approached the publisher Bessel of St. Petersburg, offering him that quartet whose success you announced to me, for publication free of charge, he

9. Issue of November 17, 1875, under the cheerful headline 'An Hour with Von Bülow: The Great Pianist's First Impression of America'.

went to Rubinstein to find out from him if that composition was worth his trouble. 'No,' my former teacher answered decisively, whereupon Bessel sent me a most decided and humiliating refusal. And the great artist has always behaved in this way with regard to my works. If I am telling you this, Monsieur, it is to make you understand the immense gratitude that I owe you, to you who were not my master and who are not even a compatriot.

Now that I own an entry card for the performance in Bayreuth, I nourish the fond hope of seeing you there and being able to repeat in person my gratitude to you. Meanwhile, let me wish you health, prosperity, and success in all your projects.
Your devoted and grateful admirer,
P. Tchaikovsky.[10]

This letter must have been music to Bülow's ears. It is not merely that Tchaikovsky is effusive in his thanks to Bülow, whom he calls 'dear protector of my muse'; the negative comments about 'that Olympian God' Anton Rubinstein would not have displeased him either, for they suggest that his archrival in the world of piano playing could not perceive musical mastery when it was placed before him. As for Tchaikovsky's innocent idea of meeting Bülow in Bayreuth for the forthcoming 1876 festival, it is clear that he had no idea of what he was proposing. The emotional maelstrom into which such a pilgrimage would have plunged Bülow was beyond contemplation, and their first meeting did not in fact take place until ten years later.

IV

The *New York Herald* infuriated Bülow when it described him as 'Liszt's son-in-law'. He had invested a lot of psychological capital in breaking away from the Liszt-Cosima-Wagner triangle, and was now his own man. Ullman had initially wanted to bill him in America as 'the pupil and son-in-law of Liszt', but Bülow had put up a fierce resistance. On December 28, 1875, he wrote the following reply to the *Herald:*

Allow me most humbly to decline the honour given me this morning by the musical critic of the *New York Herald* in calling me the son-in-law of Abbé Liszt, this honour belonging since 1870 exclusively to the composer of *Lohengrin,* Rich. Wagner Esq.[11]

10. BB, vol. 5, p. 297.
11. Ibid., p. 316. Written by Bülow in English, his letter goes on to disparage the newspaper's music critic by calling him an 'amusements reporter'. This was a pointed reference to the fact that commentary about music in the leading American newspapers, even about classical concerts, was habitually printed under the unfortunate headline of 'Amusements'.

Further aggravation was created when Bülow was tactlessly described by *The Music Trade Review* as Wagner's brother-in-law ('which is a new name for it'), the chimerical designation having arisen from the fact that both men had led Cosima to the altar. When challenged by a reader to explain what such a remark could possibly mean, the editor adroitly replied:

> We expect every day an unabridged Webster, and will try to find therein an expression which gives to a nicety the degree of relationship between a man, whose wife after being divorced from him marries again, and her new husband. Perhaps brother-in-law, or successor-in-law, would do.[12]

The controversies which always seemed to follow Bülow endeared him to the American press, which saw in him a story in its own right, quite detached from the artistic merits of his concerts. A good example of this was the little contretemps that blew up around the republication of Bülow's early piano piece "Marche Héroïque", intended as a kind of welcome to mark his arrival in the United States. The gesture was made by Charles Ditson, a prominent music publisher in Boston and New York with a large store on Broadway, who doubtless thought that it would flatter the vanity of the great virtuoso to be reminded of one of the fruits of his youth, while at the same time making a tidy profit for Mr. Ditson himself. The attractive title page ran:

MARCHE HÉROÏQUE
for piano
composed by
VON BÜLOW

Alas for poor Ditson, he did not know that Bülow had long since disowned the work and would never have authorized its republication. Moreover Ditson was in breach of copyright, because the legal owner was the firm of Schott in Mainz. A furious Bülow dashed off a letter of protest which

---

12. MTR, January 3, 1876, p. 6. The witty designation of Wagner as 'Bülow's successor-in-law' might well have provided Bülow with some private humour. He himself had furnished similar examples, to the amusement and sometimes the consternation of those in his circle. The previous year, he had attended a party in the house of Eduard Dannreuther in London, and was approached by a lady who wished to impress herself on him. She began the conversation with the question, 'Oh! Monsieur von Bülow, vous connaissez Monsieur Wagner, n'est-ce pas?' Dannreuther was aghast, and the drops of perspiration burst out on his forehead as he wondered what Bülow might say. Bülow made a low bow towards the lady, and, as if it were the most natural question in the world, replied, 'Mais oui, Madame, c'est le mari de ma femme' (SPD, p. 264).

was published in *The Music Trade Review* under the headline 'The Copyright Question', beneath which was printed an editorial insertion calculated to give Mr. Ditson heartburn: '[Bülow] accuses American Publishers
of Piracy'. Far from defending his "Marche Héroïque", Bülow described it
as 'a wretched piece', a remark which was tantamount to accusing Ditson
of lack of taste, in addition to everything else that he lacked. Bülow had
no compunction about sawing off dead branches, even if he himself happened to be sitting on one. He further pointed out that the piece was not
actually composed by him, that he had dashed it off in a great hurry
while making his debut in Hungary in 1853, and that it consisted of
themes drawn from Ferenc Erkel's *Hunyady László* (a popular opera in Pest
at that time), vital facts of which no mention was made on the new title
page obligingly provided by Ditson. Scenting another good story, *The
Music Trade Review* despatched a reporter to interview Ditson in his New
York office. Ditson lost no time in shifting the blame onto the firm of Peters, which had provided him with an original copy of the "Marche", but
had not informed him of its complicated legal background. Armed with
this revelation, our intrepid reporter went off in pursuit of Mr. J. L. Peters
himself, tracked him down in his office, and presented him with the
painful fact that his colleague Mr. Ditson had virtually accused him of engaging in unlawful activities. The texts of both interviews were printed
verbatim in dialogue form for the delectation of the reader and the certain embarrassment of both music publishers.[13]

13. Ibid., November 18, 1875, p. 14. The dialogue with Peters was particularly hilarious,
and a short extract is given here.

>   *Reporter:* Don't you think Von Bülow has a right to be angry at the way he has been
>   treated?
>   *Mr. Peters:* Not a bit! If the piece is bad, why did he write it?
>   *Reporter:* Yes, but the title was altered. The original did not state that it was 'composed' by
>   him.
>   *Mr. Peters:* I don't care about that. If he thinks he has been injured, why doesn't he appeal
>   to the government for redress, and not abuse the publishers and call us 'pirates'? We don't
>   make the laws.
>   *Reporter:* How can Von Bülow appeal to the government? What good would it do?
>   *Mr. Peters:* Now, understand me clearly. You probably think that I make money by reprint-
>   ing foreign authors' works and not paying them for doing so.
>   *Reporter:* Of course I do. Rumor says that you have made a great deal of money by doing
>   so, and are today one of the richest men in the trade.
>   *Mr. Peters:* Never mind about that . . .

And so on, leading to the absurd exchange:

>   *Mr. Peters:* 'What would you say if I told you that, although I do make money by printing
>   foreign works, I should make a great deal more if there were copyright laws?'
>   *Reporter:* 'I should say that "wonders never cease".'

Memories such as these would surely have been at play in Bülow's mind when, towards
the end of his American tour, he was asked by an interlocutor, 'Don't you agree that America
is a land of many liberties?' 'Indeed,' replied Bülow, 'and they have all been taken with me.'

V

A far more important controversy, and one that caused Bülow greater vexation, concerned his choice of pianos for the American concerts. Even before he had set foot in the New World, Bülow had been involved in discussions about the make of piano he would use for his concerts. Bechstein was unable to provide them, so Bernard Ullman had entered into protracted negotiations with both Steinway and Chickering to provide the quality instruments that Bülow demanded. The approach to Steinway fell through, but Frank Chickering stepped in with necessary guarantees, and, as we have seen, sent one of his grands to Bülow on the Isle of Wight. A storm blew up in the press on both sides of the Atlantic when it was reported that the American piano-makers Weber and Co. had offered Bülow 10,000 dollars to play their pianos but had been outbid both by Steinway and Chickering, which had offered him 20,000 dollars. Ullman published an indignant rebuttal, pointing out that no such offers had been made to him by any of these firms, and that Chickering was pleased to provide its pianos to Bülow on the basis of their merit alone.[14] Ullman did not endear himself to Steinway when he reminded everyone that the firm had paid 15,000 dollars to Leopold de Meyer and 20,000 dollars to Rubinstein in exchange for their agreements to promote Steinway pianos on their American tours. Ullman also grumbled that only Steinway artists were allowed to play in Steinway Hall, at that time the most favoured

14. Ullman's denial was reprinted from the London *Concordia* for the enjoyment of its American readers by *The Music Trade Review,* November 18, 1875, p. 15, under the headline 'The Contract between Von Bülow and the Chickerings'.

We get a hint of the poor relations that existed between Steinway and Ullman from an unpublished letter that Theodor Steinway had written to Bülow earlier in the year, in April 1875, when both men were in England. Having picked up news that Bülow had definitely decided to play on Chickering pianos during his forthcoming American tour, a disappointed Steinway told Bülow that 'Ullman's behaviour towards me in Paris was such that self-respect prohibited me from having business contact with this gentleman'. He went on to tell Bülow something of which the pianist almost certainly did not know, and that Ullman may have preferred Steinway not to disclose. 'It is another matter when my firm is dealing directly with an artist. We are glad to provide every benefit for him, but never in such a way that some impresario takes half'. After offering Bülow his personal admiration and friendship, Steinway ended his letter with this intriguing comment:

> I will go to New York via Southampton this summer in order to build a new concert grand which I have been working on for a year in theoretical models and calculations, strung with 70,000 pounds of tension and cast-iron frame. What a silly story for me; you the most important living artist will be in America and are by contract forbidden to play on such pianos. Well, another time. I am yours most sincerely,
> Th. Steinway
> Hotel Royal, London
> April 12, 1875.

See SLWA, box 262, folder 52, letter 9. From this letter we are left to conclude that it may have been Ullman himself who came between Bülow and Steinway, because of the hefty commission that he wished to siphon off into his own account.

venue for recitals in New York. From such crass commercialism Bülow always tried to distance himself. He was at first delighted with the Chickering pianos ('On other pianos, I have to play as the piano permits; on the Chickering I play just as I wish') but later started to quibble over their tone and their action. Nonetheless, this special relationship with Chickering laid the groundwork for Bülow's much-publicized concert in New York on November 15, 1875, when he inaugurated the newly built Chickering Hall, which stood on Fifth Avenue and 18th Street and represented Chickering's answer to Steinway Hall.

Built in six months at a cost of 175,000 dollars, Chickering Hall seated 1,500 people and was praised for its acoustics. When Bülow gave his first concert there, the interior decorations were still unfinished, a symptom of the haste with which the inauguration was arranged. The programme was devoted in its entirety to Beethoven. No expense had been spared to make the event a memorable one. Ullman had also engaged the services of Leopold Damrosch and his fledgling orchestra for the evening—an ensemble which, two years later, Damrosch metamorphosed into 'the New York Symphony Orchestra':

Overture: 'Consecration of the House', op. 124
Piano Concerto no. 4, in G major, op. 58
　(Cadenzas by Bülow)
　　　　　　　　Intermission
Sonata in F minor (*Appassionata*), op. 57
Variations in E-flat major (*Eroica*), op. 35
Overture: *Egmont,* op. 84

A detailed description of the evening was published in *The Music Trade Review,* which devoted three full columns to it.[15] Some keen insights were proffered, first into Bülow's approach to the keyboard, then to his style of playing, and finally to his rendering of Beethoven, which help us to round out our picture of the pianist as a platform personality:

Mr. von Bülow presents a soldier-like appearance, and we believe that in every sense he deserves to be looked upon in this light. He knows how to command as a leader, and, what is more difficult, how to obey as an interpreter.

He takes his seat rather far from the piano, puts his foot on the pedal, which he uses with wonderful rapidity and discretion, and places his hands upon the keyboard gracefully and perfectly bent,

15. MTR, November 18, 1875, pp. 15–16.

the knuckles being far over the keyboard. From the moment he touches the keys Bülow disappears, and nothing but the work, of which, as the interpreter, he becomes a part, remains.

The journal went on to produce what in the profession is euphemistically called 'a balanced review', mingling praise with censure in equal measure, often pausing to compare his playing with that of Liszt and Rubinstein, not always to Bülow's advantage. It was clear that the critic did not wholly admire Bülow's approach to Beethoven, the one composer with whom the pianist was now firmly associated. There were as well some autobiographical asides woven into the fabric of this anonymous essay, because the writer reveals that when he had heard Liszt himself play the *Appassionata* Sonata in Vienna, in the home of Tobias Haslinger, some thirty years earlier, he had stood immediately behind Liszt's chair and had been electrified. Liszt's performance had 'made us shiver and cry and held us spellbound', an effect lacking in Bülow's 'irreproachably correct' rendering just witnessed in Chickering Hall. The writer was almost certainly a pianist, because his article went on to reveal an uncommon interest in the technical aspects of piano playing:

Dr. von Bülow's mechanism is faultless, with few exceptions; his touch excessively even in all the fingers, and strong but not full; powerful from nervous exertion, not from actual strength; capable of a most charming pianissimo, which, though in some moments it reminded us of the lady who said, 'Mr. Liszt joue quelquefois si piano qu'on n'entend RIEN DU TOUT' ['Mr. Liszt sometimes plays so softly that one hears NOTHING AT ALL']; it has not the carrying energy of Liszt, not the great variety and tone-colouring of Rubinstein. The scales and shakes are of an unparalleled evenness; the shake is particularly pearly, and of an equality of both fingers rarely to be met with, though it has not the exceptional strength of Liszt's shake with the last two fingers, nor the impetus of that of Rubinstein. The same evenness, even to an astounding degree, prevails in his scales and passages in thirds. The octaves are not excessively rapid, and there are moments when their force is too much, we might say, too violently, pushed. The elasticity of the wrist is very remarkable, and enables Mr. von Bülow to play staccatos, particularly with the left hand, the like of which we have never heard on the piano; and in this instance, as well as in others, we admire as much the evenness in performance of both hands, when they have to execute the same passage together, as the thorough, we might say the counter-pointal, independence of one hand from the other.

The one sentence in the entire review which seems to sum up Bülow's significance as an interpreter was 'From the moment he touches the keys Bülow disappears, and nothing but the work . . . remains'. Selected for special praise was the Chickering piano—'the wonderful instrument which served Mr. von Bülow so faithfully, so obediently, so lovingly'.[16]

VI

Although he had been alerted by Ullman's public protest, Bülow was unprepared for the vigour with which the trade wars between Steinway and Chickering were pursued. Both companies insisted on displaying large proprietary signs next to their pianos, visible from all parts of the auditorium. In America it was a normal way of doing business. Bülow predictably objected to being used as a travelling salesman, and declared war on the signs. On one occasion he walked onto the platform and kicked the large advertisement off its stand and stamped on it. That was during a rehearsal for his Baltimore concert, on December 6. He had just arrived at the hall, made his way to the stage, and embraced the conductor Asger Hamerik, his old Danish pupil who had studied with him years earlier in Berlin, and was now the director of the Peabody Conservatory. We are told that 'this chaste but tender dalliance lasted but a moment', before it was terminated by an explosive outburst as Bülow observed a large sign hanging from the piano bearing the name of Chickering in gilt letters. He flung it downward on the stage and called out to an acquaintance in the audience, 'That jackass has sent a sign-board down with the piano'. He then lapsed into German, in which the words *Lump* and *Schweinhund* were clearly audible, appellations that referred to Frank Chickering. As the rehearsal proceeded, Bülow became ever more rattled; he was not yet done with the sign. During one of the orchestral episodes he tiptoed around the players, picked up the sign, and threw it out of sight where it landed beneath the tail end of the piano. Not yet satisfied, he took advantage of another interlude, walked up to the sign, and kicked it. As the reporter of the *Baltimore Bulletin* phrased it, 'thus was he appeased with blood'.[17] It was doubtless to put a stop to such antics that Chickering had his name painted on the side of his instruments. That did not deter Bülow, however. His audience was once astonished to see him pause in mid-concert, take out a jackknife, and scrape the name 'Chickering' off the instrument itself. At another concert in New York, on December 31, 1875, Bülow

16. Bülow had hardly left the building before the New York publisher Schuberth & Co., shrewdly anticipating the pianist's return to the same platform in a few weeks' time, and a chance to make money, designed a series of albums of piano music titled *Echoes from Chickering Hall*. There were fourteen such 'echoes' altogether, of music by Bach, Beethoven, Handel, Scarlatti, and others, 'as interpreted and played by Dr. Hans von Bülow'.

17. MTR, December 18, 1875, p. 45.

paused after the first piece and found himself on the platform minus his knife. He left the stage while two men changed the piano to 'a nameless one'.[18]

Bülow also felt constrained to give his American audiences lessons in concert decorum whenever he felt that their unsophisticated behaviour warranted it. This was especially true in the Midwest, which had little or no experience of classical piano recitals. He once berated a group of workers in the steel town of Steubenville, Ohio, who had kept their hats on during a performance of Wagner's 'Spinning Song', in Liszt's transcription. The hats were hastily removed, respect for great music restored. On another occasion he stopped in mid-performance, put on his glasses, and glared at a party of latecomers walking across the hall in squeaky shoes. Not until their perambulations had ceased did he resume playing.[19] It was perhaps more in sorrow than in anger that he once quipped, 'The further West you go, the more convinced you become that the Three Wise Men came from the East'.

All this extracurricular activity gained for Bülow yet more notoriety. A sizeable portion of his audience came not to hear the music but to observe the spectacle. Nonetheless, it was the music that lingered, and it was Bülow's integrity as an artist that won the day. America had never before witnessed such faithful renderings of the classics.

VII

If America learned to appreciate Bülow, Bülow certainly learned to appreciate America. He wrote to his friend Karl Klindworth:

> . . . I must tell you how inconceivably glad I am to have crossed the ocean. The New World is to be preferred to the Old in every respect. New Englanders are a great improvement on their forebears in the old country—more receptive, warm-hearted, and amiable in social intercourse than the 'Nibelheimer'. As regards material comforts, too, life is far pleasanter.[20]

He was impressed with the hotels, with the railways, with the architecture of Boston, New York, and Chicago especially, and above all with the

---

18. *The Arcadian,* January 8, 1876.

19. These and other anecdotes culled from the American press have been usefully gathered together in LFP, pp. 244–249, which provides a stimulating overview of Bülow's first American tour.

20. BNB, pp. 49–50.

enormous wealth of the business tycoons and their willingness to invest millions of dollars in artistic enterprises. Everything in America, he told his mother, was half a century ahead of Europe. Over the railway system he waxed positively lyrical. 'Railroad cars are like cabins, wonderfully heated, and with excellent beds of a quality undreamt of in Germany and its environs. One can fully undress, one is awakened at the right time by a black porter who has cleaned one's shoes overnight, and one can even wash oneself'.[21] The abundance of water in the hotels of Chicago, Cincinnati, and Philadelphia, and the marble bathrooms with their shining brass fittings, aroused his admiration and prompted him to declare that by comparison Germany was a backward country. Moreover, he was attracting national newspaper coverage of the kind that musicians in Europe could only dream about. In brief, Bülow felt valued, and that was precious to him.

His letters brimmed with observations about America and Americans. In Philadelphia he went to the telegraph office to despatch a cable, and was bemused when the clerk offered to expedite this service in exchange for a concert ticket to one of his concerts.[22] On New Year's Eve, he was in New York and was just about to leave his hotel when he heard a gunshot. 'Just think of it—twenty steps from me in the hotel, one Yankee shot another one dead'.[23]

With Chicago Bülow was particularly impressed. No other city in America struck him as being so dynamic and resilient. In 1837 it had been a small cattle town of 4,000 dwellers on the shores of Lake Michigan; by 1875 it had become a large metropolis of 350,000 inhabitants, many of them recent immigrants from Germany. The Great Fire of Chicago in 1871 had destroyed 17,000 houses. Bülow was amazed that within five years everything had been rebuilt on an even larger scale, and few remnants of the disaster remained. Inevitably he became aware of the racial discrimination that characterized American society, and he expressed 'great sympathy for his black human brothers', from whose ranks he elevated the barber and the waiter far above their counterparts among immigrant Germans. That last comment was published in a wide-ranging, reckless interview he gave to the *Chicago Times,* to mark the seventy-fifth concert of his tour, and it did nothing to endear him to the large German-speaking population of Chicago—a city where he was scheduled to give

21. BB, vol. 5, p. 303.
22. Ibid., p. 323.
23. Ibid., p. 330.

four recitals in the imposing McCormick Hall during the first week of February 1876.[24] At the appointed hour the *Times* reporter met Bülow in the lobby of his hotel and was immediately greeted with an interrogation:

Do you smoke?
Yes.
Permit me (handing a delicately carved ivory case full of cigarettes).
They are real Russian I assure you.

Bülow then paced back and forth, puffing on his cigarette, while the reporter relaxed in an armchair. The occasion was once more ripe for disaster, and Bülow obliged. He had apparently learned nothing from the ill-conceived interview he had earlier given to *The New York Sun,* and he again aimed some poisoned darts at the German press in America, and more particularly at those German music teachers who, having left the fatherland and settled in America, now posed as experts in classical music without really knowing anything about it. 'They have done more harm in their ignorant grafting of musical errors upon the people of this country than they can ever atone for', said Bülow between puffs:

Ill-taught themselves, they have perpetuated error in their pupils. . . . They are a set of beer-drinkers, too many of them. Bah! If they expect to find inspiration in the bottom of their beer glasses they will wait a long time, I can tell you. The souls of the masters do not lie at the bottom of beer mugs.

Bülow would have been well advised to stop there, but with that reckless abandon that so frequently overtook him when he got the bit between his teeth, he proceeded to branch out into uncharted territory. He attacked the Puritans for dampening music in early America; he attacked the Jesuits for destroying the French Republic of Napoleon III; and he attacked those who attacked Prince Otto Bismarck, the leader of a newly

24. Completed in 1873, as part of Chicago's reconstruction after the Great Fire, the McCormick Concert Hall was named after its wealthy benefactor, Cyrus Hall McCormick (1809–1884), who had made his fortune as the inventor of the mechanical grain reaper, which had opened up the vast prairie grain fields of the Midwest. McCormick Hall was located on the corner of Kinzie and Clark Streets and had a seating capacity of 2,200. After its inaugural concert on November 13, 1873 (in which one of the featured artists was the famous Polish violinist Henryk Wieniawski) the *Chicago Times* went into raptures about the city's new auditorium, and told its readers that it surpassed both New York's Steinway Hall and Boston's Music Hall in its acoustical properties. 'It should be a matter of pride to every citizen that at last Chicago has an auditorium where music can be heard to its best advantage'. Issue of November 14, 1873.

McCormick Hall, Chicago. A lithograph from 'The
Land Owner', October 1873.

united Germany. The low point of the interview occurred when he addressed the question of American women:

> I like them. They have much smaller feet and hands than the Eu-
> ropean women, and that is an essential to me in a handsome
> woman. . . . Another thing about American women that delights
> me, is the size and character of the ear. That is one of the first
> things I look at. A handsome ear is a wonderful feature about a
> woman. When it is well rounded and finely chiseled, it is a mag-
> net to any man of taste. . . . I like thin women—tall, slender, and
> graceful. You can't get me to utter any treason against American
> women, for I have surrendered all discretion.[25]

Why Bülow's taste in women was of the slightest concern to the readers of the *Chicago Times,* only the reporter to whom these insights were
vouchsafed would know. But it is not without psychological interest to
observe that both of Bülow's wives met these exacting standards, being
extremely 'tall, slender, and graceful'—as, incidentally, did the particular
American woman he had been pursuing for the past two months, and
who is shortly to enter our narrative.

25. *Chicago Times,* February 6, 1876.

The New World also appeared to have revitalized Bülow. His health had improved, and although that would not last, there were times when he was positively elated at the return of his youthful energy. He also renewed some friendships from the old days—with William Mason, with the members of the Schuberth publishing firm, with Leopold Damrosch, and (a pleasurable surprise for him) several of his old pupils from Berlin who turned up unexpectedly to his recitals. Halfway through his American tour he was so uplifted that he put pen to paper and informed Cosima of an idea that had been slowly forming in his mind and had now become a firm resolve. He was going to apply for American citizenship and turn his back on Europe for good:

> Chicago
> February 6, 1876
> . . . I regret that the 'roving life' which I lead (indeed without distaste for it or excessive fatigue) does not allow me to explain fully the news—still unknown to my mother and others—that I do not intend to recross the Atlantic, that I have found my real fatherland here ('Wo ich nütze ist mein Vaterland',[26] we once read in the *Wanderjahre*); in fact, I consider myself henceforward dead and buried as far as Europe is concerned, and I am now taking the first steps to obtain a citizen's rights in this free country. I propose to spend the last quarter of my life in my own fashion and for my own satisfaction—which I find in the prosperity of my art—and leave the rest to the grace of God.[27]

He enclosed with this letter some of his recent press cuttings which would have told her everything she needed to know about his success in America and his reasons for wanting to stay there. Cosima received the news in Bayreuth, on February 24, and wrote in her diary, 'In the evening [I] receive a letter from Hans, who has decided to remain in America. Will I ever, if only to my Siegfried, disclose the pit of sorrow which has been dug inside me?'[28] Bülow's plan to become an American citizen did not materialize, however. Several months after his return to Europe, and Cosima herself had inquired about the matter, he wrote to her from Glasgow, 'Believe me, it is not my fault that I have failed to expatriate myself; destiny put real obstacles in the way of my leaving Europe definitively for America. So here I am in Europe, and here I stay'.[29]

---

26. 'Where I am needed, there is my country', from Goethe's *Wanderjahre*.
27. BNB, p. 515.
28. WT, vol. 1, p. 894.
29. BNB, p. 517.

VIII

Bülow's brief dalliance with the baroness Romaine von Overbeck in the American capital is a subject about which there is more to be learned than the official record reveals. The encounter shows him to have been completely incapable of handling his emotional life after it had been shattered by Cosima's betrayal of him a few years earlier. Bülow was introduced to Romaine on December 9, 1875, by the German ambassador to the United States, Kurd von Schlözer, during a postconcert reception at the German embassy in Washington. Schlözer had been a close personal friend of Franz Liszt during an earlier posting to Rome, in the mid-1860s, a period when Liszt had taken holy orders in the Catholic Church. Schlözer had long followed the career of Liszt's most prominent pupil, and he wanted to open the doors of Washington's wealthy and famous to him. Five years earlier, Romaine had married an Austrian baron, Gustav von Overbeck, and there were already two young sons of the union.[30] Because the baron, who was a naval officer, spent long periods abroad in pursuit of a mercantile career (he was eventually given command of the steamship *America,* headed an expedition to Borneo, and was later named Austrian Vice-Consul to Hong Kong), Romaine must have given every appearance of living an independent life. She was a talented amateur pianist and Schlözer considered her playing polished enough for her to have become a professional. Bülow was at first doubtless pleased to find a ravishing woman who could talk about the piano and its repertoire with intelligence, and in his native tongue. But as their conversations unfolded he was quickly swept away by her charms, and appears to have built up some false hopes of a permanent liaison.

The barest review of the facts of Romaine's life ought to have been sufficient to convince Bülow that his dreams stood no chance of becoming reality. Romaine came from one of the most distinguished families in the nation's capital. Her grandfather was Samuel F. Vinton, a well-known former congressman from Ohio; while her mother, Madeleine Vinton, had honed her social skills arranging her politician-father's dinner parties and official engagements. Romaine's father, Daniel Goddard, died while she was still young. This was an important turning point in her life because her mother went on to contract a distinguished marriage to Rear Admiral John A. Dahlgren, a naval hero of the Civil War. It was the rear admiral who led Romaine to the altar for her wedding to Baron von Overbeck in 1870, one of the social events of the season. Among the guests were President and Mrs. Grant, members of the Cabinet and Congress, and the chief justice of the United States. Bülow's letters to Romaine reveal his

30. Gustav and Oscar. A third son, Alfred, was born in Europe.

agitation at the thought of parting from her. Five days after their first meeting, and just before leaving Washington, he wrote, 'If I don't see you again in two weeks in New York, I'll kill myself'.[31] He confided to Ambassador Schlözer, who had brought them together, that his dearest wish was to change her name from O[verbeck] to B[ülow],[32] but he lacked any sensible plan to detach her from the baron. Romaine evidently made two trips to New York during his sojourn there, in December 1875. By January 7, 1876, he told Romaine, who had meanwhile returned to Washington, 'I adore you so much that I turn not only crazy, but what is worse, dumb like a simpleton'.[33] In his desperation he even wrote to his mother with the absurd idea of having her enter into an intrigue with his diplomat brother-in-law, Viktor Bojanowski, and have him pull some strings with the German government to have Baron Overbeck's return to Washington obstructed.[34] Although Romaine may have been flattered by Bülow's attentions, she kept both her head and her heart intact, knowing that she had much more to lose than Bülow himself if his infatuation with her ever became public. We do not have her replies to his messages, but it is not hard to read between the lines of a letter written by Bülow (whose tour had once more taken him back to Boston) dated January 12, 1876, reproaching her with the words, 'I imagine that as a child you amused yourself by tormenting flies and butterflies, considering that you excel with virtuosity in making me suffer, me who loves you, me who adores you so—superlatively'.[35]

Bülow's obsession with Romaine ended, as it was bound to end, when he learned that she was planning to join her husband in Europe. By then Bülow was in Cleveland, and he could only write helplessly that he was ready to abandon his career as an artist and follow her from the New World back to the Old. What he proposed to do once he had caught up with her he had no clear idea. Of lawyers and divorces he had already had his fill. He managed to extract from Romaine a promise to meet him in Baltimore a few weeks later in order to hear a programme of his orchestral works at the Peabody Institute. When she failed to turn up, Bülow knew that he had been abandoned. There was a marked change in the tone of his letters to her. He abruptly dropped the intimate 'tu' for the formal 'vous', and from 'Chère Adorée', she was relegated to 'Madame'. Thereafter she disappeared from his life, or at least from that part of it he

31. BB, vol. 5, p. 326.
32. Ibid., p. 325.
33. Ibid., p. 332.
34. Ibid., p. 348.
35. Ibid., p. 333.

was presently devoting to America.[36] Bülow had been wounded, was once more in despair, and was still only halfway through his American tour.

IX

Back in New York, Bülow once more found himself embroiled in controversy. Reengaged at Chickering Hall, it was his misfortune to share a concert with a singer, Miss Rosa McGeachy. Her voice was not the greatest; it grated on the ears of many like sandpaper on steel. She having finished her aria, it was Bülow's turn to walk onto the platform. He went to the keyboard and played the baritone recitative from Beethoven's Ninth Symphony, 'Freunde, nicht diese Töne'—'Friends, not these sounds'. The musicians in the audience appreciated the joke and burst into applause. The nonmusicians were bewildered, and sought illumination through the correspondence columns of *The Music Trade Review*, which was happy to provide it.[37] The journal was especially critical of Miss McGeachy, whose name it variously mangled as 'McQueechy' and 'McReachy', rising to the heights of absurdity with 'McScreachy'. Such insults might today be regarded as libellous. But in the 1870s the New York press took no prisoners.

The newspapers were far better disposed towards another singer with whom Bülow appeared, Miss Lizzie Cronyn. This twenty-four-year-old Canadian-born soprano he had met on the voyage across the Atlantic, and had been captivated by the beauty of her voice and the unaffected charm of her personality. Miss Cronyn was returning home after five years of study on the Continent and she had already appeared at La Scala.

When she boarded the *Parthia*, bound for Boston, she was completely unknown, and faced an uncertain future. By the time she disembarked, she had been taken up by one of the world's most famous musicians, who had moreover decided to appear as her 'accompanist' in some of his own recitals. The question might well be asked, Why did Bülow need to appear with a supporting artist at all, and especially with a singer, the sort of performer he generally despised? The simple answer was that both he and Ullman knew that in order to attract the great public to his concerts,

---

36. Romaine crossed Bülow's path again several years later, after she had settled in Berlin and had acquired an apartment on Bellevue Strasse. By then she was separated from the baron, who had made money in the Far East and had remained behind in Hong Kong. Romaine occasionally travelled from Berlin to Meiningen to hear Bülow conduct the orchestra there in the 1880s, and he encouraged the friendship that was later to develop between her and his daughter Daniela. Bülow had by then remarried, and his passion for Romaine had cooled, but the old chivalry often reasserted itself in such forms of address as 'Dear Baroness of my soul!' and 'Chère noble amie!'

37. MTR, February 3, 1876, p. 113.

Two Washington recitals, with Lizzie Cronyn. December 7 and 9, 1875.

with their heavy emphasis on the German classics, above all on Bach and Beethoven, some kind of foil was necessary not only to lure people into the concert hall, but to keep them there once they had occupied their seats. The solo piano recital had not yet won full acceptance in America; in fact, there were many small towns in the Midwest which were yet to enjoy such an experience. Any number of famous singers would have been happy to have Bülow as their accompanist; he would not only have refused to share the platform with them, however, but would have made their life miserable in the refusing. Lizzie Cronyn was different. Her very lack of fame worked to her advantage and allowed her to fulfill her subservient role with grace, while at the same time giving Bülow the pleasure of introducing her talent to a larger public. She was moreover a modest presence on the platform. She dressed simply in white with a wreath of

PROGRAMME.

First Concert.

PART I.

I.—J S. BACH (1685-1750.)
  (*a*) Fantaisie chromatique et Fugue.
  (*b*) Gavotte in D Minor.
II.—L. V. BEETHOVEN (1770-1827.)
  Sonata. Opus 31, No. 3 in E Flat.
  Allegro—Scherzo—Minuetto—Presto.
III.—G. ROSSINI. "La Separazione."
  Miss LIZZIE CRONYN.

PART II.

IV.— F. MENDELSSOHN (1809-1847.)
  (*a*) Four Songs without words. (19, 21, 34 3.)
  (*b*) Prelude and Fugue. Opus 35, No. 1.
V.—F. CHOPIN (1810-1849.)
  (*a*) Nocturne. Opus 37, No. 2 in G Major.
  (*b*) Valse Brillante. Opus 42.
  (*c*) Berceuse. Opus 57.
  (*d*) Polonaise. (Opus 53.)
VI.— (*a*) GORDIGIANI. "O, Santissima Vergine "
  (*b*) RUBINSTEIN. "Thou'rt Like unto a Flower."
  Miss LIZZIE CRONYN.
VII.—F. LISZT (1811- .)
  VENEZIA E NAPOLI. Gondoliera e Tarantella.

PROGRAMME.

Second Concert.

PART I.

I.—L. V. BEETHOVEN (1770-1827.)
  Sonata Appassionata. Opus 57, in F Minor.
  Allegro assai—Andante con moto—Allegro e Presto.
II.—R. WAGNER (1813- .)
  (*a*) Spinning Song (from the " Flying Dutchman.")
  (*b*) Grand March (from "Tannhauser.")
  Arranged by LISZT.
III.— (*a*) MERCADANTE, La Prece Dell'Orfana.
  (*b*) GOMEZ, Canzonetta (from Salvator Rosa.)
  Miss LIZZIE CRONYN.

PART II.

IV.—(*a*) SCARLATTI (1683-1760.) Cat's Fugue.
  (*b*) J. S. BACH (1685-1750.) Sarabande et Passepied.
  (*c*) G. HANDEL (1684-1759.) Chaconne.
  (*d*) MOZART (1756-1791.) Menuet et Gigue.
V.— F. SCHUBERT (1797-1828.)
  (*a*) Two Impromptus. Opus 90, No. 3 and 2.
  (*b*)Ave Maria,   }
  (*c*) Valse-Caprice. } Arranged by LISZT.
6.—(*a*) MOZART. Aria, "Voi che Sapete," Nozze di Figaro.
  (*b*) ROSSINI. L'Invito, (Bolero.)
  Miss LIZZIE CRONYN.
7.—F. LISZT. 1811- .)
  (*a*) Ricordanza, Etude de Concert.
  (*b*) Mazurka Brillante.
  (*c*) Hungarian Rhapsody. No. 12.
  (Dedicated to JOACHIM.)

Two Washington recitals, with Lizzie Cronyn. December 7 and 9, 1875.

flowers in her hair, and she sang from the heart without affectation. As for her repertoire, that may well have been chosen for her by Bülow. It was notably lacking in the popular ballads of the day, and consisted in the main of operatic arias by Mozart, Bellini, Donizetti, Spohr, and others. *Dwight's Journal* summed up the situation perfectly when it reported that Bülow accompanied her 'with the protecting, tender appreciativeness of one pleased to show how pure a pearl he had found'.[38]

X

The American tour ended abruptly on May 9, 1876, with a concert in St. Louis, from where Bülow embarked on the fifty-hour train journey back to New York in a state of utter exhaustion. Arrived in New York, he sought medical help. The doctors gave him a series of treatments they labelled

38. DWJ, February 5, 1876, p. 174. And there was money to be made from this 'pure pearl'. Shortly after Bülow left America, there appeared a souvenir of their collaboration, a *Book of Miss Cronyn's Favourite Songs, as Accompanied and Edited by Hans von Bülow*. See the entry in the Complete Catalogue of Bülow's Compositions, Transcriptions and Editions, pp. 480–81.

'experimental', because they had little idea of what was wrong with him. His condition was described as 'nervous prostration'.

For this vague diagnosis Bülow's doctor charged him 120 dollars; Bülow complained that for 85 dollars he could have bought a fashionable three-piece suit, which would at least have been a more lasting souvenir than his doctor's bill. According to the *New York World*, Bülow, while practising, had fallen to the floor in a fainting fit, and suffered a memory lapse of such severity that when Bernard Ullman entered the room Bülow failed to recognize him, and he wept when Ullman's identity was revealed. This suggests that Bülow may have suffered another stroke, a diagnosis made plausible by the findings of the autopsy that was carried out on his body many years later, and pointed to chronic hemorrhaging of the brain.[39] Even a man of normal health might have buckled under the strain to which Bülow had subjected himself. What we know for certain is that his American journeys had taken him to more than thirty towns and cities across the continent, involving thousands of miles of travel, and that his health was shattered. He was obliged to cancel the remaining 33 concerts of the 172 that Ullman had planned for him, some of which were already being announced at the very moment that Bülow himself lay prostrate in his hotel room. As a result, he had to forfeit one-quarter of his fee of 100,000 francs for breaking his contract. But at least one of his objectives had been reached: he had raised 75,000 francs for his children, an uncommonly large sum of money, and dutifully made much of it available to Cosima to spend on their welfare as she wished. As Bülow approached the end of his American tour, filled as it was with stress and deprivation, he privately described it as 'nauseating slavery, which I have entered because of vile Mammon'.[40]

Ullman appeared not to understand the gravity of Bülow's condition. Even as the pianist was receiving medical attention, we find his dauntless manager suggesting another American tour the following year—'for fifty concerts I will give you 40,000 francs and all expenses'.[41] He advised the ailing Bülow to reexamine his contract where he would surely find a 'sickness clause', allowing him the odd day's rest if he felt unwell. He also lectured Bülow on the choice of his programmes, telling him not to play too much Bach and Beethoven, because they 'have a very harmful effect on the takings'. Bülow must have shuddered at such crass commercialism. 'You will not succeed in moulding [the Americans] to your way of thinking', Ullman went on. Bülow must abandon his sense of mission, he continued,

39. See pp. 465–66, of the present volume.

40. Unpublished letter to Eugen Spitzweg, written from Columbus, Ohio, and dated April 28, 1876. Original in the Music Division of the Library of Congress (call no. ML95.B905).

41. BB, vol. 5, p. 370.

because the low taste of the Americans would bring about its defeat. Then came the capitalist's credo. 'Take America for what it is: the country in which to make money, and nothing else'.[42] When he read that, Bülow knew that it was time to return to Europe. After failing to book a passage via Liverpool on his preferred Cunard line, he settled for the French steamship the *St. Laurent*. Because of his weakened condition, he joined a married couple with whom he was distantly acquainted, and departed America's shores in their company at the beginning of June.[43]

As for the hope that his gruelling workload would clear his mind of depression, that remained unfulfilled. He spent several days in London to be with his sister, Isidora, and consult the medical doctors there, but his gloom only deepened. They advised him to seek a further cure at Bad Godesberg, but he was so weak that Isidora was obliged to accompany him to the watering spa. He spent much of July and August immersed in mineral baths and undergoing daily massage, the only treatment that seemed to help him. From Godesberg he moved to Hanover, where he spent time in the company of his friend and fellow Liszt pupil Hans von Bronsart, who was now the intendant of the Royal Court Theatre there. Bronsart, together with his pianist wife, Ingeborg Starck (who had also been a pupil of Liszt), had transformed the artistic life of the city. In the old Weimar days, Liszt had dubbed Bülow and Bronsart as 'Hans I' and 'Hans II', a mark of affection that had been retained. The pair had remained friends during the intervening years, and the Bronsarts offered Bülow a comforting environment as he slowly found his feet once more. The depth of melancholy into which he had descended by the late summer of 1876 is revealed in his correspondence with Carl Bechstein. Alarmed by one of Bülow's letters, Bechstein travelled to Hanover and walked into Bülow's garden just in time to prevent him from shooting himself.[44] The immediate cause of the crisis was a quarrel with Bronsart himself. Anyone else would have shrugged off the incident. But the altercation had penetrated Bülow's troubled soul and gave him no peace.

Liszt was well informed of his former son-in-law's uncertain health, and of the rumours swirling around Bülow after his return from America,

---

42. Ibid.

43. The couple, identified only as Herr Wertheimber and his wife, were acquaintances of Ullman. Perhaps it was on this particular transatlantic crossing that Bülow was prompted to come out with another *bon mot*. Whenever he dined in the ship's restaurant he had little choice but to listen to the onboard orchestra, an ensemble of indifferent achievement. He sighed to one of his travelling companions, 'How I envy the players. They are able to dine in peace without having to listen to the music!' (BBLW, p. 288).

44. BNB, p. xxii. Du Moulin Eckart added dramatic detail to this incident when he reported that Bechstein 'wrested the revolver from Bülow's hand'.

one of which had him incarcerated in Endenich undergoing treatment for insanity. In a letter to Princess Carolyne, dated September 26, 1876, Liszt wrote:

> When someone told you that Bülow had taken refuge in a lunatic asylum with a very high reputation, near Bonn, where Robert Schumann ended his days, they were mistaken. No trace of insanity with Bülow—but great exhaustion as a result of excessive work and of labours beyond measure. He disregarded a slight stroke which took him unawares in London last year. The doctors then advised him to take care of himself—whereupon he left as rapidly as possible for America, and there, in a period of 6 or 8 months, played more than a thousand pieces of music at 140 public concerts! On returning to London, he finally followed the doctors' orders, by betaking himself to Godesberg, near Bonn, there to undergo a *Stahlbadkur* [chalybeate bath cure] under the direction of the celebrated Dr. Finkelburg . . .[45]

XI

For the next several months Bülow's career lacked direction. At first he languished in Hanover, watched over by the faithful Bronsarts. Later he drifted through a number of spas, taking water cures at such diverse places as Bex, Bad Kreuznach, and Baden-Baden. At Bex he endured a course of twenty-five cold water immersions, and with his usual stoicism reported to Bronsart that a better description for 'Paradise Bex' would be the opposite—a 'purgatorium'—but then, with a clever play on words, he reflected that the true opposite of purgatorium would be a 'constipatorium', which was also a better expression to describe his present condition. From the cold waters of Bex he plunged into the warm waters of Bad Kreuznach, where he spent much of June and July 1877.

It was at Bad Kreuznach that Bülow received a welcome invitation to direct the Glasgow Choral Union for a period of two months, towards the end of the year. The memory of his earlier visit to Glasgow, in 1875, coming as it did in the middle of his present tribulations, was so pleasant to him that he accepted the invitation with alacrity. No sooner had the directors of the Glasgow Choral Union received Bülow's written assent, however, than fortune complicated his life by smiling on him a second time. On August 15 he received an urgent message from Bronsart, offering him the conductorship of the Hanover Court Theatre, which had unexpectedly fallen vacant. What to do? He could hardly withdraw from

45. LLB, vol. 7, pp. 156–157.

Glasgow. Bülow spent 'two sleepless nights' pondering the alternatives offered him. On August 17 he sent a telegram to Bronsart,[46] proposing a compromise: he would accept the position in Hanover, and even open the season at the Court Theatre in October, if he could be released for the two months of November and December 1877, in order to fulfill his prior commitment to Glasgow, from which he was unwilling to withdraw. He reminded Bronsart of his family motto, 'All the Bülows are honourable', and with wry humour told his old friend that only on February 1, 1878, would it be possible for Bronsart to appoint himself 'Bülow's Chief'. In brief, Scotland must come before Hanover. He generously suggested that if, after further reflection, Bronsart decided to withdraw the offer and approach someone else, it would not cause any misunderstanding between the two friends. Bronsart happily accepted this compromise, and appointed an assistant conductor, Karl Herner, to take over during Bülow's absence in Scotland.

---

46. BB, vol. 5, p. 423.

A Scottish Interlude,
1877–1878

Bülow and the Glasgow Choral Union

> These Scots are ideal human beings, just as, on the whole, this city
> appears to me infinitely homely, and homogenous.
> —Bülow[1]

I

Bülow's direction of the Glasgow Choral Union for a ten-week period from early November 1877 to January 1878 is a virtually unknown episode in his career. The invitation was due in no small measure to the powerful sponsorship of Thomas Logan Stillie, the chief music critic of the *Glasgow Herald,* and one of the supporters of the Choral Union itself. Stillie was a wealthy Scottish merchant who had made a fortune as head of a calico company and had then retired from business while still young in order to cultivate his musical interests. On account of his uncommon erudition, his wide European travels, and his knowledge of foreign languages, he had been appointed to the *Glasgow Herald,* in which position he wielded much local influence. We recall that Stillie and Bülow had met on one of the conductor's earlier visits to Glasgow, in January 1875, and that Stillie had covered the rehearsals and concert in glowing detail. It was Stillie himself who wrote to Bülow in the summer of 1877, offering him the hospitality of his comfortable Glasgow home for the duration of his two-month stay in the city. In a chimerical reply Bülow thanked Stillie for 'that very seductive offer', and then turned him down. He pointed out that his somewhat odd lifestyle could only be accommodated at a hotel 'where

1. BB, vol. 5, p. 466.

one may rule without scruple of giving trouble'. His uncertain health bothered him, he explained, and he feared that it might make him an impossible houseguest. By way of ameliorating whatever negative effect his refusal might have on Stillie, Bülow expressed the hope that he might 'be allowed to enter your charming, hospitable house and to have the honour and pleasure of talking, of exchanging thoughts or vice-thoughts (on my side) with you and Mrs. Stillie'.[2]

From Robert Craig's unpublished 'Early History of Glasgow's Choral Union', we learn that Bülow's appointment came about almost by chance because the selection committee's first choice, Arthur Sullivan, was not prepared to accept the low fee. Therefore:

> a daring attempt was made to invite Dr. Hans von Bülow who was then considered the greatest conductor living. An exceptionally gifted musician and artist, he offered to come for an eight week's engagement for £10 per concert, four or five per week, which would include preliminary rehearsals, travelling expenses between neighboring towns, and a fortnightly performance on the piano. . . . It was a bold step to take but it succeeded.[3]

Bülow set out for England towards the end of October 1877, and after resting for a day or two at his sister's house in Sydenham, he boarded the 'Scotch Mail' train in London and travelled north to Glasgow. In those days this express train did the journey of 400 miles or so in just over ten hours, a feat that Bülow found so remarkable that he called the vehicle 'the Flying Dutchman of the nineteenth century',[4] a perspicacious observation if one recalls that the route would one day be covered in half the time by 'the Flying Scotsman'.

II

Bülow's relationship with the Choral Union was one of the most collegial he ever enjoyed with any musical organization. The first rehearsals went 'very smoothly', and the orchestra contained no 'invalids', as he put it. He joked to his sister that his 'maiden speech' was so satisfactory 'that even I was able to praise it',[5] a veiled allusion to the fact that he delivered

---

2. Bülow's unpublished letter, written in English and dated 'Kreuznach, 26 July 1877', is preserved in the Mitchell Library, Glasgow, call no. MS. 46/2.

3. CEH, vol. 5, pp. 147–148.

4. BAS (Part 2), p. 172.

5. BB, vol. 5, p. 468. In its issue of November 21, Glasgow's stalwart publication *The Bailie* captured the general buzz surrounding Bülow. With his arrival in the city, it declared warmly, 'Glasgow may be said to be going through a musical curriculum'.

it in English. He was especially delighted with the city's newly built St. Andrew's Hall, which held 2,800 people and which he described as both comfortable and splendid.[6] The inaugural concert took place on Tuesday, November 13, 1877, and consisted of a performance of Handel's *Messiah* conducted by the regular director of the Choral Union, Henry Lambeth. It heralded a rich period of music making in the new auditorium. Two days later there followed the world premier of George Macfarren's dramatic cantata *The Lady of the Lake,* based on the poem of Sir Walter Scott. Bülow lavished praise on Macfarren (who was at that time both principal of the Royal Academy of Music and professor of music at Cambridge University) and described him as the premier composer in Britain. Macfarren had already lost his eyesight and had to dictate all his compositions to an amanuensis, an achievement that Bülow admired. He volunteered his services to make a piano reduction of the choral parts of the cantata and he helped Macfarren with the preliminary rehearsals. Bülow's opening concert took place the following evening, Friday, November 16. It was devoted in its entirety to Beethoven, beginning appropriately with the overture *The Consecration of the House:*

Overture: *Consecration of the House,* op. 122
March and Chorus, from the Incidental Music to 'The Ruins of Athens', op. 113
Aria: 'In questa tomba' (soloist: Madame Janet Patey)
Symphony no. 8, in F major, op. 93
Intermission

Overture: *King Stephen,* op. 117
Romance in G major, for violin and orchestra, op. 40
    (Soloist: John Carrodus)[7]
Aria: 'Nature's Adoration', op. 48, no. 4
    (Soloist: Madame Janet Patey)
Fantasia for Pianoforte, Chorus, and Orchestra, op. 80
    (Soloist: von Bülow)

The hall was packed with Scottish dignitaries, including the Marquis of Lorne and his wife, Princess Louise, the fourth daughter of Queen Victoria. Under different circumstances this opening concert might have been the highlight of their week. But it was undoubtedly overshadowed by the fire that had broken out a short time earlier in Inverary Castle, where

---

6. St. Andrew's Hall remained Glasgow's premier concert venue until it was destroyed by fire in 1962.

7. At the last moment Carrodus became indisposed, and Bülow played Beethoven's Variations in F major, op. 34.

they had been staying as guests of the Duke and Duchess of Argyle. They had been summarily roused from their beds before dawn, just in time to watch the flames burst through the roof of the great central tower,[8] and witness the duchess (who had recently suffered a stroke) rescued and carried to safety at the height of the blaze. At the moment of Bülow's concert, the royals were enduring the rigours of the Buchanan Hotel, in central Glasgow.

III

Bülow was impressed with the inaugural organ recital, played by the Liverpool organist W. T. Best. He described Best as a great virtuoso and the new organ as a splendid specimen of its kind, adding that in terms of its range of colour and nuance there was nothing to compare with it in Germany.[9]

In the midst of all this music making, Bülow found that he very much enjoyed his independence. He had discovered private quarters at 144 Holland Street, within easy walking distance of St. Andrew's Hall, to which he could repair at short notice whenever he wanted to savour the solitude he so often craved between rehearsals. Moreover, he had much preparation to do. His programmes for the Choral Union were divided into two quite separate series. The main orchestral concerts were given at weekly intervals, the content was serious and weighted towards the classics. The 'Saturday Popular Concerts', by contrast, were meant to be musical entertainments for the man in the street. Bülow accepted the fact that while he was in Scotland he was a pioneer, one of his chief tasks being to forge a supportive public for the new orchestra and its new hall. He described himself at this juncture as a showman, and was not above conducting Gounod's 'Funeral March of a Marionette' wearing black gloves—an act of mock piety intended to make the audience laugh. He positively revelled in a performance of the finale of Haydn's *Farewell* Symphony in a darkened hall, each player's desk illuminated by candlelight. The players extinguished their candles one by one and left the platform, until only Bülow himself remained, and he too picked his flickering candle and slowly left the platform. 'Capital!' he exclaimed in a letter to

8. *The Times*, November 13, 1877, p. 5. See also the account in the *Glasgow Herald*, October 13, 1877, p. 4.

9. BB, vol. 5, pp. 469–470. W. T. Best's recital took place on November 19. The four manual organ was built by the firm of T. C. Lewis; it was the largest instrument this builder ever constructed (with 4,503 pipes, 64 stops, and 14 couplers). Bülow later said that he found the recital so inspiring that had he been younger he would have risked jeopardizing his career as a pianist in order to study the organ, and '*not get annoyed by rivals in petticoats*' (*The Figaro*, December 1, 1877).

Jessie Laussot.[10] As if to remind the Glaswegians that they lived in the 'Second City of the Empire', and were fully entitled to regard themselves as the equals of Londoners, Berliners, or Parisians, standing shoulder to shoulder with them at the centre of Europe's artistic life, Bülow built his 'Saturday Popular Concerts' around nationalistic themes. There was a 'French Night', an 'English Night', a 'Scottish Night', a 'German Night', a 'Popular Night', and a 'Cosmopolitan Night'. There was even a 'Universal Suffrage Night', in which the members of the public voted on pieces they wanted repeated from earlier concerts.[11] Altogether there were nine of these marathon events, which took place on consecutive Sunday evenings. Some of the repertoire was repeated in Edinburgh and Dundee.[12]

IV

Bülow always insisted on supporting the aspirations of young composers. When he heard that the orchestral overture *Cervantes* by the thirty-year-old Alexander Mackenzie had been twice rejected by the Choral Union, Bülow immediately put it into his programme for December 1, 1877. Mackenzie tells us that he travelled from Edinburgh for the final rehearsal and found that Bülow had drilled the players so hard that they were almost in a state of mutiny. It did not augur well for the concert. Mackenzie's apprehension deepened when, after yet more drilling, Bülow turned to him with the words, 'You will conduct it yourself tonight!' Mackenzie pleaded that he had not brought any dress clothes, whereupon Bülow

10. BB, vol. 5, p. 480. This concert took place on December 8, 1877. The *Glasgow Herald* reported that 'the darkening of the hall was perhaps a little overdone . . . but the effect was so droll that the large audience . . . fairly shrieked with laughter as the conductor finally sought his way out by the light of the solitary candle that was left to him'.

11. The final choice of works for this 'People's Concert' caused consternation in the columns of the *Musical Times*. It reported:

Wagner	Overture to *Tannhäuser*	279 votes
Rossini	Overture to *William Tell*	213 votes
Moscheles	'Fantasie on Scottish Airs'	126 votes
Hérold	Overture to *Zampa*	95 votes
Haydn	*Farewell* Symphony (last mov.)	118 votes
Mozart	Overture to *The Magic Flute*	100 votes
Liszt	'Hungarian Fantasie'	105 votes
Mozart	'A Musical Joke'	117 votes
Myles B. Foster	Overture to *Rob Roy*	94 votes

After surveying this bleak landscape, the correspondent of the journal added, '. . . It is scarcely credible that Dr. von Bülow and his committee accepted the vote in good faith, and carried out the behest of their patrons. But we hope that they will not do it again' (MT, February 1878). We doubt that the correspondent of the *Musical Times* survived long enough to see it, but the tradition established by this 'Plebiscite Concert' would continue in Glasgow for the next seventy years.

12. These nine programmes, which in sheer length and novelty of repertoire had few earlier parallels in the concert halls of Britain, are reproduced in BB, vol. 5, pp. 464–467. They are also described in some detail in CEH, pp. 164–182.

Bülow in the 1870s. 'Un Garde Offizier en miniature'.
A photograph.

wheeled round to a lady sitting in the stalls and called out, 'Has your husband a dress-suit that he will lend to my friend?' The lady nodded in the affirmative. It was Mrs. Stillie, the wife of the music critic. Unfortunately for Mackenzie, who was thin, Stillie was round, which left much to be desired as far as the elegance and fit of the garment was concerned. Mackenzie's recollection of the performance itself was lost in the sickening trauma of everything surrounding it. But it must have satisfied Bülow, because two nights later Mackenzie conducted the work again in Edinburgh, with Bülow sitting in the front row of the stalls, wearing a bright scarlet Turkish fez, complete with tassles, and leading the applause.[13]

13. MMN, p. 92. Bülow's unusual headwear might well have mystified many in the Scottish audience that night. It was an amusing reminder of the five years that Cervantes had spent as a slave in Algiers, and is a typical piece of Bülow *drôlerie*. A small iconography could be compiled of Bülow striking such comical poses, incidentally, which tells of a playful and unexpected sense of humour, often directed against himself. See the ribald photograph of his spoof on 'the three Bs', taken on an earlier trip to Britain, in which Bülow is 'B-sharp', Buonamici is 'B-flat', and Bache is 'B-natural' (in BBM, p. 207). During Bülow's tour of America, in April 1889, the eccentric photographer Napoleon Sarony had no difficulty in persuading Bülow to visit his studio on Broadway, and half recline upon an ornate marble

Mackenzie also rounds out our impressions of Bülow as a personality on the podium. When he first saw Bülow mount the platform and face the orchestra, he was surprised by the short, dapper figure with its jerky movements. He reported that the somewhat sallow face, pointed goatee beard, military mustache, and carefully tended short hair, reminded him of a 'Garde Offizier en miniature'. Bülow did not even look like a musician, Mackenzie observed. But the moment he lifted the baton a transformation took place. His face became rigid, and he clenched his teeth in concentration as the piece proceeded, exhibiting a total command of the ensemble.[14]

V

Bülow continued to promote Elizabeth Beesley's career. On November 28, 1877, she appeared at a 'Gentlemen's Concert' in Manchester, where she was once again billed as 'a pupil of Hans von Bülow'. *The Athenaeum* reported that she played among other things 'Liszt's Hungarian Rhapsody, and at the end of the work she was recalled with such a display of enthusiasm as is not often heard in the Concert Hall'.[15] Bülow brought her to Glasgow for a performance of the same work in one of his 'Popular Concerts', on December 29, which was repeated by popular request on January 5. At Bülow's urging, Elizabeth Beesley made her Edinburgh debut on March 9, 1878, although he was by then back in Germany.[16]

Bülow's productive association with Glasgow came to a close on January 5, 1878, with the aforementioned 'Universal Suffrage' evening in St. Andrew's Hall. This farewell concert attracted an overflow audience of 3,100,[17] 300 more listeners than the hall was designed to accommodate, and it was a fitting tribute to his evangelical work in Scotland. There were

---

bench between two young ladies of fashion, while wearing his bowler hat at a rakish angle. Nor must we forget 'Bülow the guitarist', showing the musician sitting hunched over an instrument he appears singularly unready to play (reproduced in MLHvB, p. 128).

14. MMN, p. 89. Mackenzie had been present at Bülow's first piano recital in Scotland, almost three years earlier, and had received a similar impression on that occasion. At the end of the recital, he wrote, 'I rose with a profound sense of admiration at the intellectuality of his interpretation' (MMN, p. 88).

15. Issue of 1877, pp. 743–744.

16. *The Scotsman* reviewed this recital in its issue of March 11, 1878. It was a demanding concert, worthy of Bülow himself and doubtless prepared with his help, containing works by Bach, Beethoven, Liszt, Chopin, Henselt, Rheinberger, and Sterndale Bennett. The critic referred to Elizabeth Beesley's 'power of wrist and finger with which very few lady pianists are gifted, added to a facility and certainty of execution of the very highest order'. Selected for special praise were her performances of Bach and Beethoven, and the fact that the whole recital was played from memory—'a feat which is truly extraordinary'.

17. CEH, p. 180.

The inscribed baton presented to Bülow in gratitude for his work with the Glasgow Choral Union, 1877–1878. A photograph.

many who would have liked Bülow to stay on, but the eight-week period specified by his contract had expired, and he was expected back in Hanover. During the intermission, a little ceremony was convened in the North Hall, in appreciation of his services. Mr. John Matheson, the chairman of the Festival Executive Committee, made a fine speech of thanks in which he referred to Bülow's 'peerless conductorship'. The Committee had planned to present Bülow with an elaborately engraved baton, as a souvenir of his appointment. Alas, it was not ready in time and had to be forwarded to him after his return to Germany. The silver plaque on the outside of the case bears the inscription:

> Presented to Dr. Hans von Bülow by the Glasgow Musical Festival Executive Committee, as a souvenir of the Admirable Musical Results of the Glasgow Orchestral Concerts, 1877–78, attained under his conductorship.[18]

In his gracious reply, Bülow observed that whatever success the concerts had achieved belonged to the exceptional players that the Executive Committee had engaged for the season—a sentiment that drew loud applause.

VI

As he boarded the train for London, and Glasgow slowly receded into the distance, Bülow had the satisfaction of knowing that his brief presence in the city had made a difference. Music making of high calibre had taken place and Scotland would remember it. It is not possible to write about the early history of classical music in Scotland without giving Bülow's work with the Glasgow Choral Union pride of place. The orchestra that was formed at the time of Bülow's work with the Union later became known as the Scottish National Orchestra, an ensemble of distinction that is alive and well today. After spending his forty-eighth birthday with his

18. The baton later came into the possession of Bülow's pupil Frederic Lamond, who presented it to the University of Glasgow when the honorary degree of LLD was conferred on him in 1937. It is now preserved at the Hunterian Museum, in the University of Glasgow.

sister and her family in Sydenham, on January 8, Bülow got back to Hanover on January 14, where Hans von Bronsart was waiting to greet him at the railway station and bring him up to date with the latest happenings at the Court Theatre. The pleasant Scottish interlude was over.

It is unlikely that Bülow understood the full extent of the problems that awaited him in the Hanover Opera House. Even before he had left, in late October, the storm clouds had started to gather. His ambitious repertoire, involving a number of operas never before staged at this theatre, together with his radical plans for overhauling the orchestral Subscription Series, which ran in tandem with the operas themselves and worked the players hard, threatened to overwhelm the small company. It had the potential to create havoc, and havoc duly arrived.

At Hanover, 1877–1879

I have sacrificed the best two years of my life for nothing![1]

—Bülow

I

Bülow had never sought an appointment in Hanover, but in the summer of 1877 the musical establishment there had been visited by a double misfortune. On May 20 the assistant conductor Jean-Joseph Bott had fallen from the podium in a state of intoxication and had crashed onto the front row of the stalls during the middle of a performance of Liszt's oratorio *Saint Elisabeth*. The work was stopped in its tracks and the insensible Bott was carried into the wings, with an injured right leg. Liszt himself was in the audience, quickly mounted the platform, and directed the rest of the performance.[2] Bott was forced to resign, his reputation tarnished, and not long afterwards he sank into obscurity as the director of a local music conservatory in Magdeburg. A few weeks later, fate struck the small opera house again. On August 15, the principal conductor Karl Fischer, who had been the Court Kapellmeister since 1852, was felled by a massive heart attack as he was dining at the Union Hotel, and the opera house was left in disarray. Within hours of hearing of Fischer's death, Bronsart wrote to Bülow offering him the conductorship. 'Would you be willing, hand in hand with me, to lead the opera here to a higher level of artistic significance?'[3] As we have seen, Bülow was in Baden-Baden at that moment, taking a water cure, and it was from this unlikely location that he had given his cautious assent.

---

1. BNB, p. 67.
2. This performance of *Saint Elisabeth* was part of an ambitious two-week festival that Hans von Bronsart, in his capacity as the Royal Theatre intendant, had organized in Hanover for the annual meeting of the Allgemeiner Deutscher Musikverein.
3. BB, vol. 5, p. 422.

II

Bülow raised his baton for the first time in Hanover on September 29, directing the orchestra in the first of three subscription concerts. He began with Weber's *Euryanthe* Overture and ended with Beethoven's Symphony no. 5, in C minor. In the second subscription concert (October 13) he presented Glinka's Overture 'A Life for the Czar' and Saint-Saëns's symphonic poem *Phaéton* (the first time that these works had been heard in Hanover), and he concluded the concert with Schubert's 'Great' C major Symphony. Bülow also appeared as a soloist in this particular concert, playing Beethoven's *Emperor* Concerto and some smaller pieces of Chopin. A notable event took place on October 20 (the third of the subscription concerts) when Bülow gave the premier performance of Brahms's newly published Symphony no. 1, in C minor, in its revised form.[4] He dubbed it 'Beethoven's Tenth', somewhat to Brahms's consternation, but the epithet has remained. Even as the subscription concerts were in progress, Bülow brought various operas to the Hanover stage, including Beethoven's *Fidelio* (October 4), Donizetti's *Lucrezia Borgia* (October 11), and Auber's *La muette de Portici* (October 21). His practice of rehearsing everything from memory was new to Hanover, and caused a stir.

Amidst this flurry of activity Bülow learned that nobody had yet done anything to honour the memory of his predecessor at Hanover, the venerable Karl Fischer, so he arranged an extra concert on October 18 to help pay for a memorial stone for Fischer's grave. It was a striking beginning that augured well both for Bülow and for Hanover. Alas, the honeymoon was not to last, and Hanover eventually turned into one of the more turbulent periods of Bülow's career.

Having launched the season at Hanover, Bülow spent the months of November and December in Scotland with the Glasgow Choral Union, in fulfillment of his earlier promise to the Scots, an account of which was given in the previous chapter. By mid-January 1878 he was back in Hanover and plunged into a crushing workload which affected everybody in its path. He began rehearsals for three more impending orchestral subscription concerts, already scheduled for January 19, and February 2 and 16. More important, during the five weeks that followed he presented six operas which were all new to Hanover:

MEYERBEER   *Le Prophète* (17 February)
MOZART   *Entführung aus dem Serail* (23 February)

---

4. Brahms had conducted the original version from manuscript in Karlsruhe on November 4, 1876. He had meanwhile added some last-minute touches to the symphony before publishing it the following year.

SPOHR	*Jessonda* (28 February)
WAGNER	*Rienzi* (8 March)
MOZART	*La clemenza di Tito* (for the birthday of the Kaiser, 22 March)
BOIELDIEU	*Johann von Paris* (30 March)

And this was just the beginning. Between the months of October 1878 and April 1879, Bülow conducted all nine symphonies of Beethoven; a group of symphonies by Haydn, Mozart, and Schubert; nine assorted overtures by Beethoven, Mendelssohn, Berlioz, Glinka, Schumann, and others; concertos by Beethoven, Joachim, Rubinstein, and Saint-Saëns; and the *Missa solemnis* by Cherubini. In reviewing this wide-ranging repertoire, which was ancillary to his main work in the opera house, *Dwight's Journal of Music* uttered the understatement of the year when it remarked, 'Here is prodigious activity and no mistake'.[5]

Inevitably the singers and players began to chafe beneath so heavy a burden, borne within so short a space of time. While usual for Bülow, this sort of activity was not at all usual for the players, used as they were to working with conductors of a more amiable disposition. To make matters more complex still, Bülow reformed the seating arrangement of the orchestra, not once but twice, until he had achieved the desired sound.[6]

III

The two years that Bülow spent in Hanover reestablished him as Germany's leading conductor. He rented living quarters in the old Rudolph Hotel, on the corner of Bäringstrasse and Georgstrasse, where he was looked after by a faithful manservant named Heinrich ('Ein Mädchen für alles', as Bülow jovially described him[7]). Later he moved into the more spacious Union Hotel. Once ensconced there he hung a sign outside his door that has meanwhile become famous:

---

5. The issue of July 5, 1875, p. 104, contains the complete repertoire.
6. Bülow had inherited an unusual seating plan from Joseph Bott, who had placed the entire string quartet to the left of the conductor's podium, while grouping the woodwind, brass, and percussion sections to the right—an arrangement that had been endorsed by Bott's mentor, the venerable violinist Louis Spohr. Bülow was dissatisfied with the sound, and reassigned the players. To his left he placed the first violins, woodwinds, and horns; to his right he placed the second violins, violas, brass, and percussion. The cellos and double bass players he placed along the back. The orchestra pit was cramped, and the players complained; but by the beginning of the 1879 season the pit had been enlarged (involving some further readjustments) and the sixty-four-piece orchestra gradually accustomed itself to the 'Bülow sound'. For a fuller account of the various upheavals the orchestra endured at this time, see FHB, pp. 47–48.
7. Best translated in this context as 'a jack-of-all-trades'.

HANS von Bülow, Kapellmeister.
VORMITTAGS nicht zu Hause
NACHMITTAGS nicht zu sprechen[8]

Although Bülow's reputation as a disciplinarian had preceded him, the players and singers at Hanover never got used to his banter and his bile, which he apportioned according to merit. As they assembled for their morning rehearsals, they could never be sure what to expect from their mercurial maestro—who regularly placed them in the unusual position of rejecting anything which fell short of perfection. There were players in the Hanover Orchestra who hated Bülow for the pressures under which he placed them, and they watched him apprehensively for any sign of a bad mood when he turned up for work. Erich Rosendahl, the Hanover Theatre's most reliable chronicler, is amusing to the point of comedy on this topic. 'Whenever the Herr Kapellmeister appeared at the morning rehearsal, clad in those wide yellow trousers that the entire theatre troupe called Krakelhose, (or scraggly pants), through which he had thrust his legs a bit too far, everybody knew that the barometer was set for "stormy".'[9]

On such occasions Bülow would work himself into a lather as he pulled the recalcitrant orchestra along behind him. His baton once went sailing through the air, and landed in the middle of the players. They sat on their chairs like statues, too nervous to move. Bülow, too, remained immobile, glaring at them and waiting for some poor wretch to break the tension and come forward with the stick. When nothing happened, he left the podium, retrieved the baton, smiled wryly at the orchestra, and simply said, 'Let us continue!' Bülow himself was the only person allowed to dispel the tension that he had created. The stories from those times abound, and we would fail as Bülow's chronicler if some of them were not related here. During an operatic rehearsal, the prima donna started to sing out of tune and the ensemble became so discordant that Bülow stopped the orchestra and invited them to retune their instruments. Then, turning to the soprano (instead of to the oboe, as is usual) he bowed deeply and said in his most sardonic vein, 'Would you mind, Madame, giving us *your* A?'[10] He could be equally ironic with the female chorus. He once became so irritated with the ceaseless chatter of these ladies that he called out to them, 'Ladies, I have to draw your attention to the fact that the Capitol has already been saved!'[11]

---

8. 'Mornings—not at home. Afternoons—not available'.
9. RGH, p. 136.
10. DM, Heft 7, January 1910/11, p. 213.
11. BBLW, p. 291. This esoteric allusion was to the classical legend that Rome was saved from the enemy at the gate by the cackling of a flock of geese.

During his Hanover years Bülow is said to have had a large picture of a ballerina hanging on his office wall. When asked if this was because he admired her art, Bülow replied, 'Quite so. She is the only member of the company who does not sing out of tune'. The *corps de ballet,* in fact, was usually looked upon with favour by Bülow, perhaps because it was rarely in a position to give him those purely musical headaches which originated in the orchestra pit. While conducting an opera one night he was so charmed with the work of the dancers on stage that he invited the entire troupe to join him at his hotel for dinner, giving instructions to the head waiter that they could order whatever they wished. Here he fell victim to his own caprice. From the *première* down to the *coryphée* they all ordered lobster, the most expensive dish on the menu. Bülow had to foot a bill of nearly 300 dollars—a small fortune in Hanover at that time—an incident which caused a stir in the small community.[12]

IV

On May 25, 1878, life in Hanover was enlivened by the arrival of Liszt, who stayed for a whole week with Bülow and Bronsart. He had come to discuss the forthcoming annual festival of the Allgemeiner Deutscher Musikverein (an organization of which he was the president), to be held in Erfurt during the period June 22 to 26. Until the very last moment Liszt had been uncertain whether Bülow would even agree to take part, and he was reluctant to issue the invitation himself. It was only when he learned indirectly from Carl Riedel (the conductor of the famed Riedel Choral Society in Leipzig) that Bülow had expressed willingness to participate in the Erfurt celebrations that Liszt decided to thank Bülow in person and arrive at some firm decisions about the repertoire. Liszt had not seen Bülow since their last meeting in Rome, in June 1874. During the four years that had meanwhile elapsed he had followed his old pupil's meteoric career closely, and had been concerned about his state of health. Ten days before setting out for Hanover, in fact, Liszt had written an unusually diplomatic message to Bülow which set the scene for his visit:

Dear Unique One,
Just this minute I received a note from Riedel that tells me that you will have the great kindness of lending distinction to the next 'Tonkünstler Versammlung' in Erfurt. I would not have ventured to ask you for this favour but am very grateful to you for granting it.
On Saturday, 25 May, I hope to meet you again in Hanover.

12. *The Etude,* July 1888.

Semper ubique [ever and everywhere]
Your F. Liszt
15 May '78, Weimar[13]

Whatever concerns Liszt may have harboured about Bülow's physical condition were put to rest when he witnessed him conduct a performance
of Wagner's *Rienzi* (on May 26) which, thanks to Bülow, was now in the
Hanover Theatre's standard repertory.[14] The details of the Erfurt festival
then preoccupied everybody for the next couple of days. The small town
had just opened a new theatre, with 1,100 seats; and adjoining it was a
new concert hall, well suited for recitals.

In Erfurt Bülow was reunited with a number of his old friends and colleagues, including the composer Felix Draeseke, the critic Otto Lessmann,
the conductor Max Erdmannsdörfer, and a number of orchestral players
from the combined ranks of the Weimar, Erfurt, and Sondershausen orchestras. The main works conducted by Liszt were his own Psalm Thirteen
for Tenor and Orchestra, and his Symphonic Poem *Hungaria*. Max Erdmannsdörfer conducted Liszt's Two Episodes from Lenau's 'Faust', a topical choice when we recall that the meeting between Faust and Mephis-
topheles, according to the old legend, had taken place in Erfurt's village
inn, not far from the concert hall. Bülow's chief contribution was to appear as soloist in Bronsart's Piano Concerto no. 1, in F-sharp minor, with
Liszt conducting. He also appeared with the cellist Friedrich Grützmacher
and the violinist August Kömpel in a performance of Bronsart's Piano
Trio in G minor, which had been revised and published the previous year.
Bülow was delighted when his promotion of Bronsart's music captured
the attention of Breitkopf and Härtel who asked for all the composer's
manuscripts to be sent to them.

At the end of the festival, Liszt was in an expansive mood. He insisted
on taking Bülow back with him to Weimar, accompanied by Bronsart and
his wife, and by Otto Lessmann. In Weimar they attended a concert performance of Berlioz's *Damnation of Faust,* and the following afternoon

13. Hitherto unpublished. Holograph in the Surrey History Centre, England (ref. 2185/
JB /87/26).
14. Immediately after the performance Bülow was moved to write in his music calendar: 'Historic date!' Thirty-four years earlier, as a fourteen-year-old boy, he had heard *Rienzi*
brought to life in Dresden under Wagner's baton, in the presence of Liszt. With dry humour
Bülow went on to point out in a letter to his mother that 'today, son-in-law no. 1 conducted
in Hanover the very same first-born composition of son-in-law no. 2 for the magician of
Rome, Pest, and Weimar' (BB, vol. 5, pp. 503–504). See also page 36 of the present volume.

there was an informal soirée in Liszt's home, the Hofgärtnerei, during which Bülow delighted Liszt with performances of his old master's *Ricordanza* and the Eighth Hungarian Rhapsody. That evening they went across to Frau Emilie Merian-Genast (the sister-in-law of Raff) where Bülow and Kömpel, in a nostalgic frame of mind, played Raff's—'Volker's Abschied'—for violin and piano. For two or three days the party of friends revelled in one another's company, and the experience had a beneficial effect on Bülow. He was sufficiently relaxed to have a heart-to-heart chat with Adelheid von Schorn, whose acquaintance he had first made in Weimar some twenty-five years earlier. In her memoir of the Erfurt festival, and of Bülow's subsequent visit to Weimar, Schorn recounted a story that Bülow enjoyed telling against himself. He once visited a lady who was not very sympathetic towards him. In the course of the increasingly animated conversation she began to tease him. He told her, 'I am like my clock. If one winds me up, I go'. Whereupon he picked up his hat and left.[15]

Bülow stayed on in Weimar a day or two longer than the others, and Liszt enjoyed his company. Shortly after Bülow had left, von Schorn visited Liszt and they chatted about Bülow 'whom he loves very much. His character he considers very highly, and demands of others that they accept his weaknesses calmly, just as he does himself'.[16]

V

Bülow took frequent advantage of the liberal terms of his contract in Hanover, giving occasional recitals elsewhere in Germany and even returning to Britain for brief periods between the autumn of 1878, and the early part of 1880, to play in London and the provinces in order pick up more English money.[17] These trips represented colourful extensions to his earlier visits to Britain. In November 1878, for instance, he crossed the English Channel for a six-week tour which embraced London, Brighton, Liverpool, Manchester, Bristol, Birmingham, and Glasgow. Why abandon Hanover at such a time, even as a temporary expedient? Why take

15. SZM, pp. 347–348
16. Ibid., p. 348.
17. Bülow's concerts in Britain were now under the exclusive control of Narciso Vertigliano, who took over George Dolby's agency when the latter finally retired in 1880. 'Vert', as he liked to be addressed, was known in the business as 'the veritable Napoleon of Managers', a designation that would have appealed to Bülow. Vert's nephew Pedro Tillet joined him at the agency, which years later was metamorphosed into 'Ibbs & Tillet', one of the most successful British concert agencies of the twentieth century, with a roster of artists second to none. See FI, pp. 1–12.

on the aggravation that concert tours of the British provinces invariably seemed to bring his way? The answer to our questions will surprise no one who has followed the story of Bülow's life thus far.

In the summer of 1876 the first Bayreuth Festival had incurred a large deficit of 120,000 marks after mounting the world premier of *The Ring*, and its future was now in doubt. Until the books were balanced there could be no question of arranging another festival (the second Bayreuth Festival, in fact, did not take place until 1882). In an attempt to liquidate the debt, Wagner undertook to conduct a series of eight marathon concerts of his music in London's Albert Hall, in May 1878. He and Cosima stayed for the whole of that month as guests of Edward Dannreuther in Bayswater. A huge orchestra of 170 musicians was assembled (105 in the string section alone), and some distinguished singers who had sung leading roles at Bayreuth were engaged as well. Although the concerts attracted large audiences, the profits were small. After the musicians and singers had been paid, Wagner had returned to Bayreuth with the derisory sum of 700 pounds in his pocket. Bülow smouldered with discontent at what he considered to be this snub on the part of the German nation against Wagner and the Bayreuth enterprise. He referred witheringly to 'shabby Germany' and railed against his fellow citizens for refusing to be parted from their money in support of a cause he considered sublime. Bülow had yearned from the depths of his soul to attend Bayreuth in 1876, in order to witness the miracle of *The Ring* for himself. His illness in the summer of that year, following his return from America, had mercifully prevented him from facing a crushing realization: even if he had been well enough to go, his presence in the small town would have stirred up a hornet's nest of resentment among the Wagner family. Bülow's ambivalent relationship with Bayreuth, which was presently a closed city for him, is a complex topic to which we will return. For the moment, only one thing needs to be noted. In January 1878, once the full extent of Wagner's financial débâcle was made known to him, Bülow set himself the preliminary task of raising 10,000 marks for the recently established Bayreuth Festival Deficit Fund.[18] We use the word preliminary with caution because no one has ever been able to state with certainty just how much money Bülow raised for Bayreuth across the years. It is enough to know that after the British tours of 1878—1879 were over, Bülow was reported

18. As early as August 7, 1878, we find Bülow telling Carl Bechstein that raising money for Bayreuth 'amounts to a moral necessity for me' (BNB, p. 386). By January 1879 he was able to inform Karl Klindworth that he planned to raise 10,000 marks, a target that within a few months had increased to 40,000 marks. For the year 1879 alone, incidentally, there are receipts in the Bülow archives in Berlin amounting to more than 10,000 marks paid into the Bayreuth Deficit Fund (DSB, NL HvBülow, F IV, 11).

to have deposited the sum of 16,817 marks into the Fund,[19] and that was just a beginning. In February 1880 we even find him entering the heart of darkness itself, when he gave a benefit concert in Munich, a city that still harboured ghosts of times past. He was overwhelmed when he received a standing ovation, with the audience shouting 'Hier bleiben!' [Stay here!]. Ten years had elapsed since Bülow left this pit of despair. 'This new generation is worth more than the old one', he observed. 'Almost half the orchestra members began their studies under my direction, and have become not only intelligent and excellent artists but "gentlemen".'[20]

This victory in Munich netted 2,400 marks for Wagner. It emboldened Bülow to move on to Bayreuth itself, where he gave a solitary benefit concert on February 15. It was the only occasion on which he is known to have visited the town, and the reason it was possible for him to do so was because the Wagners had left for a protracted stay in Italy the previous month, and there was no possibility of meeting them. Bülow was greeted at the railway station by Friedrich Feustel (the Bayreuth banker appointed by Wagner to oversee the financial affairs of the Festival) and his cohorts—including the mayor and Hans von Wolzogen, the editor of the *Bayreuther Blätter*. They positively fawned over Bülow, doubtless seeing in him their last best hope of clearing the festival deficit. They even arranged for him to tour the Bayreuth Festival Theatre, an experience that made 'a grandiose impression on me', as he later expressed it.[21] Meanwhile he informed Klindworth, 'You know I intend to raise 40,000 marks in all', a challenging target that must have filled Feustel's heart with gladness when it was made known to him. By September 6, however, we find Bülow admitting to Klindworth that because he was still 12,000 marks short of his goal, he had decided to make good the difference out of his own pocket. The sum of 40,000 marks was duly despatched to the Bayreuth Deficit Fund. It was a magnificent contribution, and Feustel and his colleagues could be forgiven for indulging in the small outbreak of joy that followed. Bülow had just eased their burden by one-third. Alas, they had reckoned without Wagner himself. We now know that Wagner's pride refused to allow him to accept the gift, and he returned it to Bülow after discovering that a substantial portion of it had come from Bülow's private purse. Since this matter has been much disputed, we should draw attention to a letter that Cosima wrote to Daniela, on March 16, 1881, which not only offers proof positive of Wagner's refusal to accept Bülow's gift, but goes on to tell Daniela that Wagner had requested that the money be

19. *Musical Review,* February 5, 1880.
20. BB, vol. 6, p. 10.
21. Ibid., p. 11.

A Bülow recital in benefit of the Bayreuth Festival Fund in Dresden, March 10, 1879. A concert billing.

invested for her and the other children.[22] Had anyone else met with this sort of rebuttal, they would have drawn a swift and obvious conclusion: namely, that Wagner did not want to be helped by his wife's former husband, especially in so public a fashion, and the river of benefaction would have dried up immediately. But we are not dealing with anyone else; we are dealing with Bülow. He seemed determined to make Wagner and Bayreuth dependent on him. The benefit recitals would continue. We even find Bülow sending money to Bayreuth after Wagner had died, and was no longer in a position to refuse it.

The many recitals that Bülow gave in behalf of the Bayreuth Deficit Fund have never been properly chronicled. The following list is based on surviving concert programmes for the years 1878–1880, preserved in the Deutsche Staatsbibliothek, and it is almost certainly incomplete.

1878	
October 23	Berlin Singakademie
1879	
January 22	Berlin Singakademie
February 10	Bremen
March 10	Dresden Hotel de Saxe
March 11	Leipzig Gewandhaus
March 26	Berlin Singakademie
April 9	Cologne
October 23	Berlin Singakademie
November 24	Cologne
December 12	Berlin Singakademie
December 17	Hanover Stadttheater
1880	
January 4	Leipzig Gewandhaus
February 12	Munich Odeon Theatre
February 16	Bayreuth
April 13	Munich Museum
April 15	Mannheim Court Theatre
April 17	Karlsruhe Museum

Wagner was fully aware of these concerts, which were widely advertised across Germany; yet he appears to have shown scant regard for what Bülow was doing. The blood and toil that the pianist invested in them evidently counted for nothing.

22. CWBD, p. 171. Bülow set out the figures in a letter to Hans von Wolzogen, dated 'September 10, 1880' (BB, vol. 6, p. 28) who in turn must have made it known to Wagner that a substantial part of the gift of 40,000 marks came from Bülow's own pocket.

VI

Bülow's appearance in London's St. James's Hall, on November 20, 1878, was notable because he played the last five piano sonatas of Beethoven in one recital, in chronological order—the first time such a thing had been attempted in Britain. This evangelical project had been forming in Bülow's mind ever since he had moved to Hanover, and he had only recently found the opportunity to put it into practice. He had launched the programme a month earlier, on October 23, in Berlin's Singakademie, and had donated the funds to the Bayreuth cause. He entertained no illusions about the popularity of such a programme.[23] Its purpose was to win converts to the difficult music of Beethoven's final period, a mission that Bülow pursued with fervour across the years. It may be useful to remind the reader that before Charles Hallé had appeared in London, in 1848, no Beethoven sonata had ever been publicly performed in that city. The first sonata that London heard from Hallé's fingers was the one in E-flat major, op. 31, no. 3, at one of John Ella's 'Musical Union' concerts; it aroused such interest that it was soon followed by the one in D major, op. 28, the *Pastorale*.[24] It was still an uphill battle though. When Bülow announced that he would play the last five sonatas of Beethoven at one sitting, it is a fair guess that few in the audience had ever heard them.[25] This concert in St. James's Hall was delivered from memory, as usual, and although we are told by one particularly observant gentleman of the press that it contained some minor blemishes, they were 'so trifling as to be distinguishable only by those who came looking for them'.[26] The hall was not full, or, to borrow a diplomatic phrase from this same wordsmith, the audience 'though fit, were few'.

At Bülow's Glasgow recital, given in The Queen's Room on November 22, he was again faced with rows of empty seats, although for a different reason.[27] This depressing spectacle was the result of the financial collapse

23. Bülow had floated the idea with Bechstein earlier in the year, and when he had failed to arouse the piano-maker's enthusiasm he complained, 'Berlin must have sunk very low if it cannot listen to my reading of Beethoven's complete testament: the sonata cycle of opp. 101, 106, 109, 110, and 111. Well, if the middle classes cannot listen . . . let them walk out'. Bülow then raised the admission price (BNB, pp. 386 and 388).

24. HLL, pp. 103–104.

25. Seventeen years earlier, in 1861, Charles Hallé had played all thirty-two sonatas of Beethoven in this same hall. He diminished his burden, however, and that of his audience, by unfolding them across eight recitals, and he included some vocal numbers for contrast, and later some of the Beethoven violin and piano sonatas as well. This feat he repeated in 1862. By the time that Hallé arrived on the scene, Arabella Goddard had played the *Hammerklavier* Sonata in public four times. But it was left to Bülow to offer the last five sonatas in one helping.

26. MMR, December 1878, p. 191.

27. BB, vol. 5, p. 533.

of the Bank of Glasgow the previous month, which had lost more than 7 million pounds. Fraud was involved, and several directors were ultimately sent to jail. Many ordinary Glaswegians were rendered penniless, and could no longer afford the luxury of attending concerts. Bülow consoled himself with the thought that he played well, even though few were there to hear him. It was an irony that would not have been lost on him that this box office fiasco coincided with Saint Cecilia's Day. The patron saint of music does not always look after her own. Bülow had a better attendance in Edinburgh a day or two later, where he once more played the last five sonatas of Beethoven.

Then came Newcastle, London, Brighton, Liverpool, Birkenhead, and Manchester, in that order. Birkenhead was one of the low points of the tour. Bülow was joined by a group of local musicians for a performance of Hummel's Septet, a work he admired. The reading had hardly got underway when it became apparent that the horn player had consumed too much whisky, and the ensemble hovered on the brink of disintegration, with Bülow anxiously filling in the missing phrases. He later wrote that while the hornist in his inebriated state saw only half the notes, he also saw double the rests, so the audience benefitted by hearing rather less of this worthy than would otherwise have been the case.[28]

From Brighton he wrote a letter of thanks to Bechstein for providing four grand pianos for the tour. One instrument remained behind in London, while the other three were shuttled back and forth to various cities, there to await Bülow's arrival. He told Bechstein:

> Brighton, last of November 1878
>
> All four grands are glorious, just what I always dreamed you would produce in the end. . . . It seems to me that this last short but energetic tour—eleven concerts behind me, six (including today's) still to come—will at last bring your name the recognition it deserves. Certainly, you appear to be becoming dangerous to your competitors. Steinway spends no end of money advertising in just those towns and on those days when I play 'you'.[29]

This brief tour of England ended on a note of low comedy. Bülow boarded the night train from London to Dover only to discover that it was delayed. When he finally arrived at Dover's dockside his steamer had put out to sea ten minutes earlier. Bülow tells us that with the help of a

28. *The Musical World*, February 1, 1879, p. 67.
29. BNB, p. 392.

generous tip he managed to board another ship to Calais, but his luggage was 'left in the lurch' at the Belgium border, together with all his money.[30] He got back to Hanover exhausted, on Sunday afternoon, December 8, minus his personal possessions, just in time to conduct a performance of Auber's *La muette de Portici* that same evening.[31] Only later, after an animated exchange of telegrammes, was his luggage released to him.

VII

Bülow's final season at the Hanover Opera House turned into the most demanding yet—both for him and the players. His 'music-calendar' shows that he began rehearsals on August 26, 1879, and drove himself and the performers to the brink of exhaustion for the next two months. Wagner's *Rienzi, Tannhäuser,* and *Lohengrin* were all performed in September; as were Mozart's *Don Giovanni,* Weber's *Freischütz,* Beethoven's *Fidelio,* and the Brahms *Requiem.*[32] The orchestral concerts also flourished, and attracted an increase of 150 subscribers over the previous year, with two extra concerts to accommodate the overflow. 'Hanover is becoming the world's music centre!' Bülow exclaimed ironically.[33] It could not last. The theatre was a ticking time bomb, and no one was quite sure when it would go off.

If Bülow's brief tenure at Hanover is remembered by the wider world today, it is for his famous confrontations with the Heldentenor Anton Schott which have entered the history books. While Bülow was popular with neither the orchestral players nor the singers, it was with Schott that he had his most memorable encounters. In light of the precipitous decline in their later relationship, it may surprise some readers to learn that Bülow considered Schott to have a good and promising voice, and at first wanted nothing more than to improve him through a bit of coaching here and there. For such aspirations Schott had little patience. In earlier life he had been a cavalry officer, more used to giving orders than to receiving them. Once, during a rehearsal of Berlioz's *Benvenuto Cellini,* Bülow took Schott to task over some trifling matter. While the cast was enjoying a well-deserved break, Bülow overheard Schott complaining to a fellow singer that 'an artillery officer should not flaunt his rank', an obvious reference to how an officer and a gentleman should behave in the presence of those he is privileged to command. We are told that Bülow bit his lip so hard that he almost drew blood and repressed his first ri-

30. BB, vol. 5, p. 539.
31. BNB, p. 393.
32. BB, vol. 5, pp. 591–592.
33. BNB, p. 391.

poste, doubtless depriving the world of one of his finer insults. After a pause for reflection, he managed to bark back, 'Indeed, I understand nothing about artillery'.[34] But the seeds of revenge had been planted in Bülow's mind, and he awaited an opportunity to puncture Schott's vanity. In the third act of *Rienzi* the Tribune makes an entry on stage, sitting astride his horse. As a former cavalry officer Schott allowed his various riding skills to exhibit themselves to special effect, but at the expense of his singing. Bülow rounded on Schott and cried out sarcastically, 'Herr Schott, do you take me for the circus director Carré?' (Oskar Carré's circus, based in Amsterdam, was famous for its performing animals.) It was now Schott's turn to take offense at the notion that the imposing military figure he wished to cut on the Hanover stage might be mistaken for a member of Carré's troupe. At the next rehearsal Schott appeared once more on his horse, but with a riding crop in his hand with which he swished the air, as if to mock Bülow's authority and make it appear that the conductor really was directing a circus. The stage manager, Alexander Liebe, was absent that day, otherwise the infuriated Bülow would have sought permission to fire Schott on the spot.

Relations between the Heldentenor and the conductor now went into a headlong decline. Like any other opera house in Germany, it was customary at Hanover for the singers to receive floral tributes at the end of each act, which were thrown from the stalls onto the stage by their adoring fans. On one occasion, one of these 'vegetables of fame', as Bülow disparagingly called them, landed at the feet of Anton Schott after a performance that Bülow found particularly distressing. 'Look at the beautiful bouquet that lies at my feet', Schott taunted Bülow. 'Yes', cried Bülow. 'It lies at the very spot on which you made a mess of things!'[35] In September 1879, during a rehearsal of Wagner's *Lohengrin*, Schott sang so unrhythmically that he parted company with Bülow's baton. Bülow saw his chance, and making creative use of Schott's earlier comment on what constitutes acceptable behaviour for officers, came out with his celebrated line, 'You are no Knight of the Swan [Schwan], but a Knight of the Swine [Schwein]'.[36]

<hr />

34. This depiction of Bülow as an 'artillery officer' was an inside joke on the part of Schott, which the modern reader cannot be expected to appreciate. There was another Hans von Bülow (1816–1897), an artillery officer who had distinguished himself on the field of battle in the Franco-Prussian War of 1870–1871, and who now enjoyed the rank of inspector general of artillery for the whole of Germany.

35. DM, 1910/11, p. 213 ('*auf der Sie gepatzt haben*'). Bülow himself was once presented with a laurel wreath at the end of a recital. He declined it with the words, 'I am not a vegetarian'.

36. These and other anecdotes stemming from Bülow's time at Hanover may be found in RGH, pp. 135–138.

When placed in this context, Bülow's comment, 'A "tenor" is not a voice but a disease', takes on the character of personal experience. However, it was Bülow who left Hanover, and not Schott. While it must have cost Bronsart dear, he was obliged to accept the fact that the only way to keep the peace was to let the conductor leave. The last opera Bülow directed for Hanover in an official capacity was Mozart's *Don Giovanni*, on October 23, 1879. Two days later he tendered his resignation. He told Klindworth that Bronsart had refused to accept his ultimatum setting out his conditions for remaining in the city. 'The Amitié between us is over'.[37] It must have given Bülow some quiet satisfaction to know that while the players and the administration were happy to see him go, the Hanoverians themselves were of a different mind. A petition containing 1,200 signatures from the general public was sent to the king, urging that Bülow be allowed to stay in his post.

If Schott thought that the departure of Bülow gave him free play on the Hanover stage, he was quickly disillusioned. Almost immediately he ran afoul of Bülow's successor, Ernst Frank. The Heldentenor then discovered that he had 'jumped from the frying-pan into the fire'.[38] To be battered by Bülow or fried by Frank was not much of an option, and Schott's days were numbered. He, too, was released from his contract with Hanover two years later, in 1881.

---

37. BNB, p. 67.
38. RGH, p. 138.

Britannia Scorned,
1878–1879

Encounters and Skirmishes in
'The Land without Music'

A journey in a fog
—Bülow[1]

I

When Bülow left Britain, in January 1878, in order to resume his duties in Hanover, his reputation throughout the country stood at its zenith. Had he never gone back, he would have continued to carry the admiration of the nation with him. He did go back, however, and built up resentment among the English because of his sharp tongue and abrasive comments. Undoubtedly his nerves were fretted by the ongoing tensions in the Hanover theatre; and his tribulations could hardly have been eased by the arrival of a dismal English winter, making travel through the provinces, much of it at night, a difficult business. For whatever reason, the moment he set foot in Britain again, in November 1878, he began to hold forth in a series of musical 'Travelogues' for publication in the Leipzig *Signale*, which were critical of musical life in this country. They appeared under the general title of 'Autocritical Notes of a Journey in a Fog', and were translated into English and reprinted in British journals.[2] Bülow sent

1. The title of Bülow's travel diary in England. BAS (part 2), p. 180.
2. Notably in *The Musical World* and *The London Figaro*. They were also reprinted in *Dwight's Journal of Music* for the benefit of American readers. These polemical 'Travelogues' were written at the invitation of Bülow's longtime colleague Bartholf Senff, the editor of the Leipzig *Signale*. Such 'letters from abroad' had a long literary tradition. Liszt had written his 'Letters of a Bachelor of Music', while travelling through Switzerland and Italy in the 1830s.

his despatches from such diverse places as Sydenham, Sheffield, Manchester, Bristol, Liverpool, Birmingham, Glasgow, Birkenhead, and London—anywhere that his tour happened to take him. Of musical life in England he was generally dismissive. He derided the amateur status that music was given within the social fabric of the country. Nothing and no one was spared. Sir Julius Benedict, Sir William Sterndale Bennett, August Manns—all fell victim to his rapier comments. Of a composition by Sterndale Bennett he declared that it sounded so much like Mendelssohn that it could have been written by Julius Benedict.[3] And when he heard that Benedict had arranged a concert in benefit of Benedict himself, Bülow called him 'Sir Julius Benefit', a comment made yet more piquant by the fact that Benedict's father had been a local banker in Stuttgart, which raised questions as to why his musician son was now attempting to live at the public's whim. August Manns, the conductor of the famous Crystal Palace Concerts, with whom Bülow had already appeared, he damned with particularly faint praise (and by default the whole of musical London) when he remarked that 'in the country of the blind, the one-eyed man is king'.[4] Put another way, this meant that whenever the public was unmusical enough, it was possible for incompetents to avoid detection and rise to the top. He was particularly contemptuous of the way in which orchestral players were hired by the hour, racing from one engagement to another in order to make a living, the same faces often appearing in different orchestras on consecutive nights, and frequently absent from rehearsals—or worse, present at rehearsals and absent from concerts. He quoted with approval Berlioz's witticism that in London the musicians were so busy rehearsing that 'they do not have time to perform'. His rage against the incompetence of certain individual musicians boiled over in a letter he wrote to *The London Figaro*. He reminded his readers that the emperor Napoleon III had an axiom to the effect that 'you only really destroy something if you replace it'. And he went on to recommend that in the interests of good music 'W.C.', 'A.M.', and 'Dr. W' should be replaced immediately by Henry Gadsby, Charles Hallé, and Arthur Sullivan.[5] He was equally critical of certain English cities. Of Sheffield he remarked that 'you

---

And George Sand had also contributed to the genre in her 'Lettres d'un Voyageur'. One of the earliest of Bülow's missives was mailed from Glasgow, as early as November 1877, during his tenure with the Glasgow Choral Union, and was largely complimentary of his Scottish hosts. It was the later ones, begun in 1878, on which the English musical establishment began to choke, and brought about Britannia's retribution.

3. BBLW, p. 282.

4. BAS (part 2), p. 165.

5. Issue of November 10, 1877, p. 7. We surmise that 'W.C.' was William Cusins, who had succeeded Sterndale Bennett as the conductor of the Philharmonic Society concerts; 'A.M.' was undoubtedly August Manns, the conductor of the Crystal Palace concerts; and 'Dr. W.' was Dr. Henry Wylde, the principal of the London Academy of Music.

only know about the sun from hearsay',[6] and held its smoke-clouds responsible for the want of colour in the music of Sterndale Bennett who, as he put it, had had the misfortune to be born there. Because this gifted composer had died only three years earlier, there were many who thought the comment tasteless, and it did not sit well. Bülow even turned his critical gaze on London, and described it as a mere 'station on the road to Scotland'.[7]

II

Some of the sharpest arrows in Bülow's quiver were aimed in the direction of August Manns. Manns had at first been cordiality itself with regards to Bülow, and had engaged him as a soloist on several occasions for the round-the-year Crystal Palace Concerts he directed—though never as a conductor, a fact which appeared to work like a corrosive on Bülow's sensibilities. Manns had been a military bandmaster in the Prussian army before settling in England, and, as Bülow saw it, had brought to his adopted country no more than the mechanical attributes required to ensure that his ensemble could start and finish together—somewhat like recruits on the parade-ground. Bülow now attacked 'poor Mr. Manns's' conducting abilities in the columns of *The London Figaro*. At first the good-natured Manns let it pass. But since the attacks continued, and having had as many 'twittings as he cared to take', as he put it, Manns retaliated with a lengthy polemic of his own in *The Musical World*.[8]

From a careful reading of the text we learn something about which Bülow himself remained silent throughout his dispute with Manns. Bülow had offered to conduct the Crystal Palace Orchestra without a fee, and Manns had turned him down. An entire comedy of errors was at play in the background, but the chief facts of the matter can be simply stated. Manns had engaged the great violinist Pablo Sarasate to be one of his soloists. Bülow, somewhat unwisely, but acting out of both friendship and admiration for Sarasate, wrote the violinist a letter in which he offered to replace Manns as his conductor. 'It will cost the Crystal Palace Company nothing', Bülow assured Sarasate. Bülow then suggested that Sarasate himself should carry these joyful tidings to Manns, and to the directors of the orchestra, while he, Bülow, simply sat back and awaited their call. In the carrying out of such a delicate mission Sarasate's courage failed him, and instead of requesting Bülow's services as if it were a personal

6. BAS (part 2), p. 191.
7. *The London Figaro*, November 10, 1877, p. 7.
8. Issue of January 12, 1878, pp. 42–44. The article bore the inflated title 'Dr. Hans von Bülow's Prescriptions for the Cure of Anti-Bülowism'. Manns also had this article published privately as a separate pamphlet for circulation among his friends.

St. James's Hall, Piccadilly. A lithograph.

favour, he showed Bülow's unfortunate letter to Manns. Manns was at a loss to understand why Bülow, who was at that moment living with his relatives, the Bojanowski family, in Victoria Park Lodge, in Sydenham, just a stone's throw away from Crystal Palace, did not simply walk across the road to his office and approach him directly, and he refused Bülow's offer. 'My readers know what followed', wrote Manns. '*The London Figaro* was advised to destroy and replace me as soon as possible in the interests of good music.' Manns also published Bülow's private letter to Sarasate for the whole world to see, an act that must have enraged Bülow.

What weakened Manns's position throughout this long wrangle was that while Bülow had seen him conduct a number of times at the Crystal Palace Concerts, Manns had not yet observed Bülow at work on the podium. And without that Manns was unable to move from his present position of defence to one of attack.

All that changed on the evening of November 19, 1878, when Bülow gave an orchestral concert in St. James's Hall, and Manns arrived looking for trouble. Manns tells us that he paid 10 shillings for two tickets, and 'had my full money's worth'. Part of the value Manns obtained for the price of admission was a conducting climax '. . . in Liszt's *Totentanz,* in a quick movement in triple-time, for which my noble confrère performed the wondrous feat of making about two hundred and fifty beats per minute: a task which none of the "Fabrikdirigenten aller Orten"[9] could have accomplished; because they, in their lazy mode of time-beating, would—as I at least invariably do—have preferred to mark the full bars only'. Manns reserved his most humourous observations for Bülow's interpretation of Beethoven's Fifth Symphony, 'which, one may safely say, has never had its like on terra firma'. If Victorian England knew nothing else about Beethoven, it knew that the first four notes of this symphony represented 'Destiny knocking at the door'. So Manns took that as his point of departure:

It was a grand idea of my noble confrère to prefix three silent bars at the beginning of the first movement. I wonder if some New German-principled conductor could add four bars more in order to vex Destiny—who, as we know, is waiting to knock at the door—into a still greater fury than Herr von Bülow did last Tuesday. That Destiny was made impatient through being compelled to wait three bars before it could proceed with its knocking at the door became evident to all who were present; for it did knock with a vengeance after the first beat, and rushed off with such a furious impetuosity that my noble colleague got fairly frightened, and was compelled 'to pull up' which had the disastrous effect of destroying, for the rest of the movement, the plastic pose of his left arm, because the left hand had to assist the right one in tightening the reins of infuriated Destiny. It was accomplished most beautifully and made its mark on my impression. . . .

To sum up in a few words . . . in St. James's Hall [Bülow] showed me by actual deeds what he had told me last year in his uncalled-for letters to the Leipzig *Signale,* in words of unbridled conceit and arrogance, namely, HOW I OUGHT—NOT TO DO IT.
August Manns
Crystal Palace, November, 1878.[10]

9. 'Factory-made conductors from all over the place'—Bülow's unflattering description of his peers on the podium.

10. *The London Figaro;* reprinted in *The Musical World,* December 21, 1878. Manns's description of Bülow's baton swishing the air with three silent bars before the opening notes of the Fifth Symphony will raise eyebrows, because not even an amateur military bandmaster would have done such a thing. What Manns singularly fails to mention, and we must point out, is that Bülow was conducting an orchestra made up in large part of advanced pupils from the Royal Normal College and Academy of Music for the Blind, and their professors. While the leader (Carl Deichmann), and a few musicians placed at strategic points in the ensemble, could see him, some of the players were partially blind, and others completely so, and they had memorized their parts. One of the soloists was the blind violinist Prince Alexander of Hesse, a pupil at the Academy, who played Beethoven's Romance in

III

It goes to the heart of Bülow's complex personality that he was incapable of observing the conflict of interest in which these skirmishes placed him. Here he was, a frequent visitor to a foreign country that had given him some of its highest honours, and he was repaying them by lampooning their provincial ways for the amusement of his German readers. His comments eventually drew the ire of the *Musical Times,* which loosed a broadside against him in March 1879:

> Dr. von Bülow has been writing to a German paper from England some things about England, which display his usual good taste and amiability. As far as we know, nobody invited this virtuoso to come amongst us; but he did come, and, having constituted himself a guest, proceeded to sneer at his hosts. A few examples of his politeness will suffice. Finding himself in Sheffield under a canopy of smoke, he bethought him of Sterndale Bennett, and wrote, 'It is said that the English Toledo or Solingen can boast of knowing the sun only from hearsay. In this report I always believed that I could find an explanation of the style of composition affected [*sic*] by the late Sir W. S. Bennett, who first beheld the darkness of the world amid the ocean of smoke-clouds at Sheffield, and whose want of colour is as remarkable as his correct drawing, which latter obtained for him, as we know, the surname of the miniature Mendelssohn'. This was graceful about a dead artist in the place of his birth, but Dr. von Bülow is above all ordinary considerations. Engaged to play at the Liverpool Philharmonic, he sent a transcript of the pro-

---

F major, for violin and orchestra. The soloist in Liszt's *Totentanz* (receiving its first British performance on this occasion) was Bülow's old colleague and former pupil Frits Hartvigson, who was the senior professor of piano at this same institution.

In its issue of November 20, *The Times* published a lengthy review of the concert. It differs so radically from Manns's polemic that it is as if the two observers were attending quite separate events. Further doubt is cast on Manns's veracity by Herbert Thompson, the music critic for the *Yorkshire Post.* Years later he wrote, 'I well recollect what a revelation was afforded when von Bülow in 1878 volunteered to conduct a concert on behalf of the Norwood Academy for the Blind and gave a wonderful interpretation of the C minor Symphony'. *Yorkshire Post,* March 8, 1907.

Incidentally, the Academy of Music for the Blind was located in the London suburb of Norwood, in the vicinity of the Crystal Palace, Manns's own place of musical residence. In earlier years there had been a partnership between the Crystal Palace Orchestra and the pupils of the Academy, which had meanwhile been severed. Why Manns chose to review this particular concert and make no mention of the handicap under which the pupils played, can only be explained by the fact that he was goaded beyond endurance by Bülow, and this was the only orchestral concert on Bülow's London itinerary at the time of the dispute. Incidentally, the following afternoon, November 20, Bülow returned to this same hall and played the last five piano sonatas of Beethoven. See p. 258.

gramme to Germany, with the sneer, 'The ostrich-like stomach of the English public is worthy of all respect, is it not?' Next he girded at Sir Julius Benedict's 'urbanity', laughed at the orchestra as containing 'tolerably heterogeneous elements', and a 'disturbing contingent of Falstaffian recruits;' while the rehearsals, he declared, were conducted in a 'liquoring-up kind of way'. Whether all this and much like it be true or untrue is beside the question. It is hardly for Dr. von Bülow, who comes here to pick up English money, to say it. This is not the first time he has lampooned us, nor probably will it be the last. He will no doubt perform another journey 'in the fog', as he calls it, and write more letters to his friend Herr Senff. Contemplating this, he need not be afraid of popular retribution. Englishmen are used to ridicule, and they know that he laughs best who laughs last'.[11]

It might have cheered the anonymous writer of this piece to know that Bülow's criticisms of his fellow Germans were yet more damning than the ones he was levelling against the English. He talked of 'the beery complacency with which Herr Richter conducted *Meistersinger*'. And when he described Max Bruch as 'a Hiller who has turned out well', neither composer benefitted from the comparison. He mocked the second-rate operatic German composers who had come forward to claim Meyerbeer's crown by dividing them into two classes: those who added to the repertoire of the hurdy-gurdy, and those who borrowed from it.

Nor did he fear to lock horns with the Berlin Hochschule für Musik, whose director was Joseph Joachim. In an article in the Leipzig *Signale*, in November 1877, Bülow attacked this institution because of its official policy of banning the music of Liszt, and for punishing those students who ignored the ban. Bülow went straight for the two people responsible for this practice. Ernst Rudorff, the head of the piano department, he castigated for 'the incredible fact of forbidding the pupils of the institution, to their most serious detriment, not only from studying, but even from rendering themselves acquainted with Franz Liszt's works for the piano'. And Bülow then issued a challenge to Joseph Joachim himself: 'Will the Director please point out to me a piece by Herr Rudorff which contains such good, specific music as, to take just one example, the 3rd of the grand master's Twelve (Transcendental) Studies [the *Pastorale*, in F major]?'[12] It is surprising to find Bülow holding up the *Pastorale* Study as an example of Liszt at his best, when he must have known that there were many other

11. MT, XX, 140, March 1879.
12. These and other tidbits had already been published in the articles that Bülow wrote for the Leipzig *Signale*, between October 27 and November 4, 1877; republished in three issues of *Dwight's Journal of Music*, January 19 through February 16, 1878.

keyboard pieces of Liszt which were far more effective. But perhaps the choice was deliberate. Knowing how Bülow's mind worked, he may well have been saying that even inferior Liszt was better than superior Rudorff.

IV

It might be supposed that Bülow's relations with the English establishment could hardly get worse. But they did. Engaged to perform the Tchaikovsky Piano Concerto at a New Philharmonic Society concert, on June 22, 1879, Bülow withdrew after the first rehearsal because of the incompetence of the German-born conductor Wilhelm Ganz.[13] Ganz was one of those conductors of whom it may be said that he appeared without trace. He had only recently succeeded to his position in succession to Henry Wylde, and Bülow probably had little idea of what he was getting into when he agreed to play the Tchaikovsky concerto with Ganz at the helm. This work he knew intimately but it was not yet familiar to British ears—nor, evidently, to those of Ganz. At the first rehearsal it became clear within minutes that Ganz had no idea of what to do with the score, so Bülow took him aside and gave the 'would-be conductor' two-and-a-half hours' worth of private instruction—to no avail. So Bülow simply abandoned his fee of 30 guineas and walked away. Under Ganz, he observed acerbically, the New Philharmonic Society ought to be renamed the New 'Misharmonic' Society.[14] Bülow might well have been content to let the matter rest there. Indeed, he allowed it to be put about that he had become indisposed at the last moment, an explanation that was meant to shield Ganz himself from criticism; but his nonappearance inevitably attracted the attention of the press, as did the growing suspicion that Ganz himself might have been to blame. The conductor had earlier given a performance of questionable merit of Berlioz's *Fantastic* Symphony, and Bülow was asked by the editor of *The Musical World* to respond directly to the only question that most concerned his readers: Did he abstain from playing because of his own incapacity or because of the 'incapacity' of Ganz? Bülow's caustic reply, published in his own English, ran:

> London W., July 1, 1879
> Dear Sir:
> Not having had the displeasure of witnessing the execution of Berlioz's Symphony alluded to in *The World*—April 30—I cannot testify

---

13. It will not have escaped attention that it was nearly always the German-born conductors who drew Bülow's ire. We have seen him attack in turn Carl Bergmann, August Manns, Julius Benedict, and now Wilhelm Ganz. The one thing they all had in common was that they were fellow countrymen, and he despised their laissez-faire approach to the profession—a legacy of what he considered to be their lax German training.

14. BB, vol. 5, p. 574.

to what happened on that occasion. But from my personal experience of Mr. Ganz as a time beater I have no hesitation in admitting that the substance of that criticism stated but the exact truth.

As to your question, whether I abstained from playing at the last New Philharmonic on account 'of the incapacity of Mr. Ganz', I can only say that his incapability of reading a score is such, that he could not even correct the parts of the single instruments, although he had only to look at the score before him with marks ('Eselsbrücken' we call them in German[15]) which in a private lesson of two hours and a half in my room I had added, in order to put him at least 'at the foot of the tree'. I owed it to my friend Tchaikovsky, the composer of the concerto, not to act as an accomplice in the murder of his work under a leader, who seems unable to read an orchestral accompaniment of any importance, nay, unable of being himself conducted by a most intelligent and quick conceiving band, let alone conduct it.

Therefore I was forced to retire, allowing however from a feeling of 'charité mal ordonnée' my non-appearance to be attributed to sudden indisposition. People being inclined to construct this feeling as a want of respect to the public on my part, I avail myself of the opportunity to state the plain truth.[16]

This is vintage Bülow. One is left to wonder whether such enmity could really have been generated by a single, chaotic rehearsal, or whether other factors were quietly at work. When Bülow seated himself at the keyboard, in fact, and waited for the unfortunate Ganz to raise his baton, he was still smouldering from a thoughtless comment made earlier by the conductor: 'Of all living Kapellmeisters Bülow is the first pianist, and of all contemporary pianists the best conductor.'[17] This shining accolade loses much of its lustre when we think it through, and Bülow had thought it through. Ganz had chosen his comparison groups with reckless abandon. To be the best pianist among the stick-wavers of Bülow's time was faint praise. But to be the best conductor among the pianists was to occupy a position so low as to open oneself to mockery. As Bülow observed mordantly, 'Ambition, what more dost thou desire?'[18]

V

Throughout much of this hustle and bustle Bülow escaped London whenever possible and sought refuge in the home of his sister and the

15. Literally a 'crib sheet', useful to donkeys.
16. BB, vol. 5, p. 577.
17. *The Musical World,* January 11, 1879, p. 19.
18. Ibid.

Bojanowski family in Sydenham. There he was able to invite friends and acquaintances and relax in their company. The English writer C. M. Barry, who happened to be their neighbour, was a regular guest and left some lively recollections of his encounters with the conductor.[19] Barry recalled one occasion when Bülow sent him the following handwritten invitation:

> My sister, Mme de Bojanowski, will be charmed if you would eat your mutton with us on Friday at 6 o'clock. No dress, of course. I hope to have the pleasure of seeing you before at 5, in order that we may talk *de omnibus rebus musicalibus et quibusdam alteris*.[20]

Unfortunately, Bülow's invitation failed to arrive because he had forgotten to write the all-important word 'Sydenham' on the envelope. The town was not yet a suburb of London and had a separate postal address. Barry was already in the middle of dinner at his own house when a servant from the Bojanowski establishment knocked on the door, bearing a message from Bülow to the effect that he and his sister were about to start dinner, and where were Barry and his wife? Barry diplomatically responded that although he had not received an invitation, he and his spouse would be glad to join Bülow later that evening. It was one of those awkward situations that could easily have led to an explosion on Bülow's part and disturbed the neighborhood for weeks afterwards. Not until Bülow's invitation was returned to him from the 'dead letter office', a few days later, did he realize that the error was entirely his. He forwarded it to Barry and attached his card bearing the message, 'Mea culpa, mea maxima culpa! Sicut figura docet'.[21] It was the beginning of a long and collegial friendship during which Barry got to know Bülow well. From Barry we learn that Bülow enjoyed showing off various card tricks and other games. 'On calling on him one morning in Sydenham,' writes Barry, 'I found him engaged with two ladies in playing a game with draughts called "Go bang!" After having always proved victorious with them, he at last asked me to have a game with him, when, by some lucky fluke, and to our mutual astonishment, I beat him at the first go off'.[22]

Barry also observed the fractious side of Bülow's nature. During an encounter at a Richter concert, Bülow expressed disagreement with a notice that Barry had recently published about the overture to Berlioz's *Les francs-*

19. In three issues of *The Musician* (September 1897). See BPR.

20. 'We'll talk about all things musical, and whatever else'.

21. 'My fault, entirely my fault!' To which Bülow has added the words, 'So goes the phrase,' as if to link it to the Roman Catholic liturgy.

22. BPR, p. 331.

juges, the second subject of which he had pronounced 'heavenly'. Bülow disagreed, dismissing the theme as 'barely removed from being common-place'. It was hardly the basis for a confrontation, but with Bülow one could never be certain. Barry decided to steer the conversation towards a safer topic, and knowing that Bülow had just returned from Berlin (this was in 1881), asked him whether he had been present at the recent pre-mier there of Wagner's *The Ring*. Barry had provided the gunpowder; Bülow obliged him by striking the match:

> 'No', he replied. 'Why should I hear *The Ring*? I think I know it as well as anyone else, and besides, Mr. Barry, I am surprised that you, knowing my present relations with Wagner, should allude to such a subject'. He had often previously spoken to me in the calmest way and with the utmost enthusiasm for Wagner. I tried to excuse myself by saying that I had seen it mentioned in the newspapers that he had just been in Berlin, and was curious to know whether he had taken the opportunity of witnessing a performance of *The Ring*. He burst out afresh: 'Then go to your d[amne]d newspapers; I am not a bureau for information!'[23]

For years the issues of Wagner and Bayreuth remained a smouldering volcano on whose sulphuric fumes Bülow was liable to choke. When Carl Bechstein picked up rumours of a possible meeting between the pair, as early as 1873, and had innocently passed them along to Bülow, he was met with a scorching rejoinder. 'A Meeting with Herr Wagner at Cologne? No, no, my dearest Beflügler, not in this century. How could you suppose it? . . . I can only say with respect that I do not care a damn. The expe-riences I have had in life have taught me once and for all how certain things should be dealt with!'[24]

But that, of course, was not true. Bülow never appears to have learned 'how certain things should be dealt with'. His way of handling dispute and disagreement was to avoid diplomacy altogether, and plunge into a military campaign instead. He reversed the famous aphorism of Clause-witz, that 'war is an extension of diplomacy by other means', and simply went to war, leaving diplomacy to take care of itself.

---

23. Ibid. The Berlin premier of *The Ring* took place in the Prussian capital's spacious Vik-toria Theatre, in May 1881, under Anton Seidl. Bülow had given an all-Liszt recital in Berlin the previous month in order to draw attention to Liszt's seventieth anniversary, which oc-curred later that year. Wagner was in Berlin, supervising rehearsals of his tetralogy, but he and Bülow never met.

24. BNB, p. 325.

Vistas from the Summit, 1880–1894

The Meiningen Years, 1880–1885

I: The Meiningen Miracle

> Learn to read the score of a Beethoven symphony *accurately* first,
> and you will have found its interpretation.
> —Bülow[1]

I

Nowhere had the turbulent events leading up to Bülow's dramatic resignation from Hanover been more closely watched than at the tiny ducal court of Saxe-Meiningen. As comedy turned into calamity, the reigning duke, Georg II, saw a golden opportunity to attract Bülow to his domain. He had, in fact, long wanted to place the mercurial conductor in charge of the Meiningen Court Orchestra. Georg now acted with extraordinary despatch, as a glance at the dates will show. Bülow abdicated his duties at Hanover on October 25. Within ten days the duke's formal offer had reached him, and he had bound himself to Meiningen. It was an inspired decision on both sides.

The main condition on which Bülow insisted before taking up the baton in the small town was simple: freedom to continue the development of his own artistic career, whether as pianist or conductor. That privilege was readily granted in a letter dated November 5, 1879.[2] 'You are a 'Freiherr' in the fullest meaning of that word, and in every respect', he was assured in a happy play on words. The letter went on to offer the absurdly low salary of 5,000 marks per annum, but pointed out that the Meiningen

---

1. SRR, p. 121.
2. BB, vol. 6, pp. 1–2.

Bülow's decree of appointment to Meiningen, February 10, 1880.

season only lasted for seven months, from November to May each year, and Bülow was in any case free to come and go as he wished. After making sure that he would have plenipotentiary powers over the orchestra, with unlimited rehearsals, and freedom to choose the repertoire, Bülow accepted the offer. The decree of appointment, signed by Georg II, is dated '10 February, 1880'.[3]

II

Who was Georg II, Duke of Saxe-Meiningen, and how had he been able to attract Bülow to his tiny dukedom? Born in 1826, Georg had been destined by his father, Duke Bernhard, for a military career. His early love of the theatre had weaned him away from the life of a soldier, and when, at the age of forty he inherited the dukedom, he devoted himself entirely to a study of the theatre. He was thirty-four years old before he took as his first wife the nineteen-year-old Princess Charlotte of Prussia (sister of the kaiser) in 1850. There were four children of this love-match, two of whom died in infancy. Charlotte herself died giving birth to the fourth, when she was twenty-four years old. The duke remarried in 1859, taking once again a much younger wife, the twenty-year-old Feodore, Princess zu Hohenlohe-Langenburg. There were two sons of this later union. Feodore died in 1872, aged thirty-three.

It was the duke's morganatic third marriage, to the actress Ellen Franz, that was to prove the most durable.[4] Attracted to the theatre from her youth, Ellen overcame parental opposition and became a professional actress. We recall that she was briefly a piano pupil of Bülow's in Berlin, in the late 1850s, and got to know Cosima. By the time that she was twenty years old she was playing leading roles in the Gotha Theatre, from where her career took wing and she appeared in Stettin, Oldenburg, and Mannheim. It was at Meiningen that she achieved her greatest success, and caught the eye of the theatre-loving duke. After the premature death of his second wife, the duke proposed marriage to the thirty-four-year-old Ellen. On the eve of their wedding, in March 1873, Georg bestowed on her the title 'Baroness Helene of Heldburg', and handed control of the theatre to her. Theirs was a true artistic partnership which lasted for the rest of their lives. From her newly elevated position at the court, Helene worked assiduously with Georg II to make Bülow's transfer to Meiningen possible.

3. The document is preserved in the Meininger Museen, Br. 302/1.
4. Ellen had an English mother (Sarah Grant, who came from Essex) and a German father. She was brought up speaking both German and English.

III

Bülow took up his post at the end of September 1880, and moved into the Sächsischer Hof Hotel, a few minutes' walk from the theatre. Prior to the first rehearsals he inspected the concert hall, oversaw the reorganization of the music library, arranged for some of the decrepit seats and music-desks to be repaired, and introduced a different seating plan for the players. He even installed a thermometer to ensure that the temperature of the hall remained constant, and so preserve the intonation of the orchestra.

Meiningen in those days was a sleepy town of about 9,000 inhabitants, hardly predestined to become a centre of musical excellence. The combined personnel of the theatre and orchestra barely amounted to a hundred people. The audience was essentially middle-class, consisting of court officials, lawyers, doctors, civil servants, military officers, and their families. Bülow called Meiningen at various times a 'village', or a 'nest'; he lamented the lack of social life in the small town, which boasted a mere five droshky cabs, observing that there were no restaurants, no bookshops, no first-class tailors, no Bohemian life such as one might enjoy in Munich. And he shrewdly remarked that without such things, without a bit more community life, the formation of a large, appreciative audience in Meiningen would be difficult. Bülow knew that there was but one solution. If the world would not come to Meiningen, then Meiningen would have to reach out to the world. That is why he eventually proposed taking the orchestra on tour in order to display its talents in such cities as Berlin, Leipzig, Hamburg, and Frankfurt, and eventually to other countries including The Netherlands, Austria, and Hungary. It was an idea that brought lasting fame to the small dukedom—and to Bülow himself. But first there was work to be done.

The rehearsals began on October 1, and they were closed to the general public. Between then and December 20 not a single note of music other than Beethoven's was sounded in Meiningen. For twelve weeks Bülow drilled the orchestra daily, moulding them to his will. Duke Georg, his curiosity aroused, curtailed a hunting trip so that he and his wife could witness Bülow and the orchestra at work. Georg is known to have attended about forty of these rehearsals. Bülow told him, 'Study, work, rehearsals, that is what needs to be done in the first place; it is the foundation-stone of the building'.[5] They were not so much rehearsals as study sessions, each player becoming a student of Beethoven's music and en-

---

5. Unpublished letter dated 'October 4, 1880'. Staatsbibliothek Meiningen. Quoted in EBMJ, p. 54.

tering into an intimate relationship with the master's scores. Bülow's 'Academy of Players' was exclusive, and had but one purpose: to get to the heart of the music. On November 7 the orchestra emerged transformed, and launched a series of seven Beethoven concerts in which all nine symphonies were performed from memory,[6] as well as a number of other Beethoven works. It was an achievement unmatched by any other orchestra. The series culminated in a double performance of Beethoven's *Choral* Symphony on December 19. It was the first time that Bülow had attempted such a thing, although it would not be the last. Eduard Hanslick observed that it was like baptizing the infidels with a fire hose. The image is not a bad one. Bülow was ever the evangel, and the Beethoven symphonies were for him the equivalent of holy water.

Looking back over the first twelve weeks in Meiningen, Bülow summed up his achievement by paraphrasing Jules Verne, 'A Journey round Beethoven in 80 days'.

IV

Bülow's rehearsal methods attracted attention. He gave an interview to the *Weimarer Zeitung* in which he identified what he called the 'Meiningen Principles':

> I am working according to the Meiningen principles:
> separate rehearsals for wind and strings—the latter being divided into 1st and 2nd violins, violas, cellos, and basses [i.e., five sectional rehearsals for strings alone]. Every dynamic nuance is studied; every stroke of the bow; every staccato prepared until it is exactly together; musical phrasing and punctuation rehearsed in every detail. 'In Art there are no trivial things,' is my maxim.
>
> This system, which has been in effect since October 1, seems to work well. In any case, I hope to obtain better artistic results than have hitherto been obtained anywhere in Germany. The concentration on Beethoven's music (from October 1 until December 20

---

6. Nov. 7: Symphonies nos. 1 and 2
   Nov. 14: Symphony no. 3 (*Eroica*)
   Nov. 21: Symphony nos. 4 and 5
   Nov. 28: Symphony no. 6 (*Pastorale*)
   Dec. 5: Symphony no. 7
   Dec. 12: Symphony no. 8
   Dec. 19: Symphony no. 9 (*Choral*) (a double performance).
   Other important Beethoven works included in the series were the Choral Fantasie, op. 80; the Violin Concerto, op. 61; and the Triple Concerto, for Piano, Violin, and Cello, op. 56, in which Bülow himself took the piano part.

not a note by any other composer will be played) seemed to me to
be a necessary condition for this experiment, which seeks to found
a 'style', to form the proper taste in both playing and listening'.[7]

One of the best decisions taken by Georg II some years earlier had been
to close down the Meiningen Opera, and transfer its resources to the theatre, with compelling results. The orchestra was now free to concentrate
on purely instrumental music. Unencumbered by duties in the opera
house (a common fate for overworked orchestral players in the German
principalities) they were ready to achieve distinction by the time that
Bülow was brought in to direct them.

At Meiningen Bülow was able to realize a long-cherished dream: to
make his conducting an extension of his piano playing. He had sometimes talked of the piano as 'a ten-fingered orchestra'. He now came to
regard the orchestra as a multi-fingered piano, which through rigorous
rehearsals would learn to respond to his every musical impulse. As to
Bülow's insistence that the ensemble play everything from memory, he
would doubtless have justified his radical demand by observing that he
was not asking the players to accept anything that he himself was unwilling to do. The value of his approach soon became evident. By looking
the entire orchestra in the eye, so to speak, and have them reciprocate,
he was able to attend to every aspect of phrasing and nuance—an obvious impossibility if everyone is staring at the notes on the page. It drew
from Bülow another of his timeless aphorisms, 'It is better to have the
score in one's head, than one's head in the score'.[8]

V

When Bülow took over the orchestra it consisted of a mere thirty-six
players. One of his first tasks was to persuade the duke to hire eight more.

7. Issue of December 16, 1880. Bülow borrowed the term 'Meiningen principles' from
the theatre. The polished stage productions of the Meiningen troupe, admired all over Europe, were the result of the rigorous discipline that Georg II had imposed on his actors.
However sumptuous the production, it never overwhelmed the integrity of the play itself.
And however talented the individual actors, they subordinated themselves even to minor
roles for the sake of the whole. 'There are no minor roles, all roles are major', was one of
Georg's maxims, and it is clear that Bülow had it in mind when he paraphrased it during
the interview he gave to the *Weimarer Zeitung*, quoted above: 'In art, there are no trivial
things'. The Meiningen troupe was famous for its crowd scenes and its lighting effects, yet
these were not the usual diversions meant to distract from the plot, but were subsumed to
it. This is the context in which Bülow's appropriation of the term 'Meiningen Principles'
should be understood: (1) Integrity to the musical text; (2) each orchestral player a soloist,
but none more important than the others; and (3) the virtuosity of the team placed in the
service of the composer to such a degree that it simply disappeared during performance,
and became part of the composition itself.

8. SRR, p. 121.

During his five-year tenure, the orchestra never exceeded forty-eight players. Quality not quantity was Bülow's watchword. He constantly tried to enrich the sound of the ensemble, and to this end he introduced the five-string bass, the Ritter alto viola,[9] and the pedal timpani. Bülow also experimented with some unusual orchestral effects. In order to obtain clearer articulation of the bass-line, he would sometimes divide his string basses —one half playing legato, the other half playing *detaché*. This made the bass-line cut into the ear with unexpected clarity. Again, in order to make crescendos more effective, he would gradually increase the number of strings until the climax was attained, not so much by raising the decibel level as by thickening the texture. He also recruited some of the leading players in Germany, including the outstanding hornist Gustav Leinhos (who had played for Wagner at the world premier of the *The Ring* in Bayreuth, in 1876), and Friedrich Hilpert, who became his principal cellist. But the orchestra always contended with limited financial means. When Bülow replaced the oboist with a better one, he himself volunteered 300 marks from his own pocket in order to prevent this additional burden from falling on the Court.[10]

Among the players already installed in the orchestra was the virtuoso clarinettist Richard Mühlfeld (for whom Brahms would later write his Clarinet Quintet and the two Clarinet Sonatas). Nor must we forget the orchestra's leader, Friedhold Fleischhauer, who had arrived in Meiningen as early as 1864, and was to retain his position for more than thirty years, stepping down in 1896, shortly before his death. By then he was an iconic figure, one of the best-known concertmasters in Germany. Bülow learned both to respect and to trust him, and often played chamber music with him. The Fleischhauer String Quartet was renowned for its performances of the Viennese classics, and they were sometimes invited to Wahnfried in order to give private concerts for Richard Wagner.[11]

Mention must also be made of the violinist Alexander Ritter, whom Bülow brought to Meiningen in 1882 as the assistant concertmaster. Their friendship, which went back to the time when as boys they were pupils at the Dresden Gymnasium, had not faded. After the Ritter family had temporarily fled Dresden during the uprising of 1849, Alexander had pursued

---

9. Hermann Ritter (1849–1926) had first exhibited his larger *alto viola* in 1876. Wagner was interested in this deep-toned instrument, and included it in the Bayreuth Festival Orchestra for the performances of *Parsifal*, in 1882.

10. BBLW, p. 136.

11. On March 28, 1877, for example, Cosima wrote to Fleischhauer, 'Dear Concertmaster Fleischhauer, Would it be possible for you to come here next Thursday, April 1, with the three other gentlemen of the Quartet? We would be pleased if you wanted to come to us once more to make music'. (From the family archive of R. Fleischhauer [EBMJ, p. 71].)

his violin studies at the Leipzig Conservatory with Ferdinand David. His chief interest, however, was composing. In 1854 Liszt had offered Ritter an appointment among the first violins of the Weimar Orchestra. The offer was timely because it coincided with the impecunious Ritter's marriage to the actress Franziska Wagner, a niece of Richard Wagner. Liszt even undertook to find living quarters for the honeymoon couple in Weimar. Two years later Liszt helped Ritter secure the conductorship of the Stettin Orchestra, a job that he held for a mere two seasons because his championship of modern music made him enemies in the small town. For a long time thereafter Ritter had led an itinerant life, playing the violin for a living but preferring to set aside as much time as possible for composing. He settled briefly in Schwerin where Franziska was engaged as an actress. The couple lived in straitened circumstances on her income until they both managed to find employment in the Stadttheater in Würzburg—he as a violinist and she as an actress—which remained their home for nineteen years. Here Ritter began to compose an important series of chamber and orchestral works, which remained utterly neglected until Richard Strauss introduced them with much success to the next generation. In order to supplement his meagre resources Ritter opened a music shop in Würzburg where he might well have ended his days—as a salesman. This was the situation in which Bülow found the fifty-year-old Ritter when he brought him to Meiningen and rescued him and his wife from the genteel poverty into which they had declined.

To this roll-call of names would later be added two of distinction: Richard Strauss and Johannes Brahms. After having featured the teenage Strauss's music in some of the Meiningen concerts, Bülow appointed him as his assistant conductor in 1885, when Strauss was barely twenty-one years old. As for Brahms, he became an honorary member of the Meiningen ensemble, so to speak, when he accepted Bülow's generous invitation to come to Meiningen as often as he wished, and use the orchestra to rehearse his own music. We shall have more to say about both composers presently.

VI

We mentioned that Bülow's rehearsals were closed. He greatly disliked them being disrupted by visitors, even royal ones, and such interruptions could give rise to some droll moments. One day the duke and his adjutant, Herr von Kotze, entered the theatre. Bülow immediately stopped the orchestra and enquired of the duke what were his wishes. The duke replied that he merely wanted to listen to whatever was being played. It happened to be the Berlioz *Harold* Symphony, a complex work. Bülow explained that he was unable to conduct it for the duke because the orchestra had

The old Meiningen Court Theatre, before the fire of 1908. A contemporary photograph.

only just begun to learn it. 'Never mind', the duke replied affably, 'I'll just listen'. Bülow: 'I am very sorry, Sir, the performance is not polished enough; I cannot play it for Your Highness'. The duke: 'But Bülow, don't be funny. It does not matter how it is played, I shall be glad to listen'. Bülow, bowing stiffly for the third time: 'I am really sorry. At the stage we have reached with the Symphony it would do, at the most, for Herr von Kotze!' Imagine the scene. On the stage, the grinning orchestra; in the centre, Bülow in impeccable court attitude; below them the duke and the poor victim, Herr von Kotze.[12]

On another occasion the duke unexpectedly turned up with some out-of-town visitors. This time Bülow adopted a different tactic. He stopped the orchestra and began to drill a pair of bassoons in a highly repetitious passage. On and on went the mournful sounds, without respite, finally forcing the guests to withdraw and seek refuge outside the auditorium.

VII

Having rehearsed the Meiningen Orchestra to perfection, Bülow now arranged to exhibit it to the world. No serious attempt has yet been made to chronicle in detail the tours that the orchestra undertook during the five years that Bülow was in command, but the Meiningers eventually

12. SRR, p. 125.

swept through Germany, Austria, Hungary, and The Netherlands, leaving astonishment and incredulity in their wake. Cities such as Berlin, Vienna, and Leipzig had never heard anything like it. They may have possessed more famous orchestras, but these ensembles were led for the most part by simple time-beaters who lacked the ability to make them play as one. Then Bülow and his small band of Meiningers appeared, seemingly out of nowhere, declaring war on much larger armies and winning impressive victories along the way. Liszt expressed it well when he observed that 'the little Meiningen phalanx, thanks to its present conductor, is in advance of the largest battalions'.[13]

It all began in January 1881 when Bülow took the ensemble to the nearby towns of Bamberg, Erlangen, and Nuremberg, in order to test its newly won repertoire on different audiences. Heartened by its early success, the orchestra penetrated yet more deeply into Southern Germany, and in March they played in Jena, Halle, Schweinfurt, Bamberg, Ansbach, Regensburg, and Würzburg, returning once more to Nuremberg. They aroused such enthusiasm that some listeners accompanied the players from one town to the next—perhaps the first time that an orchestra had generated a travelling 'fan club'.

As interest in these first tours grew, Bülow was emboldened to take the orchestra to larger cities, including Dresden, Hamburg, and Leipzig. In January 1882 the Meiningen players arrived in Berlin and gave nine concerts in two weeks, from January 4 to January 18. The first six concerts were given in the Singakademie, and were entirely devoted to the music of Beethoven. The last three concerts took place in the Central Skating Rink—a venue that would later be transformed into the famous Philharmonie, and become the home of the Berlin Philharmonic Orchestra.[14]

The critic of the *Berliner Volkszeitung* spoke of a miracle,[15] while the correspondent of the *Musikalischen Wochenblatt* talked of a 'phenomenal effect'. After a performance of the *Eroica* Symphony, on January 5, Bülow informed Georg II that the orchestra was now a sovereign entity in Berlin, and had touched off a revolution in the country's capital. And he added that if such a word sounded too much like a *coup d'état* to the duke's ears, then it could still be regarded as 'an epoch-making success for the entire world of music'.[16] The concert on January 8 was of particular interest. This all-Brahms programme contained the newly composed Piano Con-

13. LLB, vol. 2, p. 357.
14. The full repertoire of all nine concerts may be found in HMIB, p. 61.
15. Issue of January 6, 1882.
16. Unpublished letter dated 'January 6, 1882'. Meininger Staatsarchiv call no. Ha 12.

Bülow and the Meiningen Court Orchestra in Berlin, January 1882. A photograph.

certo no. 2, in B-flat major, with Brahms himself as the soloist. It was the first time that Berlin had heard this masterpiece.

VIII

Brahms, in fact, had already begun to enjoy a special relationship with the Meiningen Orchestra. Bülow had first met the composer years earlier in Hanover, in January 1854. Joachim had brought them together, and the three young musicians had spent some stimulating hours together. Bülow confided to his mother, 'I have got to know Robert Schumann's young prophet Brahms pretty well; he has been here a couple of days and is constantly with us. A very lovable, candid nature, and something really of God's grace, in the best sense, in his talent!'[17] Joachim showed Bülow the manuscript of Brahms's recently composed C major Piano Sonata, a work that was dedicated to him. Bülow was so impressed with the piece that he copied out the first movement, and on March 1, 1854,

17. BB, vol. 2, p. 166. These references to a 'young prophet' and someone of 'God's grace' are direct allusions to Schumann's famous article on Brahms which had recently been published in the NZfM (October 23, 1853). Schumann had there talked of one who would not reveal his mastery slowly, 'but like Athena, would spring fully armed from the head of Zeus. And now he has come, a young man over whose cradle Graces and Heroes stood watch. His name is Johannes Brahms'.

Bülow performs the first movement of Brahms's
C major Piano Sonata in Hamburg, March 1, 1854.

he played it in Hamburg's Apollo-Saale. Until that time no pianist other
than Brahms himself had played his music in public. The fact is worth
observing, if only because it dispels the popular notion that Bülow's conversion to Brahms was the result of some later antipathy towards Liszt
and Wagner. Bülow had followed Brahms's subsequent development with
keen interest, had embarked on a deep study of his music (especially the
piano music, which turned up with increasing regularity in his recital
programmes), and had gradually formed the opinion that Brahms was

the true heir to Beethoven, the one composer capable of continuing the great tradition of German music, which had begun with Bach and continued through Haydn, Mozart, and Schubert. Somewhat to Brahms's embarrassment, Bülow began openly to refer to the 'three Bs'—Bach, Beethoven, and Brahms—an alliteration that has meanwhile become enshrined in the narrative of music history.[18] As for his earlier proclamation that Brahms's First Symphony was 'Beethoven's Tenth', that was by now an accepted term of endearment among Brahms's many followers.

Bülow had already given Brahms a standing invitation to visit Meiningen whenever he wished, in order to rehearse his music at leisure, and Brahms was taking full advantage of this remarkable opportunity. On October 17, 1881, he had turned up with the still unpublished manuscript of the Second Piano Concerto in his luggage, and Bülow had put the work into full rehearsal. He reserved a room for Brahms in the Sächsischer Hof Hotel, at his personal expense, and arranged for a piano to be installed there for the composer. Brahms became acquainted with Georg II and Baroness Helene, and his relationship with the royal couple developed into one of warm friendship. They were proud of the lustre that Brahms shed on their small town, and encouraged him to visit Meiningen often. The duke even extended invitations to visit them at the Villa Carlotta, their summer estate on Lake Como. In gratitude for such friendship, Brahms dedicated to the duke his *Gesang der Parzen* ('Song of the Fates') op. 89, for chorus and orchestra, which was first performed in Meiningen on Georg's birthday, April 2, 1883.

'It was a graceful act of Bülow's', wrote the composer's Viennese friend Theodor Billroth, 'to invite Brahms to Meiningen, so that he might work . . . in absolute leisure there, with no public, and without any view to a concert'.[19] Bülow devoted countless hours to Brahms's music, rehearsing it in the composer's presence, including it in his out-of-town concerts,

---

18. Bülow, in a fit of apostolic fervour, once inscribed an autograph book with the words, 'The three greatest composers are Bach, Beethoven and Brahms. All the others are cretins'. When Moritz Moszkowski saw this entry, he wrote underneath it, 'The three greatest composers are Mendelssohn, Meyerbeer and Moszkowski. All the others are Christians!' (GAW, pp. 15–16).

19. NB, p. 133. The deep affection which Bülow developed for Brahms comes out strongly in a letter he wrote to Marie Schanzer, who was about to become his second wife. 'You know how much I think of Brahms; after Bach and Beethoven, he is the greatest, the most exalted of all composers. I consider his friendship my most priceless possession, second only to your love. It marks an epoch in my life; it is like a moral conquest. I believe that not a musical heart in the world, not even that of his dearest friend Joachim, experiences so deeply, has immersed himself so far in the depths of his soul, as mine. Oh, his Adagios! Religion!' (BB, vol. 6, p. 176).

and even handing the baton to Brahms to conduct the perfectly drilled ensemble.

IX

In keeping with the agreement he had first secured from Georg II, Bülow readily combined the Meiningen tours with his second career as a concert pianist. It would take us far afield to chronicle the recitals he gave, side by side with his orchestral concerts, and would add little value to our commentary. But one excursion stands out, and that was his memorable visit to Budapest in February 1881, to give two piano recitals in the Vigadó, on February 14 and 18, respectively. The first was devoted entirely to works by Liszt, the second to the last five sonatas by Beethoven. Liszt, who attended both concerts, described them to his friend Baroness Olga von Meyendorff:

> February 26, '81
> Budapest
> Last week's musical event here was Bülow's two concerts. The first consisted of fifteen or so pieces by me (*Liszt Abend*), excluding any transcription and even any Rhapsody. This exclusion was significant. Such feats bear the stamp of Bülow.
>
> The second concert consisted of Beethoven's five last sonatas. The same programme for the Vienna concerts. There, as here, the hall was crowded (the demand for tickets could not be met), and there was enthusiastic admiration for the astonishing genius—for multiple talents developed to this point constitute genius—of the transcendent virtuoso.
>
> One can strictly apply to him the phrase of former years, 'He is music personified, from alpha to omega. . . .'
> Yours ever
> FL[20]

Liszt's evident pleasure in the *Liszt-Abend* was due in no small part to the fact that Bülow had delivered a recital consisting entirely of original compositions. (A copy of the handbill is displayed on page 292.) For years it had been a refrain among Liszt's critics that while he was a brilliant arranger and transcriber of operas, symphonies, and songs, he lacked creative genius of his own. By excluding Liszt's crowd-pleasing arrangements, Bülow wanted to show the critics that they were wrong. Liszt, for his part, had long since stopped defending himself against these fatuous observa-

---

20. WLLM, p. 397.

tions. His self-mocking response to Alfred Jaëll, who had expressed a desire to play Liszt's E-flat major Piano Concerto, cannot be bettered:

> What is the matter? Cannot you hear the ever-increasing rumblings of the Goliaths of learned criticism, the yappings and croaks, the protests and invectives from the newspapers of all sizes . . . which declare in unison a truth which is truer than true: that LISZT has never been and never will be capable of writing four bars . . . that he is sentenced without remission to drag around the ball and chain of transcription in perpetuity.[21]

That thoughtless phrase 'the ball and chain of transcription' may still be heard among the chattering classes, and it is interesting to see that Bülow felt it to be a part of his mission to free Liszt from those imaginary shackles.

As for Bülow's all-Beethoven recital that same week, the open letter that Liszt wrote at the invitation of Dénes Pázmándy, the editor of the French-language *Gazette de Hongrie,* is worth recalling:

> You want to know my impression of yesterday's Bülow concert? Certainly it must have been the same as yours, as that of us all, that of the whole of the intelligent public of Europe. To define it in two words: admiration, enthusiasm. Twenty-five years ago Bülow was my pupil in music, just as twenty-five years earlier I myself had been the pupil of my respected and beloved master Czerny. But to Bülow it is given to do battle better and with more success than I. His admirable Beethoven edition is dedicated to me as 'the fruit of my teaching'. Here, however, the master learned from the pupil, and Bülow continues to teach by his astonishing virtuosity at the keyboard, as well as by his exceptional musical learning, and now too by his matchless direction of the Meiningen orchestra. There you have the musical progress of our time!
> Cordially,
> F. Liszt
> Budapest
> February 15, 1881[22]

'There you have the musical progress of our time!' It is a fine phrase. Bülow's response to Liszt's letter, and to its praise of his piano playing, his

---

21. *La Revue musicale,* no. 4, 1904.
22. LLB, vol. 2, p. 306.

Bülow's all-Liszt evening, 'consisting of fifteen or so pieces by me.' The repeat performance in Vienna on February 21, 1881.

direction of the Meiningen Orchestra, and his edition of Beethoven's keyboard music has not come down to us. But Liszt's comments must have pleased him, coming as they did from a man he continued to revere.

The following week Bülow took both recitals to Vienna's Bösendorfer Saal. Hanslick's condemnation of the 'all-Liszt' recital on February 21, and especially his lacerating description of the B minor Sonata as 'a steam-driven mill that nearly always runs idle', has long since entered the lexicon of musical invective. Bülow's response was to take the recital first to Weimar, on April 4, 'for the benefit of the Grossherzoglichen Musikschule', and then to Berlin, on April 27, where he played it in the Singakademie and gave the Berliners, in effect, a long-delayed second helping of the Sonata.

The Meiningen Years, 1880–1885

II: Enter Marie Schanzer

> Oh, how I would like to be a different, a better man, in order to—serve you!
>
> —Bülow[1]

I

Behind the public euphoria surrounding Bülow's success with the Meiningen Orchestra, an elation of a very private kind had taken possession of him. In the early part of 1882 he had fallen in love with a young Meiningen actress named Marie Schanzer, who eventually became his second wife. The story is fraught with complication, and it would require a Balzac or a Dickens to do it proper justice. But the chronicle of Bülow's life cannot continue much further without dwelling on this young woman, and the central role she was to play in his affairs.

Marie Schanzer was twenty-seven years Bülow's junior.[2] She was born in 1857, the same year that he had married Cosima. She entered into matrimony with Bülow in the full knowledge that her path would not be easy. In her memoir of him she points out that they had first met in the spring of 1877, when she was barely twenty years old, and he had seen her acting in the title role of Lessing's 'Minna von Barnhelm' in the Karlsruhe

---

1. BB, vol. 6, p. 194.
2. The Schanzer family came from Cracow. Marie's distinguished father was Stanislaus Schanzer, the Austrian Minister for Defence, and her mother was Amalie Hnatek. Marie's younger brother, also named Stanislaus Schanzer (1859–1929), pursued a distinguished naval career, eventually becoming an admiral in the Austrian navy. Bülow tells us that Marie only learned to speak German in her tenth year. She also had an unmarried sister, Mlle Amalie Schanzer, who lived in Cracow and looked after their ailing mother.

Marie Schanzer in April 1885, age twenty-eight.

Court Theatre. As a result of the favourable impression she made on him, he arranged shortly afterwards to have her invited to take part in a production in Hanover, and their friendship deepened. It was only after Marie's appointment to the Meiningen Theatre, however, that they encountered each other on a regular basis, and developed a professional admiration for each other that gave way first to attraction, and then to love. In January 1882, Bülow surprised Marie by meeting her in Hamburg, where she was fulfilling a guest engagement in the theatre, a visit that resulted in the couple's precipitous engagement, although it was not formally announced until March.[3] Bülow's proposal must have thrown

3. Just how impetuous the engagement was can be gathered from a letter that Bülow wrote to Brahms. On January 15, after giving a matinee performance of Brahms's D minor Piano Concerto in Hamburg, with Brahms conducting, he spontaneously invited Marie ('the slim brunette with soul-bewitching eyes') to go with him that same evening to the theatre to see a performance of his favourite opera *Carmen*. In Bülow's phrase, 'On the evening of our Hamburg matinee, the dynamite exploded' (BB, vol. 6, p. 174). The account fits in with everything that we know of Bülow's susceptibility towards the opposite sex. When he and Marie walked into the opera house they were acquaintances; when they walked out again they were in love, and soon to become engaged.

the young woman into turmoil. She was tolerably familiar with his past, and with the débâcle of his first marriage. And she had seen his volcanic outbursts, both on the podium and off, and knew that he was always poised on a knife-edge. She also knew that he desired a home of his own, and she was overwhelmed that this famous man wanted her to provide it.

Protocol demanded that Bülow inform his patron, Georg II, about his engagement. He broke the news in mid-March, by which time the marriage plans were well under way. The reply that he received from the duke's wife, the baroness Helene von Heldburg, must have given him pause. Perhaps he had hoped for a letter brimming over with all the tactful euphemisms traditionally reserved for such happy occasions, and as a bonus written perhaps in French, the language of diplomacy. Instead the baroness wrote to him in her native English, and did not varnish her prose:

Meiningen, March 10, 1882
Dear friend!
You can fancy how thunderstruck we were by your last news, and although I have, as you say, *'alle Köpfe voll zu thun'*,[4] I can think of nothing and nobody but you! I have not yet spoken to your lady-love, because I dare not—I should perhaps not be able to hide from her my anxiety, my fear for your happiness, and who knows what would come of our interview. No, I dare not take that responsibility on myself. I am thunderstruck, I cannot deny it, at your earnestly thinking of marrying again—not her only, but anybody. I think marriage in any case such a risk that, to tell you the truth, I cannot understand anybody's running it a second time, let the result of the first have been, as it may.[5]

And you, such a difficult person to live with (there, it is out, don't be vexed with me) I cannot help being dreadfully afraid for you! As to 'love', that has less to do with a happy marriage, I think, than one usually believes—people may love each other devotedly, and yet make each other desperately unhappy—living together happily depends on so many things—but here I am preaching about married life to you! Of course, if you are smitten so deeply, all reasoning will be useless. Only one thing we beg of you—don't marry her, don't make it irrevocable *in a haste,* judge for yourself, more than you can have done in two or three evenings. If it is for your happiness, all right but do not bind yourself irrevocably in a hurry —engagements may be broken off without any great harm to either party, but marriage—oh dear, oh dear!!

4. 'More than enough to think about'.
5. While Bülow was digesting the baroness's thoughts on second marriages, he could not have failed to appreciate their oddity, coming as they did from a third wife.

'Gefällt es Cäsar aus Güte gegen Cäsar mich zu hören, so rath'
ich ihm, es gut mit sich zu meinen, und sich Zeit zu lassen![6] . . .'
If you *insist* on my speaking with her about it, I will do so. Send me
a line.
Your very anxious old friend,
E. v. Heldburg.

Bülow had evidently given much thought to the choice of a second
bride. Marie was a tall brunette, very good looking, and exquisitely
groomed, as befitted a professional actress. Richard Hoffman, the Anglo-
American pianist, described her as 'a woman of unusual culture, charm,
and intelligence'.[7] She was deeply read, and had mastered a number of
important theatrical roles which had brought her to prominence.[8] She
was also well organized in her private life, a quality that Bülow prized.
When some years later Claire de Charnacé met her in Versailles for the
first time, she was struck by her voice, and the clear articulation of her
words, typical of someone who was at home on the stage. Madame de
Charnacé also made a shrewd observation: 'it is strange that the very
small Bülow should twice have allied himself with women of the greatest
height'.[9] Bülow, in fact, barely came up to Marie's shoulders. Did he see
in her a second Cosima? This is not such a peculiar notion in light of
what we have to relate.

6. BB, vol. 6, pp. 152–153. These lines, written in German, are paraphrased from Shakespeare's *Julius Caesar*, which the baroness knew to be one of Bülow's favourite plays. They
come from Act 2, Scene 4: '. . . If it will please Caesar to be so good to Caesar as to hear me,
I shall beseech him to befriend himself'. Bülow could not have failed to recall that the warning comes from the Soothsayer's speech, just before Caesar is stabbed by Brutus. The essential point being urged on Bülow by the baroness, and presented here within the context of
Shakespearian drama, was that he needed to allow himself more time if he was to avoid
being betrayed by someone who claimed to love him. That Marie was able to bring herself
to publish this letter in her edition of Bülow's Collected Letters is a tribute to her scholarly
detachment. Almost certainly unknown to her, however, was Bülow's response to a further
conversation that he had shortly afterwards with Helene about his choice of bride. She
asked him if Baroness Romaine von Overbeck would not make a better wife for him, with
whom she knew he had at one time been deeply infatuated, who was now separated from
her husband, and who had recently visited Meiningen. He replied, 'You are 26,000 times
right that she would make a far more suitable wife for me. But as a Catholic, unable to divorce her husband, as well as poor health and three children . . .'. From an unpublished letter dated March 16, 1882. Thuringen Staatsarchiv, Meiningen HA 1.
7. HMR, p. 151.
8. During her Meiningen years Marie played leading roles in Schiller's *Maria Stuart*
('Queen of England'), Goethe's *Iphigenie* ('Iphigenie'), and Shakespeare's *Romeo and Juliet*
('Juliet'). Bülow's pupil George Hatton saw her act the role of Juliet and told Bülow that 'the
applause after her scene where Juliet takes the sleep-potion was more spontaneous than
I have yet heard in the theatre here'. Hitherto unpublished. Meiningen Stadtbibliothek,
MM. XI 4333/V Briefe 293/3.
9. VMA, Ms F 859, carton 9, p. 1.

Bülow consulted a number of friends about the wisdom of his engagement, including his agent, Hermann Wolff, who tactfully pointed out that since Bülow was now already engaged, any commentary on the matter would be superfluous. Hermann's wife, Louise, was somewhat more outspoken, and made it known that she was convinced that Bülow wanted to remarry out of spite, that his second marriage was the result of wounded pride, that it was nothing but an attempt to assuage the psychological injuries that he still bore from the breakup of his first marriage. That was a harsh judgement, belied by the love and affection that the newly engaged couple were now expressing towards each other in their letters. On the other hand, Bülow himself came out with several frank admissions at this time which lend weight to the idea that this was to be an unusual union. He told Hermann Wolff that he did not want to lead a typical German marriage, with its eternal 'squatting together'.[10] To Eugen Spitzweg he was more explicit. 'My wife will remain on the stage, act under the name of Frau Schanzer, and travel with the Meiningen acting troupe, while I rehearse in Meiningen and go back and forth'. And he added, 'We definitely will not live under one roof and will definitely not see one another for more than half the year. That is how I understand—the "Artist's marriage"'.[11] In brief, theirs was to be a marriage of convenience, cemented together by mutual admiration and respect. This frank admission was confirmed during a chance conversation that Bülow had at this time with an old Weimar acquaintance, Adelheid von Schorn, who was on her way to visit relatives in Nordheim, and had to change trains at Meiningen. As she alighted, whom should she see standing on the platform but Bülow, who took her back to his apartment and conversed with her for almost three hours. Bülow told her that after the wedding, Marie would return to her own lodgings at the other end of town. It was, he added, the only way to a perfect marriage. Adelheid assumed that Bülow was joking, and was about to laugh out loud when Bülow seized her hand, and said, 'Do not laugh, I am completely serious'.[12]

But there was one other admission from Bülow which is so startling that it requires elaboration. He told a number of people that it would be 'expedient' to change his father-in-law, an allusion to his growing ambivalence towards Liszt.[13] This particular point was made so forcefully, and with a cynicism so blatant, that it could hardly hide the deeper truth

10. S-WW, p. 70.

11. BB, vol. 6, p. 163. Bülow's desire to see his wife continue with her career was enlightened. Contrast that with Mahler, who obliged his wife to abandon her activities as a composer; or, for that matter, with Mendelssohn, who discouraged his sister from composing.

12. SZM, p. 423.

13. S-WW, p. 69; see also SZM, pp. 423–424.

that it was crafted to mask. Bülow's marriage to Marie represented psychological freedom for him, a final loosening of the old ties that had bound him to Liszt for more than thirty years, and through Liszt to Cosima and Richard Wagner as well.[14] A scrutiny of the correspondence makes it clear that through his remarriage Bülow glimpsed the possibility of visiting the Bayreuth Festival, and perhaps attending a performance of *Parsifal,* the much-heralded world premier of which was to take place on July 26, three days before his wedding. Even though he was now giving recitals across Germany in support of the Bayreuth enterprise, he had set foot in the city but once. That, as we have seen, was for a benefit concert on February 15, 1880, at a time when the Wagners and the children had already left for an extended stay of six months in Italy; Bülow gave the concert and departed after one day. Bayreuth, he had persuaded himself, was effectively barred to him as long as he remained single. As the divorced husband of Richard Wagner's second wife, with his first two daughters resident in the Wagner household and the paternity of the third one still in contention, the embarrassment of his presence would have roiled everyone in Wahnfried and made it socially impossible for them to function together in the small town. But his new marriage would change all that, so he reasoned. It would restore the balance of the social norms, so to speak. Bülow felt certain that he could go to Bayreuth with a young new bride on his arm, and face down whatever residual difficulties awaited him there.[15] From everything we know of his elated state of mind in the spring and early summer of 1882, he would beyond question have looked forward to such an encounter, and would have enjoyed introducing his daughters to their beautiful new mother-in-law—and for a profoundly important reason. It would have put paid once and for all to the growing insistence on the part of Cosima that these daughters be formally adopted by Wagner. This is a saga that has rarely been told, but it must be introduced at this point, otherwise we shall miss one of the essential

---

14. It is a fact that, as far as Liszt was concerned, Bülow delayed breaking news of his marriage until the last possible moment. He did not write to his old master about it until May 22, 1882, and then simply described Marie as 'an actress, the daughter of Polish parents'. Was the date of this unpublished letter fortuitous, or did Bülow deliberately choose it to coincide with Wagner's sixty-seventh birthday?

Liszt, incidentally, was not to meet Marie Schanzer for another eighteen months, on December 1, 1883. On that day he travelled from Weimar to Eisenach, in the company of his acolyte Felix Weingartner, where Bülow and the Meiningen Orchestra were scheduled to play a Beethoven concert. They encountered Bülow and his new wife on the railway platform, as they got off the train bearing the entire Meiningen Orchestra. And that is where the first introductions took place.

15. Bülow himself said as much when, a few years later, he made this extraordinary confession to Cosima's half-sister, Claire de Charnacé: 'I had to re-marry . . . I married again in order to repair my links with Bayreuth' (VMA, Ms F 859, p. 10).

threads in the tangled tapestry of Bülow's life at the very moment he proposed matrimony to Marie Schanzer.

II

About a year before Bülow acquired his new bride, he and Cosima had
been compelled to meet after a separation of more than twelve years in
an attempt to resolve Bülow's intransigence towards the idea of allowing
Wagner to adopt Bülow's daughters, a notion that he found offensive.
Daniela and Blandine had been brought up in the Wagner household
since their early childhood, they called Wagner 'Papa', and both Cosima
and Wagner thought it reasonable that these girls should bear the Wagner name. But Bülow did not think it was reasonable at all. Across the
years he had provided very large sums of money for the education of these
girls, and at great physical and mental cost to himself had reluctantly
toured Europe and America to raise the necessary capital, which Cosima
had been pleased enough to receive in order to protect Wagner himself
from assuming this burden. No amount of correspondence between
Cosima and Hans had sufficed to resolve the issue of Wagner's adoption
of these children, so in July 1881 the pair had finally agreed to meet in
Nuremberg in order to thrash it out. They had not set eyes on each other
since the painful autumn of 1868, and their parting. The first of their two
meetings was a turbulent one that lasted for two-and-a-half hours, with
neither side giving ground to the other. Cosima wrote in her diary on July
10: 'Hans with me from 4 to 6:30pm. Attempt to quell the violent outbursts and overcome his unfairness to Daniela. Unsolvable task!'[16] Bülow
asked Cosima to stay on until the following morning so that he could
explain his point of view more thoroughly, but this second meeting
was worse than the first. Hans told her that he could no longer tell
whether white was black or black was white. He was overcome by a nervous twitch, while Cosima herself was ravaged by a toothache that she
had brought with her from Wahnfried. They parted in discord. Cosima
returned to Bayreuth in tears, her mission unfulfilled, while Bülow went
back to Meiningen thoroughly shattered by this bruising encounter with
his former wife, but having the satisfaction of knowing that his daughters would continue to bear the name of Bülow until they married.

The situation with regards to the third daughter, Isolde, was yet more
sensitive. Bülow had stubbornly gone on insisting that she was his child
too, even though he knew her to be Wagner's—as a review of the evidence

16. WT, vol. 2, p. 685.

presented on an earlier page makes plain.[17] By law she had always been known by the name placed on her baptismal certificate at the time of her birth in Munich, in April 1865—'Isolde von Bülow'—willingly recorded by a mother who was at that time lawfully married to Hans von Bülow, and willingly witnessed by a father who was hell-bent on preventing his disintegrating marriage from total collapse.

During Bülow's first reunion with Daniela, in April 1881, after a lapse of almost twelve years, the pair must have discussed many aspects of the family's complicated history which until then she had heard only from her mother's side. Soon afterwards, Daniela's letters to her sister started to arrive at Wahnfried addressed to 'Fräulein Isolde von Bülow', a practice that must have fretted the Wagner household, to say nothing of Wagner himself. However much Wagner, Cosima, and Isolde herself in later life, may have wanted the law to recognize her as a Wagner, Bülow's permission was required to effect the transition. And that permission was steadfastly refused. Wagner badly wanted to give his name to Bülow's own two daughters as well, for whom he felt genuine affection, although he had no biological claim to them. Bülow's response was not only to keep Daniela and Blandine within his fold, but to oblige Isolde to remain there too. There were times when Wagner was beside himself with what he regarded as a deliberate attempt on Bülow's part to torment him; but on the issue of giving up his parental rights to Wagner, Bülow remained implacably opposed. Wagner was frequently left to ponder the full meaning of the motto on Bülow's family crest: 'All the Bülows are honorable'. When Bülow was of a mind to do it, he could wield chivalry like a blunt instrument.

This was the complex situation in which Bülow found himself when he first began to turn his mind to the question of obtaining a second wife. One way to prevent Wagner from becoming the stepfather of his two daughters was to find them a stepmother. And in July 1882, through his marriage to Marie Schanzer, Bülow did just that.[18]

III

As if this little drama were not enough, another one of a very different order had been quietly unfolding in the background, and suddenly came

---

17. See p. 122.

18. It is an indication of Bülow's determination to remarry, that even as he was giving consideration to 'the slim brunette with the soul-bewitching eyes', his old flame Baroness Romaine von Overbeck had started to hover around him once more, and with his encouragement was attending some of his concerts in Meiningen. They refreshed their correspondence, and Bülow took to calling her 'adored angel'. Romaine's proximity to Bülow at this time had obviously caught the eye of Baroness Helene, resulting in her earlier question to Bülow, 'Would not Romaine make a better wife for you?'

to dominate everything else. Bülow was taken completely by surprise when Cosima informed him, in the early spring of 1882, and before his own nuptials·to Marie Schanzer had been announced, that Blandine was planning to get married. The previous November the Wagner family had begun their prolonged visit to Palermo, in Sicily, in order to allow Wagner some necessary leisure after the rigours of producing *Parsifal*. Daniela and Blandine explored the social life of the island, and at one of the balls organized by prominent families in Palermo, Blandine met the thirty-two-year-old Count Biagio Gravina, and became engaged to him. She was still only nineteen years old, and needed Bülow's permission to enter matrimony. Bülow had not seen his younger daughter since she was six years old, and felt somewhat isolated from her. Nor had she ever shown much interest in him; across the years she had usually left it to others to transmit news of herself to her father.[19] He was nonetheless dispirited that Blandine herself had not written to him about a matter so vital to her future happiness as her own wedding, but had rather left it to her mother and Daniela to act as her intermediaries. So he simply telegraphed back to Cosima, 'You have full powers, Madame'. Quite naturally, Cosima regarded this terse message as somewhat inadequate, and she rashly urged Bülow to take a more practical interest in his daughter's affairs. That was enough to prompt the hard-pressed Bülow to let off some steam. He contacted Daniela and informed her, in legalistic vein, that because he feared compromising her sister's plans by writing a letter in which he would be forced to express his displeasure openly, he preferred instead to follow the advice of the sage, 'If in doubt, abstain'. To this assertion he added another, namely, that her mother's messages on the topic fell on him 'like bullets in the midst of my musical and social chaos'. It is true that Bülow was experiencing musical and social chaos aplenty at this time, but by likening Cosima's comments to gunshots on a battlefield he aroused her anger. His extraordinary letter ended with the injunction, 'My dear Daniela, I appoint you my plenipotentiary in this affair. Justify my confidence in you'.[20] Bülow must have known that such a proposal was a legal impossibility; his firstborn could have no jurisdiction over the matrimonial decisions of his second-born. As for Cosima, she noted in her diary that Bülow's letter in its offensiveness 'transcends everything so far experienced'.[21]

Wagner was enraged by the missive. Coming so hard on the heels of his offer to adopt the daughters, and Bülow's stormy rejection of that

19. Bülow's correspondence with Blandine remains unpublished. If it ever sees the light of day it would surely proffer some insight into their problematic relationship. When Count Du Moulin Eckart travelled to Italy in the hope of getting Blandine's permission to include a selection of these letters in his *Neue Briefe*, he was met with a refusal.

20. Unpublished. See SBM, p. 286.

21. WT, vol. 2, p. 840.

offer, he now urged Cosima to break off all connections with her former husband. That was hardly a practical solution, of course, so Daniela now became the go-between, and her letters show that she played her role with tact and sensitivity. She began by giving Bülow a lot of necessary information about Blandine and Count Biagio Gravina, which did much to mollify him. Gravina was well connected, being the second son of the Prince of Ramacca, one of the oldest families in Sicily. He had made a positive impression on Richard and Cosima, and despite the fact that he was thirteen years older than Blandine and lacked any visible means of support, he promised to keep her in style. Bülow was at last prevailed upon to write to Gravina ('it is so devilish hard to write to a complete stranger on intimate matters,' he told Daniela, 'particularly when one has received so little encouragement to do so'[22]), and the wedding was set to take place at Wahnfried on August 25. Among the many practical matters to be addressed by Bülow before that date arrived was how to transfer Blandine's dowry of 50,000 marks still on deposit at Frege's bank. 'Ask your dear mother *how* she wishes me to hand it over', he urged Daniela.[23]

If Bülow thought that the doors of Wahnfried would now be thrown open, that he would be invited to walk Blandine down the aisle and give her in matrimony to Count Gravina in front of the entire Wagner clan, and in the presence of his new wife, he had badly misjudged matters. In mid-May he learned from Daniela that he would not be welcome in Bayreuth, that his presence at the wedding would 'present some difficulties to Mamma'. This news was deeply wounding to him, and he accepted it with difficulty. It was compounded by the disappointing realization that he would not be able to hear *Parsifal* after all. The fund-raising recitals he had given in aid of the Bayreuth enterprise evidently counted for nothing. As he ruefully expressed it to Daniela, 'It is after all by no means necessary for me to be among the listeners to *Parsifal*: the fifty thousand francs which I contributed have of course no value, as they come from an independent, non echo'.[24] Wagner, in brief, was happy to accept Bülow's money, but wanted no part of his presence.[25]

---

22. BNB, p. 585.
23. Ibid.
24. BNB, pp. 587–588.
25. One or two scholars have asserted that Bülow attended the premier of *Parsifal* incognito. There is not a scintilla of evidence to support the idea. Perhaps it stems from a reading of a letter Bülow wrote to Daniela on May 19, 1882, in which he casually floats the notion of going to one of the August performances, 'incognito' (ibid., p. 588). But we now know that he spent most of that month in Klampenborg, on honeymoon with Marie, before returning to Meiningen very ill. For the rest, had Bülow stepped foot inside Bayreuth while the festival was in full swing, there is no way that he could have masked his identity;

Bülow's relations with the Wagners were now at their lowest ebb. Not only had he been rebuffed in his attempt to attend Blandine's wedding, and through it perhaps to gain entree to the Bayreuth Festival Theater, but he had succeeded in alienating nearly everybody in sight because of his initial displeasure at the thought of having Count Gravina as a son-in-law. The one exception was Daniela, to whom with the passing years he became ever more devoted, and she to her father.

Two years elapsed before Bülow and the Gravinas were finally united. In July 1884 they passed through Meiningen and stayed with Bülow as his houseguests for two days. He consulted Daniela about how best to treat 'Their Sicilian Majesties', enquiring after their culinary likes and dislikes. A genuine reconciliation seems to have taken place, for after the Gravinas had left, Bülow told Daniela that 'your brother-in-law came up to all that I had been led to expect . . . he is as aristocratic as he is intelligent. What more can one want?' And in a typical twist of phrase, Bülow flattered his firstborn by telling her, 'Blandine is worthy of her sister: need I say more in her praise?'[26]

IV

Two weeks before his own wedding Bülow begged Marie to consider with care the enormity of the step that she was about to take. The complications in his family life, the chains that bound him to the past, his volatile temperament—all these things had to be weighed in the balance. 'Am I really lovable enough?' he asked her.

> Have you not told yourself that you must love me, that you want to love me, have deluded yourself and decided to carry through with it simply because of your character, as a *point d'honneur,* so to

---

he would have been recognized at once, and word would have spread through the small town like wildfire.

If further proof were required that Bülow never went through with his plan to attend the Bayreuth festival during that fateful summer of 1882, it is provided in a letter written by Walter Bache to Bülow himself. Bache, who had attended the performance of *Parsifal,* gives a detailed account of every aspect of the production. He reports on the warmth of the orchestral sound under Wagner's direction, on the remarkable performance of the leading singers—Materna, Winkelmann, and Scaria—and on the effectiveness of the stage sets. He even describes the ten minutes of ceaseless applause which only ended when Wagner appeared on stage to make a speech (BBM, pp. 268–269). The transmission of such details would have been pointless if Bülow had witnessed the performance for himself. Bache's letter served but one purpose: to offer some small compensation to Bülow who was not there.

26. BNB, pp. 626–627.

say? Or are you just in love with love, in love with an individual as unqualified for love as I am, just because I came along at the right time, carrying the banner of this all-conquering emotion?[27]

He implored her to withdraw from the marriage unless she was absolutely certain about it. His own feelings he made abundantly clear when he told her, 'You will hold command over me completely, to the extent that I hold command of myself; I look forward with joy to the various manifestations of your will, and will try to behave in every way as your property'. And to this promise of total subservience he added the words, 'Oh, how I would like to be a different, a better man, in order to—serve you!'[28]

What, it may well be asked, did Marie get in exchange for the load of care that Bülow brought to the altar? First, a promise that a marriage to him need not stand in the way of a career for her, a career to which she had devoted years of her life and which neither he nor she wanted to see pointlessly sacrificed on the altar of matrimony, the usual fate for a woman in Marie's position. Second, financial and material security. Bülow was now earning handsome fees in his triple capacity as concert pianist, conductor, and teacher. Despite the crippling monetary obligations that he had voluntarily assumed towards his daughters at the time of his divorce, most of those obligations had been discharged and there was enough money left over to keep a new wife in some luxury. Finally, Marie became overnight a baroness. This elevated her position in society, an advantage that was not lightly to be dismissed. Marie had the poise and the education to bear such a title with dignity. And Bülow himself was soon to write, 'My wife enjoys playing the role of baroness'.[29]

V

Bülow and Marie were married in Meiningen on July 29, 1882, and left on what was supposed to have been an extended honeymoon at the Danish resort of Klampenborg, where years earlier he and Cosima paid occasional visits. That may have been a fatal error. Surrounded by memories of his past Bülow fell apart, and in the middle of his honeymoon had to seek medical help for his nervous condition. It was Marie's dramatic introduction to married life with Bülow. The symptoms, according to her, were similar to the ones he had endured while he was on his tour of America in 1876, characterized mainly by violent headaches and fatigue.[30]

27. BB, vol. 6, p. 193.
28. Ibid., p. 194.
29. S-WW, p. 70.
30. BBLW, pp. 140–141.

This testing experience showed Marie, as she herself was later to show the world, that despite all the odds she was the ideal partner for Bülow. Instead of fleeing from the trauma, as many another young woman might have done, she held fast. But her plight was revealed in a letter she wrote to her sister on August 24, in the midst of the crisis at Klampenborg and barely a month after the wedding. 'Hans is too ill, too old, to take romantic walks through the wind and the weather with his wife. Tomorrow at the first rehearsal [in Meiningen] I will hear what prospect of deliverance I will have'.[31] That telltale word 'deliverance' speaks volumes. She was referring to the sort of care that Bülow might require in the months ahead, and what this might mean for her own freedom. The test would be how Bülow handled himself on the podium.

On this last point both Bülow and Marie remained silent. In fact, there is an unprecedented hiatus of four months in Bülow's published correspondence, from the end of August to the end of December 1882. What was he doing? Where did he go? From some small scraps of information that Marie shared with her family, we gather that Bülow virtually stopped conducting until the following year. She told her sister, 'Above all, it is now my aspiration to make separate housekeeping unnecessary, but to establish an orderly, comfortable household'.[32] That was a sure sign that Marie had become Bülow's caregiver, and the modern notion of two separate dwellings for the newlyweds had been abandoned. On September 24, she broke some further news to her father in Vienna. 'I have now temporarily given up my position [in the theatre] for I could not leave my husband in this condition. It was a difficult decision for both of us'.[33] Her leave of absence from the Meiningen stage is further proof of the seriousness of Bülow's condition. Cosima was meanwhile following this crisis with apprehension. She wrongly thought that Bülow was incarcerated in a mental asylum—a misleading piece of news that was conveyed to her in a particularly brutal fashion by Wagner, and it struck her like a physical blow. One entry in her diary runs, 'I flee to my room and see Hans before me, alone in that institution, and I feel like screaming, screaming to some god to help me! . . . I do not think that I shall ever have, or deserve

---

31. BAB, p. 384n1.
32. Ibid. Adelheid von Schorn, who had passed through Meiningen in June, and from whom we already gleaned something about Bülow's unusual ideas on marriage, passed through the city again in September. Bülow was not at home, but Adelheid met Marie Schanzer for the first time. Adelheid tells us that when Bülow's young bride had realized the seriousness of his illness, it had become obvious that she could not look after him while living in a separate household. Within one day she had moved her bags and baggage into Bülow's house, and thenceforth lived with him (SZM, pp. 424–425).
33. BB, vol. 6, p. 202.

to have, another happy moment'.[34] Bülow may have been tormented by the ghosts of his broken marriage to Cosima, but Cosima's torments were worse, driven as they were by her lifelong guilt at having left him.

VI

The vale of tears that represented the first few months of Marie's marriage to Bülow ended in a crisis for which neither was prepared. On February 13, 1883, news of Wagner's death was flashed around the world. Bülow had been confined to his bed for most of that day suffering from a bout of 'neuralgia', and it was not until the evening of the fourteenth that Marie finally summoned the courage to break the news to him, and only then in the presence of his doctor. She wrote to her mother, 'The news of Wagner's death has had such a shattering effect on my husband that since then the atmosphere has been one of the most profound melancholy'. Even she, she went on, had no idea of the depth of the love that he bore Wagner, and Bülow told her that he felt as if his own soul had died with Wagner's fiery spirit, and that only a fragment of his own body was left to wander the earth.[35] When Bülow learned that Cosima, para-

---

34. WT, vol. 2, pp. 975–976.

35. BAB, pp. 389–390. Max Kalbeck, in his massive biography of Brahms, gives a description of Bülow's violent reaction to Wagner's death that stretches our credulity. Brahms had arrived in Meiningen on February 12, the day before Wagner had died. Bülow managed to rouse himself from his sickbed, and in the company of Marie and some of the orchestral players, went to the railway station to meet Brahms. The next day the telegramme with its black border arrived from Bayreuth, and Marie had to choose the best moment to hand it to her husband. She waited until the evening of the fourteenth, and the arrival of Bülow's doctor. According to Kalbeck, Brahms was present when Bülow read the telegramme, screwed it angrily into a ball, and then threw himself to the floor in convulsions, biting and clawing at the carpet. Brahms was so disconcerted, Kalbeck continues, that he thought Bülow had lost his reason (KJB, vol. 3, p. 377). Kalbeck gives no source for this graphic scene, nor indeed could he have done so because we now know it to be pure invention. Marie von Bülow confirms that Brahms was not even with Bülow on the evening of February 14, let alone in his sickroom. (She deals with this matter at some length in BAB, p. xiv.) She points out that during these bouts of physical suffering, Bülow's way was to isolate and impose total silence on himself. At such times he liked to quote the comical Viennese saying, 'Compared to my silence, the grave is the purest tea-party' (BNB, p. 651).

It is no part of our present task to question the general reliability of Kalbeck's biography of Brahms, which, because of its impressive length—2,000 pages—gained for itself an authority among an earlier generation of scholars which has not stood the test of time. We know that Kalbeck provided his readers with a number of fantasies masquerading as facts, particularly those having to do with the impoverished young Brahms playing the piano in the saloons and brothels of Hamburg to make ends meet—a story which became an instant fixture in the Brahms literature, and prompted all manner of psychological theories explaining the composer's ambiguous relations with women in later life. (For more information on this absorbing topic see AJBL, pp. 2 and 3.) The point at issue is a simple one. If Kalbeck could go so grievously wrong in telling the story of his hero's life, is it likely that whatever he has to say about a peripheral figure such as Bülow (whom he hardly knew) is any more reliable?

lyzed with grief, was refusing to be parted from Wagner's body, he sent her his fabled telegramme, bearing the terse message, 'Souer, il faut vivre' (Sister, one must live).

The home that Marie eventually created for Bülow on Charlotten-strasse in Meiningen was the first he had enjoyed since the breakup of his marriage to Cosima. It was an elegant dwelling, facing the *Englischer Garten,* a stone's throw from the theatre. For the remaining twelve years of his life Marie provided Bülow with a woman's touch, and made his life softer. She became both his helpmate and his soul mate, and she sustained him through a variety of tribulations. There would be separations, for they willingly gave each other much personal freedom. That this placed the relationship under stress cannot be denied, and it led on one occasion to a situation so grave that it nearly resulted in a permanent rupture. But that crisis passed, and in his union with Marie, Bülow found much contentment.

The Meiningen Years,
1880–1885

III: Paths of Glory

Let me become your pupil, even if I must pay my tuition with blood
. . . I put myself in your hands. . . .
—Gustav Mahler[1]

I

Despite the Byzantine complications in Bülow's private life from which we have just emerged, his work with the Meiningen Orchestra remained constant. The European tours continued to absorb his time and involve him in his best work, and it is to them that we must now return. When the history of these long and arduous journeys comes to be written, the ones pursued in 1884 will be seen to rank not only among the most numerous but also the most memorable. The orchestra stood at the peak of its form, and it was gathering laurels wherever it appeared. In January alone, the ensemble gave twenty concerts in various cities in South Germany; and in February, after enjoying a brief respite in Meiningen, they swept through North Germany in a grand orbit that took them to Göttingen, Hamburg, Kiel, Lübeck, Bremen, and Berlin. Finally, in November and December, they rounded off the year by giving no fewer than thirty-two concerts in five weeks, moving through Bavaria, Austria, and Hungary—playing along the way in such cities as Munich, Graz, Pressburg, Vienna, and Budapest.

Some of these concerts merit attention. Gustav Mahler was present when the ensemble gave an all-Beethoven programme in Cassel, on January 24, and was electrified by the precision of the playing and by Bülow's

1. BMB, pp. 28–29.

command of the orchestra.[2] The admiration that the twenty-three-year-old Mahler subsequently had for Bülow has gone largely unremarked. Mahler was at that time the second conductor at the Court Theatre in Cassel. The day after the concert, and with all the impetuosity of youth, he tried to gain admittance to Bülow's hotel, but was refused by the porter. He returned to his apartment and expressed his gratitude to the older conductor in an impassioned letter:

> At yesterday's concert, when I beheld all that beauty which I had imagined and hoped for, everything became clear to me. I thought, 'Here is your home; here is your master. Your wandering must end now or never!' . . . Take me with you, in any capacity you wish. Let me become your pupil, even if I must pay my tuition with blood . . . I put myself in your hands, and if you will accept me, I do not know what would mean greater happiness to me. If you will grant me a reply, I am prepared to subscribe to anything you demand. Oh, at least give me an answer![3]

At the concert in Pressburg, on November 21, the seven-year-old Hungarian prodigy Ernst von Dohnányi was in the audience. More than fifty years later, he told a Hungarian Radio audience that he still recalled this concert, a memory on which Ilona von Dohnányi later elaborated when she wrote in her biography of her husband that 'this was the beginning of his aspirations toward conducting symphony orchestras'.[4]

When the orchestra arrived in Vienna on November 20, for the first of its three concerts in the Great Hall of the Musikverein, the eighteen-year-old Busoni was there. One of the works in the programme was Beethoven's *Egmont* Overture. The performance was severely criticized by the music critic of the *Fremdenblatt,* a judgement that Busoni thought unfair.

---

2. This all-Beethoven programme included the *Egmont* Overture, the Grosse Fuge, and the Eighth Symphony.

3. BMB, pp. 28–29. Bülow's reply was brusque. He told Mahler that it would be at least eighteen months before he could do anything to help, because he presently lacked any proofs of Mahler's talents as a pianist, conductor, and chorus master, and 'at this time I cannot give you the occasion to furnish me with them'. This was no more than the plain truth. But Bülow inexplicably forwarded Mahler's letter to Kapellmeister Wilhelm Treiber, the first conductor at the Cassel Court Theatre, which complicated Mahler's position there during the remaining months of his contract. The letter, dated 'January 28, 1884', is housed in the Cassel Theatre archives.

4. The radio address was delivered on January 30, 1944 (DSL, p. 12). Dohnányi's childhood reminiscence would have been made still more vibrant for him by the fact that in March 1899, as a twenty-one-year-old composer-pianist standing on the brink of his career, he was awarded the Hans von Bülow Grand Prize, just established by Ludwig Bösendorfer, for the early version of his Piano Concerto in E minor.

At the second Vienna concert, Bülow said nothing. But at the third, given on December 1, Bülow walked onto the platform with a copy of the *Fremdenblatt* in his hand, turned to the audience, and remarked:

> Since I am a stranger [*Fremder*] here, I feel it my duty to return the amiability of the Viennese public by reading the *Fremdenblatt;* and in fulfilling this duty I discovered that its music critic was much disturbed by my interpretation of the overture to *Egmont.* I therefore think it better not to perform that work, as I had announced, and I shall substitute the Academic Festival Overture by the master, Brahms.

Bülow had no sooner finished speaking than the call came from all corners of the hall, '*Egmont, Egmont!* We want *Egmont!*' Knowing Bülow as we do, we can say that he had judged the situation to perfection. He brought his baton down on the first chords of *Egmont* not only in defiance of the local critic, but also in response to an overwhelming demand of the audience, thus rendering the critic's words sterile. He might have left it there, but he could not resist chiding the audience as well, telling them, 'In 1810 you would with equal insistence have demanded an overture of Weigl'.[5] The critic of the *Fremdenblatt,* Ludwig Speidel, was in the hall and was humiliated by Bülow's speech. Brahms was present as well, sitting in a box with the music publisher and impresario Albert Gutmann, who tells us in his memoir of this occasion that as he accompanied Brahms back home, the composer turned to him with the words, 'God protect me from my friends!'[6]

II

As the orchestra made its triumphal way along these paths of glory, it was occasionally joined by Brahms. Bülow was happy to hand his friend the baton and have him direct the perfectly drilled players in performances

---

5. Bülow was reminding the audience that in the Vienna of 1810, their forebears had preferred music by the conservative Joseph Weigl to the revolutionary Beethoven.

6. Among the various accounts of this colourful scene that we have at our disposal, the main ones may be found in BB, vol. 6, p. 327; DFB, pp. 57–58; and GAW, pp. 23–24. Albert Gutmann, the author of this last source, and the person responsible for arranging the Austrian tour, provides some entertaining details of the Meiningen Orchestra's concerts in Vienna. He at first doubted that they would be successful in the Great Hall of the Musikverein, because the orchestra was so small. The Vienna Philharmonic Orchestra (which was conducted at this time by Hans Richter) possessed double the number of players and filled the platform. Bülow addressed the problem in a letter to Gutmann, which began with a rhyming couplet:

'Nicht Quantität, sondern Qualität
Ist unsere Spezialität!'

Montag, den 25. Februar 1884,

Abends 7½ Uhr:

Im Saal der Singakademie

ERSTES CONCERT

(Beethoven-Abend)

der

Hofkapelle S. H. des Herzogs von Sachsen-Meiningen

unter Leitung ihres Intendanten

Dr. Hans von Bülow.

Programm.

1. **Ouverture zum Ballet „Die Geschöpfe des Prometheus",**
   Op. 43 (1801).

2. **Sinfonie No. VIII, Op. 93 (1812).**
   Allegro vivace con brio.
   Allegretto scherzando.
   Tempo di Minuetto.
   Finale (Allegro vivace).

3. **Rondino für Blasinstrumente, Es-dur (Jugendarbeit).**
   Hoboen: Herren Kirchhof und Berlig.
   Clarinetten: Kammervirtuos Mühlfeld und Kammermusikus Schwarz.
   Hörner: Herren Leinhos und Müllich.
   Fagotte: Herren Höchstein und Treckenbrodt.

4. **Grosse Quartettfuge,** Op. 133 (1825).
   Ausgeführt von sämmtlichen Streichinstrumentalisten.

5. **Ouverture** zu „König Stephan", Op. 117 (1811).

6. **Sinfonie No. V,** C-moll, Op. 67 (1807).
   Allegro con brio.
   Andante con moto.
   Scherzo e Finale.

Während der Musik bleiben die Thüren geschlossen.

Das zweite Concert findet morgen Dinstag statt.
Beginn 8 Uhr.

The Meiningen Orchestra plays an all-Beethoven concert in the Singakademie, February 25, 1884. A concert billing.

of Brahms's own works—including the Academic Festival Overture, the Second Symphony, and the First Piano Concerto—knowing that it added lustre to Meiningen's crown. By now, whenever the players returned home, they were greeted like warriors bearing trophies from distant lands. This the Duke of Meiningen had to acknowledge. An occasion presented itself on February 3, 1884, when the orchestra found itself temporarily back in Meiningen where Brahms directed them in a performance of his Third Symphony. The next day, in an unusual ceremony, the duke personally invested Brahms with Meiningen's highest honour, the 'Komthurkreuz' (1st class), hitherto reserved exclusively for ministers of the court. Bülow himself received no such recognition, although we recall that years earlier he had been inducted into this same order—albeit at the 2nd class level. In any case, at this point in the tour a further decoration would have meant little to him. Like the good general that he was, he knew that it was possible to be decorated for winning battles and still lose the war, and he was about to take the war to the Prussian capital itself.

The arrival of the orchestra in Berlin, during the last week of February of this immemorial year of 1884, rivetted the attention of the musical world. The ensemble created a sensation by giving three consecutive concerts in the Singakademie (February 25, 26, and 27), each one of which featured Beethoven's Grosse Fuge from the String Quartet, op. 133, played by the entire string section from memory, standing up. This was a movement that lay beyond the capacity of most of the leading string quartets of the day, let alone an orchestra. But there was more to come. Two days after the Singakademie concerts the orchestra appeared in the Central Skating Rink in an unusual programme consisting of nine German overtures, headed 'Deutscher Styl':

SPOHR   *Berggeist, Faust, Jessonda*
WEBER   *Euryanthe, Freischütz, Oberon*
WAGNER   *Rienzi, Meistersinger, Tannhäuser*

After the last strains of *Tannhäuser* had died away, there was a storm of applause which moved Bülow to deliver an impromptu speech. He pointed out that twenty-five years had elapsed since he had first conducted this work in Berlin, when it had been hissed off the stage. He was happy to see that a new generation of listeners had shed the encumbrances of their forefathers and could listen to this music without prejudice.[7]

---

7. Bülow was referring to the concert he had conducted in Berlin on January 14, 1859, when he had asked 'the hissers to leave the hall'. See pp. 87–88.

III

Bülow now had Berlin at his feet. On March 4, he was invited back to the Skating Rink in order to conduct one of the Philharmonic Popular Concerts. At these affairs people paid a modest 75 pfennigs for their tickets and sat at tables, the women knitting and the men drinking beer. One of the works on the programme was Bülow's own *Triumphmarsch*, from his incidental music to *Julius Caesar*. But Bülow had prepared a little surprise. Instead of his *Triumphmarsch* he substituted the March from Meyerbeer's *Le Prophète*, because he had a point to make. As the applause subsided, Bülow turned to the audience to thank them for their indulgence in allowing him to change the programme. He then remarked, 'I recently heard that piece in the "Circus Hülsen" so deplorably massacred, that it was for me a necessity to perform it properly'.[8] There was a roar of approval, and people stamped their feet and clinked their beer mugs.

At the Royal Opera House, a stone's throw away, the reception was vastly different. Intendant Baron von Hülsen, Bülow's old nemesis, was incensed that both he and the Royal Opera House had once more been publicly humiliated by Bülow, and he seized the moment. He instructed Baron von Schleinitz at the 'Ministerium des königlichen Hauses', to despatch a formal letter of protest to the Meiningen Court, where Bülow's employer, Duke Georg II, was presently basking in all the reflected glory coming out of Berlin. The letter informed the duke that the title of 'Royal Court Pianist', which had been enjoyed by Bülow since 1858, was forthwith revoked.[9] Because the royal families of Berlin and Meiningen were intimately connected through Duke Georg's first marriage to the kaiser's sister, Princess Charlotte of Prussia, Meiningen was deemed to have been insulted as well. For days the press argued about the merits of the 'Hülsen-Circus' affair. As for the irascible Bülow, he gave himself a new title, one of which he was infinitely more proud, and had it printed on his visiting-cards: 'The People's Pianist'.

Hülsen may have thought that the score was settled. Bülow knew otherwise. Three years later more retribution rained down on the Royal Opera House, this time with effects infinitely more diverting. Although it takes us somewhat ahead of our narrative, the story belongs here because it was all part of Bülow's sustained campaign against what he considered to be the *Schlamperei* of the Berlin Opera.

On February 28, 1887, Bülow attended the first performance of Rüfer's opera *Merlin*, doubtless hoping that standards at the Royal Opera House

8. BB, vol. 6, p. 257.
9. The correspondence between Berlin and Meiningen on this tangled topic is preserved in DSB, NL H.v.Bülow, E III, 6.

(Eine Erinnerung an die Meininger Konzerte)

Worte: Doch ewig stört uns das Gelärme,
        Das Grunzen, Plärren und Gegirre
        Der musikalischen Geschirre.
        Die eine Schaar im schwarzen Fracke,
        Mit krummen Fingern, voller Backe,
        Vom Meister Zappelmann gehetzt,
        Hartnäckig in Bewegung setzt.
                    Busch: „Maler Klecksel".

'Hans von Bülow conducting the Meiningen Orchestra'. A caricature from the 'Wiener Lust' by Hans Schliessmann, Vienna 1884.

had improved. He was so appalled at what he witnessed that he sharpened his earlier jibe and now likened the organization to the Renz Circus, famous for its animal shows, one of the most popular entertainments in Berlin. The newspapers pounced on the story, there were peals of laughter across Germany, and an apoplectic administration of the opera house demanded that Bülow issue a public apology. Bülow complied by apologizing not to the Opera, but to the Renz Circus for having linked its name to that of the opera house. For that further insult, Bülow was banned from the building in perpetuity. His photograph was distributed among the ushers with instructions to eject him on sight. Doubtless wishing to test the effectiveness of the ban, Bülow turned up at the opera house in the company of the Bechstein family, together with his wife. He had already handed in his coat at the cloakroom and was engaged in conversation with a group of acquaintances when he was approached by a liveried usher and asked to leave the premises. A verbal skirmish ensued, during which Bülow demanded to know on whose authority this lackey was acting. Reinforcements were summoned, so Bülow donned his coat, offered his arm to his wife, and walked away.[10] The Berliner *Lustige Blätter* contributed to the general brouhaha when it published a full-page cartoon of Bülow being asked to leave the opera house by its new intendant, Count Bolko von Hochberg, who had assumed the position after the recent demise of Hülsen. 'Please leave the premises, mein Herr!' Hochberg is demanding, pointing a menacing swagger-stick in Bülow's direction. 'Very well', replies Bülow, 'I'll go to the Renz instead'.[11] Meanwhile, Ernst Renz, who was revelling in this priceless publicity, published an announcement in the Berlin newspapers inviting Bülow to visit the circus at any time. 'Whenever you wish to come, we are open'.

The main purpose of this later visit to Berlin, in fact, was to allow Bülow to perform a series of Beethoven recitals in the Singakademie, between March 2 and 10. According to an annotation in Marie von Bülow's personal copy of the programme, a demonstration was mounted against Bülow outside the building on the evening of March 2.[12] As he walked onto the platform the atmosphere was electric, for the audience expected a speech full of sarcasm and invective against the opera house and Count Hochberg. It did not come. Instead, Bülow sat down at the piano and began to improvise on a short quotation from Mozart's opera *The Marriage of Figaro,* a melody known to every schoolgirl in Germany: 'Will der Herr Graf ein Tänzchen wagen?'—'Does the Count want to risk a little dance?'

---

10. One of several accounts of the *Ausweisung* [or 'expulsion'] of Bülow from the Royal Opera House may be found in the *Vossische Zeitung,* March 1, 1887.

11. Issue of March 10, 1887.

12. DSB, Mus. Db 1815.

Figaro inquires. 'He has only to say so, and I'll play him a tune he won't forget'.

Mark Twain has reminded us that against the assault of laughter nothing can stand. The audience exploded in mirth.[13]

IV

From the beginning of his tenure at Meiningen, Bülow had taken an interest in Richard Strauss, who was still in his late teens. Strauss's debt to Bülow was incalculable, a fact made evident in the touching memoir that Strauss wrote about his mentor many years later, when he himself was at the height of his fame.[14] Bülow gave the world premier of the young composer's Serenade for Thirteen Wind Instruments in Berlin (1881), helping to launch Strauss's career. He also made room on his concert programmes for Strauss himself to conduct his own orchestral works, including the youthful Symphony in F minor and the tone poem *Macbeth*. Bülow dubbed him 'Richard the Third', the joke being that since Wagner was 'Richard the First', and therefore unique, there could be no 'Richard the Second'. The mock title was nonetheless a compliment to Strauss's growing musical powers.

Strauss himself has told us the diverting story of how his first, traumatic conducting engagement was brought about by Bülow. In 1884 Bülow commissioned the twenty-year-old composer to write a new work for the Meiningen Orchestra. The result was the Suite in B-flat major for Thirteen Wind Instruments, which Strauss submitted to Bülow that summer. Bülow was so pleased with this composition that he decided to include it in the orchestra's forthcoming tour. By chance this happened to include Munich, Strauss's native city, and in view of that fact Bülow thought that it would be appropriate to let Strauss himself conduct the work in front of a circle of the young man's local admirers. Strauss was duly flattered, but explained to Bülow that he had never before held a baton in his hand and wanted to know when he could rehearse. 'There will be no rehearsals', Bülow replied abruptly. 'The orchestra has no time for such things on tour'.

13. 'Mag er's nur sagen, ich spiel ihm auf.' Figaro's lines come from act I, scene 2. The droll phrase 'ich spiel ihm auf' is rich in colloquial meanings, including 'I'll lead him a merry chase.'
14. SRR, pp. 118–126.

Richard Strauss in 1890. A photograph.

Strauss was stunned, but Bülow was adamant. The great day arrived, but when Strauss went to pick up Bülow from his hotel he found the maestro in a dreadful mood. This visit to Munich had evidently stirred some bad memories. Bülow railed against the Bavarian capital; he railed against Baron von Perfall (his old adversary, the intendant of the Munich Opera House); he railed against all the appalling personalities who had driven Wagner out of the city fifteen years earlier; and he railed especially against the Odeon Theatre, which he called a combination of a church and a stock exchange. The abuse against Munich continued all the way to the auditorium, and Bülow's curses were still ringing in Strauss's ears as he mounted the podium to make his debut. He tells us that he conducted his Suite under the influence of a slight coma, with little recollection of what happened, save that he made no blunders. Bülow did not even hear the performance, but paced angrily up and down in the artist's room, smoking one cigarette after another. After the performance there was an explosion backstage. Franz Strauss, Richard's father, had entered the artist's room, visibly moved at the success of his son's debut as a conductor, wanting to thank Bülow in person. Bülow pounced on the elder

Strauss and bellowed, 'You have nothing to thank me for. I have not forgotten what you have done to me in this damned city of Munich. What I did today I did because your son has talent and not for you'. Everybody fled before the onslaught, including Franz Strauss. The incident ruined Richard's debut. He only realized much later that Bülow was still a prisoner of the past, and the old rage against Cosima, Wagner, and the little people in Munich who had almost ruined his life in the late 1860s had come boiling to the surface the moment he had set foot inside the city. Bülow later went out of his way to make amends to Strauss senior, who subsequently bore him no grudge.

V

As for Richard Strauss, Bülow paid him the finest compliment by appointing him assistant conductor of the Meiningen Orchestra. In the summer of 1885 Franz Mannstädt resigned, and left Meiningen in order to take up a position in Berlin.[15] Weingartner, Nicodé, Mahler, and Zumpe were all interested in the vacancy. 'We're swamped with applicants', Bülow told Marie.[16] His choice nonetheless fell on Strauss. Although the young man was lacking in practical experience, Bülow sensed his enormous potential. Would the orchestra accept the authority of one so young? Would Strauss, in turn, accept the discipline of daily rehearsal schedules, and the requirement to learn unfamiliar scores quickly? The players were privately polled by the hornist Gustav Leinhos, who found them eager to work with the youthful composer whose music they had come to admire. Georg II had still to put the seal of approval on this appointment, and he was at that moment on a private visit to England. Bülow therefore suggested that Strauss join him in Frankfurt, where he was about to commence teaching his summer masterclasses at the Raff Conservatory. There, he told Strauss archly, the young man would be able to make a diplomatic 'conquest' of Princess Marie of Meiningen, one of the duke's daughters, who was herself an accomplished pianist (she had earlier studied in Berlin with Ehlert and with Bülow himself) and was already enrolled in the course. Strauss duly arrived in Frankfurt and began attending the classes on June 9. The next day he was introduced to Princess Marie by Bülow, and impressed her by playing her his newly composed 'Improvisations and Fugue'. Bülow quickly turned the situation to Strauss's advantage and sent off a powerful recommendation to Georg II, in which he included the positive reactions of Princess Marie to the young man's playing.[17] On June 18 Strauss received the message for which he had been

15. Ibid., pp. 119–120.
16. Letter of May 5, 1885. BB, vol. 6, p. 359.
17. BB, vol. 6, pp. 367–368.

waiting: an official confirmation of his appointment as Bülow's assistant conductor for one season, with a modest remuneration of 1,500 marks.

Not long afterwards Bülow left on tour, and placed Strauss in charge of the Meiningen Choir, an amateur group of more than a hundred singers. One of the members was Marie von Bülow, who kept her husband informed about the young man's progress. She told Bülow that Strauss was already so popular with the sixty or so ladies in the choir that after a rehearsal of Mozart's *Requiem* they all broke into a round of applause. A few days later she was approached by the Princess of Hesse, who remarked, 'This is certainly something very different from that Mannstädt fellow'. Strauss was very tall, so Marie jovially nicknamed him 'our wee Strauss', and reported that he had already made some conquests among the ladies at the Casino Ball, where he had danced until he dropped, 'although the "slyboots" won't breathe a word about them'. Strauss was also allowed to rehearse the orchestra in some of Brahms's works, including the Violin Concerto and the A major Serenade. No wonder that he wrote so enthusiastically, 'Herr von Bülow is kindness itself to me, and I like my new career very much'.[18]

Strauss made his official debut as Meiningen's new 'assistant conductor' on October 18, 1885, sharing the podium with Bülow at the second subscription concert of the season. Bülow himself opened and closed the programme with performances of Beethoven's *Coriolan* Overture and the Seventh Symphony, respectively; Strauss conducted his own Symphony in F minor and appeared as soloist in Mozart's Piano Concerto in C minor, K. 491. In this triple capacity of conductor, pianist, and composer, the twenty-one-year-old achieved a notable triumph. Bülow was delighted with his young protégé and told his Berlin agent, Hermann Wolff, 'Strauss: *homme d'or*. Symphony *capital*. His playing, like his conducting debut— downright breathtaking. If *he* wants, he can step into my shoes tomorrow, with S.H.'s consent'.[19] Strauss had composed his own cadenza for the Mozart Concerto, which so impressed Bülow that he tried hard to persuade Eugen Spitzweg, the director of the publishing firm of Joseph Aibl, to publish it, but the latter lacked the courage to do so. Strauss is not remembered today as a pianist, but this early episode reminds us that he could just as easily have taken up a career as a concert pianist.

Strauss has left us many anecdotes about his early association with Bülow, but few more amusing than the following. Having thoroughly rehearsed the Meiningen Orchestra in some works of Brahms, so that the

18. Letter to Hermann Levi. SRS, pp. 95–97.
19. BB, vol. 6, p. 384.

Meiningen.

Herzogliches  Hoftheater.

Sonntag, den 18. October 1885:

Zweites Abonnements-Concert

der

Herzogl. Hofkapelle,

unter Leitung der Herren Intendant **von Bülow** und Hofmusik-
direktor **Richard Strauss**, sowie auch solistischer Mitwirkung
des Letzteren.

PROGRAMM:

1) **L. v. Beethoven:** Ouverture zur Tragödie „Coriolan", Op. 62.
2) **W. A. Mozart:** Clavierconcert mit **Orchester**, C-moll.
    Allegro. — Larghetto. — Allegretto. —
    Clavier: **Herr Richard Strauss.**
3) **Richard Strauss:** Sinfonie F-moll, Op. 12.
    Allegro ma non troppo, un poco maëstoso. — Scherzo. Presto. —
    Andante cantabile. — Finale. Allegro assai, molto appassionato.
    (Unter Direktion des Componisten).

Zehn Minuten Pause.

4) **L. v. Beethoven:** Siebente Sinfonie, A-dur, Op. 92.
    Poco sostenuto ed Allegro vivace. — Allegretto. —
    Scherzo (Presto ed assai meno presto). — Finale (Allegro con brio).

Flügel aus der k. k. Hofpianofortefabrik von BECHSTEIN in BERLIN.

Preise der Plätze:

Fremdenloge 3 M. Erster Rang 3 M. Sperrsitz 3 M. Parquetplatz 2 M.
Zweiter Rang 2 M. Sitzparterre 1 M. 20 Pf. Orchester 2 M. Stehparquet 1 M. Amphitheater 80 Pf.
Stehparterre 80 Pf. Gallerie 50 Pf.

Während der Dauer eines Musikstücks bleiben die Thüren geschlossen.

Anfang: 4½ Uhr.   Ende: 6½ Uhr.
Kasseneröffnung: 4 Uhr.

Der Billetverkauf findet bei Herrn Hoftheaterkassier **Helbig** (Marienstrasse 1) und
an der Herzoglichen Hoftheaterkasse statt.

Druck von H. Marbach in Meiningen.

Richard Strauss makes his official debut as Bülow's assistant conductor in
Meiningen, October 18, 1885. A playbill.

master himself could conduct them, Bülow decided to conclude the programme with Brahms's 'Academic Festival Overture', a work that calls for an enlarged percussion section. In order to show respect towards Brahms, and to avoid recruiting the extra percussion players from the ranks of the overstretched string section, Bülow elected to play the cymbals himself, and directed Strauss to play the bass drum. Unfortunately it transpired during the rehearsal that neither musician was able to count rests. Strauss eventually used a full score. But Bülow kept losing count after eight bars or so, and had to keep running over to the trumpeter to ask, 'To what letter have we got?' He would then start counting all over again. As Strauss put it, 'I do not think that a greater mess has ever been made of the percussion parts than on the evening when the two conductors took a hand'.[20]

VI

Bülow somehow managed to keep his concert fingers in shape, although it was remarked by some that his piano playing now lacked the polish of his earlier years.

   Much of the month of April 1885 was spent in Paris, where Bülow had been invited to give four concerts. On April 12 he appeared in the Théâtre impérial du Châtelet, and performed the G major Piano Concerto of Beethoven, with a large orchestra conducted by Eduard Colonne. He also played some solo works by Rubinstein and Chopin. The Parisians regarded him as a relic from the past. They admired his musicianship and his memory; but he was for them a sort of musical Rip van Winkle, a virtuoso who had gone to sleep a generation earlier and had suddenly reawakened to find himself in an unfamiliar world. *Le Ménestrel* covered the first concert in depth, and reported that there was scarcely a seat to be had in the spacious auditorium. 'Bülow plays less in the style of a virtuoso than in that of an excellent musician', we read. 'One feels that he identifies himself with the works he plays'. The paper then went on to say, somewhat artfully, that 'had the playing been less analytical, less scrupulous, less attentive to detail, it would have been entirely enjoyable'.[21] A warmer response was published in the journal *L'Art musical*, whose music critic was the Russian composer César Cui. Filled with enthusiasm for what Bülow had achieved in St. Petersburg earlier in the year, 'dragging the city out of its musical lethargy', Cui wrote an impassioned appreciation of Bülow's

---

20. SRR, p. 124.

21. *Le Ménestrel*, April 12, 1885. Once again we encounter a criticism that had pursued Bülow throughout much of his career: namely, that his performances sometimes became trapped in their interior details. For the discerning listener, however, it was the interior details that mattered.

career for the benefit of his French readers. He drew attention to Bülow's 'uprightness', 'selflessness', and 'someone with no ulterior motives'; and concluded that 'Bülow has just proved that true artists have not yet entirely vanished'.[22] He made special mention of Bülow's promotion of the music of Brahms (who was virtually unknown in Paris, and whom Bülow featured in three of his Paris concerts).[23] The fourth concert took place in the Salle Pleyel on April 22, and aroused so much interest that he gave in to public demand, returned to the same venue a week later, and presented a fifth.

Attending these concerts was Claire de Charnacé, whom Bülow had not seen since the days of the Munich crisis and his divorce, seventeen years earlier. She invited him to her home in Versailles. They talked of Wagner, of Cosima, of the wreck of Bülow's first marriage, and of the stability of his second. Claire expressed regret for having allowed herself to be turned into Cosima's unwitting dupe during the latter's surreptitious trip to Venice in the company of Wagner. This memory opened the door to many topics. Claire was introduced to Marie von Bülow and was struck by her resemblance to Cosima. Of Marie's impeccable diction she recalled that it came from 'someone who has studied the art of declamation'. Claire was later moved to write a nineteen-page memoir of her encounter with Bülow, which provides details of his private life not readily available elsewhere.[24]

VII

Bülow's resignation from Meiningen had much to do with a misunderstanding with Brahms, whose recently composed Fourth Symphony had been so rigorously rehearsed by the Meiningers that when the composer arrived in the city to conduct the world premier (on October 25, 1885) there was little more for him to do than inspire the perfectly prepared orchestra to achieve a magnificent performance. Strauss was a daily witness to the loving care that Bülow lavished on the symphony. At the concert Brahms was described as mounting the podium wearing his decorations—the 'Grand Cross' and the 'Commander's Cross'—and being warmly received by the audience. A repeat performance was given in Meiningen on November 1, this time under the direction of Bülow, which was generally held to have been a superior rendering, because Brahms's phlegmatic baton technique was no match for that of Bülow.

22. *L'Art musical*, April 15, 1885, p. 50.
23. The Brahms repertoire that Bülow introduced to French audiences at this time included the Sonata no. 3, in F minor, op. 5; the Scherzo in E-flat minor, op. 4; and the complete Caprices and Intermezzos, op. 76.
24. VMA, Ms F 859, Carton 9.

The trouble arose shortly afterwards when Bülow took the orchestra—and the symphony—on tour to more than a dozen different cities in Germany and The Netherlands. Brahms joined them, but instead of coming along as a passive companion, as Bülow had expected, he calmly insisted on conducting his new symphony, often at the last minute, leaving Bülow with little option but to comply. It was a state of affairs that slowly began to grate on the conductor's nerves, because he had put so much of himself into the rehearsals. Brahms knew that Bülow particularly wished to conduct the work in Frankfurt, because of the latter's connection to the Raff Conservatory, and it was Bülow's clear understanding that he would do so. As Brahms casually told Clara Schumann, 'I cannot exactly refuse to allow Bülow to travel about with it a bit'.[25] But Frankfurt was a city where several of Brahms's own friends lived, including Bernhard Scholz and Clara herself, and Brahms effectively shut Bülow out. The conductor was supposed to have introduced the symphony to the Frankfurters on November 3, 1885, the first concert of the great winter tour, but Brahms insisted on taking over the baton. When the orchestra returned to Frankfurt three weeks later, for its closing concert of the tour, on November 24, the Fourth Symphony was once more announced, and Bülow fully expected to conduct it. But Brahms broke away from the tour and returned to Frankfurt ahead of Bülow in order to conduct a semiprivate performance of the work with the Frankfurt Museum Symphony Orchestra, stealing from Bülow whatever thunder was left with which to impress the Frankfurters when he himself arrived in the city. Determined not to suffer a further indignity on November 24, Bülow removed the symphony from the programme. Marie von Bülow scrawled above her copy of the printed handbill the words 'BRAHMS—CONFLICT. Letztes Meininger'.[26] The item 'Fourth Symphony' of Brahms she crossed out and substituted the title of Beethoven's Seventh Symphony, Bülow's last-minute choice of a replacement. To the outside world it looked like a simple gaffe, but to Bülow it hid a betrayal so grave that it led to a break in their friendship that lasted for more than a year.

Bülow was affronted that Brahms appeared to see no reason not to continue the warm relationship he had come to enjoy with the Meiningen Orchestra, and especially with the duke and his wife, and to go on assuming that he could safely rely on Bülow for future services to himself and his music. In this he was profoundly mistaken. Bülow refused to be taken for granted. He cut off all possibility of that happening by tendering his resignation to the duke and leaving Meiningen. This was an extreme step, but the principle involved was clear enough to Bülow, and Brahms

25. Letter dated 'end of October, 1885', LSB, vol. 2, p. 294.
26. DSB, Mus. Db 1815 Rara.

Bülow and Brahms. 'Executive' and 'Legislative'.

had ignored it. It was expressed in some precise words after their rapprochement three or four years later, when Bülow inscribed a photograph
of himself and Brahms with their respective appellations, 'Executive and
Legislative'. Bülow conducted the music, Brahms composed it.[27]

Bülow may well have been disappointed not to receive more support
for his point of view than Georg II was prepared to grant him, and this too
undermined his position. It is a fact that the correspondence between
Brahms and the royal couple showed such warmth of feeling that they
might well have regretted Bülow's departure somewhat less than that of
Brahms.[28] Helene, especially, may not have been unhappy to see Bülow go.
According to Richard Strauss, to whom Bülow handed over the baton, she
was always somewhat jealous of the fame of the orchestra which, thanks
to Bülow, now overshadowed that of the theatre, her special project.

27. See the photograph above. Beneath the picture Bülow has written a further inscription 'Hans von Bülow zu freundlichen Erinnern an Mainz, 16. Nov' ('In friendly remembrance of Mainz, November 16'). Bülow had played in the city on that date, and appears to
have given the picture to Brahms in Hamburg, two days later.
28. Their extensive exchange of letters is published in MHBB.

Bülow's decision to leave Meiningen was made somewhat easier for him by the fact that Marie Schanzer had recently been fired from the theatre. The story is a long one, the fine details of which need not detain us. It is sufficient to know that the ensemble of actors had gone to Dresden to fulfil a guest engagement. On December 5, 1884, Bülow had turned up there with the orchestra, having just given thirty-three concerts in thirty days. Without warning, and without first seeking formal permission, Marie left Dresden and travelled back to Meiningen with Bülow, leaving the production in the lurch. It brought to a head a long-simmering conflict between Marie and Baroness Helene. Because of her many important roles, Marie was regarded by some as a 'star' of the Meiningen troupe and this Helene could not abide. It went against the grain for which the troupe was justly renowned: the Meiningen Theatre offered no sanctuary for 'stars'; no actor was greater than the part being played. With growing impatience Helene and the theatre director, Ludwig Chronegk, recognized that they had found in Marie Schanzer someone with more temperament than the troupe could handle. The display of independence at Dresden was for Chronegk the last straw. Helene even congratulated Chronegk on his decision to terminate Marie's contract, telling him, 'Would that we had never taken her on! I regard her as a bad woman'.[29] From the beginning of 1885, Marie had been unemployed, her annual salary of 3,000 marks withdrawn.

Just before Bülow left Meiningen the duke wrote to him, 'There remains, therefore, nothing more for me to do than to declare my sincere thanks for all the unforgettable hours which you prepared for us, as well as for the fame you have brought my orchestra. Your memory will always be honoured by us, and we would also like your memory of the good hours you spent with us in friendship to continue'.[30]

Far more important than these appreciative words of Georg II was the remarkable tribute that the members of the Meiningen Orchestra sent to Bülow when they learned that he was about to leave them:

Highly Esteemed Herr v. Bülow!
The Meiningen Court Orchestra would not like to see you depart from their midst, highly esteemed Master, without at least having

29. ESG, p. 340. '. . . eine böse Frau'. This was a loaded expression that perhaps only Chronegk would have appreciated. Earlier in the season Marie had been cast as the 'Böser Geist' (or 'evil spirit') in Goethe's *Faust*. Evidently both Helene and Chronegk saw Marie playing this role offstage as well as on. Chronegk's letter terminating Marie's contract is dated '9th December, 1884'. Meininger Stadtbibliothek, call no. 291/13.

30. Hitherto unpublished. DSB, Georg II to Bülow, Mus. ep. 181, dated November 25, 1885.

taken this opportunity of expressing their deep feeling, warmest and most profound thanks, for all the high and glorious things that you accomplished during the term of your activity here, which brought honour and fame to our revered art; for all the artistic gifts that you poured out from the rich cornucopia of your genius; and above all, for having dignified us with the honour of cooperating with you in the great work of reform, which has moved and delighted the whole world of music.

The great enthusiasm and gratitude which we bear for you, our great master and benefactor, with every drop of our blood, we will demonstrate by regarding it our most sacred duty to uphold in the purest form the traditions that you have established with your interpretations of the immortal works of our great composers, particularly those of Beethoven, so that in time to come you can look back with pleasure and satisfaction at the living memorial that you yourself have erected here. With the assurance of its everlasting respect, a heartfelt 'Lebewohl' and a joyful 'Auf Wiedersehen' is proclaimed for you by the grateful Meiningen Court Orchestra. Meiningen, 1. 12. 1885[31]

Few conductors have received such a glowing salute. Despite all the toil and sweat to which Bülow had subjected them, the players had not only come to respect him but to admire him as well.

VIII

Bülow lost no time in putting distance between himself and Meiningen. He left on a six-week conducting engagement with the St. Petersburg Russian Musical Society, which kept him out of Germany from early December 1885 to mid-January 1886. He was greeted in person by the leaders of the Russian School—Balakirev, Cui, Glazunov, Borodin, and Rimsky-Korsakov, with whose *Antar* Symphony he scored a notable success.[32] But perhaps his greatest conquest was with the music of Tchaikovsky, who spent an entire day in Bülow's company and went through the score of his newly composed *Manfred* Symphony with the conductor.[33] Tchaikovsky also attended Bülow's rehearsal of his Suite no. 3 in G major, which

---

31. BB, vol. 6, p. 399. The tribute bears the signatures of all forty-eight orchestral players, headed by that of their new director, Richard Strauss. The original document may be consulted in the Library of Congress (call no. ML422.B9 M4 Case). Bülow sent his formal reply to Strauss himself, 'since your name stands at the head of the signatures . . .' (BB, vol. 6, pp. 399–400).

32. R-KMM, p. 234.

33. BAB, pp. 445 and 471.

Bülow presented at the concert on December 26. Bülow readily agreed to return to St. Petersburg in March and April of 1886.

Meanwhile, the German newspapers, always on the lookout for trouble whenever Bülow was involved, happily broke news of the recent quarrel between him and Brahms, and of his subsequent resignation from Meiningen. The story was taken up by the *Journal de St. Petersburg,* and was published in its issue of November 22 (Old Style)[34] at the moment of Bülow's arrival in the city. He replied:

> Sir,
> May I venture to ask you to issue a correction about a 'piece of gossip' borrowed from a Berlin newspaper, reproduced in the number of 22 November [4 December] from the *Journal de St. Petersburg,* and which affects me too closely for me to let it pass?
>
> There was no *incident* in Cologne in which I was involved, there has been no *quarrel* between Herr Brahms and his humble admirer; the only true statement in it is my resignation as Intendant of the Ducal Orchestra in the service of His Highness the Duke of Saxe-Meiningen, a resignation that became necessary, since, not possessing the gift of being everywhere at the same time, I had to choose between the honour of conducting the symphonic concerts of the Russian Musical Society of St. Petersburg, and the pleasure of taking the ducal orchestra across Germany and the neighbouring countries.
> Hans von Bülow
> St. Petersburg, 24 November [6 December][35]

Anyone familiar with the facts of the matter knows this explanation to contain some sophistry. The friction between Brahms and Bülow, with the E minor Symphony at its centre, had become a subject of public comment even as the orchestra wended its way through the Rhineland cities. The *Journal de St. Petersburg* specifically mentions Cologne. The ensemble had, in fact, arrived in Cologne on November 23, 1885, where, according to the printed programme, Brahms's Fourth Symphony was performed 'under the personal direction of the Master'. (It was the ninth occasion that Brahms had taken over the direction of his new symphony from Bülow.) Moreover, it was at Cologne that Bülow learned of the aforementioned 'unofficial' performance slipped in by Brahms in Frankfurt, because the following day (November 24) the orchestra and its two con-

---

34. December 4, New Style.
35. BB, vol. 7, pp. 3–5.

ductors were both in Frankfurt where the crisis broke.[36] The report in the Russian press, then, contained a good deal of truth. It was pride alone, fuelled by a temporary outbreak of anger against both Brahms and the duke, that had compelled Bülow to walk away from Meiningen. But that anger had now subsided, and he wanted to normalize his relations with Brahms especially. Bülow probably thought it worthwhile to publish a white lie—well illustrated here as an untruth issued because its motives were honorable—in an attempt to put the matter to rest. It would never be put entirely to rest, however. The quarrel with Brahms was a bell that could not be unrung.

IX

Bülow took his formal leave of Meiningen on January 29, 1886. His farewell concert was given in benefit of the 'Widows and Orphans Pension Fund', his only motive for returning to a city with which he was essentially done.[37] It featured his own symphonic poem *Nirwana* and Beethoven's *Eroica* Symphony. He also appeared as soloist in Rubinstein's G major Piano Concerto. Richard Strauss wrote to his father about the *Eroica*. 'It was a performance such as I shall never hear a second time . . . I was so moved that after the last movement I cried like a child in the orchestra room; I was alone with Bülow there and he put his arms round me and gave me a kiss that I shall never forget as long as I live'.[38]

Brahms wrote his old friend a letter of reconciliation, which he tactfully addressed to Marie von Bülow in the hope of sparing Bülow further unpleasantness. Six months elapsed, and Brahms received no reply. Then, out of the blue, he got a birthday telegramme on May 7, 1886, signed by a group of friends and admirers, including Bülow. Brahms saw an opportunity to heal the rift and now wrote directly to Bülow himself, inquiring whether Marie had ever shown him that earlier letter. Not only had Bülow not seen it, but Marie bluntly denied ever having received it.[39] Brahms told Bülow that it would be difficult for him to repeat its heartfelt contents for fear of reopening old wounds, but that its purpose had been 'to set aside a misunderstanding which lay more heavily on my heart than

36. See the account given in GBLW, p. 158. All these performances of the Fourth Symphony were played from manuscript, and we surmise that Brahms took the score and orchestral parts ahead with him to Frankfurt. The symphony was not published until the following year, in October 1886.

37. Nonetheless, the interest that Bülow took in this charitable organization was powerful enough to attract him back to Meiningen on a further occasion, when he conducted a concert in benefit of the same Widows and Orphans Pension Fund on April 10, 1887.

38. SBE, pp. 84–85. See also SRS, pp. 109–110.

39. 'No such letter ever reached my hands' (BB, vol. 7, p. 34).

you might presume'. But he could hardly have endeared himself to Bülow by going on to add that 'concerts and anything connected to them just don't count as very serious matters with me'.[40] The rupture between Brahms and Bülow was healed about a year later, when Bülow visited Vienna in January 1887. He found a calling card from Brahms waiting for him, on which a few notes of music had been scribbled. They came from Act II of Mozart's *Zauberflöte,* and accompany Sarastro's words, 'Soll ich Dich, Teurer, nicht mehr sehen?' ('Shall I, dear one, see thee nevermore?'). Bülow called on Brahms that same day, 'chatting with him for a bewitching hour'.[41]

Richard Strauss left Meiningen in April 1886, a few short months after Bülow himself. When he was not conducting he could be found in the theatre, unexpectedly enjoying a season of classical plays, because in 1886 the troupe did not undertake any tours. When Strauss went to take his formal leave of the duke and his wife, Helene turned to him with the words, 'The Duke and I regret to lose you so soon. You were . . .' (Strauss was just about to make a gratified bow, expecting a compliment on his conducting, when Helene completed her sentence) '. . . the best *claqueur* we've had in our theatre for a long time'.[42] His appreciation of the theatre, it seems, was valued more highly by Helene than his work with the orchestra.

What Bülow had long suspected now came to pass. Brahms himself came very much to the fore. In 1886 Duke Georg appointed Fritz Steinbach (on Brahms's recommendation) to direct the orchestra. Steinbach lost no time in turning Meiningen into a centre for Brahms, in much the same way that Bayreuth had become a centre for Wagner. When Steinbach took the ensemble on tour, the four Brahms symphonies were placed at the heart of the repertoire. As for the orchestra itself, the marvellous machine that Bülow had created began slowly to unwind. And after Steinbach's own departure from Meiningen, in 1902, the glory days were over.

40. AJBL, p. 634.
41. BB, vol. 7, p. 73.
42. SRS, p. 104. Unknown to the duke and his wife, Strauss had been busily engaged in an intense correspondence with Bülow, and had already decided that he was going to leave Meiningen, while at the same time seeking his mentor's advice about the wisdom of doing so. With Bülow's approval Strauss finally accepted the position of 'third conductor' at Munich.

Bülow the Pedagogue

The Frankfurt Masterclasses, 1884–1887

> The interpreter should be the opposite of a grave-digger: he should
> bring what is buried into the light of day.
> —Bülow[1]

> So you are a piano teacher? But are you not the music teacher to the
> whole world in general, and to musicians in particular?
> —Adolf Brodsky[2]

I

For four summers, from 1884 through 1887, Bülow gave masterclasses at
the Raff Conservatory in Frankfurt-am-Main, in aid of the Raff Memorial
Foundation. Because these classes flowed directly out of his Meiningen
years, this is the proper place to consider them, together with their influence on the history of piano pedagogy. The fact that Bülow was willing to sacrifice so much of his time to an activity that he held in near
contempt, and which he had once described as 'slavery of the most an-
nihilating kind', speaks volumes about the high regard in which he held
Raff himself. But in order to understand why Bülow became attached to
Frankfurt at all, we have to go back a few years.

Joachim Raff had been appointed the first director of the newly created
Hoch Conservatory of Music in 1878, an institution that had been
brought into existence by virtue of a massive endowment of 900,000 gold

---

1. BAS (part 2), p. 274.
2. Unpublished letter to Bülow, dated December 18, 1884. BKHB, p. 79.

marks bequeathed by the Frankfurt merchant Dr. Joseph Hoch. Raff had held the position with distinction until his death from a heart attack in June 1882, at the relatively early age of sixty. At the time of his death more than 200 students were enrolled at the Conservatory, and Raff himself had become a revered figure. His funeral was an imposing affair. The entire student body helped to form the long procession of mourners as it wended its way towards Frankfurt's city cemetery. Bülow had rushed from Meiningen on hearing the news, but got to Frankfurt too late to see his old friend lowered into the ground, and he paid his silent respects at the graveside the following day. This friendship, whose loss he felt so keenly, went back almost forty years when Bulow was a teenage student at the Stuttgart Gymnasium. 'Joachim Raff was my oldest, truest friend', he wrote despairingly. 'I could be proud of his affection, which often proved itself in practical ways'.[3] While he was in Frankfurt he learned that Raff had left his family in straitened circumstances.[4] In consequence, the composer had been buried in a modest plot, in a crowded part of the cemetery, with nothing but a small headstone to identify his remains. This situation Bülow quietly resolved to change.

During his tenure as the director of the Hoch Conservatory, Raff had brought in some distinguished faculty, including Clara Schumann (piano); Hugo Heerman (violin); Julius Stockhausen (singing); Joseph Rubinstein (the Wagner devotee who had been the pianist at the first rehearsals of *The Ring,* in 1874); and Bernard Cossmann (cello); and within a short time these musicians, all of whom enjoyed national careers, had turned the Hoch Conservatory into one of the leading musical establishments in Germany. It was a notable balancing act on the part of Raff, because these faculty members represented both the conservative and the revolutionary trends in music. Nor had Raff neglected before his death to appoint some gifted younger teachers to the faculty, including Bülow's old pupil Max Schwarz, Bertrand Roth, and Max Fleisch, who were still in their twenties.

By training and temperament Raff was a supporter of the New German School of Liszt and Wagner, and his demise created some uncertainty. Who would the new director be? What sort of curriculum would he create? Would there be hirings and firings? When in January 1883 the board of directors announced that Bernhard Scholz from Breslau was to be ap-

3. BB, vol. 6, p. 188.
4. According to Raff's daughter Helene, her father was so confident of his place in musical history that he believed his family would be able to live comfortably off his royalties. In this he was sadly mistaken, for his music soon fell into that oblivion from which it has never really escaped. RR, pp. 264–265.

pointed Raff's successor, the faculty was split right down the middle. Clara Schumann described it as 'a revolution'.[5] Scholz was an archconservative, hostile to the music of both Liszt and Wagner. He had been one of the signatories to the partisan 'Manifesto' drawn up by Brahms and Joachim, and published in the *Berliner Musik-Zeitung Echo* in May 1860, proclaiming their opposition to the radical ideas of the New German School. That had been more than twenty years earlier, but the 'War of the Romantics' was still alive and well. Frankfurt was widely regarded as a conservative, anti-Wagner city, thanks in large measure to the presence of Clara Schumann and her cohorts, who welcomed the appointment of Scholz as a highly visible supporter of her best musical friends, Brahms and Joachim. The younger members of the faculty, led by Schwarz and Roth, rebelled and refused to work under the new director. Three of their number resigned; another three were fired. Early in 1884 they formed a breakaway institute and named it the 'Raff Conservatory'. For several years thereafter the atmosphere of Frankfurt was poisoned as the two groups faced each other in open hostility.

This was the situation that greeted Bülow when he brought the Meiningen Orchestra to Frankfurt, on January 8, 1884, in order to give an all-Beethoven concert in memory of Raff. During the morning, everybody assembled at the new institute for a short memorial service, during which Bülow conducted the Funeral March from Beethoven's *Eroica* Symphony. Raff's widow and daughter were present, as were many of his pupils and a number of family friends. The creation of a Raff Memorial Fund was formally announced, and Bülow agreed to head the committee whose task was to raise money and commission a monument worthy of the composer. The ceremony had been planned as a prelude to the concert that evening, at which a capacity crowd was expected:

Coriolan Overture, op. 62
Symphony no. 1, in C major, op. 21
Rondino in E-flat major, for wind instruments
               Intermission
Symphony no. 8, in F major, op. 93
Grosse Fuge, op. 133
    (transcribed for string orchestra by Bülow)

The circumstances surrounding this memorial concert almost beggar belief, but can be substantiated. In an attempt to torpedo the concert, Bernhard Scholz forbade the faculty and student body at the Hoch Conservatory

5. LSB, vol. 2, p. 265n1.

from attending the 'rival' building, on pain of dismissal. To make sure that his orders were carried out, he arranged for an extra student concert to coincide with Bülow's appearance, and he made it mandatory for every member of the Conservatory to attend. The previous evening Clara Schumann had also put on a grand reception at her home, to which all the leading personalities in Frankfurt were invited, however remote their connections to the arts, in order to rob Bülow and his orchestra of some limelight. It was in effect a public snub.[6] Despite the opposition mounted against it, the Meiningen Orchestra that evening enjoyed one of it greatest triumphs. Bülow described it to Marie, in extravagant language, as 'Colossal, Pyramidal, Monumental!'[7] His elation was fuelled in part by the fact that on this same day he had celebrated his fifty-fourth birthday, and his success with the Frankfurt audience was the best present he could have received. The tour continued with concerts in Darmstadt, Nuremberg, Karlsruhe, Stuttgart, Mainz, Worms, and Cassel, and then headed back to Frankfurt where Bülow determined to serve his adversaries a second helping of humble pie. Clara Schumann was in the audience this time, and while she found Brahms's C minor Symphony and his *Haydn* Variations 'enjoyable', Bülow's treatment of the other pieces by Weber and Beethoven she called arbitrary. 'He rehearses as he plays, everything is plucked to pieces and dissected. The heart has nothing to do with it. Everything comes from the head, calculated. But this he did achieve: one experiences joy at the mastery of the orchestra. . . . His platform manner was as always to me shockingly unsympathetic. However, he knows how to be eminent!'[8]

Equally unflattering were the references to Bernhard Scholz and Clara Schumann that we find in the unpublished correspondence between Bülow and Max Schwarz. 'How is little Clara?' Bülow slyly enquires. 'No inclination to produce [Schumann's] Andante and Variations for two pianos in the next life with J[oachim] [R]aff'?[9] The subtext here implies that Clara shows no signs of joining the recently deceased Raff in the Great

6. One witness who was present in Frankfurt, and left an account of this dismal episode, was the pianist Frederic Lamond, who had recently become a pupil of Max Schwarz at the Raff Conservatory (LM, pp. 27–29) and later joined Bülow's masterclasses there. Marie von Bülow also mentions the débâcle in BB, vol. 6, p. 239.

7. BB, vol. 6, p. 242.

8. LCS, vol. 3, p. 448. On March 29, 1885, Bülow conducted Brahms's Third Symphony in Leipzig, the first time that Clara had heard the work. She noted in her diary that she found the performance '. . . without comprehension and feeling, the whole amounting to a cold calculation, degenerating into the crassest tastelessness' (LCS, vol. 3, p. 464). We may wonder how she came to such a conclusive judgement, lacking any previous knowledge of the work.

9. CHC, pp. 91–92.

Beyond, and playing with him a work by her husband to cement the celestial relationship. And Bülow delivered a venomous pun when he referred to Scholz and Clara as 'Hermann and Dorothea', and wished on them a *Bleichsucht* (or 'greensickness', otherwise chlorosis), creating at a single stroke an association between Goethe's famous poem and the postal address of the Raff Conservatory, which was situated at 13 Bleichstrasse.[10]

During the ten days that elapsed between the two Frankfurt concerts, Bülow's name was frequently brought forward as someone who might help put the fledgling Raff Conservatory on its feet. Max Schwarz offered him the position of honorary president of the new organization, and Bülow accepted 'with joyful pride, with prideful joy', as he put it. He went on to tell Schwarz that while he was unwilling to join the regular piano faculty ('if I am entirely healthy it makes me ill; if I am ill, it annihilates me') he wanted to help in whatever way Schwarz might find useful, providing it did not create problems for Bülow himself.[11]

This is how Bülow came to launch his masterclasses in Frankfurt. And by accepting the position of honorary president of the Raff Conservatory, he incurred the lasting hostility of everybody connected with the Hoch Conservatory, but above all of Clara Schumann and her circle. Bülow not only paid his own expenses while living in Frankfurt (he liked to stay at the Schwan Hotel), he willingly waived his fee as well, which was diverted into the Raff Memorial Fund. The eventual result was a generous contribution of 10,000 marks towards the cost of a monument which, because of many delays, was not placed over Raff's grave until May 1903. By that time Raff's body had been relocated to a more spacious plot in the Frankfurt cemetery, and Bülow himself had gone to meet his Maker.

II

The Frankfurt masterclasses have been well documented, but it is worth pausing to look at their impact on those who participated. The classes were held in the main concert hall of the Raff Conservatory, from 8:00 a.m. to 11:00 a.m. The fee for each participant was 100 marks. Bülow himself auditioned the aspiring candidates the day before the class began,

10. The informed reader will recall that the backdrop to the story of Hermann and Dorothea was the French Revolution, and the flight across the Rhine into Germany of countless numbers of dispossessed people, whose hopes of a better life under Napoleon had collapsed when the consequences of his tyrannical rule became apparent. Bülow's parallels between Bernhard Scholz ('Napoleon') and the 'revolution' at the Hoch Conservatory ('France'), with its dashed hopes of better times to come (the 'flight' from the Hoch Conservatory to the 'safety' of the Raff Conservatory), are too obvious to require further elaboration.

11. BB, vol. 6, p. 244–245.

and only a few were selected. For a small admission charge members of the general public were also admitted. All this money went into the Raff Memorial Fund. Bülow sat at a second piano, from which vantage point he would listen to the student, and then illustrate those passages that he thought needed improvement. Everything was played by him from memory; no matter what pieces the pupils brought along, he seemed to know them inside out. Unlike Liszt, who allowed his students to play whatever they liked, Bülow preferred to concentrate his attention on one composer at a time, so entire sessions were devoted to Bach (especially the Preludes and Fugues); at other times the sessions concentrated exclusively on Beethoven, Chopin, Liszt, Brahms, or composers to whose music Bülow was especially attached, including Raff and Mendelssohn. Bülow would talk at length about the works and composers under review. Analysis, history, and biography were all part of the rich mixture of ideas that poured from his mind, elevating these classes from the humdrum level of 'piano workshops' to that of a course in music philosophy. It was not uncommon for Bülow to deliver a lengthy preamble on one or another aspect of music. Even the discipline of pedagogy itself was reviewed, peopled as it was by teachers who in his view were often inferior and hamstrung by methodologies which were useless. One of his public utterances on this matter expressed the view that there really ought to be teachers to 'unteach' the piano (*Clavierverlehrer*) whose role would be to undo the damage created by the teachers themselves.

On the last day of his first season's teaching at the Raff Conservatory (July 1, 1884), and just before going home to Meiningen, Bülow allowed himself to relax by visiting the Frankfurt Zoo. As he inspected the caged animals, he was forcefully reminded of life in a music conservatory. 'Nothing reconciles me more to people like me than to be in the company of noble beasts without words', he wrote to Daniela. 'It hurt me more to part from a camel with which I had made friends . . . than from my professorial colleagues at the Raff Conservatory'.[12] As he warmed to his theme, he asked rhetorically: What else was Paradise but a zoological garden? Could he but shake hands with a tiger in that faraway place, he continued, this glimpse of eternity would help him bear any temporal torture, and he would think it ideal to be in a town where he could live opposite such a paradise—a veiled reference to what the Hoch Conservatory might have been, and was not. For him it was simply a zoo. Bülow's comments should surprise no one who has followed the story of his troubled relations with Frankfurt thus far, to say nothing of his dark view of

12. BNB, p. 626.

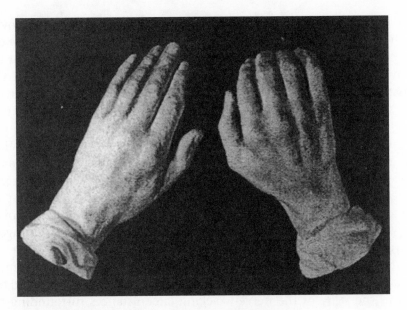

Plaster casts of Bülow's hands, taken during his lifetime.

institutionalized teaching. Yet he returned to the city time and again. His loyalty to Raff's memory left him no alternative.

Richard Strauss attended the masterclasses in the summer of 1885 (we recall that he had travelled to Frankfurt in the company of Bülow while awaiting confirmation from Georg II of his appointment as assistant conductor in Meiningen), and he left a number of firsthand accounts of Bülow's work, both as a teacher and a player. He wrote to his father, 'I attend the Conservatory every day, and I'm rapidly coming to the conclusion that Bülow is not only our greatest piano teacher but also the greatest executant musician in the world'.[13] He also extolled Bülow's performance of a part of the last movement of Beethoven's Piano Sonata in C minor, op. 111. 'It made me realize how beautiful the movement is'.[14]

Another student was the seventeen-year-old Scottish pianist Frederic Lamond, on whom these classes made an unforgettable impression. For Lamond, Bülow was a musical colossus. 'I have never heard the slow movement from Bach's *Italian* Concerto played with such feeling' he later wrote. 'In Beethoven's *Les Adieux* Sonata, various items of Brahms, Chopin, Liszt, he was unrivalled'.[15] Lamond captured Bülow's attention by insisting

13. SRS, p. 92.
14. Ibid., pp. 92–93.
15. LM, p. 43.

that he be allowed to play the *Hammerklavier* Sonata in the Beethoven segment of the course. 'Impertinent boy!' cried Bülow in front of the entire class. 'You must wait years before you attempt such a work!' But Lamond persisted, and the next day again told Bülow that he wanted to play the *Hammerklavier*. This time Bülow lost his temper, and stamped his foot so hard that the pupils, teachers, and onlookers became terrified that they were about to witness one of those eruptions for which Bulow was notorious. On the third day Lamond, almost in tears, again told Bülow that the only work he was prepared to play for the class was the *Hammerklavier*. This time Bülow smiled at the young man's audacity and agreed to hear the Scherzo. It pleased him so much that he asked Lamond to play the opening Allegro, and then the entire work. Bülow had been won over. He paid Lamond a great compliment by inviting him back to Meiningen. There Lamond played the oboe during the rehearsals of the Court Orchestra. (Lamond's first instrument during the early part of his career was actually the violin, not the piano. He was a true all-rounder.) Lamond has told us the story of the nerve-wracking circumstances surrounding his performance of the Brahms B-flat major Piano Concerto, which Bülow thrust on him at a few days' notice, and which the youth played before the assembled ducal court in the Meiningen Theatre. 'Make your bow to Princess Marie', whispered Bülow, as they walked onto the platform. Lamond, perhaps concentrating too hard on his bow, had hardly reached the piano stool before the horn came in with the first entry. He instinctively reached for the keyboard just in time to play the arpeggio in the second bar. As the work unfolded it became clear that the orchestra knew the Concerto as well as he did. Bülow had drilled them so well that they accompanied Lamond from memory. After the concert, master and pupil walked to Bülow's waiting carriage. Bülow turned to Lamond with the words, 'Bravo! You can play the Brahms Concerto anywhere and everywhere'. It was raining in torrents, and Lamond was soaked to the skin. 'But what of that?' he wrote. 'Bülow had praised me, and I was happy'.[16]

III

A cornucopia of stimulating ideas emerged from these classes which Bülow fashioned into memorable aphorisms. The best of them stand comparison with Robert Schumann's 'Advice to Young Musicians':[17]

In the beginning was rhythm.

*

16. Ibid., p. 41.
17. These aphorisms of Bülow, gathered from a variety of printed and verbal sources, may be found mainly in BAS (part 2), pp. 264–277 and in VHB.

Talent is industry.

*

There are no easy pieces, they are all difficult.

*

There are no great teachers, only great pupils.

*

Whoever cannot sing (whether the voice be beautiful or unbeautiful) should not play the piano.

*

Whoever has no feeling for space cannot paint. Whoever has no feeling for time cannot make music.

*

There are three grades of musical performance. One can play correctly, beautifully, and interestingly. But one must not play so interestingly that it ceases to be beautiful; and not so beautifully that it ceases to be correct.

*

When you make music, your permanent condition must be that you are highly dissatisfied with yourself. Then you must ask yourself, what is the reason that you are highly dissatisfied with yourself?

*

Crescendo means piano. Diminuendo means forte. You must not begin by being at once what you are yet to become.

*

Music is language. We must punctuate, phrase, divide. We must *speak* at the piano, not babble at it.

*

The bar-line is only for the eye, not for the ear. In playing, as in reading a poem, scanning must be subordinated to the declamation.

*

The key to understanding an artistic creation lies in becoming familiar with all the main things that brought it into being.

*

With Bach we must always be aware that whenever he composes keyboard music, it is the organ that strikes his imagination. With Beethoven it was the orchestra; and with Brahms it is both.

*

The Well-tempered Clavier is the Old Testament, the Beethoven Sonatas are the New Testament. We must believe in both.

*

Bach is really the true musician of the future because he will always be admired when the memory of others has long since decayed.

*

With Beethoven one must place one's technique in the shadows, not bring it into the light.

*

Memory is not a special gift; it may be trained and exceedingly strengthened.

*

Calm is the pianist's first requirement.

IV

For the development of technique Bülow recommended the studies of J. B. Cramer, and in his own selected edition of sixty of these vintage pieces he declared them to be a necessary introduction to the more difficult *Gradus ad Parnassum* studies by Clementi. Among his more interesting recommendations to the budding virtuoso was to practise the Cramer studies at different dynamic levels, and also to render them both staccato and legato, the better to secure physical control over the keyboard. Another was to work at transposing them from one key to another. He writes, 'Any really modern virtuoso must be able to perform Beethoven's

Bülow at the piano. A photograph.

[*Appassionata* Sonata] as comfortably in F-sharp minor as in F minor'.[18] Few are the pianists today who could do that. But for Bülow the advantage was obvious: greater physical control over the original. It led him to make one of his more penetrating observations: namely, that the main mechanical difficulty in playing the piano was the uneven 'territory' created by the white and the black keys—territory he called the 'arena' for the activity of the fingers. Because the keyboard presents two planes, a flat white one and an elevated black one, Bülow argued that the player's main attention should be directed towards making the fingers overcome the difference, enabling them to move as freely on the black keys as on the white. To achieve this he recommended unorthodox fingerings that would have been frowned on by a previous generation:

> [The old method] seems to have been concerned mainly with circumventing all dangers threatening the tranquil position of the hand by the changing relation between the black and white keys. . . . It rejected the freedom of movement for the thumb so necessary to perform polyphonic music and to avoid embarrassment in transposition, and it declared as the best composer for the piano the person whose inspiration was guided solely by the superficial picture of the twelve semi-tones of the keyboard as seven broad and level keys plus five narrow and elevated ones. This would certainly have given Clementi's piano fugues a definite superiority over those written by a J. S. Bach.[19]

The classes were often filled with humour. On May 30, 1887, Vianna da Motta was in attendance and recalled that a student came forward to play the 'Edward' Ballade of Brahms, op. 10, no. 1. This piece of programme music was inspired by an old Scottish saga which unfolds a dark tale of patricide, and begins with the mother's anguished question, 'Why is your sword so red with blood, Edward, Edward?' Bülow thought that the class should understand the story before hearing the Ballade, so he began: 'Edward committed a great crime. He'—here he took a long pause, and one read in his highly expressive face that he was preparing a very good joke—'murdered his wife's father-in-law'.[20] Vianna da Motta tells us that the success was so thunderous that the playing had to be delayed until the laughter had subsided.

On another occasion a young lady elected to play Liszt's Hungarian Rhapsody no. 6, in D-flat major. The piece has a certain notoriety among

18. From Bülow's preface to the Cramer Studies.
19. Ibid.
20. ZMB, p. 124; VHB, p. 69.

pianists because of the rapidly repeated octaves in the 'Friska'. Bülow told her that while she had a splendid technique, she lacked wit. When she came to the octaves, Bülow left the room. Naturally the woman stopped playing, so Bülow returned and remarked, 'Do go on. I consider my presence superfluous during this'.[21] Laughter ensued. The wit had been restored.

V

Like many teachers before and since, Bülow did not shrink from placing ideas and thoughts of a nonmusical kind into his pupils' minds if he thought that such a device would steer them towards a better interpretation. Even the more severe works of Beethoven were sometimes provided with 'imagery' not sanctioned by the composer himself. The footnotes to Bülow's edition of the *Diabelli* Variations offer many examples. In Variation XIV, he invites the player to 'summon up before his eyes the sublime arches of a Gothic cathedral'. To Variation XX he gives the nickname 'The Oracle', because of its mysterious sequence of chords. And he happily reminds the player of Von Lenz's description of Variation XIII as 'eloquent pauses'—silence, so to say, speaking more effectively than sound. The final Variation (XXXIII), Bülow asserts, could easily have been called 'Farewell to the Listener' by Robert Schumann. Bülow was equally obliging towards the general listener who came to his Beethoven recitals wanting to grapple with this most intractable of piano compositions. In his printed programmes, handed out at the door, he provided each one of the thirty-three variations with a title, among them 'Duet' (III); 'Idyll' (XVIII); 'Explosion' (XXIII); and 'Butterflies' (XXVI).[22] We should not smile too readily at such naïveté. Even today, the average writer of programme notes, whose words are intended for swift consumption in the concert hall just before the performance begins, rarely strays beyond such simple language, which the great public is invited to digest without distress.

The diary of Laura Kahrer, a document to which we have previously alluded, provides similar testimony.[23] While she did not attend the Frankfurt classes, Laura studied privately with Bülow and heard him play Bee-

---

21. ZMB, p. 68; PSB, p. 112.

22. It is stimulating to read Bülow's scathing criticism of the Breitkopf and Härtel edition of the *Diabelli* Variations, which had recently been published. He accuses the firm of 'a surprising piece of vandalism (servilely copied, of course, by the cheap Peters edition)', because one bar appeared to have been deliberately omitted from Variation XII by the editor, due to its rhythmic irregularity. He also pours scorn on Breitkopf and Härtel's inflated reputation as 'The Guardians of the Sublime Right', adding that he considers it his duty to rouse the German public 'somewhat roughly from its contented trustfulness' in this publishing house.

23. See pp. 198–99.

thoven, Mendelssohn, Schumann, Liszt, and Chopin among other composers. One performance especially stood out in her memory. Bülow had overheard her practising Liszt's *Au bord d'une source,* and had remarked to her, 'I would like to hear you play that again. I myself play it slower'. As she played, he commented in an imaginative way on the various shades of water that Liszt had depicted in this music—'here it is blue, there it becomes silver, and here the sunlight dances across the surface'—then he himself sat down to play the piece. Laura tells us that he played it with extraordinary clarity and transparency. She likened it to flying pearls of crystal which at the merest touch Bülow seemed to be able to transform into water. She then played Schumann's *Kreisleriana.* After she had finished each movement Bülow himself sat down at the piano, delivering some magisterial interpretations while at the same time pointing to the connections between the music and the stories about Kapellmeister Kreisler that had inspired Schumann. About Laura's own playing Bülow was in general full of praise. 'You have nothing more to learn technically', he told her, but he warned her to guard against the syrupy-sweetness then gaining ascendancy in so much Chopin and Schumann playing. One's playing must be healthy and masculine ('*gesund und männlich*'), he told her. With sentimentality he would have nothing to do. And he added an observation, as true in our time as in his, 'There are nowadays far too many pianists and far too few musicians'. Laura added that Bülow hardly ever looked at the keyboard as he played, would occasionally glance at his listeners, but was mostly withdrawn into himself.[24]

VI

In 1887, the twenty-five-year-old Walter Damrosch happened to read in a New York newspaper that Bülow would be holding masterclasses for advanced pianists that summer in Frankfurt, and he wrote to Bülow asking

24. R-KE, p. 315. Laura Kahrer further informs us that Bülow had an entire repertory of images to go along with the 24 Preludes of Chopin. The labels she claims he attached to them are so childish, however, and the stories spun from them so puerile, we take leave to doubt that Bülow ever intended them to do more than bring a dying performance back to life, let alone be published. Nonetheless, Kahrer did publish them, in 1911, and they appeared in an English translation shortly afterwards. The Prelude in E minor is supposed to represent 'Suffocation'; the one in F-sharp minor 'Desperation'; while the one in E-flat minor summons up 'Fear'. A new low is reached when we come to the Prelude in G sharp minor (no. 12) which is called 'The Dual'. We are invited to imagine two rivals, armed with flashing swords, fighting over the love of George Sand. One of them is Chopin (naturally), who is wounded and amidst great confusion is borne away from the scene of conflict. Nonsensical as such things appear to the modern reader, they were part of every piano teacher's methodology in the nineteenth century (and may be found alive and well in some quarters today). Most of these worthies used analogies and poetical images which should never have left the privacy of the teaching studio. The damage is done only when pupils decide to publish such stories, and then go on to claim that these confections are what the music is supposed to be 'about'.

for lessons, not in piano playing but in conducting. 'In what way do you conceive that your wish could be fulfilled?' asked Bülow, somewhat taken aback. He had never before been asked by anybody to teach conducting. There were many who doubted that this most elusive art could be taught at all. Not a single conservatory, on either side of the Atlantic, offered courses on the topic. All the leading conductors of the day—Seidl, Richter, Levi, Mottl, Hallé, Thomas, and Bülow himself—were self-taught. So Bülow's question was a good one, and the way in which he came to deal with it was instructive. Damrosch himself tells us about their daily 'lessons' together:

> He went through all Beethoven's nine symphonies with me, bar by bar, phrase by phrase, and I still have the scores in which he made certain notations of phrasing or illustrated changes of dynamics of certain instruments in order to bring out the undoubted intentions of Beethoven more clearly. He virtually analyzed the symphonies for me in the same way as in his edition of the piano sonatas, and at the close of our three months together he gave me a copy of his own score of the Ninth Symphony with all his own annotations, many of which were based on the analysis made by Wagner during his historic performance of that work at the cornerstone laying of the Bayreuth Fest-Spielhaus.[25]

Damrosch frequently went over to the Schwan Hotel in order to pick up Bülow and go for long walks with him through the parks and suburbs of Frankfurt, chatting all the while about things musical, literary, and personal. 'It was a revelation to me', observed the young man. Damrosch had recently lost his father, Bülow's old friend and chamber-music partner Leopold Damrosch, and was emotionally vulnerable. He had been thrust into the musical limelight, assuming the conductorship of the New York Symphony Orchestra and the Oratorio Society (both of which had been founded by Leopold) while still only twenty-five years old. Walter recalled the 'terrible responsibilities' which had been placed on his shoulders as a result of his father's demise, together with his gratitude towards Bülow who took him under his wing, giving him endless encouragement. Bülow was impressed that the young man was already experienced in opera, oratorio, and orchestral conducting and did not waste time giving him lessons in 'baton technique', which is concerned with externals only, and can be picked up as one goes along. It was the music that mattered, and Walter tells us that he received such a wealth of ideas regarding musical

---

25. DMML, pp. 78–79. Damrosch provides a detailed description of Bülow's interpretation of the Ninth Symphony in MHB, pp. 280–293. It is replete with music examples which incorporate changes attributed to Wagner, and accepted by Bülow.

interpretation, based on a close study of the score, that it took him years to digest it properly. He had heard all the usual stories concerning Bülow's brusque manner and biting comments, and was surprised to find him so companionable and so gentle in all his dealings towards him. This he attributed to the affectionate memory in which Bülow held his father. In his memoir about Bülow, written many years later, he made a perceptive observation about his mentor. 'He had a heart most tender and sensitive, but life had dealt this idealist so many hard knocks that he incased his heart in a shell with which to protect it from further onslaughts'.[26]

From Damrosch, too, we get a glimpse of the physical anguish under which Bülow sometimes laboured, and which took him unawares. The young man stayed for a time in the same hotel as Bülow, and had to pass the conductor's room en route to his own. One night he heard sounds of distress coming from behind Bülow's door. Bülow was kneeling by the bed, his head buried in pillows, racked with pain. Damrosch somehow got him to bed, and stayed with him until he went to sleep. 'He was in wretched health', wrote Damrosch, 'but with an iron will went through the summer's programme, accepting no financial recompense for himself, solely to help gather money through his classes towards the completion of the Raff monument'.[27]

VII

Bülow was occasionally called upon to take over the masterclasses of Franz Liszt in Weimar. Such visits are worth dwelling on because they help to round out our picture of Bülow as a teacher. The students dreaded his arrival because they knew that he regarded many of them as 'hangers-on', without any talent, who were misusing Liszt's goodness and benevolence towards them. Bülow liked to draw attention to the paradox that in the best pianist's house one could hear the worst pianists playing. In June 1880 he visited Liszt in Weimar and used the opportunity to clean out the Augean stables, as he put it. He assembled the class and addressed them in the following terms:

> Ladies and gentlemen! Do not forget that the Master was born as long ago as 1811, or that he is the essence of goodness and gentleness; and do not misuse him in this revolting way. You ladies in particular: most of you, I assure you, are destined for the myrtle rather than the laurel.[28]

26. Ibid., p. 78.
27. Ibid., p. 80.
28. BBLW, p. 273.

Some of the students left, but the braver ones remained, and the class began. Dori Petersen elected to play Liszt's *Mazeppa*—doubtless in a misguided attempt to impress Bülow, whom she knew to be intimately acquainted with the difficulties of this particular piece—a tone-picture of the Cossack chieftan 'Mazeppa', stripped naked by his enemies and lashed to his terrified horse, which streaks across the Russian Steppes in headlong flight. She was a rough and ready player, and the performance went badly. Bülow rounded on her with words that have become enshrined in the annals of piano pedagogy. 'You have but *one* qualification for playing this piece—the nature of a horse'.[29] Liszt's disciple, the composer Berthold Kellermann, was in the group of onlookers and later told Liszt what had happened. 'Bülow was quite right', declared Liszt amiably, 'but he was too hard. I suppose that you will see all those people tonight at the Sächsischen Hof? Just tell them to wait until Bülow has left, and then to come back here'.[30] Bülow could never understand why Liszt failed to appreciate what he had done. As he explained to Adelheid von Schorn, he had merely provided the same service for Liszt as he did for his own dog in ridding him of his fleas.

Nonetheless, the 'fleas' came back. There was another confrontation between Bülow and the Weimar masterclass in the summer of 1881. Bülow was in Weimar to meet his daughter Daniela, whom he had not seen for twelve years, a reunion that had been brought about largely through the intervention of Liszt himself. On July 2, however, Liszt had slipped on the stairs of the Hofgärtnerei and injured himself so seriously that he was confined to his bed for several weeks. Bülow once more recognized that he must do his duty.

'His very appearance created a feeling of apprehension', recalled Emma Grosskurth, one of the pupils in the class that day. 'It was as if a great hawk had suddenly swept down among us. Several tried to flutter to cover, to the further end of the salon, or behind the curtains that divided the rooms'.[31] Lina Schmalhausen had been playing as Bülow entered. She gathered up her music and prepared to disappear along with everybody else, but Bülow barked at her, 'No, it is you I want to hear first'. Schmalhausen oozed incompetence from every fibre, and Bülow knew it. She was a notoriously bad timekeeper and was thoroughly frightened by Bülow's presence in the room. After she had made her erratic progress through whatever piece she had brought that day, Bülow gave her a dressing-down in front of the class. 'I have heard it said', he declared in his most

29. DM, vol. 7, 1910–1911, p. 213. The anecdote comes from Alfred Reisenauer, who was in the class that day. He identifies the player only as 'Fräulein P'. Ever since the publication of the diary of Carl Lachmund, in 1995, we know it to have been Dori Petersen (LL, p. 20).

30. KE, p. 26.

31. LL, p. 20.

sarcastic tones, 'that there are people who cannot count three. You cannot even count *two!'* Schmalhausen picked up her music and fled. During this same session Dori Petersen once more found herself at the receiving end of Bülow's sharp tongue. He listened to her with growing impatience, and then cut her dead. 'I hope never to see you here again', he told her. You should be swept out of here—not with the broom, but with the handle!'[32] Bülow's bruising visits to Liszt's masterclasses were widely reported and reached the ears of Daniela, who wanted to know what was going on. He told her by way of explanation, 'Apropos of vermin, let us not rejoice too much on your grandfather's account over the little revolution at the Hofgärtnerei. I believe that in matters of insecticide "things are destroyed only to be replaced".'[33]

VIII

Bülow's presence at the Raff Conservatory brought the institution to national attention and attracted donors. In the summer of 1884, he was informed by his English acquaintance A. J. Hipkins, a representative of the firm of Broadwood & Sons, that the venerable company had arranged to send one of its imperial grand pianos to the Raff Conservatory, with a request that it be publicly inaugurated by Bülow and used for public concerts. The only stipulation was that Clara Schumann should also be allowed to use the instrument.[34] Bülow's letter of thanks to Hipkins, written in his own English, runs:

Dear Sir:
I have just now received your kind note of the 28th inst. I feel quite amazed by the imperial ways of Mr. Broadwood's generosity towards the Raff Conservatorium, which I hope will prove worthy of such an illustrious and liberal patronship. I am about sending word at once to my friend Mr. Steyl at Frankfurt that he might take the greatest care for carrying out the particular wishes of the gracious donor. I will inform Mme Schumann that the piano should always be at her disposal. As for the inauguration by public performance, I intend playing the piano at the concerts of the ducal orchestra at Frankfurt which are to take place in the first week of

32. Ibid.
33. BNB, p. 594. This was a wordplay on the dictum of Napoleon III, which Bülow was fond of quoting: 'Only that which is replaced is destroyed'. Napoleon's method, apparently, could not be applied at the Hofgärtnerei. No matter how much insecticide was used, the 'vermin' came back because Liszt was unwilling to replace them.
34. Through this piece of veiled diplomacy Hipkins evidently wanted Bülow to know that he was fully aware that the Hoch and the Raff conservatories had recently declared war on each other.

November next. Of course, I shall have the honour of giving notice of it in due time.

Pity that there are just holidays in the Conservatorium (from
the 19th July until the 1st of September) and as I suppose that most
of the Professors will be abroad. But it matters little as Mr. Steyl is
one of the surest businessmen I ever met in my life.

Hoping you are enjoying better health than my poor self who
has been and is still sickly. I remain, dear sir,
Yours most truly
Hans v. Bülow.
30 July, 1884[35]

It is unlikely that Clara Schumann ever touched the Broadwood grand,
firmly located as it was on the other side of the great divide that now ran
through Frankfurt. Although Bülow resided in the city for only a few weeks
each summer, Clara always regarded him as an interloper. Her dismissive
comment to Brahms summarizes her general attitude. 'Bülow is not to be
regarded as a teaching force—he hardly ever teaches but only plays to his
pupils, at least so I heard the other day'.[36] This was hearsay, of course, and
it happened to be untrue; she is not known to have attended a single class.

IX

A few brief comments on Bülow's many editions are called for, if only because the Frankfurt pupils often brought them along to the masterclass.
Bülow got into the business of editing at a period of transition in the
development of piano playing, and even of musical interpretation itself,
a period which bridged the new and the old approaches to performance.
His initial training at the Leipzig Conservatory had steeped him in the
classical methods of Louis Plaidy and later of Friedrich Wieck. Although
he never studied with either Moscheles or Hummel, he admired the polished, nuanced approach to piano playing for which they stood. Later,
after he had worked with Liszt and had taken on all the trappings of a
modern virtuoso, adding many big Romantic works to his repertoire, he
became a very different artist, but never lost sight of the time-honoured
principles of piano playing—a beautiful sound, clear articulation, balance
of interior voicing, fidelity to the composer's intentions—which he tried
to pass on to his students.

Some of Bülow's editorial commentaries may strike the modern pianist
as dry and pedagogical. But they represent the man and throw light on

35. Hitherto unpublished. Brit. Lib. Add. 41637 f. 188.
36. LSB, vol. 2, p. 279.

his teaching. Many of his observations (especially those in his Beethoven edition) which were initially meant to guard against a false interpretation, have meanwhile become redundant because a correct performing tradition has taken hold. In a rare moment of self-disparagement he once told his Frankfurt students that he preferred them to use the Klindworth edition of the Beethoven sonatas (which had appeared in 1878) rather than his own. He pointed out that while his edition was the first to take the task of editing seriously, others now did it much better. 'Klindworth's edition . . . does not include as much chatter [*Geschwätz*] as mine'.[37] Clara Schumann, as we might expect, harboured a strong dislike of Bülow's edition, and forbade her students to use it. It was the 'chatter' that upset her. On May 23, 1882, for example, she imparted the following thoughts to her diary: 'I have tried hard to persuade Hiller once more to write against Bülow's editions of Bach and Beethoven and to warn against them. He disfigures the works through his detailed *Analysierungen* to such an extent that one scarcely recognizes them any more and not a single trace of the student's own feeling and imagination is allowed to take root. I have always forbidden my students to use these editions'.[38]

By contrast, Bülow's edition of the Complete Studies of Chopin (opp. 10 and 25) should be revived. Its creative ideas on fingering, its highly original suggestions for mastering Chopin's challenging textures through preparatory exercises derived from the music itself, and its general tips on how to practice these difficult pieces, place it in a similar category to Cortot's more celebrated edition of these same compositions. To give just one absorbing example: In order to obtain greater physical security in the 'Black Keys' Study, Bülow recommends transposing it from G-flat major to G major—'in which the right hand would play exclusively on the white keys, whereas in the key of G-flat major it plays exclusively on the black keys'. Any pianist who can do this well, will find that his newly acquired skill conveys immediate benefits on the original.[39]

With the Frankfurt masterclasses Bülow arrived at the peak of his eminence as a pedagogue. The activity may not have brought him particular pleasure, but because he put the best of himself into it, he created memorable musical experiences for his students. They took away traditions of performance (of Beethoven especially) that dominated the field of interpretation for years to come. Bülow's classes were vastly different from those of the easygoing Liszt, because of their fierce concentration on the

---

37. ZMB, p. 40; PSB, p. 60.

38. LCS, vol. 3, p. 427.

39. Few pianists would disagree with Bülow's assertion that the Study in A-flat major (op. 10, no. 10) is the most difficult in the entire collection, because of its myriad rhythmic complexities. 'Whoever can play this Study in a really finished manner, may congratulate himself on having climbed to the highest point of the pianist's Parnassus', he observed.

mechanical details of playing. This may well have been the reason for Liszt's qualified utterance, 'Bülow is a schoolmaster, but one of aristocratic rank'.[40] For those who attended the classes it was the aristocrat and not the schoolmaster whom they remembered. At the conclusion of his account of these classes Theodor Pfeiffer declared, 'All of us who took part knew what these lessons were for us. . . . The remembrance of them will always remind us to pay sincere thanks to the illustrious artist, the peerless, the divinely inspired, our blessed teacher and master—HANS VON BÜLOW.[41]

40. ZMB, p. 8; PSB, p. vi.
41. ZMB, p. 73; PSB, p. 123.

A New Home in Hamburg, 1886 ✑

I prefer Hamburg 1001 times over Berlin!
—Bülow[1]

I

After his farewell concert with the Meiningen Orchestra, on January 29, 1885, Bülow began to search for a new home. It requires no more than a moment's reflection to understand how impossible it would have been for him to remain in the small town and rub shoulders on a daily basis with his successor, Fritz Steinbach. For Bülow it was a pressing matter to find a fresh base from which to project himself, first and foremost, as a concert pianist.

But where to go? And where to live? Of one thing he was certain. During whatever years remained to him he would refuse to bind himself to a minor principality such as Hanover or Meiningen. These provincial towns had consumed some of his best years, and he was no longer young. The fifty-six-year-old Bülow had become a city man. His principal residence must be in a large international metropolis. Berlin was impossible. The love-hate relationship he enjoyed with the place went back to his turbulent sojourn there, twenty-five years earlier. Frankfurt was riven by partisan factions that glared at each other from the two conservatories, and we have already learned enough to know that Bülow's presence there had roiled the opposing parties for years. Leipzig and Dresden were alternatives from which in his youth he had been glad to escape, but to which he had no desire to return. At his time of life, they offered bridges to nowhere.

Bülow's decision to settle in the Hanseatic city of Hamburg was an inspired one. It was a bustling metropolis with a population of 600,000

1. HB-CM, unpublished letter dated January 21, 1887.

people. As Germany's largest seaport, and home to a great shipbuilding industry, it was wealthier even than Berlin. Hamburg was Germany's gateway to the world. Its major shipping lines ferried passengers back and forth across the ocean on a daily basis, especially to the New World. By the mid-1880s its booming economy had produced a large middle-class population with a disposable income, together with a number of artistic organizations on which that income could be lavished. Hamburg's opera house, under the leadership of its new intendant, Bernhard Pollini, was becoming nationally known. The Hamburg Philharmonic Society, it is true, was in the doldrums, but could be rescued with the right person in charge. Hamburg was a success story waiting to happen. While Bülow's choice of this city as his permanent domicile appears in retrospect to have been inevitable, it did not look that way at first. As the year 1886 began to unfold, however, some chance factors came into play which were to bind him to the place for life. Meanwhile, in order to accommodate his nomadic lifestyle, he took rooms in the Waterloo Hotel whenever he was in town.

II

Although Bülow presently lacked a permanent orchestra, his life was hardly idle. He returned to his piano playing with renewed zeal, gave recitals in various parts of Germany, and brought to fruition a concept that he had long cherished. During these first summer months he developed his famous 'Beethoven Cycle'—a series of four recitals, to be given on successive evenings, comprising the main sonatas and sets of variations that Beethoven had written for the piano. Bülow wanted to show his listeners something specific: namely, Beethoven's creative development across a lifetime. Gone were the days when he had the desire, let alone the energy, to play a thousand pieces from memory in a single season, sacrificing himself on the altar of Mammon, as he had so graphically put it during his American tour of 1875–1876. Ten years had elapsed, and his attitude towards programme building had changed.

This heroic sequence of Beethoven recitals deserves scrutiny. Bülow's choice of music covered a period of twenty-eight years; and he played everything in chronological order, attaching a date to each work, in order to emphasize the notion of progress.[2] He selected twenty-five works for his purpose, ranging from music inspired by Haydn and Mozart to music that foretold the future. He started with one of the earliest sonatas, the

---

2. We recall that as early as 1852 Wilhelm von Lenz had published his influential book *Beethoven and His Three Styles,* which analyses the composer's music according to its chronological development.

one in A major (1795), and came to a magisterial conclusion with Beethoven's last work for solo piano, the hugely demanding *Diabelli* Variations (1823). Actually the word 'conclusion' is not quite accurate. Bülow had a further point to make. After playing the hour-long *Diabelli* Variations (which itself was preceded by the formidable *Hammerklavier* Sonata) he returned to the platform as if with a spontaneous idea: a performance of the posthumously published 'Rage over a Lost Penny'—a charming miniature. It was a symbolic reminder that Beethoven continued to address his listeners from beyond the grave, so to speak. Each recital lasted from two to three hours, and of course everything was played from memory. Such an undertaking would tax the powers of any pianist today. Here is the entire series, which Bülow first presented at the Leipzig Gewandhaus, in October 1886:

FIRST RECITAL
Friday evening, October 15

Sonata in A major, op. 2, no. 2 (1795)
Sonata in F major, op. 10, no. 2 (1797)
12 Variations on a Russian Dance Song (*Das Waldmädchen*), in
A major (1802)
Sonata in C minor (*Pathétique*), op. 13 (1798)
Sonata in E major, op. 14, no. 1 (1799)
Sonata in G major, op. 14, no. 2 (1799)
Six Variations on an Original Theme, in F major, op. 34 (1802)
Sonata in D major (*Pastorale*), op. 28 (1801)

SECOND RECITAL
Saturday evening, October 16

Sonata quasi Fantasia, in E-flat major, op. 27, no. 1 (1801)
Sonata quasi Fantasia, in C-sharp minor (*Moonlight*), op. 27, no. 2
(1801)
15 Variations and Fugue in E-flat major (*Eroica*), op. 35 (1802)
Sonata in D minor (*Tempest*) op. 31, no. 2 (1802)
Sonata in E-flat major, op. 31, no. 3 (1802)
32 Variations in C minor (1805)

THIRD RECITAL
Monday evening, October 18

Sonata in F minor (*Appassionata*), op. 57 (1806)
Sonata in F-sharp major, op. 78 (1809)

Sonata in E-flat major (*Les Adieux*), op. 81 (1810)
Fantasia, op. 77 (1810)
Sonata in E major, op. 109 (1820)
Sonata in A-flat major, op. 110 (1821)
Sonata in C minor, op. 111 (1822)

FOURTH RECITAL
Tuesday evening, October 19

Sonata in A major, op. 101 (1816)
Sonata in B-flat major (*Hammerklavier*), op. 106 (1819)
33 Variations on a Waltz-theme by Diabelli, in C major, op. 120 (1823)
Rondo a capriccio ('Rage over a Lost Penny') in G major, op. 129 (posth.)

Bülow's presentation of the last five sonatas in one evening was already legendary. But this Beethoven Cycle was different. It required the listener to have what Germans call *Sitzfleisch*—staying power. These concerts were diametrically opposed to Anton Rubinstein's 'historic recitals' in which the Russian bear presented his audiences with a chronological smorgasbord of musical history, covering a 300-year period from William Byrd to Chopin and even to Rubinstein himself. Rubinstein's recitals were unusual and enormously popular, but they revealed little about how things came to be as they were. Bülow went for what mattered: the story of one creator's life of the mind, so to speak, through a presentation of 'style in motion'. The sophisticated listener could hear Beethoven's musical character changing before his very ears, as the composer remoulded the classical structures of the past, slowly emerged with a new harmonic language, and eventually drove the keyboard itself to the brink of impossibilities.

After its Leipzig premier, Bülow took his Beethoven Cycle to such far-flung places as Vienna (1887), Berlin (1887), Hamburg (1887), Munich (1887), and London (1888); later he presented it in New York (1889), Boston (1889), and Chicago (1890). These incursions—there is no better word to describe their evangelical nature—will be reviewed as we come to them. They bestowed on Bülow a lasting place in the annals of piano playing.

III

On January 21, 1887, Bülow unveiled his Beethoven Cycle in Vienna, in the Great Hall of the Musikverein. Hugo Wolf reviewed these recitals negatively, and talked of 'Beethoven vivisection'. He told his readers that

Bülow's performances of Beethoven were 'cut and sawed to pieces' and that they belonged in a conservatory, not in the concert hall. It was, he said, a cruel 'Beethoven massacre'.[3]

Had Wolf already forgotten that only three years earlier he had informed his readers that Bülow was the ideal Beethoven interpreter?[4] For his abrupt shift of opinion there are two possible explanations. The first may have had to do with Bülow's increasingly open support of Brahms in Vienna, which Wolf would have found disconcerting, because Brahms was now the most visible representative of the conservative opposition in the ongoing 'War of the Romantics', and Wolf had fought that opposition tooth and nail.[5] The second may have had to do with a brief speech in praise of Czech music that Bülow had delivered in Prague, after giving a benefit concert for the Association of Czech Artists a few weeks earlier. In that speech, which was given during a banquet in his honour, Bülow had urged the Czechs to persevere in their *Deutschenhetze,* as he put it, or their agitation against the German elements among them, in order to find their national identity. Prague, which was still part of the Austro-Hungarian Empire, was considered by German nationalists to be a 'German' city, and such a public show of support for its ethnic Czech artists by a leading German conductor was regarded by many—including Hugo Wolf—as a betrayal of the ideal of German hegemony in the arts. To make matters worse, Bülow had quoted Goethe in his speech—'Wherever I can be useful, there is my fatherland'—an explosive comment to make in such explosive times. He had also styled himself 'Hanusch', the Bohemian form of his name which had been plastered across the concert hoardings of the city, using the provocative Czech spelling of 'Hanuš' Bülow. The large German population in Prague was infuriated with him, and when shortly afterwards he appeared in Dresden and Breslau, protests broke out in the audience; a recital in Graz had to be cancelled because of fears of a riot. Anxious to suppress similar outbreaks in Vienna, the city's chief of police extracted from Bülow a promise not to make any postconcert speeches in his city.[6] This was the smouldering context in which Bülow brought his Beethoven Cycle to the Viennese capital.

3. 'Bülow Abende', in the *Wiener Salonblatt,* February 6, 1887. See HWK, vol. 1, pp. 187–191; and HWK, vol. 2, pp. 113–114.

4. *Wiener Salonblatt,* February 17, 1884. See HWK, vol. 1, p. 15.

5. Hugo Wolf's opposition to Brahms has been determined for all time by his remarkable observation that a single cymbal crash of Liszt's was worth more than all the Brahms symphonies combined (*Wiener Salonblatt,* April 27, 1884).

6. BB, vol. 7, pp. 73–74. News of Bülow's troubles with the German population in Prague even reached *The New York Times.* See the issue of December 10, 1886, in which we find an article under the headline 'The Storm von Bülow Raised'.

Even while Hugo Wolf was excoriating Bülow for his Beethoven interpretations, they were creating a lasting impression on the theorist Hugo
Riemann, and making inroads into his influential theory of rhythm and
metrical structure which he was at that time developing. Riemann discharged his musical debt to Bülow by dedicating to him his own analytical edition of the Beethoven sonatas.[7]

IV

What made the emergence of the Beethoven Cycle so notable was that
Bülow had prepared it at a time when his private affairs were weighing
heavily on him. On July 4, 1886, Daniela married the art-historian Henry
Thode, a *privat Dozent* at the University of Bonn. Once again the marriage
venue was Bayreuth and Wahnfried. The ceremony took place in the
Protestant church, which was packed with guests. Rehearsals for *Parsifal*
were already in full swing, in readiness for the Bayreuth Festival due to
start two weeks later, and many visitors had descended on the small town
early, swelling the congregation. The wedding was followed by a reception
at Wahnfried attended by more than eighty specially invited guests, at
which the Burgomeister made a speech in honour of the young couple.
Both father and daughter knew that there could be no question of Bülow
attending the ceremony. Neither of them wished to revive the difficult
family scenario that had unfolded four years earlier, when he had tried
to attend the wedding of his daughter Blandine, and had found Cosima
implacably opposed to his presence. Bülow had to content himself with
telling Daniela, 'I can only be there in spirit'.[8] She was given away in matrimony by her grandfather, Franz Liszt.

Bülow approved of his new son-in-law, and delighted in this union.
Thode was cultivated, intellectual, and articulate, with a bright academic
future before him. He was thirty-one years old, Daniela was twenty-six.
On the face of it, this was a brilliant match. Even before the wedding
we find Bülow addressing Thode, in anticipation of the union, as 'My
Dear Son-in-Law' and Daniela as 'Frau Dr. Thode'. What were Liszt's own
thoughts as he led his granddaughter down the aisle? A week or two earlier he had voiced some private misgivings. 'I hope that Thode is the right
man for Daniela, who was not born for everyone, and has too much of
the uncomfortable mixture of her father'.[9] These were prophetic words.

---

7. The beautiful letter that Riemann wrote to Bülow, praising his interpretation of the
classics, is quoted in HMIB, p. 261. Riemann had earlier dedicated to Bülow his 'Phrasing
Edition' of the Mozart Sonatas, an act of homage that was born of his admiration for the
way in which Bülow's interpretations revealed a work's underlying structure.

8. BNB, p. 635.

9. LDML, vol. 2, p. 128.

The marriage would bring much misery to the couple, remain childless, and end in divorce in 1914. The grounds cited in the legal action were that the union had not been consummated.[10]

When Liszt raised his glass in Wahnfried, and toasted the newlyweds, no one could have imagined that in less than a month he would be dead. He had left Bayreuth briefly to return to his masterclass in Weimar, but had promised Cosima that he would come back later in the month in order to lend his presence to the Wagner Festival, and to the production of *Tristan* especially, an opera which had not yet been heard in Bayreuth. Liszt's unexpected demise in the town, on July 31, placed Bülow once more in a quandary. Had Liszt died in any other city there is no question that Bülow would have attended the funeral. But Cosima did not want the complications of Bülow's presence, especially in the public setting of the Bayreuth Festival. It would have raised too many questions to have the greatest Wagner conductor of the day, who had first brought *Tristan* to life twenty-one years earlier, come to Bayreuth at such a time. Already the question on many lips was: Why was not Bülow himself conducting *Tristan?* Since the Munich days there had grown up a sizable coterie of Wagnerians who looked back nostalgically to those times, and to Bülow's performances there, which they regarded as definitive, and they could not understand why the new Bayreuth production had been entrusted to Felix Mottl. With such criticism Cosima would have nothing to do, and she knew that the best way to stifle it was to have Bülow not come anywhere near the Bayreuth Festival Theatre. Dozens of prominent people in Liszt's circle had meanwhile travelled to the city for the master's funeral, including some of his best-known pupils. Among the ones who joined the sad procession bearing torches in the master's honour were Siloti, Friedheim, Reisenauer, Stavenhagen, Weingartner, Krause, and Bache. Their presence made Bülow's absence all the more regrettable.[11]

10. After the divorce Thode married again almost immediately, this time to the Danish violinist Hertha Tegner (1884–1946) with whom he had been madly in love for several years, causing Daniela herself much anguish.

11. Daniela kept Bülow informed about Liszt's final illness and death in Bayreuth. Perhaps to spare his feelings, she withheld from him the distressing sequence of events—involving medical malpractice and family neglect—that constituted Liszt's last ten days on earth, and to which she herself had been a daily witness. In a letter to Daniela, Bülow wrote, 'It was really, I quite agree with you, a divine dispensation that he should have faded out painlessly at Bayreuth. At the same time, in the interests of his posthumous fame I should certainly like to see his mortal remains removed to Hungary' (BNB, p. 640). It is evident that Daniela had become a mouthpiece for the Bayreuth publicity machine, which had already begun churning out news that Liszt had faded away painlessly, the word 'Tristan' on his lips. Liszt's death was not benign, and his last word was not 'Tristan'. It was 'Luft!' He could not breathe. A comprehensive account of Liszt's disturbing demise may be found in my *Death of Franz Liszt* (WDL).

V

There was one other burden that lay on Bülow's shoulders, this one of a purely musical nature, which makes the launching of his Beethoven Cycle in October 1886 still more exceptional. Just twelve days after he gave the concluding recital in Leipzig (October 19) he took up a new position as director of the Hamburg Subscription Concerts, which began on November 1, 1886, the preparations for which had preoccupied him for the past several months. In order to understand how this had come about, we must go back a year or so.

When Bülow's resignation from Meiningen was announced, his manager, Hermann Wolff, had come forward with a proposition. He told Bülow that he was planning a new series of six Hamburg Subscription Concerts in the coming winter season of 1886/1887, in collaboration with the intendant of the opera house, Bernhard Pollini. They were to take place in the concert hall of Hamburg's Convent Garden, and the players were to be drawn from the Hamburg Opera House itself. In order to pique Bülow's interest, Wolff told him that he could have as many as a hundred orchestral players on the platform if he so desired. Would he be interested in taking over this ensemble?

Bülow's reply is highly interesting from a musical point of view. He told Wolff:

> 100 musicians are too many. The crowd brings nothing to quality. The numbers are optically good, acoustically bad. Fourteen first violins, twelve seconds, ten violas, ten cellos, eight basses—fifty-four maximum. For every ten players, you can save on two. The same on the winds: woodwinds 9—10; brass 10—12; harp. . . . Seventy [players] in all are enough.[12]

Hamburg's Convent Garden, in which the subscription concerts were to be launched, was originally established in 1853 as one of the city's pleasure parks. It had opened its imposing ballroom in 1855, an ornate space illuminated by glittering chandeliers, which for fifteen years had hosted some of the city's fashionable balls. In 1870 the place was redesigned as a concert hall by the architect Martin Haller, with a seating capacity of 1,500. Overnight, Hamburg was provided with a superior home for its instrumental concerts, which even Berlin at that time was unable to match.

---

12. BB, vol. 7, p. 13.

The first concert took place on November 1, 1886. In order to mark the passing of Franz Liszt, Bülow dedicated the second half of the concert to the memory of his old master:

BRAHMS   *Tragic* Overture, op. 81
BEETHOVEN   Piano Concerto no. 4, in G major, op. 58
              soloist, Eugen d'Albert
DVORAK   *Hussite* Overture, op. 67

PART II (In memory of Franz Liszt, d. July 31),

LISZT   Symphonic Poem *Les Préludes*
              Piano Concerto no. 2, in E-flat major
              soloist, Eugen d'Albert
WAGNER   *Tannhäuser* Overture

Let us also note that Bülow opened his new series with a work by Brahms, the *Tragic* Overture. The city of Hamburg had been slow to recognize the stature of its famous son, and from his newfound position of artistic authority at Convent Garden, Bülow determined to do something about it. Although his quarrel with Brahms was not yet patched up, Bülow's promotion of the composer's music, both on the podium and in the recital hall, continued unabated. On November 24 of the following year, he put Brahms's Symphony no. 1, in C minor into the subscription series, a work that had not so far been heard in Hamburg. It was a last-minute decision, and he dropped Rubinstein's *Ocean* Symphony from the programme in order to do it. His reason was not without interest. Three days earlier, Brahms's venerable teacher, the Hamburg-born eighty-two-year-old Eduard Marxsen, had died. Bülow wrote to Marxsen's brother, Leopold, telling him that he wished to honour Eduard's memory through this performance;

To Mr. Leopold Marxsen
Holstengasse 122
ALTONA
Hamburg,
November 21, 1887

Dear Sir:
Deeply shattered by the dire news of the death of Music Director Ed. Marxsen, the distinguished musician, I take the liberty to convey herewith the expression of my most intimate sorrow.

Professional obligations of an irrevocable nature prevent me from attending the funeral of the revered deceased,[13] to pay him a last, sad tribute, as I would have liked to do so much.

Yet in another, surely even more solemn way, I will be able to commemorate the sad event. On Thursday, the 24th, instead of Rubinstein's *Ocean* Symphony which was originally scheduled, I shall conduct the First Symphony of Johannes Brahms, with the verbal announcement that through this work of his outstanding student,

EDUARD MARXSEN

as his teacher has created for himself, and for all time, an eternal monument: that this will be the requiem for the noble spirit of the deceased.

With foremost respect
yours very devotedly
Hans v. Bülow[14]

It is unlikely that Brahms saw this letter, and he did not attend the memorial concert. The symphony made a lasting impression on the Hamburg public, however, and Bülow knew that all he had to do was to go on letting Brahms's music speak for itself.

Two or three days prior to this concert Bülow received a message from Alexander Wheelock Thayer, the biographer of Beethoven, requesting permission to attend the rehearsal of 'Beethoven's Tenth'. Thayer had followed Bülow's career as the foremost Beethoven interpreter with care, and finding himself in Hamburg he reached out to the conductor. Bülow was familiar with Thayer's groundbreaking biography of Beethoven, a copy of which he kept in his library and frequently consulted. His reply, written in his idiomatic English, runs:

Hamburg
22 November 87
[Tuesday] Evening

Dear Sir,
It would be as much honour as pleasure for myself your witnessing my rehearsal of Brahms's first symphonie but alas!—there is but

---

13. Bülow was fulfilling a conducting engagement in Bremen.
14. Hitherto unpublished. Moldenhauer Archives, Box 11, Library of Congress.

one short rehearsal on Thursday morning from 10 to 12 o'clock, in which half the time is to be consecrated to the soloist, and thanks to the blessed opera business[15] I must content myself by solely pursuing fragments, washing 'disjerte membra' [disjointed limbs] of the aforesaid work. Had I known of your desires I had informed you [beforehand] that the principal rehearsal of the orchestral works was settled upon yesterday morning.

Notwithstanding should you like to be present at our last rehearsal to morrow after to morrow [*sic*], please call at Convent Garden five minutes to ten o'clock. But you must take into consideration that we are to play in a large hall under wretched acoustical circumstances. 'A l'infortuné du pot'.[16]

I remain dear Sir,

   Hans v. Bülow

(simply 'Director' of his own business)[17]

VI

Bülow's glancing reference to 'the blessed opera business' reveals another side of his professional activity in Hamburg which had begun to dominate much of his time.

Shortly after the subscription concerts got underway, Bülow was approached by intendant Bernhard Pollini to conduct thirty operas at the Stadttheater, beginning in January 1887. This ambitious proposal appealed to Bülow, not only because Pollini gave him a free hand in the choice of operas, but granted him plenipotentiary powers in matters of stage production as well. In retrospect it may have been a politically incorrect arrangement for Pollini to have made, because he had just appointed the twenty-three-year-old Felix Weingartner as 'first conductor', and we know from subsequent events that the young man felt threatened by Bülow's proximity. The Hamburg Opera House was presently becalmed in a sea of ineptitude, and Pollini recognized that in order to get things moving again, it required the sort of whirlwind that only Bülow knew how to generate. His choice of repertoire included Spohr's *Jessonda*, Bizet's *Pearl*

---

15. Bülow was rehearsing Mozart's *Don Giovanni* for the Hamburg Theatre that same day.

16. Freely translated as, 'You'll have to take pot luck'.

17. Hitherto unpublished. Library of Congress, call no. ML95.B905. Alexander Thayer had lived in Germany for many years, and had acted as the U.S. Consul in Trieste during the period 1866–1882. His life of Beethoven appeared in German long before it was published in English: vol. 1, 1866; vol. 2, 1872; and vol. 3, 1879. Bülow's mischievous salutation at the foot of his reply to Thayer, 'simply "Director" of his own business', seems to refer to the fact that Thayer had addressed him with a formal title that was not his to receive.

Fishers, and a complete Mozart cycle.[18] The opera on which Bülow lavished much attention, and one which garnered critical acclaim, was Bizet's *Carmen,* not least because it was given without cuts, an unusual practice at that time.

The first performance of this landmark production took place on January 12, 1887, and it was generally agreed that Bülow's interpretation of the opera was definitive, that his somewhat slower tempos revealed beauties that other conductors glossed over. Because Bülow was prevented by prior engagements from conducting the next two performances in nearby Altona, it fell to Weingartner to take his place.[19] Weingartner claims to have experienced 'acute discomfort' when he first witnessed Bülow's interpretation of *Carmen.* He tells us that he became convinced that Bülow was perpetrating a huge joke on the public, and was foisting meaningless nuances and *Luftpausen* onto the opera merely to see what someone of his fame could get away with. Weingartner was equally disconcerted that the critics talked of 'Bülow's *Carmen*' and not Bizet's. This was a cardinal sin for the younger man, whose own conducting style was marked by self-effacement to the point of redundancy. Weingartner therefore felt himself duty bound to make some fundamental changes to the two performances vouchsafed to him during Bülow's absence. They chiefly concerned a return to the swifter tempos generally adopted in this opera, and a somewhat more frivolous approach to the plot. When Bülow returned to Hamburg, he observed that it had taken only two performances to reduce a noble opera to the level of a cheap operetta, and he chastised Weingartner for incompetence. Weingartner may have enjoyed the title of 'first conductor', but he was insecure in his new position, and Bülow's words lacerated him. They set Weingartner (sensitive and ever litigious) against Bülow for life. Their relationship, in any case, had never been easy. Two years earlier, Weingartner had applied for the job of assistant conductor under Bülow at Meiningen, when the position had been vacated by Franz Mannstädt, and he had been turned down in favour of the even younger Richard Strauss. During their interview in Berlin, Bülow had bluntly informed Weingartner that he could not make use of his services 'because you are too independent for me'.[20] Weingartner seems to

---

18. Within the three-week period October 29 to November 23, 1887, Bülow conducted Mozart's *Don Giovanni, Idomeneo, Cosi fan tutte, Der Schauspieldirektor, Il Seraglio, Titus,* and *Die Zauberflöte.*

19. Bülow, as we have seen, had set out for Vienna in order to give his Beethoven Cycle.

20. WUD, p. 22. We come across this phrase in the first German edition of his book *Über das Dirigieren* (1896), where it is tinged with some emotion. Weingartner tells his readers, 'I was in need . . . I had to earn my own bread . . . I visited Bülow in Berlin, met him in the street in front of his apartment, and we travelled a short distance together in a carriage. He spoke immediately about my application and said quite literally the following: "I cannot use

have taken this comment to heart and to have used the *Carmen* production to show just how independent he could be. The lifelong grudge that he harboured against Bülow as a result of the 'Carmen episode' achieved its most vindictive expression in his book *On Conducting*, page after page of which is devoted to excoriating Bülow's work on the podium.[21] It remains

---

you. You are too independent for me. I want to appoint someone who will only do absolutely what I want. You could not do that, and would not want to do it" (p. 30). Whereupon the interview was terminated. This scene occurred more than a decade before Weingartner put pen to paper, yet its corrosive nature had evidently burned itself so deeply into his mentality that he bore its impression for life.

By his own account Weingartner was unhappy in Hamburg. He began to drink heavily, and started to gamble. There was a violent confrontation between him and Pollini, who removed him from a performance of *Fidelio* and gave the opera to the conductor Karl Schröder instead. Weingartner resigned with bruised feelings and left Hamburg, first for the Mannheim Opera House and later for Berlin, in pursuit of happier times which continued to elude him.

21. Marie von Bülow took particular exception to Weingartner's frivolous charge that Bülow had distorted *Carmen* as a joke in order to prove that a famous name could dupe the critics, and she provided a spirited rejoinder in 1908 (see BB, vol. 7, pp. 82–83). She pointed out that artistic integrity was the most important thing in Bülow's life, and he would never have sacrificed it in the way that Weingartner so casually claimed. Not content to attack Bülow's conducting, Weingartner also made some gratuitous criticisms of the two cadenzas that Bülow had provided for Beethoven's G major Piano Concerto, describing them as 'soulless and unmelodious'. These cadenzas, he claimed, made him doubt whether Bülow had any understanding of Beethoven at all—a foolish comment when we recall the lifetime that Bülow had devoted to presenting entire cycles of the symphonies and the piano music, arousing the admiration of Liszt, Richard Strauss, Mahler, Bruno Walter, and many other knowledgeable musicians whose opinion was diametrically opposed to that of Weingartner. Unlike Bülow, Weingartner left recorded evidence of the special relationship he felt he enjoyed with Beethoven. His Beethoven recordings unfold the text, the whole text, and not much more than the text.

There is one other fact that helps to explain Weingartner's general unhappiness with Bülow and, we suspect, with himself as well. Four years after the *Carmen* episode, Weingartner was appointed Court Conductor in Berlin, and he tried to influence the programmes of the Berlin Philharmonic Orchestra, which by then had come under Bülow's control. He was publicly rebuked by Bülow for his trouble. To someone of Weingartner's disposition, so quick to criticize but unable to accept criticism himself, the torment must have been acute, and we must bear it in mind when reading his book. It is also worth adding that immediately after Bülow's death, Weingartner sought an urgent meeting with Hermann Wolff, the Berlin Philharmonic's manager, putting his own name forward to take over the orchestra in succession to Bülow, and requesting an inflated salary of 15,000 marks (S-WW, p. 90). Wolff preferred to solve the crisis by engaging a series of guest conductors until a permanent one could be found. These guest conductors included Richard Strauss, Ernst von Schuch, Felix Mottl, and Rafeł Maszkowski from Breslau—all of whom Weingartner considered to be so inferior that in his autobiography he claimed it was their poor work on the podium that had prompted him to write his book on conducting a year or two later (WBR, p. 217). The arrogance of that statement appears to have eluded him. Meanwhile, even as he approached Wolff for the philharmonic appointment, he was busily suing Henry Pierson of Berlin's Royal Opera House for slander, a legal tangle from which he was forced to extricate himself by withdrawing the suit and paying all the costs himself (WBR, pp. 211–212).

For the rest, the title of Weingartner's book *On Conducting* is really a misnomer, and would better be styled *About Conductors*, because he writes about Wagner, Berlioz, Habeneck,

only to add that the first edition of Weingartner's book was conveniently published in 1895, just one year after Bülow died, thereby depriving the world of an explosive rejoinder from Bülow himself.[22]

VII

During these first months in Hamburg there had been a sensational development in Bülow's private life. To the outside world it was a closely guarded secret, and it remained that way until long after his death.

One of the wealthy Hamburg families into whose home Bülow was regularly invited was that of a prominent businessman, Eduard Gorrissen, who had earlier been the Turkish consul-general for Germany, based in Istanbul. The Gorrissens were cultivated patrons of the arts, and they arranged musical soirées in their home. It was there that Bülow met and fell in love with their daughter Cécile Gorrissen-Mutzenbecher, who was nineteen years his junior. Some account of Cécile's life is called for because this was no passing affair, and it held out the prospect of becoming a potential catastrophe for both parties. When she was only seventeen, Cécile had married Gustav Mutzenbecher, a wealthy Hamburg businessman who was twenty-three years her senior, in 1866. There were two daughters of the marriage—Luise and Mathilde. Cécile contracted tuberculosis in 1871 and spent the next several years travelling to resorts in Switzerland, Paris, Würzburg, and Reichenhall. In 1876 she obtained a legal separation from her husband on grounds of his infidelity. The following year, in 1877, she was granted a divorce, and settled in Wiesbaden with her younger daughter Mathilde and the latter's governess Fräulein Voigt. The elder daughter, Luise, remained behind with her father Gustav who, as part of the divorce settlement, provided Cécile with an annual allowance of 25,000 marks and a further sum of 25,000 marks to furnish her

---

Mendelssohn, and Weber, among others, while not providing a single word about baton technique. But his most vituperative comments are reserved for Bülow, and they are so extensive that even the casual reader must suspect a personal vendetta, one which stained Weingartner's autobiography as well. In her aforementioned rebuttal of 1908, Marie von Bülow posed this rhetorical question: 'How is it possible that in the twelve years since the appearance of Weingartner's brochure not a single voice has been raised in protest against this disparagement of the dead Bülow?' Although it comes more than a hundred years late, we are happy to answer the call, and we place this footnote on the record as a matter of simple justice. Weingartner's account may be found in WUD, pp. 22–24, and p. 37, and in his autobiography (WBR, pp. 162–163). See also p. 12 of the present volume.

22. The text actually began a modest life in the *Neue Deutsche Rundschau* earlier that same year, before it appeared in book form, subsequently going through five editions.

Cécile Gorrisson-Mutzenbecher. A photograph.

own establishment.[23] Cécile was therefore independently wealthy. In the winter months she frequently returned to Hamburg to stay with her parents, and she became a regular concertgoer. That is where she first got to know Bülow, in the summer of 1886, just as he was bracing himself for his forthcoming Beethoven Cycle and the Hamburg Subscription Concerts.

Bülow often played the piano at the Gorrissens, including four-hand music with Cécile herself. Their unpublished correspondence reveals an intimate relationship more than capable of compromising his marriage to Marie Schanzer, who still lived in Meiningen.[24] He told Cécile that he regarded himself as her 'spiritual husband', and that she was 'the concubine of my soul'.[25] In December 1886 he sent her his photograph, which

23. MCM, p. 13.
24. We doubt that Marie ever saw the correspondence, although she eventually learned of its existence. In her own edition of Bülow's *Briefe* Cécile appears in the index of volume VII under the pseudonymous entry 'X—Frau Cäcilie *grande dame*'. Copies of more than 100 of Bülow's unpublished letters to Cécile are preserved in HB-CM.
25. HB-CM. Unpublished letter of April 1, 1887.

Bülow inscribes his picture for Cécile Mutzenbecher,
musically entwining his initials around hers: H-C-B.
December 4, 1886.

he inscribed with the musical motto 'H,C,B'—representing the names
'Hans, Cécile, and Bülow'.[26] Cécile accompanied him on a number of his
concert tours, staying in the same hotel, although she remained a discreet companion. When she returned to Wiesbaden in the late spring of
1887, Bülow could not bear to be parted from her and followed her there.
He resided in her house in Wiesbaden for a part of May and June 1887,
and even disclosed his whereabouts to Marie. Because Bülow was at this

26. The inscription that Bülow has written for Cécile in the photograph reproduced
above, runs:

'Wer nicht die Welt in seiner Freundin fuehlt,
verdienet nicht dass sie sein Herz ihm stiehlt'.

['Whoever does not experience the world in his lady-love,
Does not deserve to have her steal his heart'.]

time conducting his summer masterclasses in nearby Frankfurt, Cécile was able to attend them as an observer. One weekend in May he took Cécile, her daughter, and the latter's governess by steamer on a romantic journey down the Rhine to Bonn, to attend a music festival.[27] It was brash behaviour because he was so easily recognized in public. Soon Bülow was referring to Cécile as 'my adored Egeria'; he apostrophized her as 'Eurydice' and himself as 'Orpheus'. He went on to designate her his 'Saint Cecilia', after the patron saint of music, and signed one letter with a loving pun on her name, 'your completely devoted Cécilidolator'.[28] This was incendiary language which was almost certainly reciprocated. At Cécile's request, Bülow destroyed her letters to him although she preserved his to her. Just how much Marie knew of the affair, and just how intimate Bülow allowed it to become, remain matters of speculation. In the summer of 1887, Bülow's temporary bachelor estate came to an abrupt end when Marie joined him in Hamburg. It was such an obvious breach of their earlier understanding to keep their professional lives separate that we are left to assume that Marie perceived Cécile to be a direct threat to her marriage. The unexpected arrival of his wife from Meiningen forced Bülow to make some hasty decisions. Their house on Charlottenstrasse was closed down. He bought a luxurious apartment in Hamburg, on the second floor of 10 Alsterglacis, with a magnificent view of the Lombard Bridge stretching across the Inner Alster Lake, which became their permanent home.

It was now more difficult for Bülow to pursue Cécile, but the unpublished correspondence shows that he thought himself capable of rising to this reckless challenge. By 1888, his letters had reached a crescendo of passion, and we find him addressing her as 'dear, dear, darling', and 'much adored Cécile'. The following year he allowed himself to pen her this astonishing sentiment: 'Why did you not deign to make my acquaintance before my marrrriage!'[29] Was he serious, or was he simply offering her the

---

27. MCM, p. 23. In mid April Bülow had set out on a two-week trip to Italy—first to Venice and then to Florence—the chief purpose of which had been to witness the reburial of Rossini's remains, which had been exhumed from the cemetery in Paris and transferred to St. Croce in Florence. That he missed not having Cécile with him we have no doubt. There was, in fact, an uncanny role-reversal at play during this spring of 1887. It was a mirror image of the old *Meistersinger* days, twenty years earlier, when Cosima had sought solace in Wagner's arms at Tribschen and later in Venice, leaving Bülow to suffer his solitary uncertainties in Munich. And now we have Marie suffering her own uncertainties in Meiningen, while Bülow and Cécile pursued their bliss in romantic locations down the Rhineland—a trip almost certainly forged in Bülow's imagination a month earlier while passing through Venice, the city where Cosima had conceived Siegfried.

28. HB-CM. Unpublished letter dated 'Bremen, March 15, 1887'.

29. Bülow's own distortion of the word 'marriage'. Unpublished letter of July 9, 1889. HB-CM.

Bülow's Hamburg apartment, no. 10 Alsterglacis, with a view of the inner
Alster Lake, inset. A photograph.

flattering words that every woman in Cécile's position longs to hear.
Whatever the case, Bülow was by now on a collision course with reality,
incapable of maintaining the fiction of a double life, but incapable of
ending it. In the event, it was ended for him. The three-year intermezzo
with Cécile was brought to a standstill in November 1889, when Marie discovered the extent of the deception. She was contacted by a woman whom
Bülow described as a 'chief poison-mixer' from Hamburg.[30] Marie confronted Bülow and forced him to terminate the relationship by threatening to divorce him, a prospect from which he shrank. His despair stands
revealed in his correspondence with his daughter Daniela—the only person to whom he was close enough to confide his misery: 'I must make
every sacrifice to keep my wife from—running away from me, not only
on practical grounds, but because our *common sorrows* have bound me
so closely to her that, at my age, I could not survive the parting. That is
the fact'.[31] He apologized to Daniela for pulling her into his troubles. 'I
have no friend, no confidant, not a soul about me who is on my side',
he lamented. He then sent her to Wiesbaden to see Cécile, although the
exact nature of his commission remains unknown. All of Daniela's com-

30. BNB, p. 677.
31. Ibid. This wrenching letter was published in 1927, well within Marie's lifetime. Her
reaction to it remains unknown.

Bülow's music room in Hamburg, 1887–1894. A photograph.

munications to him on this subject, he warns her, must be sent to his
Berlin hotel, because letters to Hamburg are not safe—an indication that
his correspondence might be intercepted by Marie. He had become completely ensnared in that tangled web we weave, when first we practice to
deceive.

Bülow never saw Cécile again. At the moment of their parting she
wrote him a letter of farewell, the emotional contents of which indicate
that the attachment may have been even stronger on her side than on
his. 'From you I received the strength and the will to live. You never knew
how deep this attraction was, how unique you were for me in life. I rest
content to love you in silence. I bury this love in the depths of my heart'.[32]
Cécile died in Berlin, in 1907, and like Bülow was cremated in Hamburg.

---

32. Dated 'Wiesbaden, Donnerstag (21) November 1889', this is one of the few letters
from Cécile that Bülow did not burn. It is reproduced in MCM, p. 73. There is little doubt
that this was the letter that Bülow forwarded to Daniela just four days later, together with
the one from the 'poison-mixer' from Hamburg. By inviting his daughter to form her own
opinion about the nature of his infidelity—inviting her to assume that Cécile's letter proved
that it was his mind and not his body that had been unfaithful—Bülow demonstrated yet
again how hopeless he was at understanding female psychology. For the rest, to attempt to
distinguish between degrees of infidelity was a Jesuitical exercise in which Marie could not
be expected to indulge.
    Bülow gave Marie his sacred word, as he put it, not to visit Wiesbaden again. This obliged
him to cancel a recital he was to have given there, consisting of the last five Beethoven
sonatas. He offered it instead to Frankfurt, in aid of the Schopenhauer memorial statue
(BNB, p. 678).

VIII

Even as Bülow's love affair with Cécile was moving towards its denoue-
ment and consuming him with private worries, his public life took wing.
In January 1887, the ever-persistent Hermann Wolff had approached him
with a proposal that would yet again change the course of his career.
Would Bülow be interested in assuming the conductorship of the Berlin
Philharmonic Orchestra? The ensemble was in crisis and Wolff had moved
in to prevent its collapse. The story of how Bülow took command of the
ailing orchestra, and turned it into an ensemble of international distinction, has become an essential part of the Berlin Philharmonic's history. It
also happens to represent the crowning achievement of Bülow's career.

The Berlin Philharmonic, 1887–1892

I: The Eagle's Wings

> I can only justify my existence [in Berlin] by introducing reforms.
> —Bülow[1]

I

When Hermann Wolff took over the Berlin Philharmonic Orchestra, it consisted of little more than fifty disillusioned players who had recently broken away from the popular Benjamin Bilse Orchestra and were struggling to arrange concerts on their own. Bilse had been the conductor, manager, and owner of the orchestra since its inception in 1868, and he was now putting on three or four popular concerts a week in the old Berlin Concerthaus on Leipzigerstrasse. Some of the concerts were devoted to classical music, others to light entertainment. At Bilse's concerts one sat at tables and drank beer with one's friends while listening to whatever the orchestra was playing that evening. Once a week the Bilse Orchestra even played dance music, the Berlin Concerthaus having been turned into a dance hall for the occasion. Bilse was nicknamed the 'musical sergeant from Liegnitz' (his birthplace) because of his mechanical bearing on the podium and his rough-and-ready manner with the players. Among Bilse's more memorable characteristics was his preference for conducting with his back to the orchestra, out of deference to the audience. Better to turn his back on his players than commit the social gaffe of turning it on his paying customers.[2] A shrewd businessman, Bilse recompensed his musicians with miserly wages while working them hard.

---

1. BB, vol. 7, p. 143.
2. BMP, p. 42.

The last straw for them was when he arranged to send them on tour to Warsaw and booked them as '4th class passengers' for the long train journey through East Prussia and Poland. Against such shabby treatment the orchestra rebelled. They tried to negotiate with Bilse, but the profit-driven maestro refused to budge. Fifty-four of his seventy players walked out and formed their own orchestra. They elected their own board of directors, paid themselves out of their own box-office receipts, and drew up a constitution in the presence of a notary, each player assuming personal liability for the financial fate of the ensemble. And they reserved unto themselves the power to hire and fire their conductors. Most of the players were under thirty years of age, and they were willing to give as many as six concerts a week for a salary of 150 marks a month in order to maintain their independence and keep the enterprise going. It was an unprecedented attempt to form what has been well described as 'the first musical republic',[3] a democratic way of doing things that has meanwhile been copied by other orchestras. They appointed as their first conductor Ludwig von Brenner, who kept the fledgling orchestra going for its first season. This was not easy. Bilse fought to preserve his territory, and his own concerts proved to be just as popular as ever, and possibly more lucrative. The Philharmonic brought in Franz Wüllner for a short series of concerts, and then Joseph Joachim and Karl Klindworth. These men may have been splendid musicians, and the last two had national reputations, but they lacked charisma on the podium. Moreover, their concerts lost money.

In order to pay off a mounting debt, the orchestra undertook a series of tours under its temporary director, Franz Mannstädt, and readily signed a lucrative contract to play for six weeks each summer in the casino of the popular seaside resort of Scheveningen, Holland. On September 1, 1886, disaster struck when the casino went up in flames. For the players it was a catastrophe. They lost not only their personal possessions, but most of their instruments as well. Not a sheet of music remained, save one charred page of a waltz by Johann Strauss. It was titled 'Freut Euch des Lebens'— 'Let Life Be Joyful'![4]

II

Perhaps the best move that the Philharmonic made during these early years was to ask the impresario Hermann Wolff to manage them.[5] Wolff

3. SBP, p. 39.

4. Ibid., p. 42.

5. The Hermann Wolff Concert Agency had opened its doors on Berlin's Leipzigerstrasse in 1880, and was already an organization of distinction. It represented many of Europe's leading soloists—including Eugen d'Albert, Emil Sauer, Joseph Joachim, Max Pauer, and Anton Rubinstein. Later on such luminaries as Arthur Nikisch, Wilhelm Furtwängler, and

saw at once what was lacking. Fifteen years had passed since Berlin had been declared the capital of a unified Germany, yet from a musical point of view it could not begin to compare with Leipzig, Dresden, or Vienna. Wolff knew that there could never be a better time to turn the Berlin Philharmonic into a world-class ensemble, and he cast around for a conductor capable of releasing the orchestra's vast potential. Five years earlier, when the fledgling Philharmonic was still in financial distress, its future uncertain, Bülow and the Meiningen Orchestra had appeared in Berlin, capturing the headlines. The critic of the *Berliner Zeitung* had written, 'Perhaps the success will cause certain circles to give the great conductor a different podium than he has in Meiningen'. And he added archly, 'We probably don't need to express ourselves in clearer fashion'.[6]

On January 13, 1887, Wolff wrote a confidential letter to the one man he knew to be capable of putting the Berlin Philharmonic on the musical map:

> Geehrter Herr von Bülow! As you will gather from the contents of this letter, absolute and unconditional discretion is required in connection with the same. At last both Joachim and Klindworth are laying down their directors' batons. The Philharmonic Society, however, will continue to survive in another form. . . . Would you undertake the direction of eight or ten subscription concerts?[7]

So anxious was Wolff about the fate of the Berlin Philharmonic that he pursued Bülow to Vienna in order to appeal to the conductor in person. Wolff tracked his quarry down at the Hotel Imperial on January 21, and implored him to accept the Berlin appointment. That same day Bülow wrote to Cécile Mutzenbecher:

> Wolff arrived this morning—big Philharmonic revolution in Berlin. Joachim as well as Klindworth are dropping out too. Wolff has taken the whole business into his own hands and begs me not to

---

Ferruccio Busoni were added to its roster. Bülow had been a 'Wolff artist' from the beginning, and developed a close relationship with his manager. Because Wolff had earlier studied the piano under Franz Kroll, he possessed an insider's knowledge of the discipline (unlike Bülow's previous managers), and this quality Bülow respected. Prior to opening his agency Wolff had also been the editor of the *Neue Berliner Musikzeitung,* as well as the associate editor of the *Musikwelt,* which gave him an overview of the entire profession. The history of the Wolff Concert Agency, and Bülow's own association with it, has been told in affectionate detail by Wolff's daughter Edith Stargardt-Wolff in S-WW.

6. Issue of January 6, 1882.
7. S-WW, p. 59.

abandon him. I told him, 'In April we'll talk about it again'. I shall do what you tell me to do. By the way, I prefer Hamburg 1001 [times] over Berlin![8]

Bülow was in no hurry to accept the Philharmonic position. His hands were already full with the subscription concerts and operas in Hamburg, a city he had no intention of abandoning. He had moreover also undertaken to conduct a season of concerts in Bremen, beginning in the autumn, which he refused to relinquish. Throughout much of the summer of 1887 Wolff and Bülow argued back and forth until all Bülow's conditions had been met.

Bülow finally told Wolff, 'I can only justify my existence [in Berlin] by introducing reforms'.[9] And introduce reforms he did. Briefly, he cut a lot of dross out of the repertoire, which gave the orchestra more time to rehearse only the best music, and he shortened the concerts. He refused to preside over the three-hour marathons that were still popular with the man in the street, consisting as they did of a smorgasbord of pieces meant to satisfy all tastes, even the lowest. Programme building became of paramount concern to him, and one of his chief conditions was that it must remain within his total control. Bülow knew that if he lost that he lost everything. And Wolff wisely yielded this ground to him. The choice of soloists Bülow was happy to leave with Wolff ('I have always considered this to be your special domain').[10] He meanwhile had Wolff send him all the orchestral scores for the first season so that he could mark them with his own bowings and expression marks, and then have everything copied into the individual parts 'so that at the first rehearsal nothing goes so wrong that we are prevented from setting to work on the music right away'.[11] He had already made it clear that 'with me it cannot be a question of just playing things through'. And he added, not entirely in jest, that if things were not to his liking in Berlin he would go on strike (!)—a glancing reminder to Wolff of the ultimate weapon available to someone of his left-wing social persuasions.[12] But it never came to that.

III

Bülow's first concert with the Berlin Philharmonic took place on October 21, 1887. It was deliberately severe, and no soloist was engaged. The event was to be a showcase for the orchestra and conductor alone:

8. HB-CM. Hitherto unpublished letter dated 'January 21, 1887'.
9. BB, vol. 7, p. 143.
10. ACB, p. 21.
11. BB, vol. 7, p. 142.
12. Ibid., vol. 7, pp. 141–142.

HAYDN	Symphony no. 102, in B-flat major
MOZART	Symphony no. 41, in C major (*Jupiter*)
	Intermission
BEETHOVEN	Symphony no. 3, in E-flat major (*Eroica*)

The concert created a sensation, and the Presto Finale of the Haydn symphony had to be repeated. The critics spoke of the 'novelty of perfection' and 'the eagle's wings which every orchestra under Bülow's direction seems to develop'.[13] Otto Lessmann's fine words summed up the feelings of many who attended the concert: 'To every man his due, but the crown goes to Herr von Bülow above all conductors of our time'.[14]

Lessmann spoke truer than he knew. Bülow was now conducting three separate orchestras—in Berlin, Hamburg, and Bremen—each with its own season of concerts. His cycle of Mozart operas at the Hamburg Opera House was also well underway. His life at this time he described in Napoleonic terms as 'my musical winter campaign in three cities'.[15] It was not surprising that within a few weeks he had developed an inflamed right shoulder for which he engaged the services of a personal masseur to knead the muscles every day.[16] In December 1887 he was obliged to conduct Beethoven's Ninth Symphony in Bremen mainly with his left arm. Two weeks later the right shoulder was still too weak for him to play the Brahms B-flat major Piano Concerto in Berlin; he made the laconic observation that 'certain arm-movements still hurt a lot'.[17] Time and again he walked onto the platform knowing that he not only had to make music, but that in order to make this possible he had to conquer the frailties of his own body as well. Only the members of his inner circle were aware of the struggle it cost him. The public at large saw only the charismatic figure on the podium, compelling the players to recreate one magical performance after another.

IV

The careful planning of each successive season in the Philharmonie became a preoccupation for Bülow, and brought out the best in him. Berlin had never before witnessed such an array of talent. During his first three seasons (1887/1888, 1888/1889, and 1889/1890) the following soloists

---

13. *Berliner Börsen Courier*, October 1887, no. 289.

14. *AMZ*, October 28, 1887.

15. BB, vol. 7, p. 164; HHB, p. 241. The table on p. 395 offers a useful summary of his 'musical winter campaign'.

16. HB-CM. Hitherto unpublished letter dated 'January 8, 1888'.

17. HB-CM. Hitherto unpublished letters dated 'Berlin, January 8' and 'Berlin, January 22', 1888.

appeared under Bülow's direction: among the pianists were Eugen d'Albert, Alfred Grünfeld, Bernhard Stavenhagen, Emil von Sauer, Ernst Pauer, Anna Haasters (a pupil), and Teresa Carreño; while among the violinists were Adolf Brodsky, Gabriele Wietrowetz, Stanislaus Barcewicz, Carl Grigorovich, Ludwig Bleuer, and Emile Sauret; the female singers included Amy Sherwin, Pauline Metzler-Löwy, Emma Fursch-Madi, Fanny Moran-Olden, and Mathilde Brandt-Görtz. Nor did the 1890/1891 season shine less brightly than its predecessors. Bülow added three more stars to his galaxy when he invited onto the platform Ignace Paderewski, Carl Halir, and Lilli Lehmann. Later still would come such renowned violinists as Joseph Joachim and Jenö Hubay.

We mentioned Paderewski. His concert took place on December 8, 1890, and featured the Polish pianist as the soloist in his own newly published Piano Concerto in A minor, op. 17, a work that had aroused Bülow's interest. This was Paderewski's first and only appearance at the Philharmonie, and it was the occasion of a curious incident that took root in the literature and has never been formally dislodged. Paderewski expressed much bitterness against Hermann Wolff, whom he accused of plotting against him and obstructing his career after he had refused to accept Wolff as his manager. More seriously, Paderewski implied that in consequence of this refusal, Bülow had sabotaged the performance of his concerto by encouraging the orchestra to play badly. He also reported that Bülow walked off the platform during one of the solo items that the conductor had specifically invited Paderewski to play, instead of sitting in his chair listening, as was the custom at that time, an act that the pianist interpreted as a further sign of disapproval. This elaborate story Paderewski honed across the years, until he allowed it to appear in the 'authorized' version of his memoirs in 1938, when he was not only at the height of his fame as a concert pianist, but was still basking in the after-glow of having served as prime minister of Poland.[18] When the story was brought to the attention of Marie von Bülow she denied that the incident ever took place. She pointed to the obvious fact that 'no conductor, not even the most obscure and insignificant, could have behaved thus, not to speak of Hans von Bülow, the most conscientious amongst the great'.[19] This denial contains the ring of truth. For Bülow to have sabotaged any concert he directed would have meant the sacrifice of everything that he stood for and would have robbed his professional life of its meaning. Not long afterwards, in fact, Bülow invited Paderewski to repeat the concerto

18. PM, pp. 164–172.
19. IPAM. Hitherto unpublished letter to Harry Anderson, dated 'Berlin, February 9, 1932'.

in his Hamburg series, took him to his home for lunch, and lavished much hospitality on him, a clear enough indication that there was no animosity of any kind in their early relations. On that occasion Paderewski met Marie von Bülow, and conversed with her in their native Polish.[20]

Bülow led Teresa Carreño onto the concert platform of the Philharmonie on November 23, 1891, for a performance of Tchaikovsky's Concerto in B-flat minor. It was a time of growing political tension between Germany and Russia, as a result of which Bismarck had earlier ordered that no Russian notes could be accepted by the state's banking system. The decision caused some consternation in Germany, because anyone in possession of Russian currency now had worthless paper in hand. As Madame Carreño got into her stride, and the concerto began to unfold in all its majesty, the lights in the hall suddenly went out and the performance came to a standstill. Bülow turned to the audience, and declared, 'I am afraid, ladies and gentleman, we must stop for a moment, for in these dark times those Russian notes (pointing to the music) will be of little use to us!'[21]

V

Bülow's programmes introduced a formula for the Berlin Philharmonic that survived, with some modifications, until recent times. The core content was generally 'Germanic', the favoured structure being an overture, followed by a concerto, and, after an intermission, a major symphonic work. Naturally there were exceptions to this plan, but the plan itself was like a theme across which the variations unfolded. Contemporary music was not excluded and Bülow's Berlin concerts featured in plentiful measure the music of Tchaikovsky, Saint-Saëns, Glinka, Wagner, Berlioz, Richard Strauss, Max Bruch, Dvořák, and others. But while their presence in his concerts fluctuated, the German classics hardly ever did, and there was scarcely a programme that did not contain at least one work from the First Viennese School—Haydn, Mozart, Beethoven, and Schubert—with generous allotments of time given to Mendelssohn, Schumann, and Brahms, their natural successors. Whatever else he did, Bülow regarded it as his sacred mission to present the classical masterpieces of the past, in a temple specially adapted for the purpose—the old Philharmonie.

---

20. Just before lunch, the following absurd exchange took place. Bülow turned to Paderewski and asked, 'Tell me, Paderewski, what you best like to eat. Is there any dish you especially prefer? If so, we shall prepare it with pleasure'. Wishing to be tactful, Paderewski told Bülow, 'At luncheon I must tell you that I prefer your company above all else!' 'Oh, cannibal', Bülow cried, 'cannibal!' [PM, p. 172].

21. BA(1), p. 216.

The Berlin Philharmonie, formerly the Central Skating Rink. A drawing by G. Theuerkauf, 1888.

What shall we say of the Philharmonie? We used the word 'temple' just now, and think it appropriate. From the beginning the city had lacked a proper auditorium for the new orchestra, so the players had taken over an old roller-skating rink on Bernberger Strasse, installed proper seating, and converted it into the 'Berlin Philharmonie', a hall that was remodelled twice in the course of its long history, and eventually came to be regarded as one of the great concert halls of Europe. Individual chairs were set up in rows, with a single aisle running down the middle (and how noisy those chairs could be!). The ornamental decorations of the interior, with its impressive chandeliers and busts of the great composers lining the walls, created an impression of opulence that belied the hall's humble origins. Between the two world wars there were many calls for a newer, more modern auditorium, but there were always voices raised in defence of the venerable building which, in the words of Wolfgang Stresemann, had become ennobled by the music that had sounded within its walls.[22] The Philharmonie was destroyed by Allied bombs in January 1944 only a few days after Wilhelm Furtwängler conducted a concert there.

22. SBP, p. 8.

And what of the 'sacred mission'? It was nothing less than a struggle for the soul of the music. What made Bülow's conducting so exceptional was that his work on the podium became an epic battle between life and death—the life or death of the composition before him—and audiences had never before witnessed such a phenomenon. The young Bruno Walter attended one of those early Berlin concerts. From his seat above and behind the kettledrums he had a direct line of vision to the conductor's podium, and experienced an epiphany. He later recalled:

> I saw in Bülow's face the glow of inspiration and the concentration of energy. I felt the compelling force of his gestures, noticed the attention and devotion of the players, and was conscious of the expressiveness and precision of their playing. It became at once clear to me that it was that one man who was producing the music, that he had transformed those hundred performers into his instrument, and that he was playing it as a pianist played the piano. That evening decided my future. Now I knew what I was meant for. No musical activity but that of an orchestral conductor could any longer be considered by me, no music could ever make me truly happy but symphonic music. Before the evening was over I told Father that I would be glad zealously to continue my piano studies and be publicly active as a pianist later, just as Bülow was, but today the die had been cast, today I had recognized what I had been born for. I had decided to become a conductor.[23]

During the course of his five-year tenure, Bülow conducted more than fifty concerts with the Berlin Philharmonic Orchestra, and when he finally stepped down in April 1892, gravely ill, it had become an ensemble of international distinction. It was taken over in turn by Arthur Nikisch and Wilhelm Furtwängler, both of whom inherited a number of the players who had first started their fledgling careers under Bülow, and with them many of the traditions that Bülow had established. In such circumstances, comparisons became inevitable. Not long after the forty-two-year-old Arthur Nikisch had succeeded Bülow, the German critic Ferdinand Pfohl made some interesting distinctions between them. He had witnessed both conductors on the same podium numerous times, and his observations merit thought. 'Nikisch is a poet; Bülow was a philosopher', he remarked. And he continued:

---

23. WTV, p. 39. Bruno Walter was about twelve years old when he began attending the Bülow concerts. He was a piano student at the Stern Conservatory in Berlin.

Nikisch is a great colorist; Bülow was more like a draftsman than a painter. A symphony under Bülow resembled a landscape in winter: a frost-clear picture, full of sharp lines and the brightest lighting effects. A symphony under Nikisch is a picture of spring, the landscape in all the fullness of spring.[24]

Wilhelm Altmann, the violinist and musicologist, attended many of Bülow's concerts and left a compelling account of his work on the podium. He tells us that Bülow beat time with a strongly measured, almost four-square motion, so that everyone knew exactly what his baton intended to convey. He never wearied of stressing the *exact* Piano or the *exact* Forte that these general dynamic indications conveyed, and he constantly called for their relative distribution within the orchestral fabric. He loved to contradict the listeners' expectations with uncommonly sharp accents on weak beats, shaping the phrase in opposition to the bar-lines. And when a new phrase was about to enter he would sometimes allow a so-called *Luftpause,* or an intake of breath, to take place.[25] During rehearsal, if the shape of a phrase did not please him, he would sing it out or even go over to the piano and play it, until his intention was understood. Even the soloists had fully to comply with his wishes in this respect.[26] Such rigour occasionally aroused opposition. There were those who saw in Bülow's baton not a magic wand but a scalpel. Max Kalbeck, in his biography of Brahms, went so far as to picture him as a scientific horror. He tells us that Bülow 'responded to the tender structure [of a Beethoven Adagio] not as a lover, but as an anatomist. Instead of caressing the beautiful sound-body with the baton, he dissected it'.[27] For the rest, Bülow's approach to conducting was the same as his approach to piano playing. The music was unrolled like a map, down to the smallest detail. Inevitably, the age-old question arises: Who was more important, Bülow the pianist or Bülow the conductor? Each was surely contained within the other.

24. PAN, pp. 31–32.

25. It was Bülow's incorporation of the *Luftpause* into orchestral music that disturbed many musicians, because they were unused to it. Yet the *Luftpause,* and its second cousin the agogic accent, are among the more expressive devices available to the interpreter, and are employed by soloists all the time. Bülow was modelling himself on the great singers, who must needs breathe if they are to survive the song. One can still hear something of the tradition in the Brahms recordings of Bruno Walter, and in light of this conductor's early admiration for Bülow it is legitimate to assume that he was influenced by his predecessor.

For the rest, Bülow regarded musical performance as a form of speech, and even spoke of 'a musical punctuation', with commas, semicolons and periods. Walter Damrosch provides two telling examples of Bülow's use of the comma in the first movement of Beethoven's Ninth Symphony in DHB, pp. 283 and 286.

26. ACB, p. 671.

27. KJB, vol. 3, p. 495.

For as long as the art of conducting itself survives, comparisons between Bülow, Nikisch, Furtwängler, and those who came after them will continue to be made. But in one respect Bülow was incomparable. The size of his repertory and his flawless memory placed him beyond the reach of his successors, even the most illustrious. The rehearsals provided one graphic illustration after another of Bülow guiding the players through the complexities of a composition, correcting wrong notes here and false dynamic markings there, without so much as a glance at the score. That is why the Berlin players so often referred to Bülow as 'our great teacher'. The rehearsals were not there solely for the purpose of putting polish on a performance. They were there to give the players a deeper insight into the creative process. In brief, they amounted to a seminar on musical composition. Bülow was exemplary in his support of modern music, too. To scrutinize the Berlin years alone is to reveal the fact that practically the whole of modern music, as it then existed, passed through his hands. Among the giants of the nineteenth century, who were already deceased when Bülow came to Berlin, the names of Wagner, Berlioz, Mendelssohn, and Schumann featured prominently in his programmes. It is when we come to the living that we begin to appreciate the tireless efforts he made to bring the latest music to his Berlin audiences. The roll call includes Brahms, Tchaikovsky, Dvořák, Max Bruch, Grieg, Carl Goldmark, Mikhail Glinka, Charles Villiers Stanford, Joachim Raff, Eduard Lassen, Jules Massenet, Anton Rubinstein, and Moritz Moszkowski. And at this juncture the list becomes very esoteric indeed. Who hears a note today of Siegmund Noskowski, Robert Radecke, Robert Kahn, Heinrich Hofmann, and Carl Reinthaler? Yet the Berliners did, under Bülow's all-inclusive baton.

VI

Toward his friend and acolyte Richard Strauss, Bülow continued to be particularly generous. Bülow had followed his rising star with admiration, from the days of their earliest encounters in Meiningen. Now, from his commanding position in Berlin, Bülow conducted several of Strauss's early works, including the Symphonic Fantasy *Aus Italien,* and the tone poems *Macbeth* and *Don Juan.* He also began rehearsals for *Tod und Verklärung,* a work which he finally decided should be conducted by the composer himself (February 23, 1891). All these works projected Strauss onto the international stage and helped to establish his early reputation as the *enfant terrible* of modern music. In gratitude for such friendship, Strauss dedicated to his mentor his Symphonic Fantasy *Aus Italien,* which Bülow introduced to the Berlin public as early as January 23, 1888. For this performance Strauss travelled to Berlin, and in an ecstatic letter to his father he wrote, 'The Berlin Philharmonic Orchestra is the most intelligent, the most splendid, and the most alert orchestra that I know. . . . I do not

Bülow conducts at the Berlin Philharmonie. A lithograph, ca. 1892.

believe that I will hear my Fantasy played more beautifully. . . . The whole concert was glorious'.[28] Over the preparation of *Don Juan*, Bülow took special care. He conducted the work from manuscript on January 31, 1890, at the Seventh Berlin Philharmonic concert of the season. Strauss took the liberty of sending him a detailed set of metronome markings which could be studied with profit today, and he added, somewhat disarmingly, 'where they do not fit in with your own conception, I implore you urgently just to disregard them'.[29] Bülow did, in fact, disregard them and Strauss was displeased with the result, as we learn from a letter he wrote to his parents the following day.[30] Nonetheless, the critic Otto Lessmann spoke of this pivotal work's 'unique creative strength', and described the performance as 'masterly'. Bülow, he went on to tell us, vigorously applauded the composer who was present, and in so doing led the opinion of the public. 'Herr von Bülow loves this sort of thing, to create an atmosphere'.[31]

The twenty-four-year-old Sibelius was in the Philharmonie that evening, and took away some lively memories of *Don Juan*. The Finnish com-

28. SBE, p. 103. Strauss goes on to speak in glowing terms of Bülow's performances of Beethoven and Wagner in the same concert. 'The *Leonore* Overture under Bülow was a pure revelation, the *Meistersinger* Overture, da capo; glorious, splendid'.

29. BSC, pp. 91–92.

30. SBE, p. 127.

31. *Vossische Zeitung*, February 1, 1890.

poser was already attracted to the idea of programmatic tone poems, and soon began to compose his own. His *Lemminkäinen* Suite is based on the amorous escapades of the legendary Finnish hero of that name—a kind of Nordic 'Don Juan'. Sibelius, who was studying in Berlin, attended the entire season of Philharmonic concerts under Bülow. What lingered were his memories of Bülow's interpretations of the Beethoven symphonies, and Sibelius made copious annotations in his miniature scores. He also attended a piano recital in the Singakademie in which Bülow played the last five piano sonatas of Beethoven.[32]

The rise of Czech nationalism in the nineteenth century, and the Teutonic backlash that it provoked, caused Bülow to be criticized by his fellow Germans for featuring Dvořák's music in his programmes—especially the highly partisan *Hussite* Overture. The work was really a tone poem connected to the life and work of Jan Hus, the Bohemian religious reformer, who had been burned at the stake for heresy. The Czechs were looking for heroes, and found one in Hus. When Hermann Wolff questioned the wisdom of performing the *Hussite* Overture in Berlin, Bülow replied bluntly, 'I will answer for everything I conduct. Next to Brahms, the most important composer is Dvořák'. Wolff was simply being prudent; the demonstrations mounted against Bülow in Dresden and Breslau a year or two earlier were still fresh in the memory. Dvořák was grateful for Bülow's pioneering work in his behalf and he offered the conductor the dedication of his Symphony no. 5 in F major. Bülow replied:

> Most honoured Master!
> A dedication from you—next to Brahms the most divinely gifted composer of the present time—is a higher decoration than any Grand Cross from the hands of any prince. With my most heartfelt thanks I accept this honour.
> With sincere esteem,
>
> Your devoted admirer,
> Hans v. Bülow
> Hamburg, November 25, 1887.[33]

32. TS, pp. 58–59.
33. DKD, vol. 6, p. 135. Bülow was already the recipient of many compositions bearing his name on the dedication page, including:

> Richard Strauss: Symphonic Fantasy, *Aus Italien*, op. 16.
>   Improvisations and Fugue, for piano (1884).
> Tchaikovsky: Piano Concerto in B-flat minor, op. 23.
> Liszt: Hungarian Rhapsody no. 14, in F minor.
>   Fantasie on Hungarian Folk-themes, for piano and orchestra.
>   *Totentanz*, for piano and orchestra.

Dvořák later visited Berlin, and was in the audience to acknowledge the applause after Bülow gave a performance of the Symphony no. 7, in D minor, in October 1889.

His enthusiastic pursuit of 'ethnic' music led Bülow toward some esoteric repertoire—from Scandinavia, Russia, and even Ireland. In January 1888, he conducted the German premier of Charles Villiers Stanford's *Irish* Symphony in the Hamburg Subscription Concerts. Stanford tells us that he travelled to Hamburg in order to attend the rehearsals, and sat in the darkened hall of Convent Garden beneath the balcony, without Bülow's knowledge. He was astonished to observe how deeply Bülow had entered into the spirit of the symphony, which he rehearsed and conducted from memory. Stanford later wrote, 'He conducted superbly. It was a lesson to the composer how to make it sound right!'[34] The work was so well received that Bülow invited Stanford to accompany him to Berlin, where he repeated the symphony in the Philharmonic concerts a few days later. When Stanford got back to London he went over to see the composer Hubert Parry, who later reported that 'he praised Bülow to the skies. Said he was a better conductor than Richter'.[35]

VII

As we survey Bülow's work with the Berlin Philharmonic, one thing must inevitably be borne in mind. It took place while he was fighting a mortal battle against the frailties of his own body, a battle that he would eventually lose. It is unlikely that Bülow enjoyed more than two or three consecutive weeks of normal health during his entire tenure in Berlin. He was beset with colds, influenzas, and a variety of neuralgic pains so severe that he was sometimes obliged to take to his bed until they had subsided;

Complete Transcriptions of the Beethoven Symphonies, for solo piano.
Joachim Raff: Drei Klavier-Soli, op. 74.
  Overture: Eine fest' Burg ist unser Gott, op. 127.
  Piano Concerto, op. 185.
Gabriel Fauré: Piano Quartet no. 2, in G minor, op. 45.
Charles Villiers Stanford: Piano Trio no. 1, in E flat major, op. 35.

Later would follow Brahms's Sonata no. 3, in D minor, for violin and piano, op. 108; and Eugen d'Albert's Piano Sonata in F-sharp minor, op. 10.

34. DCVS, p. 193, in a letter Stanford wrote to Alfred Littleton, dated January 31, 1888.

35. DCVS, p. 194, quoted from the unpublished diary of Hubert Parry, entry dated February 11, 1888. This comparison between Richter and Bülow is of more than passing interest, and was later taken up by Stanford in his article 'Conductors and Their Methods'. He took issue with Wagner's assertion that if you wanted perfection in orchestral performance you should have Bülow conduct the rehearsals and Richter conduct the performances. 'I venture to think that the position of these artists should have been reversed', Stanford responded. It was Bülow's electrifying temperament, he argued, that lifted him above Richter's 'standpoint of common sense', and made him the ideal interpreter.

and he imbibed an alarming variety of medications to help them on their way. It is a source of wonder that he could function at all. Bülow conjures up the mythical figure of Sisyphus, who was condemned by the gods to roll a boulder uphill in perpetuity, because they also saw to it that it always came rolling down again. Each concert for Bülow was a boulder of Sisyphus. Time and again he walked onto the concert platform not knowing how he might survive the experience. It is arguable that from a purely psychological point of view, the challenge of rolling the boulder uphill drew from him some deep reserves of energy which might otherwise never have been available to him on the concert platform, and enabled him to turn his greatest drawback into his strongest virtue. 'One must imagine Sisyphus happy', declares Albert Camus in his beautiful *Myth of Sisyphus,* adding perceptively, 'the struggle itself towards the heights is enough to fill a man's heart'.

Bülow continued to spend his summer months at various watering-spas, of course. This custom, by now long established, enabled him to recover his strength and resume the struggle the following season. In the summer of 1888 he went to take the waters at Scheveningen. On August 7 he received a cable from his nephew Viktor von Bojanowski informing him of the death of his mother. The eighty-eight-year-old Franziska was, in Bülow's words, 'blind and half-decrepit',[36] and her passing was not entirely unexpected. Viktor and his father assumed the responsibility for making all the funeral arrangements, and informed Bülow that his presence was not vital. Bülow insisted on abandoning his cure, however, and travelled to Berlin in order to join his sister and her family for the sad ceremony. Franziska's demise must have been a relief for the Bojanowski family, who had looked after this increasingly querulous woman during her declining years. As for Bülow, his mother's death reminded him of his own mortality. He was only fifty-eight at this juncture, but already saw himself as having passed through the portals of old age.

VIII

In Hamburg Bülow continued his pioneering work in behalf of Brahms. A year had elapsed since he introduced the composer's First Symphony to the Hamburg public, and Bülow considered the time ripe for further action. He persuaded Dr. Carl Petersen, the venerable mayor of Hamburg, to have the Freedom of the City of Hamburg bestowed on Brahms. A friendship had sprung up between Bülow and the eighty-year-old mayor,

---

36. HB-CM. Unpublished letter dated August 8, 1888. Viktor's terse cable ran, 'Your mother went to sleep quite peacefully during the night—my wife and daughters are in Cudowa-Schlesien—can I carry out your last wishes?'

Hamburgische Gewerbe- und Industrie-Ausstellung 1889.

Erstes Fest-Concert

unter gütiger Leitung des Herrn

Dr. Hans von Bülow

Montag, den 9. September, Abends 7½ Uhr in der Festhalle.

Solisten:

Frau Marie Wilhelmj, Concertsängerin aus Wiesbaden (Sopran).
Frau Ernestine Heink-Rössler vom Hamburg. Stadttheater (Alt).
Herr Carl Dierich, Grossherzogl. Mecklenb. Kammersänger aus
   Schwerin (Tenor).
Herr Franz Schwarz, Grossherzogl. Sächs. Hof-Opernsänger aus
   Weimar (Bass).
Chor ca. 400 Damen und Herren. — Orchester 110 Musiker.

PROGRAMM.

I.

1. L. v. Beethoven: Kyrie und Gloria a. d. Missa solemnis für Soli-
   stinnen, Chor und Orchester op. 123 (1823).

II.

2. Joh. Brahms: Deutsche Fest- und Gedenk-Sprüche für Chor
   a capella op. 109 (Manuscript).
   Unter gef. Leitung des Herrn Director Julius Spengel.

3. R. Wagner: Huldigungsmarsch. König Ludwig II. von Bayern
   gewidmet (1864).

III.

4. F. Mendelssohn: „Lobgesang". Symphonie-Cantate für Solo-
   stimmen, Chor und Orchester op. 52 (1840).
   Symphonie: Allegretto maestoso e vivace — Allegretto agitato —
   Adagio religioso.

The opening concert of Hamburg's Trade and Industry Exhibition, September 9, 1889.
A concert billing.

and the conductor used his political skills to have Petersen get a resolution passed by a reluctant Senate to award Brahms its highest honour. Only fourteen people had ever been selected for this distinction, and they included Field Marshal Blücher, General Moltke, and Prince Otto von Bismarck.

Bülow knew that the accolade would mean much to Brahms, who had often complained that since he had begun to amount to something in the world, his name had been virtually ignored in the place of his birth. When Petersen broke the good news to Brahms, in May 1889, the composer replied that it was 'the most beautiful honour and the greatest joy' that anyone could have given him.[37] The private ceremony took place on September 14 in Petersen's spacious home, and Brahms travelled to Hamburg to receive the illuminated scroll of citizenship in person. The service was witnessed by Bülow and by Brahms's friend Julius Spengel, the distinguished director of Hamburg's *Cäcilienverein* and an enthusiastic promoter of the composer's large-scale choral works. In gratitude for the distinction bestowed on him, Brahms dedicated to Petersen his newly composed *Deutsche Fest- und Gedenksprüche,* op. 109, which received its premier performance on September 9 during Hamburg's so-called 'Trade and Industry Exhibition', held during the week of Brahms's visit, and conducted by Spengel himself. Characteristically, Brahms never offered any public thanks to Bülow for arranging the honour, although shortly before it was announced he dedicated to Bülow his newly-composed Sonata in D minor, for Violin and Piano, a worthy response.

Bülow celebrated his sixtieth birthday in Hamburg, and on January 8, 1890, the congratulatory telegrammes poured in. More than fifty of them are preserved in the Berlin archives.[38] Aside from family members, they came from such diverse sources as Bernhard Pollini, Johannes Brahms, Friedrich Simrock, Richard Mühlfeld, Adolf Brodsky, Alfred and Heinrich Grünfeld, the playwright Henrik Ibsen, and organizations such as the music school in Würzburg, and of course the Berlin Philharmonic Orchestra. There was also a scroll of honour from the city of Hamburg, in acknowledgement of everything that Bülow had done for the artistic life of the community. A cable from Romaine Overbeck, in English, ran, 'Heartfelt Congratulations and many happy returns of the day'. Bülow was delighted to receive from Brahms a gift of the autograph copy of the composer's Symphony no. 3, in F major, a work he had done much to

37. BB, vol. 7, p. 252.
38. DSB, Mus. NL E IV.

promote, and for which he had a particular affection.[39] Perhaps the gesture that moved Bülow most deeply, however, was the gift of 10,000 marks sent to him by his friends and admirers, with the stipulation that it be donated to any musical cause of his choice. Bülow eventually took the advice of Brahms and awarded it to the impoverished Friedrich Chrysander in recognition of the scholar's monumental edition of Handel.

In the spring of 1890, Bülow learned from Daniela that her stepbrother, Siegfried Wagner, the twenty-year-old son of Cosima and Richard Wagner, had been attending some of the Berlin Philharmonic concerts incognito. Siegfried was now a student of architecture in Berlin, and was showing more than a passing interest in Bülow, whom he had not yet met. Bülow lost no time in asking Hermann Wolff to make complimentary tickets available to the young man. Wolff even arranged to bring the pair together for a meeting in the artists' room, and we learn that Bülow was enchanted by Siegfried's personality. It was the only time the pair ever met.[40]

IX

There was as yet no endowment fund for the Berlin Philharmonic, and the lack of financial security weighed on the future of the ensemble. In the summer of 1890 Bülow turned his attention to the creation of a pension plan for the players. He conducted an extra concert during the 1890–1891 season specifically to raise money for this purpose, which yielded the promising figure of 14,409 marks. By the end of the fiscal year (July 31, 1891) more than 18,000 marks had been deposited in the fund.[41] None of this would have been possible without the loyal support of the Berlin audience, which across the years had turned out in ever-growing numbers to sustain Bülow and the orchestra. Eventually Bülow opened his rehearsals to the public as well, which not only helped to swell the coffers, but increased the affection with which the Berliners regarded their orchestral director. For a modest charge, anyone could get into the Philharmonie the day before the concert and witness Bülow putting the Berlin Philharmonic through its paces. It was a wonderful learning experience for students and teachers alike, who would sometimes bring their scores, particularly when the works were unfamiliar. Almost from the beginning

---

39. Brahms inscribed the manuscript with the words, 'Seinem herzlich geliebten Hans v. Bülow, in treuer Freundschaft. Wien, 8. January 1890'. ('To his sincerely loved Hans v. Bülow, in faithful friendship. Vienna, January 8, 1890'.)

40. BBLW, pp. 170–171.

41. As early as November 1885, those directing the affairs of the orchestra had lamented the absence of a pension fund, and had sought to remedy the matter by placing a statute in the orchestra's constitution, but preliminary attempts to get things started had faltered. For details see ACB, p. 26n1.

of Bülow's tenure his audience instinctively sensed that they were witnessing history, and because these fleeting times would never return, they had to be cherished.

Bülow's close relationship with his Berlin audience was not achieved without some stress and strain along the way. At a Philharmonic concert in January 1892, a half-dozen latecomers, who had been held up at the cloakroom during the intermission, made a noisy entrance in the middle of the third movement of Beethoven's Symphony no. 2, in D major. The chairs scraped on the floor of the old Philharmonie with as great a decibel level as the roller skaters who had once occupied the building. At the end of the movement Bülow made a very long pause, turned and glared at the offending listeners, who happened to be sitting near the front, and cried out, 'Unmusical public!' striking the empty music desk before him with such force that the ensuing crack resounded through the Philharmonie like a pistol-shot. Bülow, too, could create decibels to the discomfiture of the public if he wanted to. His outburst was greeted with some grumbles and protests from the audience. Bülow then commenced the finale. At the end of the concert the applause was mixed with some hissing. Bülow returned to the podium, bowed sardonically, and thanked the audience for its participation in the performance. The tension evaporated, as it usually did, at this sign of ready wit.

Not only ordinary music lovers but also professional musicians attended the open rehearsals. It must have been on one such occasion that the following incident occurred. Bülow was taking the orchestra through the *Eroica* Symphony. Seated in the hall was another conductor, there to capture the details of 'the Bülow reading' for himself. With pencil poised, he diligently marked in his copy of the score every point that Bülow deemed worthy of attention. Towards the end of the first movement, where the added trumpet reinforces the main theme,

the trumpeter articulated the last four notes in such a blatant manner as to remind the listener of a certain well-known waltz. Bülow stopped the orchestra and said, 'Do not make this passage sound like 'The Blue Danube'. The other conductor, all ears, earnestly jotted down the words, '*Not* to sound like The Blue Danube'. When Bülow heard about it, he sent the conductor a copy of his score of *The Flying Dutchman* Overture, the rehearsals of which had recently provoked him. At a particularly difficult point in the score, Bülow had written, 'Curse them here!'

The newspaper critics Bülow continued to despise because of their self-importance, and he lost no opportunity to expose their musical ignorance. On one occasion Bülow, at a public rehearsal in the Philharmonie, remarked upon a printing error in the second horn part of the Breitkopf edition of the Beethoven symphonies. A well-known critic, who was present, waited until the end and came forward to ask Bülow to confirm the exact bar number of the mistake. Bülow opened the score at random, pointed to the horn part, and said, 'There it is'. The critic looked briefly at the bar in question and then said, 'Quite right, of course, of course'. Bülow had correctly sensed that the knowledge of this 'authority on music' did not even extend to transposing the horn parts, and dismissed him with a sarcastic smile.[42]

Young composers whom Bülow decided to feature in the concerts were encouraged to present themselves at the rehearsals, and even to direct the orchestra themselves, whenever that was deemed to be helpful. We can only admire the resourcefulness of the budding symphonist who, in an attempt to save time, distributed seventy pencils among the players and told them to mark their copies according to instructions he proposed to deliver verbatim. The next day, Bülow took over the podium and distributed seventy erasers, advising the orchestra to delete everything that they had earlier written down.

Perhaps the most famous of these 'rehearsal concerts', one arranged for a special event that was not part of the regular Philharmonic series, occurred on March 6, 1889, when Bülow conducted Beethoven's Ninth Symphony twice in one evening. Such a thing had not been done in Berlin before (although we recall that Bülow had already done it in Meiningen and Vienna), and the occasion attracted widespread attention. Bülow's intention was to make this most intractable of Beethoven's symphonies better known to the Berlin public. Even Kaiser Wilhelm indicated that he wanted to attend, but at the last moment he was prevented by illness from doing so.[43] Brahms travelled all the way from Vienna to

---

42. SRR, p. 121.

43. S-WW, pp. 65–66. Bülow's letters to Daniela make it clear that he had originally intended this double performance of Beethoven's Ninth Symphony to take place in Hamburg on December 17, 1888, to mark the composer's birthday. But other engagements, notably his concerts in Bremen, got in the way, so it was postponed. He told her, 'Had I undertaken to conduct the Ninth (which has repeatedly thrown me) on that December 17, I should at

witness the phenomenon. Strauss journeyed from Munich in the company of Alexander Ritter. Long before the performance all the tickets had been sold. Naturally there was the usual rehearsal the day before, and as the symphony reached its triumphant conclusion, the packed audience went wild with enthusiasm. Until that moment Bülow had not intended to conduct the symphony twice at the rehearsal as well, but he suddenly changed his mind. He turned to the large gathering and said, 'If the orchestra and the audience agree, we will repeat the Symphony because today the real music lovers are here, and tomorrow the snobs will come'. A storm of applause broke out and the symphony was duly repeated. It made sense to Bülow that since the symphony was being performed twice for 'the snobs', it had to be performed twice for the 'real music lovers' as well. But such logic resulted in the Berlin Philharmonic, to say nothing of the soloists and chorus, having to perform the Ninth Symphony four times in just over twenty-four hours. The critic Eduard Hanslick questioned the value of such an undertaking, describing it as an *'ästhetische Rosskur'*—a drastic aesthetic treatment—for whatever it was that ailed the Berlin public. But this grudging comment overlooked the deeper fact that it had hitherto been rare to hear this symphony once, let alone twice in swift succession. Indeed, it was only with the arrival of the gramophone record, some years later, that the general public stood the remotest chance of getting to know the symphony well.[44]

It is hardly possible to talk about Bülow's performance of Beethoven's *Choral* Symphony without mentioning the sterling work of his young colleague, the chorus master Siegfried Ochs. Ochs had formed the 'Siegfried

---

this moment certainly be lying on my nose with all the arrangements for the second half of the season irreparably destroyed' (BNB, p. 666). This symphony was always an Everest for Bülow, and if he conquered it more effectively than his contemporaries, it was because he let nothing else stand in the way. As it happens, Hamburg did not lose the event to Berlin. It eventually got its own double performance of Beethoven's Ninth the following season, in celebration of 'the birthday of the Messiah of acoustics', as Bülow put it, the two renditions flanking the birthday itself—the first taking place on December 16 and the second on December 18, 1889. Bülow was delighted that each one of the 224 ladies in the vast choir wore a white carnation in his honour.

Incidentally, modern scholarship has thrown doubt on the exact date of Beethoven's birth. December 17 was the date of his baptism, making December 16 the probable date of his birth. But even that remains an open question. Bülow and his contemporaries were untroubled by such uncertainties.

44. The first complete recording of Beethoven's Ninth Symphony was not released until December 1923, in an acoustical pressing issued by Polydor (69607/13), which occupied fourteen sides of seven 78 rpm discs. Bruno Seidler-Winkler conducted the 'Berlin New Symphony Orchestra', with the BSO chorus. It was intended to mark the centennial anniversary of the symphony's premier performance in Vienna, in 1824. Weingartner's better-known electrical recording, with the London Symphony Orchestra, appeared in 1926.

Ochs'schen Gesangverein' in 1882, when he was only twenty-four years old, shortly after being dismissed from the Berlin Hochschule für Musik. He had come to prominence reviving the choral music of Schütz, Bach, and Handel. Ochs's work on the podium attracted Bülow's notice, because he admired his attention to detail. Within five years the Gesangverein had grown into the Berlin Philharmonic Choir, with more than 400 members. Between the years 1889 and 1892 it gave numerous concerts with Bülow in the Philharmonie, including the Ninth Symphony.

The Old Berlin Philharmonie: A photograph taken before World War I.

All this activity in Berlin becomes more phenomenal still when we recall that Bülow continued to conduct the Hamburg Subscription Concerts as well as the Bremen Subscription Concerts, and he was constantly commuting among the three cities. Hamburg remained his home; but whenever he conducted the Berlin Philharmonic he stayed in the 'Akanischer Hof Hotel' on Königgrätzer Strasse, just a three-minute walk to the concert hall. Since the programmes were rarely the same, Bülow spent many an hour studying his scores in railway carriages, marking the orchestral parts, and engraving each page on his memory. The season of 1887/1888— 'my musical winter campaign in three cities'—was especially gruelling. A burden that few modern conductors would care to shoulder is revealed in the following table. Indeed, as some of these worthies rove around the world, we might well enquire what their briefcases actually contain. A few standard repertory works perhaps, a baton, a change of shirt, an airline ticket to the next city, and space for little else.

1887–1888
'My Musical Winter Campaign in Three Cities'

HAMBURG	BREMEN	BERLIN
Six Subscription Concerts	**Seven Subscription Concerts**	**Ten Philharmonic Concerts**

HAMBURG

Six Subscription Concerts

November 2
All-Beethoven

November 24
Brahms,
Mendelssohn, Grieg

January 10
Beethoven, Brahms

January 26
Stanford, Beethoven

February 24
Saint-Saëns, Wagner,
Mendelssohn

April 13
Hummel, Wagner,
Beethoven

Opera Season

In addition to the Hamburg orchestral concerts (above), Bülow also conducted twenty-three opera performances in the Hamburg Opera House, including a series of Mozart operas:

Don Giovanni
(October 29)
Idomeneo
(October 31)
Figaro
(November 5)
Titus
(November 11)

These operas were repeated throughout the season.

Concurrently, Bülow also directed performances of Bizet's *Carmen* and *Pearl Fishers;* Spohr's *Jessonda;* and Cherubini's *Wasser-träger.*

BREMEN

Seven Subscription Concerts

October 11
Beethoven, Brahms

December 9
Beethoven's Choral
Symphony in bene-
fit of the orchestral
pension fund

January 17
Beethoven, Richard
Strauss

January 31
Mendelssohn,
Schumann

February 28
Soloist in concertos
by Hummel and
Beethoven

April 10
Wagner, Beethoven

April 17
Haydn, Mozart,
Rubinstein, etc.

BERLIN

Ten Philharmonic Concerts

October 21
Haydn, Mozart,
Beethoven

November 14
Mendelssohn,
Chopin, Goldmark,
Brahms

December 5
Meyerbeer,
Schumann, Raff,
Saint-Saëns, Handel,
etc.

January 6
Wagner, Brahms,
Reinecke, Bach, etc.

January 23
Richard Strauss,
Wagner, Saint-Saëns,
Beethoven, Liszt

February 6
Beethoven, Brahms,
Stanford, Weber

February 20
Bazzini, Weber,
Tchaikovsky, Bruch,
etc.

March 5
Haydn, Davidoff,
Berlioz

March 19
Brahms, Mozart,
Saint-Saëns, Wagner,
etc.

April 6
Hummel, Taubert,
Moszkowsky,
Schubert, etc.
(Bülow also played
Beethoven's *Diabelli*
Variations in this
concert!)

X

Bülow continued to sustain his second career as a pianist. He spent most of the month of June 1888 in London, where he had been invited to give his Beethoven Cycle in St. James's Hall—this time spread across a period of three weeks: June 4, 12, 19, and 26. A distinguished audience awaited him, for nothing like this had been heard in England before. Hans Richter was there, as were Sophie Menter, Vladimir de Pachmann, Sir Charles Hallé, Sir George Grove, and Pablo de Sarasate, as well as members of London's high society. *The London Times* recognized Bülow as a pianist with a mission, 'that mission being the active advocacy of all that is highest and purest in art'.[45] The newspaper went on to point out that this Cycle served an educational purpose, which could 'not fail to leave [its] trace on the spirit in which Beethoven is taught and studied in England'. This was a prescient observation. Sitting in the audience was the young Tobias Matthay, who later became one of the best-known piano pedagogues of his generation—the mentor of Myra Hess, Irene Scharrer, and Moura Lympany among others—whose influential theories of piano playing were self-confessedly based on his empirical observations of the three great pianists who passed through London in the 1880s: Liszt, Rubinstein, and Bülow. Matthay took his scores along to all the Bülow recitals. His personal copy of Bülow's Beethoven edition is of more than passing interest because it contains several annotations which tell us how Bülow performed certain passages.[46] In the Finale of the *Appassionata* Sonata, for example, Bülow made the canon between the two hands more audible than was customary (mm. 158–164) by inserting accents at the following places:

45. Issue of June 5, 1888.

46. These scores are now in the possession of the American Matthay Association, presently based in Dayton, Ohio.

XI

Bülow returned to Germany in early July. As was now his custom, he searched for a summer refuge at a watering-spa, and his choice fell once more on the coastal resort of Scheveningen in The Netherlands. Within the unlikely location of the Scheveningen *Kurhaus,* between drinking the waters and undergoing a daily massage, Bülow engaged in a lively correspondence with Hermann Wolff, studied his musical scores, and readied himself for another season of concerts in Hamburg and Berlin.

His recent success in London, and the deep impression he had created there with his Beethoven Cycle, unexpectedly came to dominate his future plans. Word of Bülow's accomplishment had crossed the Atlantic and attracted the attention of Frederick A. Schwab, the music critic of *The New York Times*. Schwab, a German-born journalist who had lived in America for many years, had witnessed Bülow's rise to preeminence in Germany and was determined to attract him back to the New World. This 'return of a legend' was in the best traditions of American business enterprise, and it appealed to the entrepreneur in Schwab. Would Bülow be willing to travel to America and present his Beethoven marathon before audiences in New York and Boston? And would he be willing to conduct one of the New York orchestras, since America had not yet heard him in a role in which he was widely regarded as the greatest living master? Nothing could be done before March of the following year, Bülow told Schwab, after the orchestral season in Berlin had ended. And his decision must hinge on getting the right financial terms, and above all on finding the right pianos. So Schwab set to work, and succeeded in both endeavours.

Return to America, 1889–1890

> This country is a veritable Canaan. Saint Liberty is the mother
> of all good and beautiful things.
> —Bülow[1]

I

Bülow set sail for America from Bremen on board the steamship SS *Saale*, on March 14, 1889, accompanied by his 'two Maries'—his wife and their young friend Marie Ritter. 'What a marvel this floating town is,' Bülow enthused over the state-of-the-art passenger liner. 'The most Bismarckian order reigns overall, and in everything'.[2] Eight days later, after a smooth crossing, the little party was in New York. They checked into the old Hotel Normandie, situated on the east corner of Broadway and 38th Street, not far from the Metropolitan Opera House, where Bülow was scheduled to conduct his opening concert.

When he began negotiations with Bülow, Frederick Schwab was the music critic for *The New York Times*, a position he had held since 1875. His career deserves some passing mention for it was tinged with notoriety, although it is unlikely that Bülow was at first aware of it. By acting as Bülow's impresario, Schwab was placing himself in a highly public conflict of interest. It raised eyebrows, with the notable exception of those of

---

1. BNB, p. 669.
2. HB-CM. Unpublished letter dated March 14, 1889. Built in Glasgow in 1886, for the North German Lloyd shipping line, the SS *Saale* carried 1,240 passengers—150 first class, 90 second class, and 1,000 third class. The name of the ship's commander was Captain Richter. These statistics would be largely irrelevant to a life of Bülow were it not for the fact that on Friday, March 22, the last day of the transatlantic crossing, Bülow gave a benefit concert 'for the Seamen's orphanage of the Norddeutscher Lloyd, Bremen'. Was this the first piano recital ever presented on the high seas? According to the ship's log, the vessel was still 177 miles out to sea on March 22, 1889. A rare copy of the programme is preserved in the Deutsche Staatsbibliothek (Sig. Db. 1815. Mus. NL, HvBülow F IV, 11). Marie Ritter, incidentally, the young companion whom Bülow and his wife took with them to America, was the niece of his boyhood friend Alexander Ritter.

The 'S.S. Saale'. A photograph.

Schwab himself, whose journalistic career had always been marked by scandal, gossip, and good old-fashioned corruption. In earlier years, as the chief drama critic of *The Times,* he had been accused of accepting bribes in exchange for positive reviews. He had also pursued an affair with the celebrated actress Adelaide Neilson while cheerfully reviewing her plays, and even acting as her agent. *The Times* had been forced to dismiss him when a group of managers from the Broadway theatres threatened to re-move their advertising from the newspaper, but he had somehow man-aged to bounce back as its music critic.[3] If Bülow became aware of these rumours he dismissed them, for he knew that few people were so well ac-quainted as Schwab with the musical life of New York. Moreover, Schwab had found some wealthy backers to bring Bülow to America, and had con-vinced them that they would make money. He had also signed a contract with the piano firm of Knabe & Co., committing Bülow to the exclusive use of their instruments while he was in America.

II

Nearly thirteen years had elapsed since Bülow was last in the New World, and the country had undergone vast changes. Greater New York had grown into a city of three-and-a-half million people, and was now the second largest in the world, refreshed by wave after wave of European immigrants. The five boroughs—Queens, the Bronx, Brooklyn, Richmond, and Manhattan—were on the point of merging into one huge metropo-

3. In its issue of May 25, 1878, the *Dramatic News* fired with both barrels when it wrote '[Schwab] did not hesitate to take money from managers at every available opportunity, ostensibly for work done, but in reality to purchase favorable opinion. In fact by his public and private acts he brought dishonour on his calling'. See also ROD, pp. 13–20.

A New York street scene, 1885. 42nd Street at Madison Avenue.

lis, with Manhattan at its centre, a fact made inevitable by the completion of the Brooklyn Bridge in 1883, which now dominated the New York skyline. Another feature of that ever-changing silhouette, not present at the time of Bülow's earlier visit, was the Statue of Liberty, dominating New York's Upper Bay, which had been dedicated by President Grover Cleveland in 1886. Manhattan after dusk was now beginning to look like a fairyland. Much of Broadway was illuminated at night with electric street lighting; Madison Square was bathed in the light of powerful arc lamps placed on top of a 160-foot-high tower. The effect was described as 'that of pale moonlight'.

The telephone had meanwhile been invented and had made instant communication possible between diverse parts of the continent. This, together with the rapid growth of the American railway system, whose thousands of miles of tracks now stretched from sea to shining sea, had made the introduction of 'time zones' inevitable. Until 1883 the railways had relied on local 'sun time', making the accuracy of their hundreds of timetables a dubious undertaking. At noon, on November 18, 1883, the nation's telegraph lines had transmitted Greenwich Mean Time (GMT) to all the major American cities, and the authorities had adjusted their clocks.

This simple act had transformed the commercial life of the nation. It galvanized the stock market, to take one simple example, whose continuously fluctuating stock prices, and the times of their trade, were now instantly available in all parts of the country. Bülow, whose own life was so tightly structured, delighted in these scientific marvels, that enabled him to communicate information instantly, and allowed him to predict with pinpoint accuracy the time that his train would pull into the local railway station—however remote the destination.

In 1883, the Metropolitan Opera House had opened to great fanfare, and was now central to the musical life of the city. Every mature opera of Wagner (with the exception of *Parsifal*) had been given there during the 1880s, under the direction of Anton Seidl. The city also boasted two professional symphony orchestras. The New York Philharmonic Orchestra had been founded as early as 1842 and tended to specialize in the German classics, a natural reflection of the repertoire that its long succession of German conductors had brought to the podium—George Loder, Theodor Eisfeld, and Carl Bergmann among them. By contrast, the New York Symphony Orchestra, founded in 1878 by Bülow's old colleague Leopold Damrosch, promoted the more modern music of Liszt, Wagner, and Berlioz; after the death of Damrosch, in 1885, the orchestra had been taken over by his son, Walter, who, as we learned earlier, had for a time received conducting lessons from Bülow. Nor must we forget the eighty-piece Theodore Thomas Orchestra, which in the view of many occupied pride of place in America's musical life, for it not only gave regular concerts in New York but extended its reach along the fabled 'Thomas Highway' to Philadelphia, Chicago, Boston, and across the border into Canada.

As for Bülow himself, his image was quite different from that of the brilliant concert pianist who had roamed the country in 1875–1876. He was returning to America as the chief conductor of the Berlin Philharmonic Orchestra, and was generally regarded as the preeminent executive musician of his time—one, moreover, whose piano playing, especially of Beethoven, had ripened and become the stuff of legend. New Yorkers were to hear him in both roles.

III

Bülow's opening concert took place at the Metropolitan Opera House, on March 27, where he had been engaged to conduct an orchestra of eighty players drawn from the combined ranks of the New York Philharmonic and the New York Symphony orchestras. It was the happy idea of Frederick Schwab to turn the event into a fund-raising concert, in benefit of the 'Workingmen's School and Free Kindergarten'. Whatever the merits of this particular charity, it had the desired effect of attracting a capacity audience of more than 2,000 listeners. This was the first orchestral concert that Bülow had ever conducted in America, and many of New York's musical elite were there, including Damrosch, Seidl, and Thomas.

BERLIOZ	Overture to *Benvenuto Cellini*
MASSENET	Aria from 'Hérodiade'
	sung by Emma Fursch-Madi (soprano)[4]
BRAHMS	Symphony no. 4, in E minor, op. 98
	Intermission
SAINT-SAËNS	Two fragments from 'Samson and Delilah'
	sung by Emma Fursch-Madi
BEETHOVEN	Symphony no. 8, in F major, op. 93
WAGNER	Overture to *Tannhäuser*

The New York Times began its lengthy review with a description of Bülow on the podium:

No doubt there were many curiosity seekers at the Metropolitan Opera House last evening. These saw a wiry little man, with a strikingly-intellectual head and a picturesquely-nervous manner, conduct an orchestra with a marvelously-expressive variety of gestures. Those who had concerned themselves less with curiosity than with art recognized once again the existence of a powerful musical force in Dr. Hans von Bülow. It is 12 years since he was here before, but he is still an active man, brimming over with energy, and as masterful in spirit as ever.[5]

This otherwise laudatory article, written by W. J. Henderson, contained two important reservations. The first had to do with the orchestra. Because the players were drawn from two different organizations, Henderson observed, they were unused to working with one another. Impressive though the results were, more rehearsals might have allowed the ensemble to respond to the unusually wide range of expressive gestures coming from the podium. The other reservation had to do with Bülow's interpretation of Beethoven's Eighth Symphony, or rather its third movement. Henderson reminded his readers that the Tempo di Menuetto is clearly marked ♩ = 126 by the composer. So why did Bülow adopt a tempo

---

4. Emma Fursch-Madi (1847–1894) was a favourite with the New York public, and at the time of Bülow's arrival in New York she was regularly appearing in leading operatic roles at the Met.

5. Issue of March 28, 1889.

of ♩ = 93? 'We should like to know his reasons', he intoned in *The Times*, 'for performing this movement so slowly'. Bülow made no public reply, although he could easily have reminded everyone that even during Beethoven's lifetime the composer's metronome markings were regarded as notoriously unreliable, and Beethoven himself had sometimes changed his mind about them.[6] For the rest, the thought of the hapless Henderson holding a score of the Beethoven symphony in one hand and a stopwatch in the other presents an image best left undisturbed.

It is worth pausing here to add some detail to this 'Beethoven controversy', which briefly held New York's intelligentsia in thrall. Bülow, after all, was now identified as the greatest Beethoven interpreter of his generation. *The Times* had raised a legitimate issue in asking why he had departed so radically from the published metronome mark of the Tempo di Menuetto. We earlier remarked that Bülow made no public reply. A day or so after the concert, however, he made one privately to Henderson, 'in the course of an hour's chat', and the critic published Bülow's comments in a lengthy article in *The New York Times* on April 1. Bülow also wrote a personal letter to Henry Krehbiel, the powerful critic of The *New York Tribune*, in which he put forward a compelling defence of his position. Krehbiel, a keen admirer of Bülow, had evidently taken it upon himself to contact Bülow about a matter that seemed to be getting out of hand. He was at that moment devoting thousands of words to Bülow's New York concerts[7] and Bülow doubtless thought that he owed Krehbiel the courtesy of an explanation. His letter is a document that retains much interest for modern conductors. The nub of the problem for Bülow was clear: because the designation 'Tempo di Menuetto' cannot be reconciled with Beethoven's metronome mark of ♩ = 126, one of them has to go. Bülow abandoned the metronome. His thesis falls into five parts, and can be paraphrased as follows:

1. Did Beethoven himself put ♩ = 126 in his score?
2. Was the metronome he used the same as it is now, seventy years later?
3. Compare this movement with the Menuetto of the Piano Sonata in E-flat major, op. 31, no. 3 (♩ = 88) or the Menuetto from Mozart's *Don Giovanni*:

---

6. Beethoven published his first eight symphonies without any metronome marks at all. It was only about five years after the composition of the Eighth that he supplied them in a supplement to the *Allgemeine Musikalische Zeitung,* on December 17, 1817. By then he was profoundly deaf, and could only reconstruct his music in his imagination.

7. They are to be found in KRNY, vol. 4, pp. 176–185; and vol. 5, pp. 63 and 65.

4. It is impossible to obtain clarity in the Trio at a speed of ♩ =
    126. The triplets in the cello accompaniment sound like 'cater-
    wauling knee-fiddles'.
5. There is a want of dignity in the drums and trumpets, which,
    Bülow continued, should be played with 'fiery stateliness'.

He tells us that he derived his conception from Richard Wagner (who had never believed that Beethoven's metronome
marks were authentic) and from Louis Spohr (who had played
the symphony under Beethoven's direction at its premiere in
1814). The interpretation he offered to New Yorkers, Bülow
argued, was rooted in tradition.

What also struck Bülow with force was a point ignored by his interlocu-
tors. Beethoven does not simply call this movement a 'Menuet'. He provides instead the even more emphatic title 'Tempo di Menuetto'. If language means anything at all, that can only denote 'to be played in the
tempo of a Menuet'. As Bülow saw it, if you do not understand the difference between a piece called a Menuet, and a piece that must be played
in the tempo of one, you do not really understand the problem.[8]

8. Wagner devoted a good deal of space to this same distinction in his book *On Con-*
ducting, pp. 25–28, which formed the basis of Bülow's own conception. We also find Wagner discussing the same matter in *Mein Leben* (WML, p. 329). The entire debate about the
correct tempo of the Menuet of the Eighth Symphony was a very old chestnut, in fact, and
it would be surprising if Henderson thought that he was raising anything new. A widely
publicized contretemps had arisen over exactly the same issue ten years earlier, in London.
The critic of the *Monthly Musical Record* had attacked August Manns for traditionally taking
the Menuet too *fast* at his Crystal Palace Concerts. Manns had written a spirited rejoinder
in which he defended Beethoven's published metronome mark of ♩ = 126. See MMR, January 1, 1878, pp. 5–7. It seems that whenever they were in search of good copy, the critics
could have things both ways.

IV

It was to Bülow's piano playing that attention now turned. Schwab had arranged for him to give his Beethoven Cycle in New York's Broadway Theatre, and to accomplish all four recitals within five days, giving the pianist one day's rest at the halfway point.[9] A severe downpour of rain drenched the city on the afternoon of the first day, April 1, but it could not keep the crowds away. The 2,000-seat auditorium was packed, for the audience, which contained many of the city's musical elite, knew that they were witnessing something unique. According to Henry Krehbiel, who reviewed the entire cycle for The *New York Tribune,* there were so many professional and amateur musicians in the audience, and such an array of scores, 'that the recitals seemed a good deal like a post-graduate course in Beethoven interpretation'. Krehbiel went on to declare that these four recitals constituted 'the most eloquent exposition of the principal piano sonatas and variations of Beethoven that had ever been vouchsafed them'. Bülow was now in his sixtieth year, and some listeners thought he had lost something of his digital flexibility. It is true that he no longer possessed either the strength or the opportunity to practise with the unrelenting persistence of former years. Occasionally his fingers would stumble, and now and then he might even drop a phrase. But none of this mattered in the context of these magical afternoons. As Krehbiel expressed it, 'The old master was not performing as a virtuoso, but interpreting as a disciple of the supreme musical creator of the century'.[10] Against this, we should recall that at his final recital (on April 5) Bülow summoned the strength to play the Fugue from the *Hammerklavier* Sonata as an encore.

The following day Bülow was asked to write an endorsement for the Knabe piano, which was serving him so well and with which he was obviously pleased:

'The Knabe Pianos which I did not know before have been chosen for my present concert tour in the U.S. by my impresario and accepted by me on the recommendation of my friend Bechstein ac-

---

9. Monday, April 1; Tuesday, April 2; Thursday, April 4; and Friday, April 5. It will be recalled that Bülow always ended his Beethoven Cycle with the posthumously published 'Rondo a capriccio in G major'—popularly known as 'Rage over a Lost Penny' ('Die Wut über den verlornen Groschen'). At his concert on April 5, this was translated for the benefit of his American audience as 'The Anger over a Missing Dime'! It was not the only occasion when something was lost in translation. At Bülow's recital in the First Baptist Church in Brooklyn, on March 29, Liszt's two Concert Studies *Waldesrauschen* and *Feux-follets* were also mangled in translation, emerging as 'In the Woods' and 'Dance of the Hobgoblins', respectively.

10. The *New York Tribune,* April 2, 1889.

Music Hall.

———•·—

MONDAY, APRIL 15,
TUESDAY, APRIL 16,
WEDNESDAY, APRIL 17,
THURSDAY, APRIL 18,

At 3 P. M. Precisely,

DR. HANS VON BÜLOW

IN THE

BEETHOVEN CYCLUS

UNDER THE MANAGEMENT OF

MR. FREDERICK A. SCHWAB.

———

THE KNABE PIANO USED IN ALL BÜLOW CONCERTS.

E. W. TYLER, 178 Tremont St., Sole Agent.

Im April 1889 spielt Bülow in Boston an vier aufeinander folgenden Abenden
erneut seinen Beethoven-Zyklus

Bülow's 'Beethoven Cycle' in Boston's Music Hall, April 1889. A concert billing.

quainted with their merits. Had I known these Pianos as now I do I would have chosen them by myself as their sound and touch are more sympathetic to my ears and hands than all others of the country.

New York, 6th April, 1889.
Dr. Hans von Bülow
To Mr. William Knabe and Co.

Once again we are given a hint as to the qualities Bülow most valued in pianos. These included a responsive touch, a reliable action, a range of colour, and above all the capacity to project the multiple layers of sound that constituted the hallmark of his playing. The same day that he signed this endorsement, Bülow fell down the marble staircase of the Normandie Hotel and injured his right leg. He wrote that it turned 'the colour of bishop's violet' and that he would bear the signs of it for weeks. For a time he walked with a limp and whenever he changed positions it was hard for him to suppress a groan.[11] This was the condition in which Bülow gave some additional Beethoven recitals in Brooklyn, and other boroughs of New York during the week following.

So memorable was the opening Beethoven Cycle in Manhattan that the irrepressible Frederick Schwab informed the public that he had, as a result of its response, arranged for Bülow to repeat the concerts in Boston's Music Hall later that month. The fact that the Boston recitals had actually been planned weeks in advance was a bagatelle with which Schwab had no intention of confusing the public. With all the false modesty that he could muster, he credited the public itself for the wave of success on which these concerts were sweeping towards Boston:

> Mr. Frederick A. Schwab has the honour to announce that, encouraged by the success of the BEETHOVEN CYCLUS in New York— every seat in the Broadway Theatre having been sold for the four concerts before the first performance—he has arranged for a repetition of Dr. HANS VON BÜLOW'S matchless recitals of Beethoven's masterworks for the piano, at the Boston Music Hall, on the afternoons of Monday, April 15, Tuesday, April 16, Wednesday, April 17, and Thursday, April 18, at 3 o'clock.

The Boston recitals aroused the same sort of enthusiasm as the ones in New York. As Bülow walked swiftly across the stage of Boston's great

11. HB-CM. Hitherto unpublished letter, dated April 7, 1889.

Music Hall towards the Knabe grand piano, many memories were stirred. Everybody knew that it was on this same platform that he had made his American debut almost thirteen years earlier. After acknowledging the uncommonly warm applause from his 'modern Athenians', Bülow sat down at the keyboard and began the Cycle, as usual, with Beethoven's Sonata in A major, op. 2, no. 2. This time Frederick Schwab had given him just four days to accomplish the marathon, with no day of rest.[12] Once again it was the musical connoisseurs who turned out in large numbers, and made these recitals so memorable. It prompted the critic of the *Boston Daily Advertiser* to come out with a phrase that lingered long after the last chords of Bülow's playing had faded away. 'Hundreds of young pianists if asked this week, "Who is your teacher?" may truthfully respond, "Dr. Hans von Bülow"'[13]

V

While he was in Boston, Bülow made more history. He cut his first cylinder recordings for Thomas Edison, who had despatched his chief recording engineer, Theodore Wangemann, to the city in order to set up his complex apparatus on the stage of the Music Hall. Bülow recorded what he called 'Chopin's last Nocturne'—presumably the one in E major, op. 62, no. 2. 'Five minutes later', he told Cécile Mutzenbecher, 'it was re-played to me—so clearly and faithfully that one cried out in astonishment'.[14] Wangemann also played other cylinders for Bülow, including parts of a Schumann symphony that had been recorded by the Theodore Thomas Orchestra, and also Lilli Lehmann's entrance as Brynhilde in Wagner's *Die Walküre*. Bülow went into raptures and described Edison's cylinders as 'acoustical marvels'. He was not satisfied with his own recording, however, claiming that the presence of the machine had made him nervous.

Bülow had long wished to meet Edison himself. On Saturday, April 13, he and Marie made a detour to Orange, New Jersey, while they were en route to Boston, in order to pay their respects to the great man. There they found the inventor resting, utterly exhausted, after having worked straight through without sleep for five days and nights. The couple was greeted instead by Edison's young wife, Mina Miller, a woman half his age, whom Bülow described as the inventor's 'nymph-companion'. Did

12. The Boston recitals took place on Monday, April 15; Tuesday, April 16; Wednesday, April 17; and Thursday, April 18. See the playbill on page 407.

13. Issue of April 19. *The Musical Courier* was equally enthusiastic, and in its issue of April 24 described Bülow's Beethoven cycle as a 'Beethoven Cyclone'.

14. HB-CM. Hitherto unpublished letter dated 'Boston, April 15, 1889'. In many editions of Chopin's Nocturnes, the 'last' one is the posthumous one in E minor. Bülow does not tell us which one he played.

Bülow and Edison ever meet? Bülow is silent on the matter. Many years later, however, Marie was asked about this visit to Orange, and she recalled that not only had they met Edison, but that Bülow had actually recorded a Chopin mazurka for him; the results, however, were 'pitiful'.[15]

There is a detailed description of Bülow's encounter in Boston with Theodore Wangemann and the Edison phonograph in the *American Art Journal* for April 27, 1889. Wangemann went to Boston for the express purpose of recording Bülow's recitals—not only taking them in, as the *Journal* adroitly put it, but taking them down as well. It seems entirely possible, then, that Bülow recorded far more than the solitary Chopin nocturne about which he went into raptures with Cécile. For according to this same *Journal*'s music critic, 'behind the screen there was a big-mouthed phonograph taking in the afternoon's music'. The implication is that other piano pieces were recorded as well. Because each cylinder was unique, and could not at that time be replicated, it was Edison's practice to buy them up. What became of them? Their whereabouts is unknown. In one of the great understatements of nineteenth-century music criticism the *Journal* added that 'a great future is before the Phonograph'.

Reports of Bülow's nervousness in the presence of Edison's phonograph, and of his 'cry of astonishment' as he listened to the playback, crossed the Atlantic and led to a colourful embellishment in the *Musical Times*:

> After playing upon the pianoforte, from which issued sounds compared to the soft and dreamy gurgle of a brook, the far-off sighing of the night wind and the roar of the cataract, [Bülow] is described as placing the phonograph tubes to his ears; now a look of surprise creeps over his features, his face becomes ashy pale, he staggers back from the machine exclaiming: 'Mein Gott! Mein Gott! It is bewitched'. Recovering from what was almost a faint, he begs to be sent home at once, saying that his nerves are completely unstrung, and he must have rest.[16]

With nerves unstrung or not, the next leg of Bülow's tour took him to Philadelphia and another repetition of his Beethoven Cycle. Once again hundreds of music students and teachers formed the bulk of his audi-

---

15. From an unpublished letter of Marie von Bülow, dated 'Berlin, February 9, 1932'. IPAM, Anderson Scrapbook. See also HB-CM, Bülow's unpublished letter to Cécile Mutzenbecher on the same topic, dated 'Boston, April 15, 1889'. See also note 20.

16. MT, August 1, 1889.

ence, and most of them brought their scores to the concert. The *Philadel-phia Evening Telegraph* wrote:

> Here was an opportunity not often to be enjoyed by earnestly musical people—a chance to learn something to be stored for future use, to be taught how to enjoy. The strange combination made the occasion unique. Music teachers and students could be seen by the hundreds in the house, following on the books in their laps the work of the intense little man at the piano-forte.[17]

From Philadelphia, Bülow returned to New York to begin rehearsals for what the enterprising Schwab had grandly billed as Bülow's 'farewell' to America, adding that the conductor's final appearance would mark 'the close of a series of Concerts absolutely unprecedented in respect of artistic impressiveness and material success'. That last phrase 'material success' was Schwab's delicate way of telling everybody that he had made a handsome profit. In earlier days Bülow, who was violently opposed to the American way of mixing music and Mammon, would almost certainly have made a public protest from the podium, but he remained silent. In fact, for the entire duration of this American trip he made neither a single speech nor wrote a single letter to the newspapers. For this we must undoubtedly thank Marie von Bülow, whose constant presence at his side had a calming influence on him. On May 2, Bülow once more mounted the podium of the Metropolitan Opera House and conducted an orchestra of more than 100 players for his 'farewell' programme. The auditorium presented a rather unusual spectacle. It was still decked out with streamers and bunting left over from the centennial celebrations, held three days earlier, of George Washington's inauguration as the first president of the United States on April 30, 1789. Surrounded by these remnants of patriotic fervour, Bülow brought down his baton on an all-German programme:

BRAHMS	*Tragic* Overture, op. 81
HAYDN	Symphony no. 102, in B-flat major
MEYERBEER	*Struensée* Overture
	Intermission
BEETHOVEN	Symphony no. 3, in E-flat major (*Eroica*), op. 55
WAGNER	Overture to *Die Meistersinger*

At the rehearsal, which Bülow conducted as usual from memory, there occurred an amusing altercation with the orchestral librarian, Russell by name. Bülow was about to begin the *Tragic* Overture, when he noticed

17. Issue of April 25, 1889.

that there was no contrabassoon sitting among the players. 'Where is the contrabassoon?' he called out to Russell. 'Why is there no contrabassoon engaged?' Russell protested in vain that he had not been told to engage a contrabasson. A major conflagration seemed all but assured. Suddenly, Bülow's anger melted away and he began the rehearsal. His insider's knowledge of what each instrument was supposed to do was on full display that day, and impressed all who witnessed it. It must have impressed Russell too, who sat through the entire session in a state of high anxiety, wondering what sort of outburst was in store for him. As the rehearsal ended Bülow called Russell over, slipped him a five-dollar bill, and whispered, 'Do not say anything; it was my mistake, there is no contrabassoon in the Brahms Overture'.[18]

VI

This final concert captures our attention for a different reason. Wangemann had set up four phonographs on the platform, and recorded the programme in its entirety. Bülow left the country two days later, and never heard the playbacks. Today the whereabouts of these wax cylinders, like the ones the conductor made in Boston three weeks earlier, is unknown. Three years after the recordings were made, curiosity as to their fate was still very much alive, as witness this comment in *The Century Magazine*:

> . . . At Herr von Bülow's farewell concert in this country two years ago [*sic*], a phonograph was employed to make a record of the whole concert, and particular care was taken with Beethoven's symphony, the *Eroica*. The learned conductor left the country before the phonograms, the results of the evening's work, could be prepared for his hearing, but these results surprised and delighted a host of musical experts. . . .[19]

Were these cylinders destroyed, or are they still lurking in some archive, waiting to be rediscovered? If they ever came to light, would time have taken its toll on the cylinders themselves, the original quality of which 'surprised and delighted the host of musical experts' who heard them? We shall probably never know, and the fact that Bülow himself never heard them, and never even referred to them in his correspondence, suggests that the matter was of small importance to him. It is a matter of

18. DMML, pp. 88–89.
19. Issue of May 1893, p. 153. *The Musical Courier* also confirmed that this concert was recorded: 'An Edison phonograph was an inanimate witness at this concert, and took down the performance of the entire programme, which now can be reproduced with startling and undeniable truthfulness as often as the respective wax cylinders are put into Mr. Edison's great apparatus' (issue of May 8, 1889, p. 367).

importance to posterity, however, and the restoration of the *Eroica* recording especially would provide a remarkable opportunity to assess for ourselves Bülow's reputation as a Beethoven interpreter.[20] Of this concert *The New York Times* wrote:

> The marvellous rhythmical energy which characterized every number, the reposeful symmetry of each interpretation, and the balance preserved among the voices of the band, were quite as noticeable in the work of the orchestra as they have been in the doctor's pianoforte playing. Even when old convictions were disturbed there was no cessation of interest.[21]

Once again the writer was W. J. Henderson, and once again his review contained a major qualification. Among the 'old convictions' that Bülow had disturbed was the tempo of the Overture to *Die Meistersinger*. Henderson found it far too fast, and went on to observe that 'neither Richter nor Seidl . . . plays this music with anything approaching the speed that Dr. von Bülow adopted last night'. The *Musical Times,* on the other side of the Atlantic, rallied to Bülow's defence. Its American correspondent, who had covered the concert for British readers, referred loftily to those American critics 'who have fallen into the habit of regarding Seidl as the great Wagner apostle', and the journal went on to remind its readers that Bülow had conducted the world premier of *Die Meistersinger* with the approval of Wagner himself.[22] Bülow once more refused to be drawn. He appeared to have made a bonfire of his vanities. His unusual silence earned him a commendation from the *Musical Times,* which, doubtless reflecting on some of the upheavals that Bülow had earlier caused in Britain, could not help observing that 'the Doctor distinguished himself . . . by being continually in a good humour, and he sailed away leaving a surprising popularity behind him'.[23]

As Bülow boarded ship on May 5 and set sail for Bremen, he had the satisfaction of knowing that this visit to America had been both an artistic and a financial triumph. Unlike his earlier visit, it had also generated

---

20. In 1932 the recording expert Harry Anderson wrote to Marie von Bülow asking if she herself was in possession of these 'Schallplatten'. In her reply she said that she was not. (Hitherto unpublished letter, dated 'Berlin, February 9, 1932'. IPAM, Anderson Scrapbook.) Anderson went on to ask Marie to confirm a rumour that Bülow might also have made a recording in Berlin. She replied, 'I was not present there and my husband never mentioned it (we lived not in Berlin but in Hamburg then)'. Ibid.

21. Issue of May 3, 1889.

22. Issue of June 1889. See, in passing, Wagner's complimentary remarks about Bülow's premier performance of *Meistersinger* in 1868, p. 151.

23. Issue of June 1889.

an ocean of goodwill, especially among the younger generation of musicians for whom he was now an icon and who clamoured for his return.
The trip had netted Bülow the handsome sum of 13,000 dollars, plus a
further 12,000 dollars for Schwab and the speculators who had brought
him over. Even as the New York skyline disappeared from view, Bülow
knew that he would be back. An invitation had already been issued for
him to return to America the following spring, and by early July the contract had been signed.[24] By then Schwab had retired to Europe, the better
to enjoy the fruits of his many speculations. Bülow's new tour would be
managed by the American impresario Leo Goldmark.

VII

On March 12, 1890, the Bülows crossed the Atlantic for a second time on
the SS *Saale* from Bremen, and headed directly for Boston. The crossing
was rough and, as Bülow put it, 'not without its dangers'; consequently,
they arrived in Boston a day-and-a-half late, and Bülow's first concert
had to be rescheduled. Boston itself was paralyzed by a late winter snow-
storm, the streets were blocked, and most traffic came to a standstill. The
Bülows cocooned themselves in the comfortable Parker Hotel and waited
for the inclement weather to die down. The headline in *The Boston Globe*
confirmed what they already knew. 'Twas a Tempestuous Day for Craft Off
the Coast'.[25]

Bülow was billed to give three piano recitals in Boston's Music Hall,
on March 24, 27, and 31. Because of the winter storm, the first one was
transferred to April 5. The opening concert on March 27 was typical of
the varied repertoire presented to his 'New Athenians':

BACH	Chromatic Fantasie and Fugue
MOZART	Sonata in F major
MENDELSSOHN	Variations sérieueses, op. 54
SCHUMANN	Faschingsschwank aus Wien, op. 26
CHOPIN	Nocturne in E-flat major, op. 9, no. 2
	3 Mazurkas opp. 50
	Polonaise in F-sharp minor, op. 44
	Tarantella, op. 43

The other two concerts were equally unremitting and included big works
such as Brahms's F minor Sonata, op. 5, Schumann's C major Fantasie,

---

24. HB-CM. Unpublished letter dated 'July 8, 1889'.
25. Issue of March 20, 1890.

op. 17, and Schubert's Sonata in A minor, op. 42. Bülow was refusing to spare himself, despite his failing health.

While Bülow was in Boston, he learned of Bismarck's dismissal as chancellor of Germany by Kaiser Wilhelm II. According to Marie von Bülow he was completely stunned by the news, regarding it as a 'personal catastrophe'.[26] For two years he brooded over this matter. The volcano finally erupted in his famous speech, delivered from the podium of the Berlin Philharmonie before a largely hostile audience, in which he 're-dedicated' Beethoven's *Eroica* Symphony to Germany's true hero, the Iron Chancellor. The colourful story is told in detail on a later page.

Bülow was now awaited in New York, where memories of his Beethoven recitals the previous year were still fresh. He had been engaged to give four matinée concerts in the Broadway Theatre during the afternoons of April 1, 2, and 3, and May 2. On this occasion hardly a note of Beethoven was to be heard.[27] He concentrated instead on some of the bigger works of Brahms, Chopin, and Schumann. Obviously pleased both with himself and his public, Bülow wrote enthusiastically to Hermann Wolff, 'Yesterday I surprised even myself with the Schumann Fantasie, op. 17, whose colossal effect here I could hardly dream of!' He enclosed some cuttings from the New York press, which confirmed his own high opinion of his playing. According to the *Tribune,* 'Some of his work in the last sonatas of Beethoven excepted, this performance [of the Fantasie] was the loftiest exhibition of pianoforte-playing which the redoubtable doctor has given in New York. . . . A more eloquent reading of the Fantasie could scarcely be imagined'.[28] *The New York Times* agreed: 'He played admirably. His rendering of the 'alla marcia' in the Schumann Fantasie showed what a grand store of reserve power he possesses'.[29] It was left to *The New York Sun* to sum up the general feeling when it reported on his last recital. 'His stupendous achievements in piano work and his marvellous

26. Bismarck was dismissed as chancellor on March 18, 1890. Two days later he resigned from the Reichstag as well. In a letter to Helen Raff, Bülow later observed, 'Since 20 March of this year, my patriotism has suffered very badly' (BB, vol. 7, p. 301).

27. The solitary exception was Beethoven's short two-movement Sonata in F major, op. 54, which he played at his second concert, and we believe that Bülow chose it for a purpose. The sonata begins with a menuet—the only one in Beethoven's entire output to do so. Moreover, the movement is headed 'In tempo d'un Menuetto'—like the Menuet of the Eighth Symphony. In light of the dispute over Beethoven menuets in which he had been involved on his previous visit, it seems that Bülow was determined to have the last word. In his own edition, the movement moves at a modest $\bf \rfloor = 104$.

28. Issue of April 4, 1890.

29. Issue of April 4, 1890.

grasp of the intellectual forms of music grow upon the listener with every repeated hearing. He is one of the musical monuments and bulwarks of this century and our public grieves to say "farewell" to such a noble apostle of the divine art'.[30]

Fresh from his New York triumphs Bülow moved on to Chicago, where he had been engaged to play his four-day Beethoven Cycle in the city's Central Music Hall, commencing on April 14, 1890. The *Chicago Herald* expressed the feelings of many when it reported:

> . . . as this will probably be the last opportunity that Chicago people will ever have of listening to the masterly playing of this distinguished artist, the event is of very great importance to patrons of the highest grade of musical art. Dr. von Bülow, the most perfect interpreter of Beethoven the world has ever known, and who knows no rivals except Rubinstein and d'Albert, is now sixty years of age, and this is to be his farewell tour of the United States.[31]

From Chicago, Bülow's farewell tour took him in turn to Cincinnati (April 21), St. Louis (April 23), Pittsburgh (April 25), Washington, D.C. (April 29), Baltimore (April 30), and Philadelphia (May 3), and in every city his audiences continued to express goodwill and even affection towards him.

VIII

Bülow had now been in America for nearly seven weeks, and hardly a day had passed on which he had not given a recital. By the first week in May he was back in New York to begin rehearsals for his final orchestral concert at the Metropolitan Opera House, announced for Saturday, May 10. Once again he led a large ensemble of players, drawn this time from the ranks of the Theodore Thomas Orchestra, for which some additional players had been recruited.

MENDELSSOHN	Symphony no. 3, in A minor (*Scottish*), op. 56
BRAHMS	Piano Concerto no. 2, in B-flat major, op. 83
	soloist, Eugen d'Albert
	Intermission
WEBER	*Oberon* Overture
BACH	Concerto for two pianos, in C minor
	soloists, d'Albert and Bülow
BEETHOVEN	*Leonore* Overture no. 3, op. 72

30. Issue of May 3, 1890.
31. Issue of March 23, 1890.

The presence in New York of Bülow's old colleague Eugen d'Albert was a happy coincidence. They had worked together in Europe a number of times. With the possible exception of Bülow himself, d'Albert understood the Brahms concerto better than any other pianist alive. *The New York Times* called his performance 'superb' and drew attention to d'Albert's 'marvellous range of tonal power from the most subtle pianissimo to the most sonorous forte'. At the work's conclusion, 'the pianist was called out half-a-dozen times'.[32] For the Bach concerto, Bülow pared down the accompaniment to two string quintets—a mere ten players. He himself directed the performance from a favourite Knabe piano. For contractual reasons, d'Albert remained at his Steinway.

This all-German programme was Bülow's fitting farewell to the New World. America would not hear him again. A day or two later he boarded the SS *Fulda,* together with his 'two Maries', and sailed back to Germany.

32. Issue of May 10, 1890.

The Berlin Philharmonic, 1887–1892

II: 'Glory, Honour, and Good Fortune'

> May God preserve you to us in long, long untroubled youthful vital-
> ity and vigour—you, most revered Master, to whom all we young
> ones look up as our sole and only protector . . .
> —Richard Strauss[1]

I

Much of what Bülow was doing after his return from America was men-
aced by the uncertain state of his health. Sometimes his neuralgic pains
caused him little more than a minor inconvenience; but at others his
symptoms broke out with ferocity and his headaches and sinus pains
('like gout in the head') forced him to seek urgent treatments at various
spas, where he consulted a multitude of doctors and subjected himself to
a variety of water cures, massages, and mineral baths. He also underwent
'galvanic' therapy—the application of mild electric shocks to stimulate
the muscles and the nervous system. In July 1890, for instance, he travelled to Heidelberg for a course of galvanic treatment administered by
Professor Wilhelm Erb, the celebrated neurologist and professor of inter-
nal medicine at Heidelberg University. And in November 1890 he mentions that he tried to get rid of his 'maddening neuralgia' with antipyrin—
a contemporary analgesic with a chemical base drawn from coal tar that
was administered hypodermically and which in some patients resulted in
a temporary increase in the heart rate followed by profuse sweating. For
a time it held first place in the treatments of neuritis and rheumatism. But
among the unfortunate side effects was that it raised both the arterial

1. BSC, p. 89.

tension and the blood pressure, the last things that Bülow needed. This modish treatment brought him no long-term benefits either.

His orchestral concerts in Berlin and Hamburg continued unabated, despite his reliance on whatever medications his doctors could prescribe to keep him going. At the turn of the New Year 1892 he received a warm message of support from the players of the Berlin Philharmonic Orchestra, wishing him 'many, many more years of health and contentment', as well as 'glory, honour, and good fortune!' An inspection of his concert programmes reveals that his workload continued unabated. He invited violinist Jenö Hubay and pianist Eugen d'Albert to share the platform with him, both in Berlin and Hamburg; and he continued to introduce unknown music to his audiences, by such composers as Gernsheim, Gade, and Rheinberger, mixing their compositions with more standard fare from his beloved Viennese classics. As the shadows deepened it brought him immense pleasure to receive the Freedom of the City of Hamburg, on February 22, a distinction that acknowledged the yeoman's service he had undertaken in helping to bring the city to the forefront of musical life in Germany.

II

On the evening of March 28, 1892, Bülow gave his fiftieth concert with the Berlin Philharmonic Orchestra. It marked his formal retirement from the position of artistic director. He deliberately chose an all-German programme, consisting of the 'three Bs', as a proper way to say farewell to the Berlin public: Bach's Suite for Strings and Flute; Brahms's Serenade, op. 16; and, after the interval, Beethoven's *Eroica* Symphony. But there was something else on his mind that evening, and it made his farewell unforgettable. This was the occasion on which Bülow made a speech, during which he 'undedicated' Beethoven's *Eroica* Symphony and rededicated it to Bismarck, causing a storm in the newspapers. Two years earlier, it will be recalled, news had been brought to him in Boston of Bismarck's dismissal by the young Kaiser Wilhelm. Bülow had often spoken truth to power, sometimes from the podium, but never before had he done so to such compelling effect.

After delivering an uplifting performance of the *Eroica*, shouts arose from all parts of the hall, 'Bülow, Speech!' Bülow had already made it known that he intended to address the audience at the conclusion of the concert, and word quickly spread that this was to be a farewell speech. As he returned to the podium a respectful silence fell across the auditorium. Everyone thought that they were going to hear the usual platitudes, consisting of dewy-eyed sentiments that are all too often employed in the service of a farewell address. Tonight they would get a shock; Bülow had something different in store for them. He began by reminding his audience

Bülow's 'farewell' concert with the Berlin Philharmonic Orchestra, March 28, 1892. A concert billing.

Bülow addresses his audience from the podium.
A silhouette.

that Beethoven's original intention had been to dedicate the *Eroica* Symphony to Napoleon, the hero of the people. But Napoleon had betrayed this trust by having himself crowned emperor of France, an act that showed him to be no better than the monarchs he had deposed. Beethoven had then torn up the title page of the symphony and had dedicated it instead to his patron, Prince Lobkowitz, Bülow continued, but musicians everywhere found this dedication to be unsatisfactory in the context of such a heroic work. Bülow now came to the nub of his speech. He informed his audience that he had a better idea to propose:

> We need only to think that in a few days, in the course of this week, an important celebration for the whole of the German nation stands before us. In the course of this week a day arrives that is more important than Sedantag,[2] an anniversary whose only pur-

---

2. 'Sedantag' had been celebrated annually across Germany to mark the victory of Prussia over France in the War of 1870, a war whose chief architect had been Bismarck himself.

pose is yet again to provoke neighbourly hate. We musicians, with heart and brain, with hand and mouth, we consecrate and dedicate the heroic symphony of Beethoven to the greatest spiritual hero to have seen the light of the world since Beethoven. We dedicate it to Beethoven's brother, to the Beethoven of German politics, to Prince Bismarck! Prince Bismarck—Hoch![3]

There was a stunned silence. Then pandemonium broke out. Frenetic applause and cheers were mingled with catcalls, jeers, whistles, and shouts indicating displeasure. Everyone in the audience knew of Kaiser Wilhelm's confrontations with Germany's venerable Chancellor Bismarck, the creator of the German Empire, and that the chancellor had been forced to resign because of them. The German people were still in a state of bewilderment over this issue, and no one had yet come forward to break the ominous silence that had descended on the political scene and begin a public debate. Until Bülow, that is. He had had the audacity, through his speech, to praise Bismarck and by implication to criticize the kaiser. Bülow already knew that the kaiser had advised those in government circles who disagreed with the way things were going in the Fatherland to 'shake the dust of Germany from their feet'. Because the din of the audience showed no sign of abating, and because much of it was coming from the kaiser's supporters, Bülow showed his contempt for them by taking out his handkerchief and dusting his shoes. His speech, and the special attention that he devoted to his footwear, became leading stories in the German newspapers.[4]

The decisive battle had been fought at Sedan on September 1. And the day that was even more important than this national anniversary? On April 1, just a few days after Bülow's speech, Bismarck would celebrate his seventy-seventh birthday.

3. BB, vol. 7, pp. 378–381. The 'Eroica' speech also contained some potent comments on the words of the French Revolution—Liberty, Equality, Fraternity. Bülow pointed out that these words were everywhere spoken and nowhere realized. Even without any mention of Bismarck, the speech contained enough inflammatory material to draws the ire of the political right wing. There was, for instance, an admiring reference to the ideas of the nihilistic philosopher Max Stirner, whose book *Der Einzige und sein Eigenthum* ('The Ego and Its Own') had provoked the intelligentsia because of its rejection of religion, state, and even of family, and played a notable role in the intellectual development of both Karl Marx and Henrik Ibsen. The whole of Berlin knew that a week or so earlier Bülow had unveiled a memorial plaque outside Stirner's old house on nearby Philippstrasse, for which he himself had put up the money. Bülow also paid for a new granite headstone to be placed over the philosopher's grave in the Sophienkirchhof, which had fallen into neglect. The 'Eroica' speech, then, amounted to a political manifesto, with Beethoven's revolutionary symphony pressed into service. The *Berliner Reichsbote* went so far as to doubt that Bülow, after making such a speech, would ever be able to conduct in the city again.

4. S-WW, pp. 76–78.

He received threats of violence, but this was nothing new for him and he remained unruffled. The next day he telegraphed Marie, who had remained behind in Hamburg, 'Did my duty'.[5] The audience may have come to hear the 'three Bs', as Bülow had so famously dubbed them, but when they left they knew that he had affixed a fourth name to that list: Bismarck![6]

III

News of Bülow's speech reached Bismarck's ears within hours. It was brought to the former chancellor that same night by Professor Ernst Schweninger, a medical doctor who was present at the concert and who was staying as a guest at Bismarck's home in Friedrichsruh, on the outskirts of Hamburg. It was there that Bismarck expressed a desire to meet Bülow. On April 1, three days after the rededication of the *Eroica* Symphony, Bülow and Marie went to congratulate the German leader on the 'important celebration' to which Bülow had referred in his speech: Bismarck's seventy-seventh birthday. It was one of those moments at which one wishes a camera had been present. The two men looked at each other —Bismarck with his famously long pipe and Bülow with his cigarette. Bismarck thanked Bülow for his public expression of high regard during the Berlin Philharmonic concert. As they chatted, he could not help noticing that Bülow was dressed in mourning. The reason, explained Bülow, was that his brother-in-law, President Bojanowski, had recently passed away,

---

5. BB, vol. 7, p. 382.

6. Before taking his leave of Berlin, Bülow had one last labour of love to fulfil. On April 4 he conducted Beethoven's Ninth Symphony in a benefit concert for the Berlin Philharmonic Orchestra's Pension Fund. The Leipzig *Signale* wrote that 'Bülow was never so celebrated as on this evening. One saw that his recent musical-political speech had not left the slightest trace of unpleasantness'. This was proved when Bülow went to the railway station on April 6 to catch his train back to Hamburg. A large crowd of well-wishers had assembled on the platform to bid him goodbye, and it was there that a touching scene took place. As the throng surged around him a woman rushed out of the crowd at the last moment and planted a farewell kiss on the unsuspecting Bülow's cheek. Her name was Marie Rudolph (known to everyone locally as 'die Zeitungsmarie') and she owned the seltzer booth on Berlin's Potsdamer Bridge, from where she also sold newspapers. She was a fixture in the area, and she had a large circle of loyal customers, including many artists, who used to converse with her as they picked up their newspapers. She remembered everybody, and even before the customer asked for a particular journal, she had it ready to hand. Bülow often chatted with Marie Rudolph on his way to the concert hall, found her well informed about the arts and politics, and invited her to his concerts. The *Nationale Zeitung,* well aware of Bülow's dislike of public demonstrations of affection, described the kiss as 'a historic *fait-accompli*' (issue of July 13). A charming correspondence ensued between Bülow and 'Zeitungsmarie', and Bülow sent her a photograph inscribed with some socialistic words he knew she would appreciate: 'Der Bürgerin von Berlin Fräulein Marie Rudolph, Hänschens Gönnerin, zum freundlichen Erinnern an den 6. April 1892, Dr. Hans von Bülow, Bürger von Hamburg'. ('To the citizen of Berlin, Fräulein Marie Rudolph, Hänschen's patron, in friendly remembrance of April 6, 1892, from Dr. Hans von Bülow, citizen of Hamburg'.)

whom he described as 'a true servant of the prince'. To which Bismarck gave a democratic rejoinder that delighted Bülow, 'Let us call him a fellow-worker!'[7]

That same evening Bülow conducted an all-Beethoven concert in honour of Bismarck's birthday, this time in Hamburg:

Symphony no. 1, in C major, op. 21.
Ballet Music from *Prometheus*
Overture to *Egmont*
> Intermission
Symphony no 3, in E-flat major (*Eroica*), op. 55

The performance of the *Eroica* Symphony was just as spellbinding as the one in Berlin, and Bülow delivered his rededication speech once more. The Hamburg audience, unlike the one in Berlin, proved to be wholly receptive to his comments. They were proud of the fact that Bismarck had taken up retirement in their city. In celebration of the chancellor's birthday, the printed programme contained the bold declaration, 'In Memory of a great man'. This sentence, of course, had been part of Beethoven's original salutation before he tore Napoleon's name off the title page. On the reverse side of the programme Bülow printed a eulogy in the form of his 'Bismarck Hymn'. At the top of the page the name 'Bonaparte' has been crossed out and the name 'Bismarck' substituted. Beneath the rededication Bülow has reproduced the music of the Finale's so-called 'Prometheus' theme, and provided a nationalistic text containing a word-play on Bismarck's name. The last two lines may be freely translated as, 'Bismarck in you we trust, You united us!'[8]

7. ZBG, p. 33.

8. At the foot of the page Bülow has written the impish comment, 'The correction is vouched for by the plagiarist Hans von Bülow'. He presented the original handwritten copy to Bismarck, as a birthday gift. Our understanding of the Bismarck affair is greatly increased when we recall that Bülow had first met the Iron Chancellor in the home of Dr. Carl Petersen more than two months earlier, when the latter had hosted a dinner party in the chancellor's honour, in January 1892. We are told that as Bismarck entered the room with his wife, all the guests rose in a half circle and bowed. Bülow tried to kiss Bismarck's hand, but Bismarck disarmed him and kissed him on the cheek instead! During the dinner, Marie von Bülow was seated next to Bismarck, who asked about her origins. Mindful that her answer might lead her into a political minefield, she nervously admitted that she was Polish. 'In politics the Poles are dangerous', the chancellor replied. But he added gallantly, 'The Polish women through their charm exercise great power over the men' (PBHF, pp. 69–73). Bülow was sitting opposite his idol, transfixed by the evening's conversation. He later said that he felt he was in the presence of true greatness. This private encounter with Bismarck provided Bülow with a stimulating incentive to honour the chancellor in public a few weeks later, and go through with his 'Bismarck speech' in the Philharmonie.

Bülow's 'Bismarck Hymn', set to Beethoven's 'Eroica' theme.

Gustav Mahler attended this concert, and as he was leaving he told an acquaintance, 'Never forget this evening! You have never heard anything like it before, and never will again; it is supreme perfection!'[9]

IV

Mahler had taken up his duties as the director of the Hamburg State Opera in March 1891, and remained there for six years. He frequently attended Bülow's concerts, and was often to be seen sitting on the front row of Hamburg's Convent Garden Concert Hall, score in hand, following every nuance of Bülow's interpretations, some of which he himself would soon adopt. Mahler admired the iron control that the older conductor exerted over his players. As for Bülow, he saw in Mahler a kindred spirit. He was among the first to appreciate what Mahler was trying to do in Hamburg, having himself already rescued from near-disaster some of the sorry productions that passed for the Hamburg Opera at that time. After attending a performance of Beethoven's *Fidelio* conducted by Mahler, Bülow sent the young conductor a laurel-wreath bearing the inscription, 'To the Pygmalion of the Hamburg Opera—Hans von Bülow'. It was meant to imply that Mahler, like Pygmalion of classical times, had breathed life into an inanimate object. Mahler kept it hanging on the wall of his study. According to Bruno Walter, it was the only such tribute that he ever preserved.

Bülow several times made a public show of support for Mahler. He would occasionally hand him the score of a lesser-known work from the podium. At other times, as he accepted the applause, he would bow in Mahler's direction. It is to Bruno Walter that we owe this strange anecdote. Bülow walked towards the podium, and noticed Mahler sitting in his usual place in the stalls. 'Instead of acknowledging the applause', wrote Walter, 'he hurried down the steps of the platform and offered Mahler his baton, inviting him to take his place on the platform'. Mahler became embarrassed and declined the offer. So Bülow returned to the platform and conducted the concert himself.[10] Mahler was Bülow's first choice to take over the Subscription Concerts whenever he himself was indisposed. The two men also socialized. During Mahler's first season in Hamburg, he was an occasional dinner guest at the Bülow home, until the latter's illness made it impossible for him and his wife to do much entertaining.

Towards Mahler the composer, Bülow's attitude was markedly different. He failed to understand Mahler's music, and when Mahler finally overcame his deference towards Bülow and approached him with a request

9. GM, p. 247.
10. WTV, p. 79.

to include his 'Songs of a Wayfarer' in one of the Hamburg Subscription Concerts, Bülow turned him down. He told Mahler that although he had made a serious attempt to 'penetrate the strange style of the songs' it had proved in vain. It would serve neither the interests of the composer nor the singer, he continued, to have him conduct these pieces. Bülow could have left it at that, but he was greathearted enough towards his younger colleague to have Hermann Wolff, the manager of the concerts, invite Mahler to rehearse and conduct the songs himself.[11]

Mahler has described in detail the scene in which he went to see Bülow, in September 1891, with the score of the still incomplete *Resurrection* Symphony under his arm. He played through the 'Todtenfeier' movement to Bülow on the piano, with Bülow standing near the window at the other side of the room. After several minutes Mahler glanced up from the keyboard only to see Bülow with his hands clasped over his ears. It was for Mahler a moment of deep trauma. Somehow he finished the performance, and there was a deathly silence. Bülow finally spoke. 'If this is still music,' he complained, 'then I do not understand anything of music anymore!'[12] From that moment Mahler, who was still struggling to find his way as a composer, realized that he could not rely on the brightest musical intelligence from the previous generation of conductors to help him find his way. Bülow may have done more pioneering work in behalf of modern music than any other conductor of his time, but in his twilight years, and dogged by illness, he had become more conservative in his tastes. Meanwhile, Mahler put his *Resurrection* Symphony aside. It would be revived under dramatic circumstances, less than three years later, in which the dead Bülow himself would play a central role.

V

With the Bismarck incident still fresh in everyone's mind, Bülow decided that there was one other wrong he wished to right, this time of a purely musical nature. A few days after his meeting with Bismarck, Bülow wrote a letter of atonement to Giuseppe Verdi, expressing remorse for having been so foolish, eighteen years earlier, as to publicly criticize the Italian composer's *Requiem*, and in such abrasive language.[13] The injustice meted

---

11. The letter is dated October 25, 1892. See BB, vol. 7, p. 407. That same day, Bülow also wrote to Mahler informing him of the proposal he had just made to Wolff: namely, that Mahler himself conduct the songs. Part of this letter is reproduced in BBLW, p. 176. The background to the situation is well presented in GM, pp. 261–262.

12. Mahler's account was given some years later to the Czech composer Josef Bohuslav Förster, and may be found in JFP, pp. 356–357. See also RHM, pp. 261–262.

13. See pp. 195–96.

out to Verdi had long preyed on Bülow's mind. As Verdi had grown in stature, and the *Requiem* was universally recognized as a masterpiece, Bülow had come to realize that his position was untenable. On April 7, 1892, he fell on his sword:

Hamburg, April 7, 1892.
Illustrious Maestro,

Deign to hear the confession of a contrite sinner! Eighteen years ago the writer committed a crime of making a great—a great journalistic howler against the last of the five kings of modern Italian music. How often he has bitterly regretted it. When he committed that mistake (for which your magnanimity will perhaps have made allowances) he was out of his senses, if you will forgive the mention of the extenuating circumstances. His mind was blinded by fanaticism, by an ultra Wagnerian prejudice. Seven years later he gradually came to see the light. His fanaticism was purged and became enthusiasm.

Fanaticism is an oil-lamp; enthusiasm electric light. In the world of the intellect and of morals the light is called justice. Nothing is more destructive than injustice, nothing more intolerable than intolerance, as that noble writer Giacomo Leopardi says.

Having reached this 'point of knowledge', how much I congratulated myself on it, and how much my life was enriched by it! And how much that field of most precious joys—the artistic ones—has grown because of it! I have started to study your greatest works: *Aida, Otello* and the *Requiem,* of which a recent performance, though it was a poor one, moved me to tears. I have now studied them not only according to the letter which kills, but according to the spirit which quickens. And so, illustrious master, I have come to admire you and to love you.

Will you absolve me and exercise the royal prerogative of forgiveness? I must confess the mistake of the past, and because I am able to do it, set an example to younger brethen who have gone astray.

Faithful to our Prussian motto, *Suum cuique,* I cry: Long live VERDI, the Wagner of our dear allies.[14]

Hans von Bülow (nato 8 Gennaio 1830).

Verdi's reply was equally magnanimous:

14. This was a political reference to the Triple Alliance between Germany, Austro-Hungary, and Italy.

Genoa, April 14, 1892.

Illustrious Maestro Bülow,

There is no shadow of sin in you, and there is no need to talk of penitence and absolution.

If your opinions have changed, you have done well to say so; not that I should have dared to complain. For the rest, who knows? Perhaps you were right in the first place.

However that may be, your unexpected letter, coming from a musician of your worth and standing in the world of art, gave me great pleasure. And that, not out of personal vanity, but because it shows that really great artists can form judgements without prejudice about schools and nationality and period.

If the artists of the North and South have different tendencies, well, let them be *different*. Every one should maintain *the peculiar characteristics of his own nation*, as Wagner has most happily said.

Happy you, who are the children of *Bach*. And we? We too, children of *Palestrina*, once had a great school—and today? Perhaps it is corrupt and in danger of falling in ruin!

If we could only turn back to the beginning!

I am sorry not to be able to attend the Musical Exhibition in Vienna, where I would have not only the good luck to find myself among so many distinguished musicians, but also the grand pleasure of shaking your hand. I hope that my weight of years will be taken into account by the gentlemen who so kindly invited me, and that they will forgive my absence.

Your sincere admirer,

G. Verdi[15]

VI

Bülow remains the only conductor in the long and distinguished history of the Berlin Philharmonic who walked away from that post. One or two of his successors died during their tenure, and one or two others did not have their contracts renewed. But Bülow simply left. It is true that he was suffering from poor health, but that alone would not explain his decision to leave the orchestra. Nor was the Bismarck speech and worries about his physical safety in Berlin a sufficient reason to abandon the city. 'Cowardice is foreign to me', he wrote, 'and I feel it is my duty to carry out my promised support of the Pension Fund I helped to establish'.[16] This prom-

15. BB, vol. 7, pp. 386–388. This correspondence was published almost at once for the whole world to read, and very likely without Bülow's knowledge, by Verdi's publisher G. Ricordi, in the firm's house journal 'Gazzetta Musicale di Milano', August 7, 1892, issue no. 32, pp. 507–508.

16. SBP, p. 55.

Bülow in June 1892. A post-concert pose.

ise was fulfilled within the next few weeks when he returned twice to Berlin, the first time to conduct an orchestral concert and the second time to give a piano recital, the proceeds on both occasions going to the Pension Fund. These concerts were completely sold out, and the audience rewarded Bülow with standing ovations for abiding by his convictions. When he left Berlin a large crowd of people assembled at the railway station to voice their support and shouts of 'Come back! Come back!' arose from all sides. 'Before I come back I must leave!' Bülow quipped.[17]

The true reasons for Bülow's departure from the Philharmonic cannot be found in the mere externals of his life in Berlin, a city he actively disliked. They run deeper than that, and go to the heart of who he was as a man and as a musician. In a private comment he made to his former pupil Buonamici, shortly after he had left the Philharmonic, he remarked that he was 'bored with the monotony of the sublime'.[18] And to this unexpected assertion Marie von Bülow added that at the time of his greatest

17. BB, vol. 7, p. 384.
18. Ibid., p. 366.

triumphs in Meiningen, Hamburg, and Berlin, he had often remarked, 'I expect even more now'. Where, exactly, he expected to find 'even more now', and what form it would take, we cannot know. What is clear is that he was searching for new peaks to conquer. He had served five seasons in Berlin, and had brought the orchestra to a marvellous level of perfection. For a man of Bülow's temperament, the prospect of facing a life of tautology was worse than pointless. The job was done; he must move on.[19] The orchestra, for its part, could hardly comprehend that he wanted to leave them, and begged him to stay. They wrote a letter in which their devotion to their conductor stands revealed. 'Just as the pupil respectfully approaches his master, or the son his father, so the Philharmonic Orchestra approaches you with confidence and love . . .'.[20] Bülow could not be swayed, however. Richard Strauss was brought in to take over the concerts for the following season, one of several temporary conductors who came to the rescue at the moment of crisis. It was to be three years before the orchestra found a worthy successor in Arthur Nikisch.

After the hurly-burly of Berlin, Bülow and Marie sought a temporary respite in Italy, a visit which Bülow sensed he would be making for the last time. They were met in Northern Italy by Daniela and her husband, Henry Thode, and lingered for a few days in their company, while Bülow relived the memories of happier times in a country that had once restored him to health. Bülow and Marie then travelled down to Naples from where they took ship and crossed the Tyrrhenian Sea. Arrived in Palermo, Bülow was reunited with Blandine and her husband, Count Biagio Gravina. He had not seen the couple since their fleeting visit to him in Meiningen, in the summer of 1884. There were now three children of the union,[21] and

---

19. Confirmation of Marie's observations may be found in the unpublished letters of Bülow to Cécile Mutzenbecher. More than two years earlier he had confided to Cécile a surprising desire to retire from his position. The spectre of his sixtieth birthday had begun to haunt him, he told her, a point in life that he regarded as the gateway to old age. However meagre his lifetime achievement, he continued, he did not want whatever he had attained to go uncrowned by default. In brief, it would be better to get out while still at the top of his form. And he added poignantly, 'I do not want old age to become for me synonymous with *decrepitude* as it was with the Great Ones: Liszt, Rubinstein, Joachim . . . (yes indeed, the latter as well, do not doubt it). This year, if all goes well, thanks to the last tour in America, I will be in a position to live modestly . . . on the income from my work'. He asked Cécile not to breathe a word 'of this completely private confidence' to anyone, especially to his agent, Hermann Wolff. 'I plan to disappear from the public arena, to leave it to younger people than me'. And as if to confirm that all his major tasks had been accomplished, he added revealingly, 'Between ourselves, Brahms will not be writing any Fifth Symphony, so what is the use of repeating what is ended?' (HB-CM, unpublished letter, dated 'Hamburg, September 26, 1889').

20. BB, vol. 7, p. 365. Bülow also received a petition from the general public, urging him not to leave the Berlin Philharmonic. It was signed by over 600 well-wishers. The original document is preserved in the Deutsche Staatsbibliothek (Mus. NL H.v.Bülow F IV, 5).

21. Manfredi (b. 1883), Maria Cosima (b. 1886), and Gilberto (b. 1890). A fourth grandchild, Guido, was born in 1896, after Bülow's death.

'Hans von Bülow'. An oil painting by Franz von Lenbach. Munich, June 1892.

Bülow found himself occupying the unaccustomed role of grandfather. He enjoyed relaxing in the Gravinas' imposing residence at Ramacca, which they had named 'the Villa Blandine'. It was a source of profound joy when the family was joined by Isolde, who had not seen Bülow for twenty-four years.[22] In mid-May, Bülow and Marie returned to the Italian mainland and journeyed to Florence, where they were joined once more by Daniela and Henry for a nostalgic reunion in the home of Jessie Laussot. In Jessie's home, surrounded by family members and close friends, Daniela persuaded her father to go to the piano and play one of his favourite Beethoven sonatas, *Les Adieux*. The performance transfixed the small group of hearers and Daniela described it as 'movingly beautiful'. Standing at the end of the piano, the architect Adolf Hildebrand clasped a sketch-pad firmly in his hand, and made a drawing of Bülow's face as he played. This likeness inspired the bronze relief set within the memorial stone designed for Bülow's last resting place in the Hamburg cemetery.[23] The journey back home took Bülow and Marie through Monaco, and from there to Munich, where he sat for the painter Franz von Lenbach.[24] The result was a regal oil painting, executed in May and June 1892, which captures far better than a photograph Bülow's commanding presence on the podium, even though the face shows the ravages of terminal illness.

VII

By mid-June 1892 the Bülows were back in Hamburg, only to find themselves confronting a crisis of a different kind. Earlier that year the city had been struck by cholera, and the disease had reached epidemic proportions. It had begun in the spring of 1892, and now held the city in its deadly embrace. The social life of Hamburg came to a partial standstill, and Bülow's daily activities were disrupted along with everyone else's. Restaurants and cafés remained empty, as people avoided human contact. Tradespeople were kept at arm's length and were dealt with through

---

22. In a communication to Daniela dated 'May 18, Palermo' he addresses his first-born as 'My Precious Cordelia', and tells her that 'Regan and Goneril are amusing me so well—partly because they are so charming and talk so much about you . . .'. Through this allusion to Cordelia, Regan, and Goneril, Bülow sees himself playing the role of King Lear, with Daniela as his favourite (BNB, p. 710). Bülow did not live to witness the tragedy that was all too soon to overtake his daughter Blandine and tear the Gravina family asunder. Through some reckless land speculations, Count Gravina lost money, fell into depression, and in 1897 he committed suicide. Blandine was only thirty-four years old at this time, and was left with uncertain resources and four small children to care for. She never re-married, and never formally re-joined the Wagner circle in Bayreuth, living another forty-four years mainly in Italy. She died in Florence, in 1941.

23. RWHB, p. XLI. See also p. 438.

24. BNB, p. 710.

Hamburg's cholera cemetery during the epidemic of 1892.

the windows rather than allowed through the front doors. Trains were sprayed with carbolic disinfectant as they entered and left Hamburg's railway stations. Bismarck's train, too, was sprayed when it crossed the Austrian border en route to Vienna, as an amusing cartoon in the magazine *Kladderadatsch* showed.[25] In the high-rise tenement buildings, where thousands of poorer families lived in slum conditions, the authorities carried out a mandatory cleansing programme. So-called disinfection squads patrolled the city, accompanied by policemen to give them force of law, and they moved into private apartments and doused everything with carbolic. The medical authorities issued continuous warnings that every household must boil its drinking water. Large water-carriers containing thousands of gallons of boiled water patrolled the city streets and people lined up with buckets at prearranged collection points. As the epidemic gained hold, there was a general exodus out of the city. The Bülows decided to spend some time in Skodsborg, a small Danish resort about fifteen kilometers north of Copenhagen, a quiet backwater with historic buildings and a *Kurhotel,* where Bülow received regular massages. Bulletins describing the mounting crisis in Hamburg were brought to him each day. The death toll climbed above one dreadful peak after another. By August 27 there were 1,105 new cases, and 455 deaths; by August 30 a further 1,000 cases.

25. Issue of September 25, 1892.

On September 2 the highest number of deaths was recorded for a single day—561. Out of 17,000 people who were infected between mid-August and mid-November, 8,700 of them died.[26] Infected people had to be transported from their homes and placed in police cells on cold floors because the hospitals could not accommodate them. 'Is there no Moltke here, then?' exclaimed the *Hamburger Nachrichten,* outraged at the lack of organization.[27] It was in Skodsborg that word was brought to Bülow that particularly distressed him. The music critic of the *Nachrichten,* Dr. Paul Mirsch, had returned to Hamburg from a summer holiday, and within a few brief days had contracted cholera and died. Bülow could not shake off the thought that this relatively young musician had succumbed so swiftly, and the image hung over him like a shroud. He hardly needed the encouragement of his Hamburg physician to stay away from the city, and after prolonging his sojourn in Skodsborg, he and Marie continued on to the relative safety of Berlin.[28]

26. The statistics may be found in EDH, p. 295.

27. Issue of September 7, 1892. Moltke was the victorious Prussian general of the Franco-Prussian War of 1870.

28. On August 26, the *Vossiche Zeitung* complained that there were still only eleven ambulances in the whole of Hamburg. City officials called for volunteers to deal with the dead and the dying, and within two days that number jumped to thirty—although these makeshift vehicles were ill-suited for their grim task. A Viennese journalist, Karl Wagner, who served as a volunteer ambulance-man at the height of the epidemic, left a graphic description of those times:

> The vehicles which were to be used were horse-drawn coaches from which the upholstery had been removed, so that patients, whom we had to wrap in blankets, were carried on the bare wooden seat-frames. Almost inconceivably, five to seven large holes had been cut in the floor of the coach, through which the patients' excretions flowed onto the street!!! To begin with I fetched a 14-year-old girl, an old woman, and a boy; the woman died on the way. . . . The dwellings I entered were begrimed with dirt, so that I was more nauseated by them than by the cholera itself. During my service I transported 132 patients, of whom almost half died on the way. (EDH, p. 329.)

The creation of a so-called 'cholera cemetery' on the outskirts of town was particularly distressing. The municipal cemetery could not accommodate all the dead. Bodies were barracked in makeshift wooden buildings—warehouses of death. From late August, one could observe an endless procession of horse-drawn carts crisscrossing their way through the city in order to pick up the corpses and make for the cemetery gates. There they were unceremoniously bundled into mass graves which were quickly covered over by volunteers armed with shovels who worked around the clock. One of the most moving accounts of these times was left by the pastor of Hamburg's St. Michaelis Church, Georg Behrmann, who would later officiate at Bülow's own funeral. He visited the dead and the dying in their homes, children and adults alike, and even identified the corpses of those in his parish where no family members had survived to take on this sad task. He recalled the bright chimes of the water wagons, sounding death and hope at the same time. He never forgot the night of August 27. Because of the stifling summer heat he had to keep his ground floor window open, and became a helpless witness to the macabre stream of ambulances ('a procession of death') that passed through his district en route to the final resting place (BE, pp. 275–285).

VIII

As it happened, there was a good reason for the Bülows to sit out the month of September in the German capital. On October 4, 1892, the newly built Bechstein Hall was opened to great fanfare. This was an event of great importance to Berlin's musical life and Bülow had been invited to play a leading role in it. The hall was the brainchild of Hermann Wolff and Carl Bechstein, who had long discussed the feasibility of bringing to the city a facility that it had hitherto lacked—a midsized auditorium with a more intimate atmosphere than that offered by the Philharmonie. This 500-seat auditorium, which possessed excellent acoustics, was designed to accommodate piano and lieder recitals, as well as small chamber groups. Carl Bechstein was now sixty-six years old, a pillar of Berlin's musical establishment, his pianos renowned throughout Europe. It was fitting that his firm should have a concert hall bearing his name in which his instruments could be heard under ideal conditions; and it was fitting, too, that Wolff should have access to a recital hall where his distinguished soloists could play the greatest chamber music before a select audience. Located on a small side street, not far from the Philharmonie, Bechstein Hall served as a perfect foil to the main orchestral concerts. Many a visiting soloist, after playing a concerto with the Berlin Philharmonic Orchestra, prolonged their stay in Berlin by a few days in order to give a recital in Bechstein Hall.

Three inaugural concerts were planned as part of the opening festivities, and they took place on October 4, 5, and 6. Hermann Wolff issued invitations to Berlin's intellectual and artistic elite. Not only musicians, but artists, writers, scientists, and politicians flocked through the doors. At Bechstein's express invitation the opening concert was given by Bülow, who got up from his sickbed in order to fulfil what he considered to be a solemn duty to honour his old friend. He was in such pain that while he was in the artist's room, and about to walk onto the platform, he exclaimed, 'Whoever were to put a bullet through my head right now would be my friend'.[29] His programme made no concessions to his frail condition:

MOZART	Fantasia in C minor, K. 475
BEETHOVEN	Sonata in E-flat major (*Les Adieux*), op. 81a
F. KIEL	Variations and Fugue in F minor, op. 17
SCHUMANN	Faschingsschwank aus Wien, op. 26

29. BB, vol. 7, p. 403.

CHOPIN   Nocturne in G major, op. 37, no. 2
Impromptu in F sharp major, op. 36
Scherzo no 3, in C sharp minor, op. 39
Berceuse, op. 57

This recital was Bülow's swan song as a pianist. The other two inaugural concerts, incidentally, given later that week in Bechstein Hall, featured the Joachim String Quartet with Brahms, and Anton Rubinstein with the violinist Carl Halir.[30]

'Hans von Bülow'. A pencil drawing by Franz von Lenbach. Munich, 1892.

IX

Bülow was now at the pinnacle of his fame, but his artistic triumphs had been bought at the expense of his physical condition, and his headaches worsened. Although he was gravely ill, he was persuaded by Hermann Wolff to return to the Philharmonic Orchestra and conduct the final concert of the season on March 13, 1893. It required an iron will for Bülow to

30. See S-WW, p. 146.

do this. He had spent the last several weeks in Berlin's Pankow Hospital for Nervous Diseases, seeking treatment for the control of his pain. In Marie's notebook he had jotted down the following imperative: 'Mach, dass ich das nächste Concert dirigieren kann'.[31] The will became father to the deed. As the small doors behind the orchestra opened and Bülow's dapper figure emerged, he was greeted by a tumultuous ovation. He mounted the podium and bowed to the audience in acknowledgement of this jubilant greeting. His face was white and he had aged; and he was almost certainly medicated, a fact of which the audience (and possibly the players, too) knew nothing. They cared about only one thing: Bülow was back in the Philharmonie:[32]

The programme was severe and consisted of three symphonies.

BEETHOVEN	Symphony no. 4, in B-flat major, op. 60
HAYDN	Symphony no. 96, in C minor
	Intermission
BRAHMS	Symphony no. 3, in F major, op. 90

As the last strains of the Brahms symphony died away, there were shouts for a speech above the applause. In a quiet voice Bülow addressed the audience. 'Allow me to acknowledge this deeply felt demonstration of affection, first of all on behalf of the orchestra for its excellent performance'. There was a slight pause, while he silently reflected on the more turbulent moments with his Berlin audiences across the years. Then he added softly, 'And also to accept it for myself, as an amnesty offered for [my] earlier, mistaken extravaganzas'.[33]

31. 'Make it so that I am able to conduct the next concert'. These words were written down on January 8, his sixty-third birthday. BB, vol. 7, p. 411.

32. In their determination to find a remedy for his condition, Bülow's doctors had already introduced him to an array of pharmaceutical products. At the end of February he was receiving injections of codeine to relieve his neurological pains. When this did not work, his doctors switched to chloral hydrate. The effect of this drug was to induce a euphoric, trance-like condition, during which the patient could at least gain some sleep. Chloral hydrate had been introduced into medicine as early as 1869, and it was popular among artists and the intelligentsia because of the hypnotic mood of well-being it produced in the user. Among its adherents were Dante Gabrieli Rossetti, Friedrich Nietzsche, and the writer Karl Gutzkow. And all this was going on at the time of Bülow's final concerts with the Berlin Philharmonic Orchestra.

For an absorbing account of Bülow's bizarre relationship with the medical profession during the last year or so of his life, see Isolde Vetter's informative *Hans von Bülow's Irrfahrt durch die Medizin*, in BKHB, pp. 100–118.

33. BB, vol. 7, p. 422.

Because of his deep commitment to the Philharmonic Pension Fund, which he had helped to establish, Bülow made the effort to mount the podium one last time, on April 10, 1893. He chose an all-Beethoven programme:

Overture: *Fidelio,* op. 72
Symphony no. 5, in C minor Symphony, op. 67
Intermission
Symphony no. 7, in A major, op. 92
Overture: *Leonore* no. 3, op. 72

At the conclusion of the concert he was so weak that he was unable to speak, so he sat down at the piano and played 'Auf Wiedersehen' from Mozart's *Zauberflöte.* This music appears in Act I, where the 'Three Ladies' attending the Queen of the Night join Tamino and Papageno (whose mouth has been padlocked, rendering him uncharacteristically silent) in a quintet. They repeat several times the words, 'So lebet wohl. Wir wollen gehn. Lebet wohl! Auf Wiedersehen'. ('Farewell. We wish to go. Farewell, until we meet again!' [Exit].) The audience grasped the situation at once. Papageno could not speak, Bülow could not speak. Since he was unable to take his leave of them, they would have to take their leave of him. As Bülow rose from the piano and quietly left the platform, they knew that they would never see him again.[34]

34. This last public appearance of Bülow calls for comment. As is well known, there are four overtures to Beethoven's opera, the *Fidelio* overture itself and the three so-called *Leonore* overtures. To open and close the programme with overtures from the same opera does not appear to make much musical sense. There was, in fact, some symbolism at play. The deeply political social commentary that lies beneath the story of Beethoven's *Fidelio* concerns the struggle and eventual triumph of individual liberty over tyranny. Even as 'Leonora' (disguised as 'Fidelio') is helping to dig her husband 'Florestan''s grave, deliverance is at hand. Among the last sounds that the Philharmonie audience heard under Bülow's direction was the off-stage trumpet call, as it split the air, carrying its blazing message of hope for mankind. Bülow's farewell to the podium demonstrated that he remained a man of the people. That trumpet call was meant not just for him but for everybody.

The Last Days and Death of Bülow, 1893–1894

'Exegit monumentum aere perennius'.[1]
—Horace

I

Word quickly spread that Bülow was seeking treatment as an occasional patient at the Pankow Hospital for Nervous Diseases, where his doctors were conducting some exploratory tests. This led to speculation on the part of the general public that Bülow had lost his reason, and that he had been incarcerated in an asylum for the mentally insane.[2] It has been well said that a lie can make its way around the world at once, while truth is still putting on its boots. Pankow was, in fact, an advanced centre for the treatment of neurological disorders, with a medical faculty which was among the best in the field. Towards the end of April 1893, shortly after his final appearance at the Philharmonie, Bülow agreed to enter the institution as a full-time patient. Even so, it was clear that the doctors who examined him had no idea what was wrong with him, and they subjected him to a variety of unpleasant and largely unnecessary treatments. His immediate symptoms were obvious, for they had driven him to Pankow in the first place: an unremitting pain at the base of the skull, shooting pains of the facial nerve, and some excruciating, if intermittent agonies in

---

1. S-WW, p. 89. 'He erected a monument to himself more durable than one of bronze'.
2. These false reports were picked up almost at once by New York's *The Spirit of the Times*, and published in its issue of January 28, 1893. They were still being repeated by *The New York Times* in its obituary notice of Bülow, on February 14, 1894. By the following month, March 1894, this canard had reached a point where *The Etude* was informing America's pianists that 'von Bülow's insanity has been acute'. Meanwhile, the British press, equally eager not to let the facts get in the way of a good story, was busy publishing its share of deceits. The London *Daily News* even went so far as to say that Bülow's mental illness had forced the doctors to place him under restraints (issue of February 14, 1894). Constance Bache castigated this newspaper in a spirited reply. See MMR, March 1, 1894.

the lower trunk. The doctors treating him also knew of the minor strokes that he had suffered across the years. His periodic fainting fits would also have been a part of the complex medical picture.

In the absence of any clear idea of what to do with their distinguished patient, the Pankow doctors began to experiment on him. The general consensus was that the pains of the facial nerve were caused by infected sinuses, and Bülow was subjected to an unpleasant operation through the left nostril in order to puncture the sinus cavities on that side of the face and drain them. A few days later the wound was cauterized in order to help the healing process. Bülow described this latter procedure as 'horrible enough, still certainly gentler than the bone-sawing place [*Knochensägerei*]', an image on which it does not do to dwell. Shortly afterwards a similar operation was carried out through the right nostril.[3] Cocaine was administered to relieve the pain of these operations. Bülow was in any case given regular injections of morphine while at Pankow in order to ease his general discomfort, and there is some circumstantial evidence to suggest that he became addicted to these opiates. The nasal operations were carried out by someone whose identity was obscured by Marie von Bülow in her edition of her husband's letters, and was merely described by her as 'Dr. Y'. In her memoir of Bülow, however, published in 1925, more than thirty years after his death, Marie identified this 'expert' as Dr. Wilhelm Fliess, a colleague of Sigmund Freud, whose modish theory of 'nasal reflex neurosis' had just become popular among Berlin's intelligentsia.[4] The hypothetical link that Fliess had established between the nose and a variety of neurological symptoms, and the operation that he had devised to sever that link, would today be dismissed as quackery. Fliess was convinced that the membranes of the nose held the key to neurotic symptoms arising from sexual repression. He was later to carry out a similar operation on Freud himself who broke with Fliess when it became evident that the latter's scientific work amounted to little more than psychopathology. Marie von Bülow appears to have been outraged that Fliess was called in to treat her husband without her knowledge, and in a letter to her friend Toni Petersen she relieved herself of some anti-Semitic comments at Fliess's expense.[5] Bülow's baffled doctors would eventually suggest a course of hypnosis, to which he readily agreed, but which, in the understated words

3. BAB, p. 564.
4. Wilhelm Fliess (1858–1928) had published his book *Neue Beitrage und Therapie der nasaelen Reflexneurose* in Vienna, in 1892, just one year before he began to treat Bülow, and he was already a figure of controversy. Marie was determined not to have Bülow's symptoms dismissed by the world at large as psychosomatic in origin, which explains her desire to obscure Fliess's identity. For some interesting, and far from flattering, commentary on Fliess and his theories see JSF, vol. 1, pp. 318–319 and 339.
5. BKHB, p. 107.

of Marie, 'made no impression on my husband'.[6] Beleaguered he might be, but his willpower was too strong to capitulate to the mind of another.

He was a difficult patient. He saw his medical condition with greater clarity than did his doctors, argued with them, and brought much *Galgenhumor* to bear on his situation. In an amusing play on the words 'laudanum-laudamus', he headed one of his letters to Marie 'Te Deum Morphinium laudamus!' [We Praise Thee, O Morphine!]. Another he headed 'Pankow-Paradies' but added, as if not wishing to tempt Providence by making fun of his plight, 'mein Gott, ein privater momentaner Jammerschrei! ['my God, a private moment of lamentation!']. He must often have thought of the dark aphorism, passed on to him ten years earlier by one of his physicians in Gurnigl. 'Death is the bridge to a better life. You have to give the toll-charge to the doctor'.[7] He came to despise his doctors and the empty prattle that passed for a diagnosis, and he wrote to Marie, 'Do you remember the last lines of Kent's in *King Lear?*'[8] He knew that she would, and would also understand why he embraced them. They run:

He hates him
That would upon the rack of this rough world
Stretch him out longer.

Marie saw him for the first time in four weeks when she came to pick him up from Pankow, on May 23. She could not help observing how much older he looked.[9] The following day they had a final consultation with one of the Pankow physicians who observed that Bülow had such a pronounced distrust of his treatment as to make it impossible to pursue it. Overriding the objections of his doctors Bülow discharged himself. That same day Marie took him back to their Berlin apartment, and thereafter became his primary caregiver. She would be called upon to see him through some unimaginable crises in the months to come.

II

Bülow's final sufferings now turned into one long Calvary. The neuralgic pains, which were at first centered at the back of the neck, spread slowly across the entire head. It sometimes felt, in his words, like a 'crown of

6. BAB, p. 569. On August 18, 1893, we even find Marie planning to take Bülow to Paris for a consultation with Jean-Martin Charcot, the celebrated neurologist at the Salpêtrière hospital. She was unaware that Charcot had died two days earlier.

7. 'Der Tod ist die Brücke zum besseren Leben.
   Das Brückengeld hat man dem Ärzte zu geben'. BB, vol. 6, p. 213.

8. BB, vol. 7, p. 437.

9. BAB, p. 566.

thorns'. In an attempt to find some necessary tranquillity, he and Marie travelled in June to the health resort of St. Blasien in the Black Forest, not far from the Swiss border. On June 24 Marie reported that his distress was such that 'the poor man clasped his hand to his mouth in order not to scream! I believed already that insanity might break out at any moment'.[10] From St. Blasien the pair moved to Aschaffenburg, the picturesque 1,000-year-old town in Bavaria, but Bülow was in no condition to admire the beauties of what Ludwig I used to call 'my Bavarian Nice'. By now his body weight had dropped alarmingly and he could barely walk. On September 14, a particularly bad day, he was unable to endure the pain and he 'whimpered the whole day for morphine'. Marie described the source of the pain as 'occipital'. She was torn with doubts about whether she should continue to be responsible for allowing him to suffer in such a way. As she witnessed his struggles, she even wondered whether not only Bülow but she herself would end her days in a mental asylum.[11] The doctor came, and 'hardened by scepticism', did not think that the pain was so bad that Bülow could not bear it. On October 3 Bülow woke up shivering, unable to breathe properly. He went back to bed in the afternoon, and was visited by the doctor who diagnosed pneumonia. 'Imagine my shock', wrote Marie,

> It is a mystery how, with all the precautions, we allowed that to happen. In all the 14 months of suffering, I could not even approximately have sensed this news. But after 24 hours we were already able to take a deep breath . . . and today [Bülow] was permitted to get up for a few hours because lying in bed is detrimental to his other conditions.[12]

For a time there was a suggestion by his doctors that Bülow might in earlier years have contracted malaria, perhaps in Italy or in America, and the patient was given quinine; but this was only one of several false diagnoses. On October 17 he was again visited by a doctor who urged Marie to put a piano in Bülow's room, despite opposition from the patient himself. It is an interesting piece of information for it tells us that Bülow had given up his piano playing in response to his debilitating illness. Marie finally prevailed on Bülow, a piano was installed, but he did not touch it for a couple of days. On the twenty-third she left the apartment to pursue some errand, and when she returned the housemaid exclaimed, 'The Herr Baron is playing really beautifully once again!'[13] Marie could not help

10. BB, vol. 7, p. 443.
11. BAB, p. 570.
12. Ibid.
13. Ibid., p. 571.

smiling at such rustic naïveté. Here was one of the world's great pianists struggling to find his concert fingers, with a Bavarian housemaid as his sole critic. Thereafter Bülow played the piano for at least an hour each day, and the experience seemed to bring him pleasure. On November 12 he was examined by another neurologist, Professor Julius Michel, who not only confirmed severe neurasthenia but also diagnosed Bright's disease, a general failure of the kidneys,[14] which explained the pains in the lower trunk. This last news came, in Marie's words, like a death sentence. It was withheld from Bülow in order not to rob him of hope. Left untreated, Bright's disease would have had the inevitable effect of raising the blood pressure, which in turn would have aggravated all the other symptoms from which Bülow suffered.

Bülow and Marie had now been away from Hamburg for nearly six months. That is a very long time, and it cannot be entirely explained by Bülow's increasingly desperate need to alleviate his symptoms. In June 1893 they had received news that cholera had once more broken out in Hamburg. Thousands of wealthier people were again fleeing the city. The newspapers reported that entire hotels in the Harz Mountains and Thuringia had been reserved for the summer by people fearful that this year's outbreak might exceed last year's in scale. In the event it did not, but caution was still the better part of valour. No one trusted the Hamburg politicians, who had deliberately downplayed the severity of the previous outbreak and might now be downplaying this one.[15] A decisive factor in keeping the Bülows away from Hamburg may have been news that Gustav Mahler had gone down with cholera. He had returned to the city after taking a short summer break, and had moved into new lodgings which turned out to be infected. For several days Mahler hovered between life and death, but was nursed back to health by his sister Justine.[16] Marie wisely decided that they were better off staying in the relative safety of Aschaffenburg until winter arrived and the crisis had passed.

14. Ibid., p. 572.
15. Confirmation that this was so comes from an unexpected quarter. Mark Twain, who was in Germany at the time of the earlier outbreak of cholera, had railed against the Hamburg newspapers for their complicity in keeping the brutal facts from the reader. 'I know now that nothing that can happen in this world can stir the German daily journal out of its eternal lethargy', he wrote. 'One might imagine that the papers are forbidden to publish cholera news'. TCE, pp. 572–573.
16. GM, vol. 1, p. 280. The son of Mahler's new landlady had died, and almost simultaneously the boy's grandmother had become seriously ill. That same night, even as the boy's corpse was being removed from the house, Mahler experienced stomach pains and violent diarrhea. The doctor who treated him the next day diagnosed cholera, but was persuaded by Justine not to send her brother to a hospital, where he might well have died, but to allow her to care for him herself.

III

By December 1 Bülow and Marie were back in Hamburg with the spectre of death hanging over them. They celebrated his sixty-fourth birthday in their apartment, enveloped in a pall of gloom. Four days later, on January 12, Marie heard of a miracle cure in Egypt, and hope was revived. On January 19 they received a visit from Richard Strauss, who confirmed the 'Egyptian cure'; he himself had convalesced there the previous year.[17] He recommended that Bülow should journey to Cairo without delay in order to enjoy the benefits of the dry climate and undergo a course of treatment at Helwan, a famous watering resort on the Nile, with a sanatorium run by German doctors. The hope now was that the wonder-working rays of the Egyptian sun might succeed for Bülow where other cures had failed.

On the afternoon of Monday, January 29, 1894, Bülow and Marie travelled to Berlin's Anhalter railway station, there to await the arrival of the train that would take them on the first leg of their long journey to Cairo. They arrived early, and made their way to the waiting room where they were joined by a group of loyal friends, come to bid Bülow a last farewell. Bülow's widowed sister Isidora von Bojanowski was there, as were Hermann Wolff and his wife, Louise; also present were Richard Strauss, Stanislaus Schanzer (the brother of Marie), Frau Emmy Bock, and the musician-writer Eugen Zabel, who later left a detailed account of this scene.[18] The ever-devoted Toni Petersen had barely strayed from Marie's side for the past few weeks, and she was there, together with another longtime admirer of Bülow, Frau Henriette Lazarus, the widow of a Viennese medical doctor, who now lived in Hamburg. The train pulled into the station. Bülow was so weak that he could barely stand. Hermann Wolff and Herr Schanzer placed his arms around their shoulders and Bülow literally dragged his feet as they led him to the carriage. In Zabel's words, one almost had the impression that they were carrying a corpse. Wolff and his wife were weeping, and even the normally imperturbable Richard Strauss was visibly moved. Through the window of the railway-carriage Bülow somehow managed to wave his hand, smile, and blow a kiss to his

---

17. On his return journey from Egypt, Strauss had stayed with Bülow's daughter Blandine and her husband, Count Gravina, in their villa at Ramacca in Sicily. In a letter to Bülow dated June 4, 1893, in which he gives details of his Egyptian sojourn, Strauss is obviously aware that Bülow himself was undergoing a lengthy course of medical treatments, for he writes, 'Amidst the mummies of ancient Egyptian princesses there percolated to me here and there news of the progressive mummification of the Philharmonic concerts, then suddenly came the good news that you were conducting again and I saw the spirits of Beethoven and Haydn arise rejuvenated from the rock tombs which had been designated for them'. BSC, p. 102.

18. ZBG, pp. 54–55.

friends as the train moved away and disappeared in a cloud of smoke. His 'Flight into Egypt', as his friends wryly described it, had begun. Aside from his wife, Bülow was accompanied on the long journey to Cairo by Toni Petersen, Frau Lazarus, and family friend Frau Schiff, because he now needed round-the-clock care.

The small party travelled first to Vienna and then to Trieste, where they were briefly reunited with Daniela who took her final parting of her father on February 2. As she accompanied him onto the deck of the ship which was to take them on the next leg of their long journey, she observed that he looked like a sick, tired, but infinitely patient child. He leaned on her arms for support because he could scarcely stand, let alone walk. His last words to her were a benediction. 'God bless you, my child! I know that he will bless you'.[19] 'In all my misery', Daniela added, 'I thanked God for such grace'. The vessel then bore the sad party down the Adriatic Sea to the port of Brindisi. From there they took ship to Alexandria, crossing the Mediterranean Sea. Early on the morning of February 7 they docked at Alexandria, boarded the train, and got to Cairo around 12:30 p.m. During the train journey 'Hans was quiet', wrote Marie, 'as he always is now, but not in discomfort, and he read some newspapers'.[20] It was a gruelling journey for a dying man to have undertaken, sustained by one last hope.

IV

'One calls that a *cachet*', remarked Bülow approvingly, as he caught his first glimpse of the river Nile in all its majesty. But the Egyptian sun, whose warmth they had crossed a continent to find, was nowhere to be seen. They had booked accommodation in the Hôtel du Nil, thanks to the good offices of Bülow's nephew Viktor von Bojanowski, but owing to some oversight they were not able at first to obtain adjoining rooms, an absolute necessity for them. Eventually this was sorted out, and they settled in. The first night, February 7, was very disturbed. Bülow got out of bed disoriented, opened the door to the corridor, and wandered around lost. On the morning of Thursday, February 8, Toni Petersen led him onto the terrace, but it was windy and cloudy, and they came back indoors. Still the fabled Egyptian sunshine failed to materialize. Bülow took a little lunch with Marie and Toni, and after dessert he lay on the sofa and tried to light a cigarette. He put a matchstick into his mouth by mistake and

19. MHB, pp. 496–497. These highly uncharacteristic words were doubtless forced from Bülow's lips by the gravity of his condition. They were relayed by Daniela to Du Moulin Eckart, who placed them in his biography.

20. BB, vol. 7, p. 458.

tried to light it with another. Marie helped him and he smoked. Because he showed a passing interest in Egyptian coins, Marie went to the other room to fetch Toni to explain them to him. That same day he was examined by a German physician, Dr. Wild, whose job it was to take charge of the patient and arrange the onwards journey to the sanitarium at Helwan. During the examination it was noticed that his body appeared withered on one side and the eyelids kept drooping as if in sleep. The doctor delivered his opinion to Marie, but out of earshot of Bülow.[21] Dr. Wild then left to make arrangements for the patient to be transferred within a day or two to Helwan, which lay about twenty kilometers south of Cairo. Bülow, helped by Toni, got dressed and then went out onto the terrace of his hotel room to await the warm sunshine, while his wife went to fetch some linen from an adjoining room. Suddenly she heard a heavy fall, and a rattling in the throat. Bülow had suffered a massive stroke and had collapsed to the floor. The body was blocking the door, preventing Marie and Toni from entering. They reached him through an occupied neighboring room. He appeared unconscious, was laid on the bed, and was violently sick. Half-an-hour passed before the doctor returned and arranged for an Austrian nurse to spend the night with Bülow. A few hours after collapsing, he tried to leap out of bed. Marie asked, 'What do you want?' 'Unhindered movement', he replied, a response worthy of inclusion in a book of famous last words. On Friday afternoon a conveyance arrived to take them to the Protestant nursing hospital called 'The Victoria'. Marie climbed in with Bülow, while the doctor went ahead in another vehicle. There were Arabs on donkeys along the street, observed Marie. 'This was our first outing in Cairo!'[22]

By the time they got to the hospital, Bülow was half asleep and as cold as a bag of ice. The Protestant sisters put him to bed and established a twenty-four-hour vigil. At 10:00 a.m. the following morning, Bülow was examined again and the doctor asked, 'Where are you, Herr Baron?' 'At Dr. Wild's', came the reply. 'Who is that?' persisted the doctor. 'Dr. Wild—the sisters—my wife', murmured Bülow brokenly. It was Sunday

21. There would have been little that Dr. Wild could have told Marie that she and Bülow himself did not already know. Bülow had brought with him a letter written by his Hamburg physician, Dr. Alfred Saenger, written the day before he and Marie had set out on their long journey to Cairo. It was addressed to the Cairo doctors, and contained a detailed list of the symptoms from which Bülow had suffered for the past several years. According to Saenger, Bülow suffered from an accumulation of urine in the blood, a result of kidney disease; a discharge of white plaque from the left eye, the socket of which was partially collapsed; and intermittent neurological pains, for which morphine was administered. Saenger was reluctant to overprescribe morphine, but often acceded to Bülow's requests for it. Hitherto unpublished. DSB, Mus NL HvBülow, F IV, 2. dated Hamburg, 28/i, 1894.

22. BB, vol. 7, pp. 458–459.

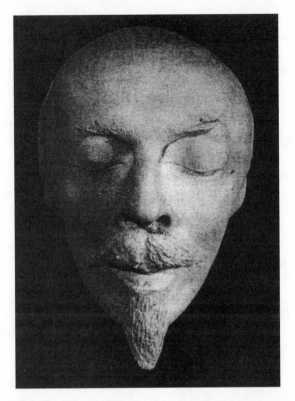

Bülow's death mask, taken by H. Tschirigi on February 13, 1894, Cairo.

morning, and as the singing of the sisters' choir from the adjoining chapel drifted down the corridor, Bülow caught the strains and inclined his head slightly, as if listening. It was the last music he ever heard.

Early on Monday morning, February 12, the pallor of the face became dark. To the doctor's question, 'How are you?' came the incomprehensible response, almost like a gentle breath, 'Schl . . .'. Afterwards not another word. Injections, doctors, consultations, all to no purpose. For three hours, there was a great heaving of the chest. At 7:00 p.m. the breathing became gentle, like that of a sleeping child. At 7:35 p.m. it ceased. In Marie's words, there was another gentle gurgle, then everything was quiet—for ever.[23]

The morning after Bülow's death an autopsy took place in accordance with his oft-expressed wish. Just before the dissection, Marie arranged for

---

23. Marie's account of Bülow's death lacks one poignant detail, and it was characteristic of her not to mention it. February 12, 1894, the day of Bülow's death, was also her thirty-seventh birthday. She celebrated it in a foreign country, watching her husband expire.

a death mask to be made, together with casts of Bülow's hands; and she also had photographs taken of the body on the deathbed.[24] The initial findings included deterioration of the kidneys, advanced calcification of the arteries, bronchitis, and cardiac hypertrophy. The pathologist, Dr. P. Kaufmann, assured Marie that a recovery would not have been possible, that the sudden death of her husband should be regarded as a release from hopeless martyrdom. These platitudes she did not need. With great resilience she instructed that Bülow's brain be removed and sent to Frankfurt for forensic examination. It was preserved in alcohol inside a zinc container for the long journey home, and its despatch was arranged through the German consulate in Cairo, which also cabled news of Bülow's death around the world.[25] On arrival in Frankfurt, the brain was inspected by the chief pathologist, Dr. Ludwig Edinger. It would be some months before Marie learned the truth. The immediate cause of Bülow's death, and the origin of so much of his suffering, was a tumour at the back of the neck, pressing on the base of a nerve close to the brain stem. The tumour was found to be quite old, 'probably dating back to the time of his youth'. And the report added, 'It is possible that we are dealing with the remnants of a meningitis which had been overcome early in his youth'.[26] There were also signs of chronic hemorrhaging, although Edinger complained that the cut made by Dr. Kaufmann as he removed the brain from the skull obscured the site of the bleeding. The brain itself weighed 1,425 grams, somewhat larger than normal.[27] The main irregularity observed in the structure of the organ was that the so-called Sylvii cleft was conspicuously shortened.

Immediately after the autopsy the body was embalmed and sent back to Germany on the passenger ship *Reichstag,* which arrived at Hamburg on March 22. From there Bülow's remains were taken to Hamburg's imposing St. Michaelis Church and for the next seven days thousands of mourners came to view the coffin and pay their last respects. They were not confined to Hamburg but came from Berlin and other cities as well. There were representatives from the Berlin Philharmonic Orchestra, the Hamburg Philharmonic Orchestra, the Bremen and Meiningen orchestras, musical

---

24. The plaster death mask was made by H. Tschirgi, and the photograph was taken by F. Dremen.

25. The manifest, prepared by the German consulate in Cairo for the customs service, indicates that the death mask and the zinc container holding the brain were carefully packed in cotton-wool before being sent back to Germany. Despite these precautions, the brain suffered some minor bruising in transit. (See the autopsy report on p. 466.) The death mask is on display in the Deutsche Staatsbibliothek, Berlin.

26. Dr. Edinger's report is dated September 23, 1894. See BB, vol. 7, pp. 490–491. See also Marie's own observations on p. 459 of the same source.

27. The average weight of a mature human brain in males is 1,409 grams, or 49.7 ounces.

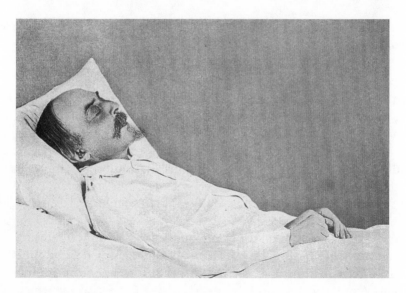

Bülow on his deathbed. February 12, 1894.

colleagues who had known Bülow across the years, and simple music lovers who travelled to Hamburg in great numbers in order to say farewell to a man they admired.

Even as Bülow's remains were on the high seas bound for Hamburg, Gustav Mahler had conducted a memorial concert in the city's Convent Garden, on February 26. The programme consisted of the following works:

BACH	Prelude for Organ and Chorus: 'Wenn ich einmal soll scheiden'
	A Commemorative Address
BRAHMS	Two Choruses from *Ein Deutsches Requiem* 1. 'Selig sind, die da Leid tragen' 2. 'Denn alles Fleisch ist wie Gras'
BEETHOVEN:	Symphony no. 3, in E-flat major (*Eroica*), op. 55

Let us note in passing Mahler's deliberate inclusion of the 'three Bs'—the triumvirate in German music to which Bülow had constantly drawn attention. The performance of the *Eroica* Symphony, especially, was acclaimed for its nobility. 'Bülow's spirit lived in it', wrote Ferdinand Pfohl in the *Hamburger Nachrichten*.[28] As we shall see, Bülow's death and funeral

28. Issue of February 27, 1894.

were to have a profound effect on Mahler, who was to play an important role in the memorial service itself.[29]

V

On the morning of March 29, at 9:00 a.m., the great doors of the St. Michaelis Church were opened for the funeral service. The coffin had been placed on a huge, elevated catafalque in front of the main altar, and was buried beneath layers of flowers and surrounded by hundreds of candles. About 500 wreaths from distinguished musicians were displayed, including Moritz Moszkowski, Eugen d'Albert, Teresa Carreño, Siegfried Ochs, Johannes Brahms, Gustav Mahler, Max Reger, Richard Strauss, and a host of others. Laurel wreaths and rose bouquets from leading musical organizations also adorned the catafalque, including ones from the Berlin Philharmonic Orchestra, the Hamburg and Bremen orchestras, the Allgemeiner Deutscher Musikverein, the Royal Music School in Munich, the Richard Wagner Society, and the St. Petersburg Conservatory, which bore the inscription 'To the Great Master, our honorary member, Dr. Hans von Bülow'. The vast church contained about 2,500 seats, and they were all filled before the ceremony began. Shortly before 10:00 a.m. Marie von Bülow, dressed in deep mourning, emerged from the vestry together with other family members, and they took their places on the left side of the church near the coffin. Among the relatives were Daniela and Henry Thode; Bülow's sister Isidora and her children Viktor and Wjera; and Siegfried Wagner, who represented the Wagner family. Marie von Bülow was accompanied by Toni Petersen, who had barely left her side throughout the long ordeal. Bülow's daughter Blandine and her husband, Count Gravina, did not attend.[30] Neither did Brahms, Richard Strauss, and Eugen

---

29. Immediately after Bülow's death the whole of musical Germany rallied to his memory. Even before his corpse had arrived back in the Fatherland, memorial concerts were being held across the country, not just the 'official' commemoration conducted by Mahler. They included:

1894	
Meiningen	February 20
Hamburg	February 26 (conducted by Mahler)
Munich	March 3
Wiesbaden	March 9
Cöthen	March 12
Augsburg	March 14
Frankfurt	March 16
Raff Conservatory	March 20
Wagner Verein (Berlin)	March 22

At most of these concerts Beethoven's *Eroica* Symphony was performed, either in full or the 'Funeral March' movement from it.

30. See the evening edition of the *Hamburgischer Correspondent* on March 29, 1894, p. 3, under the headline, 'Trauerfeier für Dr. Hans von Bülow in der grossen St. Michaeliskirche'. A comprehensive list of mourners may be found in *The Musical Courier* (April 25, 1894,

d'Albert, and their absence occasioned some negative comments in light of Bülow's early recognition of their talents and his unceasing efforts in their behalf. The grandeur of the service, punctuated as it was by the tolling of the great cathedral bells, impressed all who witnessed it.

The service was led by the pastor of St. Michaelis, Dr. Georg Behrmann, who commenced with a reading of Psalm 90, a text which concerns the frailty and mortality of man. He then quoted some words from the First Book of Corinthians: 'Death is swallowed up in victory. O death, where is thy sting? O grave, where is thy victory?' Behrmann knew full well that Bülow was not a religious man, a fact for which he made allowance in his long eulogy, of which the following is a brief extract:

> For a man who was exceptional, some exceptional words from the Holy Scripture are fitting. For a man whose significance lay in the wonderful gifts with which God had endowed him, this saying is suitable: 'Lord, Thou hast wrought all our works for us'.[31] To him was given a talent so individual, so rich, that we cannot find its equal among his generation. But the gifts of God are at the same time a responsibility: 'For unto whomsoever much is given, of him shall be much required'.[32] We are therefore permitted to turn our saying around: 'What Thou hast given us, we should make use of'. So his life became a struggle for the perfection of his own artistic development; and, to be sure, of all his strengths, yes, even a struggle against the natural dwindling of his powers. At the same time the victory of his musical ideals was a goal which hovered clearly before him, and to which he held fast.[33]

The musical forces were large, and the emotion-charged performances would have pleased Bülow. The ceremony began with Bach's chorale-prelude *O Haupt voll Blut und Wunden* played on the organ by Alfred Burjam, the resident organist. The choir then sang the closing chorus from Bach's *St. John Passion,* 'Ruht wohl, ihr heiligen Gebeine',[34] followed by a

---

pp. 11–13) whose correspondent provides one of the most detailed eyewitness accounts of the funeral service itself. Lost in the vast crowd was one mourner whose presence in the church would have been appreciated by Bülow: Marie Rudolph ('Zeitungsmarie') had temporarily abandoned her newspaper stall in Berlin and travelled to Hamburg to pay her last respects.

31. Isaiah 26:12.

32. Luke 12:48.

33. SRW, p. 462. Behrmann's eulogy was translated and reprinted in *The Musical Courier,* April 25, 1894.

34. 'Rest in peace, thou holy bones'. A detailed account of the obsequies at Bülow's funeral will be found in SRW, pp. 461–477.

movement from Brahms's *Ein Deutsches Requiem*. Perhaps the most moving part of the service came when the women and children of the choir sang a setting of Friedrich Klopstock's poem 'Auferstehen' ('Resurrection').

The coffin was borne out of the church by a company of Hamburg beadles in full dress uniform, complete with breeches, three-corned hats, and dress-swords ('like a Holbein painting', as one observer put it), and was placed on a waiting hearse drawn by four black horses. This touch of pageantry was brought about because of Bülow's position as a Freeman of the City of Hamburg. As the 'Dead March' from Handel's *Saul* rolled through the church the mourners emptied onto the street outside. About forty carriages formed the long funeral procession, which now set out for the Ohlsdorf crematorium, where Bülow's remains were to be consigned to the flames in accordance with his wishes. Along the way it slowly passed in front of the opera house where Gustav Mahler had assembled the orchestra on the terrace for a performance of Siegfried's 'Funeral March' from Wagner's *Götterdämmerung*. The day's events had had a profound effect on Mahler, who later revealed that he was inspired to compose the finale of his *Resurrection* Symphony—which ends with a choral setting of the same Klopstock poem 'Auferstehen' he had heard during the funeral service.[35] At the gates of the crematorium the procession was

---

35. The information comes from Mahler himself. See the letter he wrote to the critic Arthur Seidl, dated February 17, 1897. The words of the poem run:

> Rise again, yea, thou shalt rise again,
> My dust, after short rest!
> Immortal life! Immortal life
> He who called thee will grant thee.
> To bloom again art thou sown!
> The Lord of the Harvest goes
> And gathers in, like sheaves,
> Us who died!

> Aufersteh'n, ja aufersteh'n wirst du,
> Mein Staub, nach kurzer Ruh!
> Unsterblich Leben! Unsterblich Leben
> Wird der dich rief dir geben.
> Wieder aufzublühn wirst du gesäht!
> Der Herr der Ernte geht
> Und sammelt Garben
> Uns ein, die starben!

The psychoanalyst Theodor Reik, a colleague of Freud, put forward the interesting notion that Bülow—who had harshly rejected the first movement of this symphony (the so-called *Todtenfeier*—or 'funeral rites') a few months earlier, a rejection which had brought the composition of this symphony to a temporary standstill—was unconsciously perceived by Mahler to be an authoritarian father figure and rival, whose death now resulted in an emotional breakthrough for the younger musician. Reik reconstructed Mahler's unconscious death wish against Bülow as follows: 'As certain as you are now dead because I wished it, will my work, which you rejected, be victorious and become immortal' (RHM, p. 271). The traumatic scene in which Mahler played through the *Todtenfeier* movement to Bülow on the

Hans von Bülow's last resting place. Ohlsdorf Cemetery, Hamburg. Memorial stone by Adolf Hildebrand.

met by members of the 'Cremation Society' (*Feuerbestattungsverein*) who offered a last farewell to their comrade.[36]

Bülow's cremation took place the following day, March 30. Again it was a time for eulogies and mourning. A distinguished group had assembled for this final farewell, including Hermann Wolff and his wife, Louise; the choral conductor Siegfried Ochs; Burgomeister Carl Petersen and his daughter Toni; the chairman of the Hamburg Philharmonic Orchestra, Dr. Hermann Behn; and the Berlin poet Otto Ludwig. A choir from the

---

piano, in November 1891, only to observe him with his hands over his ears, is central to this analysis. (See p. 428.)

36. BBLW, pp. 189–190; and BB, vol. 7, pp. 459–460. Hans and Marie were convinced supporters of cremation at a time when it was far from acceptable to the religious authorities in Germany, or anywhere else in the Western world for that matter. When Bülow was cremated, there were only two crematoria in the whole of Germany—at Gotha and Ohlsdorf. In his second will (March 1889) Bülow had already identified Gotha as his only option. In a letter to his daughter Daniela, we find him referring to 'my incineration in Gotha' (BNB, p. 672). But when in August 1891 Hamburg built its own crematorium, it made sense to have his remains disposed of there. According to the records of the Ohlsdorf Cemetery Bülow was only the sixty-seventh person to be cremated, even though the facility had been in use for three years. In the year of Bülow's death there were forty-eight cremations, twenty-eight of those coming from the Hamburg area, the remaining twenty from various parts of Germany.

Hamburg Stadttheater, accompanied by Gustav Mahler on the harmo-
nium, sang a Schubert chorus and a choral transcription for male-voice
choir of the 'Song of Thanksgiving' from Beethoven's String Quartet in
A minor, op. 132. At the conclusion of the service, Marie von Bülow
and her inner circle watched as the coffin bearing Bülow's remains disappeared within the crematorium. According to contemporary reports,
the burning of the body took one-and-a-half hours.[37] The ashes were
buried in consecrated ground the following day. An impressive memorial
stone by the sculptor Adolf Hildebrand marks his final resting place. Unveiled in 1897, it is still the only memorial to Germany's most influential
conductor. It shows Bülow's bust in left profile and supports an urn containing his ashes.

VI

Some mention must be made of the unfortunate absence of Richard
Strauss from the funeral ceremony. Strauss was already scheduled to conduct a concert with the Hamburg Philharmonic on February 26, as part
of the regular Subscription Series normally conducted by Bülow himself.
In view of Bülow's death, a blow Strauss felt so keenly, he readily agreed
to a request from the orchestra's chairman, Dr. Behn, to alter the programme in favour of one that would best honour Bülow's memory. Strauss
submitted what he called 'a purely symphonic funeral celebration'—
Héroïde funèbre or *Orpheus* by Liszt, *Nirwana* by Bülow, the *Eroica* Symphony by Beethoven, and Wagner's *Tristan* and *Meistersinger* preludes.
And he added that he would be happy for Gustav Mahler to follow him
on the podium to conduct the Funeral March from *Götterdämmerung*.
These entirely appropriate suggestions were turned down for partisan reasons, probably because Behn was out of town. Strauss found himself in
the middle of a wrangle that broke out among Bülow's conservative supporters, who wanted no part of a concert containing music by Liszt and
Wagner. Where, they wondered, was the music of Brahms? Strauss was
asked to conduct the Brahms *Deutsches Requiem* instead, but by this time
he had had enough of those who had appointed themselves guardians of
Bülow's memory, and he refused to conduct the concert. He was reported
to have said, 'I do not conduct music for dilettantes'. This arrow flew past
its mark and struck the Brahms *Requiem* instead, and Strauss had to deny
that he had ever criticized the work of Hamburg's great composer. In the
event, the memorial concert was conducted by Gustav Mahler, who included two numbers from the *Requiem*.

---

37. The correspondent of *The Musical Courier* observed 'ominous looking black clouds
issuing from the smoke stack, which told of the fulfillment of the artist's wish for the cremation of his remains' (issue of April 25, 1894, p. 12).

❈ Concerthaus — Conventgarten. ❈

Montag den 26. Februar 1894, Abends 7½ Uhr pünktlich

IX. ABONNEMENT-CONCERT

GEDENKFEIER FÜR

HANS VON BÜLOW

Dirigent:

Kapellmeister Herr Gustav Mahler

(Mit gütiger Bewilligung des Herrn Hofrath Pollini).

Unter Mitwirkung eines Chores von Damen und Herren, unter Leitung des Herrn **Julius Spengel.**

Orgel: Herr **Carl Armbrust.**

PROGRAMM.

1. Praeludium für Orgel u. Choral: „Wenn ich einmal soll scheiden". . . . . . . *J. S. Bach.*

2. Gedenkrede.

3. Zwei Chöre aus: „Ein deutsches Requiem" *J. Brahms.*
    I. „Selig sind, die da Leid tragen".
    II. „Denn alles Fleisch ist wie Gras".

4. Sinfonie No. 3, Es-dur (Eroica) (1804) . *L. v. Beethoven.*
    Allegro con brio. — Marcia funebre (Adagio assai). — Scherzo (Allegro vivace). — Finale (Allegro molto).

X. (letztes) Abonnement-Concert: Montag den 12. März 1894.
Dirigent: *Eugen d'Albert.*
Solisten: Frau **Teresa d'Albert-Carreño** und Frl. **Katharina Rösing** (Gesang).

Bülow's memorial concert, conducted by Gustav Mahler. February 26, 1894. A concert billing.

In order to understand the painful dilemma in which Strauss found himself, one must read in full the four-way correspondence which he was at that time pursuing on the matter of Bülow's memorial concert, between Cosima Wagner, Daniela Thode, Henry Thode, and later Dr. Behn—all of whom offered him different shades of well-meaning advice.[38] Strauss saw that this was one of those proverbial roads which are paved with good intentions but lead straight to hell, a destination he wished to avoid. It was doubly unfortunate for Strauss that the thoroughly false impression gained ground that he had also refused to conduct at the funeral service as well. It is enough to report that Strauss honoured Bülow's memory for the rest of his life. In his 'Erinnerungen an Hans von Bülow' he calls Bülow the 'model for all the illuminating virtues of the interpretative artist', a remark that reverberates long after the concerts devoted to Bülow's memory have fallen silent.

VII

Shortly after Bülow's death an appeal was launched 'in the name of the German nation' for a permanent monument to be erected in Hamburg, the city in which he wanted his ashes to repose. 'As the leading champion of German art he won new glory for the German name', the citation read. 'It is the solemn duty of the German people to erect a monument to him'. The document was signed by many prominent people from the arts and the sciences, including the physicist Hermann von Helmholz; the poets Klaus Groth and Friedrich Spielhagen; the painters Adolph Menzel and Franz von Lenbach. Among the musicians were Johannes Brahms,[39] Joseph Joachim, Gustav Mahler, Felix Mottl, Richard Strauss, and Felix Weingartner. This monument was never built. Bülow, for his part, would surely have preferred the wisdom of Cato the Elder (234–149 BC): 'I would rather have men ask why I have no statue, than why I have one'.[40]

For many years that is where matters rested. When Edith Stargardt-Wolff, the daughter of Hermann Wolff, published her touching memoir of Bülow and her father in 1954, sixty years after Bülow's death, she con-

---

38. Selections of these letters were published in SRS, pp. 344–348.

39. On the day of Bülow's cremation Brahms sent a donation of 1,000 marks to the Pension Fund of the Berlin Philharmonic Orchestra.

40. By October 1895, the subscription fund had reached the sum of approximately 18,000 marks. The Berlin Philharmonic gave a benefit concert but only succeeded in raising 1,658 marks—'a rather poor sum for a capital for which Bülow did so much' (MMR, November 1, 1895, p. 260). The Hamburg Orchestra did better, raising 5,135 marks at a similar concert that same year. The imposing statue originally envisaged for the city of Hamburg never materialized. Whatever money had been collected was put towards the commemorative site in the Ohlsdorf Cemetery, created by Adolf Hildebrand.

soled herself for posterity's dereliction by dwelling on the winged words of Horace, which we quoted at the head of this chapter. Almost a quarter-century passed. Then, in 1978, thirty of the world's leading conductors and composers came forward to finance the restoration of Bülow's memorial stone in the Ohlsdorf Cemetery, which had fallen into neglect. It was a fitting gesture, and symbolized something profound. These musicians understood his value; his work had made theirs possible. Their names are engraved on a granite tablet placed at the foot of the memorial stone.

In Honour of Hans von Bülow

G. Albrecht • D. Barenboim
L. Bernstein • K. Böhm
P. Boulez • A Ceccato
C. Davis • Ch. v. Dohnanyi
A. Erede • M. Gielen
H. Hollreiser • E. Jochum
H.v. Karajan • R. Kubelik
K. Kondraschin • F. Leitner
L. Maazel • I. Markevitch
J. Mrawinsky • E. Ormandy
G. Rozhdestvensky • G. Solti
P. Sacher • W. Sawallisch
M. Schostakowitsch
H. Stein • O. Suitner
K. Tennstedt •H. Zender
F. Strauss für Rich. Strauss
Berliner Philharmoniker
JDK Interessenverband
Deutscher Komponisten 1978

Each one of the musicians whose name is engraved on this tablet also provided a written tribute to Bülow. Their responses were collected and published in facsimile that same year, and issued in a commemorative volume titled *Hans von Bülow as Famous Conductors See Him.*[41] Particularly noteworthy was the homage paid by Pierre Boulez:

Hans von Bülow is the great model for the role of the conductor as it is understood today. It was he who gave it concrete form and significance.

41. See BUD.

Lorin Maazel, too, gave voice to the general sentiment concerning Bülow's place in history:

> Every conductor is still a pupil of Hans von Bülow. He was a master of his profession and demanded no more of his musicians than he did from himself.

VIII

Even while the arrangements for the funeral were taking place, Bülow's second will had been opened, its contents widely circulated. It had been drawn up in August 1887, with a codicil dated March 10, 1889.[42] Edith Stargardt-Wolff was not wrong to describe this will as 'inconceivable'. In it Bülow declared, 'With my first wife Cosima von Liszt I have four daughters, the first two of whom are already married, and have already received their inheritance. To the two younger ones, Isolde and Eva, I bequeath respectively 40,000 Marks, which I have deposited in the banking house of Frege & Co. in Leipzig'. The whole world knew this to be untrue, because Bülow had often told his friends that Isolde was only half his, and Eva was not his at all.[43] Why the deception? In order to understand Bülow's convoluted thinking, we have to go back to that last, painful meeting between him and Cosima in Nuremberg, in July 1881, when at Wagner's behest she had tried with might and main to secure Bülow's agreement to have the three older daughters—Daniela, Blandine, and Isolde—legally adopted by Wagner. With such a proposal Bülow would have nothing to do. We recall that although Isolde bore Bülow's name on all her legal documents, she had been brought up in the Wagner household with the other children from her infancy. We are left to assume that the codicil Bülow attached to his will was intended as a posthumous retaliation against Wagner. It was as if in death Bülow wanted to rehabilitate Cosima, who had caused him so much pain in life, by telling the world that she had not been an adulterous wife, and henceforth the burden of paternity was

---

42. The codicil was filed just four days before Bülow and his wife boarded ship for New York and the second American tour. The will itself was registered in Hamburg's City Hall (*Acten des Erbschaftsamts*) under the call number 'F 1894 Nr. 1458 (fol. 57)'. According to the Hamburg Staatsarchiv, whither the testament was eventually transferred, several pages were legally removed from the file, in response to a *Retent*, or a lien, in the year 1920.

Whose interests would have been served by the removal of these pages? We are left to speculate that Bayreuth may have had a hand in the matter. Isolde von Bülow had died a few months earlier, and although she had lost her legal battle to be formally accepted as Wagner's daughter, despite Cosima's testimony that no other conclusion was possible, Bülow's words to the contrary had made a mockery of the whole process, and were best expunged from the record.

43. S-WW, p. 88.

to be lifted from Wagner's shoulders and placed on his own.[44] The date of Bülow's second will lends force to this argument. By any yardstick of normal human behaviour, the proper time to have made out a new testament would have been on the occasion of his marriage to Marie Schanzer, in July 1882. But Bülow bided his time—not only until after the death of Wagner the following year, but after the death of Liszt as well, in 1886. Whatever testimony they might have brought to the family squabble had now gone to the grave with them. There is one other small matter that the observant reader will not fail to notice about this controversial clause. When Wagner had refused to accept the sum of 40,000 marks raised by Bülow for the Bayreuth Deficit Fund, he had returned the money with a request that it be 'invested for the children'.[45] Never in his worst imaginings could Wagner have envisaged that Bülow would, in that spirit of perversity so central to his character, go on deliberately to interpret 'the children' to mean not only Daniela and Blandine but Isolde and Eva as well. We do not know whether Bülow was familiar with the cynical aphorism of Marie d'Agoult, Cosima's mother, 'Forgiveness is a form of contempt'. In any event, Bülow's second will may be interpreted as a wonderful example of contempt in action.[46]

44. Adolf von Gross, the Bayreuth banker who had become a tower of strength to Cosima after the death of Wagner, and was now playing a key role in setting the shaky financial affairs of the Bayreuth Festival in order, travelled from Bayreuth to Hamburg because he wanted to ensure the smooth transfer of the money that Bülow had bequeathed to Isolde and Eva. That Bülow, after so many years of silence on the matter, now claimed paternity over Eva as well as Isolde was a preposterous assertion made plausible in his eyes by one simple fact. Eva was born in February 1867; Cosima did not finally desert Bülow, leave Munich, and take up permanent residence with Wagner at Tribschen until November 1868. It was up to the world to wrestle with these dates as best it could. If Bülow now wanted to assert paternity over Eva as well as Isolde, was there a court in the land which could deny him that right? This part of Bülow's will was a piece of legalistic mischief making, and he must have known it. It was not merely the rehabilitation of Cosima that Bülow's logic-chopping thought process had as its goal; it was also a *coup de grâce* delivered against Wagner. One can hardly imagine the furore that would have arisen if Wagner had outlived Bülow and had learned of the latter's plans to rearrange the family circle. Some such fantasy may well have sustained Bülow and given him quiet satisfaction as he went to meet his Maker—and, who knows, to meet Wagner too, in whatever heaven is reserved for musicians.

45. CWBD, p. 171.

46. Other beneficiaries mentioned in Bülow's will were his mother (who had already predeceased him) and his sister Isidora. Bülow also left money to the pension funds of three orchestras: Berlin, Hamburg, and Bremen. In addition he left a donation to the ongoing Liszt *Stiftung*. Marie inherited everything else. It was a considerable legacy which kept her in reasonable comfort for the rest of her days. Aside from money, she acquired all his manuscripts, his vast correspondence, jewellery, medals, the Hamburg apartment, and household effects. (*Le Ménestrel*, Sunday, April 1, 1894). These generous provisions help us to explain why Bülow's second will was drawn up in August 1887, a date that was hardly arrived at by chance. Marie had just rejoined him in Hamburg, after her discovery of his affair with Cécile Mutzenbecher.

IX

And what of Marie von Bülow? She outlived her husband by more than forty-seven years, dying in Berlin on August 30, 1941, aged eighty-four. Her remains were transported from Berlin to Hamburg where she was cremated at Ohlsdorf and her ashes placed close to those of Bülow. During the years immediately following Bülow's death, she devoted much time to editing and publishing his letters and articles. But that work was essentially finished by the year 1908, although she later went on to produce a short biography of Bülow. Still in possession of a fine figure and handsome looks, the old lost longing for acting returned. She appeared in a number of silent movies, directed by some of Berlin's leading moviemakers. Among the films in which she was cast in supporting roles were *Wenn Menschen reif zur Liebe werden* (1916), directed by Fern Andra; *Der Knabe in Blau* (1919), directed by Friedrich Wilhelm Murnau; and *Monte Carlo* (1921), directed by Fred Sauer.[47] As her black-and-white image flits before us on the silver screen, we begin to see why Bülow found her so attractive. He would surely have rejoiced in the fact that having willingly sacrificed much of her career for him during his lifetime, she had now gone on to achieve a modest immortality of her own, albeit in a direction he could hardly have imagined.

Throughout the years remaining to her, Marie became a familiar figure on the Berlin musical scene, attending all the important concerts of the Berlin Philharmonic Orchestra, conducted first by Arthur Nikisch and then by his successor, Wilhelm Furtwängler. What were her thoughts as she witnessed these two great conductors directing the ensemble her husband had raised from obscurity? Few would disagree with the comment she made in 1932 to an American correspondent, 'They reap what he has sown'.[48] In 1914 Marie founded a charitable salon, called the 'Künstlerhilfe'. Every Wednesday afternoon her elegant home in Charlottenburg was opened to the public, where distinguished artists volunteered their services and gave recitals in benefit of those in need, especially for the bereaved families of soldiers killed in the trenches of World War I. The players were happy to do it for one simple reason: they had been asked by Marie von Bülow, a name that still evoked powerful memories among Berlin's musical intelligentsia.

---

47. Marie appeared in at least twenty-nine movies. Other titles include *Fridericus Rex* (1922); *Nonne und Tänzerin* (1919); *Das Bacchanal des Todes* (1917); and *Das Tagebuch einer Verlorenen* (1918). In some of these films she was billed as Maria von Bülow.
48. IPAM. Letter to Harry Anderson, dated 'Berlin, February 9, 1932'.

On January 8, 1930, the one hundredth anniversary of Bülow's birth, Marie turned her regular soirée into a memorial for her late husband. Her salon was packed for the occasion, and was filled with memorabilia. One Berlin newspaper observed that the occasion was so lifelike that it was almost as if Bülow himself were in the room. A short programme of Bülow's pieces was played, including the song-cycle 'Die Entsagende' and the piano piece 'Rêverie fantastique'. Marie also gave a reading from one of his essays. That same day there was a Bülow memorial concert at the Lessing Museum, at which Marie again spoke. On January 9 the Dresden Philharmonic Orchestra broadcast a memorial concert containing works by Liszt, Brahms, Beethoven, and Bülow himself, after which Marie delivered a radio address about Bülow's life and work which was heard across North Germany.

As early as 1912 Marie had started to donate portions of her vast Bülow legacy to the Deutsche Staatsbibliothek. The first installment had included his music library, the death mask, casts of his hands, a collection of his batons, and bound albums of photographs. Other installments continued to be made at intervals, until 1940. By far the most important acquisition was made in 1935, consisting of 5,144 letters, of which Marie had only been able to publish 1,925 in her eight-volume *Briefe und Schriften*. The remaining 3,000 or more remain unknown to the world at large, although they cast revealing light on the music and musicians of the time.[49] In December 1939 Marie expressed concern about the delay in cataloguing what was by now a considerable collection; it was one of many messages she had addressed to a succession of archivists. On December 15, 1939, she received an assurance that despite many difficulties everyone was working 'with great intensity' on the project. Marie was eighty-two years old at that time, World War II had broken out, and she herself had less than two years to live.[50] The task of cataloguing the collection remains unfinished to this day.

---

49. Shortly after Bülow's death, Marie began the Herculean task of contacting many hundreds of people in possession of his letters with a request to copy and publish them, including Baroness Helene von Heldburg from Meiningen. The baroness advised Marie to wait 'bis die Generation, die mit ihm jung war, nicht mehr ist' (until the generation that was young with him is no more). In her reply, Marie pointed out that she had no children, and if she were to leave a will containing instructions that required great care in its implementation, and if moreover she were to die suddenly, she would not know to whom she could entrust this solemn task. In short, she was the only person who could carry it out (BB, vol. 6, p. viii).

50. For Marie's correspondence on this matter, see DSB, Mus. NL HvBülow H 1. Akte über den Bülow-Nachlass.

Appendix I

Bülow's Autopsy Report

I

On the morning of February 13, 1894, an autopsy was carried out on Bülow's body in Cairo, by Dr. P. Kaufmann. His report is preserved in the Deutsche Staatsbibliothek.[1] Marie von Bülow published a part of it in the final volume of her edition of Bülow's correspondence, to which she added some interesting introductory remarks. The question arises: Why was she so intent on sharing such graphic details with the rest of the world? The answer is not hard to find. During the final years of Bülow's life there were those whose favoured explanation for his occasionally erratic behaviour was to declare him mentally unsound. Marie realized that the best way to silence such rumours was to provide medical evidence to the contrary.[2] She wrote:

Given the interest which the scientific world nowadays takes in the autopsies of eminent people, it may seem justified to provide the results which have been determined from the most competent professionals. At the beginning of the report on the post mortem of Hans von Bülow's body, Dr. P. Kaufmann who carried it out summarized the diagnosis as follows: 'Chronic hemorrhaging, nephritis, incipient shrinkage of the kidneys, cardiac hypertrophy, bronchitis, Bulbar paralysis?' This question mark was followed by the comment, 'To be examined microscopically'.

---

1. DSB, Mus NL HvBülow F IV, 2.
2. Although she does not say so, the image of poor Oda, Bülow's mentally retarded younger sister, would almost certainly have been in her thoughts as she pressed Dr. Kaufmann for more details about Bülow himself.

465

Marie concludes her remarks by telling her readers that 'the brain, the weight of which was 1425 grams, was sent to Dr. Ludwig Edinger in Frankfurt-am-Main for a detailed examination'.[3]

Several months elapsed, and Dr. Edinger responded to Marie's request as follows.

II

DR. LUDWIG EDINGER'S REPORT ON THE AUTOPSY OF HANS VON BÜLOW'S BRAIN. Dated Frankfurt a.M. 23 September, 1894.

The brain given to me was hardened in alcohol and somewhat bruised in transit, so that a sufficient examination of the surface was not possible at first. Because, however, a number of irregularities in the brain convolutions became conspicuous, the two cerebral hemispheres were very carefully preserved so that they could later be compared with the brains of other musicians yet to be collected.

The arteries were everywhere strongly calcified, even the middle ones. A few pieces were taken out of the cerebral cortex, carefully cut and dyed; then the upper part of the spinal cord, the marrow, the *Vierhügel* and parts of the cerebellum were cut into the finest sections, which were similarly prepared as microscopic specimens through dyeing.

As far as the preservation of the cerebral cortex made a judgement possible, it could be considered normal. Nothing was revealed which could point to a diseased brain, or even a diseased cortex.

The hemorrhage, which the dissection of the brain stem had made evident, has not been found again. It fell directly on one of the incision areas which Dr. P. Kaufmann had made for the sake of preservation. And since it had been so exposed, it was eliminated in transit through the hardening process. It must have been a very recent hemorrhage (perhaps the ultimate cause of death), otherwise traces would have been found in my sections. . . .

An explanation has now been found for the terrible pains in the back of the head, which Bülow suffered all his life. A tumour which is certainly very old, probably dating back to the time of his youth, was the source of the pressure on the two upper nerves on one side of the neck, close to the brain stem. This growth had seriously compressed the base of the nerve close to the brain stem. Essentially confined to its site of origin, this growth, which did not protrude,

3. BB, vol. 7, pp. 490–492.

was certainly likely to produce the most intense neuralgic pains in the back of the head. Most of the root fibres of the two upper neck nerves on one side were implicated. It is possible that we are dealing with the remnants of a meningitis which had been overcome early in his youth. Here, too, there were no specific protrusions. The brain stem, and also the spinal cord, were healthy, as far as their preservation allows this conclusion. The fact that all the blood vessels in the brain and in the spinal cord had been so seriously hardened, had in his last years certainly led to the result that his nervous system, which was so abnormally saturated with blood, was quickly exhausted. This is perhaps the reason for the frequent attacks of fatigue.

The hardening and calcification of arteries of this age, which occurs frequently with intellectual work, was far advanced, and it easily affects the kidneys, together with other functions.

The result of my examination thus far, satisfactorily explains some things observed in [Bülow's] life, and leaves others of greater psychological interest unanswered.

Prof. Dr. L. Edinger,
Director of the Dr. Senckenberg Institute of Neurology in Frankfurt a.M.

III

Fourteen years after the autopsy report came into her hands, Marie von Bülow was preparing the final volume of her husband's correspondence for publication. She contacted Dr. Edinger again and pressed him for some further thoughts on the cause of Bülow's death. He provided the following postscript to his earlier remarks, pointing to some physical characteristics displayed by the brains of the musically gifted, shared by Bülow:

POSTSCRIPT:
Frankfurt a.M., 1 June 1908:

I am now finally in a position to inform you about the autopsy of the hemispheres of the master's cerebrum. In the year 1906, Dr. S. Auerbach very carefully examined, in my institute, the brain of Prof. Koning, an eminently musically gifted violinist.

He discovered a curious enlargement of the back part of the left first gyrus, of the kind that could not be found among a hundred other hemispheres. The enlarged position here is exactly where we can locate, for other reasons as well, the function of advanced psychological hearing. Now, I examined Bülow's brain again and compared it, gyrus for gyrus, with a normal brain structure. There it became evident that the strong enlargement of the left upper temple gyrus, which was already considerable in Koning's case, was much more pronounced in the case of Bülow; the 'Sylvii cleft' was significantly shortened through the development of the brain, a development which had also taken place at its back rim in the area of the Gyrus Supramarginalis; and the upper temple Gyrus itself had multiple partitions. In the right brain hemisphere, none of this was evident. I have attached the re-constructed drawings to the comprehensive treatise which Dr. S. Auerbach has published in 1906 in the Archive for Anatomy and Physiology, under the title *Beitrage zur Lokalisation des musikalischen Talentes im Grosshirn und am Schädel.*

It is not without interest to add that Stockhausen's brain, which Dr. Auerbach examined in my institute as well, has revealed enlargements which are similarly located.

Marie now had at her disposal all the necessary expert medical opinion she required to rebut the allegations of Bülow's mental instability that had swirled around his reputation since his death in 1894, and she published the autopsy results in 1908. By placing them on the record in so public a fashion she made it impossible for future newspaper gossip and innuendo to survive the comparison.

Appendix II

Complete Catalogue of Bülow's Compositions, Transcriptions, and Editions[1]

(A) ORIGINAL WORKS

Piano

op. 2. Arabesques en forme de variations sur un thème favori de l'opéra 'Rigoletto' de Verdi. *Dedicated to Mons. J. N. Dunkl.* Pest, 1853; Rószavölgyi. Mainz, 1855; Schott cat. no. 13793.

op. 3. Marche héroïque d'après des motifs hongrois populaires. Pest, 1853; Mainz, 1855. Schott cat. no. 13832.

op. 4. Mazurka-Impromptu. *Dedicated to Countess Elisa Mycielska.* Breslau, 1855; revised edition, Breslau, 1862. Leuckart cat. no. 1018.

op. 6. Invitation à la Polka. Morceau de Salon. *Dedicated to his friend and co-disciple Dionys Pruckner.* Breslau, 1855/1862. Leuckart cat. no. 1044.

op. 7. Rêverie fantastique. *Respectfully dedicated to Princess Marie de Hohenzollern.* Breslau, 1855/1862. Leuckart cat. no. 1047.

op. 11. Ballade for piano. *Dedicated to his friend Louis Ehlert.* The motto at the head of the score runs: 'O poète! je vais dans ton âme blessée/Remuer jusqu'au fond de ta profonde pensée' ['O Poet! I am going to stir your profound thought right to the core of your wounded soul.']. Victor Hugo, from 'Les Voix intérieures'. Mainz, 1854. Schott cat. no. 14076.

---

1. The first worklist was compiled by Marie von Bülow, in BAS (part 2), pp. 291–300. For the most exhaustive catalogue, complete with annotations and commentaries, see Hans-Joachim Hinrichsen in HMIB, pp. 371–402.

Cadenzas to Beethoven's Piano Concerto no. 4, in G major. *Dedicated to the Royal Music Director, Herr Adolf Hesse.* Breslau, 1859. Leuckart cat. no. 1284.

op. 12. Chant polonaise (à la Mazurka). Transcription of G. F. Truhn's 'Der Letzte Pole', op. 7. *Dedicated to Mons. Th. Avé Lallemant.* Hamburg, 1860. Böhme cat. no. 946.

op. 13. Mazurka-Fantasie. *Dedicated to Cosima von Bülow, née Liszt.* Breslau, 1860. Leuckart cat. no. 1377. Orchestrated by Liszt in 1868.

op. 14. Elfenjagd. Impromptu. *Dedicated in friendship to Louis Köhler.* Leipzig, 1860. Heinze cat. no. GH 35.

op. 17a. Souvenir de l'Opéra 'Un ballo in maschera' de Giuseppe Verdi. Morceau de cour. *Respectfully dedicated to Her Majesty, Queen Auguste of Prussia.* Berlin, 1864. Bote & Bock cat. no. 6213.

op. 17b. Capriccio à la Polacca sur des motifs de la musique de 'Struensée' de Meyerbeer. Morceau de Concert. *Dedicated to Anton Rubinstein by his sincere admirer Hans von Bülow.* Berlin, 1869. Schlesinger cat. no. 5732.

op. 18. Trois valses caractéristiques. *Dedicated to Madame Marie de Mouchanoff, née Comtesse de Nesselrode.* Leipzig, 1865. Peters cat. nos. 4484–4486.
1. Valse de l' 'Ingénu'
2. Valse de Jaloux
3. Valse de Glorieux

op. 19. Tarantella (1865). *Dedicated to his pupil Paul Kuczynski.* Leipzig, 1865. Peters cat. no. 4483.

op. 21. Il Carnevale di Milano. Ballabili e Intermezzi. *Dedicated to the celebrated artist Signora Elvira Salvioni, with the greatest admiration.* Leipzig, 1870–1871. Senff cat. no. 1086.

op. 24. Au sortir du Bal. Valse-Impromptu. Berlin, 1857–1858. Bote & Bock, cat. no. 3794.

op. 25. No work was assigned to this number.

op. 27. La certa. Impromptu pour le piano (1879). *Composed for and dedicated to Countess Marie Dönhoff, née Princesse Camporeale.* Munich, 1879. Aibl cat. no. 2292.

op. 28. Königsmarsch. Munich, 1880. Aibl cat. no. 2398.

Orchestral

op. 10. Musik zu Shakespeare's *Julius Cäsar.*
  (a) Ouverture héroïque
  (b) Marche des Impériaux

Dedicated to His Majesty Napoleon III, Emperor of the French, with the most profound and enthusiastic respect of the composer. After several revisions published in Mainz, 1867. Schott cat. no. 18950/2.

op. 16 Ballade for large orchestra: *Des Sängers Fluch* (Uhland). *Dedicated to his Royal Highness Grand Duke Friedrich von Baden, with grateful respects.* Berlin, 1863. Peters cat. no. 327.

op. 20. Nirvana, Symphonic Stimmungsbild, for large orchestra. *Dedicated to his friend Carl Ritter in Florence.* First version 1854–1859. Revised as 'Nirvana: Orchesterfantasie in Ouvertürenform'. Munich, 1881. Aibl cat. no. 2389.

op. 23. Vier Characterstücke for large orchestra (1868).
  1. Allegro risoluto
  2. Notturno
  3. Intermezzo guerriero
  4. Funerale

Originally entr'acte music for *Julius César. Dedicated to Hans von Bronsart, in friendly devotion.* Leipzig and Weimar, 1872. Seitz cat. no. 291.

Vocal

op. 1. 'Sechs Gedichte' (Heine and Sternau), for Soprano or Tenor, with piano accompaniment. *Dedicated to Frau Rosalie von Milde, Court Opera singer to the Grand Duke of Saxony.* Leipzig, 1853. Kahnt cat. no. 56.
  Vol. 1 (Heine)
  1. Ein schöner Stern
  2. Wie des Mondes Abbild zittert
  3. Ernst ist der Frühling

  Vol. 2 (Sternau)
  1. Frieden
  2. Noch weißt du nicht, daß ich dich liebe
  3. Hast du mich lieb?

Op. 5. 'Fünf Lieder', for high bass voice with piano accompaniment. *Dedicated to Julius Stockhausen.* Hamburg, 1857. Schuberth cat. no. 115.

1. Freisinn: 'Lasst mich nur' (Goethe)
2. Der Fichtenbaum: 'Ein Fichtenbaum steht' (Heine)
3. Wunsch: 'O könnte doch' (Meissner)
4. Nachts: 'Blüthen öffnen' (H. Grimm)
5. Volkslied: 'Die schönste Rose' (Immermann)

op. 8. Song-cycle: 'Die Entsagende' (Carl Beck), for mezzo soprano. *Dedicated to Madame Jessie Laussot.* Weimar, 1857–1864. Kühn cat. no. 30; revised Berlin 1873, R. Sulzer cat. no. 600.

1. Verbleibst ihm dennoch hold gewogen
2. Ach, Lust und Leid!
3. Ich glaubte, die Schwalbe träumte
4. Wenn Gott mir auch vergönnte
5. Gott hilf!
6. Wiegst traurig dein Gezweig

op. 22. 'Sonett' von Dante Alighieri für eine Singstimme mit Piano (1865). 'Tanto gentile e tanto onesta'. Transcribed for Piano by Franz Liszt (1875) (cf. Searle catalogue 479).
Dedicated to Countess Julia Masetti. Berlin 1865. Schlesinger.

op. 26. Due Romanze per mezzo soprano in chiave di sol con accompagnamento di pianoforte. *Expressly composed for and dedicated to signorina Lillie von Hegermann-Lindencrone, nata Greenhough.* Milan, 1878; Lucca cat. no. 24713/24714. London, 1879; Augener & Co. cat. no. 8816.

1. Adieu (Alfred de Musset)
2. Préférence

op. 29. 'Fünf Gesänge' (August, Graf von Platen), for four-voice mixed chorus. *Respectfully dedicated to Professor Carl Riedel and his Choral Society.* Berlin, 1881. Bote & Bock cat. no. 12502.

1. Tristan
2. Vogelfreiheit
3. Genuß der Stunde
4. Lenzestriebe
5. Osterlied

op. 30. 'Drei Lieder' (Poems by A. Freiherrn von Loën), for Soprano and Piano. *Dedicated to Fräulein Antoinette Foerst, Court opera singer to the Grand Duke of Saxony.* Leipzig, 1884. Sulzer cat. no. 437.

1. Du bist für mich ein holdes Heil'genbild
2. Immer fühl' ich deine Nähe
3. Wenn an des Weltmeer's Klippen

Works Without Opus Number

'Du Tropfen Tau' (Oskar v. Redwitz). Lied with piano accompaniment (NZfM, vol. 36, no. 12). March 1852. Leipzig 1853, C. F. Kahnt. No cat. no. available.

'Bundeslied des Allgemeinen deutschen Arbeitervereins' (Georg Herwegh) for four-part male chorus. Published under the pseudonym 'W. Solinger', as an anthem for Ferdinand Lassalle's German Workers' Party. Zurich, 1864.

Romanze für Tenorstimme zum dritten Act von Halévy's 'Musketiere der Königin'. *Composed for Herr Heinrich Vogl, Court Opera Singer.* Munich 1869. Aibl cat. no. 1922.

'Der König von Thule' (Goethe) for voice and piano accompaniment (ad libitum). *Dedicated to Fräulein Johanna Meyer, actress in the Royal Court of Bavaria.* Munich 1869. Aibl cat. no. 1925.

'Vision' (Dante's Purgatorio, V. 130–37) *from the Album of Countess Silvia Baroni-Pasolini in Faenza.* 1870 (NBMZ 46). See also Briefe, vol. 4, pp. 563–567.

'Innocence'. Albumblatt für das Pianoforte. *Dedicated to the royal opera singer Frau Julie Koch.* Hanover, 1879. Simon cat. no. 96.

Three Scottish Folksongs, for Voice with piano accompaniment (German and English texts). *Dedicated to Fräulein Helene Arnim, concert singer in London.* Munich, 1879. Aibl cat. no. 2379.
    1. To Mary in Heaven (Robert Burns).
    2. The Sun rises bright in France.
    3. The Snow-white Rose.

Bayerische Volkshymne (M. Oechsner), for four-part mixed chorus (1880). Aibl cat. no. 2394a/b.

'Abend am Meer' (Alfred Meissner), for four-part chorus Leipzig, 1882. Eulenberg cat. no. 218.

An den Sonnenschein. 'Neuer Klang zu altem Sang'. For soprano or mezzo soprano, with piano accompaniment. *Respectfully dedicated to Mrs. Max Sonnenschein of Prague ('To the Sunshine'), as a jocular reminder of their travels in North America, in 1889.*[2] New York, 1889. Schirmer cat. no. 7577.

---

2. Dedicated not to Max Sonnenschein, as stated in previous catalogues, but to Max's wife. See the title page of the printed music.

Liebeslied. 'Nicht lange täuschte mich das Gluck' (Heine), for voice and piano (1879). Briefe vol. 6, pp. 417–422.

'If Order is Heaven's First Law', for voice and piano (probably composed in 1876, during Bülow's first tour of America). Commissioned by Mrs. Madeleine Vinton Dahlgren for her publication *Etiquette of Social Life in Washington* (See *Die Musik,* IX, 1910).

(B) Arrangements, Transcriptions, and Instructive Editions

BACH, Carl Philipp Emanuel
  Rondo in B minor. Berlin, 1860. Schlesinger cat. no. 4927.
  Six selected keyboard sonatas. 2 vols. Leipzig, 1863. Peters cat. nos. 4380–4385.

BACH, Johann Sebastian
  A selection of keyboard pieces undertaken for Bote & Bock, Berlin, 1860–1866.
  1. Italian Concerto (BWV 971). Berlin 1860. Cat. no. 4702.
  2. Sarabande and Passepied, from the English Suite no. 5, in E minor (BWV 810). Berlin, 1862. Cat. no. 3023.
  3. Two Bourrées from the English Suite no. 1, in A major (BWV 806) and no. 2, in A minor (BWV 807). Berlin, 1863. Cat. no. 5997.
  4. Two Gavottes from the English Suite no. 6, in D minor (BWV 811) and no. 3, in G minor (BWV 808). Berlin, 1861. Cat. nos. 3021 and 3022.
  5. Chromatic Fantasia and Fugue, in D minor (BWV 903). Berlin, October 1863. Cat. no. 5995.
  6. Fantasie and Fugue in A minor (BWV 904). Berlin, 1866. Cat. no. 7024.
  7. Four pieces from the Partita in B minor (BWV 831):
     (a) Gavotte; (b) Passepied; (c) Bourrée; (d) Echo. Berlin, 1866. Cat. no. 7025.

English Suite no.4, in F major (BWV 809). I: Preludio. II: Allemande. III: Courante. IV: Sarabande. V: Menuetto. VI: Gigue. Munich, 1873. Aibl cat. no. 2080.

Fantasie in C minor (BWV 906). Munich 1873. Aibl cat. no. 2081.

Overture (Suite) for Flute and String Orchestra (BWV 1067). Leipzig, 1892. Aibl cat. no. 2549.

BAZZINI, ANTONIO
Overture to King Lear, op. 68, transcribed for piano, four hands. (The original orchestral work was dedicated to Bülow.) Milan ca. 1879. Lucca cat. no. 26161.

BEETHOVEN, LUDWIG VAN
Military March in D major, a concert version for solo piano. Dedicated to Carl Tausig. Leipzig, 1869. Senff cat. no. 797.

Sechs Menuetten, concert version for solo piano. Dedicated to Theodor Ratzenburger. Leipzig, 1869. Senff cat. no. 840.

Vols. 4 and 5 of the 'Instructive Edition of Classical Piano Music', issued by J. W. Cotta. Stuttgart, 1872. Cotta cat. nos. 23 and 35. *'Dedicated to the master Franz Liszt, as the fruit of his teaching, by his grateful student Hans von Bülow'.* These volumes contain:
1. Piano Sonatas, from op. 53 to op. 111.
2. Variations opp. 35, 76, and 120.
3. Polonaise, op. 89.
4. Eleven Bagatelles, op. 119.
5. Six Bagatelles, op. 126.
6. Rondo a Capriccio, op. 129.

BERLIOZ, HECTOR
'Benvenuto Cellini', opera in 3 acts.
(a) Grande Ouverture. Transcribed for piano (four hands). Berlin, 1855. Schlesinger cat. no. 3090.
(b) 'Humourous Quadrille' drawn from motives from the opera. *'Dedicated to Fräulein Alma Börs'.* Hanover, 1879. Simon, cat. no. 98.
(c) Six lyrical pieces with piano accompaniment. Hanover, 1881. Simon, cat. no. 111.
    1. Cavatina and Rondo of Teresa (Frau Vizthum-Pauli)
    2. Recitative and Romance of Cellini (Herr Anton Schott)
    3. Buffo Aria of Fieramosca (Herr von Milde)
    4. Rondo of Ascanio (Fraulein Riegler)
    5. Arioso (Benediction) of the Cardinal (Herr von Reichenberg)
    6. Pastorale of Cellini (Herr Anton Schott)

CHOPIN, FRYDERYK
Selected Studies from opp. 10 and 25. Instructive Edition. Foreword in German and English (translated by G. F. Hatton). Munich 1880. Aibl cat. no. 2392.

Complete Studies, opp. 10 and 25. Instructive Edition. Foreword in German and English (translated by Constance Bache). Munich 1889. Aibl cat. nos. 2605 and 2606.

Four Impromptus, opp. 29, 36, 51, 66. Munich, 1885. Aibl cat. no. 2545.

Tarantelle, op. 43 (transposed from A flat major to B major!) Munich, 1886. Aibl cat. no. 2563.

CRAMER, JOHANN BAPTIST
50 (later 60) Selected Studies, Munich 1868. An instructive edition prepared for the use of the piano class in the Royal Music School, Munich. Aibl cat. no. 1921.

DOPPLER, FRANZ
Fantaisie concertante on motifs from the Hungarian opera *'Ilka'*, for violin and piano, by Edmund Singer and Hans von Bülow. Dedicated to Messieurs Leo and J. Kern. Mainz 1853–1854. Schott cat. no. 13606.

FIELD, JOHN
Rondo in E flat major (Finale from the Sonata, op. 1). Munich 1876. Aibl cat. no. 2198.

GLUCK, CHRISTOPH WILLIBALD
Dance movements from his operas, arranged for piano solo. *'Respectfully dedicated to the illustrious reformer of the dramatic art of stage-production, His Highness Georg II, Duke of Sachsen-Meiningen'*. Munich 1879–1880. Aibl cat. nos. 2373 (vol. 1), 2376 (vol. 2), 2377 (vol. 3), 2378 (vol. 4).

Volume 1. *Orpheus*
  Pantomime (Todtenopfer)
  Sarabande (Reigen der Seligen)
  Aria (Euridice's Schattenwandlung)
  Bourrée (Chortanz)
  Menuetto
  Gigue
  Gavotte
  Hirtentanz
  Chaconne

Volume 2. *Alceste*
  Priestermarsch
  Opferhandlung

Divertissement (in four movements)
Gigue
Festmarsch
Sarabande
Gavotte

Volume 3. *Iphigénie in Aulis*
Waffentanz
Sarabande
Menuetto
Anglaise
Passepied
Marsch (Auftritt Achille's)
Passepied
Gavotte
Tambourin
Menuetto
Sclaventanz

Volume 4. *Armida*
Huldigungsmarsch
Pavane
Tanz mit Chor
Menuetto pastorale
Gavotte
Furientanz (Dance of the Furies)
Bourrée
Tanz mit Chor

Iphiginia in Aulis (Richard Wagner's version of 1847), transcribed for piano. Leipzig 1858. Breitkopf & Härtel cat. no. 9793.

GOTTHARD, JOHANN PETER
Gavotte in G major. London 1873. Lucas, Weber & Co. cat. no. 205.

HANDEL, GEORG FRIEDRICH
Selected keyboard works. Berlin 1862–1866. Bote & Bock.
Chaconne in F major, HWV 485 (cat. no. 3024).
Aria and Variations in D minor, from the Suite in D minor, HWV 428 (cat. no. 5998).
Three Gigues (E minor, HWV 429; F minor, HWV 433; B major, HWV 440) (cat. no. 5996).

Prelude and Fugue in F minor, from the Suite in F minor HWV 433 (cat. no. 7022).

Prelude, Fugue and Capriccio, from the Suite in D minor, HWV 428 (cat. no. unavailable).

HANDEL, G. F.

Twelve Easy Piano Pieces, for use in obligatory keyboard instruction. An instructive edition prepared for the use of the piano class in the Royal Music School, Munich. Munich 1868. Falter & Sohn, cat. no. 1645.

Gigue in G minor. 3rd mov. from the Suite in G minor, HWV 439. Munich 1876. Aibl cat. no. 2200.

HAYDN, JOSEPH

Fantasy in C major, Hob. XVII:4. Munich 1876. Aibl cat. no. 2197.

LISZT, FRANZ

'Vom Fels zum Meer'. German Victory March. Arranged for keyboard (four hands). Berlin 1865. Schlesinger cat. no. 5282.

Fantasy on Hungarian Folksongs, arranged for two pianos. Leipzig 1864. Heinze cat. no. 99.

Concerto Pathétique (Grosses Konzertsolo), arranged for two pianos. Contains a thirty-nine-bar expansion of Liszt's own arrangement for two pianos, which had already been published in 1866. Leipzig 1884. Breitkopf & Härtel cat. no. 16341.

MENDELSSOHN, FELIX

Capriccio in F sharp minor, op. 5. Munich 1880. Aibl cat. no. 2319.

Rondo Capriccioso, op. 14. Munich 1880. Aibl cat. no. 2396.

MEYERBEER, GIOCOMO

Grande Scène du Mancénillier de l'Opéra 'L'Africaine', for piano solo (published under the pseudonym 'W. Solinger'). Berlin 1866.

MONIUSZKO, STANISLAS

Polonaise charactéristique. Munich 1880. Aibl cat. no. 2385.

MOZART, WOLFGANG AMADEUS

Fantasie in C minor, KV 396. Munich 1880. Aibl cat. no. 2386.

Gigue in G major, KV 574. Berlin 1869. Schlesinger cat. no. 1695.

Menuett in D major, KV 355. Berlin 1869. Schlesinger (no cat. no. available).

SCARLATTI, DOMENICO
Eighteen selected keyboard pieces, grouped as suites. 3 volumes. Leipzig, June 1864. Peters cat. nos. 4458, 4459, and 4450.

'Cat's Fugue', K.30. Munich 1876. Aibl cat. no. 2194.

SCHUBERT, FRANZ
'Gott in der Natur' (Poem by Gleim) D. 757, for four-part women's chorus, op. 133. The piano accompaniment transcribed for small orchestra. Vienna/Leipzig, 1876. Cranz cat. no. F.S.23800.

Impromptu in G-flat major, D. 899 no. 3 (transposed into G major!). Munich 1880. Aibl cat. no. 2318.

WAGNER, RICHARD
Tannhäuser. March and Chorus, transcribed for piano (four hands). Paris 1860(?). Flaxland cat. no. 356.

Tannhäuser. Overture, transcribed for piano (four hands). Paris 1860(?). Flaxland cat. no. 391.

Fantaisie concertante on motifs from the opera *Tannhäuser,* for piano and violin by H. von Bülow and Edmund Singer. *'Homage to Franz Liszt'*. Mainz 1858. Schott cat. no. 13579.

A *Faust* Overture, transcribed for piano solo. Leipzig, 1866. Breitkopf & Härtel cat. no. 10775.

Tristan und Isolde. Piano reduction of the full score. Leipzig, 1860. Breitkopf & Härtel cat. no. 9942.

Prelude to *Tristan und Isolde*. Transcribed for piano solo. Leipzig, 1861. Breitkopf & Härtel cat. no. 10326.

Prelude to *Tristan und Isolde*. Transcribed for piano (four hands). Leipzig, 1860. Breitkopf & Härtel cat. no. 10117.

Die Meistersinger von Nürnberg.
(a) Overture. A concert paraphrase for piano solo. Mainz, 1867. Schott cat. no. 18975.
(b) Assembly of the Guild of Meistersingers. Fragments from Act I. A concert paraphrase for piano solo. Mainz, 1867. Schott cat. no. 18976.

(c)   Quintet from Act III. A concert paraphrase for piano solo, *'dedicated to his pupil Fräulein Alexandra von Milochevitch'*. Mainz, 1869. Schott cat. no. 19830.

Huldigungsmarsch. Transcribed for piano solo. Mainz, 1865. Schott cat. no. 18335.

Huldigungsmarsch for His Majesty Ludwig II, King of Bavaria. Transcribed for piano (four hands). Mainz, 1865. Schott cat. no. 18343.

WEBER, CARL MARIA von
Momento capriccioso in B-flat major, op. 12. Munich, 1879. Aibl cat. no. 2371.

Aufförderung zum Tanz, op. 65. Munich, 1880. Aibl cat. no. 2395.

Polacca brillante, op. 72. Munich, 1880. Aibl cat. no. 2397.

Konzertstück for piano and orchestra, op. 79. Arranged for solo piano and *dedicated to Carl Bärmann, 'teacher of advanced piano playing at the Royal Music School in Munich'*. Leipzig, 1869. Senff cat. no. 883.

Konzertstück for piano and orchestra, op. 11. Arranged for solo piano and *'respectfully dedicated to Ernst Ferdinand Wenzel, teacher at the Leipzig Conservatory of Music'*. Leipzig, 1872. Senff cat. no. 901.

Konzertstück for piano and orchestra, op. 32. Arranged for solo piano and *'respectfully dedicated to Ernst Ferdinand Wenzel, teacher at the Leipzig Conservatory of Music'*. Leipzig, 1872. Senff cat. no. 904.

A Book of Songs (1876, America)
'Miss Cronyn's favourite songs as accompanied by Dr. H. v. Bülow in his concerts throughout the United States, edited and revised by H. v. B'.

1.   Beethoven: 'La vita felice'
2.   Beethoven: 'La partenza'
3.   Beethoven: 'L'amante impaziente'
4.   Rubinstein: 'Thou seemst to me a flower'
5.   Gordigiani: 'O santissima vergine'
6.   Gomez, Carlos: 'Mia Piccirella, deh!'
7.   Rossini: 'Separazione'
8.   Rossini: 'L'invito'
9.   Meyerbeer: 'Barcarolle'
10.   Meyerbeer: 'Chant de mai'

11. Liszt, Franz: 'Comment?'
12. Liszt, Franz: 'Le désir'
13. Beethoven: 'Song of Penitence'
14. Weber: 'Cavatina' from *Der Freischütz*

SIGLA

BWV = Bach Werke Verzeichnis [Complete Catalogue of Bach's works]
D = Deutsch Catalogue of Schubert's works
HWV = Handel Werke Verzeichnis [Complete Catalogue of Handel's works]
HOB = Hoboken Catalogue of Haydn's works
K = Kirkpatrick Catalogue of Scarlatti's works
KV = Köchel Catalogue of Mozart's works
S = Searle Catalogue of Liszt's works

Appendix III

Bülow's Titles and Honours

September 16, 1853	Elevated to the German nobility on the death of his father. Thereafter he bears the title of Baron.
May 1, 1856	Honorary Membership in the Neu-Weimar-Verein
1858	Appointed Royal Prussian Court Pianist. The title was removed from him in 1884 for publicly insulting Baron von Hülsen, intendant of the Berlin Royal Opera House. Thereafter, Bülow styled himself 'The People's Pianist'.
April 12, 1860	Diploma of Honorary Membership in the Conservatory of Music in Bohemia
February 12, 1864	Degree of Doctor of Philosophy (*honoris causa*) from the University of Jena
February 13, 1864	Honorary Diploma of the Jena Academic Choral Society
September 12, 1864	Appointed *Vorspieler* to His Majesty King Ludwig II of Bavaria
October 1867	Invested by His Majesty King Ludwig II of Bavaria with the Order of the Cross of Saint Michael, First Class
February 22, 1870	Honorary Diploma as Corresponding Member of the Royal Academy of Music in Florence
March 25, 1870	Order of the Crown of Italy, confirmed by his Royal Majesty Vittorio Emanuele II, Grand Master of the Order

March 1870	President of the Cherubini Society in Florence
April 2, 1872	Diploma of the Richard Wagner Society in Munich
May 26, 1873	Gold Medal of the Philharmonic Society, London
January 6, 1874	Invested by Duke Georg II of Meiningen with the Order of the Komthurkreuz (2nd Class)
January 5, 1878	Presented by the Glasgow Choral Union with a specially inscribed baton, in gratitude for his services
January 10, 1881	Invested by Grand Duke Carl Alexander of Weimar with the Cross of Commander of the White Falcon
January 1884	Honorary President of the Raff Conservatory of Music, Frankfurt-am-Main
June 1884	Honorary Member of the Philharmonic Society, London[1]
November 20, 1885	Honorary Diploma of the Harlem Bach Association, The Netherlands
September 8, 1887	Honorary Diploma of Membership in the St. Petersburg Conservatory (member no. 203)
January 8, 1890	Honorary Diploma from the city of Hamburg, marking his sixtieth birthday
February 22, 1892	Receives the Freedom of the city of Hamburg

1. Evidently in those early days election to honorary membership of the Philharmonic Society was a distinction quite separate from that of receiving the Society's Gold Medal. Bülow received both.

List of Sources

ACB   Altmann, Wilhelm. *Chronik des Berliner Philharmonischen Orchesters (1882–1901), zugleich ein Beitrag zur Beurteilung Hans von Bülows*. Die Musik, Berlin and Leipzig, 1902.

ACLA   Agoult, Marie d'. *Correspondance de Liszt et de la Comtesse d'Agoult*. Edited by Daniel Ollivier. 2 vols. Paris, 1933, 1934.

AJBL   Avins, Styra, ed. *Johannes Brahms: Life and Letters*. Translated by Josef Eisinger and Styra Avins. Oxford, 1997.

AMZ   *Allgemeine Musik-Zeitung: Wochenschrift für die Reform des Musiklebens der Gegenwart* (Berlin). Cited by issue.

AWC   Alan Walker Collection, housed in the William Ready Division of Archives and Research Collections, Mills Library, McMaster University, Hamilton, Ontario, Canada.

BA(1)   *Bülow-Anekdoten*, mitgeteilt von Frau Marie von Bülow. *Die Musik*. Berlin, 1910, Heft nr. X pp. 210–216.

BA(2)   Bayreuth Archive. Nationalarchiv der Richard Wagner Stiftung, Bayreuth.

BAB   Bülow, Hans von. *Ausgewählte Briefe: Volksausgabe*. Herausgegeben von Marie von Bülow. Leipzig, 1919.

BAS   Bülow, Hans von. *Ausgewählte Schriften, 1850–1892*. 2nd ed. Herausgegeben von Marie von Bülow. Leipzig, 1911.

BB   Bülow, Hans von. *Briefe*. Herausgegeben von Marie von Bülow. 7 vols. Leipzig, 1895–1908. A selection of letters from the first two volumes was translated into English by Constance Bache. See BEC.

BBLW   Bülow, Marie von. *Hans von Bülow in Leben und Wort.* Stuttgart, 1925.

BBM   Bache, Constance. *Brother Musicians: Reminiscences of Edward and Walter Bache.* London, 1901.

BC   Buonamici Collection. Contains some unpublished correspondence (1870–1872) between Bülow and his Italian pupil Giuseppe Buonamici, held in the Archives and Research Collections of McMaster University, Hamilton, Ontario, Canada.

BE   Behrmann, Georg. *Erinnerungen.* Berlin, 1904.

BEC   Bache, Constance. *The Early Correspondence of Hans von Bülow.* London 1896.

BKHB   *Beiträge zum Kolloquium Hans von Bülow—Leben, Wirken und Vermächtnis.* Zum 100. Todestag Hans von Bülows. Edited by Herta Müller and Verona Gerasch. Südthüringer Forschungen nr.28. Staatliche Museen Meiningen, 1994.

BMB   Blaukopf, Herta, ed. *Gustav Mahler. Briefe.* Vienna and Hamburg, 1982.

BMP   Benedict, Milo E. *Musical People in Retrospect.* Boston, 1931.

BNB   Bülow, Hans von. *Neue Briefe.* Herausgegeben und eingeleitet von Richard Graf du Moulin Eckart. Munich, 1927. Translated as *Letters of Hans von Bülow,* by Hannah Waller. New York, 1931. [All citations refer to the original German publication.]

BPR   Barry, C. A. 'Some Personal Reminiscences of Hans von Bülow.' *The Musician.* London. Three issues: September 1, 8, and 15, 1897.

BRAB   Boekelmann, Bernard. *Recollections and Anecdotes of Bülow.* The Century Library of Music, vol. 15. New York, 1901.

BRM   Bülow, Eduard, and Wilhelm Rustow. *Militärische und vermischte Schriften von Heinrich Dietrich von Bülow.* Leipzig, 1853.

BSC   Bülow, Hans von, and Richard Strauss. *Correspondence.* Edited by Willi Schuh and Franz Trenner. Translated from the German by Anthony Gishford. London, 1955.

BUD   *Hans von Bülow im Urteil berühmter Dirigenten (Hans von Bülow as Famous Conductors See Him).* A limited facsimile edition. Hamburg, 1978.

BWL   *Briefwechsel zwischen Wagner und Liszt.* 2 vols. Leipzig, 1887.

CB   Cairns, David. *Berlioz.* 2 vols. London, 1989 and 1999.

CB-K   Conrad, Herbert. *Der Beidler-Konflikt.* Bayreuther Festspielnachrichten, pp. 76–89. Bayreuth, 1983.

CEH   Craig, Robert. *The Early History of the Glasgow Choral Union, and the Inauguration of Its Newly Formed Resident Orchestra.* 24 vols. Unpublished work held in the Strong Room of the Mitchell Library, Glasgow. Call no. TD 1556 /8/3/5.

CHC   Cohn, Peter. *Das Hoch'sche Conservatorium in Frankfurt am Main, 1878–1978.* Frankfurt, 1979.

CLBA — Csapó, Wilhelm von, ed. *Franz Liszts Briefe an Baron Anton Augusz, 1846–78*. Budapest 1911. [Liszt Ferenc levelei báró Augusz Antalhoz].

CLW — Cornelius, Peter. *Literarische Werke*. 4 vols. Leipzig, 1904–1905.

CM — Caulaincourt, Armand de. *Mémoires du général de Caulaincourt, Duc de Vicence, Grand Ecuyer de l'Empereur*. Introduction and notes by Jean Hanoteau. 3 vols. Paris, 1933.

CWBD — *Cosima Wagners Briefe an ihre Tochter Daniela von Bülow, 1866–1885:* herausgegeben von Max Freiherr von Waldberg. Stuttgart and Berlin, 1933.

DCVS — Dibble, Jeremy. *Charles Villiers Stanford: Man and Musician*. Oxford, 2002.

DFB — Dent, Edward J. *Ferruccio Busoni: A Biography*. London, 1933.

DHB — Damrosch, Walter. *Hans von Bülow and the Ninth Symphony*. Musical Quarterly 13 (1927), pp. 280–293.

DKD — *Antonin Dvořák: Korespondence a Dokumenty*. 8 vols. Prague, 1987–2000.

DM — *Die Musik* (Berlin). Cited by issue.

DMML — Damrosch, Walter. *My Musical Life*. New York, 1923.

DMSJ — Dupêchez, Charles, ed. *Mémoires, souvenirs et journaux de la Comtesse d'Agoult*. Paris, 1990.

DSB — Deutsche Staatsbibliothek zu Berlin-Preussischer Kulturbesitz, Musikabteilung mit Mendelssohn Archive. Berlin.

DSL — Dohnányi, Ilona von. *Ernst von Dohnányi: A Song of Life*. Edited by James A. Grymes. Bloomington and Indianapolis, 2002.

DWJ — *Dwight's Journal of Music* (Boston). Cited by issue.

EBMJ — Erck, Alfred, Inge Erck, Herta Müller. *Hans von Bülows Meiningen Jahre*. Beiträge zur Musikgeschichte Meiningens. Staatliche Museen Meiningen. Südthüringer Forschungen 25. Meiningen 1991.

EDH — Evans, Richard, J. *Death in Hamburg: Society and Politics in the Cholera Years, 1830–1910*. Oxford, 1987.

EMB — Ewen, David. *The Man with the Baton*. New York, 1936.

ESG — Erck, Alfred, and Hannelore Schneider. *Georg II. von Sächsen-Meiningen. Ein Leben zwischen ererbter Macht und künstlerischer Freiheit*. Meiningen, 1997.

FBZ — Fellinger, Imogen. 'Brahms und die Neudeutsche Schule.' *Brahms und seine Zeit: A Symposium*. Hamburg, 1983.

FHB — Fischer, Georg. *Hans von Bülow in Hannover*. Hanover-Leipzig, 1902.

FHF — Freifrau von Heldenburg (Ellen Franz). *Fünfzig Jahre Glück und Leid: Ein Leben in Briefen aus den Jahren 1873–1923*. Leipzig, 1926.

FI — Fifield, Christopher. *Ibbs and Tillet: The Rise and Fall of a Musical Empire*. Aldershot (England) and Burlington (Vermont), 2005.

FKN-G   *Dr. Bernhard Förster's Kolonie Neu-Germania in Paraguay*. Berlin, 1891.

GAW   Gutmann, Albert. *Aus dem Wiener Musikleben: Künstler—Erinnerungen, 1873–1908*. Vol. 1. Vienna, 1914.

GBLW   Geiringer, Karl. *Brahms: His Life and Work*. 2nd ed. London, 1948.

GHB   Gewande, Wolf-Dieter. *Hans von Bülow: Eine biographisch-dokumentarische Würdigung aus Anlass seines 175. Geburtstages*. Lilienthal, 2004.

GIS   Garrigues, C. H. N. *Ein ideales Sängerpaar, Ludwig Schnorr von Carolsfeld und Malvina Schnorr von Carolsfeld, geborene Garrigues*. Copenhagen und Berlin, 1937.

GM   Grange, Henri-Louis de La. *Gustav Mahler: Chronicle of a Life*. Vol. 1. New York, 1973.

GMM   Ganz, Wilhelm. *Memories of a Musician: Reminiscences of Seventy Years of Musical Life*. London, 1913.

GRW   Gutman, Robert W. *Richard Wagner: The Man, His Mind and His Music*. London, 1968.

HB-CM   Unpublished letters of Hans von Bülow to Cécile Mutzenbecher. Copies in the Alan Walker Collection, Box 29, Mills Library, McMaster University, Hamilton, Ontario, Canada.

HHB   Haas, Frithjof. *Hans von Bülow: Leben und Wirken*. Wilhelmshaven, 2002.

HLL   Hallé, Sir Charles. *Life and Letters*. Edited by his son C.E. Hallé and his daughter Marie Hallé. London, 1896.

HMIB   Hinrichsen, Hans-Joachim. *Musikalische Interpretation: Hans von Bülow*. Archiv für Musikwissenschaft, Band 46. Stuttgart, 1999.

HMR   Hoffman, Richard. *Some Musical Recollections of Fifty Years*. New York, 1910.

HWK   *Hugo Wolfs Kritiken im Wiener Salonblatt*. 2 vols. Mit Kommentar vorgelegt von Leopold Spitzer unter Mitarbeit von Isabella Sommer. Vienna, 2002.

IPAM   International Piano Archives, University of Maryland, College Park, United States.

JFP   Foerster, Josef Bohuslav. *Der Pilger. Erinnerungen eines Musikers*. Prague, 1955.

JKWF   Kapp, Julius. *Richard Wagner und die Frauen. Völlige Neuausgabe*. 15th ed. Berlin, 1929.

JSF   Jones, Ernest. *Sigmund Freud: Life and Work*. 3 vols. London, 1953–57.

KBWP   Karpath, Ludwig. *Zu den Briefen Richard Wagners an eine Putzmacherin: Unterredungen mit der Putzmacherin Berta*. Berlin, 1907(?).

KE   Kellermann, Berthold. *Erinnerungen, ein Künstlerleben*. Herausgegeben von Sebastien Hausmann und Helmut Kellermann. Zurich, 1932.

KFW   Kreowski, Ernst, and Eduard Fuchs. *Richard Wagner in der Kari-katur.* Berlin, 1907.

KJB   Kalbeck, Max. *Johannes Brahms.* 4 vols. Berlin, 1904–1914.

KLRWB   *König Ludwig II und Richard Wagner Briefwechsel, bearbeitet von Otto Strobel.* 5 vols. Karlsruhe, 1936, 1939.

KRNY   Krehbiel, H. E. *Review of the New York Musical Season.* Vols. 1 to 5. New York, 1886–1890.

KWL   Kloss, Erich, ed. *Briefwechsel zwischen Wagner und Liszt.* 2 vols. Leipzig, 1910.

LBLB   La Mara, ed. *Correspondance entre Franz Liszt et Hans von Bülow.* Leipzig, 1899.

LBS   Lamond, Frederic. *Beethoven: Notes on the Sonatas.* Glasgow, 1944.

LBU   Lott, R. Allen. 'Bernard Ullman: Nineteenth-Century American Impresario.' *A Celebration of American Music: Words and Music in Honor of H. Wiley Hitchcock.* Edited by Richard Crawford, R. Allen Lott, and Carol J. Oja. Ann Arbor, Mich., 1990.

LCS   Litzmann, Berthold. *Clara Schumann: Ein Künstlerleben.* 3 vols. Leipzig, 1902–1908.

LDML   La Mara. *Durch Musik und Leben im Dienste des Ideals.* 2 vols. Leipzig, 1917.

LL   *Living with Liszt: The Diary of Carl Lachmund, an American Pupil of Liszt, 1882–1884.* Edited, annotated, and introduced by Alan Walker. Stuyvesant, N.Y. 1995.

LLB   La Mara, ed. *Franz Liszts Briefe.* 8 vols. Leipzig, 1893–1905.

LLF   La Mara. *Liszt und die Frauen.* 2nd ed. Leipzig, 1919.

LM   Lamond, Frederic. *The Memoirs of Frederic Lamond.* Glasgow, 1949.

LMM   Lebrecht, Norman. *The Maestro Myth.* London and New York, 1991.

LSB   Litzmann, Berthold, ed. *Clara Schumann—Johannes Brahms: Briefe aus den Jahren 1853–1896.* 2 vols. Leipzig, 1927.

MBB   Mützelburg, Adolf. *Hans von Bülow und die Berliner Kritik: Ein Beitrag zur Zeitgeschichte.* Berlin, 1859.

MCM   Mutzenbecher, Heinrich. *Cécile Mutzenbecher und Hans von Bülow.* Hamburg, 1963.

MCW(1)   Moulin Eckart, Richard Graf Du. *Cosima Wagner, ein Lebens- und Charakterbild.* 2 vols. Munich, 1929.

MCW(2)   Marek, George. *Cosima Wagner.* New York, 1981.

MHB   Moulin Eckart, Richard Graf Du. *Hans von Bülow.* Munich, 1921.

MHBB   Muller, Herta, and Renate Hofmann, eds. *Johannes Brahms im Briefwechsel mit Herzog Georg II: von Sachsen-Meiningen und Helene Freifrau von Heldburg.* Tutzing, 1991.

MLHvB   *Meininger Landesmusiktage Hans von Bülow.* Meiningen, 1994.

MMML   Mason, William. *Memories of a Musical Life.* New York, 1901.

MMN   Mackenzie, Sir Alexander. *A Musician's Narrative.* London, 1927.

MMR   *Monthly Musical Record* (London). Cited by issue.

MT   *The Musical Times* (London). Cited by issue.

MTR   *The Music Trade Review* (New York). Cited by issue.

MW   Meyer, C. F. *Fünfzehn Briefe Richard Wagners mit Erinnerungen und Erläuterungen von Eliza Wille, geb. Sloman.* Munich/Berlin/Zurich, 1935.

NB   Niemann, Walter. *Brahms.* Translated by Catherine Alison Philipps. New York, 1937.

NPM   Niecks, Frederick. *Programme Music in the Last Four Centuries.* London, 1907.

NLRW   Newman, Ernest. *The Life of Richard Wagner.* 4 vols. London, 1933–1947.

NZfM   *Neue Zeitschrift für Musik* (Leipzig). Cited by issue.

OASE   Olliver, Marie-Thérèse Emile. *J'ai vécu l'agonie du Second Empire.* Text selected and presented by Anne Troisier de Diaz. Paris, 1970.

PAN   Pfohl, Ferdinand. *Arthur Nikisch als Mensch und Künstler.* Leipzig, 1900.

PBHF   Poschinger, Heinrich von. *Fürst Bismarck und seine Hamburger Freunde.* Hamburg, 1903.

PGS   Pohl, Richard. *Gesammelte Schriften über Musik und Musiker.* Leipzig, 1883–1884.
           1: *Richard Wagner: Studien und Kritiken*
           2: *Franz Liszt: Studien und Erinnerungen*
           3: *Hektor Berlioz: Studien und Kritiken*

PM   Paderewski, Ignace Jan, and Mary Lawton. *The Paderewski Memoirs.* New York, 1938.

PMK   Photiades, Constantin. *Marie Kalergis, née Comtesse Nesselrode (1822–1874).* Paris, 1924.

PSB   Pfeiffer, Theodor. *Studien bei Hans von Bülow.* Berlin, 1894. See also VHB.

RGH   Rosendahl, Erich. *Geschichte der Hoftheater in Hannover und Braunschweig.* Hanover, 1927.

RHB   Reimann, Heinrich. *Hans von Bülow, sein Leben und sein Wirken.* Berlin, 1908.

RHM   Reik, Theodor. *The Haunting Melody: Psychoanalytic Experiences in Life and Music.* New York, 1953.

R-KE   Rappoldi-Kahrer, Laura. *Erinnerungen an Hans von Bülow von Laura Rappoldi-Kahrer: Mit unveröffentlichten Briefen Liszts und Bülows.* Herausgegeben von Dr. Julius Kapp. Die Musik, 8/17.

R-KMM   Rimsky-Korsakov, Nikolay. *My Musical Life.* New York, 1935.

ROD   Rothman, John. *The Origin and Development of Dramatic Criticism in the New York Times, 1851–1880.* New York, 1970.

RR   Raff, Helene. *Joachim Raff: Ein Lebensbild.* Regensburg, 1925.

RWBB   The *Diary of Richard Wagner: The Brown Book, 1865–1882.* Presented and Annotated by Joachim Bergfeld. Translated by George Bird. London, 1980.

RWHB   *Richard Wagner: Briefe an Hans von Bülow.* Edited with an introduction by Daniela Thode. Jena, 1916.

RWMW   *Richard Wagner to Mathilde Wesendonck: Tagebuchblätter und Briefe, 1853–1871.* Herausgegeben, eingeleitet und erläutert von Wolfgang Golther. Leipzig, 1915.

SABG   Schieckel, Harald. 'Ahnengemeinschaft zwischen Hans von Bülow und Cécile Mutzenbecher geb. Gorrissen'. *Genealogie.* Vol. 6. Hamburg, 1962.

SB   Schemenn, Ludwig. *Hans von Bülow im Lichte der Wahrheit.* Regensburg, 1935.

SBE   Strauss, Richard. *Briefe an die Eltern.* Herausgegeben von Willi Schuh. Zurich, 1954.

SBM   Skelton, Geoffrey. *Richard and Cosima Wagner: Biography of a Marriage.* London, 1982.

SBP   Stresemann, Wolfgang. *The Berlin Philharmonic from Bülow to Karajan: Home and History of a World-Famous Orchestra.* Translated from the German by Jean Stresemann. Berlin, 1979.

SCC   Schuller, Gunther. *The Compleat Conductor.* New York, 1997.

SLBG   Stern, Adolf, ed. *Franz Liszt's Briefe an Carl Gille.* Leipzig, 1903.

SLRW   *Selected Letters of Richard Wagner.* Translated and edited by Stewart Spencer and Barry Millington. With original texts of passages omitted from existing printed editions. New York, 1988.

SLWA   Steinway Archives, at La Guardia & Wagner Archives. La Guardia Community College, City University, New York.

SPD   Stanford, Charles Villiers. *Pages from an Unwritten Diary.* London, 1914.

SRR   Strauss, Richard. *Recollections and Reflections.* Edited by Willi Schuh. Translated from the German by L. J. Lawrence. London, 1953.

SRS   Schuh, Willi. *Richard Strauss: A Chronicle of the Early Years, 1864–1898.* Translated from the German by Mary Whittall. Cambridge, 1982.

SRW   Stockmann, Bernhard. *'Ruht wohl, ihr teuren Gebeine': Die Trauerfeiern für Hans von Bülow.* Festschrift für Horst Gronemeyer zum 60. Geburtstag. Herausgegeben von Harald Weigel. Hamburg, 1993.

S-WW   Stargardt-Wolff, Edith. *Wegbereiter grosser Musiker.* Berlin-Wiesbaden, 1954.

SZM   Schorn, Adelheid von. *Zwei Menschenalter: Erinnerungen und Briefe.* Berlin, 1901.

TCE   Twain, Mark. *The Cholera Epidemic in Hamburg.* The Complete Essays of Mark Twain. New York, 1968.

TLH   *Tchaikovsky's Letters to His Family: An Autobiography.* Translated by Galina von Meck, with additional annotations by Percy M. Young. New York, 1981.

TS   Tawaststjerna, Erik. *Sibelius.* Vol. 1, 1865–1905. Translated by Robert Layton. London, 1976.

VCA   Vier, Jacques. *La Comtesse d'Agoult et son temps, avec des documents inédits.* 6 vols., Paris 1955–63.

VHB   J. Vianna da Motta. *Nachtrag zu Studien bei Hans von Bülow, von Theodor Pfeiffer.* Berlin, 1896. See also PSB.

VMA   Versailles Municipal Library Archive, France. The unpublished legacy of Claire de Charnacé (*née* d'Agoult), including her letters, notebooks, and memoirs, and 'My last meeting and my last conversation with Hans von Bülow'. MS F 859, cartons 1 to 30.

WBR   Weingartner, Felix. *Buffets and Rewards: A Musician's Reminiscences.* Translated from the German by Marguerite Wolff. London, 1937.

WELC   Walker, Alan, and Gabriele Erasmi. *Liszt, Carolyne, and the Vatican: The Story of a Thwarted Marriage.* Stuyvesant, N.Y., 1991.

WEW   Weissheimer, Wendelin. *Erlebnisse mit Richard Wagner, Franz Liszt, und vielen anderen Zeitgenossen.* Stuttgart, 1898.

WFL   Walker, Alan. *Franz Liszt.* 3 vols. New York, 1983–96. Vol. I: *The Virtuoso Years, 1811–47.* Vol. 2: *The Weimar Years, 1848–61.* Vol. 3: *The Final Years, 1861–86.*

WLLM   Waters, Edward N. ed. *The Letters of Franz Liszt to Olga Meyendorff, 1871–1886.* Translated by William R. Tyler. Dumbarton Oaks, 1979.

WLP   Waters, Edward N. *Franz Liszt to Richard Pohl.* Studies in Romanticism. Vol. 6, no. 4, pp. 193–202. Boston, 1967.

WMC   Weingartner, Felix. *Weingartner on Music and Conducting.* New York, 1969.

WML   Wagner, Richard. *Mein Leben.* Munich, 1911. Authorized English translation. London, 1912.

WT   Wagner, Cosima. *Die Tagebücher.* 2 vols. Editiert und kommentiert von Martin Gregor-Dellin und Dietrich Mach. Munich, 1976, 1977. Translated (as *Cosima Wagner's Diaries*) by Geoffrey Skelton. London and New York, 1978, 1980.

WTV   Walter, Bruno. *Theme and Variations, an Autobiography by Bruno Walter.* Translated from the German by James A. Galston. New York, 1946.

WUD   Weingartner, Felix. *Über das Dirigieren.* Leipzig, 1896. Translated (as *On Conducting*) by Ernest Newman, from the 3rd German edition (1905), London, 1906.

ZBG   Zabel, Eugen. *Hans von Bülow: Gedenkblätter.* Hamburg, 1894.

ZMB   Zimdars, Richard Louis, ed. and trans. *The Piano Masterclasses of Hans von Bülow: Two Participants' Accounts.* Part 1: Studien bei Hans von Bülow, by Theodor Pfeiffer. Part 2: Supplement, by José Vianna da Motta. Bloomington, Ind., 1993.

Index

Page numbers in italics refer to main entries